$y - 3 = 2x$

$3y - 9 = 6x$

$y = 2x + 3$

$3y = 6x + 9$

ENTERPRISE, GOVERNMENT, AND THE PUBLIC

ENTERPRISE, GOVERNMENT, AND THE PUBLIC

Stephen J. K. Walters

Associate Professor of Economics
Joseph A. Sellinger, S. J. School of Business and Management
Loyola College in Maryland

McGRAW-HILL, INC.

New York   St. Louis   San Francisco   Auckland   Bogotá   Caracas
Lisbon   London   Madrid   Mexico   Milan   Montreal
New Delhi   Paris   San Juan   Singapore   Sydney   Tokyo   Toronto

This book was set in Palatino by The Clarinda Company.
The editors were Scott D. Stratford and Caroline Izzo;
the production supervisor was Denise L. Puryear.
The cover was designed by Carla Bauer;
the cover art was illustrated by Jane Sterrett.
Drawings were done by Grafacon, Inc.
R. R. Donnelley & Sons Company was printer and binder.

ENTERPRISE, GOVERNMENT, AND THE PUBLIC

2 3 4 5 6 7 8 9 0 DOC DOC 9 0 9 8 7 6 5 4 3

ISBN 0-07-068029-9

Library of Congress Cataloging-in-Publication Data

Walters, Stephen John Kasabuski, (date).
   Enterprise, government, and the public / Stephen J. K. Walters.
     p.   cm.
   Includes index.
   ISBN 0-07-068029-9
   1. Trade regulation.   2. Competition.   3. Monopolies—Government
policy.   4. Pricing—Government policy.   I. Title.
HD3612.W35   1993
338.8—dc20   92-18843

ABOUT THE AUTHOR

STEPHEN J. K. WALTERS received his B.A. in economics from the University of Pennsylvania in 1975, worked in the research department of the Federal Reserve Bank of Philadelphia, and then began graduate study in economics at the University of California at Los Angeles. He received his Ph.D. in 1982. He is currently associate professor of economics at Loyola College in Maryland, where he has been responsible for undergraduate and MBA-level courses on government regulation of business since 1981. His published research covers such topics as antitrust economics, economic and social regulation, privatization, and academic research productivity. He also has written over a hundred general-interest articles appearing in major newspapers, and he often serves as a consultant on matters involving antitrust, contracts, and corporate valuation.

For My Mother and My Late Father, My Two Best Teachers,
For Melanie, My Teaching Partner,
and For Matthew and John, Our Pupils

CONTENTS

PREFACE

In the last two decades, economists have learned a great deal about the complex interaction of government and enterprise. The new branch of economics called public choice analysis has shed much light on the motives and effects of government intervention in markets. A heightened appreciation of the importance of the costs of transacting has led to the development of many new hypotheses concerning firm behavior. The field of mathematics known as game theory has revolutionized the way in which economists view the interaction of rivals and the strategic behavior of firms. And enough time has elapsed for scholars to study the effects of the regulatory boom of the early 1970s and the experiments in deregulation of the 1980s.

Sadly, however, many texts in the field of business and government simply have not kept up with the pace of change. While most update their descriptions of policy and law periodically, they generally have failed to incorporate new analytical tools and perspectives in their treatment of standard issues. Many texts lack any mention of such crucial topics as public choice theory, transaction cost economics, incentive-compatible regulation, privatization, nonprice predation, and behavior aimed at raising rivals' costs. In addition, many fail to explore fully the policy implications of rent seeking, the economic theory of property rights, the market for corporate control, and the Coase theorem.

I've tried to make this text up to date both descriptively and analytically. Readers will encounter the latest insights and findings of leading researchers on the topics listed above and many more. However, I have avoided higher mathematics in favor of verbal, numerical, or geometric exposition, and I have tried to make the writing crisp and readable. Readers who have had no more than an introductory microeconomics course should find the material accessible, while readers with more extensive backgrounds in economics should nevertheless find it interesting and challenging. And all readers should find that they develop a mature appreciation for both the power and the limitations of markets and of government regulation of them.

To emphasize that the analytical tools which readers will master are relevant to practical affairs, I have included abundant illustrative material throughout the book. The longer, more detailed illustrations are specially labeled as *vignettes*. The dictionary tells us that a vignette is a "short, descriptive literary sketch." I don't know how "literary" the vignettes I have included are, but they are usually written in a less ponderous style than is typical of textbooks. They appear whenever I thought it desirable to step back and address what I think are some basic but important questions readers might have (e.g., Is this analysis valid? How does it apply to the real world? How does it relate to other material I've read earlier?). I think the vignettes are long enough to provide sufficient detail to be useful, but not so long that they will cause readers to lose the thread of the main discussion.

Other Features

The text has many additional distinctive features:

- The introductory section (Part One) includes not just a discussion of the history and nature of government intervention in economic affairs and the various public-interest rationales for it, but also an entire chapter on peculiarities of the "political marketplace." What is more, important elements of public choice analysis are woven throughout succeeding chapters.
- The treatment of antitrust issues (in Part Two) balances an institutional and theoretical perspective. Readers should get enough factual or descriptive knowledge of business behavior and government policy that they know what is and is not accepted practice. But they should also master those economic models that can help us understand why consumers, business firms, or enforcement authorities do what they do and can help us predict the consequences of these actions.
- Two special chapters in Part Three (on economic regulation) provide useful case studies of key regulated industries, including provocative discussions of the impact of regulation in agricultural markets and the savings and loan industry.
- Sophisticated yet accessible chapters on social regulation (in Part Four) will enable readers to make sense of the issues that are the stuff of today's headlines, e.g., pollution control, "drug lag," hazards facing workers and consumers, and the "tort crisis."
- A final chapter summarizes and unifies the text and discusses some systematic forces that will guide the progress of regulation in the future.
- End-of-chapter summaries genuinely facilitate reader review, and end-of-chapter questions provoke thought and force readers to apply what they have learned. (Answers to the questions are provided in a separate *Instructor's Manual*.)

A Special Note to Students

Studying the interaction of enterprise and government should have a very tangible payoff: It will almost certainly make you a better manager or policymaker. In the United States, the various levels of government directly spend about

40 percent of annual national output and affect how the remainder is produced or consumed in countless ways. Clearly, then, modern managers must know a great deal about the nature and effects of government regulation, and policymakers will want to learn about the patterns of business behavior that carry the potential for social harm.

I hope, in addition, that this book will prove interesting to those who plan never to manage a firm or formulate public policy. Most often, government intervention in economic affairs signals either that market organization of productive endeavor entails some important deficiency or that there is some equally important deficiency in the political process that gave rise to the intervention. Thus, when we study the interface of enterprise and government, we confront circumstances where our most powerful institutions are, in some sense, failing us. Such study can be alternately exhilarating or deflating, but it will usually be challenging. Those who rise to the challenge will learn a great deal about ordinary human conduct and so eliminate some of the mystery about the way the world works. At the very least, this should make them happier, better-adjusted people, for in a complex, ever-changing world, ignorance definitely is *not* bliss.

I have tried to make the writing in this book as "reader-friendly" as possible. This does not mean, however, that it can or should be read at the pace of a drugstore novel. One error students commonly make in reading textbooks—especially economics texts—is that they move along too rapidly, and without appropriate stops along the way to think about what they have read. So go slowly; try to interact with the text. Ask yourself lots of questions as you read, apply the tools discussed to new situations, and evaluate whether the assertions made are consistent with your own experience. The investment of time will pay off in vastly improved comprehension.

ACKNOWLEDGMENTS

I have imposed on many friends and colleagues in the process of developing this book. I owe them all a great debt, for they have significantly improved the product and saved me from many errors of commission and omission. If some errors remain, it is entirely my own fault. Those who have reviewed or class-tested some of or all the book include: Kathleen A. Carroll, University of Maryland, Baltimore County; Christopher B. Colburn, Old Dominion University; Joseph P. Fuhr, Jr., Widener University; Rick Geddes, Fordham University; Steve H. Hanke, The Johns Hopkins University; Thomas W. Hazlett, University of California, Davis; Herbert Kessel, St. Michael's College; Benjamin Klein, University of California, Los Angeles; Mark E. McBride, Miami University of Ohio; William S. Reece, West Virginia University; Bruce Seaman, Georgia State University; William Sjostrom, Northern Illinois University; Robert J. Stonebreaker, Indiana University of Pennsylvania; Nancy Williams, Loyola College; and Peter Zaleski, Villanova University. I thank them all.

I also must acknowledge the contributions of many others who were instrumental in getting this project started and seeing it through. Becky Ryan and Bill Webber both helped convince me it was worth doing, and Nick Miggins convinced me McGraw-Hill was the best publisher for the job. Scott Stratford, Iness Snider, and Caroline Izzo have been models of efficiency and patience in guiding a rookie author through the production process. Bonnie Nauman, Mary Kontorousis, and the staff at the Milton S. Eisenhauer Library provided able assistance throughout this book's lengthy gestation period. Most of all, I would like to thank all my friends and family members, who put up with more than my usual volume of absentmindedness while I was preoccupied with this project.

Stephen J. K. Walters

ENTERPRISE, GOVERNMENT, AND THE PUBLIC

OVERVIEW: HOW AND WHY GOVERNMENT INTERVENES IN MARKETS

CHAPTER 1

WHAT GOVERNMENT DOES: REGULATORY ACTIVITIES

The penalty good men pay for indifference to public affairs is to be ruled by evil men.

Plato

If you own or manage a business in the United States, government is your not-so-silent partner. When you hire workers, the hours they can work and the wages you can pay will be affected by law. Other laws will compel you to insure them against injury and unemployment and may require you to bargain with them collectively. If you raise capital by selling stock, a government agency will control the offering. Your pricing and marketing practices will be affected by federal and state antitrust statutes. Depending on what you sell, you may be required to modify the design of your product or have it tested for safety and efficacy before you can bring it to market. The truthfulness of your advertising claims will be scrutinized. Even your product's label will be affected by government regulations. You may be required to invest in equipment that the government deems the "best available" for controlling pollution or safety hazards, or you may have to otherwise modify your production process to conform to environmental or safety guidelines. You will be required to obtain numerous licenses, and government-mandated paperwork will seem to never end. And even if you cheerfully comply with all these requirements, you may be sued if anyone comes to harm either producing or consuming your product.

By extension, government has enormous impact on the lives of workers and consumers as well. The regulatory policies of federal, state, and local governments help to shape the bargains we strike with employers, what we buy and

3

the prices we pay, and the environment we inhabit. If we wish to understand modern times, we must grapple with the complex interaction of firms, government institutions, and people.

This interaction is the central concern of this book. Of course, regulatory policy is but one part of this interaction. Government affects us also through tax policy, through the government's purchases of goods and services, through fiscal and monetary policy, and myriad other ways. Each is sufficiently important and complex to merit separate treatment; in this text, the focus is on regulation. The field is interesting as well as important. The proper role of government in a private enterprise economy such as ours has long been hotly debated. Some view the coercive powers of the government with fear and would limit its activities to a few essential areas: provision of national defense, enforcement of property rights and contracts, and care for the handicapped, dispossessed, or elderly. Others view government as an indispensable force for good, and they stand ever ready to use it to protect the populace from outcomes they deem inefficient or inequitable. While this debate is in part philosophical or ideological, it has been fueled also by economic analysis of markets and political institutions and by empirical examination of the results of various public policy experiments.

In the remainder of this chapter, we set the stage for this discussion by briefly summarizing the history of government regulation of economic behavior. Then, in succeeding sections, we describe the structure and mechanisms of regulation in the United States, and we assess whether government regulation has grown or become more intrusive in recent years.

Later chapters in Part One seek to get at the reasons for government regulation. Chapter 2 lays some foundation for this analysis by discussing how competitive markets work to allocate resources. Chapter 3 discusses possible market imperfections and their implications, giving special attention to ways in which government action might correct such imperfections. Chapter 4 puts government itself under closer scrutiny, outlining analytical tools that might help us to better understand the regulatory process and to predict what government intervention is—or is not—likely to accomplish.

HOW IT DEVELOPED: A BRIEF HISTORY OF REGULATION

The Post-Revolutionary Era

Even before a single federal regulatory agency or law existed, U.S. enterprises were regulated. Under the rules of *common law*—in which judges make laws or give to statutes their ultimate meaning—courts moved against many business practices that would subsequently be the subject of specific legislation. The courts declared agreements to fix noncompetitive prices (later the target of the Sherman Act) unenforceable. They enjoined unfair methods of competition (later the main focus of the Federal Trade Commission Act). They ruled that markets in which competition was limited "by nature"—as at docks, toll bridges, or ferries—were required to serve customers adequately and without

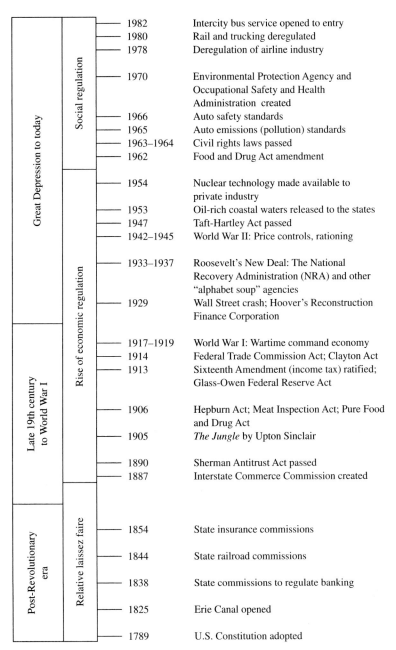

FIGURE 1.1
A TIME LINE: KEY EVENTS IN U.S. REGULATORY HISTORY. Government
intervention in economic affairs is not new, although the extent of intervention has
been greater in recent decades.

discrimination. The courts awarded damages when customers were harmed by negligent acts of business.

At the state and local levels, trade regulation was common and pervasive. Many occupations, e.g., porters and innkeepers, were licensed, and their prices were controlled by public bodies. State commissions were established to regulate the banking industry as early as 1838. State railroad commissions date from 1844 and insurance commissions from 1854. Earlier still, many states had undertaken large investment projects aimed at fostering economic development and prosperity. The Erie Canal, completed in 1825, was the brainchild of New York Governor DeWitt Clinton, who believed that linking the Hudson River with Lake Erie would fuel economic expansion all across his state. His belief proved correct, and several other states soon began building canals, roads, and rail links at a feverish pace. Many would regret it; these investments often proved to be money-losing propositions.

But the state governments have always been eager to intervene in their economies to try to stimulate growth and protect certain interests. Their behavior in this regard contributed, at least in part, to adoption of the U.S. Constitution: States' uncoordinated policies on banking and trade in the post-Revolutionary era were politically divisive and contributed to economic dislocation, if not depression. Adversity led to demands for a stronger central government, culminating in the Constitutional Convention that began in 1787.

VIGNETTE 1.1   Institutions Matter: The Confederation Period

Following the War of Independence, the former colonies were loosely tied together by the Articles of Confederation (which had been ratified in 1781). This period serves as a vivid demonstration that the *absence* of central authority and state coercive power can cause economic problems, just as excessive use of such authority and power might.

While the new nation was not nearly as weak and disorganized during the postwar period as some historians have written, the Congress of the Confederation did suffer from one glaring deficiency: It had no power to levy taxes. It could only borrow money or request it from the states. This gave rise to a major problem in the provision of an effective national defense. England still held trading posts along the southern shores of the Great Lakes and fomented Indian hostilities against pioneer settlements; Spain held Florida, the Gulf Coast, and New Orleans and similarly encouraged Indian raids and limited the export of western goods. But Congress could do little to finance an army, since each state had an incentive to turn down requests for funds in the hope it could take a "free ride" off the generosity or civic-mindedness of others. The result was that Congress was always deeply in debt, and defense was weak.

There were other problems as well. Under the Confederation, states were permitted to issue their own money and regulate trade, both internationally and with other states. Many different monetary units circulated side by side, at different exchange rates. This was inefficient; the resources that had to be devoted to keeping track of these rates and to assessing the quality of a monetary unit had more productive uses.

Rivalry between the states led to an uncoordinated trade policy. Some states sought protection for their infant manufacturing industries by levying tariffs on imports of British manufactured goods, but other states competed for this trade with low or no tariffs. This often led to retaliation, with some states imposing restrictions on goods entering from other states. New York, e.g., placed a high tariff on agricultural goods "imported" from Connecticut, New Jersey, and elsewhere. Such barriers to domestic trade inhibited development and misallocated resources.

It is uncertain how much these problems contributed to the depressed economic conditions that characterized the years from 1783 to 1787. It is clear, however, that addressing these problems would be important if the new nation was to achieve its full potential for growth and prosperity.

The Constitution, which took effect in March 1789, gave Congress the power to collect taxes, "to regulate Commerce with foreign Nations, and among the several States. . . ," and to "provide for . . . the general Welfare" of the nation. In addition, Article 1, Section 8 of the Constitution gave Congress the power to "make all Laws which shall be necessary and proper for carrying into Execution the foregoing powers." Over the years, this clause, sometimes called the *elastic clause*, has been interpreted very broadly by Congress and the courts and has enabled the federal government to expand its powers considerably as new industries grew, technology changed, and the demands of constituents evolved.

During at least the first part of the 1800s, however, federal powers to regulate remained largely unused. With the exception of two forays into central banking (the Bank of the United States operated from 1791 to 1811, and the Second Bank of the United States ran from 1816 to 1836), the federal government intervened little in the conduct of commerce. Indeed, government often proved to be more of a cheerleader for business than a regulator of it.

The Late 19th Century to World War I

By the mid-1800s, innovations in transportation technology reduced the costs of marketing output to far wider areas. This fueled industrialization and displaced many small enterprises with ones of great size—at least by the standards of the day. One result was tension and political ferment. Farmers and owners of small businesses joined forces with reformers who wrote of the dangers of growing corporate power. Eventually, the federal government altered its hands-off approach to business, although its initiatives were by no means always hostile to business interests.

The large-scale enterprises of the day and the men who ran them—decried as "robber barons" by their critics—proved enormously influential. So while Congress established the Interstate Commerce Commission (ICC) to control railroad rates in 1887, federal troops were also used to break strikes by railroad employees (e.g., in the great railroad strike of 1877 and the Pullman strike of 1894). And while the Sherman (antitrust) Act of 1890 prohibited restraint of trade and monopolization by business, enforcement of this statute was lax: Only 18 federal antitrust suits were filed before 1901.

By the turn of the century, however, farmers, workers, and reformers of various stripes became much better organized and more influential. The demands of those dubbed the "progressives" for government regulation of large corporations and consumer protection legislation began to get results. In 1903, Congress passed three bills aimed at putting more teeth into federal anti-monopoly law, and in 1906, Congress passed the Hepburn Act (which enhanced the ICC's power), the Meat Inspection Act, and the Pure Food and Drug Act. It was the beginning of the end of federal laissez faire.

In 1912, all three major Presidential candidates campaigned as progressives. During the first term of the eventual winner, Woodrow Wilson, the Sixteenth Amendment was ratified. This granted Congress the authority to levy income taxes. The growth of the federal government that would occur through much of the rest of the 20th century would have been impossible without this new power to tax. In addition, three key regulatory laws were passed. The Glass-Owen Federal Reserve Act (1913) established the Federal Reserve System to oversee the banking industry and manage monetary policy. The Federal Trade Commission (FTC) Act (1914) established the FTC to enjoin "unfair methods of competition" and "unfair or deceptive acts or practices" by business. And the Clayton Act (1914) closed some loopholes in the Sherman Act, regulating mergers, price discrimination, and several other business practices.

During World War I, federal intervention in economic affairs stepped up dramatically. Mobilization for the war effort was facilitated via creation of several federal agencies with wide discretion over the day-to-day affairs of industry. The Railroad Administration, e.g., put the railroads under complete (although temporary) federal control. The War Industries Board could allocate raw materials, tell manufacturers what goods to produce and fix their prices, and even order construction of new plants. With the armistice, however, such agencies disappeared, and the 1920s saw progressivism decline, to be replaced by a renewed government "partnership" with business.

The Great Depression to Today

Hard times invariably bring calls for government to "do something." Times were rarely harder than during the depression of the 1930s, and the federal government responded with unprecedented activism. Herbert Hoover started the ball rolling with his Reconstruction Finance Corporation (RFC), an effort to rescue the staggering finance industry, and several major public works projects. In the first term of Franklin Delano Roosevelt, federal intervention increased dramatically with the set of initiatives known as the New Deal. So many new agencies—all known by their initials—were created that people joked that Roosevelt had created an "alphabet soup" government. Many of his creations, e.g., the Securities and Exchange Commission (SEC), the Federal Deposit Insurance Corporation (FDIC), the Tennessee Valley Authority (TVA), and the Social Security Administration, remain a vital part of U.S. life today. Not all the New Deal efforts were successful—indeed, some probably exacerbated the depression—but public support for such efforts ran very high, and by the close of the 1930s it was clear that the federal government would remain deeply involved in the regulation of economic behavior.

The increased federal role was cemented during World War II. Just as in World War I, government guided the allocation of raw materials, price controls were installed, and many consumer goods were rationed. The "pitch in to win" wartime spirit meant, however, that much federal regulation was administered in a highly cooperative atmosphere; the idea was to get business to produce what was needed to win the war, not to wrap it in red tape.

When the war ended, an increased federal regulatory role remained. But business well understood, by this time, that there were benefits in regulation as well as costs. In 1947, e.g., business lobbyists helped win passage (over President Truman's veto) of the Taft-Hartley Act, which banned various "unfair" labor union practices. In 1953, oil industry lobbyists helped convince President Eisenhower to release control of oil-rich coastal waters to the states. In 1954, nuclear technology was made available—under various regulatory safeguards—to private industry.

The 1960s began a "new wave" of regulation. In previous decades, regulatory policies had focused most often on economic objectives such as lower prices, while the newer initiatives sought "social" objectives such as environmental quality, fairness or safety in the workplace, and product safety. In 1962, e.g., the Food and Drug Act was amended with stiff new requirements related to drug safety and effectiveness. Major new civil rights laws were passed in 1963 and 1964. The first automotive emissions pollution standards were imposed in 1965. Automotive safety standards were imposed in 1966.

In 1970, two major federal agencies were created: the Environmental Protection Agency (EPA) and the Occupational Safety and Health Administration (OSHA). Both would have an awesome impact on U.S. businesses. They would be joined in succeeding years by agencies charged with enhancing the safety of consumer products, regulating commodity futures trading and private pension plans, etc.

By the late 1970s, however, the rules and decisions of these agencies had become so burdensome that business lobbyists began to demand relief. They were joined by many economists, who were convinced that some regulation actually reduced the competitiveness of markets and led to unnecessarily higher costs, and by some political scientists and lawyers, who believed that regulatory agencies frequently became the captives of those they were supposed to regulate. Together, they created a "regulatory reform movement" that succeeded in rolling back regulation in several areas and, in some cases, eliminating whole agencies. In 1978, e.g., phased deregulation of the airline industry began. In 1980, the rail and trucking industries were largely deregulated. In 1982, intercity bus service was similarly opened to entry and price competition. Other agencies answerable to the President, such as EPA and OSHA, were subjected to stricter scrutiny, and they are now required to make detailed calculations of the costs and benefits of new orders before issuing them. In the view of many, such changes have made regulation more likely to achieve its stated goals and achieve them more efficiently. But these changes have also made the regulatory process more complicated. Today it is hard to follow—much less affect—this process without possessing some fairly sophisticated analytical tools.

VIGNETTE 1.2 Ideas Have Consequences: From Upton Sinclair to Rachel Carson

Policy-making frequently involves political calculation. Officeholders often listen to the entreaties of special interest groups, watch opinion polls, or "vote the mail." But ideas and information matter, too.

Consider, e.g., Upton Sinclair's novel *The Jungle*, written in 1905. Sinclair, a socialist, sought to reform capitalism by vividly portraying its failures, as in this description of the horrifying conditions of Chicago's meat packing industry:

There was never the least attention paid to what was cut up for sausage; there would come all the way from Europe old sausage . . . that was moldy and white—it would be dosed with borax and glycerine, and dumped into the hoppers, and made over again for home consumption . . . There would be meat stored in great piles in rooms . . . and thousands of rats would race about on it . . . These rats were nuisances, and the packers would put poisoned bread out for them, they would die, and then rats, bread, and meat would go into the hoppers together. This is no fairy story and no joke . . . there were things that went into the sausage in comparison with which a poisoned rat was a tidbit . . . All of the sausage came out of the same bowl, but when they came to wrap it they would stamp some of it "special," and for this they would charge two cents more a pound.[1]

President Teddy Roosevelt, an avid reader, reacted quickly to this account. He dispatched two agents to Chicago, who confirmed much of what Sinclair had said. The Meat Inspection Act, requiring federal inspection of all meats destined for interstate commerce and empowering the Department of Agriculture to impose sanitation standards, was passed soon afterward.

In a later era, Rachel Carson warned of the ecological effects of pesticides as they worked their way into the human food chain:

[C]hemicals sprayed on croplands or forests or gardens lie long in soil, entering into living organisms, passing from one to another in a chain of poisoning and death. Or they pass mysteriously by underground streams until they emerge and, through the alchemy of air and sunlight, combine into new forms that kill vegetation, sicken cattle, and work unknown harm on those who drink from once pure wells. As Albert Schweitzer has said, "Man can hardly even recognize the devils of his own creation."[2]

Critics charged that Carson overstated the dangers of insecticides such as DDT, but within a few months of publication of *Silent Spring* there were more than 40 bills in state legislatures to regulate pesticide use . Use of DDT was banned by the federal EPA by 1973.

THE NATURE AND MECHANISMS OF REGULATION

Types of Regulation

Government regulation of economic activity is typically divided into three classifications: *antitrust policy*, aimed at preserving competitive vigor in the economy as a whole; *economic regulation*, concerned with pricing and output decisions in specific industries such as railroads, gas and electric companies, or other "public utilities"; and *social regulation*, aimed at securing various

---

[1]Upton Sinclair, *The Jungle*, Robert Bentley, Inc., Cambridge, MA, 1971, pp. 135–136.
[2]Rachel Carson, *Silent Spring*, Houghton Mifflin, Boston, 1962, p. 6.

social goods such as a cleaner environment and safer products and workplaces.

Antitrust policy applies broadly to all industries, although a few have obtained partial exemptions from its strictures. At its core, antitrust is consumer protection policy. It seeks to rescue consumers (and society) from the consequences of anticompetitive or monopolistic behavior: restricted output, prices above costs, and a misallocation of resources. The application or threat of antitrust enforcement can alter the number of firms in a market, affect their pricing and output decisions, alter conditions of market entry or exit, and affect marketing practices.

Economic regulation has often been inspired by the belief—occasionally unfounded—that some markets are inherently noncompetitive, i.e., that having many firms in a particular market would be impossible or undesirable. Having many natural gas companies compete for business in a particular neighborhood, e.g., would involve colossal duplication of investment in pipes. But tolerating a single gas supplier poses the specter of monopolistic pricing. Application of antitrust policy is clearly no answer here; economic regulation is advanced as an alternative. Typically, such regulation involves government licensing of a limited number of (private) sellers in exchange for the sellers' submission to strict price regulation by a (public) commission or an authority. Frequently, such regulation is extended to other dimensions of the product, such as service quality, or even to the sellers' decisions about how to produce the product.

Social regulation is not directly concerned with the pricing or output decisions of firms or industries (although, of course, it can certainly affect these things) but with controlling what are seen as undesirable consequences of firm behavior. While economic regulation typically has a massive effect on the firms within one particular industry, social regulation applies to many firms scattered across the whole economy. Social regulation has broad power to alter firm behavior, from hiring practices to production decisions to marketing strategies. Much social regulation is based on the belief that even where competitive pricing prevails, some market outcomes will require correction. Even competitive firms, e.g., may pollute excessively or expose their workers or customers to unnecessary risks.

Administrative Structure of Regulation

The U.S. Constitution provides for three branches of government. In principle, the legislative branch makes laws, the executive branch administers and enforces them, and the judiciary interprets laws and gives them meaning. But these generalizations obscure the awesome complexity of the interaction among the branches of government. Each branch affects the behavior of the others, and in many cases areas of responsibility overlap or conflict. Judges frequently make law as well as interpret it. At the federal level, judges are appointed by the chief executive, but must be confirmed by legislative vote. Executive agencies are often run by individuals who must be similarly confirmed, and legislative committees can inquire quite forcefully into the performance of these individuals once confirmed. Many acts of Congress originate in the actions of—or in response to actions of—other branches of government. But this apparent confusion of roles is by design—part of the system of checks and balances that limit the coercive power of each branch. All three branches are heavily involved in the business of regulation.

As an illustration of the overlapping responsibilities of these branches, consider the administration of antitrust policy. The various federal antitrust laws are enforced in three ways: by suits initiated by the Justice Department's Antitrust Division, by suits brought by the Federal Trade Commission, and by private suits brought by parties alleging they have been harmed by anticompetitive business conduct. The Antitrust Division is an executive branch agency, under the direct control of the President. The FTC is an example of an *independent regulatory commission* (IRC), an entity created as an arm of Congress. Both bodies and the private parties who bring their own antitrust suits (represented by approximately 10,000 private attorneys comprising the "antitrust bar") clearly depend on the judiciary to translate antitrust goals into results.

Administration of economic and social regulation is similarly complex. Most such regulation originates with a congressional statute, but the language of such statutes is often quite vague, and it is up to the various federal regulatory agencies (and the courts) to give these statutes practical meaning.

The agencies can be of several types. Most visible are the aforementioned IRCs, commissions whose members are nominated by the President and confirmed by the Senate. Decisions of IRCs are not subject to approval by the President, nor can the President remove a commissioner except for "inefficiency, neglect of duty or malfeasance in office." Less independent are *executive branch agencies*, generally located within the major departments (e.g., Department of Labor, Commerce, or Agriculture) and headed by individuals appointed by, and directly responsible to, the President. (One executive branch agency, the EPA, is not located within a department because its activities are so far-ranging; one commission, the Federal Energy Regulatory Commission, is within the Department of Energy.) Finally, there are various quasi-independent specialized agencies (e.g., the Federal Reserve System) created by Congress to serve specific purposes.

Table 1.1 lists the major agencies involved with economic and social regulation at the federal level. The list is by no means exhaustive; there are many smaller agencies, or portions of agencies, that have regulatory roles to play.

The rules and regulations issued by the various federal agencies—even the IRCs—are subject to judicial review. Generally, the courts feel they owe deference to the findings of these agencies, which are presumed expert in their areas of responsibility. Courts can, however, set aside agency rulings that they find to be unconstitutional, "arbitrary or capricious," outside the bounds of agency authority, unsupported by substantial evidence or unwarranted by the facts, or which were reached without due observance of the procedures required by law. In practice, then, individuals or groups who disagree with an

TABLE 1.1
PARTIAL LIST OF FEDERAL REGULATORY AGENCIES BY AREA OF RESPONSIBILITY

Economic regulation	Social regulation
Transportation	Environment
Interstate Commerce Commission	Environmental Protection Agency
Federal Maritime Commission	National Oceanic and Atmospheric
Federal Aviation Administration	Administration
Federal Highway Administration	Nuclear Regulatory Commission
Urban Mass Transportation	U.S. Fish and Wildlife Service
Administration	U.S. Forest Service
Federal Railroad Administration	Bureau of Land Management
Communications	Workplace safety
Federal Communications Commission	Occupational Safety and Health
U.S. Postal Service	Administration
Postal Rate Commission	Occupational Safety and Health Review
Office of Telecommunications Policy	Commission
	Mining Enforcement and Safety
Banking and finance	Administration
Federal Reserve System	
Comptroller of the Currency	Civil rights and labor relations
Federal Deposit Insurance Corporation	Equal Employment Opportunity Commission
Federal Home Loan Bank Board	Commission on Civil Rights
Securities and Exchange Commission	Civil Rights Division (Department of Justice)
Commodity Futures Trading	Office of Civil Rights Compliance
Commission	National Labor Relations Board
	National Mediation Board
International trade	Employment Standards Administration
International Trade Commission	
U.S. Customs Service	Product safety
	Consumer Product Safety Commission
Energy	Federal Trade Commission
Federal Power Commission	Federal Aviation Administration
Tennessee Valley Authority	Food and Drug Administration
Nuclear Regulatory Commission	Food Safety and Quality Service
Federal Energy Administration	National Highway Traffic Safety
	Administration

agency's actions will often litigate the matter, alleging the agency has violated one or another of the above criteria.

The power and independence of regulatory agencies are also limited by the budget process. Agencies require funds to operate, and Presidential and congressional review of budget appropriations can exert powerful influence over agencies' actions. Programs or policies which are politically unpopular can sometimes be derailed by having their funding cut; programs which are politically popular but of dubious effectiveness will often live on. It would be naive to assume that regulators always ignore political realities when they make policy decisions.

VIGNETTE 1.3   The Power of the Purse: Congress and the FTC

Regulators' vulnerability to political considerations was made abundantly clear in the late 1970s and 1980, when a feud between Congress and the Federal Trade Commission came to a head.

The FTC, guided by activist chairman Michael Pertschuk, had begun several consumer protection programs that won applause from some consumer groups but angered those businesses targeted for stricter regulation. The businesses, working through their Washington lobbying organizations, pressured Congress to intercede.

When the FTC ignored congressional hints to ease up, Congress rolled out the heavy artillery: the power of the purse. In 1977, the House of Representatives refused to authorize the agency's funding for the normal three-year period unless "legislative veto power" over agency regulations was included in the funding bill. But the Senate refused to go along, so a temporary one-year budget compromise was worked out that kept the FTC alive. Similar one-year spending bills were passed in successive years, dispiriting the agency and limiting its ability to formulate long-term plans. As Pertschuk said in 1980, "Our morale is awful. We are damaged, no question about it."[3]

In 1980, congressional debate centered on FTC plans to regulate the business practices of funeral directors. The undertakers waged a massive lobbying effort, complaining that the FTC rules would cost them $50 million per year and cripple their industry. Not surprisingly, many in Congress took their side. After all, small businesses are major campaign contributors, and when such constituents complain, they usually get an attentive hearing.

Once again, Congress held hostage the agency's budget. For a time, it looked as if the FTC might actually die. In fact, it closed its doors for a day in May 1980, when Congress refused to authorize even temporary operating funds.

Eventually, however, a compromise was worked out. The FTC was allowed to live, but not in the style to which it had grown accustomed. Congress imposed a two-house veto of FTC rules and got the agency to drop or delay several of its more controversial proposals. The lesson was clear: In the words of one Washington lobbyist, "Agency people have learned that if they go [too far], they'll be slammed."[4]

Also note that state and local governments often have their own miniature versions of federal agencies. Many states, e.g., have their own environmental protection and occupational safety agencies and often impose requirements that are more stringent than those required by federal law. States' attorneys general also have discretion to move against business practices either that have escaped the notice of federal antitrust authorities or that federal authorities do not consider a violation of federal antitrust law. In other words, to ensure they are in compliance with all relevant regulatory policies, firms must keep their eyes on not only Washington but also the capitals of the states in which they conduct business.

---

[3]"The Assault on the FTC," *Consumer Reports*, 45 (March 1980), p. 152.

[4]Michael Thoryn, "Chastened by Congress, the FTC Carries on—Cautiously," *Nation's Business*, 68 (August 1980), p. 53.

Tools of Regulation

The methods that regulatory agencies use to accomplish their goals vary widely. In some cases, government agencies rely on little more than "jawboning" (i.e., verbal suggestions, appeals, requests, or threats) to attempt to alter private sector behavior. In others, government agencies will displace private sector firms entirely, forming publicly owned enterprises to serve specific markets (e.g., the Tennessee Valley Authority). Between these extremes are price or rate-of-return regulation, taxes and subsidies, licensing, and standards or specifications.

Jawboning The most often cited example of successful jawboning is President John F. Kennedy's treatment of the steel industry in 1962. The economy was in a mild recession, yet the major steel firms announced significant price increases. It is possible that this was the result of some sort of (tacit) collusion among the firms and might have provoked an antitrust investigation. But that would have taken considerable time. Instead President Kennedy publicly criticized the firms, harming their public image, and threatened to cancel defense-related steel orders. Very quickly, the industry rescinded the price increases; without any formal regulatory initiative, the federal government had enhanced consumer welfare.

Public Enterprises As noted earlier, some markets are optimally served by one or a few firms rather than by many purely competitive firms; in such markets, public regulation of the prices of private firms is common. In some cases, however, the firm or firms will be publicly owned and managed as well. Public enterprises are less common in the United States than in many other countries, but even here they are the norm in many industries, e.g., education, municipal transit, utilities (water, sewage, power), and law enforcement. The reasons for public ownership (as opposed to mere regulation of private firms) are many; they include absence of a viable regulatory mechanism, distrust of private firms or regulators, inability to attract private investors to a market, and bankruptcy of existing private firms.

Price Regulation Where private firms are willing or able to serve a market but competition is thought not feasible or desirable, public regulation of prices or rates of return is common. At the federal level, transportation industries are often subjected to such regulation. At the state and local levels, public authorities frequently regulate prices or profit rates in energy, communications, health care, and insurance markets.

Taxes and Subsidies On occasion, policymakers would like to alter the rate of output in a particular market. Economists have long advised, "If you want a little more of something, subsidize it; if you want a little less, tax it." This strategy has been implemented countless times. At the federal level, subsidies for agricultural products are common; taxes (or tax breaks) affect many other industries, including mining, transportation, and communications. At the state and local levels, taxes and subsidies alter the production and consumption of goods ranging from gasoline to cigarettes to housing. At the margin, tax and subsidy policy can even affect the "output" of people, via tax deductions or cash subsidies for dependent children. And economists have lately devised tax and subsidy programs aimed at altering the output of pollution, via "effluent charges" and tax credits for investment in pollution control equipment.

Licensing Many transactions pose risks for consumers; in an attempt to control such risks, government will sometimes require sellers to be licensed (or, alternatively, certified or registered) by some public or private body. Lawyers, doctors, private detectives, and vendors, e.g., are commonly licensed by state or local authorities. Possession of a license may mean that the holder has passed an examination or other test of professional ability (e.g., a bar exam), or it may just mean that the holder has visited the local licensing agency and paid a nominal fee in exchange for a piece of paper. In other words, licensing may do much or little to truly ensure that consumers are not cheated or otherwise harmed by a seller. Where licenses are difficult or costly to acquire, and where they may be revoked if the holder provides substandard service, they may serve to enhance service quality. They may also, however, serve as a barrier to entry that limits market competition, raises prices, and reduces consumer choice.

Standards One of the most common ways in which a regulatory agency affects the behavior of firms is through formal standards or mandates about how, or how much, a particular activity may be done. Less stringent are *performance standards,* which prescribe some level of attainment for a particular aspect of a product without specifying how it is to be achieved. For example, in 1975 Congress sought to conserve energy by establishing minimum fuel economy standards for all new cars sold in the United States (starting in 1978). Automakers were told how many miles per gallon their fleet of cars should achieve by certain dates, but were on their own as to how these figures should be attained. More intrusive are *specification standards,* which prescribe also the means by which a particular goal is to be achieved. OSHA, e.g., will not only tell employers that accident rates must be reduced, but also mandate the specific equipment or safety devices to be used in pursuit of this goal.

THE GROWTH OF GOVERNMENT

The Size of Government

Clearly, regulation has always been a significant part of U.S. life. Nevertheless, it is commonly alleged that government today is bigger, and its regulations more intrusive, than ever. There are some data to support such a claim.

Figure 1.2 shows total government (i.e., federal, state, and local) spending as a percentage of the gross national product (GNP) and total government

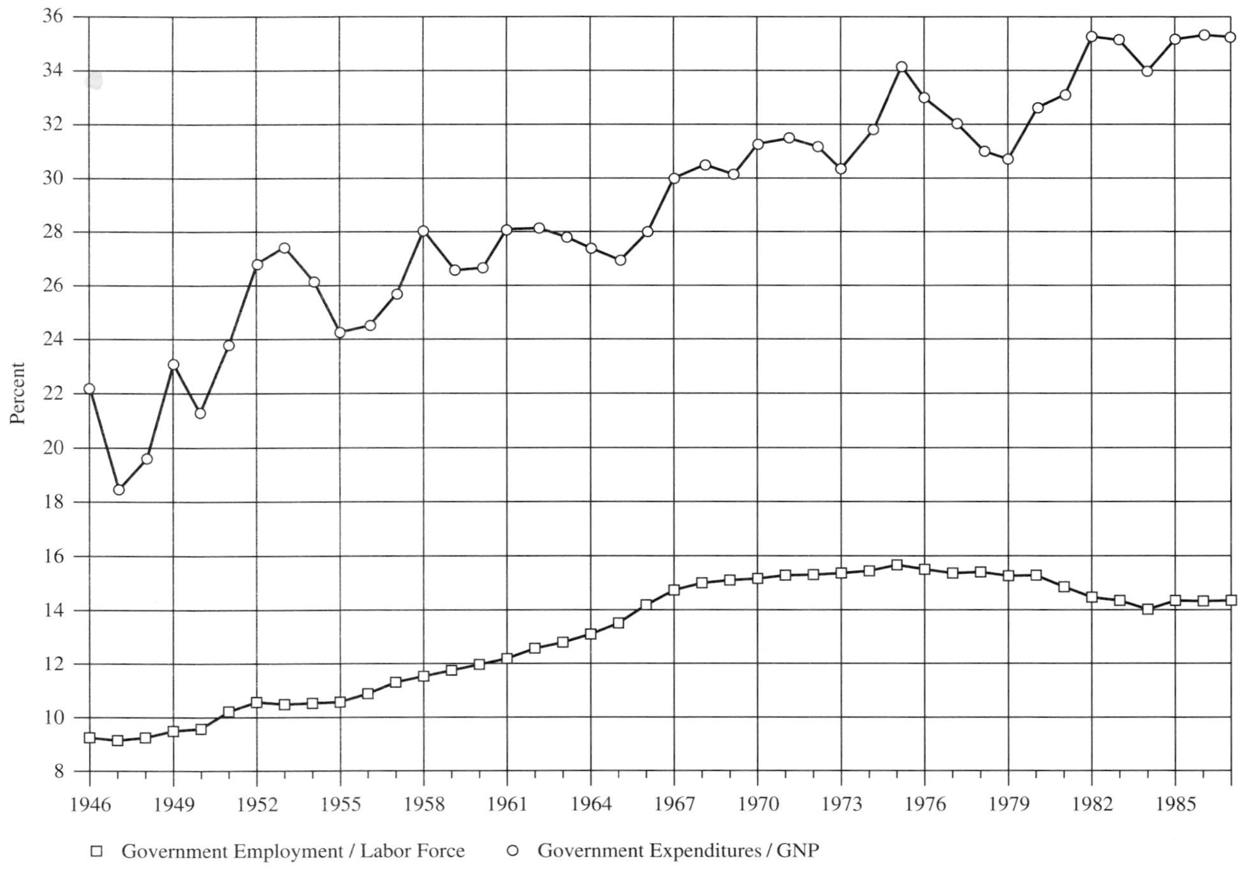

FIGURE 1.2
TRENDS IN TOTAL
GOVERNMENT SPENDING
AND STAFFING. Total
federal, state, and local
spending now claims a much
larger share of the GNP than
at the close of World War II.
Government employment also
rose in the postwar period,
although there have been
some declines since the
mid-1970s.

□ Government Employment / Labor Force   ○ Government Expenditures / GNP employment as a percentage of the total labor force for the era following World War II. The fraction of GNP spent by government has, with minor fluctuations, tracked steadily upward through this period. Currently, government spends about 35 percent of the GNP—almost double the figure for 1947. Government employment, while a much higher fraction of the labor force today than in the 1940s and 1950s, is actually below its peak of 15.7 percent of the labor force in 1975.

What of the vaunted "regulatory reform movement" of the late 1970s and 1980s? Data on federal regulatory spending and staffing show that this movement had a limited effect. Figure 1.3 shows that spending and staffing levels of various federal regulatory agencies fell somewhat during the early 1980s, but the spending cuts, at least, had been more than replaced by the end of the decade. By 1991 federal regulatory expenditures were at an all-time high, in both nominal and real (inflation-adjusted) terms. Total regulatory staffing in 1991 stood at 113,300, about 5 percent below the peak of 118,800 reached in 1980.[5]

What accounts for such growth? In part, the growth reflects the fact that we are a wealthier society. The kinds of goods that regulation can provide—environmental quality, safety, fairness—are things we demand less or think we can do without when we are less prosperous. At higher income levels, we are both able and willing to buy more of these goods, and government has been responsive to our demands.

The Impact of Government

Of course, the number of laws or regulations put in force, the number of government employees charged with implementing or enforcing them, and the budgets of regulatory agencies don't really tell us how much government affects us. But meaningful measures of the impact of government on our day-to-day lives are surprisingly scarce.

There have been several studies of the costs of *complying* with federal regulations, although by now the estimates obtained in these studies are quite dated. The most authoritative of these was conducted by Murray Weidenbaum, chairman of the Council of Economic Advisors under President Nixon. Weidenbaum calculated that administering and complying with the federal regulations in force from 1977 to 1979 cost from 3.9 to 4.3 percent of the GNP.[6] If we still spend about 4 percent of the GNP in this way, regulation costs each woman, man, and child in the United States almost $1,000 per year.

To date, no follow-up studies have been conducted to assess whether the regulatory reform movement of the early 1980s significantly affected the costs of complying with all federal regulations. Data on direct spending to comply

[5]Melinda Warren and Kenneth Chilton, "Regulation's Rebound: Bush Budget Gives Regulation a Boost," Center for the Study of American Business, Washington University of St. Louis, Occasional Paper No. 81 (May 1990).

[6]Murray L. Weidenbaum, *The Future of Business Regulation: Private Action and Public Demand*, AMACOM, New York, 1979.

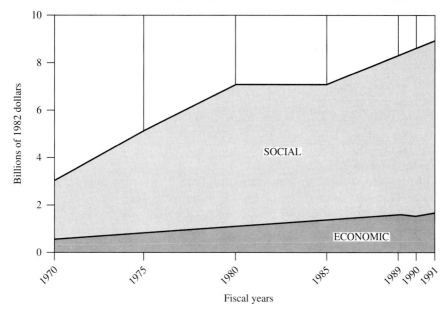

(a) Trends in regulatory spending

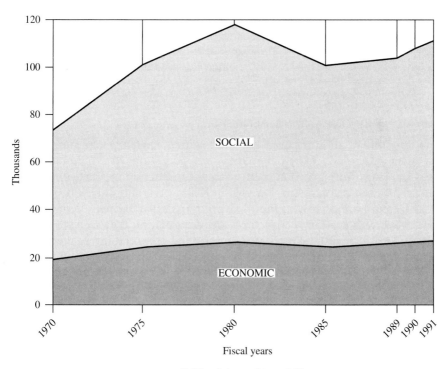

(b) Trends in regulatory staffing

FIGURE 1.3
RECENT TRENDS IN FEDERAL REGULATORY SPENDING AND STAFFING. Recent evidence suggests that declines in regulatory spending and staffing during the Reagan years may have been a temporary pause in an upward trend.
Source: Center for the Study of American Business, Washington University. Derived from the budget of the U.S. government, various fiscal years.

19

with environmental regulations alone have been tabulated by the Environmental Protection Agency, however. These data (reproduced as Figure 1.4) show that real expenditures for pollution abatement and control totaled $115 billion in 1990, about 2.1 percent of the GNP.[7] Such expenditures did, in fact, grow more slowly from 1980 to 1988—what may be termed the heyday of deregulation—but grew nonetheless, and are forecast to rise steadily in the foreseeable future.

Other recent studies have documented that the indirect impacts of regulation are nontrivial as well. Regulatory requirements force some firms to divert resources from production of tangible output to making production safer or cleaner or to satisfying regulators in other ways. Some researchers have calculated, therefore, that regulation has contributed to a slowdown in productivity growth; others have blamed it for reductions in the rate of technological innovation.[8]

That regulation is expensive or that it may have important indirect effects does not mean, however, that it is "not worth it." In principle, we regulate with full knowledge that it carries a price—often a steep one. But regulation can confer important benefits. As we will see, reasonable people may feel differently about the net effects of various regulatory efforts: some will brand them extravagant and wasteful, while others will see them as ridiculously stingy and inadequate to the problems at hand. To measure performance in this area requires some fairly sophisticated tools, which we will begin to build in the next chapter.

SUMMARY AND CONCLUDING REMARKS

Government regulation is pervasive. Almost every action that a modern business takes will be affected by regulatory considerations. Yet regulation is not new. Licensing and regulation of businesses by states and localities were common even in the colonial era. Growth in federal regulation began during the late 19th century and took off rapidly during the great depression of the 1930s. The 1960s brought a "new wave" of social regulation that was slowed a bit from 1979 to 1982 with the regulatory reform (or deregulation) movement.

The regulatory activity that will concern us in this book is of three types: antitrust policy, economic regulation, and social regulation. Antitrust is aimed at securing for consumers the benefits of competition: lower prices, greater output, and enhanced range of choice. Economic regulation usually involves the pricing and output decisions of a particular firm or industry in markets where competition is deemed undesirable or impossible by virtue of the markets' unique characteristics. Social regulation aims at controlling undesirable

---

[7]Alan Carlin, *Environmental Investments: The Cost of a Clean Environment, A Summary*, EPA-230-12-90-084, U.S. Government Printing Office, Washington, December 1990, pp. 2-2, 2-3.

[8]See, e.g., Wayne B. Gray, "The Cost of Regulation: OSHA, EPA and the Productivity Slowdown," *American Economic Review*, 77 (December 1987), pp. 998–1006; Henry G. Grabowski, *Drug Regulation and Innovation*, American Enterprise Institute, Washington, 1976.

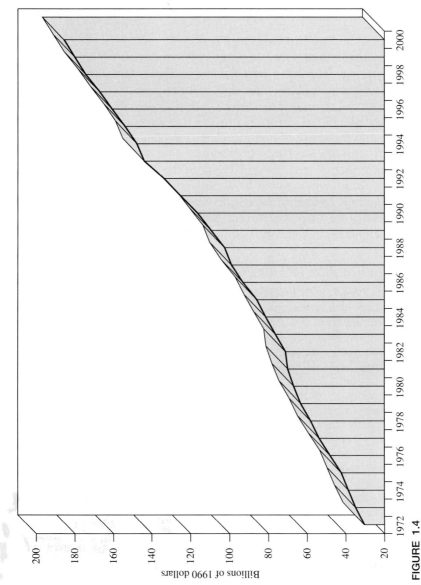

FIGURE 1.4
TOTAL ANNUAL COSTS OF U.S. POLLUTION CONTROL, 1972–2000. The costs of pollution control rose from about $30 billion (0.9 percent of GNP) in 1972 to $115 billion (2.1 percent of GNP) by 1990, and they should continue to climb into the next century.
Source: Calculated from data in *Alan Carlin, Environmental Investments: The Cost of a Clean Environment, A Summary,* Environmental Protection Agency, Washington, December 1990, pp. 2-2, 2-3.

aspects of market organization that are unrelated to competition (or its absence).

Regulations are implemented via a complex interaction of the legislative, executive, and judicial branches of government. Antitrust policy is enforced by two different agencies (one located in the executive branch, the other an arm of Congress) and by private lawsuits; all rely on the courts to carry out this policy. Economic and social regulation is conducted by a multitude of agencies of varying degrees of independence. These agencies use informal persuasion (jawboning), public ownership, price regulation, taxes or subsidies, licensing, and formal standards to achieve their policy goals.

Although the number of government rules that affect economic behavior is accumulating and the share of national output expended by government has grown steadily through the 1980s, government now employs a smaller share of the labor force than during the mid-1970s. In the late 1970s, about 4 percent of the national output was devoted to administering and complying with government regulations. Assessing the effectiveness and worthiness of such regulatory efforts must be based on careful consideration of both the direct and indirect costs and benefits thereof.

QUESTIONS FOR REVIEW AND DISCUSSION

1.1 Among the Constitution's founding fathers, Alexander Hamilton was one of the chief advocates of a strong federal government, one which would have ample power to regulate trade and industry. Writing in his 1791 *Report on Manufactures*, Hamilton argued forcefully for regulations requiring government inspection of manufactured goods, stating that inspection would "prevent frauds upon consumers at home [and in] foreign countries . . . [and] guard against successful competition from other quarters." In the *absence* of government inspection of goods, how are consumers protected against fraud by sellers? What do you think Hamilton meant when he said inspection would "guard against successful competition" from other countries?

1.2 The Articles of Confederation allowed the states to erect barriers to trade with other nations or other *states*. Explain exactly how such barriers could inhibit economic growth and misallocate resources in the new nation. Why would one state wish to prohibit "imports" from a neighboring one?

1.3 The late 19th century is sometimes called the *era of monopoly capital* because lower transport costs enabled relatively large enterprises to sell their output in new markets and displace smaller firms. For example, large iron and steel companies grew up and displaced many town blacksmiths. Is it necessarily the case that the displacement of many small businesses by a handful of large ones will diminish competition or harm consumers? Explain.

1.4 How do economic regulation and social regulation differ? Give an example of each. Recall that the income elasticity of demand measures the responsiveness of demand to changes in income; it is defined as the proportional change in the quantity purchased divided by the proportional change in income. Growth in social regulation has been especially rapid since the 1950s, a period when per capita incomes also reached fairly high levels. What can you infer about the value of the income elasticity of demand for social legislation?

1.5 The text observes that, through the budget process, the decisions of regulatory agencies are often affected by political considerations. Is this bad or good? Should regulatory policy be "democratic," or should it be framed entirely by independent (and disinterested) experts in the field?

CHAPTER 2

WHAT MARKETS DO:
COMPETITION AND
EFFICIENCY

I am not hungry; but thank goodness, I am greedy.

Punch

Although the reach of government in the U.S. economy is wide, its grasp is far more limited. Here and in other "mixed" economies where markets are regulated—but not displaced—by government, the great majority of economic decisions about *what, how,* and *for whom* to produce are made privately by individual consumers, managers and employees of firms, and owners of resources. These individuals gather information about their alternatives, make choices, and transact with each other in ongoing efforts to cope with the fundamental economic fact of scarcity.

As we saw in Chapter 1, government often guides or regulates these efforts. Government often acts as a consumer, manager, employer, or resource owner as well. But this should not obscure the primary role of markets in drawing together resources (people and their ideas, land, machines, etc.) and organizing them productively.

As you read this, you consume an incredible array of resources, from the paper and ink in this book to the steel, wood, or stone in your building to the coal or oil that provides you with electric lighting, heat, or air conditioning. And (not least!) you consume the labor and ingenuity of a huge number of people who helped form these resources into economic goods. All these goods may have been affected in some way by government. The price of the electricity that lights the room in which you read this page is regulated; the building in which you sit has been shaped in part by construction codes and zoning laws; the texture and durability of the paper on which this paragraph is printed have been affected by environmental regulations.

But the basic form of all these goods—and, indeed, their existence—owes more to markets than to government. Individuals, acting in what they perceived as their self-interest, decided to produce these goods and transacted with others in doing so. They acted voluntarily. No edict forced them to act; no authority told them exactly what to do or how to do it. Government may have told them how *not* to do it. Perhaps more important, government may have provided conditions that facilitated their productive endeavor. In a mixed economy, however, such endeavor typically arises from the initiatives of individuals transacting in markets.

Accordingly, our first task will be to develop a practical understanding of market activity. We begin with a description of economists' models of "purely" or "perfectly" competitive markets, a conception so idealized that it may have no counterpart in the real world. We then discuss more realistic models of workable competition and "contestable" markets. Throughout, we examine how competition affects social welfare and how prices and profits guide resource allocation.

"PERFECT" COMPETITION

To begin to understand something as complex as market activity, economists use highly simplified (some critics might say simplistic) models. Like engineers who build small prototypes of their creations to see how the real thing might work, economists try to approximate the workings of real markets with boiled-down diagrammatic or mathematical representations. Sometimes, of course, these models produce rather unreliable forecasts of what will happen in real life—and then we go back to the drawing board. But even in this event, a clear and comprehensible model is often a useful starting point for developing a good understanding of what will work later.

The Nature of Production Costs

Before we lay out the model of perfect competition, it is useful to review some of the generalizations that economists make about the way in which firms' costs of production typically behave. Note first that economists speak of cost conditions that apply in either the *short run* or the *long run*. Unfortunately, there is no simple mark on a calendar, say, a month or year from today, that divides the short and long runs. The distinction is based on the extent to which it is possible (or, more precisely, economically feasible) to vary the inputs used in the production process. We say we are "in the short run" if it is impossible (i.e., too expensive) to vary at least some key inputs. In the long run, by contrast, a firm has sufficient flexibility to vary all its inputs.

For example, an importer-exporter may lease a warehouse where merchandise is stored prior to shipment. As a result of fluctuating prices in some markets, the importer-exporter may wish to sell more (or less) output from time to time. In the short run, however, the size of the warehouse cannot be varied. Changes in sales volume can be achieved only by varying certain other inputs, e.g., hiring some new workers to boost output or laying off some workers if volume falls below normal levels. But the warehouse is a *fixed input*, and its rent is a *fixed cost* (i.e., this component of cost does not change with the quantity sold). Even if business is so bad that the firm temporarily shuts down, it still must pay this rent until the lease expires (or the firm finds someone who wishes to sublet the facility). In the long run, though, there are no fixed inputs or costs. In the long run, the importer-exporter can move to a larger (or smaller) warehouse or modify the production process in any way imaginable.

Short-Run Cost Curves   Panel *a* of Figure 2.1, which is based on data displayed in Table 2.1, shows how output Q and the total cost of production TC

TABLE 2.1
PRODUCTION COSTS FOR A HYPOTHETICAL FIRM.   The table shows how a hypothetical firm's total and unit costs change as output increases from 0 to 20 units per day.

(1)	(2)	(3)	(4)	(5)	(6)	(7)	(8)
Q/ day	Total fixed cost	Total variable cost	Total cost $=(2)+(3)$	Average fixed cost $=(2)/(1)$	Average variable cost $=(3)/(1)$	Average total cost $=(4)/(1)$	Marginal cost $=(\Delta 4)\div(\Delta 1)$
0	$100	$0	$100				
1	100	20	120	$100.00	$20.00	$120.00	$20
2	100	30	130	50.00	15.00	65.00	10
3	100	42	142	33.33	14.00	47.33	12
4	100	54	154	25.00	13.50	38.50	14
5	100	70	170	20.00	14.00	34.00	16
6	100	88	188	16.67	14.67	31.33	18
7	100	108	208	14.29	15.43	29.71	20
8	100	130	230	12.50	16.25	28.75	22
9	100	154	254	11.11	17.11	28.22	24
10	100	180	280	10.00	18.00	28.00	26
11	100	208	308	9.09	18.91	28.00	28
12	100	238	338	8.33	19.83	28.17	30
13	100	270	370	7.69	20.77	28.46	32
14	100	304	404	7.14	21.71	28.86	34
15	100	340	440	6.67	22.67	29.33	36
16	100	378	478	6.25	23.63	29.88	38
17	100	418	518	5.88	24.59	30.47	40
18	100	460	560	5.56	25.56	31.11	42
19	100	504	604	5.26	26.53	31.79	44
20	100	550	650	5.00	27.50	32.50	46

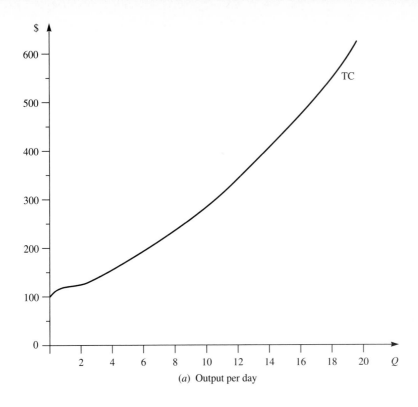

(a) Output per day

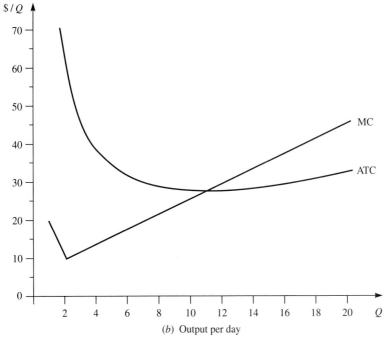

(b) Output per day

FIGURE 2.1
SHORT-RUN COST CURVES. *(a)* Our hypothetical firm's total cost (TC) as output rises from 0 to 20 units per day. *(b)* The firm's marginal cost (MC) and average total cost (ATC).

are typically related, at least in the short run. Total cost is positive even where output is zero because there are some fixed inputs and costs. Then as output rises, so does the total cost—but not by a constant amount. In this hypothetical firm, increasing output from 1 to 2 units (per day) raises the total cost only $10 (from $120 to $130), while increasing the output from 19 to 20 units raises the total cost $46 (from $604 to $650).

In general, except for the first few units of output produced (in this illustration, just the first 2 units), we expect the total cost to increase *by an increasing amount* as we raise the output. Why? Because, in the short run, the presence of some fixed inputs will constrain the productivity of the remaining variable inputs. Imagine a 100-acre farm (i.e., land is a fixed input). The farmer can get more output from these 100 acres by applying more fertilizer or water, spending more time weeding, etc. After the first few applications of fertilizer, however, additional applications will raise crop output by successively smaller and smaller amounts. (Otherwise, these 100 acres could feed the world if enough fertilizer were applied to them!) In other words, in the presence of a fixed input, additional units of a variable input will raise output only at a decreasing rate. This phenomenon is so widely observed that economists regard it as a basic law of production—the *law of diminishing returns*. In panel *a* of Figure 2.1, we are in the realm of diminishing returns from the second unit of output onward: Each extra unit of output beyond the second gets more and more expensive to produce (i.e., requires the use of greater and greater amounts of the variable input), raising TC at an increasing rate.

Panel *b* of Figure 2.1 shows two important short-run cost curves that, given information about the total cost, are easy to plot. (Again, the data underlying these curves are from Table 2.1.) We see that *marginal cost* (MC), defined as the change in total cost resulting from the production of 1 more unit of output, falls from $20 for the first unit produced to $10 for the second unit and rises afterward. Again, this just illustrates the law of diminishing returns. The *average total cost* (ATC), defined as the total cost divided by the output, falls until it reaches a minimum at a rate of output between 10 and 11 units (per day) and rises afterward. Most textbook representations of short-run unit-cost curves, including the ones that come later in this chapter, are simply stylized versions of the curves in panel *b*: MC curves that, beyond the first couple of units of output, rise smoothly and continuously and ATC curves that are U-shaped. Of course, not *all* firms will have short-run unit cost curves like these. Surprisingly many will, however.

Long-Run Cost Curves   In the long run, as we have noted, firms can combine inputs in any way they choose. They can build plants, warehouses, or other facilities of any size; adopt any existing technology; etc. After they have made their choices, effectively "fixing" certain inputs for some period, firms will likely confront short-run cost curves like those discussed above. *This means that firms' long-run cost curves can be represented as portions of the set of short-run cost curves from which the firm must select.*

Suppose, as a simple example, that a manufacturer faces only three choices

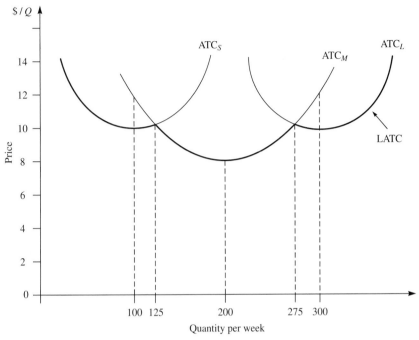

FIGURE 2.2
A SET OF SHORT-RUN ATC CURVES AND THE ASSOCIATED LONG-RUN ATC
CURVE. The selection of the appropriate plant—and accompanying short-run ATC curve—
will hinge on expected sales volume. The long-run ATC curve will be the lowest portions of
the various short-run ATC curves from which a firm may choose.

about the size of plant to build: small, medium, or large. Figure 2.2 shows the
short-run ATC curves for each: ATC_S applies to the small plant, ATC_M to the
medium one, and ATC_L to the large plant. Which plant the manufacturer will
choose depends on the normal level of sales expected. The medium plant will
be most economical if the expected sales volume is between 125 and 275 units
per week. But if the expected sales volume is 100 units per week, it would be
best to build the small plant: Then the average cost per unit would be $10 for
the small plant versus $12 for the medium one. Similarly, if the sales volume is
expected to be 300 units per week, it would be better to build the large plant than
the medium one. Thus, the long-run ATC curve, labeled LATC in Figure 2.2,
will be the "outer envelope" (i.e., the lowest portions) of the various short-run
ATC curves from which the manufacturer may choose. If we allow the manufacturer more choices about plant size, it is likely the LATC curve will look
smoother and more continuous (and less like a scallop shell, as it does here).

Given the infinite variety of ways in which firms can combine inputs in the
long run, generalizing about how long-run cost curves will look can be risky.
It's possible that most firms' long-run average cost curves are roughly U-
shaped (like the one in Figure 2.2). In general, extremely small plants have
higher average costs than larger plants do. Beyond some size, however, per-

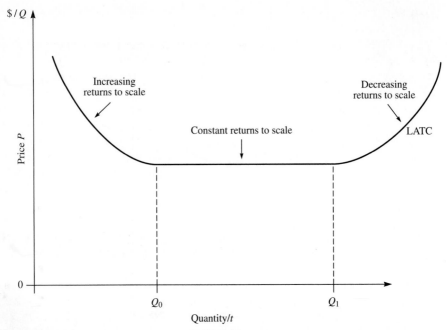

FIGURE 2.3
A LONG-RUN ATC CURVE EXHIBITING INCREASING, CONSTANT, AND DECREASING
RETURNS TO SCALE. This firm experiences increasing returns to scale up to output rate Q_0,
constant returns to scale between Q_0 and Q_1, and decreasing returns to scale afterward.

haps average costs do not vary much with the firm's size or *scale of operation.*
Thus, we may see long-run average cost curves like the one shown in Figure
2.3. Here LATC declines up to output rate Q_0, is constant between Q_0 and Q_1,
and rises afterward. In economics jargon, there are increasing returns to scale
(or *scale economies*) up to Q_0, constant returns to scale between Q_0 and Q_1, and
decreasing returns to scale (or *scale diseconomies*) afterward.

The shapes of firms' long-run average and marginal cost curves can have
important implications for the structure of markets. Suppose that a firm has a
long-run average cost curve like the one shown in Figure 2.3 and chooses a
scale of operations associated with output rate Q_1. If Q_1 is a large fraction (say,
one-half) of the normal sales volume of this entire market, the number of other
firms that can inhabit this market will be limited. This might have a significant
effect on the vigorousness of market competition.

But we are getting ahead of our story. Let's not try to identify things that
might diminish competitive vigor until we have a good understanding of
what competition is.

The Assumptions of the Perfect Competition Model

The economic model of *perfect* or *pure* competition is based on the following
set of simplifying assumptions:

1 In a perfectly competitive market, there will be a *very large number of sellers and buyers, each acting independently.*

2 *None of these sellers and buyers will be so large as to individually affect the price of the product* by varying the amount of sales or purchases.

3 The product of each seller in this market will be a perfect substitute for that of any other seller. We say that the product in a perfectly competitive market is *homogeneous,* or *uniform,* from seller to seller.

4 Resources will be able to move freely into and out of this market; there are *no barriers to entry or exit.* If an entrepreneur wishes to sell in this market, she or he can hire the factors of production necessary to do so and faces no legal or natural prohibitions on entry; similarly, those desiring to "pack it in" and leave the market can sell their assets and do so. Of course, entry and exit take time. In the discussion that follows, we will focus on short-run decision making, broadening our consideration to the long run later.

5 Within this market, there will be *no artificial restraints on prices;* prices for the product and the factors of production necessary to produce it will be able to move freely in response to changing conditions of demand or supply.

6 Sellers and buyers in this market are *fully (and costlessly) informed* about their alternatives. Sellers know where to hire factors of production and what to pay for them; buyers know the prices and product attributes of all sellers.

VIGNETTE 2.1 Is There a Perfectly Competitive Market in the House?

In the real world, many markets possess one or more of the characteristics listed above. Many introductory economics texts, e.g., use the wheat market to illustrate perfect competition. There are, after all, many thousands of wheat producers and buyers, and none is large relative to the market as a whole. What is more, wheat of a particular type grown by one farmer is likely to be indistinguishable from that grown by another.

But through most of the 20th century, this market has been far from perfectly competitive. At various times, wheat prices have been fixed by government, wheat farmers have had their incomes supplemented by government "crop insurance" or other subsidy programs, and acreage allotments have restricted entry. Similar policies have affected other agricultural markets as well. Prices of milk and of some fruits and vegetables have been fixed by government at levels far above those determined by forces of supply and demand. Many farmers obtain loans from the government at interest rates that are below market levels. In some agricultural markets, producers have been required by law to set their prices and rates of output jointly; independent action is illegal.

Even absent these institutional factors, some argue that perfect competition is impossible in agricultural markets because of the very nature of the products involved. Producers cannot be very well informed about their alternatives because it takes such a long time to take a crop from planting to harvesting. By the time a farmer brings a crop to market, what appeared to be a profitable strategy may turn out to be the opposite. Thus, the argument goes, the kinds of programs discussed above are necessary to bring order to what would otherwise be a chaotic and unreliable market. (However, this argument ignores the possibility that participating in futures markets might solve these information problems.)

If agricultural markets are not perfectly competitive, are others? Unfortunately, good examples are hard to find. Most manufactured goods are not homogeneous. In many markets, barriers to entry, whether occurring "naturally" or "artificially" erected by government, are significant. And, of course, the availability and quality of information will vary greatly from market to market.

Does that make the perfectly competitive model useless or irrelevant? Hardly. First, be aware that an assumption of perfect competition, even in markets that do not exhibit all the characteristics discussed above, may be a reasonable approximation. That is, we may find that the predictions of this model turn out to be tolerably close to reality; in this sense, the model has practical value. Second, such a model has value as a benchmark by which we may gauge the performance of markets that are not perfectly competitive. In short, we need the perfectly competitive model so that we can evaluate and measure deviations from perfection in the real world.

Competitive Behavior in the Short Run

Given the conditions listed above, each seller will be a *price taker*. That is, each seller is such a small part of the market as a whole that he or she accepts the going market price as a given and chooses only the quantity to produce. There's no reason to reduce price below the going market level, since the seller can sell all his or her output at that price. On the other hand, trying to raise price above the going market level will induce buyers to go elsewhere, reducing sales to zero. So firms in competitive markets regard price as outside their control; in effect, they regard the demand curve they face as *horizontal* at the going market price.

But isn't this statement a contradiction of the *first law of demand* (the principle that quantity demanded is negatively related to price)? Not exactly. To resolve the apparent paradox, consider the example described in Figure 2.4. In panel *a*, the market demand curve for crabs is shown. In accordance with the first law of demand, it is negatively sloped: If the price of crabs falls from $1.00 to $0.90, for example, consumers increase the quantity demanded from 60,000 to 80,000 per day. But no single crabber produces an appreciable fraction of this market output. Indeed, any individual crabber probably considers it a good day to catch 60 to 80 crabs. In panel *b*, we show the demand curve facing such an individual. Although the vertical (price) axis is the same as in panel *a*, the numbers plotted along the horizontal (quantity) axis are one-thousandth as great. Now, if an individual crabber contributes an extra 20 crabs to the market on a given day, the price must fall negligibly (a mere hundredth of a cent) to increase the quantity demanded by this amount.[1] For the individual who raises her or his catch from 60 to 80 crabs, then, the associated reduction in market price is likely to be imperceptible. Whatever the size of the individual's catch, the price will remain at (approximately) $1.00 per crab. For all

---

[1]Note that the market demand for crabs is described by the equation $Q_d = 260,000 - 200,000P$. Increasing the amount of crabs demanded from 60,000 to 60,020 would require a reduction in price from $1.00 to $0.9999.

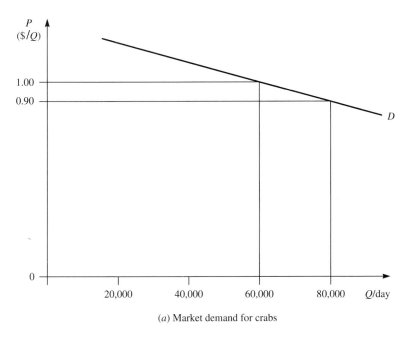

(*a*) Market demand for crabs

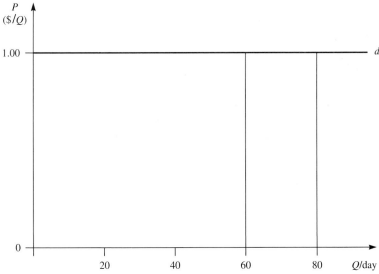

(*b*) Demand curve facing an individual crabber

FIGURE 2.4
MARKET DEMAND AND INDIVIDUAL DEMAND. Because each individual crabber contributes a negligible share of total market output, each faces an individual demand curve that is effectively horizontal at the going market price.

intents and purposes, each individual crabber faces a horizontal demand curve (or, in economics jargon, *perfectly elastic* demand).

A seller who faces a horizontal demand curve has a (relatively) simple decision to make. There's no need to fret over pricing strategy, since the seller must "meet the competition." All the seller needs to figure out (in this short-run setting) is how much to sell.

Let us assume that each seller will seek to *maximize profits*. Since profit is just the difference between revenues and costs (although, as we will soon see, economists and accountants use different measures of costs and therefore of profits), a simple rule of thumb seems a likely guide: Produce and sell any unit of output which adds more to the seller's revenues than to costs.

More formally, this rule of thumb for maximizing profit simply means that a firm should produce and sell all units of output on which there is any associated *marginal* (i.e., extra or incremental) profit. Now the *marginal profit* can be defined as the difference between marginal revenue and marginal cost:

$$\text{Marginal profit} = \text{marginal revenue} - \text{marginal cost}$$

So if the firm wishes to sell all units for which the marginal profit is positive, it will expand output until the marginal profit on the last unit sold approaches (but does not go below!) zero. At this profit-maximizing level of output,

$$\text{Marginal revenue} = \text{marginal cost}$$

That is, finding the profit-maximizing rate of output involves finding the rate of output where marginal revenue and marginal cost are equal.

For a seller in a perfectly competitive market, marginal revenue is easy to calculate and know: It is simply the going price of the product. Since competitive sellers face horizontal demand curves, each unit sold contributes the same amount to revenue—its price. Thus, for competitive firms the product price is equal to the marginal revenue, and the firm's demand curve is its marginal revenue curve. (As we will see later when we discuss noncompetitive markets, this is not always true.) Calculating marginal cost, which again equals the change in total cost resulting from the production of one additional unit of output, is sometimes a more difficult matter in the real world.

Given the necessary information about marginal revenues and costs, choosing a profit-maximizing rate of output is really very simple. Consider Figure 2.5. Panel *a* shows the market demand and supply curves for crabs; these curves interact to determine a going price of $1.00 per crab. Panel *b* shows the demand, marginal cost, and average total cost curves (labeled $d = \text{MR}$, MC, and ATC, respectively) for an individual crabber. The crabber's marginal cost curve is upward-sloping beyond an output level of 30 crabs per day, perhaps because the crabber must use increasing amounts of time, traps, or gasoline to catch each crab beyond this amount.

What is the crabber's profit-maximizing level of output? If traps sufficient to catch only 40 crabs per day are put out, some profit will be forgone; the

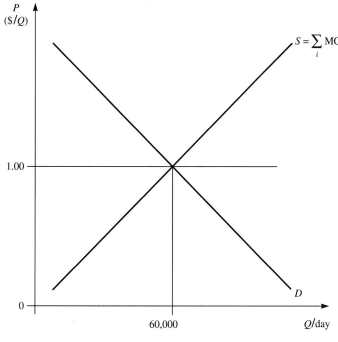

(a) Market for crabs

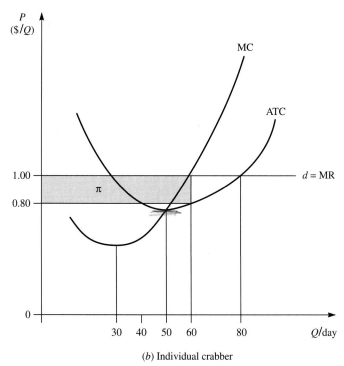

(b) Individual crabber

FIGURE 2.5
PROFIT MAXIMIZATION BY THE COMPETITIVE FIRM. Given that
the market-clearing price of crabs in *(a)* is $1, an individual crabber with
unit costs as shown in *(b)* will maximize profits by increasing production
until price and marginal costs are equal at an output rate of 60 per day.

extra revenue obtained on each crab up to the 60th exceeds the cost of catching it. However, putting out (and tending) enough traps to catch 80 crabs per day would dissipate some profit; for the 61st and successive crabs caught, marginal costs actually exceed marginal revenues. Clearly, the optimum level of production is 60 crabs per day.

The crabber's daily profit at this level of output is shown as the shaded area in Figure 2.5b. The average profit per crab equals price P ($1.00 in this example) minus the average total cost ATC ($0.80), or $0.20 per crab; this amount times 60 crabs caught per day yields a daily total profit of $12.

This may seem a meager reward for such arduous work. But note that this is *economic profit*. When economists speak of costs, they mean *all* relevant costs of doing business, including "implicit" costs such as the opportunity costs of the capital invested in the firm or of the entrepreneur's time and "explicit" costs such as outlays for a boat, gasoline, crab traps, etc. Thus, our hypothetical crabber earns $12 per day over and above that which would be necessary to pay all such costs and stay in business. This is, then, an attractive business opportunity—one which might attract the attention of other profit-seeking entrepreneurs.

Economic Profits versus Accounting Profits

In calculating profits, accountants usually focus on explicit costs (e.g., labor costs, raw-material costs, advertising expenses) and do not report implicit costs. This is because implicit costs sometimes can be measured only subjectively. To see this, suppose our hypothetical crabber has $10,000 in capital tied up in this enterprise. Clearly, there is some *opportunity cost* of using this capital in a crab business rather than elsewhere. (Recall that the opportunity cost of an action can be measured as the value of the best alternative action forgone. For example, the opportunity cost of reading this book may be the wages lost by not spending the time working in some alternative "job.") Of course, measuring the opportunity cost of capital may be tricky. One may be tempted to say, "If I put $10,000 in the bank and earn 6 percent interest, I will get $600 in a year. If there are 200 days for crabbing each year, then my capital costs are $3 per day." Of course, crabbing may be far more risky than just putting money in a bank, so perhaps a higher rate of interest (to compensate the investor for higher risk) should be used to calculate the true opportunity cost of capital for this enterprise.

In addition, the crabber might have turned down a similarly demanding and/or satisfying job paying $50 per day in order to be her or his own boss. This daily $50 forgone should also be counted as an implicit cost the crabber pays each day.

Accountants sidestep these issues entirely, leaving investors to decide whether the profits they have left after deducting explicit costs from revenues are equal to or greater than those they could have earned in some other endeavor. That is, accountants calculate profit as revenues minus explicit costs. Accounting profit can then be compared to the alternative amount that would have been earned if the entrepreneur's time and money had been invested elsewhere.

Economists, however, calculate profit as revenues minus both explicit and implicit costs. If economic profit is greater than zero, then the firm is earning a rate of return that actually exceeds the opportunity costs of all assets of the firm. What is more, a zero rate of economic profit will be sufficient to make the firm a "going concern," i.e., keep it in business. In the example above, the crabber's $12 daily profit is an amount earned *over and above* the daily $3 implicit capital costs and $50 implicit labor costs of the enterprise.

Competitive Behavior in the Long Run

Since in the competitive model buyers and sellers have full knowledge of all their alternatives, this model predicts that the positive economic profits depicted in Figure 2.5*b* will stimulate market entry. Investors will see that profit rates in crabbing exceed those in equivalently risky lines of business, and investors will begin buying, renting, or hiring the factors of production they need to share in these profits.

How will such competitive entry affect the market? To answer this question, first we must remember how the individual crabber makes decisions about how much to produce: by finding the intersection of the marginal revenue curve and the marginal cost curve. The marginal revenue curve is the crabber's demand curve, and the marginal cost curve is her or his supply curve. (More precisely, the crabber's supply curve is the portion of the marginal cost curve that lies above the crabber's *average variable cost* curve. If price falls below a seller's average variable costs, the seller will minimize short-run losses by shutting down and paying only fixed costs.) *The market supply curve is obtained by adding (horizontally) all the individual crabbers' supply curves.*

Competitive entry simply means that there will be more individual supply curves to add. As a result, *entry will move the market supply curve to the right.* This increase in supply will upset the market equilibrium shown in Figure 2.5*a*. Once the supply curve *S* starts shifting to the right, the industry price will no longer be $1.00 and industry output will no longer be 60,000 crabs per day. The equilibrium price will fall, and output will rise. As the price falls, each individual crabber will find it less profitable to devote time and other resources to this endeavor. Each crabber will reduce output slightly, moving down the marginal cost curve as the market price falls.

Where will this process stop? Entrepreneurs will have no incentive to enter this market when revenues are equal to (economic) costs, i.e., when profit rates here are equal to those in equivalently risky activities. That will be the case when the price in this market falls to equality with average total costs. At this price, crabbers will be earning zero economic profits (or, if you prefer, a rate of accounting profit approximately equal to that which could be earned in an equally risky business.)

Figure 2.6 illustrates long-run competitive equilibrium in our hypothetical crab market. The market supply curve shown in panel *a* has shifted to the

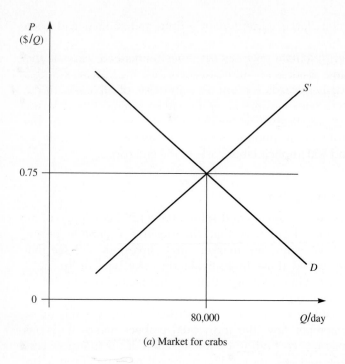

(a) Market for crabs

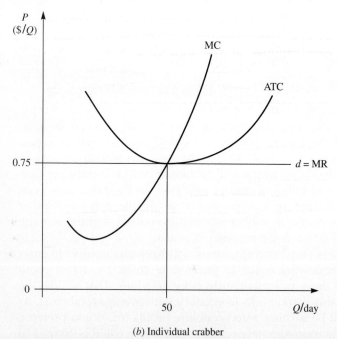

(b) Individual crabber

FIGURE 2.6
LONG-RUN COMPETITIVE EQUILIBRIUM. The lure of economic profits will bring new crabbers to the market, causing the market supply curve to shift rightward. As a result, price falls until it is equal to ATC, and no economic profits are earned.

right sufficiently to reduce the market price to $0.75 per crab, while industry output has risen to 80,000 crabs per day. Panel *b* shows that the individual crabber now finds it profit-maximizing to catch no more than 50 crabs per day. At this rate of output, the price equals (long-run) average total costs, so that no economic profits are earned.

Competition and Social Welfare

We can now step back and see how the individual firm's behavior—in both the short run and the long run—affects us.

Efficiency in Production Note first that a profit-maximizing competitive firm will have a strong incentive to adopt the most efficient, lowest-cost means of production available. In the short run, this means the firm has no incentive to waste resources so that its ATC curve is any higher than it needs to be. A firm that wastes resources is forgoing profits—or endangering its survival. In the long run, the firm will choose the technology (type of process, equipment, plant size, etc.) having the lowest possible ATC curve, and the forces of competition will force the firm to produce at the minimum point on this curve. That is, in long-run competitive equilibrium, costs are minimized and $P = $ ATC. We say, therefore, that competitive markets are *productively efficient*.

The consumer benefits of productive efficiency are many. Consumers of goods produced in competitive markets receive the largest quantity possible at the lowest feasible price (given prevailing resource costs). But consumers in other markets benefit as well. Productive efficiency in the crab market, e.g., benefits even those who shudder at the idea of consuming crabmeat. Competition, by forcing crabbers to eliminate waste and operate at precisely their optimum scale, frees up resources to produce other goods and services; this will make more of these goods and services available at lower prices.

Efficiency in Allocation Now observe that the desire to maximize profits leads sellers to choose, in both the short run and the long run, the rate of output where P (or MR) $=$ MC. In so doing, sellers ensure that the *right amount* of this good is produced. By expanding the rate of output until $P = $ MC (but no further!), sellers produce all units which society values in excess of their costs; no units are produced which would cost more to produce than they are worth (as measured by the *amount someone is willing to pay* for them). We say, therefore, that a competitive market is *allocatively efficient*: no more (or no less) output is socially preferable to the amount produced where $P = $ MC. To make this point concrete, let us consider it in detail.

Maximizing Social Surplus In market exchange, most people would pay more than the going price for what they buy. As George Stigler has written, "When a reflective man buys a crowbar to open a treasure chest, he may well remark to himself that if necessary he would have been willing to pay tenfold the price."[2]

---

[2]George Stigler, *The Theory of Price*, 3rd ed., Macmillan, New York, 1966, p. 78.

Let us return to our hypothetical crab market, shown once again as Figure 2.7. The height of the market demand curve D reveals the *maximum* price consumers would be willing to pay for each possible quantity of crabs produced. Recall that when output was 60,000 crabs per day, many consumers were willing to pay $1.00 per crab. (In fact, some consumers would have been willing to pay considerably more!) Now that competition has forced the price down to $0.75 per crab, these consumers are better off. We can even measure how much better off: These consumers save $0.25 per crab on each of 60,000 crabs they would have been willing to buy at a price of $1.00, a total benefit of $15,000.

This difference between the amount that consumers *value* output (as measured by the amount they'd be *willing* to pay for it) and the amount they actually *do* pay for it is called *consumers' surplus*. But we haven't measured all the surplus in this market quite yet. To do so, we have to deduct the market price from the demand price (i.e., from the height of the demand curve) for all units produced and consumed. That is, we have to measure the area bound by P_eFI in Figure 2.7: *The total consumers' surplus is the area under the demand curve down to the price paid and out to the amount consumed.* In this example, competitive equilibrium results in a total consumers' surplus of $40,000. Consumers get output worth $100,000 to them for a total outlay of $60,000.[3]

There is an analogous concept on the sellers' side of the market. *Producers' surplus* is the difference between the price at which a good is actually sold in the market and the minimum price a seller might have been willing to accept for it. Typically, the latter amount will be determined by the costs of production. Since the supply curve tells how much it costs to produce a particular unit of output, *producers' surplus is the area above the supply curve up to the price received and out to the quantity supplied.* In Figure 2.7, producers' surplus (at a rate of output of 80,000 crabs per day) is equal to the area bound by EP_eI.[4]

We can calculate the total gain to society resulting from the production of any amount of output by simply summing the consumers' and producers' surpluses at that rate of output. This sum is variously called the *social surplus,* or *net social benefits,* resulting from the production and consumption of a particular amount of a good. In Figure 2.7, the social surplus associated with the production and consumption of 80,000 crabs per day is the area bound by EFI.[5] In general, *social surplus is the area under the demand curve minus the area under the supply curve out to the quantity supplied.*[6]

---

[3]Suppose now that our market demand curve for crabs is described by the equation $Q_d = 140,000 - 80,000P$. Therefore, the vertical intercept in Figure 2.7 (point F) is $1.75. Area P_eFI is a triangle with height $1.00 and base 80,000; its area is therefore $40,000.

[4]If the supply curve in Figure 2.7 is described by the equation $Q_s = -70,000 + 200,000P$, then the producers' surplus will be equal to $16,000 when the output is 80,000. This is because the supply curve has a vertical axis intercept of $0.35. Area EP_eI is thus a triangle with base 80,000 and height $0.40; its area is $16,000.

[5]Since consumers' surplus has been calculated as $40,000 and producers' surplus as $16,000, social surplus is $56,000.

[6]Note that this definition holds out the possibility that the quantity supplied may be less than *or greater than* the equilibrium quantity.

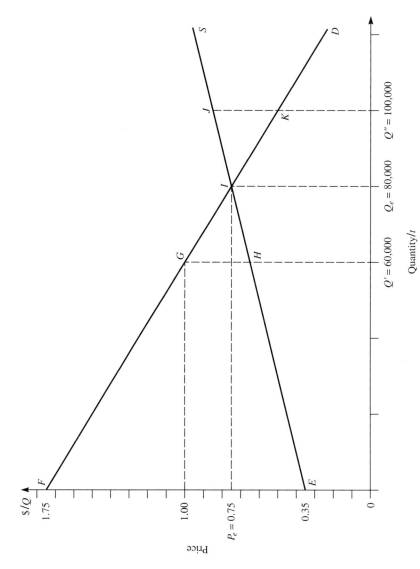

FIGURE 2.7

ECONOMIC EFFICIENCY AND MARKET EXCHANGE. In general, competitive market equilibrium prices and quantities will maximize the social surplus resulting from production and consumption. Here the equilibrium price of $0.75 per unit and quantity of 80,000 per day will generate social surplus equal to the area bound by points *EFI*.

Now observe a crucial fact: If we produce any output other than the competitive market equilibrium output Q_e (equal to 80,000 crabs per day in Figure 2.7), the social surplus in this market will be reduced. To put it another way, if for some reason we produce less (more) than Q_e, we could enjoy additional social surplus by increasing (decreasing) our output to Q_e.

If, in Figure 2.7, output was $Q' = 60,000$, the social surplus would be area *EFGH*; increasing output to $Q_e = 80,000$ would capture additional surplus equal to area *GHI*. This is so because each unit between Q' and Q_e is worth more to consumers (as measured by the height of the demand curve) than it costs to produce (as measured by the height of the supply curve). We would call any forgone surplus the *deadweight loss*, or *efficiency loss*, resulting from the decision to produce less than the optimum equilibrium output. If we produced more than Q_e, say, $Q'' = 100,000$, there would also be an efficiency loss. This is because each unit produced beyond Q_e costs more to produce than it is worth to consumers. Expanding output from Q_e to Q'' would involve production costs in excess of the value equal to the area bound by *IJK*; maintaining production and consumption at Q_e would prevent such dissipation of social surplus.

We conclude, in general, that competitive market equilibrium prices and quantities will maximize the social surplus resulting from production and consumption in any market. We therefore judge competitive equilibrium prices and quantities to be *efficient* because there is no other combination of price and quantity that would generate more social surplus. At any other combination of price and quantity, the social "pie" is smaller than it has to be.

Competition as an Ideal   Because of the characteristics just discussed, it is common to regard the model of perfect competition as some sort of ideal to be sought as a matter of policy. Since perfectly competitive markets maximize social surplus or the net social benefits of production, many have concluded that making markets "perfectly" competitive, or moving them closer to this state, ought to be a central goal of government and the courts.

But perfect competition is a model, not a goal. We must be careful not to try to make the world conform to our model. The natural sciences can serve as useful guides here. In physics, e.g., it is common to assume the absence of friction in modeling the motion of certain bodies, but physicists never suggest we should spread grease throughout the world to make it conform to their frictionless models. Economists have not always been so restrained.

Nevertheless, the model of perfect competition provides many important lessons. First and foremost, it shows that profit-seeking behavior by sellers can have profound value for buyers. Indeed, the action of competitive markets has been described as a magic "invisible hand" that harnesses the selfish interests of buyers and sellers for the good of all. Moreover, the model shows that the consequence of indifference to waste and inefficiency may be extinction. As Clair Wilcox has put it,

Competition is conducive to the continuous improvement of industrial efficiency. It leads some producers to eliminate waste and cut costs so that they may undersell others. It compels others to adopt similar measures in order that they may survive. It weeds out those whose costs remain high and thus operates to concentrate production in the hands of those whose costs are low.[7]

VIGNETTE 2.2   Can There Be Too Much Competition? The Case of Airline Safety

With the Airline Deregulation Act of 1978, Congress attempted to bring real competition to the airline industry. From 1938 to 1978, the Civil Aeronautics Board (CAB) regulated this industry, controlling conditions of entry and exit, allocating routes, and fixing fares for interstate carriers. Deregulation—and the closing down of the CAB—gave carriers great latitude to enter new markets, raise or lower fares, and abandon unprofitable routes.

Economists encouraged deregulation and have generally applauded the results. Steven Morrison and Clifford Winston, e.g., have estimated the total net benefits of deregulation to travelers and carriers to be about $8 billion (in 1977 dollars) per year. For the average passenger, the benefits per trip are $11.08 (composed of a $4.04 gain from lower fares, an $8 gain from increased flight frequency, less a $0.96 loss from slightly increased travel time.)[8] There are now many more airlines in operation than there were in 1978, the number of passenger-miles flown is up considerably, and industry employment is up.

Some, however, have argued that these benefits are more than offset by a perceived reduction in the *safety* of air travel. These critics propose two reasons why deregulation might be accompanied by reduced safety: (1) The greater frequency of flights under deregulation means that air routes and airports are more congested than ever, increasing the likelihood of collisions, or a hit. (2) Cutthroat competition and squeezed profit margins will induce airlines to skimp on maintenance and fly unsafe equipment or force pilots to fly more hours than they should.

So far, however, the safety record of the airlines is as good as or better than that under regulation. As Figure 2.8 shows, the fatal-accident rate for major airlines has fluctuated a bit, but shows a general downward trend in the era of deregulation. From 1975 to 1978, for example, immediately prior to deregulation, there was an average of 0.046 fatal accident per 100,000 departures for operators of jet aircraft; from 1979 to 1984, this accident rate fell nearly two-thirds, to 0.015 per 100,000 departures.[9]

This does not mean that deregulation has no potential to adversely affect the safety of air travel. It is possible that the number of accidents would have been lower still under regulation. But it must also be noted that factors other than competitive pressure affect safety. Specifically, air safety regulation is the domain of the Federal Aviation Administration (FAA), and (due to budget constraints) the number of FAA safety inspectors has not grown apace with the number of airlines and flights. What is more, the air traffic control system (also under FAA authority) has

[7]Clair Wilcox, *Competition and Monopoly in American Industry,* Monograph No. 21, Temporary National Economic Committee, Investigation of Concentration of Economic Power, 76th Cong., 3d Sess., Government Printing Office, Washington, 1940.

[8]Steven Morrison and Clifford Winston, *The Economic Effects of Airline Deregulation,* Brookings Institution, Washington, 1986.

[9]See Daniel P. Kaplan, "The Changing Airline Industry," in Leonard W. Weiss and Michael W. Klass (eds.), *Regulatory Reform: What Actually Happened,* Little, Brown, Boston, 1986, pp. 40–77.

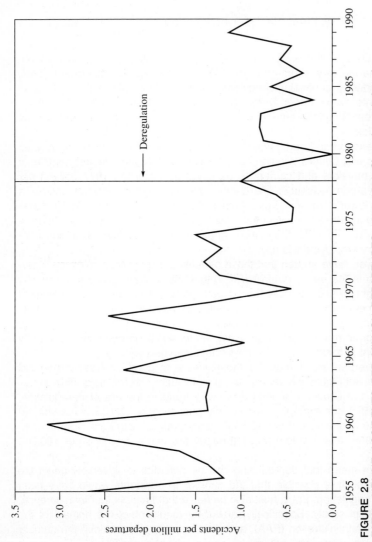

FIGURE 2.8
FATAL AIRLINE ACCIDENTS PER MILLION DEPARTURES, 1955–1990. Since deregulation, the annual number of fatal airline accidents per million departures has generally been lower than in the regulated era—although the rate has risen a bit recently.
Source: Richard B. McKenzie, *Airline Deregulation and Air-Travel Safety: The American Experience,* Center for the Study of American Business, Washington University, St. Louis, Missouri, Formal Publication 107, July 1991, p. 29.

suffered from a decline in the quantity and experience levels of controllers in the wake of an illegal strike by the Professional Air Traffic Controllers' Organization (PATCO) in 1981, which resulted in the firing of all PATCO members and decertification of their union.

Finally, an air disaster will have a negative effect on the financial well-being of the firm responsible. Several studies have documented that an airline's owners are financially "punished" if they are perceived as operating an unsafe airline: The company's stock declines significantly after a crash which appears to be the airline's fault.[10] Thus, firms have a very strong incentive to avoid such disasters—even in a highly competitive environment.

COMPETITION IN THE REAL WORLD

Desirable as the effects of competition may appear to be, we must recognize an immutable fact: *Perfect* competition, as described above, is unlikely to be a reality. While there are real-world markets with large numbers of small sellers and buyers, seldom are these buyers and sellers fully informed about their alternatives; what information they do have is often of dubious reliability and is usually costly to acquire. What is more, there will often be artificial restraints (often government-imposed) on prices or resource mobility in such markets. As noted earlier, agricultural markets, which are common textbook examples of perfect competition, are affected by restrictions on entry, price restraints, acreage allotments, and the like. As a result, economists have long searched for conceptions of competition that might prove more useful as policy guides. A few are discussed below.

Workable Competition

In 1940, John M. Clark observed that "imperfect" competition was the only type possible, but asserted that imperfect forms could "do their jobs well enough to be an adequate working reliance."[11] He began to set out criteria by which we might judge the vigor of competition, and he attempted to widen the definition of price competition as follows:

> Competition is rivalry in selling goods, in which each selling unit normally seeks maximum revenue, under conditions such that the price or prices each seller can charge are effectively limited by the free option of the buyer to buy from a rival seller or sellers of what we think of as "the same" product, necessitating an effort by each seller to equal or exceed the attractiveness of the others' offerings . . .[12]

Clark's ideas touched off an avalanche of scholarly work devoted to listing and refining the criteria for judging the workability of a competitive economy.

---

[10]See, e.g., Don M. Chance and Stephen P. Ferris, "The Effect of Aviation Disasters on the Air Transport Industry," *Journal of Transport Economics and Policy*, 21 (May 1987), pp. 151–165; Severin Borenstein and Martin B. Zimmerman, "Market Incentives for Safe Commercial Airline Operation," *American Economic Review*, 78 (December 1988), pp. 913–935.

[11]John M. Clark, "Toward a Concept of Workable Competition," *American Economic Review*, 30 (June 1940), p. 242.

[12]Ibid., p. 243.

The ultimate refinement of the list of "competitive norms" was by Stephen Sosnick; it is shown in Table 2.2.[13] Sosnick distinguished three basic headings for his list: *structural* norms, *conduct* norms, and *performance* norms. This basic approach for evaluating the workability of competition influenced policy enormously in the years that followed.

Clark and his disciples were not without their critics. Most had doubts about the operational value of Clark's approach to gauging the workability of competition. The criteria advanced were too subjective (what is "excessive concentration of power"?), too vague to put into practice (when are promotional expenditures "excessive"?), or too narrow to apply to many real-world industries. As an alternative, Jesse Markham proposed the following method of evaluating industry structure and performance:

[13]Stephen H. Sosnick, "A Critique of Concepts of Workable Competition," *Quarterly Journal of Economics*, 72 (August 1958), pp. 380–423.

TABLE 2.2
EVALUATING THE WORKABILITY OF COMPETITION.   Sosnick has listed the various structural, conduct, and performance norms for judging whether a market is workably competitive.

Structure norms

1 As many sellers as economies of scale will permit
2 Quality differences which are moderate and sensitive to prices
3 No limits on mobility or entry
4 Reasonable availability of market information
5 Sellers somewhat uncertain about whether price cutting will be followed

Conduct norms

1 Absence of collusion
2 No protection of inefficient suppliers or customers
3 No unfair, exclusionary, predatory, or coercive tactics
4 No harmful or unreasonable price discrimination (charging different prices to different consumers for essentially the same good)
5 No misleading or fraudulent sales promotion
6 Rapid response by buyers to differences in product attributes

Performance norms

1 Efficiency in production and distribution
2 Profits just sufficient to reward investment, efficiency, and innovation
3 Absence of excessive promotional expenses
4 Output consistent with efficient resource allocation
5 Business cycles not intensified by price fluctuations
6 Quality and output reflective of changes in consumer demand
7 Appropriate adoption of technologically superior products and processes
8 Appropriate regard for national security requirements, employees' welfare, and conservation requirements
9 Absence of excessive concentration of political and economic power

An industry may be judged to be workably competitive when, after the structural characteristics of its market and the dynamic forces that shaped them have been thoroughly examined, there is no clearly indicated change that can be effected through public policy measures that would result in greater social gains than social losses.[14]

Robert Bork proposed a similar definition of competition, stating that it prevails when "consumer welfare cannot be increased by judicial decree."[15]

Of course, these alternatives pose difficulties as well. As we will see later in this book, reasonable people may differ about whether there are net social gains from a policy aimed at enhancing competition or whether a particular verdict has the capacity to enhance consumer welfare.

Contestable Markets

In the early 1980s, economists William Baumol, John Panzar, and Robert Willig examined the relationship between market structure, firm behavior, and social welfare from a provocative new angle.[16] Their model, which they formalized as the *theory of contestable markets*, considers the number of *potential* as well as *actual* competitors in a market and stresses freedom of entry and exit as the key determinants of a market's "contestability." (The name refers to the fact that when entry and exit are free, we may observe a contest among potential competitors to see who will serve the market.) Contestable markets can— even with only one or a handful of actual competitors—produce results very much like those in perfect competition.

To qualify as contestable, a market must possess one crucial trait: Entry and exit must entail no *sunk costs*. This is not to say that entry and exit must be totally costless. Suppose, e.g., you go into business as a wedding photographer and buy a camera for this purpose. This may represent a sizable expenditure, but is not a sunk cost. *Sunk costs are those that are irrecoverable once a decision has been made or an action taken.* If you decide to exit the wedding photography business, you can readily sell the camera to someone else or use it in some other way (say, taking children's portraits), recovering all or most of the camera's costs. Of course, you may incur some other entry costs that really are sunk, e.g., your business cards, a licensing fee, an advertisement in the telephone book. Upon exit, such expenditures are beyond recovery.

Given the ease of entry and exit of a contestable market, existing firms in such a market are extremely vulnerable to hit-and-run attacks by outsiders. If an existing firm in a contestable market sets any price above costs (i.e., earns

---

[14]Jesse W. Markham, "An Alternative Approach to the Concept of Workable Competition," *American Economic Review,* 40 (June 1950), p. 361.

[15]Robert H. Bork, *The Antitrust Paradox,* Basic Books, New York, 1978, p. 51.

[16]See William J. Baumol, "Contestable Markets: An Uprising in the Theory of Industry Structure," *American Economic Review,* 72 (March 1982), pp. 1–15; William J. Baumol, John C. Panzar, and Robert D. Willig, *Contestable Markets and the Theory of Industry Structure,* Harcourt, Brace, Jovanovich, New York, 1982; William J. Baumol and Robert D. Willig, "Contestability: Developments since the Book," *Oxford Economic Papers,* 38 (November 1986), pp. 9–36.

positive economic profits), an entrant can go in and, before rivals respond with lower prices, collect significant gains. If rivals do respond, the hit-and-run entrant can leave the market without cost.

Long-run equilibrium in a contestable market will look very much like long-run equilibrium in a perfectly competitive market. First, economic profits will be zero (i.e., accounting profits will be approximately "normal"), for hit-and-run entry would quickly take away (through competition) any positive economic profits. Second, firms will be productively efficient. Any waste or productive inefficiency would likewise constitute an invitation to entry. Third, when a contestable market contains two or more sellers, price will be equal to marginal cost, i.e., the market will be allocatively efficient. Any $P > MC$ will invite entry; any $P < MC$ will induce one of the incumbent firms (or an entrant) to stop producing the unprofitable marginal unit of output.

In sum, contestability theory implies that there is no clear relationship between the number of actual competitors in a market and the extent to which prices resemble those we would see under perfect competition. Figure 2.9 shows a hypothetical contestable market with four firms with long-run marginal cost LMC and long-run average total cost LATC. The market supply curve S is determined as the sum of the quantities supplied by each of the four sellers at each possible price. Fearing entry, each seller sets price $P = LMC$ and produces a rate of output q which minimizes LATC. Any seller who does otherwise invites hit-and-run entry that will adversely affect market position and profitability. Total industry output Q will simply be $4q$. At this industry price and rate of output, firm profits are zero and the market is productively and allocatively efficient.

Contestable market theory, like the theory of workable competition, has its critics. Some question a few of the underlying assumptions of the model, e.g., that entry can occur instantaneously and at any scale and that exit can occur before the incumbent firms adjust prices. Most important, prominent critics such as William Shepherd argue that there are significant sunk costs involved in participation in just about *every* market; perfect contestability, they charge, may be just about as rare as perfect competition. Even when entering a new market requires no irrecoverable investment in production facilities, it may, e.g., require a seller to negotiate new contracts with suppliers or dealers, purchase local advertising, or make other resource commitments that will make a brief stay in the market quite costly.[17]

Such criticisms are important; many have led to significant modifications of the theory or more qualified statements of its policy implications. Clearly, however, the contestability framework has taken the discussion of perfect competition in new directions and offered a broader and more useful guide

---

[17]See, e.g., Martin L. Weitzman, "Contestable Markets, an Uprising in the Theory of Industry Structure: Comment," *American Economic Review*, 73 (June 1983), pp. 486–487; William G. Shepherd, "'Contestability' vs. Competition," *American Economic Review*, 74 (September 1984), pp. 572–587; Marius Schwartz, "The Nature and Scope of Contestability Theory," *Oxford Economic Papers*, 38 (November 1986), pp. 37–57.

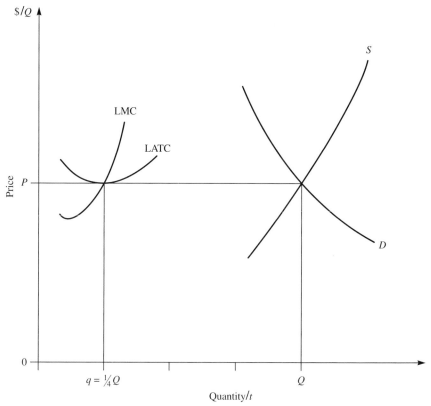

FIGURE 2.9
A CONTESTABLE MARKET. Fearing hit-and-run entry, each of the four sellers in this contestable market sets $P =$ LMC and produces a rate of output q that minimizes LATC; industry output $Q = 4q$.

for public policy toward competition (i.e., antitrust policy) than anything that came before. It has forced policymakers to look at more than just the number of sellers in an industry, or their relative market shares, before forming beliefs about that industry's competitiveness. It has also helped guide regulatory policy, even in markets which research shows are *not* contestable. In addition, by highlighting the importance of factors affecting ease of entry and exit, contestability theory has helped open a new avenue of inquiry into firms' strategies of *entry deterrence.*

VIGNETTE 2.3   Empirical Evidence on Contestability

One often cited illustration of a contestable market is the airline industry. Since planes can be bought and sold (to quickly increase or decrease capacity) or shifted from one route to another, it has been argued that the threat of competitive entry will keep fares low even where there is but a single carrier serving a particular route.

Empirical studies conclude, however, that the airline industry is not as contestable as has sometimes been suggested.

It is apparent, e.g., that new entry does occur and that established carriers reduce their fares in response; what is more, where there are few competitors, profits are high.[18] In a perfectly contestable market, the threat of entry alone keeps price as low as possible, and profits are zero. However, Steven Morrison and Clifford Winston have found that when there are at least four potential entrants, the prices of established carriers are significantly constrained; they conclude that the airline industry is imperfectly contestable.[19]

There is some evidence that behavior in other markets is quite consistent with contestability theory. Studies of the financial brokerage, telecommunications, and trucking industries have shown no significant inconsistencies with the predictions of contestability analysis; studies also suggest ocean shipping is a contestable industry.[20]

Some researchers have attempted to test contestability theory experimentally, using human subjects (usually students) competing for real money payoffs within the bounds of established "rules of the game." Don Coursey, Mark Isaac, and Vernon Smith, e.g., devised an experiment in which two participants were given money which they were required to spend to produce output in accordance with their known (marginal) cost functions. Entry and exit were completely free. The consumers' demand function was given, but not known by the sellers. A participant made a sale if her or his price was not undercut by a rival; participants got to keep any excess of revenues over costs. After repeated trials, the authors concluded that the experiments strongly support contestability theory: Even with a single producing firm, as long as entry and exit are unconstrained and collusion between players does not occur, approximately competitive prices and rates of output will result.[21]

COMPETITIVE MARKETS: OTHER VIEWS

The market system has been the dominant mode of economic organization in the western world for more than two centuries, and it has been the subject of serious analysis for nearly as long. It should not be surprising that the analysts disagree over many things, some trivial, others important.

It is fair to say that most economists consider the virtues of competitive markets to outweigh their vices. (Indeed, as we noted earlier, some economists even refer to competition as an ideal for public policy to pursue.) The fact that many people believe something, however, does not make it true. Competitive markets have their critics, and even if these critics are in the minority, the criticisms deserve consideration.

[18]Gregory D. Call and Theodore E. Keeler, "Airline Deregulation, Fares, and Market Behavior: Some Empirical Evidence," in Andrew F. Dougherty (ed.), *Analytical Studies in Transport Economics,* Cambridge University Press, London, 1985, pp. 221–247.

[19]Steven A. Morrison and Clifford Winston, "Empirical Implications and Tests of the Contestability Hypothesis," *Journal of Law and Economics,* 30 (April 1987), pp. 53–66.

[20]See, e.g., Elizabeth E. Bailey and William J. Baumol, "Deregulation and the Theory of Contestable Markets," *Yale Journal on Regulation,* 1 (1984), pp. 111–137; J. E. Davies, "The Theory of Contestable Markets and Its Application to the Liner Shipping Industry," Canadian Transport Commission, Ottawa-Hull, 1986.

[21]Don Coursey, R. Mark Isaac, and Vernon L. Smith, "Natural Monopoly and Contested Markets: Some Experimental Results," *Journal of Law and Economics,* 27 (April 1984), pp. 91–114.

Values and Fairness   The most serious objections to the theory of market competition are philosophical. The "invisible hand," the argument goes, doesn't work because competition encourages (and may even compel) people to act on their lowest instincts and values. Market competition doesn't inspire or elevate, but debases; it makes us aggressively materialistic (and rude!) and leaves us alienated and unhappy.

Other critics note that competition produces an unequal—and inequitable—distribution of income. Our income will depend, among other things, on what we are born with; neither intelligence nor family wealth is distributed uniformly, so competition will reinforce inequality. Those unable or unwilling to produce goods or services for which society will pay are, in a competitive world, quite likely to be poor (in relative if not absolute terms). Competition, if it does not actually cause poverty and inequality, will not eliminate these ills.

Such objections are difficult for economists to address, since they are outside the typical bounds of the discipline (a fact which confirms, to the critics, that the discipline needs improvement). No doubt, competitive markets yield some "goods" that many consider "bads." We can all think of things we wish were not produced in such abundance or at all. But economists are trained to think in terms of alternatives and trade-offs. We therefore have some questions for the philosophical critics of market competition. If we dislike some market outcomes, shall we jettison markets, or are there less drastic alternatives (e.g., regulation)? How much will the various alternatives impinge on personal freedoms that we hold dear? And who is the arbiter of "acceptable" taste or values? These are questions with which a society grapples in the political arena; somehow we must decide how much coercion of individual choice is tolerable and healthy.

As to the problems of poverty and inequality, economists question how much these are the result of market competition and how much they are due to other factors or institutions. Again, we invite critics to weigh alternatives. Many nonmarket societies are notoriously poor. Inequality in the distribution of income is markedly worse in undeveloped than developed countries, and no better in command economies than market economies. Many economists believe we will better address these problems if we leave markets to do their work of maximizing output—eschewing price controls, rent ceilings, and minimum wages—and then reduce poverty and inequality via direct transfers of cash. In any case, we should observe that competition is less likely to be eliminated than rechanneled. When we limit competition in the economic sphere, we move it to the political one. Will this necessarily enhance the fairness of a society?

Practical Objections   Some critics of competition take a more pragmatic track. They argue that competition will be "ruinous" or at least more expensive than the alternatives. If competition is strong enough to force firms to sell at a price equal to marginal cost, the argument goes, these firms will be balanced precariously on a knife's edge between prosperity and bankruptcy.

Aside from making life worrisome for sellers, this could cause serious economic problems—erratic fluctuations in market prices, waste, periodic deficiency, or redundancy of capacity. In this view, some protection from unfettered competition is socially desirable and necessary.

Others argue that organizing production in a small number of large firms will commonly be cheaper than in a large number of small firms, as the model of perfect competition requires. Whether because demand is inadequate to support many firms or because there are significant economies associated with large-scale firms, structuring markets competitively will, in this view, waste resources.

Some also suggest that competitive markets are inferior to noncompetitive ones as a vehicle for innovation. In competitive markets, returns are normal. But it is the pursuit of above-normal returns that inspires innovation, this reasoning goes. Noncompetitive or monopolistic markets promise greater rewards. In search of markets we can "corner," we race to be first to produce new or improved products. In so doing, we push out the frontiers of technological knowledge.

Finally, critics argue that models of market competition overlook some important realities. First, many markets are not competitive at all, but monopolistic or close to being so. Even where there are many sellers in a market, these sellers do not act independently, but are constantly scheming against the public. Second, even competitive markets will be inefficient if, e.g., producers can avoid some of the social costs of producing their goods, e.g., pollution. Third, even competitive markets will have problems producing certain kinds of goods, especially *information*.

These are important criticisms. Taken together, they suggest that there is much that markets cannot do or will do improperly; they give us ample reason to intervene in markets. A more thorough discussion of these issues is reserved for the next chapter.

SUMMARY AND CONCLUDING REMARKS

This chapter began by reviewing some generalizations about production costs and describing a model of a perfectly competitive market. This model is built on six assumptions: (1) The market will contain a large number of independent buyers and sellers, (2) none of these buyers or sellers is large enough to individually affect market price, (3) the product is homogeneous, (4) there are no barriers to entry or exit, (5) there are no restraints on product or factor prices, and (6) buyers and sellers possess all relevant information in making their choices.

Individual firms in such a market will be price takers, i.e., will face a demand curve that is horizontal at the going market price. Profit-maximizing firms will set their output rate where marginal costs equal marginal revenue, so that there is no additional profit to be made from increasing production. If this rate of output is associated with positive (negative) short-run economic profits, competitive entry (exit) will occur, bidding the price down (up) until economic profits are zero. In long-run competitive equilibrium, $P = MC = ATC$.

This result is of profound benefit to consumers. Social surplus (the area under the market demand curve minus the area under the market supply curve out to the quantity exchanged) is maximized in competitive market equilibrium. Put another way, competitive markets are allocatively and productively efficient: In long-run equilibrium, the optimum amount of output is produced at the lowest social cost.

In the real world, however, it is rare to find markets characterized by all the assumptions underlying the perfectly competitive model. Accordingly, economists have sought to define more operationally useful models of competition. The various models of workable competition focus on the presence or absence of rivalry among sellers and free choice for consumers; both are widely believed to be correlated with the number of sellers. The theory of contestable markets turned the spotlight away from the number of actual sellers in a market toward the number of potential sellers. This theory posits that ease of entry and exit can lead to competitive pricing even in the absence of a large number of sellers.

Critics of market competition argue that it caters to our basest values, encouraging materialism and defeating cooperative efforts. Others argue that it exacerbates problems of poverty and inequality. On a less philosophical level, some critics argue that competition can't work—that it will prove ruinous—or that it is more expensive than other modes of economic organization. Finally, some observe that imperfections in markets, e.g., monopoly, suggest important roles for government to play in enhancing social welfare.

QUESTIONS FOR REVIEW AND DISCUSSION

2.1 You will often hear a political leader describe his or her job as "running the country (or state or city)." Is this an accurate statement of what a government official does? Why or why not?

2.2 Instead of accepting a work-study job at minimum wage, Jovita chose to start her own business, delivering pizzas and other snacks around campus. She works an average of 20 hours per week. Her costs for goods sold, uniforms, gas, and other car expenses average $300 per week; her sales revenues average $400 per week. What is her average weekly economic profit?

2.3 Suppose we have a competitive market, but not all firms in this market are identical. To take the simplest case, suppose your firm's costs of production are lower than those of all other firms, but no one can figure out why. In long-run competitive equilibrium, will all firms in this market earn zero economic profits? Now consider another possibility: Your firm's costs are lower than those of all your rivals, and the (widely known) reason is that you are the most efficient manager in the business. Will all firms' economic profits be zero in this case? Why or why not?

2.4 The market for rutabagas is competitive. Presently, the demand for rutabagas (per day) is described by the equation $Q_d = 90{,}000 - 50{,}000P$; the supply of rutabagas (per day) is described by the equation $Q_s = -40{,}000 + 80{,}000P$.

   a What are the equilibrium price and daily output of rutabagas? What is the value of social surplus at this price and rate of output?

b Suppose that the government decides that consumers of rutabagas deserve a break and imposes a ceiling price on rutabagas equal to $0.75. What is the value of social surplus under this price control?

2.5 Suppose the market for crabs is competitive and is in long-run equilibrium. Now research produces a new form of bait to which crabs are greatly attracted; this reduces the costs of crabbing by a significant proportion. Use graphs to illustrate the short- and long-run implications of this technological innovation, tracing out the effects on prices, quantities, and social surplus (welfare).

2.6 Your roommate says, "I don't like capitalism. I can't get behind a system that's based on greed. I believe in putting people before profits." Evaluate this statement.

2.7 Suppose you learn that Robin, the smartest person in class, is earning substantial profits by tutoring first-year students in principles of economics, a course you did well in. Identify the costs you might have to pay if you entered this market. Which of these costs are sunk?

CHAPTER 3

GOVERNMENT INTERVENTION AND THE PUBLIC INTEREST

The important thing for Government is not to do things which individuals are doing already, and to do them a little better or a little worse; but to do those things which at present are not done at all.

John Maynard Keynes

As we have seen, individuals who transact in competitive markets accomplish a great deal. In such markets, self-seeking behavior is channeled in ways that are of profound benefit to society at large. Market competition can ensure that resources are allocated to their highest-valued uses, that output is produced at the lowest possible cost to society, and that consumers benefit from the widest possible array of goods and services at the lowest possible prices.

Some endorse market organization on other (noneconomic) grounds as well. An economy made up entirely of perfectly competitive markets, e.g., would have such large numbers of consumers and producers—all earning, in the long run, zero economic profits—that concentrations of economic power would be nonexistent. Such an economy would, then, be very close to a democratic ideal in which no single individual or group is so large or important as to override the wishes of others. It has also been argued that the market is inherently *meritocratic* in that it allocates rewards impersonally, according to one's contribution to output. In a perfectly competitive market economy, there would be no room for discrimination, nepotism, or political favoritism; firms and individuals making production decisions on the basis of anything other than efficiency would simply not survive.

But not all markets are competitive, and even competitive markets will fail

55

to achieve some things. These deficiencies or failures of markets form the foundation for many important *public interest* rationales for government regulation of economic behavior. In essence, these rationales assert that much government action is guided by altruistic motives—the desire to enhance social welfare by correcting one or more shortcomings of market organization. In this chapter, we introduce these *market failure* rationales, setting the stage for more detailed discussions in later chapters. We begin by outlining the consequences of an absence of competition. In succeeding sections, we catalog several other problem areas for markets: what economists refer to as *externality problems*, the peculiar types of goods known as *public goods, information problems*, and others. Wherever possible, we use the competitive market model introduced in Chapter 2 to identify why these problem areas need concern us and what they cost us. Also we describe how government might—or might not—play a part in addressing the problem in question.

MARKET FAILURE AND THE PUBLIC INTEREST

The Problem of Monopoly

In Chapter 2 we concluded that competitive market equilibrium prices and quantities maximize the social surplus resulting from production and consumption in any market. We therefore judge such prices and quantities to be *efficient* because there is no other combination of price and quantity that would generate more social surplus.

If, for any reason, a market is in disequilibrium, social surplus will not be maximized. Consider Figure 3.1 (which is very similar to Figure 2.7). If the output is lower than the equilibrium level, say $Q' < Q_e$, then surplus equal to the area bound by points GHI will be forgone. If the output is higher than the equilibrium level, say $Q'' > Q_e$, then surplus equal to area IJK will be wasted (since, for the units from Q_e to Q'', costs of production exceed the value attached to the output). Any action which eliminates disequilibrium or speeds the process of adjustment toward equilibrium recovers for society some social surplus, thus enhancing social welfare. When competition is absent, i.e., when a market is monopolistic, the result is very much like a permanent disequilibrium where output remains below the competitive equilibrium level.

Behavior and Effects   To see what harm monopoly can pose to society, let us consider a highly simplified example. Figure 3.2 shows a market demand curve D for a hypothetical good, together with the marginal revenue curve MR derived from it.[1] Suppose, for simplicity, that anyone can produce and sell this good for a constant amount per unit C.

---

[1] Recall that marginal revenue—the extra or incremental revenue associated with the purchase of one more unit of output—is generally less than price for a monopoly seller. Suppose, e.g., current sales volume is 10 units at a price of $10, and in order to sell 11 units, the price will have to be cut to $9.50. The price reduction increases total revenue from $100 ($10 per unit × 10 units) to $104.50 ($9.50 per unit × 11 units). Thus, the extra revenue associated with the 11th unit sold is $4.50, far less than its price of $9.50.

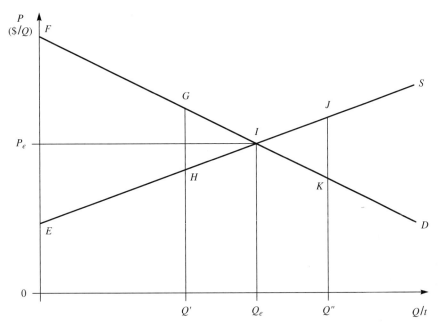

FIGURE 3.1
ECONOMIC EFFICIENCY AND MARKET EQUILIBRIUM. At output rate Q', we forgo social surplus equal to the area bound by points *GHI*. At Q'', we waste surplus equal to area *IJK*. At Q_e, social surplus is maximized.

Now consider two scenarios. First, suppose there is vigorous competition in this market. Entering the market is easy, there are many sellers of this good, consumers are well informed about these sellers and their products, and none of the sellers conspire to "rig the market" in any way. Under these circumstances, it is clear that the market price would be bid down to P_c, equal to C, and that Q_c units would be produced and consumed. Some sellers might naturally prefer to sell at a higher price (and earn above-normal profits). But if any seller attempted to set a price above P_c, consumers would simply beat a path to the door of other sellers willing to accept slightly lower prices (and profits). Thus, anyone setting a price greater than P_c is unlikely to sell any output. If we add the social surplus associated with each unit produced in this competitive market, from zero to Q_c, our total social surplus would be the area bound by points $P_c EG$ in Figure 3.2.

Now suppose competition is absent. There is only a single firm, and new firms are somehow barred from entering the market. In such a case, the profit-maximizing monopolistic seller would sell no units for which marginal costs, equal to C, exceed marginal revenues, since this would reduce profits. Thus, the monopolist would restrict output to Q_m (since C > MR for rates of output beyond Q_m), and the price that would clear the market of this amount of output would rise to P_m. Industry profits, equal to the area bound by points $P_c P_m FH$ in Figure 3.2, would be far above the normal level. More important, from an economic standpoint, social surplus would not be maximized. When

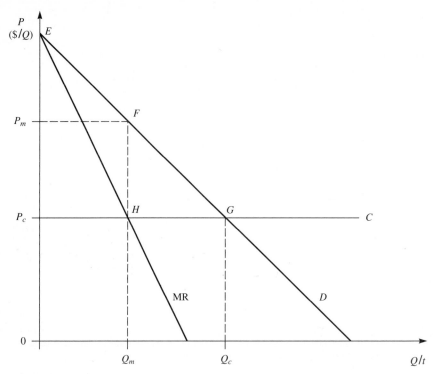

FIGURE 3.2
COMPETITION AND MONOPOLY. Competition among sellers results in a market price P_c and rate of output Q_c. If competition is absent, output will be restricted to Q_m and price will rise to P_m.

output is reduced from Q_c to Q_m by monopolistic conduct, units that are worth more to consumers than they cost society to produce would not be sold because it would not be profit-maximizing for the monopolist (or colluding firms) to sell them.[2] As a result, we would forgo social surplus equal to the area bound by points *FGH* in Figure 3.2. This area is the *deadweight social loss* associated with monopolistic conduct.

VIGNETTE 3.1   What Does Monopoly Cost Us?

It may seem curious that we restrict our definition of the social loss from monopoly to triangle *FGH* in Figure 3.2. After all, isn't the area P_cP_mFH, the monopolist's economic profits, a loss to consumers as well? The answer to this question is clearly yes, but since this amount of consumers' surplus is simply transferred to the monopolistic producer, it is not, strictly speaking, a *social* loss. Although we may object to

---

[2]One possible exception to this generalization exists when the monopolist is not constrained to charge a single price to all consumers and can *price-discriminate*. More will be said about this possibility in later chapters.

transfers on equity grounds, economists traditionally have not classified them as efficiency losses.

There have been many efforts to make a dollar estimate of the deadweight social loss resulting from monopoly in the U.S. economy. The first was by Arnold Harberger, who estimated the size of the aggregate "loss triangle" (such as area *FGH*) for U.S. manufacturing industries by assuming (1) that industry profits above the average profit rate signaled monopoly and (2) that the elasticity of demand facing all industries was unitary. Harberger concluded that elimination of monopoly in U.S. manufacturing would raise national income by a mere 0.1 percent.[3] Using different means of identifying monopolistic industries and of estimating the monopoly effect on price, David Schwartzman and D. A. Worcester (in separate studies) also concluded that the welfare loss from monopoly is small.[4]

More recent estimates of the social cost of monopoly, however, are considerably higher. In part, these higher estimates resulted from attempts to correct what the authors saw as methodological flaws in Harberger's original study. David Kamerschen, e.g., made different assumptions about the elasticity of demand in monopolized industries and concluded that the monopoly welfare loss may be as high as 6 percent of national income.[5]

But higher estimates have also resulted from the insight that a monopolist's profits may *not* be a pure transfer from consumers to producers. The idea—identified with Gordon Tullock and Richard Posner—is that considerable resources might be spent to *acquire* and *maintain* a monopoly position that yields above-normal profits.[6] In the context of Figure 3.2, if acquisition of a monopoly will enable a firm to earn economic profits (sometimes called *monopoly rents*) equal to area P_cP_mFH for a single period, the firm might be willing to spend up to that amount to obtain the monopoly (adjusted, of course, for the probability of obtaining it). If these profits could be earned for a more extended term, the firm might be willing to spend an amount equal to the present discounted value of this future stream of "rents." Clearly, spending resources to obtain or maintain monopoly status raises the social cost of monopoly because such resources could have been used to produce valued output elsewhere.

Obviously, estimating such costs is a difficult proposition. Keith Cowling and Dennis Mueller attempted to make such estimates, however, and to correct what they saw as other flaws in Harberger's welfare cost estimates as well. They concluded that eliminating monopoly could raise the gross corporate product by as much as 13 percent in the United States and by 7 percent in the United Kingdom.[7]

---

[3]Arnold C. Harberger, "Monopoly and Resource Allocation," *American Economic Review*, 44 (May 1954), pp. 77–87.

[4]David Schwartzman, "The Burden of Monopoly," *Journal of Political Economy*, 68 (December 1960), pp. 627–630; D. A. Worcester, "New Estimates of the Welfare Loss to Monopoly: U.S. 1956–69," *Southern Economic Journal*, 40 (October 1973), pp. 234–246.

[5]David R. Kamerschen, "An Estimation of the Welfare Losses from Monopoly in the American Economy," *Western Economic Journal*, 4 (Summer 1966), pp. 221–236.

[6]Gordon Tullock, "The Welfare Costs of Tariffs, Monopolies, and Theft," *Western Economic Journal*, 5 (June 1967), pp. 224–232; Richard A. Posner, "The Social Costs of Monopoly and Regulation," *Journal of Political Economy*, 83 (August 1975), pp. 807–827.

[7]Keith Cowling and Dennis Mueller, "The Social Costs of Monopoly Power," *The Economic Journal*, 88 (December 1978), pp. 727–748. These estimates have been criticized by S. C. Littlechild, "Misleading Calculations of the Social Costs of Monopoly Power," *The Economic Journal*, 91 (June 1981), pp. 348–363.

X **Inefficiency**   Some researchers have suggested that monopolies waste resources also by failing to control costs as rigorously as they would if "pushed" by more competitive conditions. The idea is simply that highly profitable monopolies will be wasteful with inputs and lazy about searching for new ways to improve efficiency. Such behavior has been dubbed X *inefficiency* to distinguish it from the allocative inefficiency discussed earlier.[8]

Anyone who has ever worked in business is likely to find the concept of X inefficiency both appealing and obvious. "Of course," such a person will say, "waste and inefficiency are pervasive in business, and the more common the bigger is the firm." Identifying *true* waste is not so simple, however. Might it simply be the case that behavior which costs a firm $X would actually cost *more* than $X to eliminate? It might, e.g., be possible to improve output by making sure that employees do not take an extra minute or two coming back from coffee breaks or do not chat while they are supposed to be concentrating on their work. But it is also possible that such an improvement in output can be bought only at the price of added personnel to monitor the employees in question, and such an expenditure might far exceed the value of the extra output. Under such circumstances, tolerating the aforementioned sources of "waste" might actually be X-efficient! True X inefficiency would involve a situation where a cost-effective alteration in the status quo exists, but the firm, insulated by its monopolistic position, has inadequate motivation to discover or adopt it.

Identifying such inefficiency, then, is problematic—especially when its source is something as hard to evaluate as potential motivation. As a result, the concept of X inefficiency has its critics. As George Stigler has written, "[p]otential motivation can indeed rewrite all history. If only the Romans had tried hard enough, surely they could have discovered America."[9]

Nevertheless, empirical evidence suggests X inefficiency exists. Researchers have compared costs in industries where competition prevails in some sectors and not in others. They've found that competition can reduce production costs by 10 percent or more and hasten the adoption of appropriate technologies.[10]

Clearly, avoiding the various kinds of welfare losses associated with monopoly is squarely in the public interest. This is (or should be) the goal of antitrust policy, the conduct of which occupies two major federal agencies (the Antitrust Division of the Department of Justice and the Bureau of Competition of the Federal Trade Commission), some state-level agencies, and occasionally private individuals pressing their own antitrust lawsuits.

---

[8]Harvey Leibenstein, "Allocative Efficiency vs. 'X-Efficiency,'" *American Economic Review*, 56 (June 1966), pp. 392–415.

[9]George J. Stigler, "The Xistence of X-Efficiency," *American Economic Review*, 66 (March 1976), pp. 213–216.

[10]See, e.g., W. Bruce Erickson, "Price Fixing Conspiracies: Their Long-Term Impact," *Journal of Industrial Economics*, 24 (March 1976), pp. 189–202; Lawrence J. White, "Appropriate Technology, X-Efficiency and a Competitive Environment: Some Evidence from Pakistan," *Quarterly Journal of Economics*, 90 (November 1976), pp. 575–589; Walter J. Primeaux, "An Assessment of X-Efficiency Gained through Competition," *Review of Economics and Statistics*, 59 (February 1977), pp. 105–108; Rodney Stevenson, "X-Inefficiency and Interfirm Rivalry: Evidence from the Electric Utility Industry," *Land Economics*, 58 (February 1982), pp. 52–65.

Related Problems: Oligopoly and Natural Monopoly

Right about now, astute readers may be nagged by some doubts about the relevance of the preceding discussion. For one thing, it doesn't appear there are very many examples of honest-to-God monopoly out there. Even the largest U.S. corporations have competitors: IBM has its dreaded rival Apple, General Motors faces Ford and Chrysler (and those upstart Japanese), and Coke keeps slugging it out with Pepsi. When we do find firms that have cornered their markets, such as the local gas, electric, or telephone companies, we often find that the government seeks not to break up these monopolies, but actually to protect them from competition. So what's all the fuss about "the monopoly problem"?

There are two answers. First, it is true that relatively few markets are pure monopolies. But economists have long felt that markets with only a few sellers—*oligopolies*—can, for various reasons, be just as bad. In fact, our worries about the monopoly problem are often worries about the extent to which oligopolies produce welfare losses like those associated with monopolies. (So we are guilty of semantic sloppiness, not irrelevance.) Second, it sometimes will be cheaper for a single seller to serve an entire market than to divide the market among two or more sellers. We'd be foolish to insist on a competitive market structure in such cases, but perhaps equally foolish to overlook mechanisms that might protect us from monopolistic underproduction and overpricing. Let us introduce each issue (leaving more detailed discussion for later chapters) and note possible policy responses.

Oligopoly   As we noted in Chapter 2, the nature of firms' long-run cost curves can have a great deal to say about the structure of their markets. It may be, e.g., that the optimal size of a firm (i.e., the size at which average cost is minimized) is so large that the market has room for only a few sellers. Where this is the case, each seller will be large enough to have a significant effect on the market price. It is quite likely that such firms will recognize that their production and pricing decisions affect each other; i.e., they will recognize their *interdependence.* They will be better off if they *all* keep output down and prices up, just as in a monopoly.

In the context of Figure 3.2, suppose there are three sellers (each with constant cost C) instead of one. Clearly, aggressive competition, which drives the price down to P_c and each firm's economic profits down to zero, promises meager rewards compared to an agreement *not* to compete. If the three sellers get together and agree to fix the price at P_m and restrict output according to some formula (each producing $Q_m/3$, for example), they each can earn positive economic profits. But, of course, consumers and society at large are victimized by such *collusion.* Just as with pure monopoly, some consumers' surplus (area P_cP_mFH) is transferred to producers, and some surplus (area FGH) goes up in smoke as deadweight loss.

Recognizing that there are potential gains from noncompetitive behavior is not the same as realizing those gains, however. At the very least, overt collusion is illegal under the antitrust laws. Obviously, making something illegal doesn't make it go away, but it can make it more difficult. In any case, several factors will make collusion problematic even if it is legal. Colluding firms might have trouble figuring out how to divide up their market, especially if costs are *not* constant and similar across firms. If the firms solve that problem, they have to keep their agreement from breaking down. Each firm will have a strong temptation to exceed its assigned output quota and cut itself a larger slice of the profit pie; detecting such cheating, and punishing it once detected, may not be easy. Finally, successful collusion may attract entry, forcing the colluders to revise their agreement or react in some other way.

Economists have been studying oligopoly for some time, on both a theoretical and an empirical level. Given the illegality of overt collusion, attention has focused on ways in which oligopolies might duplicate monopolistic outcomes even absent formal agreements about price and output. Not all the models that economists have devised (about which considerably more is said in Chapter 7) predict there will be deadweight social losses in oligopolistic markets without formal collusion, but many do. In addition, empirical studies of price-fixing conspiracies tend to find that conspiracies are more likely to occur and endure when the number of sellers is small.[11] As a result, the behavior of firms in markets with relatively few sellers draws close scrutiny from the antitrust authorities. Prices may be watched for evidence of "lockstep" movements; mergers that might confer market power on the merged firms are sometimes blocked; information exchanges and joint ventures among potential rivals are generally limited.

Natural Monopoly   In some markets, however, cost and demand conditions can be such that we may want to call off the antitrust dogs entirely. Figure 3.3 illustrates such a case, in which a single firm can satisfy market demand far more cheaply than two or more firms can. In this example, the long-run average total cost (LATC) curve slopes downward over the entire relevant range of market demand, intersecting the demand curve D at an output rate of 100,000 units per week. At this scale of operation, a single seller's average cost will be $1 per unit, so the total cost will be $100,000 per week. If two firms shared the market, each producing 50,000 units per week, the average cost would rise to $1.50 per unit, so the total cost would be $150,000 per week.

In markets like these, dubbed *natural monopolies*, we save considerable resources if we eschew a competitive market structure and organize production within a single firm. The fear, however, is that this firm will behave as a typical monopolist, restricting output and raising prices in order to earn positive economic profits—and imposing deadweight losses on society. What to do? The most common response is economic regulation aimed at ensuring that the natural monopolist's prices are kept at or near production costs. Much of this effort is expended at the state and local levels, with various commissions

---

[11]In one study, e.g., about four-fifths of the conspiracies involved fewer than 10 firms. See George A. Hay and Daniel Kelley, "An Empirical Survey of Price Fixing Conspiracies," *Journal of Law and Economics*, 17 (April 1974), pp. 13–38.

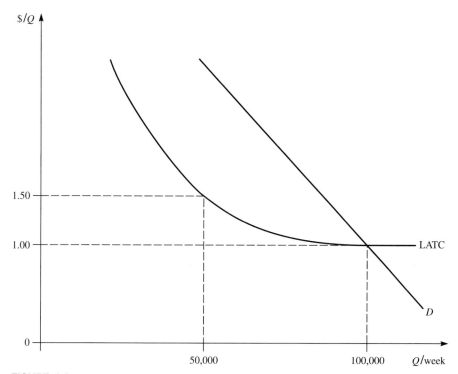

FIGURE 3.3
NATURAL MONOPOLY. Under certain cost and demand conditions, one firm may satisfy market demand more cheaply than two or more.

and bureaus controlling prices for "public utilities" deemed to be natural monopolies within some specified market area. Such regulation is, however, harder to implement successfully than one might guess (as we will see in Chapters 12 to 15). Regulators must make some hard decisions about the appropriate pricing formulas to use and must grapple with a vexing problem: Once firms' prices are tied to costs by most any formula, the firms will have incentives to inflate their costs or otherwise misallocate resources. Perhaps in response, some government entities use alternatives to direct regulation of natural monopolies, such as public ownership of the monopoly or competitive bidding for the monopoly franchise.

Externalities

Even competitive markets can be afflicted with problems. One is the existence of *externalities*, defined as costs or benefits that the market transactor imposes or confers on third parties (those "external" to a transaction) without their consent. Externalities are also sometimes referred to as *neighborhood* or *spillover* effects.

The most frequently used example of a *negative externality* is pollution, resulting from either the manufacture or use of some good, which imposes costs on individuals who neither produce nor consume the good in question. In general, when production involves such negative externalities, the competitive market equilibrium will fail to maximize social surplus.

To see precisely how, consider Figure 3.4. Once again, we have a market demand curve D and a cost curve C which, for simplicity, is horizontal. Let us suppose, however, that in this case the unit costs C that any producer would pay—for labor, land, capital, etc.—need *not* include the costs of properly (i.e., cleanly) disposing of some noxious waste product involved in the manufacturing process. To properly dispose of this waste product or to cope with it once it is improperly dumped would cost, say, $T per unit of output produced, raising the total *social* production costs to C' per unit.[12] In effect, we suppose

[12]The assumption that the costs of properly disposing of the waste product are precisely equal to the costs inflicted on third parties if the waste product is improperly dumped is a heroic one. Relaxing this assumption poses some interesting and subtle implications for what should be done about this type of problem; these are discussed in Chapter 16.

FIGURE 3.4
NEGATIVE EXTERNALITY. If producers can save $T (per unit of output produced) by disposing of wastes improperly, then competition will push price below and output above ideal levels and social surplus equal to area *FGH* will be wasted.

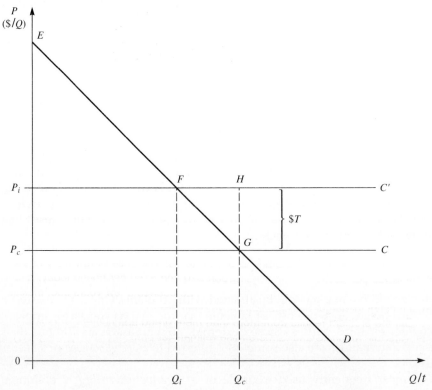

that producers, because of existing law or conventions, can get away with dumping this waste product into the air or water or some vacant lot—thereby keeping their *private* unit costs at C—instead of paying C' to do the whole job properly.

In this case, competition will likely drive output to Q_c and the price to P_c. Even if there are scrupulously honest producers who seek to dispose of all wastes properly during the production process (at unit cost C'), they will be priced out of the market by those who take advantage of existing law or conventions to improperly dump wastes, lower their unit costs (to C), and secure an insurmountable competitive advantage over the scrupulous producers.

Obviously this result is not socially efficient. In Figure 3.4, we can identify exactly how inefficient it is. In an ideal world, all firms in this market would consider their true costs per unit produced to be C' because that is how much each unit actually costs society when the costs of the pollution (or of avoiding the pollution) are factored into the bargain. The *ideal* market rate of output would then be Q_i, and the price would be P_i. By ignoring the external social costs linked to the pollution, the competitive market will overproduce and underprice this good. For each unit produced beyond Q_i, true production costs exceed the value attached to each unit, and society pays some "net social costs." Summing these costs for all the units from Q_i to Q_c, we find that the efficiency loss resulting from overproduction of this good is equal to the area bound by points *FGH* in Figure 3.4. This area measures the welfare loss resulting from the externality problem in much the same way as earlier we measured the welfare loss from monopolistic conduct. Unless the externality problem is corrected somehow, total social surplus from the production of this good is equal to the area bound by points P_iEF (which equals the amount of surplus society would enjoy had the ideal rate of output been produced) *minus* area *FGH*.

VIGNETTE 3.2   Overhunting as a Negative Externality

At one time, as many as 100 million buffalo roamed what is now the continental United States; by the late 19th century, the species was nearly extinct. In Africa today, there is a similar dangerous trend with elephants. According to some estimates, the population of elephants has been halved in the last decade, and it continues to fall at alarming rates. In both cases, overhunting is the problem. The American buffalo was virtually exterminated because of heavy demand for the lap robes made from buffalo hides; slaughtering of the African elephant is motivated by strong global demand for the animal's ivory tusks. The price of raw ivory has risen from $2.25 per pound in 1960 to between $70 and $150 per pound today, and the average tusk weighs 13 pounds (down from 25 pounds a few years ago, indicating that most of the larger bull elephants have been taken).[13]

But the problem results from more than mere greed and hunters' pursuit of profits. After all, ranchers and farmers raise animals for profit, too, but typically they do

[13]Stephen Brookes, "Ivory Proves Elephants' Downfall," *Insight,* November 21, 1988, Vol. 4 pp. 36–37.

not harvest so many at a time that the survival of the herds is threatened. The key difference is that ranchers and farmers have clearly defined, well-specified *ownership rights* to the livestock they raise. A rancher who postpones bringing cattle to market today so that the herd may grow or be replenished will be rewarded for this action: There will be more cattle to sell in the future.

By contrast, the buffalo hunters of yesteryear or the elephant poachers of today lack such property rights. Herds of elephants roam widely over large, inaccessible areas. Once a poacher locates a herd, often using a four-wheel-drive vehicle or an airplane, there is no incentive to consider the consequences of overhunting. The poacher will *not* consider leaving some fraction of the herd alive so that it might grow or replenish its numbers, because the poacher will not benefit from the existence of *future* animals. Instead, the poacher will consider only that "if I don't hunt these animals now, someone else will later." As a result, overhunting will certainly occur.

This is a peculiar—and important—example of a negative externality. By failing to consider the future implications of wiping out an entire herd of elephants, the poacher imposes a serious cost on society at large. True, the disappearance of the elephants will impose some costs on poachers as well as on the general public. But the costs to poachers of their overhunting are but a small fraction of the total social costs involved in the near eradication of a species. In the context of Figure 3.4, poachers' costs of ivory production C are far below the relevant social costs C'. As a result, too much ivory is produced at too low a price (even if the price *is* $150 per pound).

In most cases, avoiding the welfare loss associated with externality problems will require government intervention in the marketplace, whether in the form of some sort of regulatory agency or reliance on legal principles and the courts. It is true that the efficiency losses inherent in some common externalities are trivial and that intervention in such cases may be more costly than the problem it seeks to solve. It is also true that much of the intervention which has occurred has been ill conceived or inefficiently conducted. In principle, however, it is difficult to dispute the idea that where significant externality problems exist, government intervention of some kind (the right kind!) can enhance social welfare.

Public Goods

Markets may also fail to function efficiently when the good in question is a "public" good. *Public goods* are those having two rather interesting properties: (1) Consumption of the good by one person leaves no less of the good available for anyone else (i.e., the good is nondepletable), and (2) the costs of excluding those who do not pay for the public good are extremely high (i.e., the good is nonexcludable). Obviously, many goods that we commonly describe as public are not truly public goods. When I am using a particular public phone, e.g., you cannot; nor are the costs of excluding nonpayers from using public phones high. But consider the classic example of a lighthouse.

Suppose some entrepreneur builds a lighthouse that emits light signals warning ships of a nearby reef, hoping to charge each passing ship a fee for this valuable service. Suppose this fee is to be extracted by selling "subscriptions" to the service. Note that once the lighthouse is in operation, one ship's receipt of the signal in no way reduces the signal available for any other ship. Note further that the costs of excluding nonsubscribing ships may be high. The entrepreneur could place an identifying mark on subscribing ships, turning off the light when nonsubscribers approach, but such a mark might be easily counterfeited. Alternatively, the entrepreneur might memorize the silhouette of all subscribers, turning on the light only when these subscribers approach, but in foggy conditions or at night—when the signal is obviously most important—identifying subscribers may be difficult or impossible. In any case, clever nonsubscribers may simply wait until subscribers are passing by, knowing that the lighthouse signal will not be turned off as long as a paying customer is near.

Clearly, leaving the provision of public goods like lighthouses to private individuals poses some difficulties. The incentive of devious shipowners to try to take a "free ride" at the expense of subscribers appears strong. And if there are too many nonsubscribers, there is a great likelihood that the public good will be underproduced—or not be provided at all![14] This will involve the sacrifice of some of or all the potential net social benefits associated with the good, clearly an inefficient result.

Many have argued, therefore, that when a good is purely or partly public in nature, government financing—or even government production—of the good is required. Government intervention, it is said, can quickly overcome the *free-rider problem* by taxing all potential consumers of the public good an amount sufficient to see that the good is provided. Moreover, such intervention may be desirable on other grounds: Given the nondepletability of a public good, it will generally be efficient to set its price at zero. Even if free riders could be excluded, this line of argument goes, we would not want to exclude them from consuming the good or charge them any positive price for the privilege!

To see why, consider Figure 3.5, which shows a demand curve D for a hypothetical public good. The nondepletable nature of a pure public good implies that once the good has been provided to one consumer, the social cost of providing it to any additional consumer is zero. In effect, the marginal cost curve for this good coincides with the horizontal axis in Figure 3.5. Suppose the provider of this good is somehow able to exclude nonpayers and chooses to charge each payer a price P_a equal to the average cost of supplying the good to everyone who agrees to pay. This will result in total consumption equal to Q_a. Total net social benefits in this case will equal the area bound by points P_aEF in Figure 3.5. This is because total social benefits are, with output at Q_a, equal to the area bound by points $0EFQ_a$; total social costs are, on the assumptions of this example, P_a times Q_a, or area $0P_aFQ_a$. Subtracting total social costs from total social benefits thus yields area P_aEF.

---

[14]Despite these difficulties, privately constructed and operated lighthouses did exist at various times in history. See Ronald H. Coase, "The Lighthouse in Economics," *Journal of Law and Economics*, 17 (October 1974), pp. 357–376.

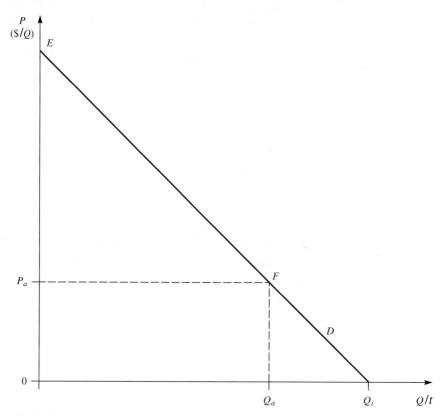

FIGURE 3.5
PUBLIC GOOD. Given that a public good is nondepletable, some social surplus will be forgone if fewer than Q_i units of the good is consumed.

But this price and quantity exclude some consumers who value the good more than the (zero) marginal cost of letting them consume it. If we allow these consumers access to the good, then there will be no less for everyone else and the social surplus associated with production and consumption of the good will expand by the area bound by points Q_aFQ_i in Figure 3.5. If society consumes any less than Q_i units of the good—assuming it has been produced—some social surplus will be forgone.

Maximizing the social surplus associated with a pure public good, in sum, requires us to offer it to any and all comers at a zero price. Even if private entrepreneurs can overcome the practical problems of excluding free riders, then, it is unlikely they will be willing to meet this condition absent some subsidy to pay the initial costs of producing the good. Thus, government intervention—if only as the payer of subsidies—in the market for public goods appears to have a strong public interest rationale. We must not assume, however, that government subsidization or production of *any* public good is in the public interest. It is true that, because of the free-rider problem, individuals will have an incentive to understate their valuation of public goods to private producers, making private provision problematic. But what assurance is there that individuals will have any incentive to properly state their preferences to some government provider, or that the apparatus of government will be properly equipped to measure these preferences accurately? Government miscalculation in the decision to provide public goods, and in the amount to provide, can lead to inefficiency of the same sort that results from reliance on private providers.

Information Problems

Embedded in most discussions of competitive markets is an assumption that consumers are well informed about various sellers and the prices and attributes of their products. On occasion, this assumption takes a rather extreme form: that information about sellers and their products is *perfect* and *freely available*. Obviously, the real world never conforms to this idealized assumption. Information is a good like any other. It is costly to produce and not always perfect. Ordinarily, markets could be relied on to produce the right amount of this good, i.e., the amount that will maximize the social surplus associated with its production and consumption. Many economists feel, however, that the market for information may be inefficient and that consumers and workers will be particularly disadvantaged in this market.

One reason that consumers may be ill informed about products they consume is that information is, in many respects, a public good. Consider, e.g., information about the safety of new automobiles. It may be possible to assess auto safety either by performing crash tests in the laboratory or by carefully studying accumulated statistical evidence on accidents and injuries in the real world. Either way, learning about the safety attributes of different kinds of cars is apt to be expensive. Once this knowledge exists, however, it will have the two key characteristics of any public good: nondepletability and nonexcludability. First, my use of this knowledge will leave no less knowledge about automotive safety available for anyone else; the marginal cost of my consumption of this good—*once it has been produced*—is zero. Second, it will be difficult or impossible to limit the use of this knowledge to those willing to buy it. This is partly because information can often be "pirated" (at the cost of a photocopy) and widely distributed to nonpayers and partly because society would likely be unwilling to exclude nonpayers where knowledge about safety is concerned.

If information (at least in some instances) is a public good, it may be underproduced. A related, though distinct, problem occurs when buyers and sellers do not have equal access to vital facts about an exchange, i.e., where there are *information asymmetries* between buyers and sellers. It is almost always true, e.g., that the manufacturer and/or seller of a particular product knows more about its quality or attributes than a prospective buyer does.

In most cases, however, consumers are aware of their relative ignorance and deal with the problem by demanding some warranty or bond (or both) from the seller before taking a chance on the product. A firm's reputation (or "brand name"), which is usually of great value, commonly serves as the firm's "bond" that its products will satisfy or its warranties will be honored. For if consumers are not satisfied by the product or feel they have been taken advantage of by the seller, the firm's reputation will be tarnished; i.e., this valuable intangible asset will depreciate or be forfeited entirely. Thus, the very fact that a product carries a "famous brand" often acts to address information problems by telling consumers that the producer has something to lose if the product proves disappointing.

Where information asymmetries are not addressed by the market, as in cases where consumers are not even aware that they are at a disadvantage, competitive market exchange will not maximize net social benefits. To see why, consider Figure 3.6, which shows a market demand curve D and a horizontal unit cost curve C. In this case, let us suppose D represents the demands of a group of consumers who are badly informed about the attributes of this

FIGURE 3.6
INFORMATION ASYMMETRY. If consumers were fully informed about the risks of this product, their demand curve D' would be to the left of the current demand curve D. The information problem leads to overconsumption of the product and reduces social surplus by area EFG.

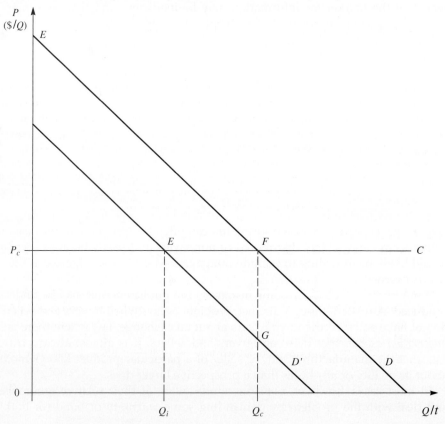

particular product, e.g., they are unaware that consuming the product carries some risk to their health. If they were properly informed about this risk, some or all consumers would either demand less of the product or be willing to maintain their current level of consumption of the product only at lower prices. In effect, then, if consumers were properly informed, their true demand curve, labeled D' in Figure 3.6, would be somewhere to the left of the current demand curve D. Absent good information, consumers will ignorantly—though perhaps blissfully—consume Q_c units of the good at price P_c. If they had good information, they would instead consume only Q_i units. The information problem reduces social surplus by the area bound by points EFG in Figure 3.6, since for every unit consumed beyond Q_i social costs per unit exceed the social value per unit.

When such information problems exist in a market, so does a public interest rationale for government intervention in that market. The government can, e.g., try to force sellers to alter their products to correct any safety problems. Failing this, sellers might be compelled to disclose key information about the products they sell. Alternatively, the government can provide information itself or subsidize those private entities which do so.

VIGNETTE 3.3   Tobacco Use and Health Warnings

Though the scientific literature contained information about the harmfulness of tobacco products in the 1850s, it was not until the 1950s that evidence linking cigarette smoking with lung cancer began to accumulate. And it was not until 1964 that U.S. Surgeon General Luther Terry published a government report bluntly concluding that smoking is a cause of lung cancer in men and a suspected cause of lung cancer in women and increases the risk of dying from pulmonary emphysema.[15] In the years since, more evidence has accumulated and more adverse effects of tobacco use have been identified. Regulatory policy, however, has not aimed at limiting availability of tobacco products but at increasing the flow of information about these products. In particular, sellers of tobacco products are required to warn purchasers about the adverse health effects of these products and are prohibited from advertising cigarettes on television and radio. In addition, public service advertisements are aimed at discouraging smoking, especially by young adults.

How has the strategy worked? There is ample evidence that the demand curve for tobacco products has shifted well to the left since the risks of smoking have become well known. Prior to 1965, surveys estimated that 44 percent of U.S. adults smoked cigarettes. By 1975, only 34 percent of U.S. adults were smokers; by 1986, that percentage had fallen to 26.5. Per capita cigarette consumption has declined every year since 1973, by a total of 23 percent. Smoking prevalence has declined from 1965 to 1985 for both women and men, for blacks and whites, and in every age group except those over 65. Since 1976, there has been a 35 percent reduction in smoking prevalence among high school seniors.

The advertising ban has contributed little—if at all—to these trends, however.

---

[15]The source for much of the information in this illustration is, U.S. Department of Health and Human Services, Office on Smoking and Health, *The Health Consequences of Smoking: Nicotine Addiction—A Report of the Surgeon General, 1988,* Government Printing Office, Washington, 1988.

Indeed, some research suggests that the advertising ban has actually slowed the rate of reduction in cigarette consumption. By rendering the so-called fairness ("equal time") doctrine inoperative, the advertising ban reduced the number of anti-smoking messages after 1970, increasing consumption over what might have occurred absent the ban.[16] Some argue, therefore, that government regulation of information has been counterproductive or at least less effective than it might have been.

Others worry that the government's focus on information is inadequate. They observe that smoking prevalence is highly correlated with educational attainment and income level. For example, only 16.5 percent of those with some postcollege education are smokers, while 33.4 percent of those with only a high school diploma smoke. This might imply that those with less education (which, of course, will also be correlated with lower income) are less able to process information about health risks. The correlation might also be explained, however, by different preferences about such risks, i.e., the rich and poor, or the educated and uneducated, might subjectively weigh the costs and benefits of smoking differently.

In some cases, of course, the government may be no better (or perhaps worse!) at assessing risks or learning of "hidden costs" associated with buying certain goods or working in certain occupations than the individuals actually involved. As a result, we must be aware that government intervention may be neither necessary nor sufficient to solve some information problems.

Merit and Demerit Goods

In some cases, it is argued, the market's own perfection is an imperfection. That is, markets sometimes serve the interests of consumers too slavishly, offering them lots of things they like that are bad for them and withholding things that would be good for consumers if only they would (or could) demand them. The latter, which we might call *merit goods,* may be things such as fuel-efficient cars or school lunches or motorcycle helmets. Their opposites, called *demerit goods,* are things such as alcoholic beverages or hallucinogenic drugs or gambling.

The idea here is simply that consumers' preferences for certain goods are, in a subjective sense, "wrong" or that consumers are not really "sovereign" but are easily manipulated by irresponsible sellers. If only consumers were wiser (or perhaps wealthier), the reasoning goes, they would buy fewer demerit goods and more merit goods. Government policy that encourages (discourages) the production and consumption of merit (demerit) goods, it is argued, is thus justified on *normative* or *ethical* grounds.

Of course, efficiency criteria are occasionally invoked in this area as well. Some merit goods are said to be (at least partly) public goods or to involve positive externalities; some demerit goods are said to involve negative externalities. Thus, when government discourages cigarette or alcohol consump-

---

[16]Lynne Schneider, Benjamin Klein, and Kevin Murphy, "Government Regulation of Cigarette Health Information," *Journal of Law and Economics,* 24 (December 1981), pp. 572–612.

tion via taxes or prohibits consumption of certain narcotics outright, these policies are sometimes justified in terms of the spillover health, welfare, or crime costs associated with these goods. Alternatively, some subsidies for some merit goods appear to be roundabout methods of redistributing income. In most cases, however, the rationales for policies of this type are ethical or moral rather than purely economic; we do them (or say we do) because they are "right," not because they are cost-effective. See Table 3.1.

ENHANCING EQUITY

Improving economic efficiency is not, of course, the only valid public purpose of government intervention in markets. Many types of intervention are aimed instead at enhancing fairness or equity. Such intervention often takes two forms: policies which *redistribute income or wealth* to individuals or groups deemed deserving or policies that secure rights or privileges (perhaps including access to certain markets) for excluded or oppressed individuals or groups.

TABLE 3.1
MARKET FAILURES AND THEIR CONSEQUENCES: A SUMMARY

Problem	Consequences
Monopoly	Seller creates "artificial scarcity" of good; underproduction and overpricing of good involve deadweight loss. May also see dissipation of rents to acquire or maintain monopoly; X inefficiency.
Oligopoly	Sellers may duplicate results of monopoly with or without formal collusive agreement; resulting underproduction and overpricing of good involve deadweight loss.
Natural monopoly	Declining average cost over entire relevant range of demand implies that production is best organized within a single firm; economic regulation often assumed necessary to protect against monopolistic pricing.
Negative externalities	Producers and/or consumers ignore spillover costs to third parties; overproduction and underpricing of good involve dissipation of social surplus.
Positive externalities	Producers and/or consumers ignore spillover benefits to third parties; underproduction and overpricing of good involve forgone social surplus.
Public good	Consumers (seeking free ride) understate true preferences for good; private producers seeking to recoup production costs charge positive price for good; resulting underproduction and overpricing of good involve forgone social surplus.
Information asymmetries	Consumers with inadequate information about risks of products may overconsume them, dissipating surplus; workers inadequately informed about job risks may oversupply, underprice labor, also dissipating surplus.

Of course, defining equity or fairness satisfactorily is difficult; in general, it concerns the extent to which the distribution of goods or rights is *just*. But what is fair or just to some may seem the opposite to others. Specifying criteria by which the equity effects of a particular policy or program might be evaluated is very difficult—certainly harder than evaluating efficiency. Philosophers have been debating such criteria for a very long time indeed and have not yet reached any clear consensus.

Nevertheless, two equity concepts can be used to develop some basic criteria for judging the distributional equity effects of public policy.

Vertical Equity   Suppose it is possible to rank all the individuals in a particular society according to their wealth or income, from highest to lowest.[17] We might then evaluate a particular policy by examining how it affects this vertical distribution of wealth or income. Does the policy redistribute wealth or income from rich to poor? Does it do the opposite?

One mild criterion for judging equity based on vertical distributional considerations might be that a policy is desirable if, all else remaining unchanged, it raises the incomes of the poorest citizens in a society. A slightly stronger version of this criterion might be that a policy is desirable if it compresses the distribution of income in a society (i.e., narrows the gap between the relatively rich and relatively poor), even if this involves redistributing income from rich to poor.

Horizontal Equity   Within each income or wealth rank (or "class") in a society are individuals or groups with comparable economic resources. We might then wish to examine how a particular policy affects these individuals or groups. Does the policy bestow benefits or inflict costs on some people with incomes of, say, $20,000 per year but not on others? Does the policy take income from some people with annual incomes of $20,000 and give it to others with the same (initial) income? One criterion for judging equity based on horizontal distributional considerations might be that policies should, whenever possible, avoid arbitrary horizontal redistributions, i.e., should impose no costs on some within a rank or class merely to benefit others of the same rank.

None of these criteria, of course, will be acceptable to all as a device for evaluating the fairness of particular policies. Judging equity effects is extremely complex, and it may well be unrealistic to assume that it will ever be amenable to rigorous, objective analytical treatment.

---

[17]Note that this is likely to be a more difficult task than one might suppose. Observe, e.g., that money income will vary greatly by age. A college student may be near the bottom of the money income rankings now, but in a few short years may vault near the top. Is such a person now a proper beneficiary of subsidies or income transfers? Observe also that much income and wealth is unmeasurable. The money income of college professors, e.g., is lower than that in many alternative occupations, but most professors remain in academia because they value the nonpecuniary benefits they receive (flexible hours, more prestige, intellectual enrichment, etc.) more than they value the increased money income they would earn in some other job. But it is impossible to rank individuals by the amount of nonpecuniary benefit they receive!

The task is made still more complicated by the fact that there is often a trade-off between equity and efficiency, i.e., that which enhances equity is often inefficient. Attempts to vertically redistribute income, e.g., often reduce the total amount of income produced. In trying to slice the pie more fairly, we may inadvertently make it smaller.

Imagine, e.g., a 100 percent tax on any earned income above the average income in a particular society, with the proceeds to be redistributed to those with income below average. Such a tax might appear to be in accord with (strong) vertical equity criteria—until its full ramifications are considered. Those with incomes officially above the average will likely reduce their work effort (since they get to keep none of the portion of their income that is above the average anyway), thus reducing total social income and average income. In the long run, in fact, such a policy might lead to near-universal impoverishment, since as average income falls, more people will be subject to the 100 percent tax on income above the average; barring repeal of the new tax, a cumulative downward spiral of reduced work effort and reduced social income would be likely, leaving even the intended beneficiaries of the policy worse off.

VIGNETTE 3.4   Government Transfers and Poverty

For decades, federal, state, and local governments have redistributed income via their taxing and spending policies. Not all redistributive programs have the alleviation of poverty as their primary goal, and not all such programs redistribute income from rich to poor. But recent data show that the net effect of government transfers of income is to *reduce the fraction of the population that is "officially" poor and reduce the degree of income inequality in the United States.*[18]

Government statisticians calculate the official poverty rate by using a three-step process. Since surveys show that low- and middle-income families spend about one-third of their income on food, the process starts by determining the cost of a nutritionally adequate food plan for families of given size. This figure is then multiplied by 3 to produce a "poverty threshold income level." The poverty rate is that fraction of the population with incomes below this threshold (which is adjusted annually to account for inflation, etc.). This official poverty rate includes consideration only of *money* income. Many government programs, however, involve not transfers of cash but transfers "in kind," e.g., food stamps, public housing, Medicare and Medicaid, and school lunches. Overlooking such noncash benefits has led to overestimates of the true extent of poverty in the United States.

For example, the official poverty statistics for 1986 identified about 1 in 7 people in the United States (13.6 percent) as poor. Adjusting these statistics for in-kind transfers reduced the poverty count to about 1 in 10 (10.3 percent). *Without* government transfers (either cash or in-kind), the Census Bureau estimates that about 1 in 5 people in the United States (21 percent) would have been below the poverty threshold.

It is also true that including the value of in-kind government transfers in calculations of income significantly reduces the degree of perceived income inequality in

[18]U.S. Department of Commerce, Bureau of the Census, *Measuring the Effect of Benefits and Taxes on Income and Poverty: 1986,* Government Printing Office, Washington, 1988.

the U.S. economy. For example, the poorest fifth of U.S. households received only 3.8 percent of aggregate national income in 1986; adjusting this figure to include the value of noncash benefits raises this figure to 4.9 percent. And the Census Bureau estimates that without government transfers the poorest fifth of U.S. households would receive only 1.1 percent of national income. Some economists would argue that the latter figure is misleading: It leaves unconsidered the likelihood that, absent a government "safety net," these individuals' participation in the labor force—and therefore their nontransfer incomes—would be greater. Indeed, some have argued that the existence of transfer programs has encouraged individuals to engage in behavior (e.g., dropping out of school) that generally leads to poverty.[19] This debate over poverty policy notwithstanding, it is clear that redistribution of income by government has a major impact on the lives of many people and on the character of the U.S. economy.

It will not always be the case that enhanced equity implies diminished efficiency. Many policies that enhance the well-being of the poor do so precisely because these policies are efficient. Ensuring that, say, the grocery business is competitive rather than monopolistic increases the net social benefits available to all, but especially enhances the welfare of the poor, since they devote a proportionately large fraction of their income to food.

We might classify policies according to their equity and efficiency effects as in Figure 3.7. Since equity and efficiency effects can both be either favorable (+) or unfavorable (−), any government policy may fall into one of four quadrants: (1) favorable equity and efficiency effects, (2) favorable equity effects but unfavorable efficiency effects, (3) favorable efficiency effects but unfavorable equity effects, and (4) unfavorable equity and efficiency effects.

Clearly, policies that fall in quadrant (1) will generally be preferred to those in quadrant (4). It might also appear that policies that fall in quadrant (1) will be preferred to alternatives that fall in quadrants (2) and (3). But the truth is that we really have no systematic way of evaluating such trade-offs. We cannot answer—with certainty, at any rate—whether it is better to pursue a policy which puts us at point A in Figure 3.7, with small increases in both efficiency and equity, or one which puts us at point B, with a large increase in efficiency but a small decrease in equity. This is because the efficiency gains associated with B may be so great that, in absolute dollar terms at least, everyone's income or wealth rises, although the increases are greatest for the rich.

We can, however, state one general principle with certainty: *In comparing or evaluating policies, we should favor those that achieve a given level of equity enhancement at the least cost in terms of efficiency loss.* In comparing policies that would put us at either point A or C in Figure 3.7 (both producing the same amount of equity enhancement, but C carrying no associated efficiency gain), we should clearly favor A.

Finally, we should remember that our menu of policy choices is rarely as limited as this discussion might imply. Often the menu will include not only A

---

[19]See, e.g., James Gwartney and Thomas S. McCaleb, "Have Antipoverty Programs Increased Poverty?" *The Cato Journal*, 5 (Spring/Summer 1985), pp. 1–16.

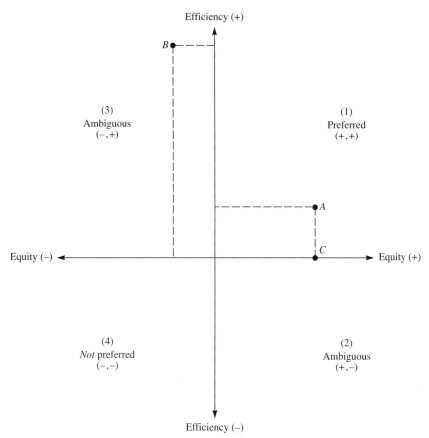

FIGURE 3.7
CLASSIFYING EQUITY AND EFFICIENCY EFFECTS. If policy *A* will enhance equity as much as policy *C* and also will enhance efficiency, we should choose *A* over *C*. Since we lack a systematic way to evaluate equity-efficiency trade-offs, we cannot say whether *A* is superior to *B*, however.

or *B* or *C*, but also a whole continuum of options (some as yet unidentified) between, above, or below these points. If it is difficult to choose between *A* and *B*, the challenge is to search for a new option (produced perhaps by a series of incremental improvements in either *A* or *B*) that will be strictly preferred to both.

SUMMARY AND CONCLUDING REMARKS

Barring certain complications, the net social benefits (or social surplus) resulting from production and exchange will be maximized when goods are traded in free, unfettered markets. But complications are fairly common in the real world. Their existence suggests a positive role for certain kinds of government regulation of economic activity. In particular, corrective action by government may be called for when (1) markets are noncompetitive or monopolistic, (2) externality problems (or spillover effects) are significant, (3) a good has the characteristics of a public good, and (4) parties to an exchange do not possess adequate information about the nature of the exchange.

In each situation, markets will, if left to their own devices, impose serious welfare losses on society, i.e., will fail to maximize social surplus. When competition among producers is absent, lost surplus, called *deadweight welfare loss,* results from an artificial scarcity of output; welfare losses may be even greater if real resources are used to acquire or maintain monopolistic advantage or if a monopolist fails to minimize production costs. In markets afflicted by negative externalities there will be overproduction, i.e., production of output that society values less than it costs to produce. When a good has the peculiar characteristics of nondepletability (my consumption of it leaves no less available for you) and nonexcludability (costs of excluding nonpayers are high), it is a public good; private production of it may be impossible or may result in its undersupply. In transactions where buyers possess less information about the good than sellers do (and are unaware of this disadvantage), it is likely that more than the optimum amount of the good will be produced and consumed.

Government intervention in the economic marketplace may also be rationalized by the desire to enhance the equity or fairness of market results. Two criteria for judging the distributional equity effects of particular policies are important: (1) Vertical equity is enhanced when the distribution of income in a society is compressed, and (2) horizontal equity is preserved when arbitrary redistribution of income within economic classes is avoided. Attempts to redistribute income often affect the amount of income produced, i.e., affect productive incentives. As a result, there is often a trade-off between equity and economic efficiency. Evaluating policies which promise greater equity in exchange for some loss of efficiency is difficult. In general, we should favor policies achieving a given level of equity enhancement at the lowest cost (in terms of efficiency losses).

That numerous rationales for government intervention *exist* does not mean, of course, that they *apply* in a particular case. Often such rationales will be invoked to justify a policy without careful thought about whether they are relevant to the problem at hand or whether the problem is really serious enough to warrant costly action at all. Often, too, such rationales merely serve as a smokescreen to hide the fact that a particular policy advances some special interest far more than it serves the *public* interest. Students should be prepared to roll up their sleeves and work hard to discover the truth lying hidden in every public policy debate. Such effort is essential, however, if we are to make a positive contribution to policy formation. As the philosopher Pascal once said, "Working hard to think clearly is the beginning of moral conduct."

QUESTIONS FOR REVIEW AND DISCUSSION

3.1 Suppose the sole right to sell textbooks on your campus is auctioned off each year to the highest bidder. That is, whoever pays the college the most for this right will obtain a monopoly on textbook sales on campus for one year. Draw a graph to describe the welfare implications of this monopoly. What will the winning bid likely be? Will the rules the college establishes for the auction affect your estimate of the welfare costs of this monopoly? Explain.

3.2 Define X inefficiency. Use a graph (like Figure 3.2) to describe how the existence of X inefficiency will affect a calculation of the welfare costs of monopoly. Are the social costs of X inefficiency likely to be large or small relative to the deadweight loss of monopoly? Explain.

3.3 Higher education is often cited as an example of a good from which positive externalities arise. Assuming this is so, use a graph to describe how the market for higher education might misallocate resources if left to its own devices. What might the government do to address this problem?

3.4 Economists often say, "There's no such thing as a free lunch." On the other hand, they also argue that pure public goods should be given away. Can you reconcile these apparently conflicting views? It is clear that public goods are costly to produce, so why shouldn't people pay for them?

3.5 Are there any information problems involved in the consumption of higher education? Explain. How are these problems addressed by private markets? How does government regulation affect these problems, if at all? Can you suggest any regulatory policies that might improve your ability to make intelligent consumption decisions in this area?

3.6 Consider the following examples of government intervention in economic life. For each, tell which form of "market failure" (if any) identified in the text might explain the intervention. *(a)* Health warnings on cigarette packs, *(b)* no-smoking regulations in theaters, *(c)* speed limits on public roads, *(d)* mandatory seatbelt use laws, *(e)* school lunch subsidies, *(f)* antigambling laws, *(g)* federally subsidized passenger rail service, *(h)* municipal police forces, *(i)* rent controls, and *(j)* agricultural price supports.

3.7 Sellers of over-the-counter (i.e., nonprescription) drugs usually know far more about the attributes of their products than do consumers. In the absence of federal regulation of the drug market, what (if anything) would protect consumers from fraud by these companies? Put another way, what (if anything) would these companies have to lose if they sold consumers a drug that proved useless or harmful?

3.8 Some studies have found that for poor families the costs of pollution control exceed the benefits received, while for high-income families benefits exceed costs. What do such studies suggest about the vertical-equity effects of some environmental policies? Based on such information, where are such policies likely to be placed on a diagram like Figure 3.7?

CHAPTER 4

CAPTURE THEORY AND BEYOND: THE POLITICAL MARKETPLACE

Some modern zealots appear to have no better knowledge of truth, nor better manner of judging it, than by counting noses.

Jonathan Swift

It is possible to invent a public interest rationale for every proposed government intervention in the marketplace. Indeed, it is de rigueur for advocates of particular policies to attempt to demonstrate how their proposals respond to one or more of the concerns discussed in Chapter 3. It is important to recognize, however, that intervention which truly has nothing to do with the public interest rationales we have enumerated—and which actually reduces welfare—can and does take place. Such action often is the result *not* of innocent mistakes, but of economic and political forces that scholars have only recently begun to describe.

The idea that government can do ill as well as good is not the invention of modern cynics, of course. Adam Smith wrote in 1776, "There is no art which one government sooner learns of another, than that of draining money from the pockets of the people."[1] And in 1861 John Stuart Mill wrote

[T]he very principle of constitutional government requires it to be assumed, that political power will be abused to promote the particular purposes of the holder; not

[1]Adam Smith, *The Wealth of Nations* (1776); Edwin Cannan's ed., University of Chicago Press, Chicago, 1976, pp. 389–390.

because it always is so, but because such is the natural tendency of things, to guard against which is the especial use of free institutions.[2]

In this chapter we examine how government might fail to serve the public interest—and how government action might, in fact, create the same kinds of welfare losses associated with market failures such as monopoly or externalities. We do this not because such failure, to paraphrase Mill, will *always* occur, but because it *might* occur and because there are systematic forces at work to encourage it. Thus, to obtain a full understanding of government intervention in the economic sphere, we must study the behavior of voters, politicians, and bureaucrats and the mechanisms by which these individuals affect economic life.

CAPTURE THEORY

Not long after public interest arguments had contributed to the creation of various federal and state regulatory agencies, economists and political scientists began to question whether furtherance of the common good was the sole—or even the dominant—goal of such agencies. One of the earliest criticisms of government regulation was that agencies created to protect society from industry misconduct might become the *captives* of the industries they were supposed to oversee, furthering the industries' interests at the expense of consumers. In the extreme, such capture might leave consumers worse off than if there had been no attempt to regulate at all.

The process by which agencies might be captured is reasonably straightforward. Even if the affected firms opposed regulation at the outset, they would soon find that regulation carries certain benefits, e.g., that it inhibits new entry into their market. This might enable the entrenched regulated firms to earn rates of profit above the competitive level. Gradually, it would dawn on the entrenched firms and their regulators that there is a coincidence of interests between them: The regulators can help the firms achieve their objectives (higher profits), and the firms can make life comfortable for the regulators by allowing them to achieve at least *some* of their objectives.

In addition, capture theorists observed that regulatory agencies require the services of individuals who are experts in the industries to be regulated. But such experts will most often be found within the industry itself and therefore may be sympathetic to the industry's interests. Alternatively, the lure of high-paying jobs with the regulated firms once their term of government service is complete may make regulators favorably disposed to such firms' interests, for clearly it will be necessary to "stay on these firms' good side" for such job offers to eventuate. The implication is that regulation will often be less stringent than the public interest requires and sometimes will actually defy the public interest.

But capture theory has its deficiencies. First, there is evidence that regulato-

---

[2]John Stuart Mill, *Considerations on Representative Government*, 1861; as quoted in James M. Buchanan, "The Economic Theory of Politics Reborn," *Challenge*, 31 (March-April 1988), p. 10.

ry agencies have not always behaved as if they were the captives of the industries they oversee.[3] Second, the theory is mute on the question of how or why some agencies might be captured while others are not, or why some agencies might be captured during some periods and not at others. Third, the theory offers no explanation as to how an agency which affects many industries will deal with what might be competing interests. The Interstate Commerce Commission (ICC), e.g., regulates not only the railroad industry but also trucking and barge lines. These are in many respects competing industries; the theory offers no rationale to explain how the agency would balance the varying goals of each or whether (or why) it will favor one over another.

In sum, capture theory should be viewed as an early, and rather primitive, explanation of regulatory failure. It is not that capture theory is irrelevant or false—the theory is not sufficiently well formulated to enable us to predict when capture might occur and to understand all the conditions that might enable it to occur. By focusing attention on such issues, however, the early literature on regulatory capture did help set the stage for later, more useful models of business-government interaction.

VIGNETTE 4.1   Did the Railroads Capture the ICC?

As we noted in Chapter 1, the Interstate Commerce Commission was organized in 1887 as the first federal regulatory agency. Despite high hopes that the ICC would solve "the railroad problem" (e.g., rationalize a rate structure under which isolated rural shippers often paid more for short-haul service than urban customers paid to ship freight long distances), the ICC is widely regarded as a costly failure. As Ari Hoogenboom and Olive Hoogenboom summarized, "The most prevalent view today is that the ICC did not live up to its promise because it was captured and manipulated by the very industry it was created to regulate."[4]

Historian Gabriel Kolko went so far as to suggest that railroads not only dominated the ICC from its earliest days, but actually fought for creation of the agency in hopes it would eliminate competition they themselves could not control.[5] And Ralph Nader's Center for Study of Responsive Law asserted that the ICC's behavior in the 1960s was exactly that predicted by capture theory. The Nader group found that ICC staffers often accepted in-kind benefits (free travel, accommodations, meals, etc.) at industry expense and that there was regular movement of ICC staff to industry employment and back again. Of the 11 commissioners to leave the ICC between 1958 and 1967, for example, 9 took jobs in firms regulated by the ICC or worked as attorneys representing firms before the ICC; the other 2 departees simply retired. The result, the Nader group concluded, was that the ICC was at best a "sleepy watchdog" guarding consumer interests.[6]

[3]See, e.g., G. William Schwert, "Public Regulation of National Securities Exchanges: A Test of the Capture Hypothesis," *Bell Journal of Economics and Management Science,* 8 (Spring 1977), pp. 128–150.

[4]Ari Hoogenboom and Olive Hoogenboom, *A History of the ICC,* W. W. Norton, New York, 1976, p. ix.

[5]Gabriel Kolko, *Railroads and Regulation, 1877–1916,* Princeton University Press, Princeton, NJ, 1965.

[6]Robert C. Fellmeth, *The Interstate Commerce Commission: The Public Interest and the ICC,* Grossman, New York, 1970.

But if the Interstate Commerce Act of 1887 was an attempt to help the railroads form a cartel, it had several major deficiencies in this regard. As George Hilton pointed out, the act provided no rate-setting powers to the ICC, did not restrict entry into railroading, and prohibited practices that might have enabled the railroads to stabilize rates at monopolistic levels.[7] Although these "shortcomings" would be at least partly corrected by subsequent legislation, especially the Transportation Act of 1920, it is clear that Congress and the ICC were not uniformly the servants of the railroads' interests. In part, this was because there were competing interest groups to whom Congress was at least occasionally sensitive. Lobbies for merchants, farmers, and manufacturers all helped shape the initial act and subsequent modifications to it, often to the detriment of railroads. The Hoch-Smith Resolution of 1925, for example, required the ICC to set agricultural freight rates with an eye toward "stabilizing" agricultural incomes—a clear invitation to give special consideration to some regions or classes of shippers at the expense of certain railroads or of other classes of shippers. Railroads' requests for rate increases were often turned down, and ICC decisions in rate appeals cases went against the railroads about half the time. Further, there is strong evidence that rates on some commodities were not set *above* railroads' costs but so far *below* costs that rail customers occasionally invented elaborate ways of evading ICC regulations and *raising* rates in order to secure suitable service.[8]

This is not to say that ICC regulation has been "balanced" or efficient. It is quite clear that ICC regulation has distorted resource allocation and generated considerable economic inefficiency. As a result, substantial modification of this regulatory structure is now underway. But it would be simplistic to chalk up all the ICC's failures to capture by the industry that the commission was created to tame.

REGULATION AS AN ECONOMIC GOOD

A better-specified theory, originating with Nobel laureate George Stigler,[9] is often referred to as the *economic theory of regulation*. Simply put, this theory treats regulation as a commodity or good. Like any good, regulation will have an equilibrium price and output determined by the interplay of the forces of supply and demand. Individuals demand regulation because they expect some tangible benefits from it. The demanders can be consumers who seek protection from monopoly or producers who seek protection from each other. The suppliers are these individuals' political representatives. Proponents of the economic theory of regulation tend to conclude (as earlier proponents of capture theory did) that producer interests typically prevail over consumer interests—or, more generally, that *special interests* will often succeed in the political marketplace.

---

[7]George W. Hilton, *The Transportation Act of 1958,* Indiana University Press, Bloomington, 1969.

[8]See Stephen J. K. Walters, "Reciprocity, Rebating, and Regulation," *Southern Economic Journal,* 51 (January 1985), pp. 766–775.

[9]See George J. Stigler, "The Theory of Economic Regulation," *Bell Journal of Economics and Management Science,* 2 (Spring 1971), pp. 3–21. The theory was subsequently refined by Sam Peltzman, "Toward a More General Theory of Regulation," *Journal of Law and Economics,* 19 (August 1976), pp. 211–240.

But how can the interests of many consumers be overridden by the interests of producers who are after all relatively few in number? How, in the political arena, can a minority rule the majority? In Stigler's model of economic regulation, political decision making is like an auction in which the highest bidder wins the right to tax everyone else. In this auction, however, *participation is not costless*. It is expensive to learn what is being auctioned and to make a bid (i.e., communicate with one's political representatives), and it is even more expensive to put together coalitions of bidders. The winning bidder is likely to be a relatively small or compact group because such groups will be cheaper to organize and therefore more likely to use the political process successfully.

To see this, consider a simple numerical example. Suppose we have a population of 100 people and a policy exists that would bestow benefits on 10 of these people at the expense of the other 90. In the ideal world of political and economic models where information is perfect and freely available and where the costs of transacting in the political market are zero, enactment of such a policy would be very unlikely. The majority of voters who would be adversely affected by the policy would know this with certainty and would (costlessly) inform political decision makers of their opposition on these grounds, and the political decision makers would block the policy. But in the real world, information is rarely perfect and never freely available, and the costs of transacting in the political market (whether this consists of writing letters to elected representatives or hiring expensive lobbyists) are certainly far from zero.

In our example, let us suppose the total value of the benefits to be transferred from the majority to the minority is $100. If this is the case, the 10 beneficiaries can expect to receive $10 each if the policy is adopted; the 90 on whom the costs of the policy fall would pay about $1.11 each. Clearly, each member of the majority has a smaller "stake" in this policy than each prospective beneficiary. Each member of the majority may have, therefore, a much smaller incentive to take political action than each prospective beneficiary does. In fact, if the costs of learning about the policy plus the costs of trying to implement or block it exceed $1.11 per person, it is quite likely that *none* of those in the affected majority will take any political action whatever! Political decision makers would scan the political landscape and see 10 very vigorous advocates of the policy—and no meaningful opposition. Note also that the prospective beneficiaries can actually raise payers' learning costs by offering *spurious* public interest rationales for the policy. To the extent that these rationales have any surface plausibility, they will increase the information costs that the majority must pay before deciding to oppose the policy.

Another factor that enhances the likelihood that the majority will be inactive is the free-rider problem, discussed in Chapter 3 in the context of the provision of public goods. In this case, even if the numerical majority are well informed about a policy's damaging effects on them, some may take no action because they may seek to "ride free" on the activity of others. Of course, if everyone seeks such a ride, no opposition will materialize. (Free-rider problems may also afflict the numerical minority, however, and impose some limits on the size of effective political coalitions.) The conclusion is that a numerical minority can, because of positive information and organization costs, rule a majority in the public policy arena.

VIGNETTE 4.2   The "Goods" We Demand from Government

Stigler identified[10] four basic "goods" which an industry (or occupation) may demand of the state:

1 Direct money or in-kind transfers. Farmers, e.g., receive both sorts of payments from the Department of Agriculture; federal outlays for "farm income stabilization" totaled $29.6 billion in 1986. Given that about 2.9 million people (hired workers and unpaid family members) worked on farms in that year, these outlays averaged over $10,000 per farmer. Most of these payments went to relatively large enterprises; farms with sales over $500,000, representing only 1.2 percent of all farms, received 13.3 percent of government payments in 1987.[11]

2 Control over market entry by new rivals. The Civil Aeronautics Board (CAB), e.g., licensed *no* new trunk airlines from its creation in 1938 to its eventual phaseout in 1984. Prior to (partial) deregulation of the trucking industry beginning in 1979, the Interstate Commerce Commission severely restricted entry into this market: In 1976, the ICC issued about 4,700 new licenses, but in 1980 the number of new licenses granted exceeded 21,000.[12]

3 Policies that affect the prices of substitute or complementary goods. At the local level, e.g., owners of existing homes often reap large capital gains by limiting or banning construction of new homes. Building codes often limit the use of new labor-saving materials, benefiting building trades unions. At the federal level, the creation and funding of the interstate highway system were of enormous benefit to the trucking industry.

4 Direct price fixing. Since limits on new entry may not be sufficient to keep prices above costs for existing firms, these firms might desire price controls administered by a body with power to curb price cutting. Thus, the CAB not only controlled entry into the airline industry and allocated routes but also set fares. As a result, in the early 1970s fares on intrastate routes (not subject to CAB rate setting) were often about half those on routes of similar mileage across state lines. In 1974, flying between San Francisco and Los Angeles (338 miles) on an unregulated carrier cost $18.75, while flying between Washington and Boston (399 miles) on a CAB-regulated carrier cost $41.67.[13]

Stigler concluded his discussion of the economic theory of regulation with a caution and a suggestion:

> Until the basic logic of political life is developed, reformers will be ill-equipped to use the state for their reforms, and victims of the pervasive use of the state's support of special groups will be helpless to protect themselves. Economists should quickly establish the license to practice on the rational theory of political behavior.[14]

As we shall see, however, the application of economic tools to the analysis of the political marketplace had already begun.

---

[10]Stigler, "Theory of Economic Regulation," pp. 4–6.

[11]Sources: *Statistical Abstract of the United States, 1988,* pp. 293, 607; *Annual Report of the President's Council of Economic Advisors,* U.S. Government Printing Office, Washington, 1987, p. 152.

[12]Thomas Gale Moore, "Rail and Trucking Deregulation," in Leonard W. Weiss and Michael W. Klass (eds.), *Regulatory Reform: What Actually Happened,* Little, Brown, Boston, 1986, p. 27.

[13]Stephen Breyer, *Regulation and Its Reform,* Harvard University Press, Cambridge, MA, 1982, p. 330.

[14]Stigler, "Theory of Economic Regulation," p. 18.

THE THEORY OF PUBLIC CHOICE

Starting in the late 1950s and early 1960s, Nobel laureate James Buchanan, Gordon Tullock, and several others began to develop an economic theory of politics, called *public choice analysis*. In part, this economic analysis of politics built on the insights of Anthony Downs, Duncan Black, and Nobel laureate Kenneth Arrow, who began to analyze majority voting rules and social choice in the early 1950s. To a great extent, however, this theory was based on principles that ruled the thinking of classical economists such as Adam Smith and David Hume, of the Founding Fathers of the U.S. Constitution, and even of political philosophers such as Hobbes and Spinoza.[15]

A central premise of public choice analysis is that political actors are just like everyone else; i.e., whether these actors are elected representatives, bureaucrats, or voters, they should be viewed as rational individuals who act in self-interest. Just as consumers maximize their utility subject to budget constraints or business owners maximize profits subject to conditions of cost and demand, we should expect political actors to maximize their well-being subject to the rules and constraints they face in the political arena. This *self-interest axiom* is in striking contrast to the public interest view of political action, which tends to view government as monolithic (i.e., not comprised of the actions of individuals at all) and selfless.

Some criticize this axiom as trivial. "Of course, politicians sometimes act in their self-interest," these critics say, "but what importance does this obvious fact have for analysis?" Public choice theorists respond, "Given this premise, we can use the traditional tools of economics to help understand government decision making."

Others, like political scientist Steven Kelman, argue that the self-interest axiom of public choice analysis is at best an excessively sweeping and cynical view of behavior in the political sphere. At worst, it may turn out to be a dangerous and self-fulfilling prophecy; i.e., the assumption that people act selfishly in political matters may be taken as an invitation to do so.[16] But public choice analysts would argue, first, that this axiom is not a suggested norm *for* behavior but a hypothesis *about* behavior. Clearly, much human action is motivated by self-interest, and a thorough and objective analyst will wish to examine whether this motive explains much of what happens in the political marketplace—quite independent of the moral issue of what *ought* to motivate human action. We can use the self-interest axiom—and others—to produce models of political behavior which have testable implications. If these implications are consistent with real-world observations, then the models are valuable as predictors and should be retained; if real-world experience refutes our hypotheses, the models will be discarded in favor of better ones. But this scientific inquiry must be guided by our best estimates of what human behavior actually *is* rather than by our wishes about what it *should* be.

---

[15] A comprehensive yet accessible survey of this theory, to which the succeeding discussion owes much, is by Dennis C. Mueller, *Public Choice II*, Cambridge University Press, London, 1989.

[16] See Steven Kelman, *Making Public Policy*, Basic Books, New York, 1987, p. 249.

Part of the value of public choice theory may lie in guiding us to institutions or rules of conduct that may save scarce resources which must now be allocated to the task of *restraining* selfish behavior. If human beings are not universally selfless, then some effort will have to be expended in convincing them to act in accordance with ethical or moral principles where these diverge from private interests. In a world of scarce resources, it will thus be desirable to develop laws or other rules which make the pursuit of private gain consistent with the attainment of the objectives of the community as a whole. As Sir Dennis Robertson has put it,

> There exists in every human breast an inevitable state of tension between the aggressive and acquisitive instincts and the instincts of benevolence and self-sacrifice. It is for the preacher, lay or clerical, to inculcate the ultimate duty of subordinating the former to the latter. It is the humbler, and often the invidious, role of the economist to help, so far as he can, in reducing the preacher's task to manageable dimensions. It is his function to emit a warning bark if he sees courses of action being advocated or pursued which will increase unnecessarily the inevitable tension between self-interest and public duty; and to wag his tail in approval of courses of action which will tend to keep the tension low and tolerable.[17]

With such considerations in mind, we turn now to some of the major propositions of public choice theory that have withstood empirical testing so far.

The Behavior of Voters

A Paradox of Majority Voting   In the political marketplace, decisions are typically based on a majority vote. A majority of voters determines which candidates are elected to office; a majority of (voting) officeholders determines which bills become law, fixes budget allocations, etc. It is common to assume that a majority voting rule will produce stable outcomes that conform to voters' preferences or at least to the preferences of the victorious majority. By following the work of Arrow and Black,[18] however, it can be shown that this will not always be the case.

Consider the following example. Suppose there are three voters (Black, Gray, and White) who collectively must choose one of three different public goods to construct (a community pool, a library, or a park). Table 4.1 shows how each voter ranks the three alternatives; each voter has well-ordered but differing preferences. Black prefers the pool to the library and the library to the park. Gray's top choice is the park; White's top choice is the library.

Obviously, if all three alternatives are on the ballot, none will command a majority, since Black, Gray, and White will all cast their votes for their top

---

[17]D. H. Robertson, "What Does the Economist Economize?" *Economic Commentaries*, Staples, London, 1956, p. 148, as quoted in James M. Buchanan and Gordon Tullock, *The Calculus of Consent*, University of Michigan Press, Ann Arbor, 1962, p. 28.

[18]See Kenneth Arrow, *Social Choice and Individual Values*, Wiley, New York, 1951, and Duncan Black, *The Theory of Committees and Elections*, Cambridge University Press, London, 1958.

TABLE 4.1

A VOTING CYCLE. Given the voter preferences shown, three rounds of (pairwise) voting aimed at determining which public good to fund will generate three different winners. Without some arbitrary vote-stopping rule, this community will be unable to make up its collective mind.

	Ranking of public goods		
Voter	Pool	Library	Park
Black	1	2	3
Gray	2	3	1
White	3	1	2

choices. But suppose that voting is "pairwise." That is, each good is matched against one of the others for a vote; the winner is then matched against the remaining good in the next round of voting, until a clear winner emerges. What will happen? If the first round matches the pool against the library, the pool will win: It is the top choice of Black, but it also gets Gray's vote because Gray's top choice (the park) is not on this ballot and Gray ranks the pool ahead of the library. The second round, then, has the pool versus the park, and now the park wins: It is the top choice of Gray but also gets White's vote because White's top choice (the library) is not on this ballot and White ranks the park ahead of the pool. Then we get a surprise in the third round: We expect that the park will defeat the library because earlier the pool defeated the library, and then the park defeated the pool. But the library wins! It is the top choice of White but also gets Black's vote because Black's top choice (the pool) is not on the ballot and Black ranks the library ahead of the park.

Note the paradoxical results: In three rounds of voting, there are three different winners. And despite the fact that each voter is able to unambiguously rank the goods from most to least preferred, there is no clear majority that can do the same thing. Majorities will rank the pool over the library, the park over the pool, and the library over the park, and then the whole cycle will start over again. There will be a "winner" only if the voting is arbitrarily stopped at some point, but that "winner" cannot be said to be the clear preference of a majority of voters. We conclude that even where individual preferences are clear and consistent, majority choices can be inconsistent and cyclical. When there are more than two choices available and voting is pairwise, majority rule may be unable to select a winner unless some arbitrary vote-stopping device is used (i.e., the community may be unable to make up its collective mind or will do so arbitrarily).

This is not to say that majority rule can *never* produce stable outcomes. When the preferences of voters and the issue to be decided conform to certain conditions, it can be shown that majority voting will produce an equilibrium. Suppose, e.g., that the issue to be decided is the amount to be spent on a public good such as national defense. Three voters (Black, Gray, and White again) have preferences like those portrayed in Figure 4.1. Each voter's preferences are "single-peaked." That is, each experiences her or his highest level of utility at some unique level of expenditure for national defense and experiences lower utility when spending for this public good is set above or below this expenditure level. Black, obviously dovish on defense, most approves of expenditure level *L*; Gray, *M*; and White, *N*. Majority-rule voting among the three alternatives *L*, *M*, and *N* would—even if voting were pairwise—produce an equilibrium level of spending at *M*. In a ballot between *L* and *M*, Black would vote for *L* but Gray and White would choose *M*. If the ballot has *M* versus *N*, then *M* wins again, since it gets Black and Gray's vote while *N* gets only White's vote. Given single-peaked preferences, then, majority rule will *not* lead to endless voting cycles; a stable equilibrium will lie at the preference peak for the median voter (in this case, Gray).

But we live in a complicated world. Not all issues involve but a single dimension of choice (such as the amount of spending on a public good), and not all voters have single-peaked preferences. As a result, the cycling problem

FIGURE 4.1
SINGLE-PEAKED PREFERENCES AND VOTING. When each voter's utility from spending on a public good is highest at some particular level and diminishes when spending is above or below this level (i.e., when voter preferences are single-peaked), majority rule will not produce a voting cycle.

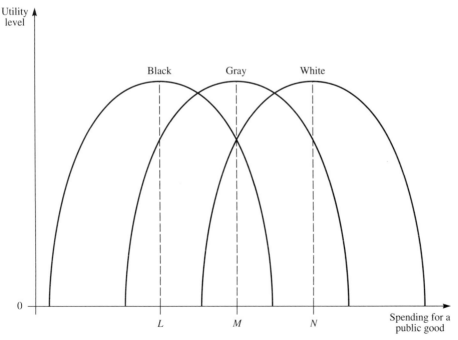

may occasionally surface.[19] Note that this does not imply that society will be paralyzed by an inability to reach consensus. Votes *will* be taken and decisions made. Where issues have many dimensions and voters' preferences are not well ordered, however, it will be impossible to say whether the decisions made are consistent with the preferences of a majority of voters. Some decisions may, e.g., be a by-product of an arbitrary cessation of voting after one or two rounds; others may be affected by the particular set of choices (i.e., the agenda) placed before voters. In such cases, it is naive to assume that the decision made will maximize social welfare or the welfare of a majority of the electorate, *because it is impossible to know (and accurately measure) what the will of the majority is.* Stated another way, certain key conditions—regarding the nature of voters' preferences or the issue under consideration—must be met before we can safely conclude that a collective decision made by majority rule is efficient or welfare-enhancing. This will be true even where people take the trouble to become well informed and to vote, and, as we will see, they frequently do neither.

Rational Ignorance and Abstention   In the economic marketplace, your spending on particular goods leads directly to the satisfaction of your wants. If you want shoes, e.g., all you have to do is find a willing seller and purchase the shoes you find most desirable at the price. In the political marketplace, however, your attempt to obtain a particular good is complicated by several factors. First, what you have to spend is not dollars but votes (although you can, of course, supplement your vote with monetary contributions to candidates or causes). And whether you get what you want in the political market will depend on not only the availability of a willing supplier but also the actions of other voters and of the representatives all collectively choose. As a result, we must be careful about the kinds of assumptions we make regarding voter behavior. There are two key issues to address: how much information voters will acquire prior to voting and whether, in fact, voting (or some other form of participation) will occur at all.

It is evident that most voters are relatively uninformed about political matters. One poll found that only 46 percent of voters knew the *name* of their congressional representative, much less how their representative felt about key policy matters.[20] And although this may be lamentable, it is also understandable from an economic standpoint. Many political issues will affect the individual only trivially, and spending time or effort to learn about such issues may not "pay." It is also true that many eligible voters rarely bother to vote. In the 1988 Presidential election, just 50.2 percent of the eligible population

---

[19]Several studies have explored, via simulation techniques, the likelihood that cycles would occur in practice. For a review of this literature, see R. G. Niemi, "Majority Decision-Making with Partial Unidimensionality," *American Political Science Review,* 63 (June 1969), pp. 488–497. If all possible preference orderings are equally likely, the probability of cycling is quite high; this probability declines if preferences are single-peaked or if some rankings are more likely than others.

[20]Louis Harris poll, published as *Confidence and Concern: Citizens View American Government,* Part 2, Government Printing Office, Washington, December 1973, pp. 215–216.

voted; only 33.4 percent voted in the off-year elections of 1986. But this, too, may be economically rational behavior: There is some cost of voting (chiefly time), and if one's vote is not expected to contribute significantly to the outcome of the election, these costs may exceed the anticipated benefits of voting.

The *rational ignorance* and *rational abstention* of voters can be better illustrated with an arithmetic example.[21] Suppose you feel that election of a certain Presidential candidate might be worth $10,000 to you. Before you rush out to vote for this candidate, however, consider: Your feeling could be mistaken, or, even if you are correct, your vote may not matter (i.e., the candidate may be elected or defeated by a sizable margin whatever you do). It is possible, then, to calculate a preelection estimate of the benefits associated with voting for this candidate by multiplying the amount of benefits you expect if the candidate is elected ($10,000) by the probability that your judgment about the candidate is accurate A by the likelihood that your vote will matter M. Let us suppose A equals 50 percent and M is 0.0000001 (i.e., there is a 1-in-10,000,000 chance that the election will be decided by your vote). In such circumstances, the *ex ante* expected benefits of voting for this candidate are ($10,000) (0.5) (0.0000001) = $0.0005. Clearly, this is a trivial expected benefit, and if the costs of voting are nontrivial or if there are no ancillary benefits of voting, such as entertainment value or psychic satisfaction associated with doing one's civic duty, you probably won't vote.

Note that if the election is expected to be very close, more voting might be expected because as M (the likelihood that a single vote will matter) rises, so do the expected benefits of voting. Note also that it may be possible to formulate more accurate assessments of candidates by gathering information. While information gathering will increase the expected value of voting by increasing A (or perhaps altering the amount of benefits expected if the candidate is elected), this act will also be costly. In the example above, suppose it is possible to increase A from 0.5 to 0.99 by buying information. Learning in this way increases the expected value of voting for this candidate from $0.0005 to $0.00099—still a trivial sum. The information is "worth" $0.00049, and unless it costs less than this amount or unless learning has some entertainment value, the information will not be acquired. It is little wonder, then, that many voters are relatively ill-informed; typically, voters do not seriously research candidates or issues, but rely instead on information that comes to them "automatically" from various media.

That voters will be rationally ignorant of many of the policies that affect them and will not always exercise their franchise to vote casts further doubt on the presumption that majority-rule collective decisions will always enhance social welfare. What is more, these characteristics of voters will certainly be of interest to politicians. As Tullock has noted,

[T]he politician, in making up programs to appeal to rationally ignorant voters, would be attracted by fairly complex programs which have a concentrated benefi-

---

[21]This illustration follows Gordon Tullock, *Toward a Mathematics of Politics,* University of Michigan Press, Ann Arbor, 1967, pp. 108–114.

cial effect on a small group of voters and a highly dispersed injurious effect on a large group of voters.[22]

How politicians choose their platforms and how they transact in the political marketplace have been the object of acute interest among public choice theorists, as we will see.

The Behavior of Politicians

The Median Voter and Political Competition   It is quite common for voters to complain that political candidates' positions on the issues are indistinct, i.e., that there are few apparent differences in the views espoused by either candidate in a two-person race. There is every reason to believe that this is no accident. Under certain conditions, political competition induces vote-maximizing politicians to espouse middle-of-the-road positions on issues and to blur distinctions with their rivals as well.

Take the simplest possible case. Suppose that (1) there are only two candidates, (2) the political decisions to be made all involve choices that are guided by a one-dimensional ideological spectrum (from left to right), and (3) voters are distributed along this spectrum as in Figure 4.2: 50 percent of voters hold positions to the left of M, 50 percent of voters hold positions to the right of M, and the distribution has a single peak at M, the median position. (Note that the area under this distribution will equal 100 percent of the vote.) Suppose further that each voter tends to vote for the candidate who is closest to her or his ideological position.

[22] Ibid., p. 103.

FIGURE 4.2
AN IDEOLOGICAL DISTRIBUTION OF VOTERS AND POLITICAL COMPETITION. If voters are normally distributed along some one-dimensional ideological spectrum and vote for candidates closest to their position on this spectrum, vote-maximizing politicians will likely tailor their policy platforms to conform to the preferences of the median voter.

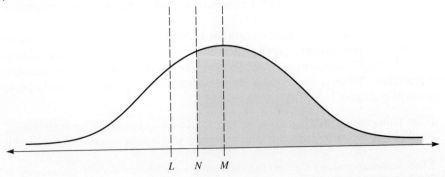

If for some reason one candidate takes position L, that candidate will lose decisively to a candidate taking the middle-of-the-road position M. The candidate at L will get all the voters to the left of L plus the voters between L and position N (which lies halfway between L and M). The candidate at M, however, will get the 50 percent of voters to the right of M plus the voters between N and M. Thus, the middle-of-the-roader in this example will win a share of the vote equal to the shaded area in Figure 4.2, far in excess of the 50 percent of the vote needed for victory. Clearly, then, there is a great incentive for politicians to adopt positions as close as possible to the median position. In this example, the only way for the candidate at L to increase her or his share of the total vote is to "move to the right," toward M. (Note that if this candidate stubbornly stays at L, a vote-maximizing rival can increase her or his share of the vote by moving to a point that is just to the right of L.) Only by staking out position M can each candidate be assured of at least 50 percent of the vote; if both candidates are at M, the election may be decided by random chance (e.g., voters pulling the wrong lever in the voting booth) or nonideological factors (e.g., which candidate is the better orator). In this simple model, then, the median position is clearly the vote-maximizing one for both candidates. As politicians seek to stake their claim to the median voter, competition will often make the candidates in a two-party race look like Tweedledum and Tweedledee.

Relaxing the assumptions of the simple model outlined above leads to some interesting implications. If some voters consider the candidates so much alike that voting is not worth the bother (voter indifference) or some voters consider middle-of-the-road positions so unattractive that voting for either candidate is undesirable (voter alienation), we will *still get the median outcome* as long as the distribution of preferences is as in Figure 4.2.[23] But a spreading out of candidates may occur if elections are in two steps, e.g., competition for a nomination within parties and then competition among or between parties. All that is required is that the distribution of preferences within a party differ from that of the population as a whole. In such a case, winning a nomination will require a candidate to stake out a position near the party median; to win the general election, however, the candidate would like to be near the population median. The optimum strategy, therefore, may be for candidates to stake out (differing) positions somewhere between their party median and the population median.[24]

If a third candidate is allowed into the race, spreading may also occur. Suppose, e.g., a third candidate stakes out a position slightly to the left of M in Figure 4.2. This would earn the third candidate slightly less than half the vote; but if the remaining two candidates stayed at M, they would split the remain-

---

[23]See O. A. Davis, M. J. Hinich, and P. C. Ordeshook, "An Expository Development of a Mathematical Model of the Electoral Process," *American Political Science Review*, 64 (June 1970), pp. 426–448.

[24]See, e.g., J. S. Coleman, "Internal Processes Governing Party Positions in Elections," *Public Choice*, 11 (Fall 1971), pp. 35–60.

der of the vote—and the third candidate would win! Of course, the other candidates would have a strong incentive *not* to remain at the median; one would likely move slightly to the right of M in order to isolate the remaining candidate in the middle. But then that candidate would have an incentive to "leapfrog" outside one of the others to isolate her or him, and so on. This spreading-out process will be limited, however, because as long as the peak of the distribution remains at M, a candidate can increase her or his portion of the vote (the positions of the other candidates remaining constant) by moving toward M.

One interesting implication of this model of political competition is that vote-maximizing politicians will be most anxious to serve the interests of the median voter. The model implies, then, that *redistributive policies will frequently transfer income not from rich to poor* (as we might prefer under various vertical-equity criteria) *but from the tails of the income distribution toward its center.* There is some empirical support for this hypothesis in the work of Werner Pommerehne,[25] who used Swiss data to test it against two competing hypotheses: an "altruistic" view that redistribution is from rich to poor and what he called a "New Left" hypothesis that redistribution is from poor to rich. Pommerehne found the data strongly supported the hypothesis that redistribution is from the tails of the income distribution toward the middle.

In the United States, however, the data show a mild rich-to-poor effect of federal redistributive policy. Suppose we rank all families in the United States by income, from richest to poorest, and then divide this ranking into quintiles (or fifths). We could then evaluate (at least partially) federal redistributive programs by seeing how much they change the various quintiles' income shares. Table 4.2 provides the necessary information. The five columns show the share of national income earned by each quintile of families, from the richest to poorest. The first row shows each quintile's pretax share of national income in 1984. For example, the richest fifth of the population earned 42.9 percent of the national income; the poorest fifth, 4.7 percent. Economist Frank Levy adjusted these figures to account for tax payments and receipts of Medicare, Medicaid, and food stamps.[26] The second row of Table 4.2 shows the results: The share of income received by the richest fifth of the population falls to 38.7 percent, the share received by the next richest quintile falls from 24.4 to 24.3 percent, and the shares received by all three lower quintiles increase, with the greatest increase (2.5 percentage points) in the poorest quintile.

Vote Trading or Logrolling   One possible deficiency of any voting system is that it may fail to take account of the *intensity* of voters' preferences on the issues. Suppose, e.g., that 49 percent of the electorate is passionately interested in the regulation of some activity that generates negative externalities, but 51

---

[25]Werner W. Pommerehne, "Budgetare Umverteilung in der Democratie: Ein empirischer Test Alternative Hypothesen," Discussion Paper 64, Konstanz (1975), as cited in Mueller, *Public Choice II*, p. 452.

[26]Frank Levy, *Dollars and Dreams: The Changing American Income Distribution*, Basic Books, New York, 1987, p. 195.

TABLE 4.2
THE EFFECTS OF FEDERAL TAX AND (CERTAIN) SPENDING PROGRAMS ON FAMILY
INCOME DISTRIBUTION IN THE UNITED STATES, 1984. Certain federal tax and transfer
programs redistribute income from rich to poor.

	Percentage of national income received by quintile				
	(1) (Richest)	(2)	(3)	(4)	(5) (Poorest)
Pretax share	42.9	24.4	17.0	11.0	4.7
Share after taxes, receipts of Medicare, Medicaid, food stamp benefits	38.7	24.3	17.7	12.2	7.2
Change (in percentage points)	−4.2	−0.1	+0.7	+1.2	+2.5

Source: Frank Levy, *Dollars and Dreams: The Changing American Income Distribution,* Basic Books, New York, 1987, p. 195.

percent of the electorate is mildly opposed to such regulation—perhaps because they are only trivially affected by the externalities and therefore are unwilling to pay any costs associated with the regulation. If a referendum is held on the issue (and if everyone bothers to gather information about it and vote—two big ifs, as we have seen), the proposal for regulation is likely to be defeated. This result may be eminently democratic, but it also may be ineffi-cient: The passionate minority may attach a far greater value to the proposed regulation than the majority attaches to its defeat. Social welfare might well be enhanced by the regulation, but since the referendum weighs all votes equally, the intensity of the minority's preferences is immaterial to the result—unless perhaps vote trading is permitted.

If voters can transact (i.e., swap support for policy X in exchange for sup-port for policy Y), then preference intensities may affect electoral outcomes. To see this, consider another simple example. Once again we have three voters (Black, Gray, and White) who this time are voting on two issues X and Y (where X is, say, whether to allow construction of an airport near town and Y is whether to spray the town with mosquito repellent). Suppose that prefer-ence intensities are not uniform among voters, i.e., that different voters attach a different value to each possible good. Table 4.3 shows how much each voter would pay for each good. Where valuations are negative, the voter would pay to see that the good is *not* produced. Gray (perhaps a frequent flier) intensely desires good X but weakly opposes Y; White intensely desires good Y (per-haps because of an allergy to mosquito bites) but weakly opposes X; Black (perhaps on ecological grounds) opposes both goods.

A simple referendum on each issue would lead to the defeat of both, even though both could enhance social welfare! Although Gray would pay $10 for good X, Black and White would vote against it even though they value its defeat by only $9. Similarly, White would pay $10 for good Y, but is outvoted by Black and Gray even though they value Y's defeat by only $9. Without vote

TABLE 4.3
INTENSITY OF VOTER PREFERENCES AND LOGROLLING. Without logrolling, both X and Y will be voted down 2 to 1. With logrolling, Gray and White may strike a bargain that ensures passage of both proposals.

	Value attached to each good or issue, $	
Voter	X	Y
Black	−5	−5
Gray	10	−4
White	−4	10

trading, the majority tyrannizes the minority on each question; but with trading, the result may be different. Clearly, there is potential for Gray and White to strike a bargain here. If Gray promises White to support good Y in exchange for White's support for good X, both proposals might pass. Production of both X and Y would make Gray and White better off, generating a net value of $6 for each. While it is true that Black would feel $10 worse off if both goods were produced, this cost would be more than offset by the $12 total gain of Gray and White. Vote trading thus enhances total social welfare in this example by $2.

Of course, vote trading among the general populace is rare. For one thing, it is—at least in most jurisdictions—illegal. But even if vote trading were not prohibited by law, such transactions are unlikely to occur in large volume for several reasons. First, an individual vote in any election is not likely to be decisive, and the transaction costs of negotiating trades will usually offset any gains. Second, secret balloting would make it impossible to determine whether agreements were honored, even if made.

But vote trading by legislators, called *logrolling*, is quite common and apparently has been so for a long time. Many analysts see no problem in this. In their view, logrolling simply allows minorities to express the intensity of their preferences for certain public goods in the same way as trading in private goods does. The community's net welfare can be improved by transactions in the political marketplace in the same way as welfare is enhanced by trade in the economic marketplace.

Note, however, that logrolling has the potential to *diminish* welfare as well as increase it. The welfare-enhancing result in the example discussed above hinges on the numbers assumed. If in Table 4.3 Gray and White are willing to pay only $8 (rather than $10) for the respective goods they most intensely desire, then vote trading will still occur but the result will *not* enhance social welfare. If X is worth only $8 to Gray and Y is worth $8 to White (all else unchanged), the trade of Gray's support for Y in exchange for White's support of X will net each $4; but this $8 total net gain for Gray and White is less than the $10 loss to Black if both X and Y are produced.

Thus, some have argued that logrolling and majority voting might beget a government that is "too large." Just as in the paragraph above Gray and White could cut a deal that would benefit them at the expense of society as a whole, special interests could use vote trading to beget many programs whose benefits are smaller—but much more concentrated—than their costs. The fear is, in Tullock's words, "If a given sum of money is to be spent on two different types of governmental activity, one of which is of general benefit and one of which benefits a series of special groups, too much will be spent on the latter."[27] Downs, however, has replied that any tendency of government to oversupply special interest legislation will be more than offset by a tendency to undersupply general interest legislation (e.g., public goods). In Downs' view, the rational ignorance of voters and free-riding behavior by voters will mean that many socially valuable programs will lack vigorous constituencies, and government will be "too small" and much of its activity misdirected.[28]

Note also that logrolling (or something like it) can occur even without any explicit vote trading by legislators or voters. Unrelated issues are sometimes addressed in a single piece of legislation, and candidates or parties often combine various policy stances into a single political platform. In the context of the example above, a party or candidate might run for office on a platform calling for adoption of both X and Y. Without even meeting or negotiating a trade of votes, Gray and White could then vote their party or candidate into office. Following this model, clever politicians often take positions that cater to some voters' most intense preferences on certain issues while deliberately opposing these voters' (less intense) wishes on other matters in order to satisfy some other group. Under certain preference orderings, the result will be lukewarm support from both groups. Such behavior is variously called *implicit logrolling*, or *bundling*.

The Shortsightedness Problem   In deciding what to do *now*, most of us calculate how our actions will affect our well-being tomorrow or next year or in 20 years. If this were not so, no one would ever go to college (which involves up-front costs in the form of tuition bills and forgone employment income in exchange for higher wages in the future) and many more of us would probably be in jail (having failed to weigh this future cost against the loot obtained from embezzlement, bank robbery, etc.). Obviously, some of us are better at such calculations than others. In addition, even the most forward-thinking individual will, given the impossibility of divining the future with perfect accuracy, sometimes make mistakes. Nevertheless, we try our best.

But politicians' evaluations of the future implications of current actions are complicated by a factor we do not face: the election cycle. If one is not reelected, the future costs or benefits of today's actions may not matter very much. Stated more formally, politicians may be biased toward policies that produce

[27]Gordon Tullock, "Some Problems of Majority Voting," *Journal of Political Economy*, 67 (December 1959), p. 578.

[28]Anthony Downs, "In Defense of Majority Voting," *Journal of Political Economy*, 69 (April 1961), pp. 192–199.

perceptible short-run benefits even if these benefits carry far larger long-term costs, for there is some chance that these costs will be identified with a successor. This bias is sometimes called the *shortsightedness problem*.

An arithmetic example should help make the nature of the problem more concrete. Suppose there are two possible policies (*A* and *B*) from which we may choose. Policy *A* requires spending $100 now, but will pay back $200 in exactly one year. Policy *B* requires no initial outlay; in fact, we *receive* $100 now, but must *repay* $200 in a year. Most of us would have no trouble determining that *A* is the better choice. If the interest rate we should use to calculate the present value of future receipts is 10 percent, then policy *A* has a net present value of $81.82. Policy *B*, by contrast, has a net present value of −$81.82.[29]

But a politician might make a different calculation—if there is an election *within* the next year. Given the possibility of electoral defeat, the politician will attach less weight to the future costs of *B* and benefits of *A*. Suppose an incumbent politician's chances of reelection are no better than 50-50, and suppose further that voters associate a policy's costs or benefits with the person in office at the time these costs or benefits are paid or received. (The latter may seem like a heroic assumption, but some policies are sufficiently complex that it may be quite difficult to correctly attribute blame or credit for their consequences—especially in view of voters' rational ignorance of the policy-making process.) To the incumbent, then, the *expected* future benefits of policy *A* are only $100 (the $200 future payment times the 50 percent chance the incumbent will be around to get credit for it), and the *expected* future costs of *B* are only −$100 (the −$200 future cost times the 50 percent chance that the incumbent will be blamed for it). To the incumbent politician, then, policy *A* appears to have a net present value of −$9.09, while *B* appears to have a net present value of $9.09.[30] The incumbent will choose *B!*

In sum, an impending election may cause incumbents to make socially inefficient—but personally rational—choices by altering the way in which they evaluate future benefits and costs. Most examples of such behavior have to do with macroeconomic policy. In 1971, for example, surveys showed that voters

---

[29]The present value (PV) of a receipt *R* received in exactly one year, if the interest rate is *i*, is simply

$$PV = R /(1 + i)$$

In this example, we can calculate the *net* present value of policy *A*, denoted NPV_A, as

$$NPV_A = -\$100 + \$200/(1 + 0.10) = -\$100 + \$181.82 = \$81.82$$

By contrast, the net present value of policy *B*, denoted NPV_B, is

$$NPV_B = \$100 - \$200/(1 + 0.10) = \$100 - \$181.82 = -\$81.82$$

[30]Now we have

$$NPV_A = -\$100 + (\$200) (0.50) /1.10 = -\$100 + \$90.91 = -\$9.09$$
$$NPV_B = \$100 + (-\$200) (0.50) /1.10 = \$100 - \$90.91 = \$9.09$$

were worried about inflation and wanted something done about it. President Nixon was warned by his economic advisers that wage and price controls might suppress inflation in the short run but would severely distort resource allocation and impose other long-term costs. Facing what he thought would be a tough election campaign in 1972, Nixon imposed controls. More recently, Reagan-era budget deficits exceeding $200 billion annually also illustrate the point.

More generally, there is the possibility of a *political business cycle.* Typically, output responds more quickly than prices to macroeconomic policy shifts. Thus, it may be possible to use expansionary monetary or fiscal policy to increase aggregate demand prior to an election. If timed correctly, the policy will produce short-run increases in income and employment before the election—and inflation increases after it. Empirical evidence on the issue is mixed. As Dennis Mueller summarizes it, "[a]lthough there exists clear evidence that some governments in some countries at some points in time have behaved as the political business cycle model predicts, the evidence is not strong enough to warrant the conclusion that this type of behavior is a general characteristic of democratically elected governments."[31]

The Behavior of Bureaucrats

External Controls and Internal Incentives   Once voters and their representatives decide which goods and services the government shall provide, this output must somehow be produced and delivered to consumers. The institutions created for this purpose—bureaus or bureaucracies—and the people who staff these institutions—bureaucrats—have been extensively analyzed from a public choice perspective in recent years.

In many respects, the theory of bureaucratic behavior is similar to the theory of managerial behavior in modern firms. In most modern firms (or at least those of relatively large size), the owners (or *principals*) hire managers (or *agents*) to conduct the firm's day-to-day affairs. But this separation of ownership and control of the firm can cause problems, sometimes called *principal-agent problems.* Specifically, it is feared that the owners of the firm will be unable to monitor all the actions of the managers they hire and that the managers will therefore have significant discretion to serve their own interests (i.e., maximize their own utility) rather than those of their employers (i.e., maximize shareholder wealth). The result will be waste, inefficiency, and misallocation of resources.

In the public sector, bureaucrats are the agents of the government, i.e., of the legislature and the chief executive. And just as with private firms, monitoring the decisions and actions of these agents is a difficult task. For three reasons, in fact, principal-agent problems may loom larger in the public sector

---

[31]Mueller, *Public Choice II,* p. 286.

than in private firms. First, the output provided by a government bureau is often intangible and therefore exceedingly hard to measure. Consider, e.g., the output of defense services, Taxpayers and their representatives can only guess how much "defense output" is being produced by measuring the inputs (soldiers, weapons, etc.) used for this purpose. Such measurement problems make monitoring the bureaucracy's actions and gauging its efficiency more difficult than for private firms, where output is measured in units and performance gauged by the profit rate. Second, these measurement problems might be amplified if government bureaus hold a monopoly in the good or service they are created to provide. Monopoly status not only removes competitive pressure that might enhance the performance of the bureau, but also denies the principal any alternative source of information about this performance.[32] Finally, the compensation formulas of bureaucrats are rarely devised with an eye toward efficiency enhancement. Private-sector principals commonly attempt to arrange salary and bonus payments so that managers' interests coincide as much as possible with owners' interests in lower costs and higher profits. In the public sector, agents typically do not benefit from cost savings or improvements in efficiency. Indeed, it is often observed that agencies that perform successfully, i.e., conduct their duties at lower-than-budgeted costs, will see their budget appropriations reduced in the next fiscal year. [33]

Taken together, these factors imply that the external controls applied to government bureaus will be relatively ineffective and that bureaus' internal incentives for efficiency will be weak. Both in absolute terms and relative to private-sector alternatives, then, public choice analysts tend to conclude that public agencies will be inefficient.

Models of Bureaucratic Behavior   An early economic model useful for predicting the behavior of bureaucrats was actually devised by Oliver Williamson to predict the behavior of managers of private corporations.[34] In the view of many, however, bureaucrats and managers face similar situations: The "owners" of the entities these agents operate are a diffuse group with neither the information nor the incentive to monitor their agents closely. Thus, neither the bureaucrat nor the manager will behave as a pure profit maximizer.

In the Williamson model, managers are assumed to maximize their own utility subject to a minimum profit constraint. Of course, what this model predicts about managerial behavior will depend in large part on assumptions about what produces utility for managers. In Williamson's view, management derives utility from two chief sources: increases in staff size and profits given

---

[32]Research by Kathleen Carroll shows that the monopoly structure of the federal bureaucracy is more limited than is generally assumed. See Kathleen A. Carroll, "Industrial Structure and Monopoly Power in the Federal Bureaucracy: An Empirical Analysis," *Economic Inquiry*, 27 (October 1989), pp. 683–703.

[33]Ronald S. Warren, Jr., "Bureaucratic Performance and Budgetary Reward," *Public Choice*, 24 (Winter 1975), pp. 51–58.

[34]Oliver E. Williamson, *The Economics of Discretionary Behavior: Managerial Objectives in a Theory of the Firm*, Prentice-Hall, Englewood Cliffs, NJ, 1964.

to stockholders over and above the minimum amount they expect. The former are deemed important because a larger staff is often correlated with higher salaries (and more job security) for managers; the latter yield satisfaction to managers in the form of pride in the organization or a feeling of accomplishment. Williamson's model predicts that costs of production in a firm managed by a utility maximizer will be higher than the minimum attainable, chiefly because of excessive staff size.

Building on the economic theory of the firm, William Niskanen produced the first formal model aimed specifically at bureaucratic behavior.[35] Niskanen assumes that bureaucrats will maximize utility by maximizing the total budget of their bureaus. In Niskanen's view, all the things that might plausibly enhance a bureaucrat's utility level (e.g., higher salary, more power, more perquisites of office) are likely to be positively related to the bureau's budget. The bureau's size will be limited, however, by the fact that it must supply that amount of output expected by the sponsor on approval of the bureau's budget—and a bureau that promises more than it can deliver will be penalized in future appropriations.

Niskanen also assumes that bureaus' unique status as monopoly producers endows them with significant bargaining advantages in dealing with appropriations committees, who are the buyers of the bureaus' output. Specifically, a monopolistic bureau may extract almost the full amount of the buyer's surplus by confronting the buyer with a single large package of programs at a single all-or-nothing price. In Niskanen's words, "[t]he primary difference between the exchange relation of a bureau and that of a market organization is that a bureau offers a total output in exchange for a budget, whereas a market organization offers units of output at a price."[36]

The Niskanen model predicts that the output of the bureau will far exceed the socially optimal rate of output. This is illustrated in Figure 4.3, which shows the sponsor's demand curve D for the bureau's product and the bureau's marginal cost curve MC. The optimal or ideal rate of output Q_i occurs at the intersection of the demand and marginal cost curves. The bureau, however, produces the rate of output Q_b associated with the largest possible budget subject to the constraint that total consumer benefits (the area bound by points $0BEQ_b$) equal total costs (area $0AFQ_b$). In effect, utility-maximizing bureaucrats "spend" the potential social surplus (area ABC, spent as area CFE) resulting from production of Q_i units of the good in order to expand output to Q_b and thus enhance their utility.

The models of Williamson and Niskanen have been modified or combined in various ways by several authors. Migue and Belanger, e.g., have criticized Niskanen in one important respect: "If Niskanen is right in assuming that the budget of the bureau is maximized, then no expenses other than those contributing to productivity are incurred since these would compete with out-

[35]William A. Niskanen, Jr., *Bureaucracy and Representative Government*, Aldine-Atherton, Chicago, 1971.
[36]Ibid., p. 25.

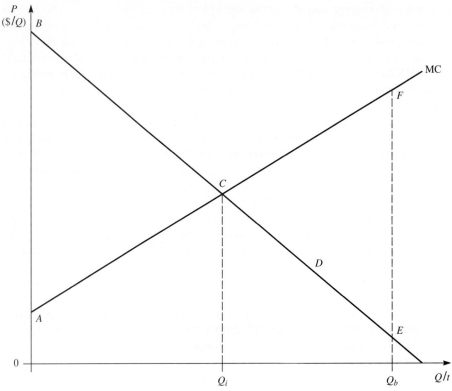

FIGURE 4.3
THE BUDGET-MAXIMIZING BUREAUCRACY. Instead of offering to produce the socially optimal rate of output Q$_i$, the bureau offers to produce Q$_b$. At Q$_b$, the bureau's budget is as large as possible subject to the constraint that total consumer benefits equal total production costs.

put."[37] In their view, any model of bureaucratic behavior must allow for the possibility that bureaucrats would expend part of their budget on utility-enhancing perquisites, higher salaries, leisure, etc. Such expenditures would raise the bureau's marginal costs of production and affect the amount of output the bureau would choose to produce. Figure 4.4 shows the result. Once again D shows the sponsor's demand curve and MC the marginal costs of which the bureau is (theoretically) capable, but the bureaucrat's costly expenditures raise actual marginal costs to MC'. The bureau once again spends all the prospective consumer surplus associated with the optimum level of output Q_i but in the Migue-Belanger model expands output only to Q_b' rather than Q_b (the Niskanen result). This is because part of the social surplus available to the bureaucrat (area ABC) will be spent as higher production costs (area AKGH), leaving fewer resources available to expand output. Thus,

[37]Jean-Luc Migue and Gerard Belanger, "Toward a General Theory of Managerial Discretion," *Public Choice,* 17 (Spring 1974), p. 29.

bureaucracies may be both allocatively and productively inefficient; i.e., they may produce a nonoptimal rate of output and do so at excessively high cost.

VIGNETTE 4.3 Are Public Enterprises Inefficient?

Empirical tests of the various economic theories of bureaucracy are complicated by the same sorts of measurement problems that plague the sponsors of the bureaus. Since most are monopolies producing intangible output, there are few benchmarks against which performance may be evaluated.

Some of the earliest—and wittiest—writings on the issue are by C. Northcote Parkinson, the originator of Parkinson's law: "Work expands so as to fill the time available for its completion."[38] So dim was Parkinson's view of bureaucratic behav-

---

[38]C. Northcote Parkinson, *Parkinson's Law and Other Studies in Administration,* Houghton Mifflin, Boston, 1957, p. 2.

FIGURE 4.4
THE ALLOCATIVELY AND PRODUCTIVELY INEFFICIENT BUREAUCRACY. If bureaucrats spend part of their budget on utility-enhancing "perks," marginal costs of production will rise to MC′ and the bureau's output will be Q_b'. Thus, the bureau will produce excessive output and do so at excessively high costs.

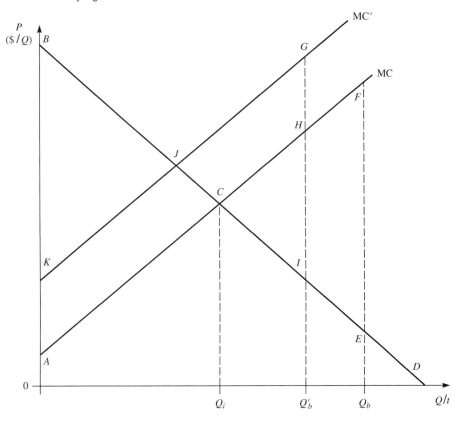

ior that he proposed two axioms: "(1) An official wants to multiply subordinates, not rivals and (2) officials make work for each other."[39] The implication is that bureaucracies will grow unchecked, even if there is nothing for them to do. And although some of Parkinson's acerbic observations were at least partly tongue-in-cheek, he provided ample data in support of his views. In the British Navy, e.g., the number of ships in commission *fell* by 67.74 percent, and the number of officers and seamen *fell* 31.5 percent between 1914 and 1928, yet the number of dockyard officials and clerks *rose* 40.28 percent and the number of Admiralty officials *rose* 78.45 percent in the same period![40]

There are many studies comparing the performance of public and private enterprises which compete in similar markets. One of the most detailed is by David Davies, who compared the performance of the state-owned and -operated Australian airline (Trans-Australian) with a private line (Anset) that flies similar routes with similar equipment. Davies found the productivity of the private line to be significantly greater on all measures for each of the 11 years studied. By Davies' estimate, denationalization (or "privatization") of the public line would reduce costs by 13 percent.[41]

In another study, Kenneth Clarkson found that private hospital administrators are more efficient than their public counterparts.[42] Mark Crain and Asghar Zardkoohi found that public water utilities' operating costs are about 25 percent higher than those of private utilities.[43] Others have reported cost savings in privately run custodial-service firms, day care centers, debt collection services, schools, electric utilities, and ship maintenance operations.[44]

Two additional studies support the hypothesis that bureaus will be both allocatively and productively inefficient. Stephen Gillespie studied how two federal agencies gather and disseminate statistical data and concluded that the costs of the programs evaluated greatly exceeded their private-sector value; i.e., the agencies had "overproduced" data.[45] And William Orzechowski, testing Parkinson's assertion that public managers will indulge a preference for excessive staff, found that public colleges employed roughly 40 percent more labor than private colleges of the same size.[46]

---

[39]Ibid., p. 4.

[40]Ibid., p. 8.

[41]David G. Davies, "The Efficiency of Public versus Private Firms," *Journal of Law and Economics*, 14 (April 1971), pp. 149–165.

[42]Kenneth W. Clarkson, "Some Implications of Property Rights in Hospital Management," *Journal of Law and Economics*, 15 (October 1972), pp. 363–384.

[43]W. Mark Crain and Asghar Zardkoohi, "A Test of the Property Rights Theory of the Firm: Water Utilities in the United States," *Journal of Law and Economics*, 21 (October 1978), pp. 395–408.

[44]James T. Bennett and Manuel H. Johnson, *Better Government at Half the Price: Private Production of Public Services*, Caroline House, Ottawa, IL, 1981. For a broad international survey concluding that state-owned enterprises are less profitable and less efficient than private firms, see Anthony Boardman and Aidan Vining, "Ownership and Performance in Competitive Environments: A Comparison of the Performance of Private, Mixed and State-Owned Enterprises," *Journal of Law and Economics*, 32 (April 1989), pp. 1–33.

[45]Stephen Gillespie, "Are Economic Statistics Overproduced?" *Public Choice*, 67 (1990), pp. 227–242.

[46]William Orzechowski, "Economic Models of Bureaucracy: Survey, Extensions, and Evidence," in Thomas E. Borcherding (ed.), *Budgets and Bureaucrats: The Sources of Government Growth*, Duke University Press, Durham, NC, 1977, pp. 229–259.

Rent Seeking

A central implication of the theoretical and empirical work of those engaged in public choice analysis is that the political marketplace, like the economic marketplace, will be imperfect. As a result of the rational ignorance of voters, free-rider problems, logrolling (explicit and implicit) by politicians, utility-maximizing behavior by bureaucrats, and numerous other factors, government action can produce transfers or losses of social surplus just as monopolies can.

Suppose, e.g., we have an industry like that portrayed in Figure 4.5, with all firms possessing constant unit cost C and facing a demand curve D. Suppose further that one or more of the factors discussed above results in some sort of government intervention that promotes monopoly power in this industry (perhaps by erecting entry barriers). Exercise of this monopoly power would produce an increase in price from P_c to P_m, a decrease in output from Q_c to Q_m, monopoly profit equal to area $P_c P_m F H$, and deadweight welfare loss equal to

FIGURE 4.5
THE COSTS OF RENT SEEKING. A monopoly would be able to earn rents equal to area $P_c P_m F H$. If it must spend real resources equal to this area to acquire monopoly power, these rent-seeking expenditures should be counted as part of the welfare costs of the monopoly.

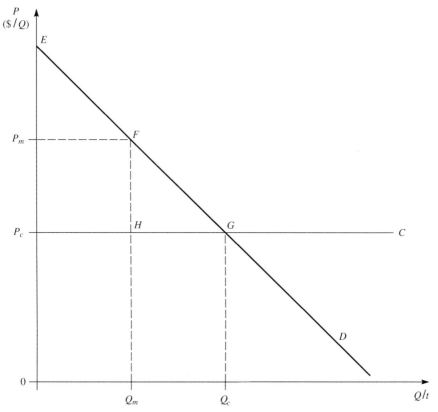

area *FGH*. Recall that these results are identical with those identified when monopoly was first discussed in Chapter 3. The only difference here is that we assume it is government intervention that has "created" the monopoly power and the resulting profits (area P_cP_mFH).

As we briefly noted in Chapter 3, economists frequently refer to such profits as *rents*. This specialized jargon is unfortunate, for it invites confusion with more common references to rent as a payment for the use of a particular building or piece of land. *Economic rents, however, are payments for goods or factors of production in excess of their opportunity costs.* In the example above, the (opportunity) cost of each unit of output produced is P_c, so each unit sold at price P_m earns the seller rents equal to P_m minus P_c.

Of course, receipt of such rents requires the seller to restrict output to Q_m; creating this "artificial scarcity" of the good imposes a deadweight welfare loss (area *FGH*) on society. But that may not be all there is to the story. If the firms benefiting from the government's grant of monopoly power must spend *real resources* in order to convince the government to make this grant, then these resource expenditures ought to be counted as part of the welfare costs of monopoly conduct—or of the government intervention that enables this conduct. If, say, the firms hire expensive lobbyists or advertising executives to convince voters and politicians of the value of limiting competition in this market, then the potential alternative output of these lobbyists or advertising executives is *lost*. (Recall the discussion of the welfare costs of monopoly in Vignette 3.1.)

Such activity—spending to acquire or maintain a market position in which rents may be earned—is called *rent seeking*. Not all rent seeking is socially wasteful. Some rents are temporary. In markets where entry is free, e.g., the lure of such rents will attract new firms and lead to lower prices and enhanced output for consumers. Rent seeking may also yield new lower-cost methods of production or result in new products that enhance consumer welfare. Even where rents are simply monopoly profits and where the monopoly power requisite for such rents is conferred by government, there need be no wasteful expenditure resulting from rent seeking. For example, the government might auction off a monopoly franchise to the highest bidder. Competitive bidding will yield a franchise price equal to the amount of rents expected once the franchise is held (or, more precisely, equal to the present value of the future *stream* of rents earned over the entire life of the franchise). If the government simply takes this amount and spends it on some worthy new program, then it ought not to be counted as a cost of rent seeking. As long as the transaction costs of conducting the auction are small, the monopoly rents can be viewed as a pure transfer—from consumers to the beneficiaries of the government's new spending.

In many cases, however, rent-seeking activity is associated with expenditures of resources that are not productive. Such expenditures can take many forms, from the obvious—spending to wine and dine policymakers in an effort to convince them to serve a particular interest—to the obscure. In her path-breaking article on the subject, Anne Krueger pointed out several subtle but important costs of government-erected barriers to international competition.[47] Many countries, e.g., protect domestic firms with strict quotas on foreign imports. Such restrictions raise the prices of imported goods above their costs; a license to import thus becomes very valuable to its holder. Where such licenses are allocated according to firms' capacities, there will often be overexpansion of capacity (even where some capacity is already idle) merely to claim a larger number of valuable licenses. Where licenses are allocated by other means, there will be wasteful expenditures aimed at influencing the probability of receiving a license, e.g., hiring a lobbyist to represent the firm in the capital city or locating the firm itself close to the capital. Where license allocation can be affected by bribes to public officials, there may be excessive competition for government jobs or for the credentials necessary to acquire such jobs.

Lest one think that such costs are trivial, Krueger has estimated that rents associated with import controls, restrictions on investment, and various price controls totaled 7.3 percent of India's national income in 1964; in Turkey in 1968, rents from import licenses alone were about 15 percent of the gross national product![48] The key question, of course, is whether such rents will be fully or partially dissipated by the kind of unproductive rent-seeking activities we have discussed. We might be tempted to think that all government-created rents will be fully dissipated if rent seekers have good information about these rents and can freely enter and exit the bidding for them (i.e., where rent seeking is competitive). But such assumptions may be unwarranted. The number of rent seekers may be limited, information may be imperfect, and there could well be less than full dissipation of rents. About all that is certain is that where government action may create economic rents, some of or all these rents are likely to be spent in advance to *obtain* them; where government action can destroy rents, some or all are likely to be spent to *protect* them.

See Table 4.4.

VIGNETTE 4.4   Taxicab Regulation, Deregulation, and Rent Seeking

As in many cities, the taxicab market in New York City is heavily regulated. Entry into this market requires a license, or medallion, issued by a city agency. Since 1937, however, the number of medallions issued by the city has remained fixed at 11,787. Obviously, population and incomes have grown considerably in the interim, leading to great increases in demand for taxicab services, but the supply of cabs has remained fixed.

The results are illustrated in Figure 4.6 (which is very similar to Figure 4.5). The current demand for cabs D is far to the right of the demand curve D_{37} that prevailed when the limitation on entry began, but the supply curve S has remained fixed. In consequence, the current market-clearing price of taxicab services (P_m in Figure 4.6) is, in real terms, much higher than that in 1937 (P_c).

If we assume (perhaps unrealistically) that the former price P_c was equal to the

---

[47] Anne O. Krueger, "The Political Economy of the Rent-Seeking Society," *American Economic Review*, 64 (June 1974), pp. 291–303.

[48] Ibid., p. 294.

TABLE 4.4
GOVERNMENT FAILURES AND THEIR CONSEQUENCES—A SUMMARY

Problem	Consequences
Special interest dominance	Numerically compact groups with a large (per-capita) stake in policy may overwhelm larger, less organized groups with a much smaller (per-capita) stake; result may be inefficient or inequitable transfers, deadweight loss.
Voting cycle	Under certain (perhaps rare) conditions it will be impossible to know what majority will is by democratic means; decisions made by arbitrary procedures.
Rational ignorance and/or abstention	High costs of gathering information and/or participating in political marketplace relative to expected benefits produce poorly informed electorate with low participation rates and contribute to special interest dominance.
Competition for median voter	Produces "look-alike" candidates, platforms; may also beget redistribution from voters at tails of income distribution toward center.
Logrolling	Can enable minority with intense preferences for certain policies to obtain them via vote trading; can beget socially inefficient or inequitable policies that otherwise would not be adopted.
Shortsightedness problem	Tendency to attach low weights to future costs or benefits of a policy (resulting from preoccupation with next election); biases policy selection toward those programs promising immediate short-term rewards.
Bureaucratic budget maximization	Absence of external controls and internal incentives gives bureaucrats latitude to maximize their utility, usually accomplished by maximizing bureau budget; this leads to nonoptimal rate of output at excessively high cost.
Rent seeking	Possibility that a policy will create (or destroy) rents will provoke interested parties to waste real resources to alter policies to their benefit.

costs of operating a cab and that these costs have, in real terms, remained unchanged, we can use Figure 4.6 to show the welfare effects of this limitation on entry. Absent the entry-barring license limitation, the supply curve would have shifted rightward along with demand, yielding equilibrium price P_c and quantity Q_c and consumers' surplus equal to area P_cEG. The entry limits yield price P_m, quantity Q_m, and the much smaller consumers' surplus P_mEF. Thus, the limits on entry rob consumers of surplus equal to the area P_cP_mFG, part of which is transferred to producers as annual rents equal to area P_cP_mFH and part of which is deadweight loss equal to area FGH. *Deregulating* the market, i.e., removing the artificial, output-restricting limit on the number of cabs, would lower prices and recover the area P_cP_mFG for consumers.

But hold on. Deregulation will not be so easy. The holders of the valuable taxicab medallions are not about to simply say, "The party's over—our rents are going to

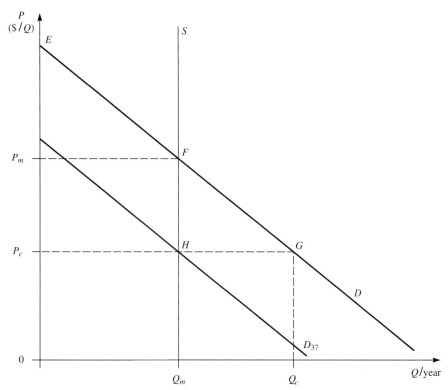

FIGURE 4.6
THE NEW YORK TAXICAB MARKET. Although the demand for cabs has increased, the supply of licenses in New York City has remained fixed since 1937, creating rents equal to area P_cP_mFH. These rents accrued to those who held the licenses at the time the supply restraints were installed—not necessarily present license holders.

disappear." For one thing, they may *not* be earning any rents! Why? Note that relatively few of the current medallion holders were actually around for the installation (in 1937) of the supply restrictions that gave rise to the rents described in Figure 4.6. Most current cab operators bought their medallions from previous holders—at prices that had climbed to $130,000 by December 1988![49] This price represents the present discounted value of the expected stream of annual profits for each cab operated in New York City. But once an operator has paid this amount for the right to operate a cab, these profits will not be profits at all, but will merely repay the operator for the up-front investment. The operator will merely earn a normal rate of return on this investment. The rents associated with the supply restrictions have, for the most part, been captured by the *initial* holders of the medallions, most of whom are now long gone (although later holders of the medallions might have earned some rents—or losses—if there have been unforeseen changes in demand, costs, or institutional rules).

[49]Carolyn Lochhead, "Cab Decontrol Is Hailed and Booed," *Insight*, December 5, 1988, Vol. 4 pp. 44–46.

Talk of deregulating the New York City taxicab market has elicited predictable howls of outrage. Current cab operators correctly claim that New York's high cab prices are *not* enabling them to earn "monopoly profits." Further, they point out that expanding the supply of licenses would be tantamount to confiscation of their property, since entry would lower real prices and erode the value of existing licenses. As one might expect, the current operators have formed a lobbying group and have promised to fight—in court—any attempts to disturb the status quo.

This makes the desirability of deregulation uncertain. True, expanding the quantity supplied to Q_c in Figure 4.6 and lowering the price to P_c could expand social surplus by area *FGH* (the amount of deadweight loss produced by the current supply restrictions). But if cab operators will spend *more* than this amount (on lawyers, lobbyists, etc.) to preserve the status quo and protect the value of their medallions, deregulation might not, on net, benefit society. As Gordon Tullock has observed, "[i]t is hard to recommend any positive action to deal with this kind of situation."[50]

SUMMARY AND CONCLUDING REMARKS

This chapter has presented several theories that predict government action may occasionally fail to promote either economic efficiency or equity.

Capture theory, an early attempt to explain government failure, suggests that regulatory agencies will sometimes do the bidding of the industries or groups that the agencies were created to regulate. A more refined theory, dubbed the economic theory of regulation, attempts to explain how such capture might occur. This theory predicts that high costs of information and of participation in the political process will make it easier for numerically compact groups with narrow, well-focused interests to use the political process to take advantage of larger numbers of individuals, each of whom may have a relatively small per-capita stake in the issue.

The use of economic tools to study the government process is called public choice analysis. The central premise of public choice theorists is that those participating in the political marketplace—be they voters, politicians, or bureaucrats—must be viewed as rational, self-interested individuals.

Public choice analysis of voters has led to the finding that majority-rule political decisions may sometimes be inconsistent; depending on the nature of the issue and the preferences of voters, it may actually be impossible to determine the will of the majority. Often voters will rationally choose not to inform themselves on many issues or not to participate in the political process at all because the costs of such activity outweigh the anticipated benefits.

Competition for votes will often lead suppliers of political goods to adopt views on the issues as close to those of the median voter as possible. Thus, candidates not only will be look-alikes, but also will often choose to supply the goods demanded by median voters more readily than those demanded by voters with more "extreme" views (i.e., voters nearer the tails of some distribution of voter characteristics). Logrolling or vote trading by politicians

---

[50]Gordon Tullock, "The Transitional Gains Trap," *Bell Journal of Economics*, 8 (1975), pp. 671–678.

enables the intensity of voter preferences to affect electoral results. Whether this enhances or diminishes social welfare, however, depends on the characteristics of these preferences. Election cycles might cause politicians to be shortsighted, adopting policies that have adverse long-term consequences and perhaps reduce welfare but which make them look good in the near term.

The bureaus or agencies that supply most government output are subject to limited external controls and have weak internal incentives to be efficient. As a result, most models of bureaucratic behavior tend to imply that these agencies will supply more output than is efficient and will do so at unnecessarily high costs or with excessive staff.

Public choice analysts tend to conclude that special interest groups will have disproportionate success in the political arena. Further, the success of these interests in using the government apparatus to transfer wealth or income from some groups to others (or perhaps themselves) may neither correct some perceived deficiency of the market mechanism nor necessarily advance the cause of distributional equity. Indeed, the very possibility of such transfers will lead some valuable resources to be wasted in their pursuit, an activity dubbed rent seeking.

Of course, the various theories of government failure discussed in this chapter are not deterministic. Sometimes agencies may be captured by the industries they are supposed to regulate or by special interest groups of another kind, but sometimes they are not. Wealth and income are sometimes redistributed in apparently inequitable ways, but sometimes the goal of greater vertical equity is served. Sometimes regulations are imposed that greatly reduce social welfare and enormous resources are often wasted in lobbying for or against these regulations, but sometimes salutary reforms occur.

It is best, then, for students to adopt a skeptical view with respect to *any* stated rationale for government action. Presume neither that government is always wise and benevolent nor that it will always fail to serve the common good; seek to discover the truth in each case.

QUESTIONS FOR REVIEW AND DISCUSSION

4.1 Suppose the wedding photographers in a particular state "capture" the legislature and convince it to erect significant barriers to entry into this profession, e.g., by requiring photographers to obtain a license and issuing licenses only to those already in business in the state. While this will make it difficult for new photographers to enter this market, it does not appear to alter the fundamental demand-supply relationships in this market, at least at present. There will still be hundreds of photographers competing for business, even if no new ones enter for a long time. So how can such a barrier affect market price and output? Use graphs to explain your answer.

4.2 Suppose a hypothetical institution of higher learning wishes to make $100,000 (per year) available to its students. Two choices are available: Either the money can be divided among all students as a tuition rebate, or it can be allocated to various student clubs or activities to "enrich campus life." The administration decides to leave the choice to the students' own elected government. Based on your understanding of the economic theory of regulation and public choice theory, which option do you think the student government will choose? What considerations will affect the choice? Explain.

4.3 The text observes that some public interest rationales for regulation may be spurious, i.e., may be attempts to defuse opposition to a policy by raising the costs of learning about its true nature. Do you know of any examples of such behavior? Describe them.

4.4 "Altruism is not a violation of the self-interest axiom, but a special case of it." Evaluate this statement.

4.5 Some have suggested that U.S. conduct of the war in Vietnam was an example of the paradox of majority voting, i.e., gave rise to a voting cycle. The idea is that there were three basic policies to choose from—we might call them "win at all costs," "middle of the road," and "pull out"—and policymakers could not effectively choose among them. Explain how this could be so, using Table 4.1 as a guide.

4.6 Recent Supreme Court decisions have put the abortion issue on center stage for many state legislatures. What does the median voter model predict about the behavior of the two dominant political parties on this issue?

4.7 Define logrolling, and explain how it enables consideration of the intensity of voters' preferences. How do bribery and logrolling differ?

4.8 There is considerable empirical evidence that some public enterprises are inefficient relative to privately owned and managed firms. Why, then, is public ownership so common? Why don't public officials substitute private ownership (and regulation, if necessary) for public ownership more frequently, given the large social savings this might entail?

4.9 Define economic rents and rent seeking. Some economists argue that agricultural price supports give rise to economic rents. Does this mean that elimination of such price supports is desirable on efficiency grounds? Explain, using graphs where desirable.

PUBLIC POLICY
TOWARD MONOPOLY

CHAPTER 5

ANTITRUST LAWS AND INSTITUTIONS: AN OVERVIEW

The trusts and combinations—the communism of pelf—whose machinations have prevented us from reaching the success we deserved, should not be forgotten nor forgiven.

Grover Cleveland

Antitrust policy is like a set of rules in a board game: It defines the types of moves players may legitimately make, but leaves the decisions about these moves to the players themselves. It is thus a fairly simple—and nonintrusive—type of government "control" of economic activity. Nevertheless, it is extremely important, for it has the potential to ensure that entrepreneurs' energies and acquisitive instincts are channeled in constructive, socially beneficial ways.

As we noted in Chapter 3, antitrust policy is inspired by our desire to avoid the costs associated with monopoly, which economists measure as the welfare losses resulting from monopolists' decisions to produce too little output at too high a price. Unfortunately, however, detecting such losses and prosecuting the behavior that gives rise to them are rarely simple and straightforward matters. These tasks require sophisticated laws and institutions aimed at eliminating harmful (or "unfair") business practices without endangering truly competitive conduct. In this chapter, we will develop a more thorough understanding of these laws and institutions. We begin by tracing the historical development of federal antitrust laws in a bit more detail than was possible in Chapter 1. In succeeding sections we review the mechanisms of antitrust enforcement, describe the penalties and remedies for violations of the antitrust laws, and note several important sectors which are exempt from antitrust policy.

Later chapters in Part Two are devoted to the various ways in which antitrust policy has been formulated and executed. Chapters 6, 7, and 8 examine the three primary areas of antitrust theory and policy: monopolization, oligopoly and collusion, and mergers, respectively. Chapter 9 examines the theory and practice of price discrimination, a tactic which presupposes some monopoly power. Chapter 10 examines a variety of potentially exclusionary or "unfair" business practices (such as resale price maintenance, exclusive dealing, and tie-in sales). Chapter 11 deals with two special topics in competition policy: patents and advertising.

THE EVOLUTION OF ANTITRUST LEGISLATION

The Sherman Act

As we noted in Chapter 1, the late 1800s saw the emergence of enterprises which seemed enormous by the standards of the day. The railroads were the first "big businesses," requiring unprecedented accumulations of land, labor, and capital. By drastically lowering transportation costs and opening up new markets, the railroads also contributed to the growth of other large-scale enterprises, especially in steelmaking, refining, and food processing. Technological advancement further fueled expansion in the optimum size of businesses. The refrigerator car, e.g., enabled meat from the packing houses of Chicago to reach a national market; the use of corrugated rollers to crack the hard, spicy wheat of the Plains states gave impetus to a flour milling industry centered in Minneapolis; mechanization greatly altered many other industries, from glassmaking to shoemaking to cigarette manufacturing. In sector after sector, small, locally based businesses were displaced by larger enterprises often located in distant cities.

The times seemed chaotic. Artisans feared displacement by machines. Farmers complained that sinister forces fixed unreasonably low prices for their produce and that railroads charged unreasonably high rates to ship it. Workers in emerging manufacturing enterprises sweated for long hours in pitiful conditions for low wages, while the "captains of industry" who employed them amassed huge fortunes. Scandals abounded; stories of stock manipulation, market rigging, and predatory behavior were common in the newspapers and pulp magazines of the day.

But while it is doubtless true that the era was marked by ample attempts to collude and conspire against the public, it is important to realize that the displacement of many small enterprises by fewer large ones was usually the result not of a conspiracy but of immutable economic and technological forces. What is more, such displacement need not have harmed consumers—and might have helped them considerably.

Consider, e.g., Figure 5.1, which shows two short-run average total cost (ATC) curves for a hypothetical industry. Here ATC_o describes production costs under an old (or small-scale) technology, while ATC_n describes production costs under a new (or large-scale) technology. Note that the minimum efficient scale of operation (i.e., the lowest rate of output at which costs will be

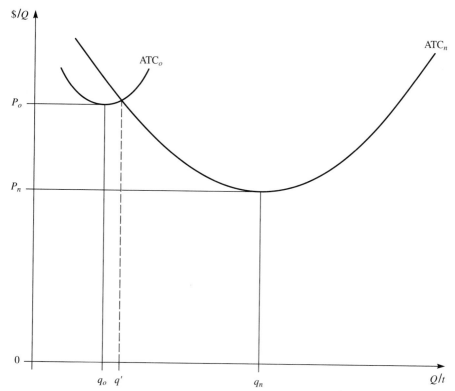

FIGURE 5.1
SCALE ECONOMIES, MARKET GROWTH, AND THE DISPLACEMENT OF SMALL FIRMS. An old or small-scale production technology (with costs described by ATC_o) will give way to a new or large-scale one once quantity demanded exceeds q' within a particular market area or once transportation costs to this area (from some distant locale where the new technology has been adopted) fall below $P_o - P_n$.

minimized) under the old technology is q_o, while the minimum efficient scale of operations under the new technology is far greater, q_n. But the new technology is not "better" (i.e., cheaper) than the old at all output levels. If, e.g., a particular town or city could absorb no more than q_o units per time period, a producer using the old technology would serve this town—*unless* output made elsewhere under the new technology could be shipped to this locale at a cost $T < P_o - P_n$. Only if transportation costs are low or if the relevant market for output grows (so that it can absorb more than q' units of output) will the new technology, which involves great economies of scale, become feasible.

For most of the early 1800s, high transportation costs made small firms using traditional technologies the rule in most U.S. communities. But, as Figure 5.1 illustrates, once transport costs fell below a certain threshhold, mass production techniques had an advantage over these older technologies in all but the tiniest or most isolated markets. Surely, the resulting changes were confusing to those affected and painful for those displaced, but it is quite likely that they enhanced consumers' welfare. For not only were the new, large-scale firms capable of producing output at much lower unit costs than those they replaced, but also in many cases these competitive regional or national firms replaced local monopolies.

None of these considerations much affected political discourse during the 1880s, however. The U.S. public felt abused by the trusts, and both major parties offered up corrective measures in Congress during 1889–1890. The one measure that eventually passed was the product of many hands. Its sponsor was John Sherman (R., Ohio), but the initial bill was much amended and almost entirely written in committee, so that the law we know today bears little resemblance to what Sherman proposed. Nevertheless, what came to be known as the Sherman Act was signed into law by President Benjamin Harrison in July 1890. Its two main sections comprise the foundation for federal antitrust enforcement. They state, in pertinent part:

> *Section 1.* Every contract, combination in the form of a trust or otherwise, or conspiracy, in restraint of trade or commerce . . . is hereby declared to be illegal.
>
> *Section 2.* Every person who shall monopolize, or attempt to monopolize, or combine or conspire with any person or persons, to monopolize any part of the trade or commerce among the several states, or with foreign nations, shall be deemed guilty of a misdemeanor. . . .

The Clayton and FTC Acts

The courts soon began to give content and meaning to this rather vague statute. As antitrust scholar Robert Bork has observed, "The years 1890 to 1914 witnessed the origin of every major theory that drives and directs the evolution of antitrust doctrine to this day."[1] There was, however, a widespread feeling that the Sherman Act was doing little to control the behavior of the trusts. Such feelings were reinforced by muckraking journalists' chronicles of corporate misbehavior and by congressional hearings on the subject.

Enforcement of the Sherman Act had indeed been spotty. The Justice Department had been provided with no extra budget or personnel for this task and by 1904 had brought only 18 antitrust suits—many against labor unions. What is more, the courts appeared not to know what to make of the law. Sometimes, the Supreme Court interpreted the act quite narrowly, at other times more expansively. The confusion of the Supreme Court is best illustrated by its first antitrust decision. In *United States v. E. C. Knight Co.* the Court found that a "sugar trust" had acquired a monopoly of sugar refining capacity, but ruled that this was *not* a violation of the Sherman Act because the law covered commerce and manufacturing was not commerce![2] Later, in *Northern Securities Co. et al. v. United States.*, the Court appeared to enjoin any consolidation of otherwise competitive firms.[3] But the decision was not unanimous, and

---

[1]Robert H. Bork, *The Antitrust Paradox*, Basic Books, New York, 1978, p. 15.
[2]156 U.S. 1 (1895).
[3]193 U.S. 197 (1904).

forceful dissents made observers unsure about the legal status of certain combinations. Such confusion led many to conclude that the Sherman Act was unworkable. Reformers and progressives were unhappy that so little "trust busting" was being done. Businesses were confused about what practices did or did not violate the law.

Toughening—or at least clarifying—antitrust policy became a major issue of the 1912 Presidential election. Lengthy congressional hearings into the matter began in 1913 at the behest of the eventual winner, Woodrow Wilson. The result was a pair of new antitrust laws. The Clayton Act (1914) expressed Congress's belief that certain business practices are (or can be) used to subvert competition and that by prohibiting these practices monopoly could be *prevented*. Its key provisions are contained in the following three sections:

> Section 2. [I]t shall be unlawful for any person engaged in commerce . . . to discriminate in price between different purchasers of commodities of like grade and quality . . . where the effect of such discrimination may be substantially to lessen competition or tend to create a monopoly . . .[4]
>
> Section 3. [I]t shall be unlawful for any person engaged in commerce . . . to lease or make a sale or contract for sale of goods . . . on the condition . . . that the lessee or purchaser thereof shall not use or deal in the goods . . . of a competitor or competitors of the lessor or seller, where the effect of such lease, sale, or contract . . . may be to substantially lessen competition or tend to create a monopoly in any line of commerce.
>
> Section 7. [N]o corporation engaged in commerce shall acquire . . . the whole or any part of the stock or other share capital . . . of another corporation engaged also in commerce, where . . . the effect of such acquisition may be substantially to lessen competition, or tend to create a monopoly . . .[5]

Section 2 is aimed at price discrimination; section 3 limits the use of "tie-in sales" or "exclusive dealing" arrangements; section 7 limits mergers. Note that none of the restrictions are absolute; the language of the statute specifies that a *substantial* lessening of competition must be in prospect before conduct is to be ruled illegal. But the statute also grants antitrust authorities the power to move against such conduct before these anticompetitive effects are actually felt—as long as the authorities feel these effects *may* eventuate.

---

[4]This section was strengthened in 1936 via the Robinson-Patman Act. The massive contraction of economic activity during the great depression of the 1930s bankrupt many firms. Small businesses appeared to be at a special disadvantage relative to larger enterprises, which often could use their "buying power" to extract concessions from suppliers and undersell mom-and-pop rivals. Although section 2 already outlawed price discrimination, the government was rarely successful in prosecuting apparent violations of this section of the law. So Congress extended prohibitions on price discrimination to cases where buyers received price concessions that enabled them to undersell competitors in the same market, restricted the use of "quantity discounts" (in which buyers of large amounts of merchandise received lower prices), and prohibited discounting of advertising rates for large customers.

[5]This section was subsequently strengthened by the Celler-Kefauver amendment of 1950. The amendment closed a loophole in the original statute by limiting mergers accomplished via asset acquisitions as well as stock acquisitions. The original language also had limited only mergers that affected competition between the merging companies; the amendment limited mergers producing a lessening of competition "in any line of commerce in any section of the country."

The Federal Trade Commission (FTC) Act (1914) expressed Congress's belief that antitrust policy would best be conducted by a specialized agency with expertise that the federal courts lacked. It established the FTC to both investigate and prosecute violations of the antitrust laws. Since President Theodore Roosevelt had in 1903 created a special unit of the Justice Department—the Antitrust Division—to enforce the Sherman Act, there would henceforth be two federal agencies "walking the antitrust beat," with substantially overlapping responsibilities. The FTC Act also contained one major policy prescription: "Section 5. Unfair methods of competition in commerce are hereby declared unlawful."[6]

See Table 5.1.

VIGNETTE 5.1   A Controversy: Whom Do the Antitrust Laws Aim to Protect?

There is some debate among economists and legal scholars as to the aim of the Sherman Act. Does it seek to protect consumers alone, or does it also protect small businesses from the depredations of large ones, even if these small businesses are less efficient than their larger rivals?

---

[6]This language was strengthened via the Wheeler-Lea Act of 1938. The courts had interpreted section 5 narrowly in early cases, applying it only to business practices that adversely affected a firm's rivals. Preventing deception of consumers was not considered part of Congress's intent. The Wheeler-Lea amendment rewrote section 5 to read: "Unfair methods of competition in or affecting commerce, and unfair or deceptive acts or practices in or affecting commerce, are hereby declared unlawful." This greatly enhanced the FTC's power to move against false or misleading advertising claims.

TABLE 5.1
MAJOR FEDERAL ANTITRUST STATUTES—A SUMMARY

Sherman Act (1890)

Section 1:	Prohibits contracts, combinations, or conspiracies in restraint of trade (e.g., collusion among rivals regarding prices or territories)
Section 2:	Prohibits monopolization or attempts to monopolize a market

Clayton Act (1914)

Section 2:	Prohibits anticompetitive price discrimination
Section 3:	Prohibits anticompetitive exclusive dealing and tie-in sales
Section 7:	Limits mergers that may lessen competition

FTC Act (1914)

Section 5:	Outlaws unfair methods of competition (leaving it up to FTC to define what is unfair in specific contexts)

Unfortunately, it is difficult to divine the "original intent" of Congress on this question. John Sherman stated that he proposed "merely to enact the common law," but the common law of the day was quite confused. Sherman's proposal was debated at great length, but Senator Sherman was so anxious to get his bill passed that he agreed to numerous objections and amendments. In any case, this floor debate proved largely irrelevant to the final language of the act, which was hastily rewritten by the Senate Judiciary Committee. The redrafted bill was hardly discussed by the full Senate, since a weightier matter (a new tariff bill) was then under review. With only a single dissenting vote, the Sherman Act passed the Senate. Facing a time limit, the House debated it even less and passed it by an unrecorded margin.

What did Congress want the act to do? Robert Bork's study of the debate led him to conclude that Congress intended to strike at cartels, horizontal mergers of monopolistic proportions, and predatory business tactics. "Other policy goals," Bork concludes, "are not to be found in the legislative history."[7] He argues that Congress was concerned with promoting consumer welfare and avoiding the deadweight welfare loss of monopoly, although, of course, Congress lacked the economic sophistication to say so in precisely those terms.

Not all antitrust scholars agree, however. Robert Lande, e.g., argues that Congress was less concerned with the efficient allocation of resources and the maximization of social surplus than with the distribution of wealth.[8] Lande asserts that Sherman's statements about the ill effects of monopolistic price increases (cited by Bork as evidence of concern for consumer welfare) show that Congress was most concerned about an inequitable shifting of wealth from consumers to producers. He believes Congress had multiple goals in passing the Sherman Act and wanted to limit the social and political power of large firms as well as prevent undesirable wealth transfers.

Whatever Congress intended the Sherman Act to do, the record is clear that it held "multiple goals" for the Clayton and FTC acts (and the subsequent amendments to these statutes). Floor and committee discussion of these statutes demonstrates a concern for the welfare of small businesses and an interest in serving various "populist" political goals. Indeed, H.R. 8442, the basis for the Robinson-Patman amendment to the Clayton Act, was actually written by the attorney for the National American Wholesale Grocer's Association, which sought to protect small grocers from the fast-growing chain stores of the day. (The chain stores were able to offer consumers lower prices by cutting out the intermediary and doing their own wholesaling).

Most scholars, however, have resisted the implication that the antitrust laws *ought* to be used to pursue such goals, e.g., to protect a small producer from the competitive superiority of a larger one. Economists especially have recognized that using the antitrust laws to protect some competitors from others will often harm consumers. Recognizing any goal for the antitrust laws other than the enhancement of consumer welfare, then, puts the courts on a very slippery policy slope, perhaps endangering the public interest rationale for these laws. Accordingly, there is considerable debate as to whether courts should even try to interpret Congress's original intent for these statutes.

[7]Bork, *The Antitrust Paradox,* p. 21.
[8]Robert H. Lande, "Wealth Transfers as the Original and Primary Concern of Antitrust: The Efficiency Interpretation Challenged," *Hastings Law Journal,* 34 (September 1982), pp. 65–151.

THE REALM OF ANTITRUST ENFORCEMENT

Mechanisms and Procedures

As we have noted, enforcement of the federal antitrust laws is shared by two agencies, the Antitrust Division of the Department of Justice and the Federal Trade Commission. But antitrust cases may also be instigated by private parties, e.g., firms or consumers who feel they have been harmed by some anticompetitive action proscribed by the antitrust laws. In addition, many states have their own antitrust statutes, enforced by their respective attorneys general.

Public Enforcement   Cases brought by the Antitrust Division often originate in complaints received from consumers, owners or managers of businesses, or press accounts. Staff attorneys, sometimes in consultation with staff economists, investigate any allegations made and decide whether a case merits prosecution. They may choose either criminal prosecution, which imposes strong sanctions aimed at deterring such conduct in the future, or civil action, by which some remedy for the alleged offensive conduct might be obtained. Once a formal complaint is drafted and a supporting report written, the assistant attorney general for antitrust (usually a political appointee) must approve the case before it is filed in one of the federal district courts for trial or settlement. The decision of the district court can, of course, be appealed to the appropriate circuit court of appeals; the appeals court's decision may be appealed to the Supreme Court. Only issues of law may be appealed, not issues of fact.

The FTC is headed by five commissioners appointed by the President and approved by the Senate. They serve seven-year terms. Antitrust matters are the domain of the FTC's Bureau of Competition; its attorneys are assisted by economists in the Bureau of Economics. (A third major policy branch, the Bureau of Consumer Protection, looks into such matters as advertising practices, marketing abuses, etc.) Most cases initiated by the FTC begin as administrative complaints issued to "respondents" (i.e., defendants) who are then tried before one or more of the FTC's own administrative law judges. Although part of the FTC, these judges are supposed to strive for independence and follow procedures very similar to those found in federal district courts. The administrative law judges' opinions may be appealed to the FTC itself. If the FTC's decisions are not satisfactory to the respondents, however, they may be appealed to the federal courts and on up to the Supreme Court. Unlike the Antitrust Division, the FTC can bring no criminal actions. It can, however, issue cease-and-desist orders that, if ignored, can provoke substantial fines. See Table 5.2.

Since the Antitrust Division and FTC have concurrent jurisdiction to enforce the Clayton Act and its amendments, there is a possibility that these agencies might waste enforcement resources by duplicating efforts in investigating complaints, etc. To avoid this, the two agencies regularly notify each other as to their work on specific cases.

The Justice Department and FTC also have devised programs to eliminate

TABLE 5.2
THE FEDERAL ANTITRUST AUTHORITIES—A SUMMARY

Antitrust Division of the Department of Justice
Has sole jurisdiction over Sherman Act cases; shares jurisdiction over Clayton Act cases.
May bring criminal suits for Sherman Act violations deemed particularly offensive (usually per se violations).
More commonly brings civil actions aimed at preventing or restraining certain conduct or restoring competitive conditions by changing the structure of the market.
Issues guidelines on mergers and other practices to reduce uncertainty about policy.
Headed by assistant attorney general for antitrust, appointed by President and approved by Senate.

Bureau of Competition of the FTC
Has jurisdiction over section 5 of FTC Act and Clayton Act.
Acts as quasi-judicial body. Issues complaints heard before its own administrative law judges; appeals go to complaint counsel to commissioners, then to appeals courts.
Can bring no criminal suits; commonly issues cease-and-desist orders enjoining certain practices.
Issues rules or guidelines on what it will consider an unfair or anticompetitive practice.
Headed by five commissioners appointed by President and approved by Senate.

doubts firms might have about the legality of specific practices. Through the years, the courts have established that some business practices (e.g., price-fixing) are so clearly harmful that no "extenuating circumstances" need be considered before judging them illegal. We say that such practices are *per se violations* of the antitrust laws. Most firms' legal advisers will be able to identify such violations and warn their clients away from them. But many practices are judged under a *rule of reason*: They may be illegal in some contexts but "reasonable" and therefore legal in others. If firms are in doubt about how some action might be viewed, they can simply contact one of the federal antitrust agencies and request a review. In addition, the agencies periodically issue formal, written guidelines indicating the kinds of practices or mergers they are likely to challenge.

VIGNETTE 5.2   Is Federal Antitrust Enforcement Efficient?

Because resources are scarce, we want to allocate them efficiently so that we benefit as much as possible from what we have. Indeed, this is a major justification for the antitrust laws. So it is interesting to ask, Do the antitrust authorities allocate their limited enforcement resources in a way calculated to produce the greatest benefit per dollar spent?

Richard Posner thinks not. After a careful analysis of historical data on antitrust enforcement, Posner (then a law professor, currently a federal judge) concluded, "The lawyers who manage the antitrust agencies . . . conduct an enterprise that, if it made shoes instead of an intangible called competition, would rightly be considered mismanaged." Posner asserted that, among other sins, the Antitrust Division "makes little effort to identify those markets in which serious problems of monopoly are likely to arise; except in the merger area, does not act save on complaint; makes no systematic effort to see whether its decrees are complied with."[9]

In a follow-up study, William Long, Richard Schramm, and Robert Tollison tried to assess whether the Antitrust Division brought more cases in those industries where the potential for improved consumer welfare was greatest.[10] They found that measures of the consumer welfare losses or excess profits from monopoly were far less important than other variables—especially industry sales—in explaining case-bringing activities. This casts doubt on the idea that the Antitrust Division was allocating its resources efficiently. In a later study using different data, John Seigfried concluded that "economic variables have little influence on the Antitrust Division."[11]

Why would the antitrust authorities pursue cases other than those where the prospective welfare gains are the greatest? In some circumstances, such cases may be overlooked because they are viewed as "bad bets," perhaps because the accused firms might have such great resources at their disposal that cases against them might be viewed as unwinnable or winnable only at excessive cost. Alternatively, the *incentive structure* of the antitrust agencies might be biased against such cases. As Seigfried has remarked, "It is probably more important to win cases than to reduce economic losses or inequities in order to move up the success ladder at the Justice Department."[12]

The self-interest axiom implies that some government attorneys will select cases that maximize their utility rather than society's welfare. Many attorneys join the government as a form of apprenticeship during which they acquire valuable trial experience before heading off to more lucrative private practice. So turnover is high. In some years, as many as one-fourth of the staff attorneys at the FTC depart, often after a tenure of less than four years. Clearly, those who view government service as a springboard will be biased in favor of uncomplicated (i.e., short) cases which carry a relatively high probability of victory and will shy away from long, involved cases—even if the latter might be more important from a social standpoint. As a result, the efficiency of antitrust enforcement will suffer.

Private Enforcement   Where federal or state authorities decide not to proceed on alleged violations of the antitrust laws—or where the authorities have *won* a suit and the damaged parties wish to recover compensation for the harms they have suffered at the hands of a monopolist—aggrieved parties may bring a *private* antitrust suit. Section 4 of the Clayton Act allows those who have been injured by anticompetitive conduct to sue in federal court. If victorious, the plaintiffs may recover compensation equal to *three times* the amount of any damages the monopolist inflicted on them (i.e., "treble damages"), plus the costs of bringing the suit.

---

[9]Richard A. Posner, "A Statistical Study of Antitrust Enforcement," *Journal of Law and Economics*, 13 (October 1970), p. 419.

[10]William F. Long, Richard Schramm, and Robert Tollison, "The Economic Determinants of Antitrust Activity," *Journal of Law and Economics*, 16 (October 1973), pp. 351–364.

[11]John J. Seigfried, "The Determinants of Antitrust Activity," *Journal of Law and Economics*, 18 (October 1975), p. 573.

[12]Ibid.

To bring a private antitrust suit, one must first establish proper *standing*. This is not always easy to do. Although the language of section 4 seems clear—it states "That any person who shall be injured in his business or property by reason of anything forbidden in the antitrust laws may sue"—some court rulings have clouded the issue. A "person" may be an individual, corporation or other business form, municipality, state, or foreign government—but not the federal government. Such "persons" need to establish that they have suffered direct injury from some violation of the antitrust laws. A consumer must show that she or he paid inflated prices for merchandise because the seller violated one or more of the antitrust laws. Note that those who suffer *indirect* effects of anticompetitive conduct lack standing. For example, the owner of a firm which alleges that a monopolist drove her or him to bankruptcy with predatory tactics has standing; the firm's landlord, who may have lost revenue because of the bankruptcy, lacks such standing.

Not all injuries, however, are compensable; the courts will inquire whether (and to what degree) the plaintiff's injuries reflect the anticompetitive effect of the alleged violation. The antitrust laws aim to prevent the diminution of competition; *antitrust injury* should therefore reflect the anticompetitive effect of any violation of these laws rather than the effects of any other factors (e.g., behavior of either the plaintiff or the defendant that is unrelated to the antitrust violation).

In measuring damages in private antitrust cases, the courts tend to ask how much wealth has been transferred from buyers to the monopolist or from potential rivals to the monopolist. That is, the courts will usually measure damages as the amount that the monopolist overcharged consumers for a good or service as a result of an antitrust violation or as the amount of profits that a business firm lost due to the violation. From an economic standpoint, however, such estimates of the damages that stem from monopolistic conduct are incorrect, for they do not accurately measure the *social* costs of monopoly.

Consider, e.g., Figure 5.2. Suppose this figure describes an industry in which price and output, respectively, are at monopolistic levels P_m and Q_m rather than the competitive levels P_c and Q_c. In this case, the monopolist would earn profits (per time period t) equal to the area bound by points P_cP_mFH. This is the amount of consumer overcharges the courts would customarily specify as damages (appropriately summed, of course, for as many time periods as the monopolistic pricing occurred). But, as we know, area P_cP_mFH is merely the amount *transferred* from consumers to the monopolist. The true social cost of monopoly, i.e., the lost social surplus associated with the monopolist's decision to restrict output and raise price, is measured by area FGH. It may be wise to award consumers area P_cP_mFH as *compensation* for the overcharges they paid the monopolist, but this area is not a valid measure of the true "damages" the monopolist inflicted on society.

Focusing on the monopolist's profits may have even less merit when the plaintiff is (or was) a potential rival of the monopolist. To say that such a plaintiff experienced damages equal to area P_cP_mFH is clearly wrong: If the monopolist had refrained from setting price P_m and instead had behaved com-

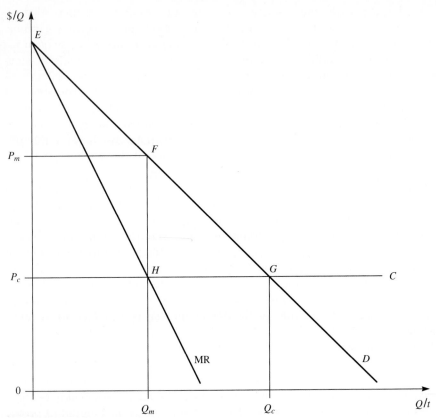

FIGURE 5.2
MEASURING "DAMAGES" FROM MONOPOLISTIC PRICING. Plaintiffs in private antitrust cases typically request damages equal to the amount of wealth transferred from themselves to the monopolist, i.e., area P_cP_mFH (summed for as many periods as the monopoly overcharges occurred). The true social costs of monopoly are equal to area *FGH*.

petitively, setting price P_c, then economic profits for the firms in this industry would have been zero. Monopolistic pricing does not "cost" the plaintiff area P_cP_mFH at all. It can be argued, then, that the assessment of damages in private antitrust suits is conceptually flawed and that this may affect the efficiency of private antitrust enforcement.

Penalties and Remedies

It is no exaggeration to say that those who violate the antitrust laws risk fairly harsh penalties, although these penalties may seem minor relative to the large social costs of anticompetitive conduct. Fines and jail terms may be imposed under the Sherman Act, and the other antitrust laws allow for the assessment of monetary damages, permit dissolution of companies or divestiture of portions thereof, or empower the courts to issue injunctions prohibiting or compelling certain actions by firms.

Fines and Forfeitures   In 1890, the Sherman Act specified fines of up to $5,000 for violators. It was soon clear, however, that this provided little or no deterrent to firms which could gain tens of millions of dollars if they success-fully monopolized markets or fixed prices above competitive levels. The limit was therefore raised repeatedly, and it is now $100,000 for individuals and $1 million for firms. Section 6 of the Sherman Act also provides for the forfeiture of property being transported in interstate or foreign commerce in violation of section 1. The FTC may also levy fines of up to $5,000 for each violation of an FTC final order, where *each day's continuance* of the violation is treated as a separate offense.

Prison Terms   Until 1959, no business manager or owner had ever gone to jail for violating the Sherman Act, although some trade union officials had done so. This pattern was broken in that year when four businessmen were given 90-day sentences by an Ohio district court. In 1960, thirty-one jail sen-tences were meted out (although only seven defendants actually served time), and nearly $2 million in fines was levied in a single case that involved price fixing by electrical equipment manufacturers.[13] Since then, criminal convic-tions that involved jail sentences have been relatively common. In 1974, an amendment changed criminal violations of section 1 of the Sherman Act from misdemeanors to felony offenses and lengthened the maximum sentence from one to three years.

Treble Damages   As noted above, plaintiffs are entitled to treble damages in private suits in which they prove antitrust injury. Often such cases *follow* a successful federal prosecution; the verdict for the government is sufficient evi-dence that the law was violated, and the plaintiff then must simply prove the amount of damages. Because the amount of damages in these cases can be so large and because damages are trebled to determine the final awards, most scholars feel that these awards are vitally important weapons in the arsenal of deterrence of monopolistic conduct. In the electrical equipment case men-tioned above, the successful government case was followed by more than 2,000 private damage suits, in which private utility companies, local govern-ments, and other plaintiffs collected nearly $500 million.

VIGNETTE 5.3   The $1 Monopoly

Not all private antitrust suits are lucrative for the victorious plaintiff. The best exam-ple is the "victory" of the United States Football League (USFL) over the National Football League (NFL). The USFL was formed in 1983 to compete with the well-established NFL. At first, the USFL avoided direct competition with the NFL, scheduling its games during the spring and summer rather than the fall. In 1986, however, the USFL shifted to a fall season and went head to head with the NFL. The strategy did not go well; the infant league was soon bankrupt.

[13]See *Final Judgment, United States v. General Electric et al.,* Civil No. 28,288 (Oct. 1, 1962).

The league's owners alleged, however, that the USFL's demise was the result of the NFL's monopolistic behavior, and they pressed a private antitrust suit against the dominant league. After a lengthy and well-publicized trial, the jury ruled that the NFL had indeed monopolized the professional football market, but awarded the USFL plaintiffs only $1 in damages (trebled to $3)![14] The verdict mystified many in the media. How could the NFL be guilty but the USFL not be entitled to a sizable damage award?

The key is to understand the concept of *antitrust injury.* During the trial, part of the NFL's strategy had been to document mismanagement and marketing blunders by the USFL. This apparently left the jury unable to determine how much of the USFL's difficulties were the result of NFL misconduct and how much the result of its own failures. Absent convincing evidence from the USFL that its losses were the result of unlawful conduct by the NFL, the jury chalked these losses up to other factors and awarded trivial damages.

Such an award is quite consistent with Supreme Court precedent on antitrust injury. In *Brunswick Corp. v. Pueblo Bowl-O-Mat, Inc.,* the Court overturned a lower-court award of damages to Pueblo for Brunswick's acquisition of bowling centers found in violation of section 7 of the Clayton Act.[15] In that case, Brunswick (the nation's largest operator of bowling centers) had taken over several centers which were near bankruptcy, and the plaintiffs argued that had Brunswick allowed the centers to close, the plaintiffs would have had increased profits. The Court ruled, however, that such damages were not compensable because they were not causally linked to illegal activities. Had the centers been kept open by a firm smaller than Brunswick (i.e., one not likely to be judged in violation of section 7), the Court noted, plaintiffs' profits would also have been lower. Clearly, it is not enough to prove a violation of the antitrust laws. To win damages, plaintiffs must show that their injuries flowed directly from the defendants' illegal acts.

Divestiture or "Deconcentration"   When sales in an industry appear excessively concentrated in the hands of a single firm, the courts may order the firm to sell off portions of its operations. In the extreme, the courts may fragment the offending firm into a much larger number of smaller enterprises. In 1911, for example, the Supreme Court dissolved the Standard Oil Company of New Jersey, judged to have monopolized the oil refining industry in the United States, into about 30 smaller firms.[16] More recently, in 1982, a settlement between the Justice Department and American Telephone & Telegraph Co. (AT&T) forced the latter to sell off 22 local operating companies, effectively breaking up AT&T. Divestiture orders are quite common in merger cases. When one firm acquires another and the antitrust authorities detect anticompetitive consequences, they usually ask the courts to order that some of or all the acquired assets (or some other portion of the firm) be sold off.

---

[14] *USFL v. NFL,* 634 F. Supp. 1155 (S.D.N.Y.) & 644 F. Supp. 1040 (S.D.N.Y. 1986), *aff'd.,* 842 F.2d 1335 (2d Cir. 1988).

[15] *Brunswick Corp. v. Pueblo Bowl-O-Mat, Inc.,* 429 U.S. 477 (1977).

[16] *Standard Oil Co. of New Jersey v. United States,* 221 U.S. 1 (1911).

Injunctions   In some cases, the remedy for an antitrust violation may simply be an injunction (i.e., an order) that requires a firm to cease certain actions or to take certain actions. For example, if price fixing is alleged or proved, the defendant may be required to cease any behavior (such as exchanging price information with rivals at trade association meetings) that facilitates such collusion. Under certain circumstances, a court will issue an injunction that prohibits a merger before it takes place (and before "untangling" the merged firms becomes a difficult matter). Where certain business practices are alleged to enhance a firm's market power, these practices may be enjoined, but the firm itself is left intact.

Antitrust Exemptions

In recent decades, Congress has devoted about as much time and effort to writing exceptions to the coverage of the antitrust laws as to refining and extending these laws. These exceptions often are more the product of a group's political influence than a result of adherence to any economic or legal principle.

Export Associations   In 1918, Congress enacted the Webb-Pomerene Act, the first of many exemptions to the Sherman Act. This law allows U.S. firms to organize "export associations" and jointly fix prices and impose territorial restraints on their foreign sales. These firms must register with the FTC when forming such an association and must not influence domestic prices or coerce firms that wish to export independently; but aside from these restrictions, these firms can act in many ways that would clearly violate the Sherman Act were they aiming at the U.S. market.

Agriculture and Labor   Section 6 of the Clayton Act exempted agricultural and labor organizations from the Sherman Act. Agriculture's exemption was further extended by the Capper-Volstead Act of 1922, the Agricultural Marketing Agreement Acts of 1926 and 1938, and some provisions of the Robinson-Patman Act of 1936. Marketers of certain agricultural products can thus openly collude to fix prices, assign output quotas, etc.—and in some cases are actually legally required to do so! Labor unions' protection from antitrust prosecution was strengthened by passage of the Norris-LaGuardia Act in 1932 and the National Labor Relations Act in 1935. Thus, unions can—unless they join or collude with nonlabor groups—engage in actions that the Sherman Act would prohibit in other contexts.

Regulated Industries   In some industries where competition is thought *undesirable* (i.e., in natural monopolies), firms may be exempted from the antitrust laws but subjected to price or rate-of-return regulation. (As the aforementioned AT&T divestiture case illustrates, however, not all regulated firms or industries are exempt from antitrust.) In principle, such regulation protects consumers from monopolistic pricing by the subject firms while at the same time securing the benefits of the massive economies of scale thought to give rise to the natural monopoly. In practice, as we shall see in later chapters, the issue of rate regulation is very complex, and the results can be unsatisfactory for consumers.

Miscellaneous   Several other industries have won exemptions from the antitrust laws. One sport (baseball) is entirely exempt; others have received partial exemptions for particular purposes (e.g., negotiation of television contracts, mergers with rival leagues). Under the Small Business Act of 1953, businesses below a certain size threshhold are allowed to engage in certain joint activities that would otherwise put them afoul of the antitrust laws.

The McCarran-Ferguson Act in 1945 provided that the antitrust laws should apply to the insurance industry only "to the extent that such business is not regulated by state law." Since most state regulation of insurance is aimed at protecting the solvency of insurance companies (i.e., ensuring adequate reserves, guaranteeing "safe" investments), this act is, for all practical purposes, an exemption from antitrust coverage. Similar exemptions have recently been withdrawn from professional associations (e.g., doctors' and lawyers' groups), however. These groups can no longer establish fee schedules or prohibit competitive pricing. Limits on advertising and other forms of competitive behavior are disappearing as well.

VIGNETTE 5.4   Avoiding Antitrust: The Importance of Interest-Group Politics

Congress is quite talented at articulating plausible public interest rationales for just about everything it does, including rescuing constituents from the clutches of the antitrust authorities. But while antitrust exemptions may be welfare-enhancing in some cases, economists suspect that they more often stem from Congress's attentiveness to special interests than from its concern for the broad public interest.

Sometimes it's easy to see how Congress would find an exemption politically advantageous. Consider Webb-Pomerene, which clearly invites firms to fix prices (and engage in other noncompetitive behavior) on their foreign sales. Since foreign consumers do not vote, the surplus transfers (and deadweight losses) associated with exporters' cartels will involve no political costs. There may be significant political benefits, however, in the form of the support (i.e., the votes or campaign contributions) of the managers and shareholders of the exporting firms.

Capper-Volstead and related laws that facilitate price-fixing in agriculture work differently. We know that price and output agreements among growers transfer some surplus from domestic consumers to producers and, in addition, impose deadweight welfare losses. Thus, such agreements involve losses (to consumers and society at large) in excess of gains (to growers). But the growers are a numerically compact group and so enjoy large per-capita gains, while the losers are so numerous and their per-capita losses so small they they are probably rationally ignorant about the issue. Even if they are not, it's unlikely (given free-rider problems, the high costs of transacting in the political marketplace, etc.) they'll be willing to do much to head off growers' demands for an antitrust exemption. Again, Congress is likely to see little political cost—and much benefit—in providing the exemption.

Labor's exemption is a little more difficult to evaluate. In the view of economists Richard Freeman and James Medoff, unions have two "faces."[17] One, a "voice-response face," enhances efficiency by giving workers an effective means of communicating with management in order to obtain optimal amounts of certain public goods associated with the workplace environment (e.g., safety). The other, a "monopoly face," reduces efficiency by giving workers the power to fix wages above competitive levels, producing welfare losses just as other monopolies do. Freeman and Medoff provide empirical evidence that the voice-response face of unions tends to be more quantitatively important than the monopoly face, so they are comfortable that labor's antitrust exemption serves the public interest. Others are not so sure, however. Robert Lande and Richard Zerbe, e.g., believe that labor's exemption is too broad. They believe that unions' voice-response function can be realized with plant-level collective bargaining and that the industrywide bargaining fostered by the exemption simply strengthens unions' monopoly power.[18] But given the political strength of organized labor, any proposal to modify unions' privileged antitrust status is probably ill-fated.

The soft drink industry has benefited from Congress's willingness to act when powerful interest groups are touched by antitrust. In 1978, the FTC ruled that eight large soft drink manufacturers had violated section 5 of the FTC Act by imposing geographically restricted sales territories on their independent bottlers. The Coca-Cola Company appealed but also pressured Congress for a special antitrust exemption relating to exclusive territorial agreements between soft drink manufacturers and bottlers. Congress provided it, in the form of the Soft Drink Interbrand Competition Act of 1980. Given the new law, the FTC had little choice but to dismiss all complaints. It is interesting to note that Coca-Cola's appeal stood a good chance; the firm had a fairly reasonable justification for its practices. But the soft drink makers judged that Congress would give them what they wanted more quickly and reliably than the courts.

SUMMARY AND CONCLUDING REMARKS

The first federal antitrust law, the Sherman Act (1890), was passed at a time when industrialization and the adoption of mass production technologies in many sectors caused many to worry about the economic and political power of "big business." Although some scholars disagree, most economists consider the Sherman Act to be aimed at securing for consumers the benefits of competitive markets: lower prices, enhanced output, and improved efficiency. It prohibits monopolization and horizontal restraints of trade. Confusion about judicial interpretation of the Sherman Act, and the feeling that antitrust enforcement was not doing enough to control anticompetitive conduct, led to the passage (in 1914) of the Clayton and FTC acts, which regulated price discrimination, certain "unfair" or anticompetitive business practices, and mergers.

The antitrust laws are enforced via court actions by the Antitrust Division

---

[17]See Richard B. Freeman and James L. Medoff, *What Do Unions Do?* Basic Books, New York, 1984.

[18]Robert H. Lande and Richard O. Zerbe, Jr., "Reducing Unions' Monopoly Power: Costs and Benefits," *Journal of Law and Economics*, 28 (May 1985), pp. 297–310.

of the Department of Justice, the FTC, and private individuals pressing their own treble-damage suits. There is some evidence that public enforcement of the antitrust laws is not entirely directed at those areas where the deadweight welfare losses from monopoly are the greatest. Private suits for damages often follow successful government suits. In private cases, a plaintiff must establish standing, prove that a violation of the antitrust laws occurred, and show the amount of these damages that actually flowed from the violation.

Antitrust penalties and remedies can include fines, jail sentences, treble-damage awards, dissolution of a firm or divestiture of part of its operations, and injunctions against certain activities. Some industries or organizations, including cartels formed for the purpose of exporting goods, unions, agricultural organizations, and some sports, are exempt from coverage of the antitrust laws and may engage in collusive activities that would otherwise be the target of the antitrust authorities.

QUESTIONS FOR REVIEW AND DISCUSSION

5.1 Some have argued that one of the virtues of the antitrust laws is that they are "self-enforcing." What do you think this means? If the Antitrust Division and FTC were both "captured" by monopolistic business interests, how would the enforcement of the antitrust laws be affected?

5.2 The text notes that the duties of the Antitrust Division and FTC overlap to some extent. In effect, then, the two agencies are competitors in the production of antitrust enforcement. Do you think such competition is a good or bad thing? Should the two agencies be allowed to communicate with each other about which cases they are investigating? Explain.

5.3 According to a study by Leonard W. Weiss ["An Analysis of the Allocation of Antitrust Division Resources," in J. A. Dalton and S. Levin (eds.), *The Antitrust Dilemma*, Lexington Books, Lexington, MA, 1974], there are significant efficiency gains from the Justice Department's antitrust enforcement efforts. Specifically, each "lawyer-year" (i.e., one lawyer working for a year) spent on prosecuting civil collusion cases produces an efficiency gain of $1,398,000; each lawyer-year spent on monopolization cases produces a gain of $958,000; each lawyer-year spent on horizontal merger cases produces $355,000; each lawyer-year spent on criminal collusion cases produces $46,000; each lawyer-year spent on exclusionary practices cases produces $14,000. (*Note:* In addition, such cases may yield equity gains in the form of redistribution of income from producers to consumers.) At the time of the study (1968 to 1970), Weiss estimated the cost of a lawyer-year to be $32,000. Assuming these calculations are correct, would you say antitrust enforcement is efficient? Would you say the Antitrust Division's allocation of its resources is efficient? Explain.

5.4 The text points out that the measurement of damages in private antitrust cases is, from an economic standpoint, flawed. Identify precisely what this flaw is. Is there any reason to be concerned about this issue? Explain. (*Hint:* How will it affect antitrust enforcement?)

5.5 Labor unions are exempt from the antitrust laws, but professional associations are not. Can you think of any reason why this distinction might make sense? Explain.

CHAPTER 6

MONOPOLIZATION

Monopolies are like babies: nobody likes them until they have got one of their own.

Lord Mancroft

For consumers, monopoly is a problem: Firms with monopoly power create an artificial scarcity of their goods in order to bid up prices and convert consumers' surplus to producers' surplus (i.e., profits). For firms, however, monopoly power will be a powerful lure, and it is quite possible that firms will devote considerable ingenuity to the acquisition and maintenance of such power. Defeating these efforts is, as we saw in Chapter 5, one of the central goals of antitrust policy.

Unfortunately, enforcing the legal proscriptions against monopoly is not a simple matter. First, it is often quite difficult to *detect* monopoly power. We rarely see a single (unregulated) firm making all the sales in a particular market. Where we do, we must ask whether competition from substitute products (or potential market entry by new producers) effectively constrains the monopoly firm's ability to charge monopolistic prices. More commonly, one firm may grow large relative to other firms in its market. In such cases, we must determine whether this firm is large enough, or dominant enough, to warrant suspicion of monopolization.

Then we must consider whether it will be worthwhile to do anything about those monopolistic firms we find. To a great extent, our decision about what to do with a monopoly will hinge on how the monopoly was created or acquired. If a firm grows to a position of market dominance via superior insight or lower production costs, should we seek an antitrust remedy? Are there tactics or strategies which enable firms to acquire or maintain monopoly power? If so, might these practices also have more constructive motives and thus be excused or forgiven in certain circumstances?

These are the issues and questions which occupy us in this chapter. Because Congress used such vague language in section 2 of the Sherman Act (which prohibits monopolization), it has been up to the antitrust authorities and the courts—often influenced by scholarly research—to chart the course of policy in this area. As we shall see, the course set has not always been straight and has almost always failed to satisfy one group of observers or another. In the next section, we discuss a popular and influential framework for understanding antimonopoly policy; then we define and evaluate various indicators of market structure. This is followed by discussion of some potential welfare trade-offs to be considered in implementing antimonopoly policy and of the ways in which monopoly might be acquired and maintained. Finally, we trace the evolution of the law on monopolization.

THE STRUCTURE-CONDUCT-PERFORMANCE PARADIGM

A preoccupation with the structure of markets (i.e., the number and size of firms, their cost and demand conditions, and the nature of their products) is at the very core of the theory of competition and monopoly. The economic model of perfect competition presupposes large numbers of sellers, each making such a small share of industry sales as to have a negligible effect on industry price. At the other extreme, the monopoly model admits only a single seller which makes all industry sales. It is probably inevitable, then, that antitrust scholars and policymakers would commonly presume that industry structure greatly affects—indeed, *guides*—firm behavior.

The idea that market structure determines the conduct of firms and that this conduct determines the quality of industry performance is often referred to as the *structure-conduct-performance paradigm*. Stated more fully, the paradigm implies that there is a direct causal link between the elements of market structure (including, in addition to the factors mentioned above, conditions of entry and degree of government regulation) and firm conduct (i.e., decisions about pricing and output, investment, marketing, and product design) and market performance (i.e., allocative efficiency, profitability, equity, employment effects, and rate of innovation).

In essence, this framework posits that the structural characteristics of an industry are stable and given, at least in the short run, and that these conditions act as constraints on firm behavior. For example, where the number of firms in an industry is great and no firm commands a large share of industry sales, the individual firm has little power to raise market price or restrict industry output. But domination of the industry by a single large firm, or the existence of a few firms selling highly differentiated products, may produce considerably different choices about price and output and, in turn, may affect industry performance.

The structure-conduct-performance paradigm has been enormously influential, among both antitrust scholars and policymakers. Empirical studies of its implications abound, and it has greatly affected the conduct of antitrust policy. But this should not be taken to imply that the framework is accepted by all or even most students of antitrust economics. Indeed, the paradigm is a subject of lively controversy.

Among the milder criticisms of the paradigm is that it has led policymakers to place excessive emphasis on the number and size of firms in their attempts to diagnose monopoly, while more important considerations—chiefly the degree of potential competition or ease of entry—are often ignored. Another criticism is that the causal link between structural variables and firm discretion over price and output is quite weak, and that inferring the latter from the former can lead to serious policy errors. Others note that in taking firms' environments as fixed and given, the paradigm misses much strategic behavior aimed at modifying these environments.

Less friendly critics claim that the paradigm's theoretical foundations are weak and that its empirical implications often are not confirmed by the data. These critics argue, e.g., that there is no clear-cut theoretical relationship between the number of firms in a market and the degree to which that market is competitive. In addition, they argue that the statistical evidence which shows relationships between certain structural indicators and measures of market performance (especially firm profitability) is unconvincing for two basic reasons. First, they assert that most empirical studies that relate structure to performance are based on flawed data (e.g., accounting data that do not conform to economists' conceptions of costs and profits, or structural data that reflect the Census Bureau's arbitrary system of classifying industries). Second, they note that correlation is not causality. In this view, a statistical link between certain structural and performance variables does not mean that structure "causes" performance of a certain kind; the linkage may reflect other influences.[1]

These are important criticisms; they will influence our discussion of antitrust policy throughout this and succeeding chapters. Even if one doubts the premises or implications of the structure-conduct-performance paradigm, however, it cannot be ignored. It has influenced, and continues to influence, legions of antitrust theorists and practitioners. In cases that involve monopolization, mergers, or collusion, consideration of the elements of industry structure is simply unavoidable. To understand antitrust policy, then, we must master the tools commonly used to describe the structure of markets. We now turn to this task.

MEASUREMENT ISSUES

Market Structure Indicators

Anyone who attempts to assess the degree of competitiveness in an industry would clearly like to know whether it holds one or 100 firms. To be truly use-

---

[1]See, e.g., Yale Brozen, *Concentration, Mergers, and Public Policy*, Macmillan, New York, 1982. For a spirited riposte to such criticisms, see Douglas F. Greer, *Industrial Organization and Public Policy*, 2d ed., Macmillan, New York, 1984, especially chapter 19.

ful, however, this knowledge must be combined with information about the size distribution of these firms. It is certainly possible that an industry with as many as 100 firms might be considered monopolized if, say, the leading firm makes 95 percent of industry sales. Attempts to combine information about the number of firms and their size have led to the development of two basic market structure indicators: the concentration ratio (CR) and the Herfindahl index.

Concentration Ratio   An n-firm concentration ratio CR_n measures the percentage of total sales in an industry made by the n largest firms in that industry. (Alternatively, concentration ratios can be based on firms' shares of industry assets, employment, or other variables.) For example, a four-firm CR, denoted CR_4, can be calculated (1) by summing the sales made by the four largest firms in the industry and dividing by total industry sales or (2) by simply summing the market shares of the four largest firms. The resulting value is then usually multiplied by 100 to express the CR as a percentage. Table 6.1 shows how various CRs may be calculated for a hypothetical 15-firm industry.

It is tempting to suppose that a CR_4 of 80 signals greater monopoly power than a CR_4 of 60 or 40. But a CR tells us nothing about the conditions of potential market entry. Indeed, the one-firm CR in a market can be 100, but if entry and exit are easy, consumers may suffer no monopolistic pricing or output

TABLE 6.1
MARKET STRUCTURE INDICATORS FOR A HYPOTHETICAL 15-FIRM INDUSTRY.   An industry with individual firm sales like those shown will have a four-firm CR of 51 and an H value of 1015.

Firm rank	Sales	Market share, %	
1	$ 2,125,000	19.98	
2	1,550,000	14.57	
3	900,000	8.46	
4	875,000	8.23	$(CR_4 = 51)$
5	800,000	7.52	
6	760,000	7.14	
7	710,000	6.67	
8	615,000	5.78	$(CR_8 = 78)$
9	503,000	4.73	
10	467,000	4.39	
11	420,000	3.95	
12	355,000	3.34	$(CR_{12} = 95)$
13	276,000	2.59	
14	198,000	1.86	
15	84,000	0.79	$(H = 1015)$
	$10,638,000	100.00	

restriction. We must remember that a CR (indeed, most any numerical indicator of market structure) is but one of many elements to consider in assessing any market's competitiveness.

Herfindahl Index   A more refined measure of industry concentration is the *Herfindahl* (or *H*) *index*, suggested by O. C. Herfindahl in his 1950 doctoral dissertation.[2] It is defined as the sum of the squares of the market shares of all the firms in the industry.

$$H = \sum_{i=1}^{N} \left(\frac{x_i}{T} \right)^2$$

where N is the number of firms, x_i is the amount of industry sales made by firm i, and T is total industry sales. (Or, as with CRs, H may be calculated by using firms' shares of industry assets rather than sales.)

As calculated above, H will be a fraction between 0 and 1 (although if firms' market shares are expressed in percent, a common practice, H will be between 0 and 10,000). Industries with many small firms will have an H value close to 0; a monopolistic industry will have an H equal to 1 (or 10,000). The hypothetical industry described in Table 6.1 has an H index value of 1015 on a scale of 10,000. Most economists tend to label industries with H index values that fall between 1000 and 1800 "moderately concentrated," those with H values less than 1000 "unconcentrated," and those with H values over 1800 "highly concentrated."

Clearly, the Herfindahl index is much like the CR. By squaring market shares, however, the index better identifies industries apparently dominated by one or a few very large firms. Consider, e.g., two industries A and B. In A, there are four firms, each with a market share of 25 percent; in B, there are also four firms, but one has a market share of 85 percent, while the remaining three have shares of 5 percent each. Both industries would be considered highly concentrated on almost any measure. But economists and antitrust authorities would say that if either industry is monopolized, it is likely B. Yet the CR measure cannot distinguish the two industries—the CR for both A and B is 100. The Herfindahl index, however, reflects a single firm's domination of B: The H value for A is 2500, while the H value for B is 7300.

Because of this feature, the Herfindahl index has become an important tool of antitrust authorities, especially (as we will see in Chapter 8) in merger cases. It has one practical drawback, however: It requires market share data for *all* firms in the industry. Sometimes, data for smaller or "fringe" firms are diffi-

[2]O. C. Herfindahl, "Concentration in the Steel Industry," unpublished Ph.D. dissertation, Columbia University, New York, 1950.

cult to obtain. In such cases, a minimum H value can be calculated by using data from the largest firms alone.

VIGNETTE 6.1   Is Aggregate Concentration Increasing?

Anxiety about the growing size of U.S. firms and the extent to which big business appears to account for ever-larger shares of national output is quite common. As we have seen, such concerns were central to the passage of the antitrust laws and periodically provoke new calls for modifications to these laws or stiffer enforcement of them. Many believe that even where CRs are not quite high enough to suggest monopolization of individual markets, excessive *aggregate concentration* is dangerous because it places too much economic and political power in too few hands (with adverse social consequences).

With an eye toward the latter issue, there have been many studies of the degree of aggregate concentration in the U.S. economy (and other economies). Aggregate market concentration is measured by summing the proportion of sales (or assets) of the largest firms in the economy, without reference to specific industries or markets. Predictably, not all the studies reach the same conclusions, for methodologies differ widely. There is, however, a general consensus that the aggregate concentration in the United States in the post-World War II era is significantly higher than it was in the earlier part of the 20th century. However, there appears to be *no* trend toward increasing aggregate concentration in more recent decades.

In U.S. manufacturing, e.g., the 100 largest firms produced 22 percent of total manufacturing net output in 1919; this share rose to 30 percent by 1954 and 33 percent by 1963, but it has remained steady since then.[3] Figure 6.1 shows the stability of concentration in manufacturing from 1963 to 1982. Whether one looks at the 50 largest firms or the 200 largest, their share of output has changed remarkably little in the past two decades.[4] Whether more recent data that incorporate the merger wave of the mid-1980s will change this remains to be seen.

Market Definition

The discussion thus far has skirted a very important issue: determining the "relevant market" for which a CR or H value may be calculated. The local McDonald's franchise, e.g., may be the only seller of Big Macs for miles. Should we calculate a CR or H value for Big Mac sales alone, or should our calculation include sales of all hamburgers, or even all fast foods? Should we limit our analysis to a few square miles or include the whole country?

The stakes here are high. Define a market too narrowly, and almost any seller may appear to be a monopolist; too loosely, and no one will appear to be one. In consequence, market definition is one of the most extensively debated issues in any monopolization case. In one Justice Department case against IBM, e.g., the participants estimated that about *half* of a six-year trial was devoted to presentation of evidence on market definition!

[3]B. Curry and K. D. George, "Industrial Concentration: A Survey," *The Journal of Industrial Economics*, 31 (March 1983), pp. 203–255.
[4]Source: Department of Commerce, 1982 Census of Manufactures, *Concentration Ratios in Manufacturing*, Table 1, p. 7-3.

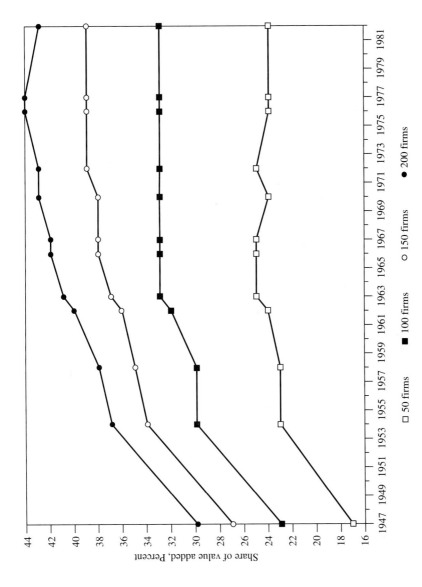

FIGURE 6.1
TRENDS IN AGGREGATE CONCENTRATION, 1947–1982. Since 1963, the share of value added (in manufacturing) by the largest 50, 100, 150, or 200 firms has been fairly stable.

□ 50 firms   ■ 100 firms   ○ 150 firms   ● 200 firms

In general, there are two key steps required to define the relevant market for purposes of devising appropriate market structure indicators. First, the *product market* must be delineated; second, the *geographic market* must be identified.

The Product Market   On occasion, goods that differ considerably in their superficial characteristics may be deemed part of the same market for competitive purposes. Alternatively, goods that achieve similar ends may be found to inhabit distinct product markets. The key here is the extent to which goods are *interchangeable* or *substitutable* in consumption.

One way to analyze substitutability in markets is to calculate the *price elasticity of demand,* sometimes called the *own elasticity of demand,* for a particular industry or good. The price elasticity of demand for a good measures how much the quantity demanded changes in response to a change in the good's price (holding constant all other variables that might affect demand). The price elasticity of demand for good X, denoted as E_{XX}, is simply the ratio of the percentage change in quantity of X demanded to the associated percentage change in the price of X, or

$$E_{XX} = \frac{\frac{\Delta Q_X}{Q_X}}{\frac{\Delta P_X}{P_X}} = \left(\frac{P_X}{Q_X}\right)\left(\frac{\Delta Q_X}{\Delta P_X}\right)$$

where Δ indicates a change in a particular variable (for example, ΔQ_X is the change in quantity demanded that results from some change in price ΔP_X).

Since demand curves are negatively sloped, E_{XX} will always have a negative value. The *greater* the absolute value of E_{XX} (i.e., the more elastic the demand), the more sensitive are consumers to changes in X's price; we can infer, therefore, that there are many close substitutes for the good. For example, the (long-run) price elasticity of demand for movies has been estimated to be -3.7.[5] This means that a 1 percent increase in the price of admission to movies will reduce quantity demanded by 3.7 percent. Since demand for movies is so highly price-elastic, it might plausibly be argued that consumers find it easy to substitute other forms of entertainment (e.g., TV, live theater, spectator sports, books) for movies. Accordingly, the relevant market might be defined to include these substitutes.

A more precise tool for gauging product interchangeability is the *cross-elasticity of demand.* The cross-elasticity of demand for a good measures the change in demand for some good in response to a small change in the price of some *other* good (holding constant all other variables that might affect demand). For example, if we have two goods X and Y, the cross-elasticity of demand for

---

[5]See H. S. Houthakker and Lester D. Taylor, *Consumer Demand in the United States: Analyses and Projections,* Harvard University Press, Cambridge, MA, 1970, p. 130.

good X in terms of the price of good Y, denoted E_{XY}, is simply the ratio of the percentage change in demand for X to the associated percentage change in price of Y, or

$$E_{XY} = \frac{\frac{\Delta Q_X}{Q_X}}{\frac{\Delta P_Y}{P_Y}} = \left(\frac{P_Y}{Q_X}\right)\left(\frac{\Delta Q_X}{\Delta P_Y}\right)$$

If X and Y are substitutes, a rise in the price of Y will cause consumers to increase their demand for X, so E_{XY} will be positive. If X and Y are complements, E_{XY} will be negative. The more interchangeable the two goods, the higher will be the value of E_{XY}. Goods with high cross-elasticities, then, are often considered to be part of the same market, even if they are different in some respects.

Both the own elasticity and the cross-elasticity of demand can be estimated by using econometric methods, assuming suitable data exist. If any problems of data availability can be overcome, another vexing issue awaits those who use elasticity measures to define a market: the question of where to "draw the line." Suppose cross-elasticities between X and all possible substitute products have been calculated and ranked from largest to smallest. Where is the cutoff point below which products will be deemed not part of the same market as good X? Unfortunately, economics provides no clear answer; there is no universally accepted way to distinguish close substitutes from distant ones. Any dividing line between them is a matter of judgment or opinion, a fact which goes a long way to explain why market definition issues are so hotly contested during monopolization cases.

VIGNETTE 6.2   "Reasonable" Interchangeability: From *du Pont* to *Grinnell*

Market definition is a key issue in many antitrust cases, but it is especially crucial in monopolization cases. In the case of *United States v. E. I. du Pont de Nemours*, the Supreme Court showed a fine appreciation of some of the economic tools useful in defining product markets.

In *du Pont*, the Justice Department alleged monopolization of the cellophane market. The government's attorneys noted that du Pont produced nearly 75 percent of all the cellophane wrap sold in the United States from 1937 to 1947 and argued that this was strong evidence of illegal monopolization. But du Pont's attorneys suggested that the firm faced ample competition from producers of other wrapping materials such as waxed paper and aluminum foil. They argued that the relevant product market included all such flexible wraps and that cellophane sales comprised just 17.9 percent of this broader market. The case turned on which market definition the Court would find more appropriate. In deciding the issue, the Court employed economists' concept of cross-elasticity:

[W]here there are market alternatives that buyers may readily use for their purposes, illegal monopoly does not exist merely because the product said to be monopolized differs from the others. . . . In considering what is the relevant market for determining the control of price and competition, no more definite rule can be declared than that commodities reasonably inter-changeable by consumers for the same purpose make up that "part of the trade or commerce" monopolization of which may be illegal.

. . . It may be admitted that cellophane combines the desirable elements of transparency, strength and cheapness. . . . But, despite cellophane's advantages, it has to meet competi-tion from other materials in every one of its uses.

. . . If a slight decrease in the price of cellophane causes a considerable number of cus-tomers of other flexible wrappings to switch to cellophane, it would be an indication that a high cross-elasticity of demand exists between them; that the products compete in the same market.[6]

The Court concluded that a broad market definition including all flexible packaging materials was appropriate, and du Pont was judged not guilty of monopolization.

In another case a decade later, however, the Court opted for a very narrow mar-ket definition. In *United States v. Grinnell Corp.*, the Justice Department alleged that Grinnell had illegally monopolized the market for "central station protective ser-vices," in which clients arrange to have their property electrically wired to detect bur-glaries or fires. The systems are monitored by a central station equipped to send appropriate emergency services. This time the Court concluded that the various substitutes for such systems were not sufficiently close to merit inclusion in the rele-vant market:

There are, to be sure, substitutes for the accredited central station service. But none of them appears to operate on the same level as the central station service so as to meet the inter-changeability test of the *du Pont* case.

. . . Watchman service is far more costly and less reliable. Systems that set off an audible alarm at the site of a fire or burglary are cheaper but often less reliable. . . . Proprietary sys-tems that a customer purchases and operates are available; but they can be used only by a very large business or by government.[7]

The Court ordered Grinnell to sell off some of its affiliates and enjoined it from acquiring firms involved in the protective services industry.

The Geographic Market   Geographic considerations will also crucially affect the specification of the relevant market. Just as with product market def-inition, defining the geographic market too narrowly may produce evidence of monopoly where none really exists; excessively widening the market area may lead to the conclusion that no monopoly exists when firms might have consid-erable local monopoly power.

Obviously, transportation costs are a key factor in defining the appropriate geographic market. If these costs are high relative to the value of the product in question, the range over which a producer can credibly compete will be limited. Consider, e.g., the market for bricks. Nationwide there are many brick producers, and the four-firm national CR in this market has been calculated at 12, conveying no hint that the brick market is monopolized. But because bricks are so heavy and costly to ship far from their place of manufacture, this mar-

---

[6]351 U.S. 377 (1956), pp. 394–395, 398–400.
[7]384 U.S. 563 (1966), pp. 573–574.

ket is more properly considered regional or local in character. One study (although now quite dated) calculated that the average *local* CR for bricks has been as high as 87 and in some markets (e.g., Philadelphia, San Francisco-Oakland) was 100.[8] In many other markets (e.g., fluid milk, soft drinks, concrete), the local or regional CR is likely a multiple of the national CR.

Sometimes legal barriers also limit the scope of markets. A state or municipality may, via licensing or other restrictions, prevent "outsiders" from entering an area and competing with (politically favored) local firms. Or natural barriers to interregional competition may exist. The newspaper market has historically been local because readers seem to prefer a good deal of local content (news, sports, classified advertising, etc.) in this product. Note, then, that both demand- and supply-side considerations will affect geographic market definition. Factors that affect both buyers (tastes, costs of transportation to or information about sellers in various locales) and sellers (shipping costs, legal barriers) must be carefully weighed in specifying the area for which market structure indicators will be calculated.

Criticisms of Market Structure Indicators

The U.S. government, through the Bureau of the Census, gathers data on market concentration in all sectors of the economy. An elaborate system assigning numerical codes to the output of every U.S. enterprise—the *Standard Industrial Classification* (or SIC) system—has been devised to facilitate reporting these data, which are much used by antitrust scholars and policymakers.[9]

Great care should be taken in using these or any other measures of market structure, however. As noted above, market definition is often a vexing matter. Just because the outputs of two firms carry the same SIC code does not make these firms meaningful competitors, for the SIC system often arbitrarily groups products that are not at all substitutable in consumption. For example, SIC code 3714 includes various motor vehicle parts and accessories (e.g., bumpers and brakes, horns and heaters) that are clearly not "reasonably interchangeable." (For what it's worth, however, the Census Bureau informs us that the four-firm CR for SIC code 3714 is 61.[10])

Structural indicators have numerous other flaws as well. As we noted above, national figures ignore regional or local concentration and may thus understate market power. However, national figures often ignore the effect that foreign competition may have in limiting domestic firms' discretion over price. Most structural measures also fail to reflect turnover in an industry. For example, a four-firm CR may remain stable at 80 for several years, but this may mask the fact that individual firms' market shares have changed dramatically during this period or that the relative positions of these firms have

---

[8]David Schwartzman and Joan Bodoff, "Concentration in Regional and Local Industries," *Southern Economic Journal*, 37 (January 1971), pp. 343–348.

[9]The SIC system is explained in Office of Management and Budget, *Standard Industrial Classification Manual*, Government Printing Office, Washington, 1972.

[10]Source: 1982 Census of Manufactures, *Concentration Ratios in Manufacturing*, Table 5, p. 7-44.

changed (i.e., that the largest firm has been knocked off its perch by the second or third largest), phenomena that might indicate vigorous competition.

Most important, concentration measures do not really describe *conduct* in the underlying market, nor do they say much about the extent of potential competition. It is possible, then, that CRs and *H* values give false clues about the degree of competition in a market. Consider, e.g., a market dominated by a large firm that prices its product competitively and earns zero economic profits. Under these circumstances, potential entrants will see little opportunity for profitable entry, so CRs and *H* values for this market will remain high and stable, providing misleading hints of monopolization. On the other hand, a monopolist who charges prices above cost might attract entry by rivals. This will lower the apparent degree of concentration in this market—and perhaps reassure antitrust authorities—but such a trend may or may not be accompanied by vigorous price competition. In sum, structural indicators do not directly measure the degree of competition of markets. While they are often helpful in considering the question of market power, they should by no means substitute for a careful examination of firm behavior and overall market conditions.

Performance Measures

Dissatisfaction with the various indicators of market structure has led many scholars to propose using performance-based indicators of monopoly power. Two of the most popular, discussed below, are named after the eminent economists who devised them: Abba Lerner and Joe S. Bain.

The Lerner Index   A price-searching (or monopolistic) firm will maximize profits by producing the rate of output that equates MR with MC; at this rate of output, $P > MC$. Price-taking (competitive) firms, however, will continue producing until $P = MC$. If we detect a difference between P and MC, then we have detected noncompetitive pricing. The Lerner index takes advantage of this fact. It is

$$L = \frac{P - MC}{P}$$

Thus, if competition forces firms to set $P = MC$, then $L = 0$. But if monopoly power enables firms to set $P > MC$, then $L > 0$ (with an upper limit of 1). The Lerner index is elegant in its simplicity: The higher L, the greater the divergence of P from its perfectly competitive level.

But the Lerner index is not without drawbacks. Chief among them is a practical problem: the requirement that MC be measured accurately. This is not an easy task. Firms do not keep data on their marginal costs. Although MC can be estimated econometrically by using firms' total cost functions, this is not a trivial undertaking. Average cost data, which are often easy to find or generate, will simply not do, for there are many reasons (having nothing to do with monopoly) why price might exceed average total cost (ATC) at some time. A demand shift may push price above ATC in a perfectly competitive market, for example, but this will induce new entry, and eventually price will return to equality with both MC and ATC. In the time it takes entry to occur, however, Lerner index values that employ ATC as a substitute for MC would hint at monopoly where none actually exists.

The Bain Index   While a monopoly will not *always* earn economic profits, it will probably do so more often than not. For this reason, Bain suggested looking at profit rates to detect monopoly power. Data on accounting profits— unlike data on MC—are usually readily available, and Bain argued that persistent excess profits are likely the result of exercise of monopoly power.[11] He recognized, however, that accounting data on profits must be adjusted to yield a valid estimate of excess or economic profits. He defined total accounting profits π_a as

$$\pi_a = TR - TC - D$$

where TR is total receipts, TC is total (*explicit*) cost (i.e., expenditures for wages, raw materials costs, etc.), and D is depreciation. We must deduct any *implicit* costs of doing business (chiefly, the opportunity cost of the owners' investment in the firm) from this amount to obtain an estimate of excess profits, or pure economic profits. Total excess profits are then

$$\pi_e = TR - TC - D - iK$$

where K is the value of the owners' stake in the firm and i is the rate of return that the owners could have earned on an equivalently risky investment. In practical terms, since π_a/K is the accounting profit rate and i is the "normal" rate of return on the owners' investment, the rate of excess profit π_e/K can be inferred by simply subtracting a normal profit rate from published profit figures. Where this rate π_e/K is persistently above zero, Bain argued, we may suspect monopoly power.

But the Bain index has been the target of much criticism. To start with, we repeat that monopoly power does not *always* guarantee excess profits; so the observation that the excess profit rate π_e/K is zero (or not persistently above zero) need not indicate that monopoly power is absent. In addition, the index is far more difficult to calculate accurately than it might first appear. Published accounting profit data are based on widely varying conventions about costs. And calculation of the "normal" profit rate will require an accurate estimate of the amount of risk faced by the firm's owners, a complicated task. What is more, the choice of accounting practices will affect the measurement of the amount of capital K tied up in the firm. Often, e.g., advertising and research

---

[11]See Joe S. Bain, "The Profit Rate as a Measure of Monopoly Power," *Quarterly Journal of Economics*, 55 (February 1941), pp. 271–293.

and development (R&D) expenditures, which probably create long-lived assets for the firm, are usually treated as current expenses. This will understate the firm's net assets and therefore overstate the rate of measured profit. Practical application of the Bain index, then, requires the utmost caution.

Beyond these methodological difficulties lurks another key issue: the presumption that persistently high rates of profit indicate monopoly power. It may be that high profit rates simply reflect the presence of some factor of production (e.g., a clever manager or superior production technology) that enables the firm to produce output at lower costs than its rivals can. If this factor of production could be identified and if it were mobile, its price would be bid up to reflect its value in production (or alternatively rivals would duplicate or imitate it and so lower their costs), and industry profits would be "normal" for all firms. In the real world, however, it is sometimes difficult to identify why some firms outperform others, even in highly competitive markets. Higher profit rates can be the result of superior insight by top management, a more dedicated labor force, luck, or countless other factors which may or may not be identifiable. To assume that persistently higher-than-normal profits are necessarily the result of monopoly power risks grave policy error.

VIGNETTE 6.3   A Closer Look at Profit Rates

Historically, the *accounting* profit rate for the pharmaceutical industry has far exceeded that of many other industries. As column 1 in Table 6.2 shows, the average accounting profit rate for drug companies from 1959 to 1973 was 18.3 percent, while the rate for a sample of other major industries averaged about 11 percent.[12] Unless the risks in pharmaceuticals are significantly greater than in the other industries in the sample, applying the Bain index here might lead one to conclude that the pharmaceutical industry is monopolized or that the firms in that industry are colluding.

Kenneth Clarkson has shown, however, that adjusting accounting data to take account of relevant economic costs can have a major impact on measured rates of return. Accountants, e.g., typically treat expenditures for research and development and advertising in the same way as they treat wages paid to workers—as current expenses rather than capital expenditures. This means that 100 percent of R&D or advertising outlays are deducted as expenses in the period incurred. Economists would argue, however, that R&D and advertising expenditures are much more like outlays for long-lived assets such as machinery or buildings: They yield benefits for months, years, or even decades into the future. If accountants treated R&D and advertising in the same way as they treat outlays for a machine—calculating its cost as the estimated amount by which it depreciates each year of its service life—firms' profit rates would look different.

Such adjustments might not make much difference in comparing profit rates across industries if all industries spent similar amounts on R&D or advertising. But

[12]The data in Table 6.2 and the ensuing discussion are from Kenneth W. Clarkson, *Intangible Capital and Rates of Return*, American Enterprise Institute, Washington, 1977.

TABLE 6.2

AVERAGE ACCOUNTING AND CORRECTED RATES OF RETURN ON NET WORTH FOR SELECTED INDUSTRIES, 1959–1973.   Adjusting accounting rates of return to take account of relevant economic costs reduces both the average profit rate within industries and the variation in profit rates across industries.

Industry	(1) Accounting rates of return	(2) Corrected rates of return
Pharmaceuticals	18.3	12.9
Electrical machinery	13.3	10.1
Foods	11.8	10.6
Petroleum	11.2	10.8
Chemicals	10.6	9.1
Motor vehicles	10.5	9.2
Paper	10.5	10.1
Rubber products	10.1	8.7
Office machinery	10.5	9.9
Aerospace	9.2	7.4
Ferrous metals	7.6	7.3
Average	11.2	9.6
Variance	7.5	2.5

Source: Kenneth Clarkson, *Intangible Capital and Rates of Return,* Washington, The American Enterprise Institute (1977), p. 64. Reprinted with the permission of The American Enterprise Institute for Public Policy Research, Washington, D.C.

Clarkson found that pharmaceutical firms typically spend far more on these things than other industries in the sample. For the period studied, drug companies spent 5.3 cents of each sales dollar on R&D and 3.7 cents on advertising. By comparison, firms in the food industry spent only 0.4 cent per sales dollar on R&D; aerospace firms spent only 0.3 cent per sales dollar on advertising.

Taking these differences into account and correcting the accounting data to reflect the true economic costs of production, Clarkson concluded that the average rate of return in pharmaceuticals from 1959 to 1973 was actually 12.9 percent (see column 2 in Table 6.2). Although still higher than the sample average of slightly under 10 percent, this difference is well within the range that might be accounted for by differential risk. What is more, the corrections substantially reduce the variance in profit rates across industries, suggesting that a good deal of the observed variation in industry profitability is illusory. If we use accounting profits as a "net" to catch monopolists, we will likely catch innocent R&D- or advertising-intensive firms as well, or instead.

MONOPOLIZATION POLICY: KEY ANALYTICAL ISSUES

So far we've focused on ways to identify monopoly through various structural indicators. As we've seen, this is not always a simple task. Assuming we clear this hurdle, however, others await. Let us now begin to consider what we should do with a monopoly once we're convinced we've found one.

The Courts' Two-Part Test

One of the things that complicates the lives of antitrust officials is that the courts generally do not consider structural evidence of market power alone to be sufficient evidence of *illegal* monopolization. In other words, all the appropriate indicators (e.g., concentration measures based on properly defined markets or performance measures based on relevant economic data) can point to the presence of monopoly, but the courts still may not find a violation of section 2 of the Sherman Act.

This is so because, from very early on, the courts have been reluctant to interpret the Sherman Act to prohibit bigness per se. Instead, in section 2 cases the courts have applied a *rule-of-reason* standard, in which they judge not only whether certain conduct has occurred or status been achieved, but whether this conduct or status is reasonable. This approach has produced a two-part test for illegality in monopolization cases. The test was briefly summarized by the Supreme Court in *United States v. Grinnell Corp.*:

> The offense of monopoly under Section 2 of the Sherman Act has two elements: (1) the possession of monopoly power in the relevant market and (2) the willful acquisition or maintenance of that power as distinguished from growth or development as a consequence of a superior product, business acumen, or historic accident.[13]

From an analytical standpoint, the courts' determination that monopoly (or bigness) by itself should not be held illegal is sensible and worthy of applause. It is after all quite possible that a firm might come to dominate a market by entirely innocent, indeed praiseworthy, means. The first firm to market a new product or improve an old one may, at least for a time, wield monopoly power (or appear to do so). Similarly, firms that are competitively superior (i.e., that have lower production costs or better insight than their rivals) might grow to dominate their markets. It would be unfortunate indeed if the antitrust laws were used indiscriminately, punishing the innovative or efficient along with the venal.

As the above passage from *Grinnell* indicates, the courts generally try to separate "good" monopolies from "bad" by looking at the "willfulness" of firms' actions in acquiring or maintaining their market power. Typically, evil intent is inferred from the presence or absence of certain conduct that goes outside the bounds of "normal business practice."

But there are clear problems here. First, there is the possibility that conduct which is merely hard-nosed competition may be judged evil and anticompetitive. Is the desire to be "never undersold" or a refusal to concede to a rival any sale anywhere an attempt to acquire or maintain a monopoly, or just good, clean competition? On the other hand, some conduct may provoke no charges of bad intent from rivals, but may be ultimately anticompetitive (e.g., where

---

[13]384 U.S. 563 (1966), pp. 570–571. This test originated in *Standard Oil Co. of New Jersey v. United States*, 221 U.S. 1 (1911).

the rivals are coconspirators in a successful collusive arrangement). Innovative activities will, almost by definition, be outside the bounds of normal practice. It will not be easy to determine which of these are benign and which are not. Finally, it is certainly possible that the *intentions* of individuals may be quite unrelated to the *effects* of their actions. Some venal capitalist consciously may seek to drive rivals out of a market in order to monopolize it and even write "smoking gun" memos to that effect, but her or his actions may serve only to lower market price, expand output, and enhance social welfare.

Such factors complicate courts' implementation of the two-part test and have made several major monopolization cases among the most controversial in antitrust law. Before wading into these controversies, however, we discuss two of the ways in which firms are commonly alleged to acquire or maintain monopolies: predatory pricing and limit pricing.

Predation

The idea that monopoly can be acquired via one or more predatory strategies is extremely popular. One such strategy, *predatory pricing,* has played a key role in many monopolization cases. In theory, a predator may cut prices below its and its rivals' costs in order to drive the rivals from the market (or, in less extreme versions, to discipline them in order to facilitate collusion). The losses accrued by the predator during the period of below-cost pricing are considered an investment to be recovered when competition is eliminated, prices are raised above costs, and economic profits are earned.

Since cost and demand conditions are not uniform across firms or across time periods, we must be cautious about what we classify as predatory pricing. If I have lower costs than you, when I undersell you, I may be engaging not in predation but in competition. Or I may set my price below my average total cost (ATC), but this may simply be a response to depressed demand conditions and another manifestation of competitive behavior: When the going market price is below ATC but above average variable cost (AVC), I will sensibly stay in business, at least in the short run, and minimize losses by producing the rate of output where price equals marginal cost.

Given these (and other) considerations, noted antitrust scholars Phillip Areeda and Donald Turner have proposed that price cuts down to AVC be presumptively legal.[14] (From an analytical standpoint, we might prefer to test whether price is below short-run MC, but since MC is often hard to measure, such a rule would be of limited practical value.) Only price cuts below AVC would be ruled predatory under this "Areeda-Turner rule." Such pricing would indicate bad intent and, when found, constitute evidence of attempted monopolization.

---

[14]Phillip Areeda and Donald F. Turner, "Predatory Pricing and Related Practices under Section 2 of the Sherman Act," *Harvard Law Review,* 88 (February 1975), pp. 697–733.

VIGNETTE 6.4   Predatory Pricing and the Areeda-Turner Rule in Practice: O. C. Hanson Sues Big Oil

In 1952, O. C. Hanson moved to Tucson, Arizona, and used his life savings of $7,000 to buy a service station. Although he suffered economic losses in every one of the next 13 years, he nevertheless expanded his holdings to include 17 service stations and a natural gas distributorship. Often his acquisitions were financed with credit that was advanced unwillingly; he would use cash from his gas sales to buy new stations rather than pay his suppliers. By 1964, he owed money to over 30 creditors; his suppliers would sell him gas only on a cash-and-carry basis. His stations were in shoddy condition, and employee turnover was high. By 1966, he closed his businesses.

But all was not yet lost: He sued the Shell, Standard, and Gulf Oil companies, alleging predatory pricing and several other violations of antitrust law. He claimed his business losses resulted from the major oil companies' attempts to drive independent dealers such as himself out of the market by keeping prices artificially low. At trial, some of Hanson's charges were dismissed, but a jury found Shell and Standard guilty of Sherman Act violations and awarded Hanson damages of $363,181.31, which, when trebled, would rise to $1,089,543.93.

Standard agreed to a settlement with Hanson, but Shell appealed and won acquittal at a new trial. Hanson appealed to the U.S. Court of Appeals (9th Circuit). The appeals court was unsympathetic to Hanson, branding him a "loser in the competitive endeavor" who sought to use "the antitrust laws as a means of shifting his losses to someone else."[15] On the issue of predation, the court went directly to the Areeda-Turner rule for guidance:

To demonstrate predation, Hanson had to show that the prices charged by Shell were such that Shell was forgoing present profits in order to create a market position in which it could charge enough to obtain supranormal profits and recoup its present losses. This could be shown by evidence that Shell was selling its gasoline at or below marginal cost or, because marginal cost is often impossible to ascertain, below average variable costs.

. . . Hanson made no effort to prove that the prices Shell was charging at either the wholesale or the retail level were below marginal or average variable costs, and for all that it appears Shell's new pricing policies were nothing more than an attempt to gain a larger share of the market because of its stronger competitive position. If its prices were above its costs, and nevertheless Shell did drive Hanson out of business, this can only be because Hanson was so inefficient that at prices at which Shell could make a reasonable profit he could not. The antitrust laws were not intended, and may not be used, to require businesses to price their products at unreasonably high prices (which penalize the consumer) so that less efficient competitors can stay in business. The Sherman Act is not a subsidy for inefficiency.[16]

The popular wisdom that predatory pricing can be a successful route toward monopolization has been challenged by several researchers. John McGee has noted that predatory pricing will likely cost the predator far more than it will cost the prey. Indeed, as the predator's market share grows, its losses may be a large multiple of the losses it imposes on its prey.

Consider, e.g., Figure 6.2. Suppose there are five firms with identical (constant) costs C facing the market demand curve D. Ordinary competition yields a price P_c and industry rate of output Q_c; suppose each firm produces $Q_c/5$.

---

[15]*Hanson v. Shell Oil Co.*, 541 F.2d 1352 (1976), p. 1355.
[16]541 F.2d 1352 (1976), pp. 1358–1359.

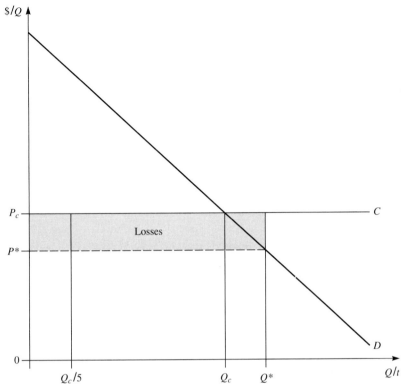

FIGURE 6.2
PREDATORY PRICING. A predatory price P^* will impose losses equal to $P_c - P^*$ per
unit sold. As a predator's share of the market grows, its share of industry losses
grows apace and may equal a multiple of the losses borne by rivals.

But now one firm seeks to drive the others out via predatory pricing, setting a
price $P^* < C$. At this price, quantity demanded will rise to Q^*. If all firms
raised their output rates equally to accommodate this increase in quantity
demanded, all would suffer losses equal to one-fifth of total industry losses,
i.e., one-fifth of the area $(P_c - P^*) Q^*$. But, of course, the other firms may be
reluctant to raise their output in order to sell at a loss. The predator then may
have to raise *its* output to maintain the predatory price P^* and clear the market. If it does so, it will be suffering greater losses than its prey—perhaps
equal to $(P_c - P^*) (Q_c/5)$ *plus* $(P_c - P^*) (Q^* - Q_c)$—from the very onset of its
predatory strategy.

Sustaining such losses will require that the predator have "deeper pockets"
than its prey. But those pockets had better be very deep indeed. For suppose
the predation convinces some of the prey to depart, leaving their share of the
market to the predator. With each departure, the predator's losses multiply.
Unless the remaining firms choose to expand their rate of output (and losses),
the predator's share of industry losses will climb steadily (from one-fifth of the

total to two-fifths, three-fifths, and so on). By the time a single holdout remains, the predator may be earning $4 (or more) in losses for every $1 loss imposed on the prey.

Once the last holdout is driven out, of course, price can be raised above costs to recoup. But for how long? Unless the productive capacity of the departed firms has somehow been destroyed, they (or new owners of their plants and equipment) may simply rise to compete with the predator, preventing it from long earning the economic profits required to make the investment in predatory pricing pay. Unless, in other words, barriers to entry or reentry exist, a predator will surely lose money.

McGee argues, therefore, that predatory pricing is a poor strategy for the aspiring monopolist. He also suspects that instances of its successful application are extremely rare (and that charges of predation often are made by those with higher costs rather than by more successful rivals, as in Vignette 6.4). After examining the various allegations of predation in one case long thought to be a textbook example of the practice (the *Standard Oil* case), McGee found that none appeared to involve actual predatory pricing.[17] Kenneth Elzinga reviewed the facts surrounding alleged predation by the Gunpowder Trust, and he reached a similar conclusion: Of the government's 14 allegations of predatory pricing, the charges could be supported in at most two instances.[18] Roland Koller examined 26 cases where firms were found guilty of predatory pricing, but he concluded that in only 7 of these was predatory pricing actually attempted and in only 4 was this strategy somehow successful.[19] Malcolm Burns, however, concluded that predatory pricing enabled the American Tobacco Company to acquire monopoly power by buying out its former rivals at distress prices over the period from 1891 to 1906.[20]

One interesting study of predation involved a controlled experiment in which human participants, acting as owner-managers of firms in a gamelike market simulation, were rewarded for making profit-maximizing decisions about entry, pricing, and output. Mark Isaac and Vernon Smith structured the experiment in a way calculated to lead some of the participants to choose a predatory pricing strategy. Only two firms were involved, and one (the larger) possessed a cost advantage over the other; this firm also possessed deep pockets (i.e., superior resources to sustain losses), and barriers to reentry were present. Despite repeating the experiment 11 times, Isaac and Smith were unable to produce predatory pricing in a structural environment that à priori they thought was favorable to its emergence. They noted that this does not prove that predatory pricing is nonexistent, but argued that those who would

---

[17]See John S. McGee, "Predatory Price Cutting: The Standard Oil (N.J.) Case," *Journal of Law and Economics*, 1 (October 1958), pp. 137–169.

[18]Kenneth G. Elzinga, "Predatory Pricing: The Case of the Gunpowder Trust," *Journal of Law and Economics*, 13 (April 1970), pp. 223–240.

[19]Roland H. Koller II, "The Myth of Predatory Pricing: An Empirical Study," *Antitrust Law and Economics Review*, 5 (Summer 1971), pp. 105–123.

[20]Malcolm R. Burns, "Predatory Pricing and the Acquisition Cost of Competitors," *Journal of Political Economy*, 94 (April 1986), pp. 266–296. Burns's findings are discussed and criticized in John S. McGee, *Industrial Organization*, Prentice-Hall, Englewood Cliffs, NJ, 1988, pp. 202–206.

design public policy as though predation were a common phenomenon should bear a greater burden of proof.[21]

But skepticism about the existence or efficacy of predatory pricing is not universal among antitrust scholars. It is clearly wrong to say the tactic will *never* be an effective strategy. For example, a firm that participates in several markets may cut its price in one in order to build a *reputation* as a predator. Such a reputation will be quite valuable; it might deter potential entry, discourage rivals from competing vigorously with respect to price or product quality, or convince them to sell out at a low price. Of course, such a reputation cannot be "hollow." If an entrant or rival believes it is not in the reputed predator's interest to cut price in a specific situation, the reputation will be irrelevant.

Entry Barriers and Entry Deterrence: Limit Pricing

Market power that is not protected from competitive entry is not really market power. You may "corner the market" for some good, but if others can easily and cheaply enter the market whenever prices are raised above costs, your ability to earn economic profits (and impose deadweight welfare losses on society) may be nil. That is why it is common to infer intent to monopolize from attempts to erect barriers to entry.

Over the years, economists have identified many barriers to market entry; predictably, there is disagreement about what truly constitutes a barrier. Most appear to favor a broad conception and would say that an entry barrier is any advantage that existing firms have over potential competitors or any factor that inhibits entry. In this view, the existence of substantial economies of scale in a market is an entry barrier.

Figure 6.3 illustrates such a situation. Suppose a firm's long-run average total cost curve LATC declines over the entire range of market demand D. If this firm sets a price P_m and output rate Q_m, it will earn economic profits equal to the shaded area in Figure 6.3, or $(P_m - \text{ATC}_m) Q_m$. Economic profits would normally attract competitive entry, but perhaps not in this case. Suppose a potential entrant assumes (optimistically) that immediately on entering it will share half the market with the existing firm. Thus, each firm will face half the market demand curve D, so that each firm's relevant demand curve becomes $D' = D/2$. But D' is everywhere below LATC, which means that there is no price at which either firm will be able to cover its costs, much less earn an economic profit. Unless the entrant believes it will have lower costs (or command a much larger share of the market) than the existing firm, it will recognize that to enter is folly.

The list of other potential entry barriers is long. It is commonly held that sizable capital costs constitute a barrier. If, e.g., entry at an efficient scale requires buildings, plant, and equipment costing billions of dollars, there may

---

[21]R. Mark Isaac and Vernon L. Smith, "In Search of Predatory Pricing," *Journal of Political Economy*, 93 (April 1985), pp. 320–345.

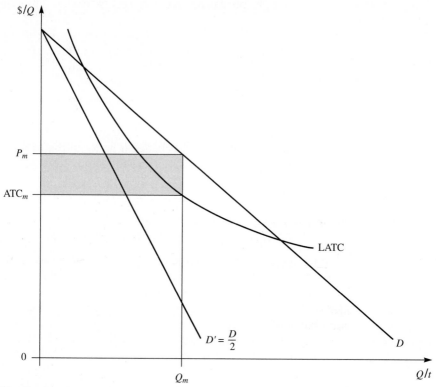

FIGURE 6.3
ECONOMIES OF SCALE AND ENTRY. Economic profits equal to the shaded area shown
would normally attract entry. In the presence of declining LATC, however, entry might not
occur. A potential entrant might judge the amount of residual demand left to it $(D' = D/2)$
inadequate to cover its costs.

be relatively few candidates for entry. Or production may require some scarce
resource (e.g., aluminum production requires bauxite). By controlling access to
this resource, a monopolist may bar entry to its market. Scholars such as
William Comanor, Thomas Wilson, and Richard Schmalensee argue also that
various marketing strategies are designed to limit entry.[22] Intensive advertising, establishment of brand names and brand proliferation, product differentiation, and frequent style changes have all been named as ways to discourage
entry of new rivals.

But it is possible to get carried away in listing things that inhibit entry.
Economists identified with the "Chicago school" of antitrust analysis take a
narrower view of what constitutes a true barrier. George Stigler, e.g., contends
that only those costs that entrants must pay but which existing firms *avoid*

[22]See, e.g., William S. Comanor and Thomas A. Wilson, *Advertising and Market Power*, Harvard
University Press, Cambridge, MA, 1974; Richard Schmalensee, "Entry Deterrence in the Ready-to-
Eat Breakfast Cereal Industry," *Bell Journal of Economics*, 9 (Autumn 1978), pp. 305–327.

should properly be considered entry barriers.[23] It may cost billions to build productive capacity and enter a particular market, but it cost the existing firms billions, too. Advertising is available to everyone, as is the right to establish trademarks or brand names, make style changes, etc. As to product differentiation, it is true that a firm which convinces consumers that its product is superior to alternatives has an advantage over entrants, but what does this imply for policy? Should we accuse firms seeking to provide high-quality products of intent to monopolize? Shall we do so only when there is reason to suppose that consumers' beliefs about superiority are false? How can we really be sure we know better than consumers? It seems strange to describe those things which consumers value (e.g., product diversity, quality, a reputation for reliability) or which exclude less efficient firms from the market as entry barriers.

One possible way for a monopolist to *deter* entry is via pricing strategy. Simply put, the monopoly firm may forgo some economic profits in the short run by setting price low enough to discourage entry, thus guaranteeing receipt of slightly lesser economic profits for a longer period. This strategy, called *limit pricing*, is illustrated in Figure 6.4.

Most limit-pricing models require the presence of some economies of scale, although these scale economies alone are not sufficient to retard entry.[24] Figure 6.4 shows a hypothetical monopolist's long-run average total cost curve LATC, which slopes sharply downward before leveling off beyond output rate Q^*. In effect, Q^* is the minimum efficient scale in this industry, i.e., the smallest scale of operation at which entry is feasible. The monopolist faces the market demand curve D and associated marginal revenue curve MR. A monopolist immune to entry would set price and output at P_m and Q_m; open competition would set price and output at P_c and Q_c.

If limit pricing occurs, however, price will be neither P_m nor P_c. Most limit-pricing models assume that potential rivals believe *the monopolist will not change its rate of output postentry.* Under these circumstances, potential entrants will gauge the desirability of entry by calculating whether there is enough market demand "left over" (after the existing firm sets its rate of output) to cover production costs at the minimum feasible entry scale Q^*. The goal of the limit-pricing monopolist, then, is to leave so little of the market to a potential entrant that the entrant stays on the sidelines.

The entry-limiting output (and associated price) is easy to calculate. The monopolist will subtract Q^* from Q_c, the rate of output at which industry profits are zero. The rate of output $Q_c - Q^*$, plus one additional unit, will be the entry-limiting output Q_l. If the monopolist produces this rate of output—and refuses to change it even in the event of entry—then a firm which enters and adds Q^* units to industry will drive the market price below P_c. All firms in the market would therefore lose money, and entry would not pay. By setting out-

[23]See George J. Stigler, *The Organization of Industry,* Irwin, Homewood, IL, 1968.
[24]See Franco Modigliani, "New Developments on the Oligopoly Front," *Journal of Political Economy,* 66 (June 1958), pp. 215–232.

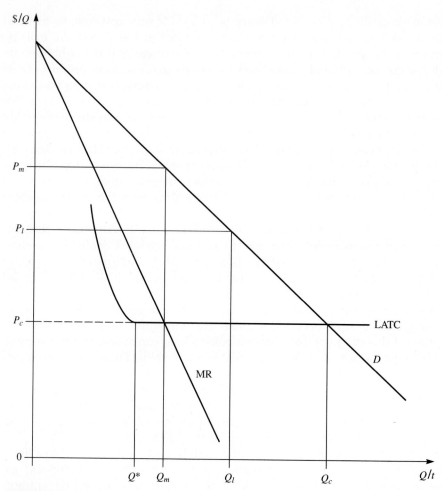

FIGURE 6.4
LIMIT PRICING. A monopoly seeking to inhibit entry might eschew P_m in favor of P_l. At P_l, the amount of residual demand left to an entrant $Q_c - Q_l$ is less than the minimum feasible entry scale Q^*.

put at Q_l and price at P_l (between the monopolistic and competitive rates of output and prices) the monopolist can earn economic profits that will persist.

Note, however, that the limit-pricing strategy rests on a threat that may not be credible. Will the monopolist *really* maintain its rate of output Q_l, come hell or high water? Suppose an entrant calls the monopolist's bluff, entering at scale Q^*. Both the entrant and the monopolist will then earn losses. Under the circumstances, it may pay the ex-monopolist to go back to the drawing board and reduce output somewhat. Reducing output below Q_l will eliminate losses altogether—and, depending on the reaction of the entrant, generate some economic profits for *both* firms. Once the monopolist's bluff is called, in other words, it will pay the firms to seek some accommodation (i.e., collude) rather than fight. Since it really does not pay the monopolist to carry out its threat, it is questionable whether any potential entrant will regard the threat as serious.

Remedying Monopoly: Should We Deconcentrate?

Suppose we catch a monopolist red-handed—and not the good kind either. Our target has acquired or maintains a monopoly through underhanded means, and we have undeniable proof of this fact. Should we now remedy the situation by dividing the large monopolistic firm into several smaller ones that (we assume) will vigorously compete with each other? The rather surprising answer is: not necessarily.[25]

To see why, consider Figure 6.5, which shows demand and cost conditions for our hypothetical monopolized market. Given demand curve D and marginal revenue curve MR, the monopolist firm with cost C_m will produce Q_m units and sell at price P_m, earning economic profits equal to the area bound by points BP_mFH and imposing a deadweight welfare loss on society equal to area FGH. If the monopolist could be broken up into several firms, all with the same unit cost C_m, we could eliminate this economic profit and recover this deadweight loss for consumers, clearly improving social welfare.

But what if the firms we created by dismembering the monopolist had *higher* costs? Suppose, e.g., that the costs in a more competitively structured industry would rise to C_c. (Query: Why *might* costs be higher after reorganizing of the single large firm?) After thus "deconcentrating" the market, the best result we could hope for is price P_c and associated rate of output Q_c.

Some might say this is fine. After all, the deconcentration has reduced price ($P_c < P_m$) and raised output ($Q_c > Q_m$), yielding substantial benefits to consumers. Unless deconcentration raises production costs considerably (i.e., above P_m), it will always improve social welfare—right? Wrong. The observed reduction in price and increase in output are just part of the story. To properly evaluate whether social welfare has improved *on net*, we must also consider the increased costs of production in the newly deconcentrated market.

To calculate the net change in social welfare that results from deconcentration, let us refer again to Figure 6.5 and calculate the total social surplus, first under monopoly and then under competition. With the monopoly producing Q_m units at a cost C_m per unit, social surplus equals the area bound by points $BEFH$ (composed of consumers' surplus P_mEF and producers' surplus BP_mFH). With several competitors producing a total of Q_c units at a cost of C_c per unit, social surplus equals area P_cEJ (which is entirely consumers' surplus).

Comparing area $BEFH$ with area P_cEJ, we see that area P_cEFI is common to both. Deconcentration, then, gets us triangle FIJ *at the expense of* rectangle BP_cIH. True, deconcentration adds the trapezoidal area P_cP_mFJ to consumers' surplus, but part of this—area P_cP_mFI—would have been producers' surplus in the monopoly situation; thus, area P_cP_mFI is not an addition to welfare, but a

---

[25]See Oliver E. Williamson, "Economies as an Antitrust Defense: The Welfare Trade-offs," *American Economic Review*, 58 (March 1968), pp. 18–36.

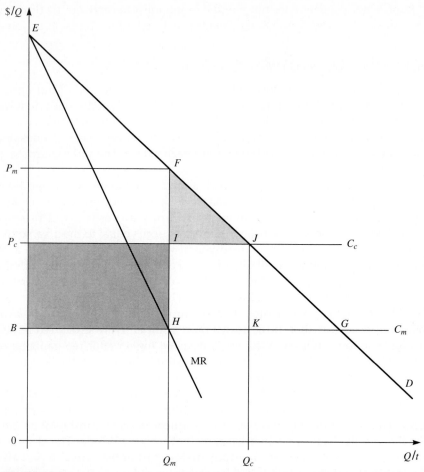

FIGURE 6.5
WELFARE IMPLICATIONS OF DECONCENTRATION WHICH RAISE PRODUCTION COSTS. If deconcentrating an industry raises costs from C_m to C_c, the price may fall from P_m to P_c but social surplus in this market may rise or fall, depending on whether area *FIJ* (the surplus gain from lower price) is greater or less than area BP_cIH (the surplus loss from higher costs).

transfer from producers to consumers. On net, society receives added surplus *FIJ minus* increased production costs BP_cIH. There is a gain in allocative efficiency but a reduction in productive efficiency. We are not indifferent to these increased production costs. Resources have alternative uses, and devoting excessive amounts of resources to this market means production in other markets must suffer. *We conclude that only if FIJ minus BP_cIH is positive will deconcentration enhance welfare; if FIJ minus BP_cIH is negative, welfare is reduced.*

Where deconcentration results in no higher production costs, of course, we need not worry about this sort of subtle "welfare trade-off." But if there is reason to suspect *any* loss of efficiency from reorganization of the industry, we

TABLE 6.3
PERCENTAGE COST INCREASES WHICH WILL OFFSET VARIOUS PERCENTAGE
PRICE DECLINES. Small cost increases can offset welfare gains from sizable price
declines; e.g., if demand is unit-elastic, a 0.123 percent cost increase will offset a 5 percent
price decline resulting from deconcentration.

	Offsetting percentage increase in costs		
Percentage decline in price	$E_{xx}=2$	$E_{xx}=1$	$E_{xx}=0.5$
1.0	0.01	0.005	0.002
2.0	0.04	0.020	0.010
3.0	0.09	0.045	0.022
4.0	0.16	0.079	0.039
5.0	0.25	0.123	0.061

Source: Originally published in 25 UCLA L. Rev. 1231. Copyright 1978, The Regents of the University of California. All rights reserved.

must tread very carefully, for small cost increases have the power to wipe out the favorable welfare effects of fairly large price declines. Consider Table 6.3. It shows, for three possible elasticities of demand, the percentage increase in cost that will offset percentage decreases in price presumed to result from the policy of deconcentration.[26] If, e.g., the price elasticity of demand in this market is 1.0 and if deconcentration will raise production costs by as little as 0.123 percent, then prices must fall by 5.0 percent to generate a net increase in social surplus. Where demand is less elastic, equal, say, to 0.5, prices must fall by 5.0 percent to offset a cost increase as tiny as 0.061 percent!

In sum, the appropriate remedy in a monopolization case must be chosen with great care. It is quite possible that some remedies (e.g., deconcentration) will produce more competitive pricing, but price reductions need not always result in improvements in welfare. Policymakers who seek to maximize social surplus must assess the likelihood and magnitude of any price reductions and weigh these against any prospective efficiency losses.

THE EVOLUTION OF THE LAW

By now it should be obvious that the theory of monopolization has undergone considerable flux over the years and that antitrust scholars are far from a united lot. Indeed, conflicting and often changing views about market definition, structure and conduct, predation, and other important issues are amply reflected in the case law on monopolization. In this section, we discuss several landmarks in the development of this body of law.

[26]The source for Table 6.3 is Wesley J. Liebeler, "Market Power and Competitive Superiority in Concentrated Industries," *UCLA Law Review*, 25 (August 1978), pp. 1231–1300.

E. C. Knight (1895)

In 1892, there were a half-dozen sugar refining companies competing vigorously in the United States. In that year, however, the American Sugar Refining Company acquired E. C. Knight and three other companies. Immediately after the consolidation, American Sugar produced 98 percent of all the sugar sold in the United States.

The Supreme Court admitted that the acquisition tended to create a monopoly in the manufacture of sugar—but then ruled that this "sugar trust" did not violate the Sherman Act. Chief Justice Fuller wrote that the act applied to interstate *commerce* and that the trust's manufacturing monopoly was outside the act's jurisdiction because "[c]ommerce succeeds to manufacture and is not a part of it."[27] This somewhat artificial distinction between manufacturing and commerce has been roundly criticized by scholars, who credit this decision with accelerating the merger wave of 1895 to 1904.

It is interesting to note, however, that the U.S. market share had fallen to 85 percent by the time the decision was rendered, and it fell to 25 percent by 1927. Entry into the sugar market was easy. Domestic raw materials were abundant, the manufacturing process was simple, and no patents protected existing producers. Thus, the sugar trust's grip on the market was weak, and there is little evidence that it was long able to wield its power to raise sugar prices: Refined sugar sold for 9 cents per pound in 1880, and its price tracked between 5.3 and 6.9 cents per pound over the entire period from 1890 to 1910.[28]

Northern Securities (1904)

In 1901 the Northern Securities Company was incorporated in New Jersey. A holding company, Northern Securities acquired a controlling interest in two railroads, the Northern Pacific (owned by J. P. Morgan) and the Great Northern (owned by James J. Hill), that linked St. Paul and Seattle.

The Supreme Court ruled that this combination of two formerly "independent and competitive" interstate railroads was a clear violation of the Sherman Act. Justice Harlan wrote that "[n]o scheme or device could more certainly come within the words of the Act . . . or could more effectively and certainly suppress free competition between the constituent companies. This combination is, within the meaning of the Act, a 'trust.'"[29]

The *Northern Securities* decision marked a turning point in antimonopoly law. By appearing to condemn all "combinations in restraint of interstate commerce," it emboldened the Justice Department to initiate several actions against large corporate holding companies, including John D. Rockefeller's Standard Oil Company.

---

[27]*United States v. E. C. Knight Co.,* 156 U.S. 1 (1895), p. 12.

[28]See Dominick T. Armentano, *Antitrust and Monopoly,* Wiley, New York, 1982, pp. 50–51; Richard Zerbe, "The American Sugar Refining Company, 1887–1914: The Story of a Monopoly," *Journal of Law and Economics,* 12 (October 1969), pp. 339–375.

[29]*Northern Securities Co. et al. v. United States,* 193 U.S. 197 (1904), p. 327.

Standard Oil (1911)

In the mid-1860s, oil refining was a small-scale and easily entered endeavor. Rockefeller bought into one of Cleveland's 50-odd refineries for a mere $4,000; nationwide, there were perhaps 200 other independent refineries in places such as Pittsburgh, Baltimore, Philadelphia, and New York, all refining crude brought from the northwest Pennsylvania oil fields. The turbulent, deflationary 1870s, however, bankrupted many of these, as kerosene prices fell from over 30 cents per gallon in 1869 to 10 cents per gallon by 1874. Rockefeller not only survived, he thrived. In 1870, his Standard Oil Company refined no more than about 4 percent of national output, but by 1874 Standard's share had grown to 25 percent, and by 1880 its market share exceeded 85 percent. Rockefeller was by then the undisputed king of the oil business.

How had this colossal empire been built? A large part of the answer is that major economies of scale were present in the industry, and Rockefeller exploited them first and best. He cut costs relentlessly, integrated into virtually every aspect of the refining business, and bought up numerous failing rivals to expand capacity. In the view of the antitrust authorities, however, the key to Standard's growth was illegal and predatory business practices. The Justice Department alleged violations of both sections 1 and 2 of the Sherman Act, accusing Standard of (1) predatory price-cutting against local competitors, (2) industrial espionage and bribery, (3) using its market position to obtain advantageous rates from railroads, (4) controlling oil pipelines and using unfair practices against competing pipelines, (5) using sham companies to fight off and kill competitors, and (6) using novel and dangerous business forms.

The Supreme Court agreed that Standard had monopolized the oil market and had done so illegally. In its decision, the Court first enunciated its two-part "intent test" for section 2 cases. By this standard, only unreasonable restraints of trade or conspiracies would be illegal. A dominant market position alone, e.g., would not be sufficient evidence of guilt. The reasonableness of a firm's actions would also be considered—especially whether these actions were "of such a character as to give rise to the inference or presumption that they had been entered into or done with the *intent to do wrong to the general public* and to limit the rights of individuals."[30] In the Court's view, Standard's bad intent could be amply inferred from "acts and dealings wholly inconsistent with . . . the development of business power by usual methods, but which necessarily involved the intent to drive others from the field and exclude them from their right to trade."[31] Standard was therefore dissolved into 34 smaller firms.

Some scholars doubt whether the dissolution accomplished much, for Standard's existing stockholders were given ownership of each of the new companies, and most of these companies had large shares of their regional markets. Others doubt whether the dissolution was even necessary. They

---

[30] *Standard Oil Co. of New Jersey v. United States*, 221 U.S. 1 (1911), p. 58 (emphasis added).
[31] Ibid., p. 76.

argue that Standard's predatory behavior was mythical[32] and that its success resulted from technical and managerial superiority that gave it great cost advantages over its rivals.[33] But all agree that by focusing judicial attention on the *intent* of accused firms, the decision had great impact on subsequent cases involving large corporations and their conduct. In the same term, in fact, American Tobacco Company was found guilty of illegal monopolization because (1) it sold upward of 85 percent of the cigarettes and small cigars in the U.S. market and (2) its bad intent could be inferred from various exclusionary or predatory tactics. It was also ordered dissolved.[34]

U.S. Steel (1920)

A year after the *Standard Oil* and *American Tobacco* decisions, the Justice Department charged the United States Steel Corporation (USS) with monopolizing the iron and steel markets. At the time, USS was the largest industrial corporation in the world. It had been formed in 1901 by combining 11 previously independent firms with a total of 60 to 70 percent of the nation's steel production capacity.

The Supreme Court ruled, however, that USS was a "good trust" and had not violated the Sherman Act. The Court lauded USS for never having been accused of abusive or predatory practices. Managed by the urbane and cultured Judge Elbert Gary (a distinct contrast to the ruthless John D. Rockefeller), USS had no corporate enemies; indeed, its competitors seemed to admire it. By the time of the decision, USS's market share had fallen to 50 percent, and the intent test enunciated in *Standard Oil* was applied in USS's favor. The Court concluded that "the law does not make mere size an offense or the existence of unexerted power an offense. It . . . requires overt acts."[35]

Donald Parsons and Edward Ray have criticized the decision. They note that there was ample evidence that USS conspired with its rivals (coordinating price and output decisions at a series of dinner meetings that became famous as the "Gary dinners"), and argue that the case should have been a section 1 collusion suit. In addition, they argue that the Court overlooked USS's control of iron ore resources, a possible source of monopoly power.[36]

Alcoa (1945)

Until 1909, the Aluminum Company of America (Alcoa) held patents that legally eliminated all competition in the emerging aluminum industry. After

---

[32]See again McGee, "Predatory Price Cutting."

[33]Armentano, e.g., argues that "Standard's position in oil refining grew rapidly because of the natural decline of small competitors; the increasing capital and innovation requirements of large-scale oil technology; [and] the economic advantages achieved through intelligent entrepreneurship. . . . It did not grow from any general reliance on alleged predatory practices" (Armentano, *Antitrust and Monopoly*, p. 64.

[34]*United States v. American Tobacco Co.*, 221 U.S. 106 (1911).

[35]*United States v. U.S. Steel Corp.*, 251 U.S. 417 (1920), p. 451.

[36]Donald O. Parsons and Edward John Ray, "The United States Steel Consolidation: The Creation of Market Control," *Journal of Law and Economics*, 18 (April 1975), pp. 181–219.

the patents expired, it excluded competitors with tactics that were viewed as underhanded. Alcoa agreed not to enter foreign markets if foreign aluminum producers conceded to it the U.S. market; Alcoa contracted with several electric companies to prevent sales of power to any other aluminum producer; it allegedly "squeezed" the profit margins of firms which purchased its aluminum ingots for fabrication into finished products.

The case also raised important market definition issues. Alcoa produced about 90 percent of the virgin aluminum ingots sold in the United States. If scrap or secondary aluminum were recognized as a ready substitute for ingots, Alcoa's market share would fall to 64 percent. And if a still broader market definition were used, Alcoa's share would fall to 33 percent—certainly not high enough to constitute a monopoly. Reasoning that Alcoa's control of ingot production gave it implicit control of the scrap aluminum market, Judge Learned Hand opted for the narrowest possible market definition. On that basis, Alcoa was a monopoly.

Hand very nearly broke new legal ground by ruling that Alcoa's monopoly was illegal on structural grounds, whatever the firm's intent. The Sherman Act, he wrote, "Did not condone 'good trusts' and condemn 'bad' ones; it forbade all."[37] But Hand hedged a bit, stating also that "[t]he successful competitor, having been urged to compete, must not be turned upon when he wins."[38] So Hand did not abandon the intent test; he modified it. He sought evidence that Alcoa intended to preserve its market position by excluding rivals, and he found it in Alcoa's aggressive expansion of capacity:

> There were at least one or two abortive attempts to enter the industry, but Alcoa effectively anticipated and forestalled all competition. . . . Nothing compelled it to keep doubling and redoubling its capacity before others entered the field. It insists that it never excluded competitors; but we can think of no more effective exclusion than to embrace each new opportunity as it opened. . . .[39]

Alcoa was not dissolved, however. Instead, the federal government subsidized entry by Reynolds and Kaiser Aluminum, selling them war plants at cut-rate prices; later still, other subsidies facilitated entry by three more firms.

IBM (1982)

IBM had been a successful producer of mechanical and electric tabulating machines since 1911. In the 1950s, IBM introduced its first computers. Technology evolved rapidly, and IBM seemed constantly to be replacing its own (and competitors') machines with faster, more powerful, more reliable, and cheaper models. Its 360 series, introduced in 1964, quickly became an industry leader.

---

[37]*United States v. Aluminum Co. of America*, 148 F.2d 416 (2d Cir. 1945), p. 427.
[38]Ibid., p. 430.
[39]Ibid., p. 431.

Viewed through the lens of the *Alcoa* decision, such aggressive "embrace of new opportunities" appeared anticompetitive to the antitrust authorities. In January 1969, the Justice Department charged that IBM had illegally monopolized the general-purpose computer market.[40] The government alleged that IBM's market share exceeded 70 percent and that its market dominance was achieved via marketing and pricing strategies designed to exclude rivals. For example, IBM quoted prices for an entire system or "bundle" of components, encouraging customers to buy the whole system from IBM and (in theory) excluding rivals who produced only a few of the components. IBM was also accused of lowering prices—perhaps to predatory levels—in markets where it faced competition and of raising them where it faced none.

In a trial that began in 1975 and lasted six years (!), IBM argued that the government's market definition was too narrow and that, in any event, its market position had been achieved via superior skill and foresight and was thus perfectly legal. Under IBM's proposed market definition, its 1972 share was 33 percent. It noted that the government's allegation that IBM's market position was protected by barriers to entry was contradicted by the facts: Many firms entered the market in the 1960s and 1970s, and not a few—discouraged perhaps by the vigorous competition—exited as well.

Observers noted that declining prices and expanding output rates in the computer market were hardly consistent with the government's claims of monopolization. When Ronald Reagan became President in 1981, his newly appointed Antitrust Division head, William Baxter (a former law professor at Stanford University), undertook a review of the case. He concluded that the government was unlikely to prevail in the suit and that even if the court decided IBM had held a monopoly in the 1960s, no structural remedy was feasible, given the emergence of new competition in the 1970s. Describing the suit as "without merit," he ordered it dismissed.

AT&T (1982)

In 1974, the Justice Department filed a monopolization suit against American Telephone and Telegraph Co. (AT&T), the largest privately owned enterprise in the world. The government sought divestiture of AT&T's manufacturing division (Western Electric) and its many local operating companies. It alleged that these phone companies were required to buy most of their equipment from Western Electric, excluding competing suppliers from this market, and that AT&T had sought to foreclose competition in the long-distance service market.

Complicating the case was the fact that AT&T's operations were heavily regulated by various state and federal commissions, since telephone service had long been regarded as a natural monopoly. AT&T argued that its submis-

---

[40]*IBM v. United States*, Civil Action No. 69 Civ. 200, U.S. District Court for the Southern District of New York.

sion to rate regulation exempted it from antitrust scrutiny and that the practices to which the government objected were necessary to maintain quality and reliability in telecommunications. But technology had changed in the decades since the creation of this regulatory structure, especially in the long-distance market that firms were clamoring to enter. Regulators were now unsure about some of the basic assumptions that had given rise to regulation and were in uncharted waters with regard to the pricing of those portions of AT&T's services and equipment that the new firms needed to compete effectively.

The case dragged on for seven years before a settlement was reached. AT&T signed a consent decree that required it to divest the local operating companies. In exchange, it got to keep Western Electric and enter some markets (e.g., for computer equipment) that a previous decree had foreclosed to it.[41]

Where We Stand Today

Recent cases like *IBM* and *AT&T* cause many to wonder whether monopolization cases have a future. The Antitrust Division spent a combined 20 years on these suits, with but a partial victory (the divestiture of AT&T's local operating companies) to show for its efforts. The cost of fishing in these waters is clearly very high; unless a large catch is ensured, we should expect rational antitrust enforcement officials to cast their lines elsewhere. In the 1980s, this forecast was dead on: From 1981 to 1988, the government pressed only three monopolization cases, the lowest number in any eight-year period in this century.

The costs of monopolization suits and uncertainty about their outcome are apt to remain great unless the intent test is abandoned in favor of a strict structural approach. At present, this is an unlikely—and probably undesirable—development. We may conclude, therefore, that most of the action in the antitrust war is likely to be on other fronts.

This may not be an altogether bad thing. Richard Posner has noted that high levels of concentration in an industry tend to dissipate by natural forces within 10 years, on average, while the typical length of a divestiture proceeding in a monopolization case is 8 years. So, "assuming that a proceeding will not normally be brought immediately upon the attainment of a monopoly," Posner argues, "it seems unlikely that administrative methods of deconcentration will work significantly more rapidly than the market."[42]

SUMMARY AND CONCLUDING REMARKS

Federal antimonopoly policy has been greatly influenced by the structure-conduct-performance paradigm, which asserts that the market structure (i.e., the

---

[41]See *United States v. AT&T*, 552 F. Supp. 131 (1982). The restructured telecommunications industry that resulted has been very controversial. The issues arising from the restructuring are discussed in detail in Chapter 14.

[42]Richard A. Posner, "A Statistical Study of Antitrust Enforcement," *Journal of Law and Economics*, 13 (October 1970), p. 417 (note).

number and size distribution of firms, cost and demand conditions, and ease of entry) determines firm conduct (pricing and output decisions), which in turn determines market performance (efficiency, equity, etc.). Two of the most commonly used indicators of market structure are the concentration ratio (the sum of the market shares of the industry's leading firms) and the Herfindahl index (the sum of the squared market shares of all firms in the industry). To have value, however, both indicators must be based on appropriately defined product markets and geographic markets.

Performance-based indicators of market power include the Lerner and Bain indices. Application of either involves practical or conceptual difficulties, so most studies of market performance (and most antitrust cases) utilize structural indicators. These studies have generally shown a positive correlation between market concentration and profitability. It has been shown, however, that this correlation can result from the competitive superiority of some firms. Superior firms will often grow large relative to their rivals, and their industries may show relatively greater degrees of concentration. Where concentration is the result of superior efficiency of large firms, a policy of deconcentration is problematic: If fragmentation of large firms raises their costs of production, any allocative efficiency gains may be offset by productive efficiency losses.

To obtain a guilty verdict in monopolization cases, evidence of structural monopoly must be combined with evidence of intent to acquire or preserve monopoly status. Such intent is often inferred from evidence that the dominant firm engaged in predatory or entry-deterring actions. For a firm to be judged guilty of predatory pricing (under the Areeda-Turner rule), its prices must be shown to be below average variable costs. Intent to monopolize may also be associated with attempts to erect various artificial barriers to entry, by entry-limiting pricing, restrictive marketing practices, acquisition of key inputs, or aggressive expansion of capacity.

QUESTIONS FOR REVIEW AND DISCUSSION

6.1 While chairman of the Federal Trade Commission in the 1970s, Michael Pertschuk was asked if he thought "bigness is necessarily bad." He responded, "Actually, I do." In what respects do *you* think big firms are bad? In what respects might they be good? What elements of the structure-conduct-performance paradigm are useful for judging whether a firm is big enough or bad enough to merit scrutiny under the antitrust laws?

6.2 Perform a structural analysis of the textbook market at your college or university. What are the relevant product market and geographic market? What substitutes exist for the textbooks sold in your campus bookstore? Is the campus store a monopoly?

6.3 Suppose you gather reliable data on firms' prices and marginal costs of production, enabling you to calculate Lerner indices for them. If the Lerner indices for two firms are equal (say, 0.50), does this mean that both are imposing equal welfare losses on society? Explain. (Hint: use graphs.)

6.4 Suppose you are an antitrust attorney and you have as a client a bankrupt businesswoman who claims that the demise of her firm was the direct result of predatory pricing by the larger companies that remain in her market. She claims she has proof of her claims: For several years, her rivals' prices were deliberately and willfully set below her costs of production. Is this proof of predatory pricing, or do you need more evidence? If so, what?

6.5 As shown in Figure 6.3, substantial economies of scale can impede entry into markets. If the conditions described in Figure 6.3 actually applied to a particular market, what policy remedy would you prescribe, e.g., a monopolization suit and deconcentration? Explain.

6.6 John D. Rockefeller was much despised by many of his competitors while Judge Elbert Gary was much admired by his. Does this suggest that Rockefeller used predation to acquire a monopoly while Gary did not, or is there another possible interpretation of these facts? Explain.

6.7 How does the *Alcoa* case differ from the *IBM* case? If you had been the head of the Antitrust Division in the early 1980s, would you have dismissed the suit against IBM? Would you have found Alcoa guilty of monopolization? Explain your answers.

6.8 In *Standard Oil* and *American Tobacco*, it was relatively easy to identify various "dastardly deeds" from which intent to monopolize could be inferred. In later cases, it has appeared more and more difficult to identify such deeds or to prove that various suspect business practices signaled bad intent. Why do you think this is so? Is this a weakness of the intent test in monopolization cases? What modifications in this test do you propose that could make monopolization cases more manageable?

CHAPTER 7

OLIGOPOLY AND COLLUSION

People of the same trade seldom meet together even for merriment or diversion, but the conversation ends in a conspiracy against the public, or in some contrivance to raise prices.

Adam Smith

Fortunately, pure monopoly is rare. There are few markets where one firm makes all or most sales; a good many of these are natural monopolies where government has licensed a single firm and regulates its prices. In many markets, however, the bulk of industry sales are made by a handful of firms.

Economists refer to markets with but a few sellers (although many buyers) as *oligopolies.* A key feature of such markets is the *interdependence* of sellers. In perfectly competitive markets, sellers are assumed to act independently because each makes such a trivial contribution to market output that rival sellers' plans may be safely ignored. In pure monopoly there are (by definition) no rivals to consider. In oligopolistic markets, however, it seems inevitable that sellers will consider the plans or responses of their rivals in setting their prices and output rates or even in designing their products and fixing advertising budgets. Such consideration might be beneficial if, e.g., it led to vows to "beat the competition." But the fear is strong that once sellers recognize their interdependence, they will undertake strategies to *limit* competition among themselves.

This fear appears to arise from two factors. First, there has long been an intuitive feeling that explicit agreements not to compete, i.e., overt collusive agreements, are possible, and likely to succeed, only when the number of conspirators is manageably small. Second, economists have produced models that suggest that even *without* the kinds of formal collusive agreements which are now illegal, prices above (and output rates below) the competitive level can evolve in oligopolies. In other words, some models predict the same kinds of deadweight losses in oligopoly that we see in monopoly even absent the kinds of "contracts, combinations, or conspiracies" mentioned in section 1 of the Sherman Act.

VIGNETTE 7.1   The Logic of Collusion: The Case of College Football

In 1938, the new entertainment medium called television broadcast a college foot-ball game for the first time. For some time afterward, schools were free to arrange broadcasting deals with any stations or networks they chose. Since the college game was quite popular—more popular, in fact, than the professional version—there was brisk demand for telecast rights. Competition among sellers, however, meant that fees for these rights tended to be quite low, and the proliferation of broadcasts damaged revenues from ticket sales. One survey showed that where televised games competed head-on with live events, attendance at the latter fell by more than 16 percent.[1]

The National Collegiate Athletic Association (NCAA) had a solution. Starting with the 1952 season, the NCAA was vested with exclusive control of all college football telecasts. It auctioned TV rights to a single network, greatly restricted the number of games telecast, limited each school to two TV appearances per year, and devised a formula for splitting the revenues from games. With minor changes, this system was in force into the late 1970s. Then a group of major football-playing schools, dissatis-fied with the limitations on network appearances and with the NCAA's fee-splitting formula, formed the College Football Association (CFA) to negotiate a separate TV contract that would be more favorable to themselves. The NCAA responded with a threat to expel the renegade schools from *all* NCAA competition. Most schools then fell in line, but two CFA members, the University of Oklahoma and the University of Georgia, sued the NCAA, alleging its TV plan constituted price-fixing, a violation of section 1 of the Sherman Act.

In 1984, the Supreme Court (affirming lower-court decisions) ruled that by limiting the number of telecasts of college games and preventing members from negotiating their own TV contracts, the NCAA had indeed violated section 1. The decision reopened the market for college football telecasts.[2] Schools and conferences scrambled to sell TV rights to their games, and the number of televised games multi-plied quickly.

Predictably, however, greater output begot lower prices. In fact, prices fell so much that collective broadcast revenues dipped as well. The NCAA's exclusive net-work contract (voided by the decision) would have brought in about $145 million in 1984–1985, but the various network and cable contracts signed instead were worth a mere $94 million. Some schools recorded spectacular declines. The University of Miami, e.g., saw TV revenue fall from an anticipated $2 million to $970,000 in 1984; the University of Pittsburgh anticipated $2.1 million in 1984 but instead earned

---

[1] The source for this datum and much of what follows is David Greenspan, "College Football's Biggest Fumble: The Economic Impact of the Supreme Court's Decision in *National Collegiate Athletic Association v. Board of Regents of the University of Oklahoma*," *The Antitrust Bulletin*, 33 (Spring 1988), pp. 1–65.

[2] *NCAA v. Board of Regents of the University of Oklahoma*, 468 U.S. 85 (1984).

$1 million. Others, however, were able to cut themselves a larger slice of the smaller revenue pie. The Big 8 Conference, e.g., received $18 million for TV rights in 1985–1986, far more than its annual allocation under the NCAA's old formula.

The affair demonstrates several key points. There are ample gains to sellers who agree to limit their output and to fix prices. But there are also some difficulties in maintaining such agreements, for not all parties will remain content with their share of the spoils from collusion. Finally, there are tangible benefits to consumers from upsetting such arrangements. For sponsors and viewers of college football games, the 1984 *NCAA* decision brought lower prices, enhanced output, and a broader selection of games. In other words, it enhanced economic welfare.

In the next section, we survey the major oligopoly theories so that readers may appreciate how oligopolistic interdependence can affect both firm decision making and market performance. We then briefly review an important empirical and policy debate in antitrust economics: the relationship of industry profits to industry concentration. Finally, we trace the development of antitrust policy toward oligopoly and various "collusive practices," from price-fixing to information sharing by trade associations to "consciously parallel behavior" by rivals.

OLIGOPOLY THEORIES

The Cournot Model

A French mathematician named Augustin Cournot devised the first systematic model of oligopoly over a century and a half ago.[3] Cournot proposed that each firm in an oligopoly would choose a rate of output that maximized its own profits and would take the output of all other firms as *fixed and given*. He showed that, where these assumptions hold, (1) there will exist stable equilibrium values for market price and output and (2) the number of sellers will affect the market price.

To illustrate the Cournot model as simply as possible, we start the analysis with two firms (*A* and *B*) facing a linear market demand curve *D*, as in Figure 7.1a.[4] Each firm has identical marginal costs of production, assumed to be zero.[5] If perfect competition were to rule, price P_c would be 0 and output Q_c would be 180 units per period. If, on the other hand, a pure monopolist inhabited this market, price P_m would be $18 and output Q_m would be 90, which is half of Q_c. (This is so because, for straight-line demand curves, the marginal revenue curve cuts the horizontal axis exactly halfway between the origin and the demand curve's horizontal intercept; here MR = MC = 0 at $Q_c/2$).

[3]Augustin Cournot, *Researches into the Mathematical Principles of the Theory of Wealth* (1838), trans. Nathaniel T. Bacon, Augustus M. Kelley, New York, 1971.
[4]For simplicity, numerical values are used below. The demand curve is described by the equation $Q_d = 180 - 5P$.
[5]While this assumption may seem wildly unrealistic, it does not affect the analysis in any substantive way. In his original formulation, Cournot used artesian wells to illustrate the model. Once such wells are drilled, the marginal costs of each unit of output are, in fact, very close to zero.

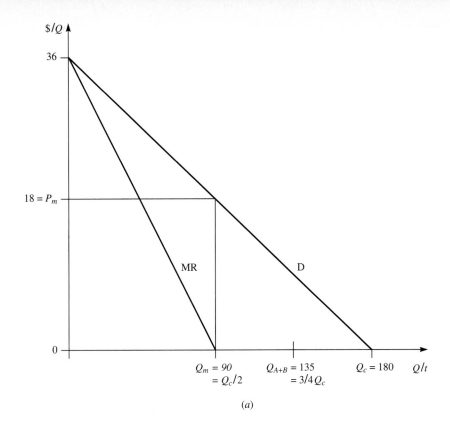

(a)

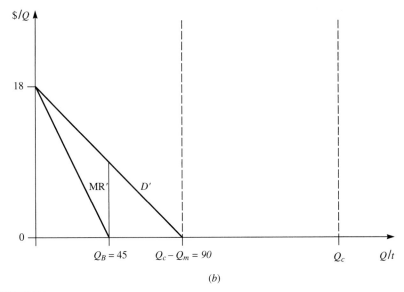

(b)

FIGURE 7.1
COURNOT DUOPOLY, ROUND ONE. Firm *A* will produce 90 units and set a monopoly price of $18 in panel *a*. Firm *B* will take *A*'s output as fixed and, based on the residual demand curve *D'* in panel *b*, will choose a rate of output of 45 units. Thus, after one round of calculations, $Q_{A+B} = 135$. But this is not yet a stable equilibrium.

In our two-firm ("Cournot duopoly") market, however, the equilibrium price and output will be at neither monopolistic nor competitive levels, but somewhere in between. To see why, suppose firm A enters the market first and decides to maximize its profits by producing $Q_A = Q_m = 90$ units. Firm B, per Cournot's assumption, takes A's output as fixed and given and views its own demand curve as that portion of the market demand curve D lying beyond (i.e., to the right of) this rate of output. This "residual" demand curve, labeled D', is shown in Figure 7.1b with its associated marginal revenue curve MR'. Firm B finds the intersection of MR' and MC (the horizontal axis, in this example) and decides to produce $Q_B = 45$ units. Industry output Q_{A+B} after this "first round" of decisions by firms A and B equals 135 units, which is three-quarters of the competitive rate of output Q_c and 1.5 times the monopoly rate of output Q_m.

But this is not yet a stable equilibrium. Note that B's decision has upset the calculations of A. If B's plans to enter and produce 45 units of output had been known to A, its profit-maximizing rate of output would have been less than 90 units (Why? By how much?). By the same token, if A's output differs from 90, B will have to go back to the drawing board and adjust its own output. Where is the stable equilibrium of which Cournot spoke? It can be shown that if each firm settles on a rate of output equal to 60 units (one-third the competitive rate of output Q_c), so that total industry output Q_e is 120 units, which is $\frac{2}{3} Q_c$, market price and output will reach stable equilibrium values. Observe that if firm A chooses to produce 60 units, the residual demand and marginal revenue curves that face firm B will dictate that it should also choose to produce 60 units per period, and there will be no pressure for either firm to change its behavior. The equilibrium price P_e will be $12 per unit, and each duopolist will earn profits equal to $720 per period.

Figure 7.2 shows this equilibrium situation.[6] In Cournot's duopoly, equilibrium industry output and price lie between the monopoly and competitive levels. That is, $Q_m < Q_e < Q_c$ (for example, $90 < 120 < 180$), and $P_c < P_e < P_m$ (for example, $0 < \$12 < \$18$). This result holds for more complicated cost functions. What is more, Cournot showed that as the number of firms in the oligopoly grows, industry output and price get closer to the competitive levels. As the example above illustrated, going from a pure monopoly to duopoly increased industry output from half the competitive level Q_c to $\frac{2}{3}Q_c$. Adding a third firm would increase industry output to $\frac{3}{4}Q_c$, a fourth firm would increase output to $\frac{4}{5}Q_c$, and so on.[7]

It is important to note that in Cournot's oligopoly model above-competitive prices (or below-competitive outputs) result even though there is no explicit collusion between firms. Rather, firms mechanically adjust their behavior until

---

[6]This equilibrium should probably be viewed as the result of simultaneous solution of a system of equations, rather than the outcome of a sequence of trials, as presented here. For a most accessible discussion, see John S. McGee, *Industrial Organization*, Prentice-Hall, Englewood Cliffs, NJ, 1988, pp. 59–67.

[7]That is, when marginal cost is constant, equilibrium output in the Cournot model will be $[n/(n+1)]Q_c$, where n is the number of firms.

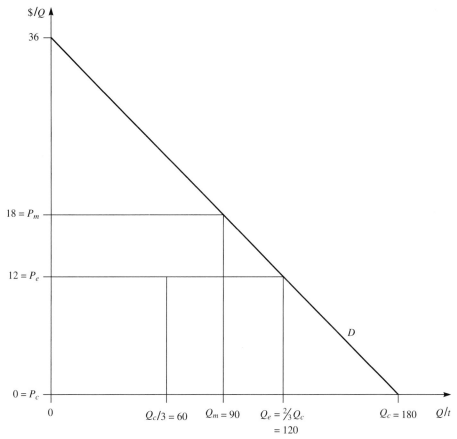

FIGURE 7.2
DUOPOLY EQUILIBRIA. In this example, Cournot duopolists find a stable equilibrium at $P_e = \$12$ and $Q_e = 120$, which is two-thirds the competitive rate of output. Bertrand duopolists wind up at the competitive rate of output ($Q_c = 180$) and price ($P_c = 0$).

an equilibrium is reached. In our two-firm example, A concedes market share to B until each makes half of all sales, but at prices that allow both firms to earn economic profits.

In a world where the assumptions firms make about their rivals' responses to their decisions (what economists call *reaction functions*) correspond to those proposed by Cournot, the linkage between market structure and performance would be especially strong. As we shall see, however, there is no shortage of alternative reaction functions for oligopolists, and even slightly different behavioral assumptions can produce enormously different implications.

Cournot's Successors

Bertrand   In 1883, Joseph Bertrand modified Cournot's model in one crucial respect: He postulated that firms would take their rivals' *prices* (rather than outputs) as fixed and given. He also assumed that products were homogeneous and consumers well informed about their alternatives, so that the lower-priced seller would capture the entire market. He showed that, on this basis, price would quickly fall to competitive levels, even with only two firms in the market.[8] Returning to Figure 7.2, suppose the first firm to enter the market sets price P_m = \$18 and sells Q_m = 90 units per period. A second firm would need only to shave P_m by a tiny amount (to, say, \$17.95) to steal all sales from the first. But the first could reply with a slightly larger price cut, and so on. The Bertrand oligopoly equilibrium results in a price equal to marginal cost (zero in Figure 7.2), i.e., the competitive result. And this result is not affected by the number of firms: P = MC whether there are 2 or 2,000 firms in the industry.

Chamberlin A major criticism of the Cournot and Bertrand approaches is that firms in these models fail to fully recognize their interdependence. They mechanically adjust output or price based on assumptions that are often contradicted. In 1933, Edward H. Chamberlin argued that intelligent managers would recognize that industry profits are maximized when price is set at the monopoly level and would be reluctant to take measures that reduce price below this level and leave all members of the industry worse off. In the context of Figure 7.1a and b, if firm A sells Q_m = 90 and a second firm B enters and increases industry output by 45 (à la Cournot), Chamberlin's firm A will immediately respond by cutting its output to 45 as well, so that total industry output returns to Q_m = 90. Firm A will do this, asserted Chamberlin, "because the *ultimate* consequences of his following through the other chain of adjustments are less advantageous to himself than to share equally with his rival the output [Q_m]."[9] Recall that, in our example, Cournot duopolists would each earn profits of \$720 per period; if, however, industry output were restricted to Q_m = 90 and the two firms shared the market equally, each would earn profits of \$810 per period. Monopoly prices and output rates would occur, in Chamberlin's view, even if there were more than two sellers; many firms would be required to generate competitive results.

Chamberlin recognized, however, that several real-world complications might defeat oligopolists' attempts to attain monopolistic results. Market frictions, e.g., time lags between the initiation of a price cut and recognition and matching of the cut, might induce firms to undercut rivals' prices in pursuit of short-term gains at the rivals' expense. Differing cost functions or uncertainty about rivals' reactions and intentions might also lead to conflicts among the oligopolists. Such conflicts might only be resolved via some formal collusive agreement among the firms. Absent such an agreement, the kind of joint profit maximization Chamberlin proposed might be impossible.

---

[8]Joseph Bertrand, "Theorie mathematique de la richesse sociale," *Journal des Savants*, Paris (September 1883), pp. 499–508. For a modern summary, see William S. Vickrey, *Microstatics*, Harcourt Brace Jovanovich, New York, 1964.
[9]Edward H. Chamberlin, *The Theory of Monopolistic Competition*, 8th ed., Harvard University Press, Cambridge, MA, 1969, p. 47.

Dominant Firms and Price Leadership One popular way to model oligopolistic firms' decisions is to designate one firm as a *dominant firm,* or *leader,* with the remaining firms in the industry following this firm's cues. The leader will commonly be the largest firm in the industry and may (but need not) have a cost advantage over its rivals. Formal dominant-firm theories can produce some surprising results. One model by Heinrich von Stackelberg, e.g., predicts that output will be higher (and price and profits lower) than in Cournot duopoly.[10]

Another model, originally formulated by Karl Forchheimer, has a price-searching dominant firm and a price-taking "competitive fringe" of smaller firms. Figure 7.3 illustrates the basic analysis. The dominant firm is assumed to know the fringe's supply function S_f and subtracts (horizontally) the fringe's potential supply from market demand D_{mkt} to yield its own "residual" demand curve D_d (that is, $D_d = D_{mkt} - S_f$). Thus, if the dominant firm sets a price above P_1, then the fringe firms will satisfy market demand entirely and the dominant firm will sell nothing. If the dominant firm sets price below P_0, the fringe will sell nothing. Once the dominant firm knows its demand curve and related marginal revenue curve MR_d, it chooses its output by equating marginal cost and revenue (i.e., finding the intersection of MC_d and MR_d). It then produces and sells Q_d units of output at price P^*. The fringe firms' collective output Q_{fringe} raises total market output to Q_{mkt}.[11]

This short-run result may cause long-term problems for the dominant firm, though. If P^* is high enough to generate economic profits for the fringe firms, then fringe firms may expand capacity or new firms may enter. This will shift the fringe supply curve S_f rightward, meaning the dominant firm will face a shrinking residual demand curve. The dominant firm may, therefore, find it worthwhile to eschew some short-term profit in order to limit such entry (recall the discussion of limit pricing in Chapter 6).

Less formal leader-follower models assert that oligopolists will be able to coordinate their actions (absent overt collusion) by adhering to certain rules of thumb or customs. In *price leadership,* e.g., changes in list prices are initiated by a specific firm acknowledged as a leader, with other firms quickly duplicating the leader's pricing policies. The presumption is that the leader keeps prices at monopolistic levels, but it may be that lockstep price movements simply reflect demand or cost shifts across a competitive industry. However, the key questions are, Will followers always find it in their interest to adhere to such customs? and What will leaders do when adherence to custom breaks down?

---

[10]Stackelberg's book *Marktform und Gleichgewicht* (1934) was published in German. It is reviewed in William J. Fellner, *Competition among the Few,* Alfred A. Knopf, New York, 1949.

[11]It is possible that the Organization of Petroleum Exporting Countries (OPEC) makes similar calculations when it chooses the amount of oil that its members will collectively pump. The OPEC member nations, taken together, can be viewed as a dominant firm facing a competitive fringe of nonmember nations (the United Kingdom, United States, etc.). Of course, once a cartel such as OPEC determines how much it collectively wishes to produce, it still faces some vexing problems about assigning output shares to members and policing members' behavior, as we will see.

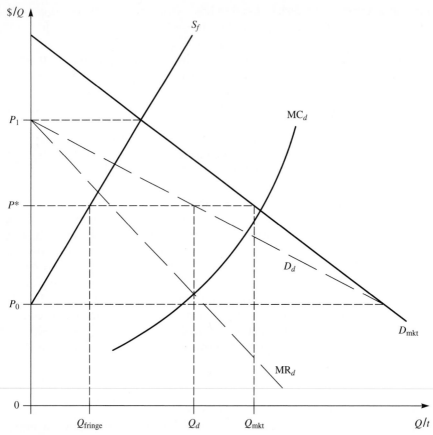

FIGURE 7.3
PRICING AND OUTPUT DECISIONS WITH A DOMINANT FIRM. The dominant firm determines the demand curve it faces D_d by subtracting the fringe firms' supply curve S_f from market demand D_{mkt}. It then finds the intersection of MR_d and MC_d and chooses output rate Q_d and price P^*. Fringe firms add output Q_{fringe} to raise market output to Q_{mkt}.

Stigler Conceding that firms wish to collude to maximize joint profits, George Stigler focused on the difficulties of policing any collusive agreement that might arise.[12] In Stigler's view, the incentive to collude is strong, but so, too, is the incentive to cheat on a collusive agreement. Consider, e.g., Figure 7.4, which shows a hypothetical market demand curve D facing three identical firms with (for simplicity's sake) zero costs.[13] Suppose the three firms have agreed to share this market equally, each selling 30 units of output (so that the total industry output equals 90) at the monopoly price of $18 per unit. Each

[12]George J. Stigler, "A Theory of Oligopoly," *Journal of Political Economy*, 72 (February 1964), pp. 44–61.
[13]Note that the market demand curve in this example remains $Q_d = 180 - 5P$, although we now add a third firm.

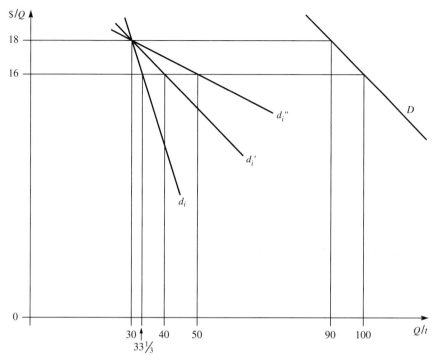

FIGURE 7.4
THE INCENTIVE TO CHEAT. Cutting price below the collusively set level of $18 will
increase a cheater's sales. A $2 cut may increase sales from 30 to 33⅓ units (i.e., along d_i)
if rivals respond with cuts of their own. If the cuts are disguised so that no response occurs,
a cheater's sales volume may rise to 40 or 50 units (i.e., along d_i' or d_i'').

firm would thus earn profits equal to $540 per period, and *industry* profits
would be at their highest possible level, $1,620 per period. But each firm may
wonder whether it could *individually* improve its situation. Suppose a price cut
to $16 will raise industry sales by 10 units, to 100 per period. Such a cut would
not make sense if it were made by *all* firms and extended to *all* consumers, for
that would cause each firm's profits to fall to $533.33 and industry profits to
fall to $1600. That is, an *open* price cut would simply move each of the firms
down along an individual demand curve such as d_i, which is simply $D/3$. Each
would sacrifice $2 in profits on the 30 units which could have been sold at $18
per unit in exchange for an additional profit of $16 per unit on an extra 3⅓
units sold per period, for a net loss of $6.67 per period. Clearly, this is a bad
idea—as Chamberlin noted.

But what if the price cuts are not open, but secret? Suppose a firm can
extend the discount selectively to new potential customers, without offering it
to its current customers or those of its rivals. Then that firm faces an individual demand curve like d_i' in Figure 7.4, which has the same slope as D. In this
case, the secret price cut will increase the firm's profits by $16 per unit times
the 10 extra units sold, a nontrivial rise of $160 per period (to a total of $700).

Even if the discount must be offered to all the price-cutter's old customers, its profits will rise by \$100 per period (to \$640). If the secret price cuts can be extended to some of the customers of the firm's rivals, stealing some of them away, the firm may see its individual demand curve resembling d''_i, which has a slope even greater than that of the market demand curve D. If the secret price cut enables a firm to attract 10 new customers *and* steal, say, 10 old customers away from rivals without the rivals' reacting or emulating the cut, profits will rise by \$260 per period (to \$800).

In sum, there can be no denying the temptation to secretly cut a collusively set price. The key—and the issue Stigler investigated—is the ease or difficulty of making such cuts and avoiding detection and response. The longer it takes rivals to recognize or respond to a price-cutter (and the less costly is the "punishment" the rivals mete out for the price-cutter's transgressions), the more likely price-cutting will be. (Note, too, that there are many ways to cut prices without appearing to do so: by varying product quality, offering favorable credit terms or free delivery, throwing in postpurchase servicing at reduced charges, etc. All will affect rivals' ability to detect cheating on a collusive arrangement.)

In Stigler's model, there is some randomness in the behavior of customers. That is, customers of firm A may switch to B for reasons having nothing to do with price-cutting by B. All firms normally expect to retain a certain proportion of their old customers and attract some proportion of the other firms' former customers or of first-time buyers. Cheating is inferred when a firm retains or attracts a *statistically disproportionate* share of buyers. Chance variations in customer behavior, then, provide a shield behind which price-cutters can hide. A firm which normally retains 80 percent of its traditional customers, e.g., may find itself retaining only 75 percent for some period. Is the loss due to price-cutting by a rival or some innocent (i.e., random) factor? *The more difficult it is to answer this question, the greater will be the incentive of collusive oligopolists to engage in price-cutting—and the closer prices will be to the competitive level.*

Stigler's theory implies that collusion is more likely, and more likely to be successful, in markets where (1) buyers accurately report purchase prices, (2) there is little "turnover" of buyers, i.e., the set of buyers is reasonably fixed, (3) sellers and buyers are few, (4) there is substantial inequality of seller firm size, (5) the product is homogeneous, and (6) demand and cost conditions are relatively stable.

VIGNETTE 7.2   How Not to Collude: The Great Electrical Equipment Conspiracy

In the late 1950s, some of the largest and best-known U.S. corporations (GE, Westinghouse, Allis-Chalmers, I-T-E) were caught red-handed in a price-fixing conspiracy. The defendants pleaded guilty to charges involving price-fixing on various electrical equipment (transformers, circuit breakers, turbine generators, etc.), and a federal judge sentenced seven executives to jail terms and fined the firms involved nearly \$2 million.[14] Subsequently, private treble-damage suits brought an additional \$400 million to the conspirators' customers.

There is no doubt that the defendants tried to rig the market. An account of their procedures reads like a spy novel, replete with code names, clandestine meetings, faked records, and complicated schemes for allocating sales. What is unclear, however, is whether the conspirators actually succeeded in raising prices much above competitive levels. Apparently, the firms double-crossed each other with regularity.

In the words of one executive, "Everybody would come to the meeting, the figures would be settled, and they were only as good as the distance to the closest telephone before they were broken."[15] In the view of another, the collusion "was a rather fruitless endeavor. It might be two days, after a meeting, before jobs would be bid all over the place."[16] Granted, such testimony may be self-serving, but there is also considerable empirical evidence that the conspiracy was a failure. Periodic "white sales" drove prices on some equipment as much as 60 percent below list during the period of alleged price-fixing. Firm profit rates were actually *lower* during the period the conspiracy was ongoing, and a lengthy study concluded that market prices were determined not by any conspiracy but by forces of supply and demand.[17]

Thus, the "great electrical equipment conspiracy" demonstrates graphically that it is one thing to try to fix prices, but quite another to actually succeed in doing so. The temptation to cheat is quite strong, and as one of the executives testified, "I think that the boys could resist everything but temptation."[18]

Game Theory and Oligopoly

Mathematician John von Neumann and economist Oskar Morgenstern published the first formal theory of strategic games in the 1940s.[19] Game theory concerns the actions of individuals (or *players*) who are aware that their actions affect each other. Many theoretic games, then, resemble the situation faced by firms in oligopolistic markets: Such firms are interdependent, know that this is so, and will consider other firms' actions in formulating their own decisions about price, output, advertising budget, etc. But while game theory is especially useful for modeling firm behavior in oligopolistic markets, it is not restricted to this use; indeed, it has been applied to a host of other tasks in the social sciences.

A full discussion of this framework is beyond the scope of this book, but some of its flavor can be conveyed with a simple and classic example, the *prisoner's dilemma*. Suppose two suspected criminals, Butch and Sundance, are

---

[14]*City of Philadelphia v. Westinghouse Electric*, 210 F. Supp. 483 (1961).

[15]*Source*: Hearings on Administered Prices by the U.S. Senate Committee on the Judiciary, Subcommittee on Antitrust and Monopoly, *Price-Fixing and Bid-Rigging in the Electrical Manufacturing Industry*, Parts 27–28, 87th Cong., 1st Sess. (1961), p. 16,884.

[16]Ibid., p. 16,962.

[17]See Dominick Armentano, *Antitrust and Monopoly: Anatomy of a Policy Failure*, Wiley, New York, 1982, pp. 148–162; Ralph G. M. Sultan, *Pricing in the Electrical Oligopoly*, Vol. 1, Harvard University Press, Cambridge, MA, 1974.

[18]*Price-Fixing and Bid-Rigging*, op. cit., p. 17,070.

[19]John von Neumann and Oskar Morgenstern, *Theory of Games and Economic Behavior*, Princeton University Press, Princeton, NJ, 1944.

TABLE 7.1
THE PRISONER'S DILEMMA.　Given the payoff matrix shown (and no "honor among thieves" or other considerations), both prisoners will find it in their best interest to confess.

	Sundance	
Butch	Confesses	Remains silent
Confesses	(−5, −5)	(0, −20)
Remains silent	(−20, 0)	(−1, −1)

apprehended and placed in separate cells, unable to communicate with each other. Each may either confess to the crimes of which they are accused or remain silent, but (we assume) both know full well the consequences of either choice. If one confesses while the other does not, the one who confesses is granted immunity and goes free, while the other goes to jail for 20 years. If both confess, both go to jail for 5 years. If both remain silent, both will be judged guilty of a petty charge (say, carrying concealed weapons) and will go to jail for only 1 year.

These consequences are summarized in Table 7.1, which is a matrix of *payoffs* to the various actions available to Butch and Sundance. In each box is the pair of sentences associated with an action each might choose; the first number is Butch's sentence, the second is Sundance's. For example, if Butch confesses while Sundance remains silent, Butch's payoff will be a sentence of 0 years, while Sundance's sentence is 20 years (numbers in Table 7.1 are negative to reflect the fact that the payoffs, in this case, are losses).

Obviously, the joint welfare of Butch and Sundance is maximized if both remain silent; they then serve a total of only 2 years in jail, far less than under any other combination of actions. But look at the problem from the point of view of one of the suspects, and assume each suspect's sole concern is his own welfare. Butch, e.g., knows that if Sundance remains silent, Butch will serve 1 year by doing likewise—or can go free by confessing. If, however, Sundance confesses, Butch knows that he'll serve 20 years if he remains silent, but Butch can cut that sentence to 5 years by also confessing. It certainly appears to Butch that *whatever Sundance does, Butch is better off if he confesses*. Of course, Sundance reasons analogously. The result is that both confess, and both go to jail for 5 years.

Many students find this outcome troubling. Since cooperating would make both Butch and Sundance better off, they argue, Butch and Sundance would find a way to do so. And perhaps this is so. Butch and Sundance might both remain silent if, e.g., they had previously arranged to have an associate impose some costs (not shown in the payoff matrix) on a partner who double-crosses the other. Or if there is honor among thieves, the psychic costs of dishonor (i.e., the shame of being known as a fink or stoolie) may be sufficient to induce cooperative behavior. And if a game is played more than once, a player

TABLE 7.2
THE DUOPOLIST'S DILEMMA. Even where there are sizable prospective returns to cooperation, it is possible that rational firms will act to their mutual disadvantage. Here joint profits are highest when prices are fixed, but the best individual strategy is to cut prices.

	Firm B	
Firm A	Cut price ($12)	Fix price ($18)
Cut price ($12)	($720, $720)	($1,440, 0)
Fix price ($18)	(0, $1,440)	($810, $810)

may signal his or her intent to cooperate, hoping the other player receives the message and does likewise; cooperative outcomes might thus *evolve*. But all such mechanisms were absent in the specification of the rules of the game above. Given the description above, confessing is not only plausible, it is, in game theory jargon, a *dominant strategy* for both Butch and Sundance; i.e., confessing will yield each player the highest possible payoff no matter what strategy the other picks.

What does all this have to do with oligopoly? It shouldn't take too much imagination to see that the considerations facing Butch and Sundance are very similar to those facing duopolists contemplating various pricing (or production) alternatives. For example, in Table 7.2, the payoff matrix for the prisoner's dilemma is rewritten to show the results of price-fixing or price-cutting behavior by firms A and B. Suppose, for simplicity, firms have but two choices: Fix price at the monopolistic level ($18) or cut price (to $12). If both firms fix price, each earns a profit of $810. If both cut price, each earns a profit of $720. If one fixes price while the other cuts price, the fixer earns zero while the cutter earns $1,440.[20] Again, the cooperative (price-fixing) choice is the one that maximizes joint profits. But, again, each firm will rationally choose *not* to cooperate (unless, again, some mechanisms exist that alter the payoffs shown in Table 7.2). For example, firm A will see that if B fixes its price at $18 per unit, A can raise its profits from $810 to $1,440 by cutting its price to $12. If, however, B cuts price, then A can protect itself by cutting price as well: Its profits would then be $720 instead of zero. No matter what B does, A calculates it will be better off by cutting price to $12. Firm B will reason in the same way; both firms will cut price. We conclude that even where sizable returns to cooperation are in prospect, it is quite possible that rational agents will choose courses of action that fail to maximize joint returns, i.e., *rivals may act to their mutual disadvantage*.

This prisoner's-dilemma result pops up surprisingly often. In arms races between countries, recruiting battles between rival colleges vying for blue-

---

[20] As earlier, market demand is described by the equation $Q_d = 180 - 5P$. This is not a repeated game, however, so profits are calculated for only a single period.

chip athletes, political bargaining, auction bidding, and many other circumstances, individuals will often undertake actions that harm everyone—at least relative to some cooperative solution to their conflict. But not all games are like the prisoner's dilemma, and not all games have such clear-cut—or destructive—outcomes.

In *cooperative* games, players can make binding commitments to each other; in *noncooperative* games, they cannot. As described above, the prisoner's dilemma is an example of the latter. Allowing Butch and Sundance to talk to each other before they decide what to do might transform the game to a cooperative one, but this would depend on the strength of any commitment the prisoners made to each other. They might agree not to confess, but if this agreement is not truly binding, they will both confess anyway when the opportunity comes to do so. Since collusion by firms is illegal, it's hard for potential colluders to make binding (i.e., legally enforceable) commitments to each other; accordingly, noncooperative game theory is most applicable to oligopoly.

Unlike Butch and Sundance in the example above, however, oligopolistic firms interact repeatedly. That is, firms do not make decisions about prices, output rates, and other variables once and for all, but continuously, at each point in time considering rivals' past actions, present characteristics, etc. This process can be modeled as a noncooperative *repeated* game, or *supergame*, in which a basic game is replicated many—perhaps infinitely many—times. Unfortunately, such games usually have many possible outcomes, depending upon what rules the players use to guide their actions and certain other variables.

Consider once again the duopolist's dilemma described in Table 7.2. We have already shown that in a one-period framework, cutting prices is a dominant strategy for both firms. But what if the game is played every day (or week, year, etc.) from now to infinity? (Although people are known to die, firms and economies have no "expiration date.") Both firms might adopt the following strategy, sometimes called the *grim strategy*:

1 In the first period, fix prices.
2 Continue to fix prices unless the other firm chooses to cut prices, in which case also cut prices forever after.

If firm *A* adopts the grim strategy, firm *B* will realize that price-cutting will yield higher profits than price-fixing in period 1, but lower profits than price-fixing forever after as *A* punishes *B*'s behavior with price-cutting of its own in periods 2 through infinity. In our numerical example, price-cutting by *B* enhances its profits by $630 (equal to the $1,440 that *B* earns by price-cutting minus the $810 it would have earned by price-fixing) in period 1, but reduces its profits by $90 ($810 minus $720) per period afterward. If the interest rate (which we use to discount future flows of dollars to their lump-sum value today) is, say, 10 percent, then the present value of price-cutting will be less than zero (−$270 to be exact).[21] Firm B will thus have no incentive to cut prices in the face of A's adherence to the grim strategy.

So fixing prices at the monopoly level (forever!) is an equilibrium outcome in this infinite game under at least one strategic rule. But alternative strategies might fail to produce such tidy results. Consider the strategy dubbed *tit for tat:*

1 In the first period, fix prices.
2 In succeeding periods, choose the action the other player chose in the previous period.

Suppose that firm A employs the tit-for-tat strategy and that firm B cuts prices in period 1 but employs tit for tat afterward. Thus A fixes prices and B cuts prices in period 1, but in period 2 their roles are reversed. In period 3, roles reverse again; the two firms alternate price-cutting and price-fixing forever.

Widening the set of actions or strategic rules available to players in such a supergame merely increases the number of possible outcomes. It is possible that price (and firm profits) will be monopolistic, competitive, or anywhere in between. The fact that *any combination of payoffs is a sustainable* equilibrium value for the firms in this supergame has been proved as the "folk theorem" (so named because no one remembers who should get credit for it).

Some interesting recent work considers the possibility that players' information sets may differ in ways relevant to their behavior, or, in the jargon, that the game is one of *asymmetric information.* For example, David Kreps, Paul Milgrom, John Roberts, and Robert Wilson (Kreps et al.) have shown that a small bit of uncertainty about the preferences of players (which translates to uncertainty about the values in the payoff matrix) can significantly affect players' behavior in repeated games.[22] Kreps et al. found that when one of the players has (or might have) a preference for cooperation, both players will cooperate (i.e., fix prices) at the beginning of the game, provided the game involves a sufficient number of repetitions. This occurs because cooperating early in the game establishes a player's *reputation* for cooperativeness, which will lead to future gains from a long-term cooperative relationship.

---

[21]Recall that the present value (PV) of a *perpetual* stream of annual payments is

$$PV = \frac{\text{annual payment}}{i}$$

where i is the interest rate. For an accessible introduction to discounting and present value, see any introductory economics text.

Here the annual "payment" is negative, −$90, and $i = 0.10$, so PV = −$90/0.10 = −$900. Thus, price-cutting gets firm B $630 today at the *expense* of a future stream of income worth $900, so price-cutting loses $270 for B. (How high must the discount rate climb to make price-cutting attractive to firm B?)

[22]David Kreps, Paul Milgrom, John Roberts, and Robert Wilson, "Rational Cooperation in the Finitely Repeated Prisoner's Dilemma," *Journal of Economic Theory,* 27 (August 1982), pp. 245–252.

Can Collusion Be Beneficial?

Not all economists believe that competition is always and everywhere good and that collusion among firms is always bad. In recent years, several researchers have explored the possibility that collusion may be beneficial or economically efficient.

Donald Dewey, e.g., theorizes that collusion is a way in which firms might seek to reduce the amount of *uncertainty* or instability they face in real-world markets. In Dewey's model, firms maximize not profits but a *utility function* with two elements: the profit rate r and the variance of this rate v. The latter is a widely used measure of market uncertainty. For given r, higher utility levels can be achieved only by lowering v; for given v, higher utility is achieved via higher r. If entry is free, Dewey argues, collusion cannot yield permanent monopoly profits. Why, then, would firms bother paying the costs of organizing and enforcing collusion? To the extent that cooperative action can reduce v, such action would produce higher levels of utility for given r. Of course, if entry is free, cooperation *might* (although, Dewey shows, it need not) produce an equilibrium characterized by lower r and lower v. This outcome might, in turn, be associated with an increase in industry output, rather than the reduction in output we normally view as the by-product of collusion. Economy-wide, Dewey concludes, legalizing collusion "will reduce uncertainty and therefore the cost of investment and marketing mistakes. In a risk-averse world, collusion by reducing uncertainty will presumably also increase the fraction of national income invested."[23]

Lester Telser has argued that cooperation among firms is not only desirable but *necessary* under certain circumstances. In Telser's view, the problems faced by real firms are far more complicated than the economic model of pure competition implies. In the real world, some goods and production processes are not infinitely divisible, firms must make decisions about (and deploy) inputs well before there is any output to sell, demand is uncertain, and the market environment is constantly changing. Pure competition may be unable to deal with such complications. Instead, Telser argues, an *optimal mix of competition and cooperation* among firms may be required to achieve efficiency.

To see the role that cooperation might play in solving some otherwise intractable market problems, consider the following situation.[24] Suppose three people—strangers to each other—are waiting at a taxi stand. All want to go to the airport, and each is willing to pay $7 for this service. Two cabs, each with two seats, show up at the same time. Each cabbie is willing to drive to the airport, with one or two passengers, for no less than $6. Clearly, social surplus will be maximized if both cabs go to the airport, one carrying two passengers and the other carrying one. This will produce social surplus of $9 (equal to total social value of $21 minus total costs of $12).

[23]Donald Dewey, "Information, Entry, and Welfare: The Case for Collusion," *American Economic Review*, 69 (September 1979), p. 593.
[24]I am grateful to George Bittlingmayer for this example.

Surprisingly, however, there is no purely competitive allocation of these gains among the cabbies and passengers, and this raises the possibility, at least, that the socially optimal outcome may not eventuate. Let us see how competition might work in this situation. Suppose one cabbie proposes a fare of $6 per person. This will mean one cabbie (whoever is lucky enough to get two passengers) gets a net profit of $6, while the other (the one left with the odd passenger) gets a zero profit. The latter would likely propose a fare of $5 per person, in the hope of filling both seats; if accepted by two passengers, this proposal would yield a net profit of $4. But then the other cabbie is likely to respond by proposing a fare of $4, and so on, down to a proposed fare of $3— below which neither cabbie will bid. What happens next? There is no single answer, which is precisely the point. After the losing bidder drops out of the competition, the winning bidder might try to raise the price to more profitable levels. But that would pull the loser back into the market, starting the process over again. Note also that if the winning bidder *does* pull away from the hotel with two passengers, each paying $3, the third passenger might wind up paying a much higher fare. (And how will the potential buyers allocate the two "cheap" seats? With a fistfight? With side payments among themselves so that each winds up paying the same fare?) But then the cabbies would vie for the position of losing bidder, for the "loser" might earn higher profits than the winner. In sum, there is an impasse here.

One possible solution involves price-fixing by the cabbies. They might agree to charge $7 per person and split the resulting profits of $9 equally between them. Alternatively, they might merge or petition the city for rate regulation. Such cooperative strategies would prevent or resolve the impasse. The key conclusion is that competition alone may not ensure a socially optimal outcome in some circumstances; cooperation may.

The cab example illustrates the problem of *indivisibilities* in production. If passengers (or seats) could be divided, the problem would evaporate: Bertrand-style competition would lead each cabbie to offer to drive 1.5 passengers to the airport at a fare of $4 per person. But obviously this is not a realistic solution. In Telser's view, many industries using mass production techniques (i.e., assembly lines) are susceptible to indivisibility problems. In the automotive industry, e.g., assembly lines operate at a given rate per hour, often around the clock. It's generally very expensive to increase or decrease this rate very much. Changes in the rate of output, then, usually require the firm to open or close an entire assembly line. Rarely is it feasible to do so for less than a day (e.g., calling workers in for a Saturday overtime shift); more commonly, output changes involve opening or closing an entire line for a 5-day, 8 hours/day shift. Clearly, opening or closing an assembly line can substantially change output relative to demand.

There are other problems for the competitive model as well. For example, when producers must pay large *fixed costs* and some *avoidable costs* (defined as lump-sum costs that are incurred at positive rates of output but not if output is zero) and face *uncertain demand*, unrestricted competition may fail to produce an equilibrium.[25] In such cases, average total costs will be declining in the industry, marginal costs will lie below average costs, and competition for buyers may prevent plants from breaking even. As a result, firms seeking to stabilize such markets may engage in various forms of cooperation (e.g., forming an exclusive sales agency, specifying output quotas, price-fixing, or allocating territories) that is anticompetitive. But such practices, in Telser's view, need not be inefficient; indeed, they may enhance efficiency in certain situations, promoting production by allowing firms to recover their costs.

These ideas of Dewey and Telser are not yet widely shared by economists and antitrust scholars. But the theories are still rather new, and there has been little time to test them empirically.[26] If evidence begins to accumulate that collusion *can* lead (at least occasionally) to enhanced efficiency, we may wish to go back to the drawing board and redraft policy toward price-fixing, for current policy is based on a presumption that such activity has no redeeming qualities.

A Partial Summation

We have viewed a portion—and a small one at that—of the mountainous array of oligopoly theories economists have developed over the past century and a half. Some of these theories suggest that in oligopoly price will exceed the competitive level, perhaps equaling the price that would prevail in monopoly. Other theories suggest that behavior and performance in oligopolistic markets may approximate or even equal that under perfect competition. Game theory has established formally that many outcomes are possible in oligopolistic markets, depending upon the strategies used by firms, the information they have at their disposal, and the characteristics of decision makers. And some recent theories even posit that collusion (and other cooperative action by firms) may help solve market problems that competition cannot.

The profusion of theories is unsatisfactory to those who seek simple and unequivocal answers to the question, What will oligopolists do? But behavior in *real* oligopolistic markets is extraordinarily varied. Collusion occurs in some oligopolistic markets but not others, is successful in some contexts but not in others, and takes many forms. Is it not reasonable, then, to expect—or even require—a corresponding proliferation of theories? It is quite possible that the various oligopoly theories are not in conflict, but are complementary.

PROFITS AND CONCENTRATION: THEORY, EVIDENCE, AND POLICY

As we have seen, some oligopoly theories (e.g., Stigler's) predict that collusion is more likely—or more likely to be successful—when sales are concentrated

---

[25]For a full discussion of these issues, see Lester G. Telser, "Cooperation, Competition and Efficiency," *Journal of Law and Economics,* 28 (May 1985), pp. 271–295.

[26]But see, e.g., William Sjostrom, "Collusion in Ocean Shipping: A Test of Monopoly and Empty Core Models, " *Journal of Political Economy,* 97 (October 1989), pp. 1160–1179.

among a few firms, implying that such markets may be more profitable than unconcentrated ones. Other theories (e.g., Cournot's) predict that the number of firms in an industry will be negatively related to industry prices and profits, even absent explicit collusion. But still other theories (e.g., Bertrand's) predict there will be no such relationship. What guidance does the statistical evidence offer here? As we have already remarked, the diversity of behavior observed in real oligopolies implies that no single theory will apply to all such markets. But do the data suggest there is one which applies to *most?*

This is one of the most extensively examined questions in economics. The discussion began with a 1951 study by Joe S. Bain, who tested the hypothesis that market concentration facilitates collusion between firms and thus enhances industrywide profits. He concluded (cautiously) that industries with eight-firm concentration ratios (CR_8s) above 70 appeared more profitable than those with CR_8s below this threshhold.[27] In the years following, scores of articles appeared in economic journals testing Bain's *concentration-profits hypothesis* with different data and more sophisticated statistical methods.[28] The great majority found a positive effect of concentration on profits.

By the late 1960s to early 1970s, the hypothesis had become doctrine. It was common to assume that market concentration signaled market power and that firms in concentrated markets could singly raise prices above costs or successfully collude with other firms in doing so. This view was so widely held that a 1968 White House Task Force on Antitrust Policy recommended revising the antitrust statutes to limit concentration, and in the early 1970s Congress considered—but did not pass—legislation to accomplish this goal. The Industrial Reorganization Act (authored by the late Senator Phillip Hart) would have created a "rebuttable presumption that monopoly power is possessed" when a firm earns an after-tax profit rate in excess of 15 percent for 5 of 7 consecutive years or where the four-firm CR exceeds 50 percent. The prescribed remedies included deconcentration of industries via sales of portions of firms' productive capacity to independent owners.

This was, however, the market concentration doctrine's high-water mark. A few antitrust scholars had always harbored doubts about the doctrine.[29] They noted that not all firms are alike; some have superior insight, lower costs, or just better luck, and such advantages will enable a firm to capture greater market share and higher profits even where competitive behavior rules. For example, Figure 7.5 shows a market in which most firms have production costs C (assume, for simplicity, constant unit costs) but one firm has lower costs C^*. The low-cost firm will (à la Bertrand) just slightly beat its competitors' prices by charging price $P_c - e$ (raising output to $Q_c + f$), capturing the entire market.

---

[27]Joe S. Bain, "Relationship of Profit Rate to Industry Concentration: American Manufacturing, 1936–40," *Quarterly Journal of Economics*, 65 (August 1951), p. 313.

[28]This literature is ably summarized, to the mid-1970s, by Leonard W. Weiss, "The Concentration-Profits Relationship and Antitrust," in Harvey J. Goldschmid, H. Michael Mann, and J. Fred Weston, *Industrial Concentration: The New Learning*, Little, Brown, Boston, 1974, pp. 184–233.

[29]See, e.g., John S. McGee, *In Defense of Industrial Concentration*, Praeger, New York, 1971.

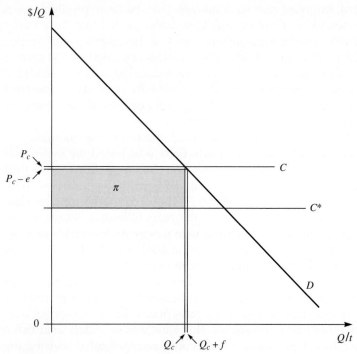

FIGURE 7.5
BERTRAND COMPETITION WITH DIFFERING COSTS OF PRODUCTION. A competitively superior firm with costs C^* will dominate an industry by lowering price just slightly below the competitive level P_c. Here the concentration ratio will be the highest possible, and the firm will show above-normal profits.

The CR here will be the highest possible, and the firm will show above-normal profits.[30] By the mid-1970s the argument that such *superior efficiency* might account for observed differences in profitability began to achieve wide currency.

One particularly influential study was authored by Harold Demsetz, who tested the efficiency explanation by analyzing how firm size affected the pattern of earnings within industries.[31] Sorting firms in a sample of 95 industries into four different size classes, he found that *within concentrated industries* larger firms tended to have higher profit rates. He argued that this indicated these larger firms had lower costs than their smaller rivals, for if costs were uniform for all firms, profit rates would be uniform, too. Superior efficiency, then, appeared to be at least partly responsible for the growth of some firms and the

---

[30]This assumes that the source of the firm's lower costs C^* cannot be identified, preventing the bidding up of its price to reflect its higher value in production.

[31]Harold Demsetz, "Industry Structure, Market Rivalry and Public Policy," *Journal of Law and Economics*, 16 (April 1973), pp. 1–10. See also Sam Peltzman, "The Gains and Losses from Industrial Concentration," *Journal of Law and Economics*, 20 (October 1977), pp. 229–263.

concentration of their industries—and researchers' subsequent finding of a positive correlation between concentration and profits.

The suggestion that efficiency accounted for part of the observed correlation between concentration and profits took the steam out of the movement for structural reorganization of U.S. industry. If large firms in concentrated industries were more efficient than smaller rivals, then chopping them up would impose some real costs on consumers (recall the discussion of the welfare effects of deconcentration in Chapter 6).

Because it's so hard to capture sources of firms' efficiency in economic data, however, the empirical question of whether the observed differences in firms' profit rates are primarily attributable to efficiency or to market power has remained cloudy. Some recent studies strongly support the competitive-superiority view of Demsetz,[32] but others conclude that both efficiency *and* market power effects might explain the higher profits often observed in concentrated markets.[33] Several studies have found that profits are unrelated to industry CRs, but positively related to firms' market shares.[34] Such a finding might mean that large firms got that way by being lower-cost producers or, alternatively, that large firms enjoy structural advantages that confer some degree of market power.

The empirical debate continues, although on a far more sophisticated level than in its early stages.[35] Data bases and statistical methods are improving, and researchers are now investigating the determinants of market structure as well as strategic elements of firm behavior (entry deterrence, product differentiation, etc.). But, in general, we no longer presume that performance can be easily inferred from market structure or that bigness is bad per se. The policy debate has shifted. Restructuring U.S. industry is no longer a "front-burner" issue—if it is on the stove at all. There is much greater emphasis on identifying and limiting strategic behavior which might inhibit entry, exclude rivals, or facilitate collusion. The cultivation of healthy competition and enhanced efficiency remain central policy goals, but today we are unlikely to employ structural remedies in pursuit of them.

PUBLIC POLICY TOWARD OLIGOPOLY AND COLLUSION

Section 1 of the Sherman Act is very straightforward, declaring illegal *every* contract, combination, or conspiracy in restraint of trade. Such a broad condemnation reflects the belief, as common in the late 1800s as today, that competition is good and that agreements among competitors to fix prices or

---

[32]See Michael Smirlock, Thomas Gilligan, and William Marshall, "Tobin's *q* and the Structure-Performance Relationship," *American Economic Review*, 74 (December 1984), pp. 1051–1060.

[33]See Roger Clarke, Stephen Davies, and Michael Waterston, "The Profitability-Concentration Relation: Market Power or Efficiency?" *Journal of Industrial Economics*, 32 (June 1984), pp. 435–450.

[34]See David J. Ravenscraft, "Structure-Profit Relationships at the Line of Business and Industry Level," *Review of Economics and Statistics*, 65 (February 1983), pp. 22–31.

[35]For a recent summary and new tests, see Richard Schmalensee, "Collusion versus Differential Efficiency: Testing Alternative Hypotheses," *Journal of Industrial Economics*, 35 (1987), pp. 399–425.

restrict output are inherently bad. Such agreements were, in fact, so widely seen as harmful that as early as 1897 they were judged illegal per se. That is, price-fixing or related practices were judged illegal in and of themselves; it was unnecessary to ask whether there were "extenuating circumstances" that might excuse them, and no test of "reasonableness" needed to be applied to them.

Of course, simple language can disguise many complex issues. Applying section 1 to *all* apparent restraints might actually choke off some beneficial trade. (Is a multiyear employment contract, or any long-term supply contract, illegal because it restrains competitive bidding while it is in force? Indeed, doesn't almost any transaction involve some subtle restraint on the freedom of one or more parties to it—or of those *not* party to it?) In addition, it may be easy to confuse competition and collusion. As Robert Bork has remarked, if everyone on a street corner raises an umbrella at the same moment, it may be collusion or it may be raining. Finally, the various forms collusion might take—and the practices that might facilitate it—may be hard to recognize. Thus, the antitrust agencies and the courts have more to do in enforcing section 1 than merely tracking down price-fixers and slapping them in irons. It is to the implementation of policy that we now turn, first discussing overt agreements among rivals and later addressing cases in which conduct is less obviously anticompetitive or evidence about conduct is less explicit.

Price-Fixing and Market Rigging

Overt price-fixing may take several forms. Rivals may draw up an explicit *contract* that specifies minimum prices, or rivals may refuse to sell directly to consumers and instead form a *sales agency* to set a single price for all participants. Alternatively, firms may avoid discussing prices and simply carve up the geographic market into various *exclusive territories;* in each territory a firm will have monopoly power. The per se illegality of such restraints reflects the belief of the courts that price-fixing and market rigging are so seldom justifiable that it is unnecessary and wasteful to spend resources arguing about their reasonableness in specific cases. Six key cases illustrate the development of the law in this area.

Trans-Missouri Freight Association (1897)   It would be hard to find a better example of overt price-fixing than this. In 1889, 18 western railroads formed the Trans-Missouri Freight Association. The members held meetings at which rates were agreed upon, and those who broke the agreements were punished. Even after passage of the Sherman Act in 1890, rate-fixing meetings continued. In 1892, the association disbanded but was replaced by a seven-member committee that continued to set rates. Challenged under section 1, the defendants never denied they had jointly fixed rail prices. Instead, they argued that (1) since railroads were regulated by the ICC, they were not subject to Sherman Act strictures and (2) the rates set were reasonable and simply prevented cutthroat competition from driving profits too low and ruining the rail industry. The Supreme Court rejected both arguments. The opinion, authored by Justice Peckham, contained the first hints of the per se rule that would develop in such cases:

> [T]he plain and ordinary meaning of [the act's] language is not limited to that kind of contract alone which is in unreasonable restraint of trade, but all contracts are included in such language, and no exception or limitation can be added without placing in the act that which has been omitted by Congress.[36]

Peckham expressed doubt about the existence of such a phenomenon as cut-throat competition, arguing that a "reasonable" rate of profit is best determined by competition, not an agreement among rivals. But even if the railroads were right that competition would undo them, Peckham said, it was up to Congress to remedy the situation (by amending the Sherman Act), not the courts.

Addyston Pipe and Steel (1899)   In 1894, six southern and midwestern firms began to fix prices on cast-iron pipe. Sales were usually to state or local governments, which held sealed-bid auctions at which the lowest bidder won the contract. Prior to such auctions, the cartel members would meet and the chairperson would announce the cartel's bid, based on consideration of the likely bids of firms (chiefly from the northeast) which were not members. The members would then hold a separate auction; the low bidder in this private auction would earn the right to submit the previously agreed-upon cartel's bid, and the other members agreed to submit higher bids. If the cartel's bid was low enough to win the contract, the difference between it and the private-auction bid would go into a fund. Periodically, the money thus accumulated was divided among the six members via a formula based on the firms' capacities.

When the Justice Department challenged the arrangement, the defendants (like those in *Trans-Missouri Freight*) argued that their prices were reasonable and the arrangement prevented ruinous competition. A unanimous Supreme Court rejected these arguments and upheld a lower-court decision in favor of the government.[37] After this verdict, the six defendant firms plus five others not involved in the case merged to form the U.S. Cast Iron Pipe and Foundry Co., which held over two-thirds of U.S. smelting capacity by 1900 (nearly twice that of the original defendants). Clearly, the merged firms were able to make joint pricing decisions. Thus, the case has the appearance of a Pyrrhic victory for the Justice Department: It eliminated a horizontal conspiracy, but provoked a merger that may have been more anticompetitive—or perhaps less efficient.[38]

---

[36] *United States v. Trans-Missouri Freight Association,* 166 U.S. 290 (1897), p. 328.

[37] *Addyston Pipe and Steel Company v. United States,* 175 U.S. 211 (1899).

[38] It is possible that the merger wave of 1897 to 1904 was partly a response to Supreme Court decisions that limited joint pricing and output decisions. See George Bittlingmayer, "Did Antitrust Policy Cause the Great Merger Wave?" *Journal of Law and Economics,* 28 (April 1985), pp. 77–118.

VIGNETTE 7.3 Was the Collusion in *Addyston* Really Harmful?

One would expect that the customers of the *Addyston* defendants would have been a bit upset to find they'd been buying from a cartel. Surprisingly, however, these customers submitted affidavits *supporting* the defendants at trial. In fact, when a stenographer possessing "smoking gun" price-fixing memoranda had earlier contacted these customers and invited them to sue for damages (to be shared, of course, with the whistle-blowing stenographer), everyone declined, leaving prosecution of the case to the federal attorney. Evidently, these customers did not regard the price-fixing conspiracy to be harmful to them. Why?

The research of George Bittlingmayer may provide an answer.[39] Bittlingmayer made a careful study of the cast-iron pipe manufacturing industry for the relevant period, and he found that cost conditions in this industry were inconsistent with viable competition among firms. Specifically, production involved significant avoidable fixed costs (i.e., costs which were not sunk); marginal costs for most plants were roughly constant and below average costs at the observed output ranges. The difficulty this posed is shown in Figure 7.6, which shows average and marginal costs for a representative firm with a capacity constraint: It cannot expand output beyond Q^*. This poses no problem if industry demand is an integer multiple of Q^*, for then each such firm will produce Q^* units and sell at a price $P^* = ATC^*$. But if industry demand is not an integer multiple of Q^*, there is no competitive equilibrium in this industry. Suppose, e.g., we have 10 firms like the one shown in Figure 7.6, but now industry demand rises from $10Q^*$ to, say, $10.5Q^*$. This would drive price above P^*, and an eleventh firm would likely enter the market with an output of Q^*, raising industry output to $11Q^*$, in excess of the amount demanded. This would drive price below P^* and lead one or more firms to exit, which would drive price back up and begin the cycle over again. One obvious short-run solution to this problem would be cooperation among firms: Each might agree to produce one-eleventh of industry demand and charge a price equal to the ATC for this output. But, of course, this is precisely the sort of agreement that will offend the antitrust authorities.

To avoid such problems in the long run, producers might have used technologies that did not entail such substantial fixed costs. But such processes most certainly involved much higher overall costs than the mass production techniques actually used, or producers would have chosen them in the first place. Perhaps this is why buyers looked upon the *Addyston* collusion with favor. They might have recognized that the cartel's prices were indeed "reasonable," i.e., lower than the prices that would have been charged by a more competitive industry using more costly production methods.

Trenton Potteries (1927)   Nearly two dozen producers of bathroom bowls and fixtures met regularly in the post–World War I period to set standard list prices for their products and try to discourage each other from offering discounts below these prices. The firms' combined market share exceeded 80 percent. At trial, the defendants argued that their prices were reasonable and competitive. Indeed, there was considerable evidence that the agreements quickly and commonly broke down and that the majority of sales were made

[39]George Bittlingmayer, "Decreasing Average Cost and Competition: A New Look at the Addyston Pipe Case," *Journal of Law and Economics*, 25 (October 1982), pp. 201–229.

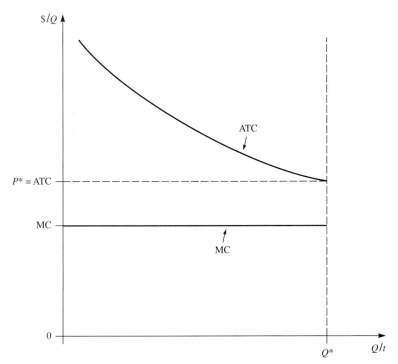

FIGURE 7.6
COST CONDITIONS IN THE CAST-IRON PIPE INDUSTRY CIRCA 1890. With significant avoid-able fixed costs, constant marginal costs, and a capacity constraint, each firm's ATC curve will be downward-sloping until the capacity constraint Q^* is reached. Unless industry demand is an inte-ger multiple of Q^*, there will be no competitive equilibrium in such an industry.

well below list.[40] Lower courts had split on the relevance of such arguments, but the Supreme Court ruled that the circumstances surrounding a collusive arrangement were immaterial. Section 1 merely required the prosecution to prove the existence of such an arrangement, not the harmfulness of the prices it established. In Justice Stone's words,

> [Price-fixing] agreements . . . may well be held to be in themselves unreasonable or unlawful restraints, without the necessity of minute inquiry whether a particular price is reasonable or unreasonable.[41]

Appalachian Coals (1933) The per se standard articulated in *Trenton Potteries* suffered a temporary setback in *Appalachian Coals*. The case was decided during the depths of the Great Depression, and it illustrates how con-

---

[40]See Almarin Phillips, *Market Structure, Organization and Performance,* Harvard University Press, Cambridge, MA, 1962, pp. 173–176.

[41]*United States v. Trenton Potteries Co.,* 273 U.S. 392 (1927), p. 397.

temporary circumstances can affect judicial decision making. The deflationary trend of the early 1930s and the high unemployment and numerous bankruptcies associated with this trend had convinced many that competition could be ruinous and that price-fixing was necessary and desirable in some circumstances.

Appalachian Coals, Inc. (ACI) was formed in 1929 as the exclusive selling agent of 137 coal producers with a combined relevant market share of about 12 percent. The coal industry had often shown negative net income since the early 1900s, and the ACI combination clearly eliminated competition among its member firms. The Justice Department moved against the arrangement even before it was put into practice. A lower court ruled in favor of the government, but the Supreme Court, clearly influenced by the industry's "deplorable" financial condition, eschewed the per se standard and articulated a "standard of reasonableness" for price-fixing cases. In the words of Chief Justice Hughes,

> [A] close and objective scrutiny of particular conditions and purposes is necessary in each case. Realities must dominate the judgment. The mere fact that the parties to an agreement eliminate competition among themselves is not enough to condemn it.[42]

The defendants argued—and the Court agreed—that their motives were benign; they intended not to fix prices but to "achieve economies in marketing" and end "destructive trade practices." Hughes noted that 130 sellers in ACI's region were not a party to the combination and found it hard to credit that the arrangement would enable effective price-fixing. ACI prevailed.

Socony-Vacuum Oil Co. (1940) Departure from the per se standard would be short-lived. In 1940, a case quite similar to that involving ACI reached the Supreme Court. A dozen major oil refining firms, including Socony-Vacuum (now Mobil Oil), were accused of buying large volumes of gasoline from independent refiners for the purpose of keeping this output off the market and supporting prices at artificially high levels. Oil refining, like coal mining, was a depressed industry during the 1930s, and the defendants argued (as ACI had) that their behavior was aimed at bringing order and stability to a weak market. The independent refiners (the defendants' "dancing partners") were generally small and possessed little storage capacity. In periods of slack demand (quite common during the 1930s) these independents would be unable to hold inventories of refined gasoline and would sell it at "distress" prices (i.e., prices below ATC) in the spot market. By purchasing this output, the defendants indirectly established a floor price for refined gasoline. Given the financial condition of the industry and the precedent of *Appalachian Coals*, this arrangement might have been found reasonable. But the

---

[42] *Appalachian Coals, Inc. v. United States,* 288 U.S. 344 (1933), p. 360.

Supreme Court reverted to a strict per se standard. In the words of Justice Douglas,

> The elimination of so-called competitive evils is no legal justification. . . . Congress . . . has not permitted the age-old cry of ruinous competition and competitive evils to be a defense to price-fixing conspiracies. . . . Under the Sherman Act a combination formed for the purpose and with the effect of raising, depressing, fixing, pegging, or stabilizing the price of a commodity . . . is illegal per se.[43]

Although Douglas made a weak attempt to distinguish the facts of this case from those in *Appalachian Coals*, it is clear that the decision repudiated the earlier case completely. Henceforth, any effort (whether direct or indirect) to fix prices would be illegal, whatever the surrounding circumstances or effects.

Topco (1972)   Topco, an association of about two dozen small supermarket chains, served as a purchasing agent for its members. The member chains also sold various products under brand names owned by Topco. The licensing agreements for these Topco-brand products specified that the member firms would sell them only in specified (nonoverlapping) areas; thus, the members could not compete with each other on sales of these items. Although the agreements did not constitute direct price-fixing, the Supreme Court had no difficulty characterizing them as restraints of trade involving competitors at the same level of the market—i.e., horizontal restraints—and judged them to be a per se violation of section 1.[44] Thus, the case extended the per se standard beyond price agreements to territorial agreements.

Trade Association Activities

Communication between rivals often serves useful purposes. In the early days of railroading, e.g., firms needed to jointly determine equipment specifications and coordinate policies regarding freight transfers from one line to another.[45] Trade associations are the usual devices to facilitate such endeavors. But, as Adam Smith noted, when rivals get together, conversation often turns toward price competition—and how to restrain it. The following four cases illustrate how much latitude the courts allow associations in discussing prices or other key competitive variables. Trade association activities are commonly judged under a rule-of-reason approach. In general, mere exchanges of information about prices are legal *unless* the exchanges take place in highly concentrated markets or there is some hint that firms are required to stick to their price announcements.

American Column and Lumber (1921)   Some 365 (of 400) members of the American Hardwood Manufacturers' Association (AHMA) participated in a

---

[43]*United States v. Socony-Vacuum Oil Co.*, 310 U.S. 150 (1940), pp. 220–221, 223.
[44]*United States v. Topco Associates*, 405 U.S. 596 (1972).
[45]For example, absent a standard gauge for track, freight would have to be unloaded and reloaded at the intersection of each line, a massive waste of resources.

program that involved the exchange of detailed daily reports on prices, shipments, and production. Any member who did not supply such data could not receive the reports of the association. The Supreme Court found the arrangement to go beyond a mere exchange of information and ruled it a subtle conspiracy to control prices. Significantly, the Court required no overt agreement to find illegality; it pointed to the association's pricing suggestions and the actual pattern of price changes as evidence of informal collusion.[46]

Maple Flooring Manufacturers (1925)   The 22-member Maple Flooring Manufacturers' Association (MFMA) circulated information in much the same way as the AHMA had. However, pricing patterns among members gave no appearance of conspiracy. Prices were not uniform, and often members' prices were lower than those of nonmembers. Also, the association made no suggestions to members about prices or production levels and did not withhold information from nonmembers. The Supreme Court ruled that no "concerted action had resulted or would necessarily result" and found the association's information exchanges permissible.[47]

The Sugar Institute (1936)   Excess capacity in the sugar industry prompted widespread secret price-cutting by producers throughout the post-World War I period. The Sugar Institute, an association of 15 large sugar refiners with a combined market share in excess of 70 percent, was formed to end such discounting. The members agreed to announce their prices in advance and adhere to them, although each member was allowed to choose prices independently. The Supreme Court found the Sugar Institute's information-disseminating function benign, but ruled that its requirement of *adherence* to announced prices was an unreasonable restraint on competition.[48]

Container Corporations of America (1969)   Exchanges of price information that involved no agreement to adhere to specified or suggested prices remained legal until 1969, when the Supreme Court found 18 manufacturers of corrugated boxes in violation of section 1 because they shared detailed pricing data. Despite the fact that prices actually declined (and the number of firms in the industry rose) during the relevant period, Justice Douglas concluded that

> The inferences are irresistible that the exchange of price information has had an anticompetitive effect in the industry, chilling the vigor of price competition. . . . Price is too critical, too sensitive a control to allow it to be used even in an informal manner to restrain competition.[49]

Justices Marshall, Harlan, and Stewart dissented, however. Justice Marshall opined that "complete market knowledge is certainly not an evil in perfectly

---

[46]*American Column and Lumber Co. et al. v. United States,* 257 U.S. 377 (1921).
[47]*Maple Flooring Manufacturers' Association v. United States,* 268 U.S. 563 (1925).
[48]*Sugar Institute v. United States,* 297 U.S. 553 (1936).
[49]*United States v. Container Corp. of America et al.,* 393 U.S. 333 (1969), pp. 337–338.

competitive markets."[50] This market, however, was far from perfectly competitive: The defendants made 90 percent of sales in the relevant market, a fact which had influenced the majority as well. Thus, the legal status of price information exchanges in less concentrated markets remains in some doubt.

Conscious Parallelism and Implied Conspiracy

Some will suspect tacit collusion whenever firms behave similarly, even if they neither meet nor exchange information. At first, the courts appeared headed toward a strict rule against *consciously parallel behavior,* even where such behavior might have been the result of independent forces and decisions. Eventually, however, a more flexible standard was developed, as the following four cases show.

Interstate Circuit (1939)   The manager of a chain of movie theaters in Texas sent identical letters to eight movie distributors. The letters asked that the distributors withhold first-run movies from any theater that charged discount prices (then, less than 25 cents) or showed first-run movies as part of a double feature. Since all distributors were named as addressees on each letter, each knew their rivals had received letters and might well comply with the request. In fact, all did. The Supreme Court judged this no accident:

> It taxes credulity to believe that the several distributors would . . . have accepted and put into operation with substantial unanimity such far reaching changes in their business methods without some understanding that all were to join, and we reject as beyond the range of probability that it was the result of mere chance.[51]

Thus, even without direct evidence of an agreement, consciously parallel actions by rivals could be evidence of unlawful conspiracy.

American Tobacco (1946)   Between 1923 and 1941, the three major tobacco companies (American, Liggett & Myers, and R. J. Reynolds) exhibited remarkable uniformity of behavior. Most changes in list prices over this period were initiated by the largest firm, Reynolds, and the others usually followed these changes within a day. The three firms also bought up low-grade tobacco which they apparently did not use in their own brands, but which was a key input for producers of economy brands. And, at the onset of the Great Depression, with raw tobacco prices *falling* precipitously, Reynolds initiated a major price *increase* that was quickly mimicked by the other two firms. When several economy brands then started to capture a large share of the market, the Big Three responded with a sizable price cut—until their market share recovered, when prices were raised again. Such actions seemed to the Supreme Court to comprise a coordinated effort to drive smaller competitors out of the market, although no evidence of overt collusion existed. But, stating that "no formal agreement is necessary to constitute an unlawful conspiracy,"

---

[50]Ibid., p. 342.
[51]*Interstate Circuit, Inc. v. United States,* 306 U.S. 208 (1939), p. 223.

the Court inferred such a conspiracy from "the action taken in concert by the parties to it."[52] Although the defendants were fined a mere $255,000, many hailed the decision as a major antitrust breakthrough. It was followed by several government victories in similar cases with larger penalties.[53] But the tide would soon turn.

Pevely Dairy (1949)[54]   The behavior of two St. Louis dairies (with a combined relevant market share of about 65 percent) was uniform in many respects. When one raised prices, the other usually followed within 2 days. Delivery schedules were also the same. A trial court ruled this an unlawful conspiracy, but on appeal a circuit court found the parallel behavior could have been entirely innocent. The court noted that both firms paid the same (government-supported) price for raw milk and both paid the same (union-mandated) labor costs. Uniform prices could be expected under such circumstances and were insufficient evidence of concerted action.

Theatre Enterprises (1954)   Movement away from the strict application of the conscious-parallelism doctrine continued with the Supreme Court's decision in *Theatre Enterprises*. A Baltimore theater (the Crest) located in a suburban mall failed to attract first-run movies despite offering generous guarantees. Movie distributors limited such films to the city's eight downtown theaters. The Crest's owners assumed the refusals resulted from the kind of conscious parallelism ruled illegal in *American Tobacco* and sued for treble damages. But the Supreme Court stated that "mere" circumstantial evidence of consciously parallel behavior was not sufficient to establish a conspiracy. The distributors argued that their uniform behavior was consistent with sound (and independent) business judgments. The Court found their explanations plausible and, absent more convincing evidence of conspiracy, ruled against the plaintiff:

> [T]his Court has never held that proof of parallel business behavior conclusively establishes agreement or, phrased differently, that such behavior itself constitutes a Sherman Act offense. Circumstantial evidence of consciously parallel behavior may have made heavy inroads into the traditional judicial attitude toward conspiracy; but "conscious parallelism" has not yet read conspiracy out of the Sherman Act entirely.[55]

In sum, consciously parallel behavior *plus more* (e.g., information exchanges, pricing or output changes unexplained by business conditions, or restrictive practices lacking some compelling business reason) would henceforth be required to infer a conspiracy to restrain competition.

---

[52]*American Tobacco Co. v. United States*, 328 U.S. 781 (1946), p. 809.
[53]See, e.g., *United States v. Paramount Pictures, Inc.*, 334 U.S. 131 (1948).
[54]*Pevely Diary Co. v. United States*, 178 F.2d 363 (8th Cir. 1949).
[55]*Theatre Enterprises, Inc. v. Paramount Film Distributing Corp. et al.*, 346 U.S. 537 (1954), pp. 540–541.

The Professions

It has long been common for professional societies to do things that, in other contexts, would be regarded as restraints on competition. Some medical or legal societies, e.g., restrict advertising or offer schedules of suggested rates, and some have had mechanisms to punish those who deviate from group norms.[56] But the societies regarded themselves as exempt from Sherman Act scrutiny because they were engaged in "public service" rather than "trade or commerce." Until the 1970s, such rationalizations were rarely challenged. Then two key decisions established that the learned professions are indeed within the jurisdiction of the Sherman Act.

Goldfarb (1975) In 1971 a couple buying a home in Fairfax County, Virginia, found that every one of the 36 lawyers they visited charged the same price for a routine title search. The fee—1 percent of the value of the home— was that "recommended" by the local and state bar associations. The couple claimed a section 1 violation. In addition to claiming exemption from the antitrust laws, the defendants argued that since their minimum fee schedule was merely "advisory," it could not constitute price-fixing. The Supreme Court rejected the notion that Congress intended to exclude the professions from section 1 coverage. And the Court noted that the associations had published guidelines stating that an attorney who regularly charged less than the suggested fees was presumed guilty of "misconduct."[57] Finding for the plaintiffs, the Court restricted the use of fee schedules in the legal profession.

National Society of Professional Engineers (1978) Under a code of ethics adopted in 1964, members of the National Society of Professional Engineers (NSPE) were prohibited from discussing fees until after a client had selected an engineer for a project. The NSPE argued that competitive bidding would lead to shoddy work and endanger public safety. The Supreme Court rejected this argument, claiming that "The Sherman Act reflects a legislative judgment that ultimately competition will produce not only lower prices, but also better goods and services."[58] The Court found the restraint on bidding a per se violation of section 1.

Other Cases Emboldened by *Goldfarb,* the Justice Department and Federal Trade Commission (FTC) pressed numerous suits against professional societies in the 1970s. Consent decrees that enjoined practices construed as price-fixing were obtained from groups representing accountants, architects, radiologists, orthopedic surgeons, and obstetricians. One additional case that affected lawyers also went to the Supreme Court. Two Phoenix attorneys had defied the local bar association's ethics code by advertising their low prices in

---

[56]See Reuben Kessel, "Price Discrimination in Medicine," *Journal of Law and Economics,* 1 (1958), pp. 20–59.

[57]*Goldfarb v. Virginia State Bar,* 421 U.S. 773 (1975).

[58]*National Society of Professional Engineers v. United States,* 435 U.S. 679 (1978), p. 695.

a local newspaper in 1976. The State Bar of Arizona suspended the two, who then sued, claiming both a Sherman Act violation and a violation of their First Amendment rights to free speech. The Supreme Court found that the advertising ban did *not* violate section 1 because the restriction had been expressly ordered by the Arizona Supreme Court.[59] But the ban *did* violate the plaintiffs' free-speech rights. Attorneys would henceforth be allowed to pitch their wares just like purveyors of beer, cars, and deodorants.

VIGNETTE 7.4   How Does an Advertising Ban Affect Prices?

Professional groups have long argued that their bans on advertising are not attempts to fix prices but are motivated by more laudable goals, such as (1) avoiding "commercialization" (which would undermine the professional's "sense of dignity and self-worth"), (2) preventing gullible consumers from being misled by advertisements, and (3) keeping rates low by avoiding the overhead costs of advertisements. It is difficult to test whether the first two rationales hold any water, but there is now ample evidence that the third does not. Allowing professionals to advertise their prices leads to much lower, not higher, rates.

In 1972, Lee Benham compared prices of eyeglasses in states that limited advertising in this market to prices in states that did not. He found that consumers in states where advertisements were limited paid from 25 to 100 percent more for their eyeglasses. States differed considerably in their restrictions on advertising, and Benham found that prices were highest in those states that prohibited *all* advertisements. Prices were lower in states that allowed some advertisements but banned mention of price, and prices were lowest of all in states with no restrictions. Thus, even "nonprice" advertising lowered prices.[60]

In 1976, John Cady compared prices of prescription drugs in states that restricted drug advertisements to prices in states that did not. He found that advertising restrictions resulted in higher prices for *all* types of drugs. He calculated that, for 1970 alone, consumers paid from $135 million to $152 million more (at prices then prevailing) than they might have if price advertising had been permitted in all states.[61]

Clearly, advertising is costly. Without it, however, consumers face formidable information problems. Knowledge about where goods are available and at what price can only be created at some cost. When advertisements are banned, acquiring such knowledge becomes more costly, and the likelihood that consumers will pay prices higher than the purely competitive level is evidently enhanced.

SUMMARY AND CONCLUDING REMARKS

In markets with few firms, called oligopolies, sellers are aware of their interdependence in setting prices and rates of output. Economists have devised many models of oligopolies, mirroring the rich variety of firm behavior in such markets. Some of these models (e.g., Cournot's, Chamberlin's) predict deadweight

---

[59]*Bates v. State Bar of Arizona*, 433 U.S. 350 (1977).

[60]Lee Benham, "The Effect of Advertising on the Price of Eyeglasses," *Journal of Law and Economics*, 15 (October 1972), pp. 337–352.

[61]John F. Cady, "An Estimate of the Price Effects of Restrictions on Drug Price Advertising," *Economic Inquiry*, 14 (December 1976), pp. 493–510.

welfare losses in oligopoly even absent formal collusion. Other models (e.g., Stigler's) start from the assumption that firms will seek to collude and then examine how collusive agreements might be reached or enforced. There is a strong incentive to cheat in any collusive agreement, and given that information about other firms' conduct is costly and imperfect, such agreements will sometimes collapse. Collusive conduct is, in general, more likely to succeed when the number of sellers (and buyers) is small, buyers accurately report purchase prices, there is little "turnover" of buyers, there is substantial inequality of seller firm size, the product is homogeneous, and demand and cost conditions are relatively stable.

The tools of game theory have been much used lately to model behavior in oligopolistic markets. Outcomes in most game-theoretic models depend crucially on the assumed strategies of the players. One-shot prisoner's-dilemma types of games suggest that even where sizable returns to cooperation are in prospect, it is quite possible that rivals may act to their mutual disadvantage. Where games are replayed ad infinitum, however, it can be shown that certain strategies will enable the players to achieve monopoly returns.

Not all theorists agree that collusion is always bad. Indeed, there is some evidence to suggest that, under certain cost and demand conditions, cooperative behavior among firms may be necessary to achieve a stable market equilibrium. Further empirical study of this and other issues in oligopoly is needed. The evidence accumulated thus far suggests that concentrated markets can be more profitable than unconcentrated ones, but that part of this may be explained by the superior efficiency of large firms in these markets.

Public policy toward overt price-fixing and market rigging is straightforward: Such behavior is illegal per se. Attempts to raise or stabilize prices via formation of exclusive sales agencies, territorial allocation, or formal or tacit agreements are illegal whether successful or not, and no inquiries about the reasonableness of such restraints will even be made under current law. Less restrictive activities, however, are commonly judged under a rule-of-reason approach. In general, mere exchanges of information about prices are legal unless the exchanges take place in highly concentrated markets or there is some hint that firms are required to adhere to their price announcements. A conspiracy to restrain competition may *not* be inferred from evidence of consciously parallel behavior alone; such circumstantial evidence must be supplemented with additional evidence of intent, e.g., information exchanges, pricing or output changes unexplained by business conditions, or restrictive practices that lack some compelling business reason. Professional groups, long left undisturbed by the antitrust laws, are now fully subject to these laws' strictures against price-fixing.

QUESTIONS FOR REVIEW AND DISCUSSION

7.1 Vignette 7.1 discusses NCAA's practice of selling exclusive broadcast rights to member schools' football games, found to be an illegal restraint of trade. But the NCAA also fixes the amount of compensation (i.e., scholarships, living expenses, etc.) that can be paid to college athletes. Evidently, given the incidence of under-the-table payments to star athletes, this compensation can be far below market-clearing levels. Review the Supreme Court's reasoning in the *NCAA* case [468 U.S. 85 (1984)], and tell whether you think the restrictions on athletic grants-in-aid should also be judged illegal. (If you think the restraints *are* illegal, you should also offer a reason why no college athlete has pressed a treble-damages private antitrust suit against the NCAA.)

7.2 Do the assumptions of the Cournot duopoly model appear realistic to you (i.e., do you think firms might really make such assumptions)? Are the assumptions of the Bertrand model more realistic? Explain. Do you think a model must be based on realistic assumptions to have value? On what other basis might the value of a model be judged?

7.3 Suppose that Congress made collusion perfectly legal and that formal cartel agreements could be written and enforced in courts of law. What obstacles to successful collusion would still remain?

7.4 In a one-period duopoly game like that illustrated in Table 7.2, price-cutting is a dominant strategy. Where this game is repeated infinitely many times, eternal price-fixing may result from one firm's adoption of the grim strategy. But what would happen if the duopoly game were repeated a finite number of times (*Hint:* What would happen in the last play of the game? What would therefore happen in the next-to-last play?)

7.5 Suppose you credit entirely the views of Dewey or Telser (or both) regarding the possible efficiency of collusion in some circumstances. Does this mean you must believe that the current per se illegality of price-fixing should be changed? Why or why not?

7.6 In 1989, several of the more prestigious universities in the United States were under investigation by the Justice Department. Allegedly, these universities shared information about future tuition levels and about financial aid offers to students who had applied to more than one of the schools. The record showed clearly that the schools' tuitions tracked very closely, often changing by identical percentages in a given year. And some students' scholarship offers were adjusted so that their net cost would be the same regardless of the school they chose. Is this sufficient evidence of price-fixing? If you were an attorney or economist working on this case, what would you need to do to establish that the schools had violated section 1 of the Sherman Act? (*Note:* In 1991, the Ivy League schools agreed to "cease and desist" such practices, but the Massachusetts Institute of Technology held out, contesting the charges.)

7.7 Explain the significance of the *Topco* decision. Can you think of any reason—other than a desire to earn monopoly profits—why the defendant firms would do what they did in this case?

7.8 Some professional groups claim that their limits on price competition (including bans on price advertising) help improve the quality of service that their members provide consumers. Devise an (economically sensible) argument in support of this position. How would you test whether this explanation (and your argument) might be valid?

CHAPTER 8

MERGERS AND ACQUISITIONS

His designs were strictly honourable, as the phrase is, that is to rob a lady of her fortune by way of marriage.

Henry Fielding

It is a rare day when the business press fails to report some actual or rumored merger or acquisition. Often the stories contain language appropriate to an adventure novel, with allusions to "raiders," "white knights," "shark repellent," and "poison pills." In part, this coverage reflects the increasing importance of takeovers and consolidations in U.S. business. As Figure 8.1 shows, the 1980s saw a stupendous increase in the frequency of corporate acquisitions. The annual number of transactions in the 1980s was approximately 3 times that in the 1970s, and the annual dollar volume of these transactions rose by an even greater multiple. Business historians have identified at least four "merger waves" in the United States, and the one we have just been through—if, in fact, it is over—is by far the greatest.[1] But part of our fascination with mergers and acquisitions no doubt stems from the extraordinary amounts of money involved in such transactions. For example, in 1989, RJR Nabisco was acquired by Kohlberg Kravis Roberts for $24.7 billion.

To some, such transactions show capitalism at its worst. In the view of these critics, mergers beget market power that will be used to jack up prices and

---

[1]The three prior merger waves are identified with the periods from 1898 to 1903, from 1926 to 1929, and from 1955 to 1968. For an interesting historical perspective, see Ralph L. Nelson, *Merger Movements in American Industry, 1895–1956*, Princeton University Press, Princeton, NJ, 1959.

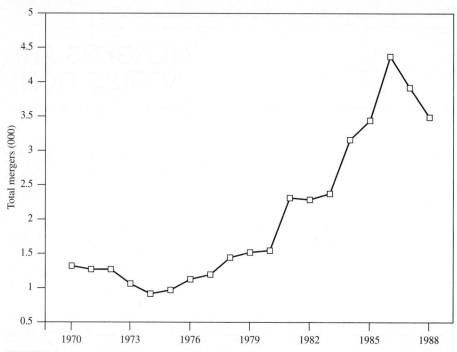

FIGURE 8.1
THE MERGER WAVE OF THE 1980s. The annual number of mergers in the 1980s was 3 times that in the 1970s, peaking at 4,500 mergers in 1986.

yield monopoly profits. Hostile takeovers force managers to emphasize short-run performance over the long-term health of their firms, and financing such takeovers burdens firms with enormous debt that makes them more likely to fail in the event of a business downturn. To others, however, mergers and acquisitions help a market economy function more efficiently. Mergers can reduce production costs, yielding tangible benefits for consumers. And, in the view of these defenders, a little paranoia can be a good thing: Managers worried about a takeover will be more likely to run a tight ship and act in the best interests of shareholders.

Mergers or acquisitions that "may substantially lessen competition or tend to create a monopoly" are outlawed by section 7 of the Clayton Act (as amended by the Celler-Kefauver Act of 1950). But, as we have already noted, concerns about the creation of monopoly power are just part of the picture here. The critics of takeover activity have long argued the need for regulations to protect the interests of shareholders of "target" firms, guard against fraud in the takeover process, and prevent acquisitions that burden the consolidated firm with excessive debt. In response, Congress passed the Williams Act in 1968. This act regulates the timing and process of "tender offers" (in which an acquiring firm agrees to buy every share of stock of a target firm at some announced price, often far in excess of the previous trading price of such stock). In the years since, about 40 states have passed further legislation regulating takeovers of firms incorporated within their borders.

In this chapter, we delve more deeply into the alleged merits and demerits of the corporate wheeling and dealing that so preoccupies business leaders and policymakers. Before we do, however, we want to clarify some terms. There are many ways by which the control of corporate assets changes hands; in what follows, we are concerned with transactions by which the assets of two (or more) previously independent firms are somehow *integrated*. There is little practical difference between a *merger* and an *acquisition*, although the former term most often is reserved to describe transactions that result in a wholly new firm, while the latter refers to transactions in which one firm is absorbed by another. Mergers and acquisitions may be either *friendly* or *hostile*. In friendly exchanges, all sides recognize some advantage in consolidation. Generally, bargaining among the affected parties produces some agreement about the terms of the exchange and the postexchange structure of the firm even before the consolidation is formally announced. (Of course, an agreement announced is not necessarily an agreement executed; the antitrust authorities may contest the transaction.) In takeovers described as hostile, the directors and managers of the target firm may regard either the proposed consolidation or its terms with disfavor; they employ various strategies to prevent the takeover entirely or delay it until the terms are improved.

Mergers and acquisitions may also be classified as *horizontal, vertical,* or *conglomerate*. Consider the production process as a ladder, with each rung a different level of production. The first rung might be obtaining raw materials; the second, refining these materials into usable form; the third, using these materials to manufacture finished goods; the fourth, selling these goods. Horizontal mergers involve firms on the same rung of this production ladder, while vertical mergers involve firms that occupy different rungs. Conglomerate mergers or acquisitions, by contrast, involve firms with little or nothing in common, i.e., firms on different ladders entirely. Of course, the lines between these classifications can sometimes become blurred. Generally speaking, however, conglomerate mergers or acquisitions are less likely to run afoul of the antitrust laws than horizontal or vertical transactions are, for the obvious reason that conglomerate transactions often pose little danger of seriously diminishing competitive vigor within some well-defined product or geographic market. Some have argued, however, that when such transactions become very large in dollar terms, the antitrust authorities should intervene to prevent aggregate concentration from increasing. Such intervention, it is argued, would prevent "overcentralization" of economic decision making and keep the scales of political power from tilting unfairly toward "big business."

In the next section, we discuss some of the rationales used to explain or justify mergers and acquisitions. We then outline public policy toward horizontal, vertical, and conglomerate mergers. Finally, we discuss Williams Act regulation of corporate takeovers and some of the empirical evidence on the economic effects of takeover activity.

MOTIVES FOR MERGERS AND ACQUISITIONS

Firms might wish to merge for many reasons, and not all are held equal in the eyes of scholars and policymakers. In the following list, these reasons are classified according to whether they are anti- or pro-efficiency, i.e., whether they will likely damage or enhance consumer welfare and the efficient functioning of the market economy. Unfortunately, real-world mergers can't always be neatly classified as bad or good. Often the potential social costs or benefits of a merger are hard to divine before the fact. What is more, many mergers *mix* costs and benefits in uncertain measure. Thus, the conduct of merger policy will be more complicated and vexing than our simple classification scheme might suggest.

Antiefficiency Motives

Acquiring Monopoly Power As we saw in Chapter 7, there is a strong incentive for competing firms to collude to restrict output, boost price, and earn monopoly profits. Such collusion is illegal, of course, but even if it were not (or if enforcement were lax), there are many obstacles to successful collusion, among them a strong temptation to cheat on any cartel agreement that might be reached. Such cheating will reduce the size of the industry profit pie, but might enable the cheater to enjoy a larger slice of this pie. One possible way to eliminate cheating is for rival firms to combine into a single entity. It might be as (or more) difficult to reach agreement about the terms of a merger as to draw up a cartel agreement, but once a merger is consummated, the incentive to cheat vanishes. After ownership shares in the merged firm are established, there is no way for one owner to gain by bidding customers away from others: If the merged firm's profit pie shrinks, all its owners suffer. In addition, detailed information about costs and capacity can be readily exchanged intrafirm, making it much easier to determine profit-maximizing prices and assign output rates across plants than would be possible in a mere cartel.

While vertical or conglomerate mergers do not appear to offer similar advantages, such consolidations can also have anticompetitive effects. Vertical mergers pose the problem of *market foreclosure*. If, e.g., a manufacturer acquires a retailer and forces the subsidiary to sell the parent's goods, rival manufacturers are said to be foreclosed from making sales to the "captive" retailer. It is also argued that vertical and conglomerate mergers can create barriers to entry, e.g., by increasing the amount of capital required for a firm to compete successfully at several levels. Both views are controversial and will be discussed in more detail later in this chapter, as we examine specific cases where such issues have been raised.

VIGNETTE 8.1 The Returns to Market Control: The Creation of U.S. Steel

By the late 1890s, the United States had surpassed the United Kingdom as the largest producer of iron and steel in the world. In terms of technical know-how and organizational efficiency, the leading U.S. firm was the Carnegie Steel Company. It was rivaled by the Federal Steel Company. Each held about 15 to 20 percent of the market for steel ingots at the turn of the century. In 1901, Carnegie, Federal, and 10 other iron and steel producers combined with numerous ore producers, steel fabricators, and transport companies to form the U.S. Steel Corporation. In its first full year of operation, the U.S. Steel Corporation produced about two-thirds of all the steel ingots, steel rails, wire nails, tin plate, and wire rods manufactured in the United States.

A 1911 study by the Commission of Corporations estimated that the premerger value of the firms involved was $700 million; after the merger, U.S. Steel estimated its value at $1,400 million. This astonishing doubling of capital values reflected the real earning power of the firm: $1 invested in U.S. Steel in 1901 was worth almost $3 by 1912, while $1 invested in a fund of all stocks grew to only $2 in the same period. What accounts for U.S. Steel's remarkable profitability? Research by Donald Parsons and Edward Ray suggests that the merger gave U.S. Steel effective control of the domestic market for iron and steel products, enabling a sharp run-up of prices.[2]

Price increases might, of course, result from other factors, such as cost or demand increases. Indeed, iron and steel price hikes of about 50 percent *prior* to the merger appear to have been the result of worldwide increases in demand. By 1901, however, U.K. prices had dropped back to more normal levels. But U.S. Steel, protected in the domestic market by tariffs (plus high transport costs) on imported iron and steel, kept its prices high. As evidence that U.S. Steel's prices were above competitive levels, Parsons and Ray note that U.S. Steel charged far less—often, 25 percent less—for its products in international markets.

Although U.S. Steel dominated the domestic iron and steel industry, it was not a pure monopoly. In the view of Parsons and Ray, however, its great size facilitated collusion aimed at restricting price-cutting by other, smaller producers. More important, U.S. Steel owned a large fraction of U.S. iron ore reserves (it produced about 45 percent of domestic ore from 1902 to 1930), plus large quantities of the finest reserves of coking coal, enabling it to inhibit entry by new producers via its control of essential raw materials. Thus, vertical aspects of the merger might have been as important as horizontal ones in giving U.S. Steel the muscle it needed to keep domestic prices above competitive levels in the early decades of the 20th century. In the opinion of Parsons and Ray, the crucial importance of the steel industry in the U.S. economy made this "the most damaging of all mergers in U.S. history."[3]

Managerial Motives: Empire Building Some corporate acquisitions may be motivated by the desires of top managers to enhance their own (rather than their shareholders') personal well-being. The payoff may come in tangible or intangible forms. Increasing the size of an enterprise under one's control may, e.g., make one feel more important or prestigious; indeed, it may even make one a celebrity. Job security may be enhanced by transforming an enterprise to one of such size and complexity that the chief executive officer is "irreplace-

---

[2]Donald O. Parsons and Edward John Ray, "The United States Steel Consolidation: The Creation of Market Control," *Journal of Law and Economics*, 18 (April 1975), pp. 181–219.

[3]Ibid., p. 215.

able." Or if compensation is tied to sales, acquiring a new branch or division may automatically qualify top managers for salary hikes.

A 1986 study by the Conference Board confirms that, on average, the bigger the company, the greater are the rewards to top executives.[4] The Conference Board sampled 883 firms; over half the variation in the pay of these firms' chief executive officers (CEOs) was explained by variation in the size of their firms. Figure 8.2 shows the relationship between firm size (as measured by sales) and executive compensation. The dark line in the figure, fitted via ordinary least-squares regression,[5] measures the general tendency of compensation to rise with firm size. The Conference Board found that in some industries (e.g., commercial banking) as much as two-thirds of the variation in compensation was explained by size alone, while for others (e.g., construction, services) size explained much less of the variation in compensation. In addition, the compensation of executives ranked second through fifth in the corporate hierarchy appeared even more strongly related to firm size than that of the CEO.

Of course, we expect that running larger enterprises is more challenging than running smaller ones; managers of big firms may simply demand higher compensation to make them willing to meet these challenges. The relevant question here is whether a firm's larger size stems from some sound business reason or the desire of top executives for more power, prestige, and income. If the latter, considerable resources will be wasted in identifying acquisition targets and transacting with them. What is more, individuals concerned with acquiring other firms (or fending off unwanted advances) may be less likely to devote their full attention to the efficient management of their own firm.

Avoiding Taxes　The tax laws may contribute to "takeover fever" in two ways. First, current law favors debt over equity financing. Firms may raise capital by either borrowing from various lenders or inducing investors to buy shares. Interest payments to lenders are, of course, deductible expenses of doing business. The dividends commonly paid to shareholders, however, are not. Even if both lenders and shareholders demand roughly the same rate of compensation for use of their funds (perhaps an unrealistic assumption: stocks are often riskier than bonds, and shareholders thus demand higher yields), it will be advantageous for firms to rely more on borrowing for their capital needs, since the after-tax cost of these funds will be lower. Often, takeovers are financed by borrowing (sometimes with high-risk, high-yield bonds called *junk bonds*). As bonds are issued and the proceeds used to buy up shares, debt is substituted for equity. The firm's capital costs fall (and it may appear more profitable), but this stems from the tax code's preference for debt over equity rather than from a real improvement in efficiency.

---

[4]Charles A. Peck, *Top Executive Compensation: 1987 Edition*, The Conference Board, New York, 1986.
[5]For an explanation of regression analysis and techniques, see any introductory statistics text.

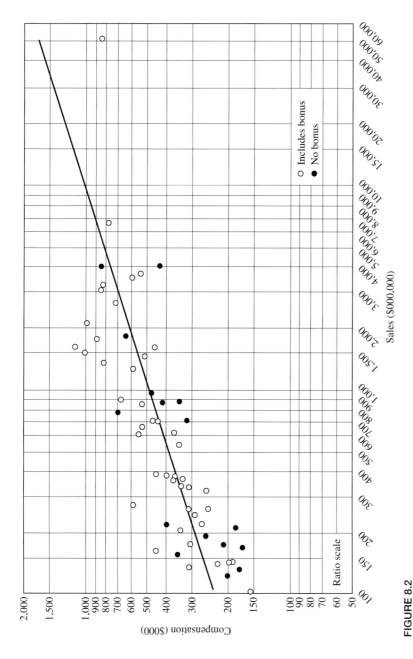

FIGURE 8.2

COMPENSATION OF THE CEO AND COMPANY SALES, 1985. Top executive compensation tends to increase with company size, providing one possible motive for corporate mergers and acquisitions. *Source:* Charles A. Peck, *Top Executive Compensation: 1987 Edition,* The Conference Board, New York, 1986.

In addition, current tax law allows firms to "step up" asset values (i.e., revalue assets at their higher purchase prices) after an acquisition. Often depreciation allowances on certain assets are used up well before these assets exhaust their usefulness. When they are revalued, the value of depreciation allowances increases, and the firm's tax liability falls.

As a result of both these mechanisms, merged firms often reduce their taxes, but, all else unchanged, this merely shifts the tax burden to other firms and individuals. Indeed, since mergers and acquisitions require the use of real resources (e.g., the talents of many attorneys, accountants, and investment bankers), when such activity is wholly motivated by the desire to shift the tax burden, it actually reduces social wealth. For this reason, many argue that limits on takeover activity are warranted or that, at the least, the tax code should be rewritten to eliminate its current bias toward debt-financed takeovers.

Pro-Efficiency Motives

Achieving Economies, Synergy   There are many ways in which mergers or acquisitions might genuinely reduce production costs. Consider an example. Company A makes ingots from molten steel; company B buys these ingots to make them into finished products (pots and pans, tools, etc.). A merger between A and B might save considerable resources. Company B could then move its craftspeople and equipment close to A's facility. Instead of reheating the ingots so steel can be poured into molds or otherwise shaped into final products, the molten steel could be taken directly from A's hearths and worked on by B's craftspeople. Time, energy, and transportation savings would result; in addition, the merged firms could devote fewer resources to bargaining with each other and writing out bills and receipts. Indeed, this integration of production facilities poses such obvious potential for savings that we would probably be surprised to see *non*–integrated firms performing these tasks.

Expanding the scale of an enterprise via merger may yield other economies. Producing more output within a single firm may enable workers to become more specialized, avoiding the waste associated with a situation where workers are "Jacks of all trades but masters of none." In some industries, automation and adoption of mass production technologies may only be feasible when a firm is large relative to the market. Large size may also enable a firm to save on purchases of inputs or transportation services. For example, after John D. Rockefeller had come to own the majority of oil refineries in Cleveland in the late 1800s, he was able to put together "unit trains" entirely made up of tanker cars. Dealing with a single shipper—especially one who put together entire trains that went out on a regular schedule—was cheaper than dealing with many, and the railroads offered Rockefeller rebates to ship his oil with them. Of course, such discounting gave Rockefeller cost advantages that enabled his firm to continue to grow relative to his rivals.

Firms with extensive product lines may also enjoy economies in marketing their goods. Consider two producers of packaged foods that sell their brands in (independently owned) grocery stores. Both producers now have sales representatives who visit the stores' managers to pitch the firms' products, take orders, handle service complaints, etc. Suppose each visit takes 35 minutes and transit between stores takes 25 minutes, so that each company's sales representative services about eight stores per workday. To produce 10,000 store visits per year, each company needs five sales representatives; together, the firms would employ 10 sales representatives. If the producers merged, so that each sales representative handled the products of both firms, a noticeable reduction in sales staff might be possible. Even if each visit now took twice as long, the merged firm could produce 10,000 store visits (accomplishing what 20,000 store visits did for the separate firms) per year with less than eight sales representatives. And if the length of each visit did not quite double (perhaps because the obligatory exchange of pleasantries on meeting the store manager could be done once rather than twice), the merger would produce even greater savings.

Of course, other savings that result from consolidation are far more subtle. In some cases, mergers beget *synergies* that yield a whole that is greater than the sum of its parts (that is, $2 + 2 > 4$). Often such synergistic effects are unexpected or mysterious in nature. For example, at the 1885 World Series of Mule Team Competition in Chicago, the winning team was able to pull 9,000 pounds; the second-place team could pull slightly less. When both teams were hitched together, however, they pulled a 30,000-pound load! At about the same time, a young manager at a company in Death Valley, California, noticed that 12-mule teams could haul loads twice as heavy as could 8-mule teams. He undertook to find the most efficient team size. The results of his experiments would eventually become an international trademark for his employer: "Twenty Mule Team Borax."[6]

Most often we identify synergies with intellectual endeavor rather than the movement of physical objects. A group of scientists, e.g., may be able to generate more new insights (per person) working together than they can working in isolation. Evidently, contact with other thinkers stimulates more creative thought. Mergers, by facilitating useful give-and-take among managers, may sometimes be productive in this sense.

Disciplining Corporate Management   Modern corporations are often far too large to be owned by a single individual or to be run by the individuals who own them. Instead, the owners of a firm (the *principals*) hire managers (their *agents*) to make day-to-day decisions about the way the firm should be run. This separation of ownership and control of large corporations may lead to problems. Owners' agents may not have the same incentive to make efficient decisions and maximize the value of the firm that the owners themselves would have. Agents might shirk work, use some of the firm's profits to feather their own nests rather than enrich the stockholders, be more averse to lucra-

---

[6]From a speech by J. W. Travis, as related by Robert M. Fulmer, *The New Management*, Macmillan, New York, 1974, pp. 132–133.

tive but risky undertakings than the owners might prefer, or fail to maximize long-run firm profits in a host of other ways. Principals, however, might fail to closely monitor their agents (and punish them for any inefficient behavior) because it is costly to do so and there is a free-rider problem: Monitoring the agents would benefit all shareholders, but only the monitors would pay the costs of such activity.

If agents *do* maximize their own well-being at the expense of shareholders' interests, it is argued, their firms will show lackluster earnings. Eventually, this leads some stockholders to dump their shares. This depresses the price of these shares until someone (often dubbed a corporate "raider") senses a chance to profit by turning the company around. This buyer accumulates sufficient shares to vote the old managers out of their jobs and replaces them with new, better-motivated managers; the performance of the firm improves; and so does the price of the firm's stock. The buyer gets a large increase in her or his wealth if this gambit is successful, society benefits from a better-run firm, and everyone is happy—with the exception, of course, of the managers who have lost their jobs. Of course, the mere possibility of such a takeover may spur agents to maximize their shareholders' wealth. Corporate raiders are, some argue, like cops walking a beat: They can have a favorable effect on behavior without actually "making a collar."

The action of this *market for corporate control* is, however, just one possible means by which managers may be prodded to be efficient. There is also a well-developed *market for managers*. In this labor market, individuals are judged by their past performance, and those who develop a reputation for lassitude or self-indulgence will find it difficult to advance. In addition, owners will often find it advantageous to link managers' pay with the performance of the firm's stock price, augmenting salaries with various stock options (which rise sharply in value if the company's stock price exceeds some target) or bonus arrangements. Finally, the above-mentioned free-rider problem may be solved in part by concentrating ownership in relatively few hands, so that each owner has a greater incentive to oversee the firm's operations. One study found that in markets where the business environment is relatively unstable—so that monitoring of agents by principals is more needed—concentration of ownership is far more likely.[7]

Financial Motives: Diversification and Bargain Hunting One of the more important axioms of investment analysis is simple enough to be summarized as a cliché: Don't put all your eggs in one basket. By diversifying, firms can reduce the variability of their earnings and thus the risk of bankruptcy.

Consider the problems faced by owners of merchant vessels in the days of sail (and in the absence of the Coast Guard and radio communications). A ship journeying to far-off ports to trade manufactured goods for tea, spices, or silk might make its owner very wealthy, but weather conditions, pirates, or hid-

---

[7]Harold Demsetz and Kenneth Lehn, "The Structure of Corporate Ownership: Causes and Consequences," *Journal of Political Economy*, 93 (December 1985), pp. 1155–1177.

den reefs could doom the ship and its crew—and bankrupt the owner. Suppose, e.g., that any ship had a 20 percent chance of sinking on a transoceanic voyage. A merchant who risked her or his entire fortune on the voyage of a single ship, then, had a 1-in-5 chance of losing all. If, instead, the merchant sold a half-interest in one ship to an investor and used the proceeds to buy a half-interest in a second ship, there would be only a 1-in-25 chance that *both* ships would be lost. And if the merchant held a one-fifth interest in five separate ships, the probability of losing everything would be infinitesimally small (0.00032, to be precise).

Note that diversification cannot raise the expected return on an investor's holdings. No matter how well diversified our hypothetical merchant may be, she or he will, on average, "win" on four of five ships and "lose" on one of five. (That is, the expected return on investment will be 0.8 times the profits on a successful voyage minus 0.2 times the cost of a lost ship, multiplied by the ownership interest in any ship or ships.) But in investment analysis we are not indifferent to risk. If two investments have the same expected return, most would prefer to hold the one with the lower risk. If, e.g., investment A is equally likely to pay us either $1 million or 0, while investment B is equally likely to pay us either $600,000 or $400,000, most of us would opt for investment B: It offers the same expected return ($500,000), but lower risk. Most of us are, in economics jargon, "risk-averse," though some are "risk-neutral" or even "risk-loving."[8]

Like an investor seeking a diversified portfolio, firms that acquire (or are willingly acquired by) others in unrelated product or geographic markets may be motivated by the desire to reduce profit risk. This, in turn, might reduce a firm's probability of bankruptcy and make it more attractive to lenders or investors.

Of course, there may be more prosaic financial motives for corporate acquisitions. The owners of one firm may believe that another is "undervalued," i.e., may think another firm's stock is worth more than its current owners do, quite apart from any consideration of the efficiency of the firm's management. Unable to resist a bargain, the owners of the first firm use its cash or shares to buy up shares in the second. Thus, what is in fact a routine speculative invest-

---

[8]Financial analysts often measure risk as the standard deviation of an expected stream of earnings, and diversification will reduce this risk when the returns to the components of an investor's portfolio are *uncorrelated*. In general, the standard deviation of returns in a portfolio that contains equal amounts of n securities with uncorrelated returns, denoted S_p, is

$$S_p = \frac{S_i}{\sqrt{n}}$$

where S_i is the standard deviation of returns of the individual securities in the portfolio. If, e.g., each individual security carries a risk (i.e., standard deviation of returns) of 10 percent, the risk on a portfolio of one security will be 10, the risk on a portfolio of two securities will be 7.07, the risk on a portfolio of three securities will be 5.77, etc. Thus, going from a portfolio of one to two securities reduces risk in this example by almost 30 percent, and adding a third security reduces risk by another 18 percent. For a full discussion of these issues, see William F. Sharpe, *Investments*, 2d ed., Prentice-Hall, Englewood Cliffs, NJ, 1981, chapter 6.

ment (an attempt to "buy low, sell high") takes the form of a consolidation or an acquisition.

In addition, firms on the brink of failure may be rescued by an acquirer (hoping, presumably, that it can improve the failing firm's performance). Or, finally, owners of small, closely held firms may wish to sell out upon retirement. Allowing such exit can be pro-competitive even though it reduces the number of firms presently in the industry, for without the possibility of easy exit the incentive to enter the industry will be reduced.

Preventing Opportunism   Relations between firms are often very complex, and occasionally a firm will be vulnerable to opportunistic behavior by another. This is often the case when one firm invests in assets that are *specialized* to a particular use or user. Specialized assets are those that have a much lower value if they must be converted to another use or made available to a different user.

Consider the following example. A miner discovers ore in an isolated area. Unfortunately, the cost of transporting the ore to market via trucks is high—so high, in fact, that at current prices he would barely break even unless some cheaper method of transport were found. Aware that it is usually cheaper to move freight that has a low value-to-weight ratio by rail than by truck, the miner approaches a railroad company about building a spur line to the area. He offers to pay a generous price—equal to what his consultants tell him would be the amortized costs of building the line plus the costs of operating it, including a tidy profit—for each carload of ore the railroad carries from his mine.

To his surprise, however, the railroad manager refuses to make a commitment to build such a line. She recognizes that such a line would be a highly specialized asset. Once constructed, it could be used only to transport ore from (and supplies to) this isolated area. She fears that the miner might renege on his promise to pay such a high price to transport ore on the line. If he "cries poverty" and says he can only afford to pay a lower price, or shuts down the mine for a while, or convinces some other railroad to build a second line and ships all his ore on it, she will be stuck with an unprofitable line. To protect against these possibilities, she draws up a contract that specifies that the miner must ship all his ore with her railroad for a period of, say, 25 years. And given that a lot can happen over 25 years, the manager insists on having a "cost escalator" clause written into the contract, under which the miner will absorb any increases in fuel or labor costs over the contract period.

But now the miner is reluctant to commit. He recognizes that the cost escalator clause is an invitation to the railroad manager to hire redundant workers (at extravagant wages). And what if there is a rail strike or other interruption in service? He would be prevented from shipping ore by any other means, which might cost him a great deal of money. The two parties are at an impasse.

Such difficulties might be resolved by having a team of lawyers draw up a more detailed contract, one aimed at protecting each party from any harm that might come from the actions of the other (whether such harm is intended or not). But lawyers are not cheap, and both the miner and railroad manager might wonder whether even the most ingenious lawyer will be able to anticipate all possible contingencies. The two parties might, therefore, avoid the costs and uncertainty of contracting by *consolidating*. The miner might exchange his ore holdings for some railroad stock, and the construction of the spur line could proceed. The merger removes each party's incentive to behave opportunistically (i.e., to alter the terms of a transaction to his or her own advantage) toward the other. One has no reason to cheat oneself. Alternatively, the miner might decide to build his own rail line. This is vertical integration—of mining and transportation—without merger.

In general, there is potential for opportunism whenever (1) trading involves specialized investments that will decline in value if the terms of trade are altered, (2) there is uncertainty or imperfect information about the future intentions or abilities of a trading partner, and (3) explicit contracts are ineffectual, perhaps because they are too costly to specify or enforce. Suppose a line of output can be sold for R, but requires the seller to pay certain nonsalvageable (or sunk) costs C_{ns} plus remaining costs C. The seller's expected profits π are then

$$\pi = R - C_{ns} - C$$

In the context of the above example, R might be the revenues associated with the miner's offer price, C_{ns} the nonsalvageable costs of laying track to the isolated mine, and C the line's operating costs. The railroad manager rationally fears that once the track is laid, the miner might reduce the price he is willing to pay, reducing the net returns on investment. Once such sunk costs have been incurred, they will be irrelevant to decisions at the margin; i.e., as long as the railroad receives revenues greater than operating costs *once the track has been laid*, it will operate the line. An opportunistic miner could reduce his payments to the railroad by an amount up to $D < R - C$ and still be confident that rail service would continue. Opportunism of this kind would reduce a seller's realized return π' to

$$\pi' = R - C_{ns} - C - D$$

which could be negative.[9] Of course, a rational seller will avoid making the investment C_{ns} without some protection from opportunism of this kind.

---

[9]Suppose, in the railroad example, R = \$25 million, C_{ns} = \$10 million, and C = \$10 million, so that π = \$5 million. Once C_{ns} is incurred and the track is built, the miner may come to the railroad manager and claim that the current price of shipping via rail will bankrupt him. Unless he is given a discount D = \$14.9 million, he will close the mine altogether. The costs C_{ns} are sunk and irrelevant here. The marginal benefits of operating trains (assuming the miner's claim is not a bluff) are $R - D$ = \$25 million − \$14.9 million = \$10.1 million, and the marginal costs are C = \$10 million. Accordingly, the railroad should make the best of a bad situation by submitting to the miner's opportunism. Submitting reduces the railroad's total net returns to −\$9.9 million = \$25 million − \$10 million − \$10 million − \$14.9 million. Allowing the line to sit idle would reduce net returns to −\$10 million, the costs C_{ns} of laying the track.

The conduct of business does not always *require* a firm to place specialized (sometimes called *specific*) assets at risk. But often production costs will be lower with such assets in place than without them. In this example, it is cheaper to transport ore by rail than by truck; if the problems of potential opportunism can somehow be solved, resources can be saved. In general, when conditions require specialized assets to achieve low-cost production, vertical integration is more likely.[10]

VIGNETTE 8.2   Integration and Asset Specificity: Some Evidence

Research has confirmed that asset specificity and the associated problem of opportunism have an important effect on firms' decisions about the way to organize production.

Kirk Monteverde and David Teece examined vertical integration in the automotive industry.[11] Designing new vehicle models and parts is a complex, lengthy process. This process will often give rise to specialized, nonpatentable know-how. Once a supplier acquires transaction-specific know-how, automakers such as GM and Ford will be susceptible to opportunistic "recontracting" by the supplier (or conceivably suppliers may be susceptible to opportunism by the automakers). Monteverde and Teece found that automakers are much more likely to produce parts "in house" where such considerations might arise, and they concluded that vertical integration by U.S. automakers is based at least in part on the desire to cope with potential opportunism problems.

In a study of the railroad industry, Thomas Palay found that when transactions involve specialized investments, carriers and shippers protect these investments in several ways, including integration, quite consistent with the theory discussed above. For example, some chemical companies ship their products in rail tank cars or hopper cars. These cars are specialized to a particular substance; using a car to carry chemical X one week and Y another will adversely affect product quality and may even be hazardous. Understandably, railroad operators are reluctant to invest in rolling stock so specialized to a single cargo or user, so most chemical companies buy their own railcars; indeed, one firm examined by Palay owned over 10,000 such cars.[12]

Scott Masten studied the organization of production in the aerospace industry. Many components of rockets and satellites (e.g., circuit boards) are custom-designed for a single use or user, while others (e.g., transistors) are more standardized. Masten found that standardized components are usually bought from outside suppliers, but market exchange of customized or specialized inputs is far more rare; users of these products usually make them themselves.[13]

---

[10]See Benjamin Klein, Richard G. Crawford, and Armen A. Alchian, "Vertical Integration, Appropriable Rents and the Competitive Contracting Process," *Journal of Law and Economics*, 21 (October 1978), pp. 297–326; Oliver E. Williamson, "Transaction-Cost Economics: The Governance of Contractual Relations," *Journal of Law and Economics*, 22 (October 1979), pp. 233–261.

[11]Kirk Monteverde and David J. Teece, "Supplier Switching Costs and Vertical Integration in the Automobile Industry," *Bell Journal of Economics*, 13 (Spring 1982), pp. 206–213.

[12]Thomas Palay, "Comparative Institutional Economics: The Governance of Rail-Freight Contracting," *Journal of Legal Studies*, 13 (June 1984), pp. 265–287.

[13]Scott E. Masten, "The Organization of Production: Evidence from the Aerospace Industry," *Journal of Law and Economics*, 27 (October 1984), pp. 403–417.

Erin Anderson and David Schmittlein studied how firms in the electronic components industry sell their products. Such firms have two choices: They can use their
own sales personnel or contract with an independent "manufacturers' representative" who might sell the products of several (noncompeting) firms. Some products in
this industry are sufficiently complex or unique that substantial training might be
required before an individual could successfully sell them. In some cases, sales personnel might even have access to "inside information" about a product that might
put the firm at a competitive disadvantage if word got out. In other words, some
products require the creation of "specialized *human* capital." Anderson and
Schmittlein found that firms use their own employees more, and independent sales-
people less, as the amount of specialized capital involved in a particular product or
firm rises.[14]

Of course, integration is not the only way to solve opportunism problems.
Alternatively, a party with the potential for opportunistic behavior might be
required to post collateral which would be forfeited if such behavior occurred.
If the collateral exceeds the party's potential gains from opportunism, the
incentive for such behavior evaporates. The posting of forfeitable collateral
bonds is commonplace in many industries, most notably in contracting for
security services (where the potential for opportunism by the security firm is
obvious). But formal bonding mechanisms can have the same shortcomings as
explicit contracts (e.g., they require detailed language to determine what types
of opportunism will result in bond forfeiture and often rely on a third party—
the courts—for enforcement); thus, they will sometimes be unworkable.

According to Oliver Williamson, however, many kinds of trading agreements may actually be informal bonding mechanisms.[15] Suppose, e.g., firm A
would be vulnerable to opportunism if it agreed to make product X for B—
perhaps because A would have to invest in certain specialized assets before it
could produce X. Firm A might protect itself by demanding that B make itself
equally vulnerable to opportunism by A; that is, firm A might demand that B
make equivalent specialized investments, perhaps to produce product Y for A.
Making the exchange of one good contingent on the exchange of some other is
called *reciprocal dealing*. In Williamson's view, reciprocal agreements can create
a "mutual-reliance relation" binding transactors together. If either tries to
engage in opportunism, the other can sever the relationship, and *both* will suffer losses. Since both firms have the capacity to harm the other in equal measure, neither does so. (This is like nuclear deterrence, where the likelihood of
"mutual assured destruction" convinces each superpower *not* to attack the
other.) Of course, the possibility of structuring reciprocal arrangements will be
greater for more diversified firms, which may suggest another motive for conglomerate mergers. More will be said about this issue later. The crucial point is
that forestalling opportunism—by vertical integration or bonding or some other
arrangement—can promote exchange and enhance efficiency. See Table 8.1.

[14]Erin Anderson and David C. Schmittlein, "Integration of the Sales Force: An Empirical
Examination," *Rand Journal of Economics*, 15 (Autumn 1984), pp. 385–395.
[15]Oliver E. Williamson, "Credible Commitments: Using Hostages to Support Exchange,"
American Economic Review, 73 (September 1983), pp. 519–540.

TABLE 8.1
MOTIVES FOR MERGER—A SUMMARY

Antiefficiency motives

Firms' desire to acquire monopoly power, foreclose markets to rivals, or raise entry barriers
Managers' desire to enhance their utility or compensation by "empire building"
Acquirers' desire to reduce integrated firm's tax liability by increasing reliance on debt financing

Pro-efficiency motives

Firms' desire to reduce costs via realization of scale or marketing economies, synergies
Acquirers' desire to realize gains from replacing underperforming management (thus, "market for
corporate control" checks managerial abuse)
Owners' or managers' desire to diversify and reduce risk, hunt for "bargains," or accommodate
retirement of one set of owners
Firms' interest in forestalling opportunism problems in supply relationships

ANTITRUST AND HORIZONTAL MERGERS

As we noted in Chapter 7, the Sherman Act's prohibition of collusive action encouraged mergers, kicking off the first great U.S. merger wave in the early 1900s. In 1914, Congress responded with the Clayton Act, the stated purpose of which was "to arrest the creation of trusts, conspiracies and monopolies in their incipiency and before consummation." Section 7 of the act banned potentially anticompetitive mergers, but it soon was shown to have huge loopholes. For example, in 1926 the Supreme Court ruled that section 7 applied only to mergers in which one firm acquired the *stock* of another, and not to acquisitions of *physical assets* (i.e., plant and equipment).[16] Subsequent cases made it clear that reform was in order if section 7 was to have any practical effect.[17]

The loopholes in section 7 were closed in 1950 with passage of the Celler-Kefauver Act. This act amended the language of section 7 to prohibit anticompetitive acquisitions of either the stock or the assets of another firm. Further, by banning acquisitions that would "lessen competition or tend to create a monopoly *in any line of commerce in any section of the country*," the act left no doubt that section 7 should apply not only to horizontal but also to vertical and conglomerate mergers.

The only significant modification of the antimerger statutes since 1950 has been the Hart-Scott-Rodino Act of 1976. The Hart-Scott-Rodino Act was inspired by the observation that it often takes years for the government to prove that a merger is anticompetitive and illegal. Over time, the merged entities become entwined in countless ways, and a divestiture of the acquired firm or firms is often difficult or impossible, like "unscrambling an egg." Hart-Scott-Rodino requires that the FTC and the Antitrust Division of the

---

[16]*Thatcher Manufacturing Co. v. FTC*, 272 U.S. 554 (1926).

[17]See, e.g., *International Shoe Co. v. FTC*, 280 U.S. 291 (1930) and *Arrow-Hart and Hegeman Electric Co. v. FTC*, 291 U.S. 584 (1934).

Department of Justice must receive 30 days' advance notice of acquisitions in which one party has worldwide sales or assets of $100 million or more and the other party has sales or assets of $10 million or more. The interagency liaison committee of the FTC and Justice Department can then decide whether to contest the acquisition or can request additional time and information to evaluate the proposal.

Key Horizontal Merger Cases

It was soon clear that the Celler-Kefauver amendment had given section 7 of the Clayton Act real force. Through the 1950s and into the late 1960s, it became steadily more difficult for rivals of any appreciable size to merge. In the 1970s, though, the tide of antimerger sentiment began to ebb slightly. And in the 1980s new merger guidelines gave firms more latitude in this area than they had enjoyed for some time.

Bethlehem Steel-Youngstown (1958) In 1956, Bethlehem Steel, the nation's second largest steelmaker with a 15 percent market share, acquired all the assets of Youngstown Sheet and Tube, ranked sixth with a 5 percent market share. The two firms argued that they sold their products in different geographic markets (Bethlehem in the east and west, Youngstown in the midwest) and were not truly competitors and that the merger would not damage competition in the steel market. In addition, they argued that as a merged entity they would be better able to compete with U.S. Steel, the nation's largest steelmaker with a 30 percent market share.

The district court rejected both arguments. It disputed the defendants' claims that no direct rivalry existed between them, and the court was suspicious of Bethlehem's contention that its acquisition of Youngstown was the only possible way it could enter U.S. Steel's midwest territory. (These suspicions proved correct: A few years later, Bethlehem would construct a large integrated steel facility 30 miles east of Chicago.) In any event, the court held that the possibility that the merged firm would be a more formidable rival for U.S. Steel in the midwest was irrelevant given that it would lessen competition elsewhere:

> If the merger offends the statute in any relevant market then good motives and even demonstrable benefits are irrelevant and afford no defense. . . .
> A merger may have a different impact in different markets—but if the proscribed effect is visited on one or more relevant markets then it matters not what the claimed benefits may be elsewhere.[18]

Such language gave a major boost to government efforts to limit horizontal mergers. Although *Bethlehem* was not appealed to the Supreme Court, its major precedents would soon be upheld in another case.

---

[18]*United States v. Bethlehem Steel Corp.*, 168 F. Supp. 576 (1958), pp. 617–618.

Brown Shoe (1962)   In 1955, Brown Shoe Co. purchased Kinney Shoe, an acquisition that combined horizontal and vertical aspects. Both Brown and Kinney were shoe manufacturers as well as retailers. Brown was the nation's fourth largest shoemaker, with a 4 percent market share, and Kinney was twelfth largest, with a 0.5 percent market share. Brown ranked third among shoe retailers by sales volume, while Kinney ranked eighth.

As the above figures hint, there was little structural evidence of monopoly in the shoe industry (although perhaps the relevant markets were not national but regional). In manufacturing, the top two dozen producers accounted for only 35 percent of market sales. And there were few evident barriers to entry in retailing, with many thousands of independent sellers competing successfully with the large chain stores. Nevertheless, the Supreme Court invalidated the merger. The Court was persuaded that in some cities Brown-Kinney's combined market share would be excessive (e.g., in six cities the firms' combined share of the children's shoe market exceeded 40 percent). What is more, the Court worried that if it approved a merger "achieving 5 percent control . . . we might be required to approve future merger efforts . . . seeking similar market shares. The oligopoly Congress sought to avoid would then be furthered and it would be difficult to dissolve the combinations previously approved."[19] Thus, the case established that horizontal mergers could be banned—even in markets where competition was vigorous—in order to forestall future increases in concentration, i.e., *to head off monopoly in its incipiency.*

PNB (1964)   In 1960, Philadelphia National Bank (PNB) attempted to acquire Girard Bank. This merger between the second and third largest of Philadelphia's 42 commercial banks would have increased the fraction of deposits held in the city's four largest banks to 78 percent. A district court ruled that the relevant geographic market was the entire New York-Philadelphia region and that the merger would not significantly reduce competition under this broader market definition. In addition, it held that mergers in the banking industry were not within the federal courts' jurisdiction, but were regulated by the states. The Supreme Court overturned this decision, holding that banks enjoyed no immunity from federal antitrust laws. Opting for a narrower market definition, the Court stated that a merger which "results in a significant increase in concentration of firms . . . is so inherently likely to lessen competition substantially that it must be enjoined in the absence of evidence clearly showing that the merger is not likely to have such anti-competitive effects."[20] In other words, mergers that yield markedly increased market concentration are presumptively bad, i.e., firms attempting such mergers are guilty until proved innocent.

Von's (1966)   In 1960, Von's Grocery Co. acquired Shopping Bag Food Stores, another Los Angeles-area food retailer. The Los Angeles market was

---

[19]*Brown Shoe Co. v. United States,* 370 U.S. 294 (1962), pp. 343–344.
[20]*United States v. Philadelphia National Bank,* 374 U.S. 321 (1964), p. 363.

unconcentrated, and neither firm was especially large; their combined market share would have been 7.5 percent. Von's argued that the merger could not harm competition in the Los Angeles area and might help it by enabling Von's to compete more successfully against the city's largest grocer, Safeway. The Supreme Court disagreed, and Justice Black's opinion illustrates how much the Court had been influenced by scholarly work that links concentration with inferior market performance and how much it had come to view the antitrust laws as a source of protection for small business rather than for competition itself:

> [T]he basic purpose of the 1950 Celler-Kefauver Act was to prevent economic concentration in the American economy by keeping a large number of small competitors in business. In stating the purposes of their bill, both of its sponsors . . . emphasized their fear, widely shared by other members of Congress, that this concentration was rapidly driving the small businessman out of the market.[21]

The number of owner-operated grocery stores in Los Angeles had fallen by one-third over the period from 1950 to 1963, and the Court saw its order that Von's divest Shopping Bag as a way to limit this trend. But as Justice Stewart noted in a stinging dissent, the number of competitors may have nothing to do with competition. Stewart criticized the majority decision as "a requiem for the so-called 'Mom-and-Pop' grocery stores" and an attempt to "roll back the supermarket revolution."[22] As subsequent events have shown, such strict application of the antimerger laws did little to slow this revolution, much less roll it back. Massive economies of scale in food retailing have made the chain supermarket a central feature of U.S. life; the contraction in the number of independent grocers has had no noticeable adverse effect on competition.

Citizen Publishing (1969)   The stringent legal standard enunciated in *Von's* effectively doomed most horizontal mergers. Competitors that sought to merge did, however, have one more card to play. In a 1930 decision, the Court had ruled that acquiring a rival headed for bankruptcy or liquidation would be viewed more generously, since the prospect for future competition between such firms was absent.[23] Under this *failing-firm doctrine,* the publishers of the Tucson *Citizen* sought to acquire the *Star,* the only other newspaper in town. The Supreme Court upheld a lower court decision that barred the acquisition, however.[24] The Court stated that for a failing-firm defense to apply, the acquiring firm must be the *only* available purchaser and must show that no successful reorganization of the target company under separate ownership is possible.

General Dynamics (1974)   By the 1970s, the courts began to show greater leniency in horizontal merger cases. The *General Dynamics* case was an impor-

---

[21]*United States v. Von's Grocery Co.,* 384 U.S. 270 (1966), p. 275.
[22]Ibid., p. 288.
[23]*International Shoe Co. v. FTC,* 280 U.S. 291 (1930).
[24]*Citizen Publishing Co. v. United States,* 394 U.S. 131 (1969).

tant milestone in this journey away from the strict application of structural criteria exemplified by *Von's*.

Through a subsidiary that dug coal from deep-shaft mines, General Dynamics had acquired a controlling interest in United Electric Coal, a strip miner. The government claimed that the combined firms held 12.4 percent of the midwestern regional market and 23.2 percent of a submarket centered in Illinois. Both figures far exceeded the threshold the Supreme Court had found objectionable in *Von's*. General Dynamics argued, however, that the government's definition of the market was faulty because it was based on current sales rather than proven reserves of coal or the portion of these reserves not yet sold under long-term contracts. By such alternative measures, United's apparent size shrank considerably: Many of its mines, their reserves depleted, had been closed by the time of the trial, and over 90 percent of its remaining reserves were committed under long-term contracts.

The Supreme Court (by a narrow 5-4 majority) found for General Dynamics.[25] Despite the fact that the government presented data showing that the number of firms in the industry was declining, the Court held that firm-specific factors ought to override evidence on industrywide structure. Accepting the defendant's argument that measures of market share should properly be based on uncommitted reserves, the Court ruled that General Dynamics' absorption of United could not meaningfully lessen competition since the latter had "presold" so much of its reserves that it was not a significant rival, whatever current sales figures said.

The 1980s: Justice Department Merger Guidelines

Movement away from the rigid application of market share rules continued in the FTC's *Pillsbury* decision.[26] And in the early 1980s, several mergers that yielded regional market shares far in excess of that which put Von's in antitrust trouble were permitted. In the oil industry, Standard Oil Co. of California acquired Gulf Oil (in a transaction worth $13.2 billion), Mobil acquired Superior Oil, and Texaco acquired Getty in 1984 alone. On the other hand, mergers between Schlitz and Heileman (at the time, the fourth and fifth largest brewers in the United States) and between Warner Communications and Polygram Records (which could have yielded Warner one-quarter of the record market) were successfully challenged.

To clarify policy in this area, the Justice Department issued a comprehensive set of merger guidelines in 1982 and revised them in 1984. Under earlier 1968 guidelines, the Justice Department had warned that it would challenge horizontal mergers in markets where the four-firm concentration ratio CR exceeded 75 percent, an acquiring firm's market share exceeded 15 percent, and the target firm's market share exceeded 1 percent. When the four-firm CR was less than 75 percent, the acquiring firm could hold up to a 30 percent mar-

---

[25]*United States v. General Dynamics Corp.*, 415 U.S. 486 (1974).
[26]*In the Matter of the Pillsbury Co.*, 93 F.T.C. 966 (1979).

ket share. The newer guidelines employ the Herfindahl index (discussed in Chapter 6) instead of the CR to measure market structure. Additional structural factors (e.g., ease of entry, turnover rates, market growth) are also considered in determining whether a merger will be challenged. In addition, the relevant market for the merging firms' product(s) is defined using a 5 *percent test*: If a 5 percent price hike causes many buyers to purchase certain substitute products, these products must be counted as part of the relevant market. Finally, the 1984 revisions stress that cost savings or *efficiencies* might be used to justify mergers that could otherwise be ruled illegal, a major departure from earlier standards. (Indeed, in earlier eras the prospect that the merged firm might have lower costs was often regarded as a reason to ban a merger, for these cost savings would put smaller rivals at a competitive disadvantage.)

In deciding whether to challenge a proposed merger, the Justice Department's first task is to define the relevant antitrust markets involved. The aforementioned 5 percent test will be crucial here, although the test can produce an excessively broad or narrow market definition in some circumstances, and the Department's analysts are free to exercise their own judgment in its application. Suppose, e.g., there is a proposed merger of two Atlanta-based producers of wood paneling. A 5 percent price increase in the price of wood paneling in the southeast might cause (1) some southeastern buyers of paneling to buy other products (e.g., drywall), (2) some southeastern producers of other products to switch over to paneling production, or (3) some producers of paneling in other regions to start shipping their goods to the southeast. Using elasticity measures, the Justice Department's analysts can estimate whether the extent of such *demand substitution, supply substitution,* or *geographic diversion* will be sufficient to make such a price hike unprofitable within a certain allotted time (usually, 1 year). If so, then the product or geographic market can be broadened to take account of such substitution or diversion. In our example, if it is found that so many consumers substitute drywall for paneling when paneling prices rise that such a price rise would be unprofitable, then the product market will be defined to include both products and the market shares will be calculated accordingly.

Given market share data for the relevant product and geographic markets, the Department assesses the competitive effects of a merger in accord with a flowchart like that in Figure 8.3. There is first a *leading-firm test*. The leading firm in an industry can acquire no firm with a market share exceeding 1 percent if the leading firm's market share exceeds 35 percent and is twice that of the second leading firm. If this test is passed, or if the leading firm in the market is not involved in the merger, then the Justice Department examines the merger's impact on market structure as measured by changes in the Herfindahl index (HI). In unconcentrated markets, where the (postmerger) HI is less than 1,000, a challenge is unlikely. In moderately concentrated markets, where HI lies between 1,000 and 1,800, challenges are likely only when the merger will produce an increase in HI in excess of 100 points. In highly concentrated markets, where HI exceeds 1,800, mergers that increase HI by 100 points will be challenged (except in extraordinary circumstances); mergers

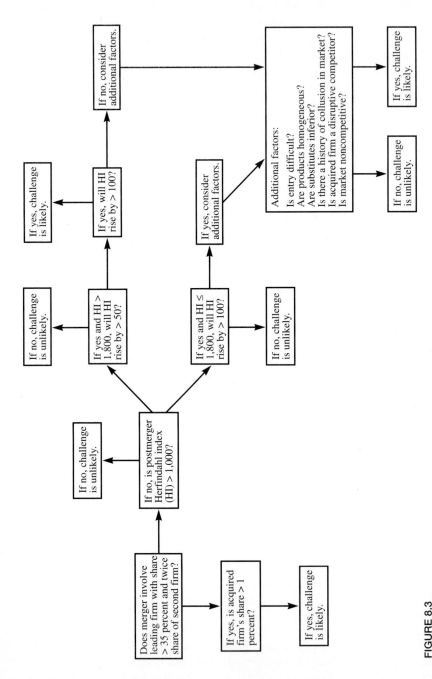

FIGURE 8.3
DEPARTMENT OF JUSTICE ENFORCEMENT POLICIES FOR HORIZONTAL MERGERS. Issued in 1982 and revised in 1984, the Justice Department's horizontal merger guidelines make it relatively easy to predict whether a proposed merger will be challenged.

that increase HI by less than 50 points are unlikely to be challenged. In between (HI rises by 50 to 100 points), challenges are likely unless entry is easy or other structural factors suggest competition is quite strong.

These guidelines, coupled with the Hart-Scott-Rodino premerger notification requirements, have made it relatively easy for merger partners to predict whether they will be the target of an enforcement action by either the Department of Justice or the FTC, greatly reducing the likelihood of costly litigation. In fact, even as the 1980s saw a sharp increase in merger activity, there was a decline in the volume of merger litigation; less than 1 percent of reported mergers provoked government enforcement actions. In many cases, antitrust authorities and merger partners sat down and worked out terms under which the deal could be made acceptable. Thus, antitrust authorities have become *regulators* in a very real sense: They affect business conduct not merely via litigation, but also by devising standards and negotiating compliance with these standards directly with the firms involved.

Note that not all antitrust scholars applaud every element of these guidelines. Franklin Fisher and Richard Schmalensee, e.g., criticize the fact that the 5 percent test is based on increases from current prices. They argue that the test might show that further price increases on some item or in some area are impossible, but that this may simply mean that the industry was already charging the monopoly price. Thus, the standard might prevent further deterioration of the competitive environment but lead authorities to miss a chance to improve this environment. Fisher is also uncomfortable with the Justice Department's willingness to consider potential efficiencies in deciding whether to challenge a merger. He worries that such cost savings are easier to promise than to deliver in fact and that phantom efficiencies will excuse mergers that are significantly anticompetitive.[27]

ANTITRUST AND VERTICAL MERGERS

In vertical mergers, the courts and antitrust authorities have long been worried about *market foreclosure*. If, e.g., a producer of flour acquires a bakery and then uses its own flour in all its baked products, rival flour producers are said to be foreclosed from competing for this bakery's business. Alternatively, if the flour producer integrates "backward" and acquires a grower of wheat, it might be accused of foreclosing rival millers from a source of supply.

In the pre-World War II era, it was common to argue that vertical mergers, because they almost invariably posed the likelihood of some degree of market foreclosure, should be judged per se illegal. In one 1947 case, the Supreme Court appeared to agree.[28] By the next year, however, in the *Columbia Steel* case, the Court eschewed such an inflexible standard, stating that "it seems

---

[27]For a useful overview of these issues, see Steven C. Salop, "Symposium on Mergers and Antitrust," Lawrence J. White, "Antitrust and Merger Policy: Review and Critique," Franklin M. Fisher, "Horizontal Mergers: Triage and Treatment," and Richard Schmalensee, "Horizontal Merger Policy: Problems and Changes," *Journal of Economic Perspectives*, 1 (Fall 1987), pp. 3–54.

[28]*United States v. Yellow Cab Co.*, 332 U.S. 218 (1947).

clear to us that vertical integration, as such without more, cannot be held violative of the Sherman Act."[29] In *Columbia*, a subsidiary of U.S. Steel had bought out a tiny competitor. The government, lacking confidence in the strength of section 7 of the Clayton Act, had pressed a Sherman Act suit. But the Court could find no significant lessening of competition in the acquisition of such a trivially small firm. Henceforth, this rule-of-reason approach would be applied to all vertical acquisitions (even after Celler-Kefauver put some bite into the Clayton Act).

Key Cases

du Pont (1957)   From 1917 to 1919, well before General Motors (GM) became the nation's largest automobile producer, the du Pont chemical company acquired 23 percent of GM's stock. Thirty years later, the Justice Department alleged that du Pont's interest in GM significantly lessened competition in the market for the paints and fabrics used in manufacturing automobiles. Specifically, the government argued that the stock link between the two firms meant that GM was obliged to buy its paints and fabrics from du Pont, effectively foreclosing other firms from GM's business.

But du Pont argued that, despite its ownership of a sizable block of GM stock, GM often bought from other companies. Indeed, du Pont supplied only about one-half of GM's fabric requirements and two-thirds of its paint requirements. And du Pont sought to sell GM other products without notable success. But the Court found this reasoning unpersuasive, for it had *prima facie* evidence that at least one competitor had been foreclosed from GM's business:

> [GM's] then-principal paint supplier, Flint Varnish and Chemical Works, early in 1918 saw the handwriting on the wall. The Flint president came to [du Pont] asking to be bought out, telling [du Pont] . . . that he 'knew du Pont had bought a substantial interest in General Motors and was interested in the paint industry [and] that . . . [he] felt he would lose a valuable customer, General Motors.' The du Pont Company bought the Flint works and later dissolved it.[30]

To the Court, this was sufficient proof that the stock link gave du Pont a competitive advantage that other paint and fabric firms did not share and thus violated section 7. (After retrial and subsequent appeal, however, it wasn't until 1961—43 years after it had begun buying GM stock—that du Pont was finally ordered to divest these shares. Clearly, section 7 could be a "sleeping giant.")

Brown Shoe (1962)   The acquisition of Kinney Shoe by Brown Shoe Co., discussed earlier in the context of horizontal merger, also had important vertical elements, since both companies were manufacturers as well as retailers. This raised the issue of foreclosure, and the Court found it clear "from the testimony of Brown's president that Brown would use its ownership of Kinney to

---

[29]*United States v. Columbia Steel Co.*, 334 U.S. 495 (1948), p. 525.
[30]*United States v. E. I. du Pont de Nemours & Co.*, 353 U.S. 586 (1957), pp. 603–604.

force [emphasis added] Brown shoes into Kinney stores."[31] Smaller, less integrated manufacturers would thus be at a disadvantage; that would be enough to invalidate the merger. It is interesting to note, however, that the Court recognized that the integration had the potential to produce some real cost savings which might reduce prices to consumers. Yet such efficiencies were given little weight:

> [W]e cannot fail to recognize Congress' desire to promote competition through the protection of viable, small, locally owned businesses. Congress appreciated that occasional higher costs and prices might result from the maintenance of fragmented industries and markets. It resolved these competing considerations in favor of decentralization. We must give effect to that decision.[32]

Ford (1972) If the moderate amount of foreclosure possible in *Brown Shoe* posed antitrust problems, it should have been no surprise when the courts invalidated the 1961 acquisition by Ford, the nation's second largest automaker, of Autolite, the second largest producer of spark plugs. Ford's purchases of spark plugs were sizable, and if Autolite's rivals were prevented from making sales to Ford, a district court reasoned, these rivals might not survive. On the other hand, if Autolite were simply ordered divested, it might have a tough time reestablishing itself as a separate firm. The district court thus ordered, and the Supreme Court upheld, a rather unique remedy: In addition to divesting Autolite, Ford was prohibited from manufacturing its own plugs for 10 years and was ordered to buy one-half its plug requirements from Autolite for 5 years.[33]

ITT v. GTE (1975) When GTE, a manufacturer of telephone equipment, purchased several telephone operating companies, ITT, one of GTE's rival equipment producers, sued. ITT argued that GTE's ownership of operating companies foreclosed ITT from sales of equipment in many parts of the country, alleging GTE's subsidiaries could buy their equipment only from their parent company. A district court agreed with ITT and ordered GTE to divest itself of one of its manufacturing divisions and several operating companies. This was the first time the divestiture remedy had been ordered in a private antitrust suit. An appeals court ruled, however, that Congress did not intend to permit private divestiture suits.[34]

Market Foreclosure Analyzed

The courts' preoccupation with foreclosure has been heavily criticized. John McGee, e.g., argues that vertical mergers do not foreclose competition as much

---

[31]*Brown Shoe Co. v. United States*, 370 U.S. 294 (1962), p. 332.

[32]Ibid., p. 344.

[33]*Ford Motor Co. v. United States*, 405 U.S. 562 (1972). To Chief Justice Warren, this remedy seemed more anticompetitive than the merger itself. See his dissent in this case.

[34]*International Telephone and Telegraph Corp. v. General Telephone and Electronics Corporation and Hawaiian Telephone Co.*, 518 F.2d 913 (1975).

as they discomfit competitors, that any real foreclosure will be the result of enhanced efficiency in the merged firm, and that the courts ought to encourage rather than discourage such cost savings.[35]

Consider Brown Shoe Company's acquisition of Kinney. If Brown has a standard U-shaped average total cost (ATC) curve, it will likely have found its optimal scale of operations—at the bottom of its ATC curve—prior to this acquisition. In Figure 8.4, this is shown as the rate of output Q_o. Forcing Kinney to carry Brown's shoes *without* reducing sales to other (independent) retailers will push Brown's output beyond the optimal level, to $Q_o + Q_k$. This will raise Brown's unit costs and prices (from P to P'). Rival manufacturers may not be able to sell to Kinney, but they will find it easy to steal other customers from Brown by keeping their price at P. Indeed, until Brown's output returns to Q_o and its price to P, it will continue to lose old customers to other manufacturers. After this shuffling of clients is concluded, all manufacturers will be left with the same share of the market. Foreclosure is not a real problem here.

If, however, Brown is (premerger) operating on a downward-sloping portion of its ATC curve, its acquisition of Kinney will enable it to permanently expand its market share. But two points must be made here. First, such an expansion in Brown's output and market share is efficient. Exploiting previously unexploited scale economies would save resources. At the least, such savings ought to be weighed against any anticompetitive effects in judging the desirability of the merger. (See, once again, Oliver Williamson's welfare trade-off model discussed in Chapter 6.) Second, the expansion would have occurred with or without the merger; it only awaited Brown's discovery that it could reduce unit costs by expanding sales. Forbidding a merger that merely hastens the inevitable may be a waste of antitrust resources.

But what if Brown's and Kinney's ATC curves are horizontal? First suppose the merger *reduces* these constant unit costs. Then foreclosure will be real: The merged firms will have an advantage over their now-less-efficient rivals and will win expanded market share. But antitrust policy is concerned with improving welfare, not protecting individual competitors. That some firms will lose market share is not sufficient reason to prohibit such a merger. Only if the merged firm will have enough market power to raise prices above competitive levels might the merger be judged harmful, and then the relevant question is whether the potential anticompetitive effects outweigh the efficiency gains. (Again, see the Williamson trade-off discussion in Chapter 6 for a framework to answer this question.)

Only if the firms' horizontal ATC curves remain unchanged will there be no efficiency benefits to weigh against any anticompetitive costs of the merger. In this case, Brown could use its control of Kinney to expand market share without putting itself at a cost disadvantage relative to rivals. But unless Brown's share of the market began to approach dangerous levels—sufficient to give it

[35]John S. McGee, *Industrial Organization*, Prentice-Hall, Englewood Cliffs, NJ, 1988, pp. 276–277.

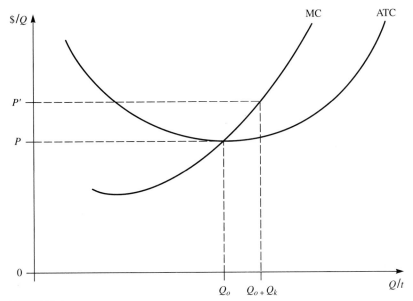

FIGURE 8.4
FORECLOSURE AND U-SHAPED COST CURVES. If a manufacturer at the optimum scale Q_o acquires a retailer in order to expand output (to $Q_o + Q_k$) and foreclose rivals, costs and prices will rise as well (to P'). Rivals will then be able to steal customers from the firm until its output returns to Q_o.

power to raise prices above competitive levels—the welfare costs of such foreclosure are quite limited. Some might argue that the elimination of some independent shoe manufacturers will produce adverse social consequences such as unemployment among managers or workers. But note: If Brown-Kinney can expand its sales without also expanding the number of managers or workers it employs, then the merger *has* in fact produced cost savings. Thus, if cost savings are not present, the merger's ill effects are entirely limited to a reduction in the number of nonintegrated firms. Preserving such firms may have social utility, but it must be remembered that any effort to do so will have costs as well. Antitrust enforcement resources have alternative uses, and they might be better used in a hunt for bigger game than this.

New Vertical Merger Guidelines

Perhaps in recognition of the factors discussed above, the Department of Justice has issued vertical merger guidelines that greatly deemphasize foreclosure considerations. In deciding whether a vertical merger should be challenged, the Department now asks whether (1) vertical integration will facilitate collusion at some level of the production process, (2) the integration will create barriers to entry, and (3) the motive of the merger is the evasion of rate regulation. One important factor in evaluating these issues is the degree of market concentration at the various stages of the production process. HI values in excess of 1,800 (indicating that the relevant market is highly concentrated) in either the primary or upstream markets are likely to produce a challenge from the Justice Department. Challenges are also likely if the acquired firm is an important "disruptive" buyer (i.e., a buyer that competes aggressively on price or other dimensions and therefore makes collusion difficult) or if integration into a secondary market will make it significantly less likely that firms will enter the primary market. Of course, these guidelines, like those for horizontal mergers, simply tell prospective merger partners what one enforcement agency is likely to do. They are not binding on courts and may, in the long run, have little effect on judicial interpretation of section 7.

CONGLOMERATE MERGERS AND HOSTILE TAKEOVERS

As noted earlier, conglomerate mergers pose fewer competitive problems than horizontal and vertical ones. One study showed that from 1951 to 1977 about 1 of every 4 horizontal mergers and 1 of every 7 vertical mergers was challenged, but only 1 of every 50 conglomerate mergers was contested.[36] Perhaps as a result, most mergers these days are conglomerate in nature.

Conglomerate mergers are often divided into three categories. In *pure* conglomerate mergers, firms in entirely unrelated markets join together. In *product extension* mergers, firms extend their operations to product lines where they have no current offerings, but where their products are similar or they might have some familiarity or expertise. An automaker's acquisition of a railroad locomotive manufacturer might be an example of such a merger. In *market extension* mergers, makers of similar or identical products extend their operations to different geographic markets. Acquisition of a Chicago cement maker by a New Orleans cement maker is an example of such a merger. (Note, however, that depending on one's definition of the relevant market, a product or market extension merger can look very much like a horizontal merger.)

Antitrust Considerations

Antitrust authorities typically raise four objections to conglomerate mergers: (1) They may lessen competition by reducing the number of *potential entrants* to a particular market, (2) they may contribute to market foreclosure by facilitating *reciprocal dealing*,[37] (3) the merged firms' deep pockets may enable them to engage in *predatory behavior* against smaller, less diversified rivals, and (4) conglomerate firms will be less likely to compete with each other because they fear that aggressive tactics in one area will beget retaliation in some other field.

---

[36]Source: Willard F. Mueller, "The Celler-Kefauver Act: The First 27 Years," U.S. House of Representatives, Committee on the Judiciary, Subcommittee on Monopolies and Commercial Law, November 7, 1979, p. 13.

[37]Recall that reciprocity was earlier defined as making an agreement to buy (sell) one good contingent on a trading partner's promise to buy (sell) some other good, i.e., "If you scratch my back, I'll scratch yours."

To address the latter two issues, the antitrust authorities have, from time to time, argued that conglomerate mergers should be limited even absent a showing of anticompetitive effect in a specific product line or geographic area. As we shall see, such efforts have not been notably successful. In cases where a conglomerate merger might impair potential competition, however, or might result in reciprocal dealing, antitrust challenges have fared better.

Key Cases

Penn-Olin (1964) In 1960, Pennsalt Chemical and Olin Mathieson embarked on a joint venture, forming a new company, Penn-Olin, to produce and sell sodium chlorate (used to manufacture paper) in the southeast. The market for sodium chlorate was highly concentrated. In the southeast, two of Pennsalt's rivals held a 90 percent market share. The government claimed that both Pennsalt and Olin Mathieson were potential entrants into this market area and that the joint venture therefore lessened competition by eliminating at least one potential rival. A district court disagreed, but the Supreme Court sided with the government, stating:

> The existence of an aggressive, well equipped and well financed corporation engaged in the same or related lines of commerce waiting anxiously to enter an oligopolistic market would be a substantial incentive to competition which cannot be underestimated.[38]

The Supreme Court ordered the district court to investigate the potential competition issue more thoroughly. Even though the district court once again ruled in favor of Penn-Olin, the case established that a possible lessening of potential competition could be a basis for a challenge to a conglomerate merger.

Consolidated Foods (1965) The antitrust authorities have always looked with suspicion on reciprocal arrangements, in part because they appear to inject an "alien and irrelevant factor" into market transactions. If *A* sells its widgets to *B* at least partly because it also makes purchases of some other good from *B*, are not other widget sellers unfairly disadvantaged in trying to make sales to *B*? On this theory, the Federal Trade Commission moved against the practice as early as the 1930s; by 1965, the Supreme Court agreed in *Consolidated Foods* that reciprocity was "one of the congeries of anticompetitive practices at which the antitrust laws are aimed."[39]

In 1951 Consolidated, a diversified food processor, distributor, and retailer, acquired Gentry, a maker of dehydrated onion and garlic products. By 1957, the FTC began investigating complaints that some firms selling to Consolidated were forced to buy their requirements of onion and garlic from Gentry. It is noteworthy that these complaints came from Gentry's chief rival, and *not* from the firms allegedly coerced into buying supplies from Gentry.

[38]*United States v. Penn-Olin Chemical Co.*, 378 U.S. 158 (1964), p. 174.
[39]*FTC v. Consolidated Foods Corp.*, 380 U.S. 592 (1965), p. 598.

The FTC argued that Consolidated's ownership of Gentry gave the latter an unfair advantage over rival onion and garlic producers. There was ample evidence that Consolidated's top executives had contacted many suppliers and suggested reciprocal trades, even threatening to stop buying from firms that did not in turn buy from Gentry. These tactics often won business for Gentry. The Court ruled that the merger thus violated section 7, for it "gave [Consolidated] the advantage of a mixed threat and lure of reciprocal buying in its competition for business and 'the power to foreclose competition from a substantial share of the markets for dehydrated onion and garlic.' "[40]

VIGNETTE 8.3   Reciprocity, Conglomeration, and Opportunism

Consolidated Foods established not only that the prospect of reciprocity could be a basis for challenging a conglomerate merger but also that the practice itself was virtually per se illegal. There is something puzzling about the case, however. If the goal here was to foreclose competition in Gentry's market, why did Gentry's customers not appear to mind? In the view of the FTC, Consolidated used its leverage over Gentry's customers to enhance Gentry's market power, perhaps eventually to obtain for Gentry a monopoly position in the onion and garlic market. If this was so, wouldn't Gentry's customers, fearing eventual exploitation by this monopoly, speak up in protest? But not only did the suppliers *not* complain, at trial they actually defended their reciprocal dealing with Consolidated/Gentry.

The puzzle is resolved on consideration of several key characteristics of the food industry. Many foodstuffs are seasonal or perishable, making production schedules fragile and dependent on prompt and regular deliveries of crucial inputs. As one of Consolidated's suppliers testified, "When we need something, we need it. If we have tomatoes in the field with no onion, we could make catsup, but it wouldn't be very good catsup. [And] we can't afford to bring our supplies of onion products in 4 to 6 weeks prior to the packing season."[41] In other words, a catsup producer's tomato crop was *specialized* to the supplier of onion. An interruption in supply, whether the result of conscious opportunism, accidents, or strikes, could produce great losses.

Firms were vulnerable to opportunism (whether conscious or not) in other areas as well. Often, e.g., processors invested in extra capacity or contracted in advance with growers for specific amounts of raw material only because certain clients promised orders. Failure to honor such promises would leave the processor holding the bag. In addition, retailers such as Consolidated often purchased products from other producers and sold them under private-label names (also called *store brands*). A supplier could stint on the quality of such goods and damage the reputation of the private-label seller.

After acquiring Gentry, Consolidated found it easier to structure reciprocal transactions that made *all* parties similarly vulnerable to opportunism by the others. The firms' mutual exposure bound them together and created a situation where none would gain—or all would lose—if opportunism (or anything else) caused a severing

---

[40]Ibid., p. 592.

[41]Stephen J. K. Walters, "Reciprocity Reexamined: The Consolidated Foods Case," *Journal of Law and Economics*, 29 (October 1986), p. 435.

of the relationship. And the parties understood the gains from their mutual-reliance relation. One witness, after discussing all the ways in which interruptions in supply (strikes, derailments, etc.) could harm his business, testified that Gentry "will keep us going. They will divert cars that may have been shipped out of the company to keep us going. These are the services we get through a very fine relationship that we have with the supplier."[42]

Consolidated's acquisition of Gentry, then, simply made it easier to create supply relationships in which the value of specialized investments was better protected and the costs of transacting were reduced. Any foreclosure of competition that stemmed from the acquisition must surely have been incidental to this purpose.

Procter & Gamble (1967)   In 1957, Procter & Gamble, a producer of household soaps and detergents, acquired Clorox, a producer of chlorine bleach. Both the detergent and bleach markets were highly concentrated, and the merging firms were the dominant sellers of these distinct, although related, goods: Procter & Gamble held 54.4 percent of the detergent market, and Clorox held 48.8 percent of the liquid bleach market. The Supreme Court agreed with the FTC's argument that the acquisition would eliminate an important potential entrant into the bleach market:

> Procter was engaged in a vigorous program of diversifying into product lines closely related to its basic products. Liquid bleach was a natural avenue of diversification since it is complementary to Procter's products, is sold to the same customers through the same channels, and is advertised and merchandised in the same manner.[43]

The Court wanted Procter to enter the bleach market with its own brand and ordered Clorox spun off.

ITT-Grinnell (1970)   In 1969, ITT, one of the nation's largest conglomerates with over 200 subsidiaries, acquired Grinnell, a producer of automatic sprinkler devices and related products. While the government alleged several anticompetitive effects of the acquisition (including possible reciprocal dealing), the main thrust of the government's case was that the acquisition, by contributing to aggregate concentration and the trend toward conglomeration, was illegal even absent proof of a lessening of competition in any specific market or area. The district court disagreed:

> The Court's short answer to this claim . . . is that the legislative history, the statute itself and the controlling decisional law all make it clear beyond a peradventure of a doubt that in a Section 7 case the alleged anticompetitive effects of a merger must be examined in the context of *specific product and geographic markets*. . . . To ask the Court to rule with respect to alleged anticompetitive consequences in *undesignated lines of commerce* is tantamount to asking the Court to engage in judicial legislation. This the Court most emphatically refuses to do.[44]

---

[42]Ibid., p. 435, note 49.
[43]*FTC v. Procter & Gamble Co.*, 386 U.S. 568 (1967), p. 580.
[44]*United States v. International Telephone and Telegraph Corp.*, 324 F. Supp. 19 (1970), p. 52.

Guidelines   On personal instructions from then-President Richard Nixon to his Attorney General, the Justice Department did not appeal the ITT-Grinnell decision to the Supreme Court. Thus, we do not know how the Court might rule in such a case. And given the current enforcement policy of the Justice Department, we are unlikely to find out any time soon. The Justice Department's conglomerate merger guidelines suggest it is likely to challenge only those mergers in which potential competition is an important issue. Even in such cases, the Justice Department is unlikely to challenge mergers where the markets involved are unconcentrated, entry is fairly easy, there are three or more comparable entrants, and the merger partners possess tolerably small market shares. The days when the antitrust authorities seek to limit corporate diversification and aggregate concentration appear to be over, at least for now.

THE WILLIAMS ACT AND REGULATION OF TAKEOVER ACTIVITY

Mergers usually involve more than antitrust issues. Even when an acquisition will have no effect on the competitiveness of the affected markets whatsoever, it is possible that the functioning of the *market for corporate control* may produce harmful effects. Corporate executives argue that fear of unwanted takeover attempts forces them to emphasize short-run performance rather than plan for the long term, and that fighting takeovers distracts them from the task of efficiently managing their firms. Alan Beckenstein has found that takeovers are frequently motivated by the desire of executives to build or maintain empires.[45] And David Ravenscraft and F. M. Scherer have found that takeovers often produce no gain in economic efficiency, but merely redistribute the tax burden or shift wealth from some shareholders (or bondholders) to others.[46]

To address at least some of the concerns arising from corporate takeover activity, Congress passed the Williams Act in 1968. Nominally, the act protects shareholder interests in takeover battles by ensuring that they have more information and time with which to make wise decisions about the disposition of their stock. Takeovers are often accomplished by tender offers: A party who seeks control of a corporation asks the stockholders of the target firm to submit, or "tender," their shares in exchange for a specified price. Usually, the offer price will be far in excess of the current trading price of the target firm's stock. This can put the shareholder in a quandary. The price may look very attractive, but might it be better still to hold the stock and see what happens? After all, once a firm is "in play," another suitor might come up with a better offer; or it might be wise to hold the stock and see if new owners might so enhance the firm's performance that its stock price eventually rises far beyond the offer price. The Williams Act stipulates that (1) any person who owns more than 5 percent of the outstanding shares of a company must file a disclo-

---

[45]Alan R. Beckenstein, "Merger Activity and Merger Theories: An Empirical Investigation," *Antitrust Bulletin*, 24 (Spring 1979), pp. 105–128.

[46]See David Ravenscraft and F. M. Scherer, *Mergers, Sell-offs, and Economic Efficiency*, Brookings Institution, Washington, 1987.

sure form with the Securities and Exchange Commission (SEC) and (2) any tender offer must remain open for 20 business days.

These modest restrictions do more than merely provide shareholders with time and information, however. They also give the management of a target firm a chance to devise defensive tactics to fend off a takeover or improve its terms. Fearing that they will be replaced if the firm offering a tender wins control of the target firm, the firm's managers may search out a second bidder, dubbed a *white knight*, who might be willing to retain the firm's management structure intact. Or, in a strategy called the *Pac-Man defense*, the target firm may initiate a tender offer for its suitor, seeking to gobble up the suitor before being gobbled itself. More generally, a firm may employ sundry antitakeover provisions in its corporate charter. *Poison pills* are aimed at making a company unpalatably expensive to a potential acquirer; a "flip-over" pill, e.g., might entitle a company's shareholders to buy $200 worth of an acquiring company's stock for $100 on consummation of a merger. Another form of *shark repellent* appears fairly innocuous: By staggering the terms of directors so that only a few come up for election each year, a company can ensure that a successful acquirer would have to wait years to gain effective control of a firm. In some cases, firms have successfully appealed to the legislatures of the states in which they are headquartered for special laws that make them harder to acquire. These antitakeover tactics, in combination with the Williams Act and various state-level regulations, increase the costs of takeovers and reduce their frequency. Whether this is desirable and whether public policy should further limit takeover activity remain subjects of lively controversy.

The Market for Corporate Control: Empirical Evidence

There is one point on which virtually all students of the market for corporate control agree: Shareholders of acquired firms benefit from takeover activity. After reviewing many empirical studies of this issue, Michael Jensen and Richard Ruback conclude that in successful tender offers the stock values of target firms increase by an average of 30 percent over levels immediately prior to the offer announcement; in successful mergers, target firms' stock values rise by 20 percent.[47]

Clearly, owning stock in a company that is the target of a successful tender offer or merger attempt can make one very rich indeed. But what is the source of these gains? It might be that the takeover will facilitate collusion or monopoly pricing in the target firm's market; the higher stock values may simply reflect the present value of future anticipated monopoly profits. Two empirical studies of a sample of horizontal mergers reject this hypothesis, however.[48]

---

[47]Michael C. Jensen and Richard S. Ruback, "The Market for Corporate Control: The Scientific Evidence," *Journal of Financial Economics*, 11 (April 1983), pp. 5–50. For a later survey, see Richard E. Caves, "Mergers, Takeovers, and Economic Efficiency," *International Journal of Industrial Organization*, 7 (1989), pp. 151–174.

[48]Robert Stillman, "Examining Antitrust Policy towards Horizontal Mergers," and B. Espen Eckbo, "Horizontal Mergers, Collusion, and Stockholder Wealth," *Journal of Financial Economics*, 11 (April 1983), pp. 225–273.

Another possibility is that acquired firms' relative stock prices rise because the acquirers redeploy the assets of the firm in ways that add to their value, i.e., in ways that make the acquired firm more efficient. Jensen and Ruback note that when tender offers or attempts at merger fail, shareholders of target firms tend to see their stock values fall slightly (although the amount of decline does not appear to be statistically significant). They argue that if stock prices rise for firms that are the object of successful takeovers but not for firms for which takeover battles fail, then it must be that efficiencies are realized only when control of the target firm's assets is transferred to the bidding party. By implication, policies or tactics that reduce the probability of a successful takeover harm stockholders of potential target firms.

On the bidders' side, the benefits of takeover activity are much smaller. Jensen and Ruback find that successful tender offers raise stock values in bidding firms by 4 percent, but successful mergers (and unsuccessful tender offers and mergers) have either no effect or a small negative effect on bidding firm share values. They argue that since target firm shareholders gain and bidding firm shareholders do not lose, takeovers create value for society. This assertion finds support in the research of Michael Bradley, Anand Desai, and Han Kim, who find that the net gains to target and bidder firms (weighted by the size of each firm) for successful tender offers from 1963 to 1984 averaged 7.4 percent.[49] They attribute these gains to synergies in the merged firms and find that these gains have been quite consistent over time (although returns to bidding firms have been lower and returns to target firms higher since passage of the Williams Act, suggesting the act has significantly affected the distribution of gains from takeover activity). They conclude that tender offers are efficient mechanisms to channel corporate resources to higher-valued uses.

Some eminent scholars disagree with this view, however. Ravenscraft and Scherer argue that the stock market will, at any given time, systematically undervalue some firms and overvalue others. In their view, a firm's stock price may be depressed because of *mistakes in the stock market* rather than mistakes by the firm's managers. The takeover market thus reflects a certain amount of bargain hunting by bidders. Increases in acquired firms' stock prices merely reflect these firms' true value and need not stem from any enhanced efficiency in these firms once they are taken over. Going beyond stock market data to case studies of individual firms and analysis of accounting data for mergers consummated during the 1960s and 1970s, Ravenscraft and Scherer found that while some mergers unquestionably produced efficiency gains, a large fraction produced no observable improvement in management efficiency—and not a few appeared to reduce efficiency. Target firms tended not to be badly run, underperforming companies, but rather quite profitable and well managed; after their acquisition, however, their performance tended to decline rather than improve. Ravenscraft and Scherer con-

---

[49]Michael Bradley, Anand Desai, and E. Han Kim, "Synergistic Gains from Corporate Acquisitions and Their Division between the Stockholders of Target and Acquiring Firms," *Journal of Financial Economics*, 21 (May 1988), pp. 3–40.

clude that the merger wave of the 1960s led to efficiency losses substantially exceeding identifiable gains.[50]

It is quite likely that debate on the functioning of the market for corporate control will continue for many years to come. Even if we accept the evidence, thin though it might be, that the net private return to shareholders of target and bidder firms is positive, many questions remain. For example, are there any *social* returns (positive *or* negative) beyond these private returns? Do positive stock returns in fact reflect efficiency gains? Do the distributional effects of the Williams Act (or the various state antitakeover laws) have any effect on the volume of transactions in the takeover market?

Resolving such issues will no doubt occupy financial and industrial economists for some time. We can rest assured, however, that with or without definitive scientific answers to these questions, there will be periodic demands for greater regulation of the market for corporate control. If one thing is clear, the free functioning of this market makes corporate executives' lives less secure and more complicated. It is therefore not surprising—although it *is* ironic—that these captains of industry plead regularly for relief from capitalism's excesses.

VIGNETTE 8.4 Staying in Charge with a Little Help from One's Friends: Public Choice Analysis and State Antitakeover Laws

When Scott Paper Company became the object of an unwanted takeover attempt in 1983, the firm's managers knew exactly how to fend off the attack. Headquartered in Pennsylvania, Scott had made many friends in the state capital over the years. So, with the help of the Pennsylvania Chamber of Commerce, Scott's managers hurriedly drafted a bill that erected several obstacles to any takeover of firms incorporated in the state, and Scott got one of the firm's friends to introduce the bill in the legislature.

The bill's language was rather obscure and its provisions labyrinthine. Even one of its cosponsors admitted to confusion about its merits, saying, "As of this moment I do not feel I have the knowledge and understanding of the bill to know whether my action for or against the bill would, in fact, be the proper action."[51] Nevertheless, the bill was made law with breathtaking speed. It was introduced in the state senate on November 16, 1983, passed by that Chamber on December 6, passed by the house on December 13, and signed by the governor on December 23—all *without any public hearings!*

This scenario has been repeated in many other states. Minnesota's legislature saved Dayton Hudson, the state's largest private employer, from a hostile takeover bid initiated by Dart Group. Arizona passed an antitakeover law at the behest of Greyhound Bus Lines, based in Phoenix. Massachusetts' law was hustled through the legislature when Gillette was the target of a bid by Revlon. And when corporate raider T. Boone Pickens evinced an interest in Boeing, that company got protection from the Washington state legislature. Recently even Delaware, the state in which

---

[50]Ravenscraft and Scherer, *Mergers, Sell-Offs, and Economic Efficiency,* op. cit.

[51]See Marc I. Steinberg, "Should the Feds Take Over State Takeover Laws?" *Business and Society Review,* 65 (Spring 1988), p. 55.

45 percent of companies listed on the New York Stock Exchange are incorporated, passed an antitakeover law.

Why are politicians so eager to pass such laws? It may be that they are sincerely worried that takeover activity leads to efficiency losses (as suggested by the above-mentioned research of Ravenscraft and Scherer).

There may, however, be a more prosaic rationale. Consider the political benefits and costs of antitakeover laws. Incumbent managers (and some employees) of target firms love such laws because they enhance job security: The harder it is for some raider to buy up the company and reorganize it (read: make heads roll), the better. On the other hand, we know that tender offers tend to increase the wealth of shareholders of target firms; these shareholders will probably be unhappy about antitakeover legislation. The key here is that most (although not all) shareholders will be outside state borders and politically irrelevant in the state legislature (even if they show up and state their opposition). The beneficiaries of antitakeover laws, however, will tend to be local and vocal. In a study of Connecticut's antitakeover law, Yale law professor Roberta Romano found that only in-state corporations and their lobbyists were involved in debate about the statute; there was no participation by the (mostly) out-of-state shareholders.[52] It's no surprise, then, that about three-fifths of states have passed antitakeover laws in recent years—with more to come.

Economists Jon Karpoff and Paul Malatesta have studied how companies' stock prices have been affected by the passage of these laws. They found small but statistically significant decreases in the stock prices of firms incorporated or headquartered in a state passing such a law.[53] In other words, the evidence suggests that state antitakeover laws deter hostile takeover bids and entrench incumbent managers at the expense of stockholders. Aware that they have less control over their "agents" in companies located in states where takeovers are more difficult or costly, some shareholders dump their shares soon after passage of an antitakeover law, depressing share prices.

SUMMARY AND CONCLUDING REMARKS

A particular merger or acquisition may arise from either the noblest or most selfish of motives. Some, no doubt, are designed to confer monopoly power on the combined entity; it is at such mergers that antitrust policy takes special aim. Under present policy guidelines, horizontal mergers are presumed to pose a peril to competition—and are likely to be challenged—when they occur in highly concentrated markets (i.e., those where the Herfindahl index exceeds 1,800) or in moderately concentrated markets (i.e., those where the HI is between 1,000 and 1,800) *and* will increase the HI by more than 100 points. Antitrust action to prevent vertical mergers is likely only in cases where the integration may facilitate collusion at some level of the production process, will raise barriers to entry, or will enable the merged firm to evade rate regulation. Antitrust action in conglomerate mergers is relatively rare, reflecting per-

---

[52]Roberta Romano, "The Political Economy of Takeover Statutes," *Virginia Law Review*, 73 (February 1987), pp. 111–199.

[53]Jonathan M. Karpoff and Paul H. Malatesta, "The Wealth Effects of Second-Generation State Takeover Legislation," *Journal of Financial Economics*, 25 (December 1989), pp. 291–322

haps a judgment that the potential for monopolistic conduct is affected little by such mergers.

But mergers may also be motivated by selfish concerns unrelated to antitrust policy (the desire of an executive to build an empire or to minimize corporate taxes) or by laudable pro-efficiency goals. Just as clearly as some mergers can beget monopoly power, they can also produce significant reductions in production costs (e.g., by producing synergies), enable firms to better manage risk, or solve potential problems of opportunistic behavior by (or toward) suppliers. For antitrust policy to be efficient, such considerations must be carefully weighed each time a merger guideline is established or a particular case is pressed.

Finally, the market for corporate control plays an important role in affecting the behavior of corporate managers. In the view of some, this role is beneficial, making managers who fail to maximize their shareholders' wealth vulnerable to takeovers. Critics of takeovers argue, however, that such activity contributes little to corporate efficiency and wastes considerable resources. Students of this market have begun applying very sophisticated analytical tools to these issues; as yet, however, the empirical debate on the effects of takeover activity is unresolved.

QUESTIONS FOR REVIEW AND DISCUSSION

8.1 Some mergers enable the combined (larger) firm to purchase its supplies or market its products at discounted prices. Some scholars call such savings *pecuniary economies* and distinguish them from "real economies" associated with mergers, such as lower production costs that result from greater specialization of labor, etc. They argue that pecuniary economies merely alter the distribution of income among firms and do not produce real reductions in the opportunity cost of production; e.g., when a firm obtains a volume discount from its supplier, its profits rise and the supplier's profits fall, and no real resources are saved. Do you agree with this assertion? Discuss the example of John D. Rockefeller's unit trains in this context. Did the rebates Rockefeller obtained from the railroads merely shift wealth, or did they reflect real economies in production?

8.2 Cecilia B. DeMille is a film producer and director. She signs Harry Heartthrob to a $5 million contract to star in her latest picture, to be filmed on location in an exotic locale. Filming begins, and everything is fine until, with about three-quarters of the schedule completed, Harry gets temperamental. Complaining that conditions at the exotic locale have made him ill, he flies home and refuses to return to complete filming—unless his fee is *doubled* to $10 million, to make him willing to suffer the discomfort of working while ill. Cecilia suspects Harry is faking. She consults her lawyers and accountants. Unhappily, they say, her contract with Harry states clearly that if he takes sick and cannot finish the project, he must still be paid for the completed portion of the schedule. In this case, that will be three-quarters of $5 million, or $3.75 million. And paying Harry off and replacing him with another star involves other costs, too; a substitute heartthrob would cost $5 million, and retaining technicians, extras, costars, etc., to reshoot Harry's scenes would cost another $1.5 million. Cecilia argues that Harry should be replaced and sued to recover these extra costs. But her lawyers caution that such a course is risky. They note that

Harry's personal physician will testify to his illness, and it would be difficult to prove that he has violated any portion of his contract. In any event, they advise, a lawsuit will take years (and will itself cost a substantial sum), and Cecilia needs to wrap up her project *now;* the longer shooting is delayed, the more expensive the project becomes. What would you advise Cecilia to do? Why? What kind of contractual terms might have prevented this situation from arising? What other (noncontractual) mechanisms might have prevented it?

8.3 Some U.S. manufacturers (taking a cue from Japanese firms) have lately adopted the *just-in-time* mode of inventory management. In brief, this involves taking delivery of certain inputs immediately prior to their use (i.e., just in time) rather than weeks or months in advance. This avoids the costs of creating warehouse capacity for these inputs and the interest costs on both the inputs and the storage capacity. Discuss whether this practice might pose any problems from the point of view of dealer opportunism. Will adoption of the practice affect a firm's incentive to merge vertically or horizontally?

8.4 Suppose we have an industry of eight firms with (appropriately defined) market shares as follows:

$$A = 20 \text{ percent} \qquad E = 11 \text{ percent}$$
$$B = 18 \text{ percent} \qquad F = 8 \text{ percent}$$
$$C = 16 \text{ percent} \qquad G = 7 \text{ percent}$$
$$D = 14 \text{ percent} \qquad H = 6 \text{ percent}$$

Calculate the Herfindahl index for this industry. Does it qualify as unconcentrated, moderately concentrated, or highly concentrated according to the Justice Department's horizontal merger guidelines? Consider now a merger between firms G and H. Is this merger likely to be challenged? Explain why or why not. What about a merger between firms F and G?

8.5 In *Procter & Gamble,* the Supreme Court gave several reasons why Procter might have found it feasible to enter the liquid bleach market *de novo* (i.e., with its own new product), competing against Clorox instead of acquiring it. Among these are possible economies of scale in advertising and distributing complementary products. Assume the Court's assertions about these economies are valid. In light of this assumption, is it logical to conclude that the acquisition of Clorox, by eliminating Procter as a potential entrant to the bleach market, necessarily damaged consumers? (*Hint:* Recall the Williamson trade-off model discussed in Chapter 6.)

8.6 Research by Ravenscraft and Scherer has found that while some fraction of mergers undoubtedly produce efficiency gains, a large fraction do not—and some reduce efficiency. Karpoff and Malatesta have detected small but statistically significant decreases in share prices of companies headquartered or incorporated in states passing antitakeover laws. What does the latter study suggest shareholders believe about the *average* effect of takeovers on corporate efficiency and performance?

8.7 The National Association of Attorneys General has put forth its own merger guidelines, suggesting that any merger that has the potential to increase prices to consumers should be prohibited. Do you think these guidelines are likely to enhance social welfare? Explain, using graphs where desirable.

CHAPTER 9

PRICE DISCRIMINATION

Let me tell you about the very rich. They are different from you and me.

F. Scott Fitzgerald

Discriminatory pricing appears ubiquitous. Take a plane trip, and you may find that the person in the seat next to you paid twice as much for her or his ticket as you did. Go to a department store on senior citizen discount day, and you will find the elderly customer ahead of you in the checkout line buying many of the same items as you are at prices 10 percent lower. Go to a movie or play, and you may qualify for a student discount that the person behind you in line will not receive.

At the least, such discrimination seems unfair. Why should another consumer pay less (or more) for a product than I? To many antitrust scholars and policymakers, discriminatory pricing poses a threat to efficiency as well. When prices favor some at the expense of others, the fear has long been that the competitive playing field will tilt in ways that harm firms and consumers alike. Accordingly, the desire to limit the ability of firms to charge different prices for essentially the same product has motivated a good deal of economic regulation and antitrust policy.

Section 2 of the original Clayton Act prohibited sellers from setting discriminatory prices "where the effect of such discrimination may be to substantially lessen competition or tend to create a monopoly." But through the 1930s the courts generally allowed quantity discounts (in which buyers of large amounts receive favorable prices from sellers), and sellers were allowed to refuse to make sales to any buyer as long as such refusals were not seen as an attempt to create a monopoly. Congress expressed considerable dissatisfaction with these "loopholes," however, and in 1936 passed the Robinson-Patman Act. This act greatly expanded the power of section 2. Previously, if a supplier gave buyer *A* a quantity discount and did not extend the same terms to buyer *B*, there was no violation of section 2 because there was no lessening of competition in the supplier's market. But Robinson-Patman made it clear that the courts should consider the effect of the quantity discount on competition between buyers *A* and *B* as well. Under the new standard, if the discount to *A* put *B* at a competitive disadvantage, the supplier's conduct could be judged illegal.

The Robinson-Patman Act aimed especially at the emerging "chains" in grocery, drug, and apparel retailing. Chain stores could use their buying power to win quantity discounts from wholesalers. Such discounts enabled them to undersell smaller independent or mom-and-pop retailers and drive them out of business. In the words of one of the act's sponsors, "[t]he day of the independent merchant is gone unless something is done and done quickly. He cannot possibly survive under that system."[1]

In such language were the seeds of enduring controversy. By aiming not merely at enhancing competition but also at protecting certain *competitors* from harm, the Robinson-Patman Act invites criticism. And the critics are many. Some argue simply that propping up small businesses by preventing larger ones from underselling them serves no valid public purpose. Indeed, they point out, this policy harms consumers by raising the prices they will pay. Others argue that price discrimination is frequently a manifestation of healthy competition rather than a way to eradicate competition. Some assert also that enforcing Robinson-Patman facilitates collusion by inhibiting price-cutting.

In this chapter, we examine the controversies arising from price discrimination in considerable detail. But before we spell out the provisions of the Robinson-Patman amendment more fully and assess its interpretation by the courts, we must better understand what discriminatory pricing is—and is not—and what its effects are. It is to this task that we now turn.

THE ECONOMICS OF PRICE DISCRIMINATION

Preliminaries: Definitions and Conditions

Price discrimination is commonly defined as charging different prices to different consumers for the same commodity. But this definition is unsatisfactory. If we observe the same product being sold at different prices to different consumers, we should not jump to the conclusion that real price discrimination is going on. We need to know more. First, we need to ask whether any observed price differences are explained by _cost differences_. There may be some added costs associated with selling to some consumers or in some locales. Usually

---

[1]Hearings before the House Committee on the Judiciary on *Bills to Amend the Clayton Act*, 74th Cong., 1st Sess., 1935, pp. 5–6.

these added costs are at least partly passed on to buyers in the form of higher prices. Or reductions in the costs of packaging or transacting may explain why lower prices are often extended to those willing to buy in bulk. Where costs of serving two customers differ, it would actually be discriminatory to charge them *identical* prices: Then the high-cost customer would be favored relative to the low-cost one.

A second, and related, question is whether goods for which we observe some apparently discriminatory prices are really *the same*. Consider one of the examples that kicked off this chapter: passengers sitting side by side on an airliner, one of whom, a vacationer, paid half as much for a seat as the other, a business traveler. Surely these passengers are consuming identical goods—the flight is equally bumpy for them, the food equally bland, etc. But perhaps not. Perhaps the business traveler bought her ticket 15 minutes before departure. If so, she is consuming not only a trip from point A to point B, but also a trip from A to B *on the spur of the moment*. She is consuming a good that differs, if only in this one crucial respect, from that of the vacationer, who bought his ticket over a month ago. The airline might have sold her seat to another vacationer, but chose not to (and risked flying an empty seat from A to B!) in the hope that someone like her would show up at the last minute, willing to pay a very steep price to fly without having made reservations a month in advance. Perhaps this detail is not enough to explain the difference between the two travelers' ticket prices, but it might be.

In sum, it's a lot harder to define price discrimination than it might appear. Once cost differences or small variations in the nature of goods sold are factored into the analysis, we can see that price differences alone are not sufficient evidence of real discrimination, and price uniformity is not sufficient evidence of the absence of discrimination. In addition, as we shall soon see, some economic models of price discrimination don't even require the presence of different consumers: Some pricing schemes can be discriminatory because they involve charging different prices for different units of a good *to the same consumer*.

Let us aim for a more meaningful definition, then. We will say that *price discrimination exists when the ratio of price P to marginal cost (MC) for a particular product (or kind of product) differs from one consumer to the next or from one unit sold to the next.* That is, price discrimination exists when

$$\frac{P_A}{MC_A} \neq \frac{P_B}{MC_B}$$

where the subscripts can refer either to different consumers to whom units of the good are sold or to different units of the good which are sold to the same consumer. Under this definition, we will see that many clever pricing schemes qualify as price discrimination, but some practices that appear discriminatory are not. In other words, we should be careful about the way we use the term.

Our more refined definition hints at the first and most important condition that must hold for price discrimination to occur: *The seller must hold some degree* _of monopoly power._ That is, the seller must face a negatively sloped demand curve for her or his product, rather than the horizontal demand curve of perfect competition. Where competition is perfect, sellers and consumers will be well informed about their alternatives and highly mobile; any attempt to charge one consumer a higher price than is offered to others will simply cause that consumer to patronize another firm. In perfect competition, then, price will equal marginal cost for all consumers or units sold (so the ratio P/MC in our definition will always equal 1).

Successful price discrimination also requires a few more conditions. The seller with some monopoly power (1) must be able to identify differences in customers' intensity of demand (or must be clever enough to devise a scheme whereby the customers reveal these differences) and (2) must prevent customers who benefit from relatively low prices from reselling their goods to customers charged relatively high prices. Some discrimination may be possible if these conditions are only loosely satisfied, but it won't be as profitable as it would be if they were perfectly satisfied. Clearly, service industries such as medicine, dentistry, and the law satisfy the last condition best—it's impossible for you to resell your appendectomy, root canal, or divorce to a potentially higher-priced buyer.

For a long time economists thought that these conditions held in relatively few cases. Today, however, we recognize that many markets provide opportunities for discriminatory pricing. In real-world markets, information is rarely perfect and freely available, resources are often less than fully mobile, and products are not homogeneous but highly differentiated. Even lacking full monopoly status, then, some firms will face negatively sloped demand curves and find it possible to practice one or more of the three basic forms of price discrimination: _perfect price discrimination, multipart pricing,_ and _market segmentation._ Let us see how they work.

Perfect Price Discrimination

Recall from Chapter 3 that a seller with monopoly power will restrict output below competitive levels in order to push price above costs and convert some consumers' surplus to profit. Consider, e.g., Figure 9.1, which shows a demand curve D and marginal revenue curve MR for a hypothetical individual as well as a monopolist seller's constant-unit-cost curve C (note that fixed costs are assumed zero, so $C = MC = ATC$). If the monopolist must choose a single price at which to sell, it will be P_m, the price that just clears the market of the monopoly rate of output Q_m. Had this market been perfectly competitive with rate of output Q_c and price P_c, our hypothetical consumer's surplus would have been the entire area bound by points P_cEG. By restricting output to Q_m, the monopolist seller converts area P_cP_mFH from consumer's surplus to economic profit. The consumer's surplus shrinks to area P_mEF, and area FGH is the deadweight welfare loss resulting from the monopolist's behavior.

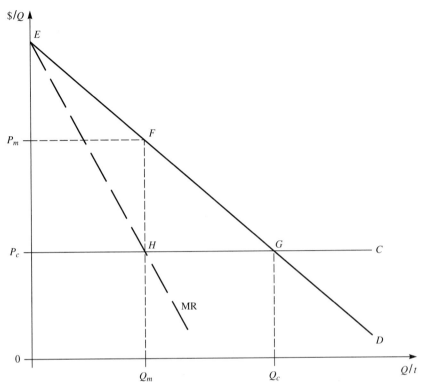

FIGURE 9.1
EXTRACTING AN INDIVIDUAL CONSUMER'S SURPLUS. A discriminating monopolist
can extract a consumer's entire surplus with a take-it-or-leave-it offer (i.e., buy Q_c units at
a total price $0EGQ_c$, or buy nothing at all) or a two-part tariff (i.e., pay a lump sum of P_cEG
for the right to buy additional units at a price of P_c per unit).

When we open up the possibility of price discrimination, however, we find
that the monopolist might be able to convert even more of the consumer's surplus to profit. Indeed, it may be possible for the monopolist to capture the consumer's *entire* surplus. A pricing scheme that leaves the buyer with no remaining surplus is called *perfect price discrimination* (or sometimes *first-degree price
discrimination*). There are at least two ways to extract an individual buyer's
entire surplus.

In one method, the seller confronts the buyer with a *take-it-or-leave-it offer*:
Buy X units of the good at a total price of Y, or buy none at all. The seller
refuses, in this scenario, to sell the buyer $X/2$ units at a total price of $Y/2$ or
any amount less than X at any price less than Y. If the seller has chosen X and
Y wisely, this offer will not be refused, for the total price Y will equal—but not
exceed—the full value the buyer attaches to X units of the good. In Figure 9.1,
the buyer values Q_c units of this good by an amount equal to the area bound
by points $0EGQ_c$. (Recall that the height of the demand curve reveals how
much the consumer is willing to pay for each unit of the good, i.e., how much

value is attached to each unit. Thus, the area under the demand curve from 0 to Q_c units measures the total value the buyer attaches to Q_c units of the good.) If the seller knows that the buyer's demand curve looks like D, the seller can simply say, "Buy Q_c units of output from me at a total price of $0EGQ_c$, or I will sell you no output." When the buyer accepts, the seller will have converted the buyer's entire surplus P_cEG to monopoly profit.[2]

Alternatively, the seller may confront the buyer with a *two-part tariff*, in which a consumer pays a lump-sum fee for the right to buy a product at some per-unit price. Suppose, e.g., that Figure 9.1 shows an individual's demand for the services of a gymnasium or country club. The monopolist seller may declare that membership in the gym or club may be bought at a price equal to the area bound by points P_cEG and that each visit to the club will cost P_c. This two-part tariff enables the seller to capture the buyer's entire surplus up front, as a lump-sum payment. The marginal fee P_c then covers the monopolist's costs for each unit of output the buyer will subsequently consume. The result—Q_c units consumed at a total expenditure of $0EGQ_c$—is the same as with the take-it-or-leave-it offer, but the seller's tactics appear slightly less heavy-handed.

So far, we have analyzed how a firm might extract an individual consumer's surplus via complex pricing strategies. If all consumers had identical demand curves like D in Figure 9.1, we would ironically observe a "discriminating" monopolist charging fairly uniform prices from one buyer to the next. But buyer preferences may differ considerably, and a perfectly discriminating monopolist will accordingly specify different prices to each consumer.

Consider Figure 9.2, which shows a negatively sloped *market* demand curve D and horizontal unit-cost curve C. In Figure 9.2, we assume each consumer wants but one unit of our product, and each is willing to pay a different price for it. If only one unit of the product exists, there is a consumer willing to pay a price P_1 for it. Another consumer is willing to pay slightly less (P_2), a third still less (P_3), and so on. If the market were competitive, $Q_c = 10$ units of the product would be produced and sold at price P_{10}. A monopolist limited to a single price might choose to sell $Q_m = 5$ units of output at price P_5, but the monopolist might do better than this if he or she can (1) sort out consumers according to their willingness and ability to pay and (2) prevent consumers from reselling the product once they possess it. If these conditions are satisfied, the monopolist can once again extract all (or almost all) the consumers'

---

[2]Students often insist that the buyer might refuse the take-it-or-leave-it offer unless she or he is left with *some* surplus, however small. For these sticklers for detail, consider the offer to be "Buy Q_c units at a total price of $0EGQ_c$ minus 1 cent, or buy nothing at all."

A more important qualification to the above discussion is that the income thus extracted from the consumer must not cause a leftward shift of the demand curve D. If the price discrimination scheme transfers so much surplus from buyer to seller that the buyer's demand for this product (and perhaps others) is significantly reduced, the size of the take-it-or-leave-it offer must be adjusted appropriately. In this and later discussions of discriminatory pricing, we implicitly assume that the income elasticity of demand for the good in question is zero, so that these income effects can, for simplicity, be ignored.

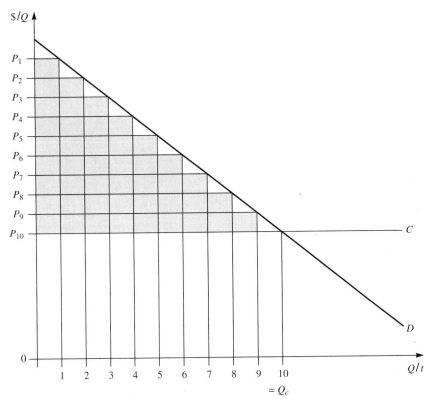

FIGURE 9.2
(ALMOST) PERFECT PRICE DISCRIMINATION. By setting a price equal to the maximum amount each consumer would pay for each unit of output, from P_1 for the first unit sold to P_{10} for the tenth, a seller can extract almost all the consumers' surplus in this market.

surplus in this market. When the consumer who is willing to pay P_1 shows up, the seller specifies that price. When the consumer willing to pay no more than P_2 arrives, that is the price the seller quotes. Each buyer will be charged precisely the maximum amount she or he is willing to pay for the product, so that in the limit none are left with any surplus. In Figure 9.2, the shaded area is captured as profit by the discriminating monopolist. Remember, though, that knowing each consumer's valuation of the good—an achievement by itself—is not enough for this scheme to work. If the buyer who pays price P_{10} can turn around and resell the good to the consumer willing to pay P_1 (presumably at some price between P_1 and P_{10}), the scheme may not be worthwhile.

VIGNETTE 9.1 Price Discrimination by Labor Unions

Some of the best opportunities for perfect price discrimination are in labor markets. Labor unions, exempt from the antitrust laws, may acquire considerable monopoly

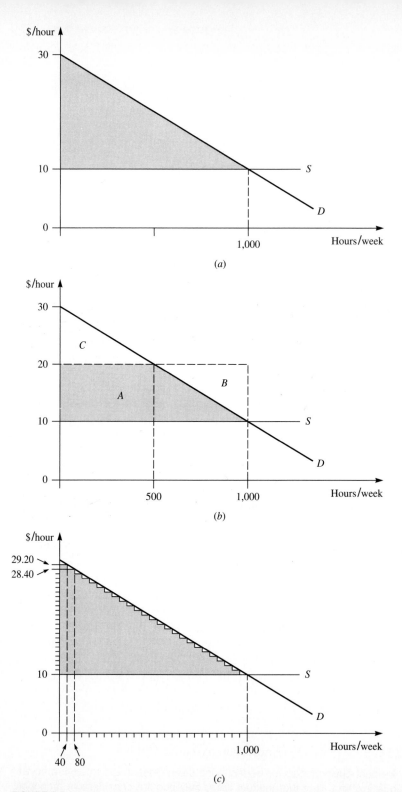

FIGURE 9.3
A PRICE-DISCRIMINATING LABOR UNION. A union might increase labor income *(a)* by using two-part tariffs, *(b)* coupling high hourly wages with minimum hour requirements, or *(c)* ranking workers according to seniority and setting higher wages for employees with greatest seniority.

power, and their exercise of this power is unconstrained by the Robinson-Patman amendment.

Consider the hypothetical labor market shown in Figure 9.3a. There is an infinitely elastic supply of labor available at a wage rate of $10 per hour and a negatively sloped demand for labor curve D.[3] If the market were perfectly competitive, there would be 1,000 hours of labor demanded and supplied each week at the competitive wage of $10 per hour, for total labor income of $10,000 per week.

A union with complete control over the supply of labor to this employer could greatly increase labor income, however. One possibility is that a union may demand that the employer make a lump-sum payment into a pension fund (or other union-controlled fund) in addition to paying a fee for each unit of labor consumed (i.e., a two-part tariff). In Figure 9.3a, the employer's surplus at a wage of $10 per hour (the shaded area) equals $10,000 per week. The union could require the employer to make a pension fund contribution equal to this amount in exchange for the right to hire workers at an hourly wage of $10. In this example, the union can double its members' income without changing the hourly wage a penny.

Alternatively, a monopoly union might demand a higher hourly wage and couple this with a requirement that a minimum number of hours per week be paid at this wage rate. At a wage of $20 per hour, e.g., the employer would ordinarily demand only 500 hours per week. But if the union demands that at least 1,000 hours per week be paid, the employer would likely accede. Total labor income under this arrangement is $20,000 per week—the same as if the union had left the wage rate at $10 per hour but demanded a lump-sum payment equal to the employer's entire surplus. In the context of Figure 9.3b, the demand for 1,000 hours of work at $20 per hour enables the union to raise labor income by the shaded area A (formerly employer's surplus) plus area B. The employer is willing to allow the union to capture area B only because it is exactly equal to area C; thus, this pricing scheme, like a two-part tariff, leaves the employer with no surplus.

A slightly less perfect form of price discrimination involves ranking employees, perhaps by seniority, and specifying a different hourly wage rate for each rank. In the limit, such a pricing scheme might look like that depicted in Figure 9.3c. The wage rate for the most senior employee might be set at $29.20 per hour. At this wage, the employer demands 40 hours per week, enough to keep occupied this employee but none others unless the wage rate is judiciously lowered. Accordingly, the wage scale drops to $28.40 per hour for the second most senior employee, to $27.60 per hour for the third, and so on, until the wage rate for the least senior employee (the one ranking 25th and last on the seniority ladder) is set at $10 per hour. By selectively lowering the price of each "worker week" to be exactly equal to the maximum amount the employer is willing to pay for an additional 40 hours of labor, the union is able to extract just about all the employer's surplus. (Observe: Total labor income under this pricing scheme would be $19,600 per week, leaving only $400 per week intact as employer's surplus.) Seniority job rights are obviously key here. This scheme would backfire if the wage scale were expressed merely in terms of years of service necessary to earn a particular wage rate, for the employer would simply substitute inexperienced workers for experienced ones whenever a worker's wage started to climb above the competitive level. To be effective, this scheme must require the employer to hire the most senior (or top-ranked) worker before hiring any other, the second most senior worker before hiring a third, and so on.

---

[3]Note that the demand for labor in this market is described by the equation $Q_d = 1,500 - 50P$.

Multipart Pricing

The information required for perfect price discrimination is often impossible to obtain. Most sellers will not know the maximum price every buyer would be willing to pay for each unit of a good. Thus, perfect discrimination may not be possible very often. But cruder schemes, in which the seller captures some fraction of the surplus of a consumer or group of consumers, sometimes called *second-degree price discrimination,* may be quite easy to implement.

In a *multipart pricing* arrangement, e.g., the basic strategy is to charge two (or perhaps slightly more) basic prices to a single consumer. Consider Figure 9.4, which shows a negatively sloped individual demand curve D and horizontal unit-cost curve C.[4] Constrained to a single price, the monopolist seller will choose $30; the individual will then buy 2 units per week, and the seller will earn weekly profits of $40 from this buyer. The seller might do better, however, by offering the buyer a volume discount. "Buy 2 units for a total of $60," the seller may say, "or buy 3 for $80." By lowering the price of a third unit to $20 (on the condition, of course, that the buyer first take 2 units per week at the higher price of $30 per unit), the seller adds $10 per week to profits.

[4]The demand curve in Figure 9.4 is described by the equation $Q_d = 5 - 0.1P$.

FIGURE 9.4
MULTIPART PRICING. The seller charges a single consumer two prices for the same good by offering to sell 2 units for a total of $60 or 3 for a total of $80. Thus, the price of the third unit is lowered to $20, and $10 is added to profits.

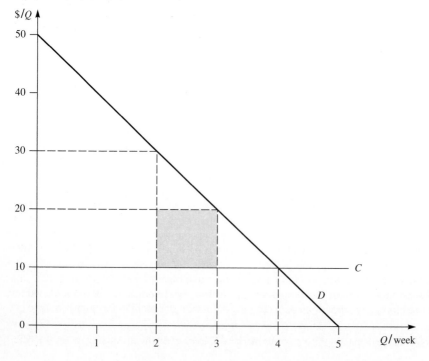

It may seem that discrimination via this kind of multipart pricing is quite common. Visit any grocery store, and you will see that many goods come in small sizes at unit prices far higher than those on larger sizes. A 1-pound box of cereal may cost $2, for example, while a 2-pound box may cost $3.50. You may suspect that this is a multipart pricing scheme: On the 2-pound box, you pay $2 for the first pound and $1.50 for the second, and both prices may exceed the seller's unit costs. Recognize, however, that there may be real differences in the costs of producing the two goods. It may be significantly cheaper (per pound of cereal) to pack, ship, and shelve 2-pound boxes than 1-pound boxes, and the price difference may simply reflect these real resource savings. That is, under our earlier definition this may not qualify as price discrimination because the ratio of price to marginal cost may be the same for each box of cereal.

Market Segmentation

Suppose it is impossible or impractical to charge all consumers different prices (equal to the maximum each will pay) for a good. A seller with market power may nevertheless be able to price-discriminate by dividing consumers into two or more groups and setting a different price for each group. Assuming one group cannot resell the good to another, this tactic, called *market segmentation* or sometimes *third-degree price discrimination* may enhance seller profits.

Consider Figure 9.5. Panel *a* shows the demand curve D_1 and associated marginal revenue curve MR_1 for one identifiable group of buyers (market 1); panel *b* shows the demand and marginal revenue curves D_2 and MR_2 for a different group (market 2). Unit costs C of serving either group are the same. The seller will find that maximum profits are earned when Q_1 units are sold in market 1 at a price P_1 while Q_2 units are sold in market 2 at a price P_2. That is, the seller should treat each group as a separate market and maximize profits in each by finding the intersection of the relevant MC and MR curves, fixing output in each market accordingly, and setting the price that will clear each separate market of this profit-maximizing rate of output.

Setting the same price in both markets will reduce profits. To see this, consider setting a single price P_1. This will maximize profits in market 1 but not in market 2. Setting a price P_1 in market 2 instead of price P_2 would involve the sacrifice of profits equal to the area labeled G (measured as P_2 minus P_1 times Q_2) in exchange for the profits measured by area H (measured as P_1 minus C times the extra amount of output sold in this market Q_2' minus Q_2). Since the marginal revenues on the extra units sold from Q_2 to Q_2' are less than unit costs, it is clear that area G exceeds area H. Similarly, setting a single price P_2 would maximize profits in market 2 but fail to do so in market 1. Reduced sales in market 1 (from Q_1 to Q_1') would involve the sacrifice of profits equal to area F in exchange for the smaller area E.

Thus, the discriminating monopolist will operate so that the extra revenue from selling one more unit in any market is just equal to the extra costs of pro-

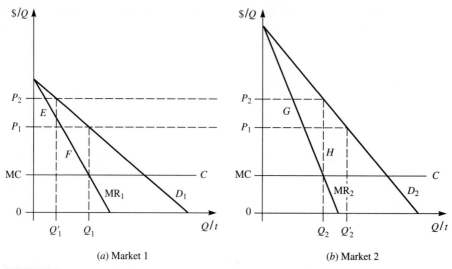

FIGURE 9.5
MARKET SEGMENTATION. It will be profit-maximizing for a monopolist to set a high price (P_2) in the segment of the market where demand is relatively inelastic and a lower price (P_1) in the market where demand is more elastic.

ducing that unit. In the example described by Figure 9.5a and b, maximum profits are found by setting prices and output rates in the two markets so that

$$MC = MR_1 = MR_2$$

Recall that the price elasticity of demand E_d measures consumers' sensitivity to changes in price. It can be shown[5] that a seller's markup of price over cost—measured as the proportion by which P exceeds MC, or $(P - MC)/P$—is related to E_d in a particular market by the following expression:

$$\frac{P - MC}{P} = \frac{-1}{E_d}$$

In words, the seller's markup is inversely proportional to the price elasticity of demand in a market. In our example, P_2 *exceeds* P_1 because demand is *less elastic* in market 2 than in market 1. (As an exercise, show that if the seller's markup in market 2 exceeds that in market 1, the absolute value of E_d is lower in market 2 than in market 1.) This makes perfect intuitive sense: A discriminating monopolist will charge a higher price in markets where consumers are relatively insensitive to price changes (i.e., where demand is less elastic) and a lower price in markets where consumers are more sensitive to price changes

[5]See, e.g., Dennis W. Carlton and Jeffrey M. Perloff, *Modern Industrial Organization*, Scott, Foresman, Glenview, IL, 1990, Chapter 5, especially pp. 101–102.

(i.e., where demand is more elastic). Market segmentation, then, is an exercise in sorting consumers according to their elasticity of demand. Consumers with relatively elastic demand will be granted discounts, while those with relatively inelastic demand will not.

Often consumers with relatively low price elasticity of demand will have high incomes, and those with more elastic demand will have lower incomes.[6] Again, this should appeal to our intuition: High-income consumers are likely to be less sensitive to price changes than low-income consumers. Thus, market segmentation will often produce discounts for low-income buyers and higher prices for high-income buyers. Discounts granted to senior citizens, students, or families might be examples of this. The very young or old will often (although not always) have lower incomes—and therefore relatively more elastic demand for a product—than those in their prime earning years.

VIGNETTE 9.2   Price Discrimination and Time

Successful discrimination via market segmentation requires considerable ability to distinguish high-price buyers from low-price buyers. Since willingness to pay will often be correlated with income, some sellers actually try to gather information on earnings before quoting prices. Some physicians, e.g., learn their patients' occupations or obtain information about health insurance coverage before billing. Colleges require disclosure of income and wealth status in students' financial aid applications. Less formally, some sales personnel—car dealers are famous for it—will try to learn a potential buyer's income status by innocently asking the buyer's occupation in prenegotiation conversation or simply by sizing up the buyer's appearance (How does the customer dress? Does he or she wear a college ring?).

In some circumstances, however, consumers can be relied on to *sort themselves out* according to their willingness to pay. Often time is a useful sorting device. Consider, e.g., cents-off coupons for grocery items. A box of cookies may sell for $1.99 normally but for $1.49 if the buyer presents the appropriate 50¢-off coupon at the checkout stand. If everyone used such coupons, there would be no point in

---

[6] To see why, note that price elasticity of demand E_d can be expressed as

$$E_d = \frac{P}{Q} \frac{\Delta Q}{\Delta P}$$

Suppose now we have two groups of consumers (high-income and low-income) for a hypothetical product. These groups differ chiefly in that high-income consumers can afford to buy more of the product at any given price; i.e., they have a demand curve to the right of that of the low-income consumers. If the slopes of the two demand curves are the same, so that the term $\Delta Q/\Delta P$ in the equation above is identical between the two groups, and if P is the same for both, then the demand elasticities of the two groups will differ only because they consume different quantities. That is, E_d for each group can be expressed as

$$E_d = \frac{k}{Q}$$

where k equals $P(\Delta Q/\Delta P)$ and does not vary between groups. It follows that if the high-income group consumes higher quantities, its E_d must be lower, and if the lower-income group consumes smaller quantities, its E_d must be greater.

having them—it would save transactions costs for the seller to simply mark down the price of the item to $1.49. But, of course, not all consumers take the time and trouble to find such coupons in newspapers or magazines, clip and save them, and take them along when it's time to shop. Those who value their time very highly will ignore the discount; those with lower time values will not. (Indeed, if it takes only 3 minutes to find, clip, and use the coupon, those who value their time at $10 per hour or more will find it uneconomical to seek the discount.)

Alternatively, sellers may use time to get consumers to sort themselves out in another way. Some goods are offered at a discount only at certain hours of the day. For example, movie theaters will often have special matinee prices on weekdays. Those who are employed during normal working hours (i.e., those who are likely to have relatively higher incomes than those *not* working at such times) will be unable to take advantage of these discounts, while the retired, unemployed, or others with more elastic demand will. Airline fares often come with time restrictions aimed at sorting business travelers (with high time value and very inelastic demand) and leisure travelers (with much greater flexibility about when and where to travel and, accordingly, greater elasticity of demand). Carriers generally offer "super saver" discount fares only to those willing to stay at a particular destination for a certain number of days, often over a weekend. This generally rules out business travelers, who tend to stay shorter periods and who wish to return home on weekends.

Finally, sellers may vary their prices over time in order to price-discriminate. Many new products are very expensive when they first come on the market, but they become cheaper as time passes. Of course, such price reductions may result from technological advances that make production more economical or from increased competition. But such pricing patterns may also be aimed at extracting consumers' surplus. Consumers who are impatient or who urgently demand a particular product (e.g., a new-generation computer, a first-run movie, the latest fashions) may be willing to pay a relatively high price to get it *now;* those with more elastic demand will wait and take advantage of future discounts. Of course, if too many consumers are willing to wait, it may actually be better for a seller to discount prices sooner rather than later, given the time value of money.

WELFARE EFFECTS OF PRICE DISCRIMINATION

The fact that price discrimination is practiced by monopolists (or those with some discretion over price) should not lead us to conclude it is always bad. Depending on how "perfect" the discrimination is, the monopolist may expand output toward the competitive level. In other words, there may be less (or no!) deadweight social loss associated with monopoly when the seller price-discriminates. Thus, allowing price discrimination might occasionally be wise—especially where prohibiting it will do nothing to destroy the market power which gives the seller the ability to discriminate in the first place.

Unfortunately, it can be very difficult to tell whether a particular instance of price discrimination improves resource allocation. Consider first the welfare effects of perfect price discrimination. In general, the chances that discriminatory pricing will enhance output are greatest here. But if the perfectly discriminating monopolist extracts sufficient income from consumers to cause a leftward shift in demand for the monopolist's product, it is uncertain how much output will be enhanced. Further, these income effects will not be limited to the monopolist's product; the transfer of income from consumers may affect resource allocation in many other markets. Or we may find that such a transfer of income is regressive, redistributing income from poor to rich. (Of course, we must recognize also that such discrimination may be progressive, for sellers of the good in question may well be poorer than buyers.) Finally, it is possible that increasing the profitability of a monopoly will increase the amount of resources expended to acquire or maintain it (i.e., will increase rent seeking). Such factors must be weighed carefully before we conclude that perfect price discrimination enhances welfare.

But, as we have observed, price discrimination will rarely be perfect. When it is not—and especially in the case of market segmentation—welfare effects of the practice are even harder to judge. Richard Schmalensee has noted that a *necessary* condition for such discrimination to enhance welfare (defined as the sum of consumers' and producers' surplus, or what we have previously called *social surplus*) is an increase in output.[7] Whether a particular segmentation scheme will, in fact, increase output depends on the shapes of the relevant demand and cost curves, however. When demand curves are linear and costs constant, as in Figure 9.5a and b, it turns out that the discriminating seller will sell the same amount of output as the nondiscriminating one (provided the monopolist sells at least one unit in the more elastic market and, again, income effects can be ignored).

When demand curves are nonlinear, however, third-degree discrimination may yield either an increase or a decrease in output. Joan Robinson has defined some conditions under which such discrimination may be expected to increase output,[8] but it is anyone's guess whether these conditions will apply in very many real-world cases. In sum, while it is quite likely that first- and second-degree price discrimination enhance output and contribute to welfare gains, we simply do not know whether third-degree discrimination commonly does so.

Allowing some kind of price discrimination will certainly improve welfare in at least one special case, however: where demand is insufficient to permit profitable operation of an enterprise under simple monopoly pricing. Consider Figure 9.6, which shows demand and cost curves for a doctor's services in a hypothetical small town. This town is composed of two groups: those with inelastic demand for doctor's services with demand curve d_1 and those with elastic demand with demand curve d_2. Total market demand for doctor's services in the town is thus $d_1 + d_2 = D$ (that is, the market demand curve D is the horizontal summation of d_1 and d_2).[9] Unfortunately, however, a

---

[7]Richard Schmalensee, "Output and Welfare Implications of Monopolistic Third-Degree Price Discrimination," *American Economic Review*, 71 (March 1981), pp. 242–247. See also Hal R. Varian, "Price Discrimination and Social Welfare," *American Economic Review*, 75 (September 1985), pp. 870–875.

[8]See Joan Robinson, *Economics of Imperfect Competition*, Macmillan, London, 1933, pp. 189–195.

[9]Note that the demand curve labeled d_1 in Figure 9.6 is described by the equation $Q_{d_1} = 60 - 0.5P$. The demand curve labeled d_2 is described by $Q_{d_2} = 120 - 2P$.

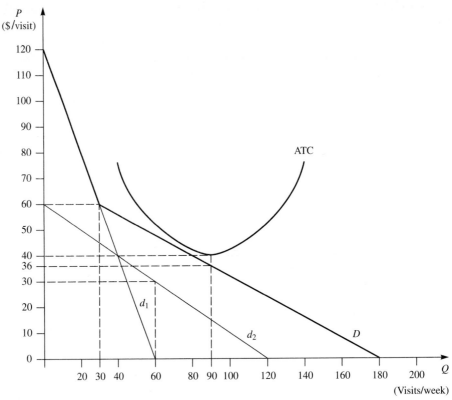

FIGURE 9.6
SURVIVAL VIA PRICE DISCRIMINATION. When ATC lies everywhere above market demand *D*, there is no single price that will enable a seller to cover costs. Price discrimination (e.g., charging those with inelastic demand $60 and those with elastic demand $30) might enable such a seller to survive, however.

representative doctor's U-shaped average total cost curve ATC lies every-where above *D*.

Thus, there appears to be no single price—even a monopoly one—that will make it feasible for a doctor to serve this town. A doctor could most efficiently serve 90 patients per week at an ATC of $40 per visit (so that total costs are $3,600 per week), but at this single price only 80 visits will be demanded (and the ATC per visit will rise). At a price of $36 per visit, 90 visits per week would be demanded, but this price is $4 less than the doctor's ATC per visit at this scale of operation. The doctor could charge a standard rate of $60 per visit, but this would result in a bigger loss still: Those with inelastic demand (along d_1) would demand 30 visits per week, generating $1,800 in revenues, but those with elastic demand (along d_2) could evidently afford no visits at all at this price. Given demand and cost conditions like these, no doctor will open an office in a town of this size—unless it is possible to price-discriminate.

But suppose a doctor can tell whether a patient falls into the group with inelastic or elastic demand (perhaps by gathering information on the income, occupation, or insurance status of each patient). Given that it will be impossible for patients to resell the doctor's services, charging different prices to each group will be feasible. If the doctor charges those with inelastic demand $60 per visit, this group will demand 30 visits per week and generate total weekly revenues of $1,800. If the doctor charges those with elastic demand $30 per visit, this group will demand 60 visits per week and generate another $1,800 in weekly revenues. All told, the discriminatory pricing scheme will generate $3,600 in weekly revenues, precisely equal to the doctor's total costs of 90 patient visits per week. This may seem unfair—after all, some people pay half as much for doctor visits as some others.[10] But most people (perhaps even those with inelastic demand for the doctor's services in our hypothetical small town) would likely agree that it is better to allow such price discrimination and have a doctor in the town than to prohibit it and have none.

POLICY TOWARD PRICE DISCRIMINATION

In the years since its passage in 1936, the Robinson-Patman amendment to the Clayton Act has been both the object of affection and the target of much stinging criticism. Some consider it to be the Magna Carta of small business, while others pray regularly for its repeal. Even the act's staunchest admirers, however, admit that it is very badly written. One critic has called it "a hodgepodge of confusion and inconsistency that any competent, order-loving lawyer must find offensive,"[11] and the Supreme Court has remarked, in more restrained terms, that "precision of expression is not an outstanding characteristic of the Robinson-Patman Act."[12] In this section, we summarize the language of the act and how antitrust scholars feel about it, and then we outline the major cases in which the courts have tried to apply it.

The Robinson-Patman Act

After its amendment by the Robinson-Patman Act, section 2 of the Clayton Act became sections 2(a) to 2(f). Sections 2(a), 2(b), and 2(f) are sometimes called the *price discrimination clauses.* Section 2(a) prohibits a seller from charging buyers different prices for goods of "like grade and quality" where the effect may be to weaken competition; 2(b) puts the burden of rebutting a charge of discrimination on the defendant; 2(f) prohibits a buyer "knowingly to induce" discrimination.

---

[10]Note that there is also an *exchange inefficiency* here. Among those with inelastic demand, e.g., a 31st doctor visit is valued at about $58. There are many among those with elastic demand who value a doctor visit by less than this—and who would therefore exchange visits they buy for $30 with those who value the visits more highly. But this price discrimination scheme would prevent them from doing so. If the doctor could devise a more perfect price discrimination scheme, of course, this inefficiency could be eliminated.

[11]John C. Stedman, "Twenty-Four Years of the Robinson-Patman Act," *Wisconsin Law Review,* 1960 (March 1960), p. 218.

[12]*Automatic Canteen Co. of America v. FTC,* 346 U.S. 61 (1953), p. 65.

Section 2(c), sometimes called the *brokerage clause,* prohibits the payment of brokerage fees unless an independent broker is involved in the transaction. It was common in the 1920s and 1930s to give large buyers who bought directly from the manufacturer a discount in the form of a "brokerage fee" equal to the amount that a wholesaler or intermediary might have received to handle the transaction. Sections 2(d) and 2(e), called the *proportionality clauses,* prohibit a seller from granting any allowance to a buyer for promotional services performed by the buyer unless the allowance is granted to all other buyers on "proportionally equal terms."

If it is established in a price discrimination case that an accused firm's prices differ among buyers, the firm has three possible defenses:

1 The price differences reflect real differences in the cost of producing and delivering goods to buyers (the *cost defense*).

2 Any discriminatory price concessions to some buyers were made "in good faith" to meet the equally low price of a competitor (the *meeting-competition defense*).

3 Sales were made to stave off bankruptcy or under distress conditions (the *distress defense*).

In cases involving the brokerage or proportionality clauses, even these defenses will be unavailing; violations of these clauses are illegal *per se.*

It is common to classify Robinson-Patman cases as either *primary-line* or *secondary-line* cases. Primary-line cases allege injury to competition (or, as we shall see, to particular competitors) in the discriminating seller's own market. Often primary-line cases involve geographic discrimination, in which a seller discounts prices in some cities or regions and not in others. Secondary-line cases allege injury to competition (or competitors) in a buyer's market. When a food processor discounts prices to large chain grocery stores and not to mom-and-pop stores, it is not feared that the food processing industry will become less competitive as a result, but that grocery retailing will become more concentrated as the chain stores' cost advantages lead to the displacement of small independent grocers.

The courts have been extremely tough on discriminating sellers in both kinds of cases. In general, to cost-justify price differences, a seller must convince the court that every penny of price difference reflects real cost differences. Although the courts have allowed a bit more latitude than this under the meeting-competition defense, a discriminating seller must nevertheless show that the competitor's price is itself lawful and nondiscriminatory.

Some Pros and Cons

Critics of Robinson-Patman (and its interpretation by the courts)[13] make three basic points:

---

[13]The literature here is awesome. For two recent discussions, see Richard A. Whiting, "R-P: May It Rest in Peace," and Marius Schwartz, "The Perverse Effects of the Robinson-Patman Act," *The Antitrust Bulletin,* 31 (Fall 1986), pp. 709–757.

1 The preservation of small businesses, clearly a central goal of the act's sponsors, is not a proper goal of antitrust. Indeed, pursuing this goal will often damage economic efficiency, the maximization of which *is* the central purpose of the antitrust laws.

2 The idea that price discrimination is always a symptom of monopoly and harmful to competition is simply wrong. Often price discrimination will be a result of healthy competition, and its practice will benefit consumers.

3 Prohibition of price discrimination leads to inefficiently rigid prices and may actually suppress price competition. Since the act and the courts have not distinguished between anti- and pro-competitive price discrimination, firms may fail to use pricing tactics that enhance competition (or disturb a comfortable collusive arrangement) for fear of prosecution under Robinson-Patman. Such fears may also "freeze" distribution channels and discourage marketing innovations.

The act's defenders[14] respond that:

1 Protecting small competitors can serve consumers' interests, for if a market is left with relatively few large competitors, collusion and economic inefficiency will soon result.

2 The antitrust laws are (or should be) concerned with more than economic efficiency and consumer welfare. Thus, even where preservation of small sellers is unnecessary on purely economic grounds (i.e., where there is little danger of monopolization or excessive market concentration in a market), it will be desirable to preserve small enterprises on social or political grounds. Smaller-scale businesses are less likely to wield undue political power, and we may thus wish to cultivate them even when their costs are higher than larger firms.

Given the stress both critics and defenders of the act place on its role as a protector of small business, it is interesting to note that there is some evidence that the act may hurt small businesses more than it helps them. Small businesses seem to have been the target of more enforcement activity than larger ones,[15] and the costs of complying with the act may be more burdensome for small enterprises. A 1977 study by the Justice Department concluded, in fact, that Robinson-Patman had not improved the ability of small businesses to survive.[16]

Judging by the number of scholarly articles opposing or favoring the act, it is probably fair to say that its critics outnumber its fans, perhaps by a considerable margin. Nevertheless, and despite the fact that scholars have identified some serious shortcomings in the way the courts have interpreted the act, there seems little likelihood that Robinson-Patman will be repealed or seriously modified any time soon. Small businesses (and the antitrust bar!) consider

---

[14]See, e.g., Clark R. Silcox and A. Everette MacIntyre, "The Robinson-Patman Act and Competitive Fairness: Balancing the Economic and Social Dimensions of Antitrust," *The Antitrust Bulletin,* 31 (Fall 1986), pp. 611–664.

[15]Source: American Bar Association, Antitrust Section, Monograph No. 4., *The Robinson-Patman Act: Policy and Law,* 1980, p. 68.

[16]U.S. Department of Justice, *Report on the Robinson-Patman Act,* 1977, p. 181.

enforcement of the act to be vital to their interests, and Congress has been very attentive to these constituencies. Perhaps in deference to the critics, the FTC and Justice Department have redirected enforcement efforts in recent years, bringing fewer Robinson-Patman cases. Private litigation in this area has, however, been on the rise. Thus, firms should consider Robinson-Patman a permanent part of the antitrust landscape and so make their pricing and marketing decisions with appropriate care. That the act is controversial—even unpopular—does not make it irrelevant.

Key Cases

Basing-Point Pricing Cases (1945, 1948) Three of the earliest Robinson-Patman cases to reach the Supreme Court involved manufacturers' use of a *basing-point pricing system.* Under this system, prices for delivered goods are equal to a list price for the goods plus a shipping charge determined with reference to a single "basing point," or point of origin, whether or not the goods were actually manufactured there. The Corn Products Refining (CPR) Company, e.g., manufactured glucose, an important ingredient in candy, in plants in Chicago and Kansas City, but made all sales at prices using the basing point of Chicago. A. E. Staley, another glucose manufacturer located in Decatur, Illinois, also used a Chicago basing point for its prices. The FTC pressed suits against both companies, alleging damage to secondary markets, i.e., that candy makers were injured by this pricing system.

Figure 9.7 illustrates how the system worked in the glucose industry. Assume that the costs of manufacturing glucose were C and were identical no matter where the plant was located. Real transportation costs, however, rose with distance traveled—along the V-shaped lines in the figure. So a Kansas City buyer of glucose *manufactured in Chicago* paid $C + T. But so did a Kansas City buyer of glucose manufactured *there!* With a single basing-point in Chicago, any particular buyer was quoted the same price by all sellers—and possibly paid "phantom" freight charges in the bargain. CPR's Kansas City customers received glucose from its Kansas City plant, but paid T in phantom shipping charges because all price quotes used Chicago as a basing point. Chicago candy makers avoided such charges.

The Supreme Court agreed with the FTC that this created a "favored price zone for the purchasers of glucose in Chicago and vicinity"[17] and that Chicago candy makers had a competitive advantage over firms in less favorable locales. The Court dismissed CPR's argument that its pricing system was not discriminatory because buyers at the same locale paid similar prices. The Court also dismissed Staley's argument that it was acting in good faith by simply meeting CPR's prices. Henceforth, meeting a competitor's illegally discriminatory price would not be an acceptable good-faith defense in Robinson-Patman cases.[18]

---

[17]*Corn Products Refining Company v. FTC,* 324 U.S. 726 (1945), p. 738.
[18]*FTC v. A. E. Staley Manufacturing Co.,* 324 U.S. 746 (1945).

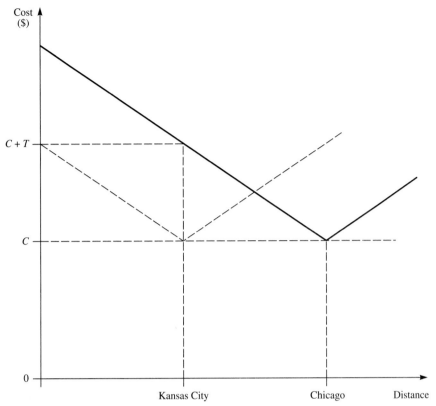

FIGURE 9.7
FINAL COSTS TO GLUCOSE BUYERS UNDER A BASING-POINT PRICING SYSTEM. With
Chicago the designated basing point, a Kansas City glucose buyer would pay phantom shipping
charges of $T for glucose manufactured in Kansas City, raising its total price to $C + $T.

The final blow against basing-point pricing was struck in the *Cement
Institute* case. Cement manufacturers had long used a multiple-basing-point
system in setting cement prices. The Supreme Court found this had
"restrained and hindered competition" and violated the FTC and Robinson-
Patman Acts.[19] The Court agreed with the FTC's view that basing-point pricing was a tool to enforce price-fixing agreements. A popular way to secretly
cut collusively set prices is to offer a buyer free (or cut-rate) delivery. In the
basing-point system, freight charges were calculated from standard, published
rate schedules. By making it easier to detect disguised price cuts (i.e., cuts in
the form of reduced freight charges), the system may have reduced the likelihood of such cuts. In addition, a firm that cut prices below approved levels
could be punished by designating its home a basing point. This would mean
the firm would receive no benefit from phantom freight revenues, while rival

[19]*FTC v. Cement Institute*, 333 U.S. 683 (1948).

firms in other cities would. Thus, basing-point pricing may facilitate collusion by providing a way to both detect and punish those who deviate from a collusive agreement.

The Court's condemnation of basing-point pricing in *Cement Institute* was so unequivocal that it seemed no such system could withstand legal challenge. Shortly after the decision was handed down, the steel industry voluntarily ended its multiple-basing-point system. But other businesses complained loudly, and congressional hearings on the issue apparently convinced the FTC to stop bringing basing-point pricing cases for a while. (Some years later, however, a private suit that alleged discriminatory basing-point pricing by plywood manufacturers was settled for damages exceeding $165 million.) Economists generally applaud the courts' hostility toward basing-point pricing, following the lead of Fritz Machlup, who in a classic 1949 book blamed the practice for distorting market prices, aiding collusion, and encouraging excessive entry and redundant capacity.[20] But a few scholars have questioned whether the motives or effects of such pricing schemes are really so bad.

VIGNETTE 9.3   Basing-Point Pricing Reexamined

Basing-point pricing certainly seems odd. It is hard to understand why candy makers in Kansas City who buy glucose manufactured nearby should pay phantom freight charges equal to the cost of shipping the stuff from Chicago. This certainly seems unfair, and it seems quite plausible that glucose makers—and cement, steel, and plywood makers as well—had some underhanded purpose in using the basing-point system. Not all scholars agree, however, that use of this system signals anticompetitive intent or effect.

David Haddock argues that basing-point pricing may be benign and have nothing whatever to do with collusion.[21] Consider the use of the practice by the steel industry. In its infancy and for some time afterward, the great bulk of steel production capacity was concentrated in Pittsburgh. Under these circumstances, it might have been logical to quote delivered prices for steel as if the steel had been produced in Pittsburgh, even if it had not. Suppose, e.g., it costs $100 (per unit) to produce steel in Pittsburgh, it costs $50 (per unit) to ship steel from Pittsburgh to Detroit, and all steel mills are in Pittsburgh. Detroit steel consumers would then pay a "competitive" price of $150 (per unit). But once a steel mill opens in Detroit, this will not change! Unless the new Detroit mill's capacity exceeds the local demand for steel at the current price of $150, the mill's owner will have no incentive to cut price below this level (i.e., the owner will behave as a price taker, accepting the current delivered price as given and expanding output until this price equals marginal cost, which may lie well above average cost). The Detroit steel producer gets to keep the saved transport costs, but this is not a symptom of collusion or indeed any failure of the competitive mechanism.

The above-normal profits earned by the Detroit producer may, of course, induce

[20]Fritz Machlup, *The Basing-point System: An Economic Analysis of a Controversial Pricing Practice,* Blakiston Co., Philadelphia, 1949.

[21]David D. Haddock, "Basing-Point Pricing: Competitive vs. Collusive Theories," *American Economic Review,* 72 (June 1982), pp. 289–306.

more firms to open steel plants there, but until productive capacity in Detroit exceeds local quantity demanded, none will have an incentive to cut price below the levels determined by "the competition" in far-off Pittsburgh. As capacity in new locales expands, of course, these may well become designated bases in a basing-point pricing system. The steel industry did, in fact, employ a multiple-basing-point system, and when buyers bought from a mill at the closest basing point, the delivered price of steel included no payment for phantom freight.

One by-product of basing-point pricing long thought to be evidence of its inefficiency is called *cross-hauling.* Suppose Pittsburgh is the sole basing point, but other cities, e.g., Chicago, have some steelmaking capacity. In this case, we may observe steel being shipped from Pittsburgh to Chicago (since the price Chicago steel buyers pay will be the same, under the basing-point system, whether the steel comes from Pittsburgh or next door) at the same time as Chicago steel is shipped to cities, e.g., Cleveland, somewhere between Pittsburgh and Chicago. Thus, steel going eastward may pass the identical product going westward under this system! It would be cheaper for all steel to stay closer to home. But Haddock argues that this kind of cross-hauling may be motivated by the desire to cultivate different sources of supply to protect against costly supply interruptions (which may result from conscious opportunism by suppliers or from unavoidable accidents, strikes, etc.). In this regard, cross-hauling may be efficient (at least in a long-run sense) and may arise even absent basing-point pricing.

In the view of Dennis Carlton, basing-point pricing may not be such a hot cartel enforcement tool either.[22] He notes that colluders must figure out a way to divide their market among them, and he suggests basing-point pricing may fail to do this. Compare basing-point pricing with an alternative: *FOB pricing.* Under free-on-board (FOB) pricing, the manufacturer quotes a price to have goods loaded onto a transport carrier; the total price then includes this FOB price plus actual freight charges to wherever the customer takes delivery. If colluding sellers agree to charge the same FOB prices at their plants and add actual transportation charges, the sellers' market will be divided neatly. A buyer will always be able to get the lowest price from the closest producer. Cheating on the collusive agreement will thus be easy to detect: If a distant firm steals a customer from a closer one, the distant firm has probably cut price below the collusively set level. Under a basing-point system, however, it would be impossible to make such an inference. For example, with a single basing-point in Pittsburgh, a Chicago steelmaker could not tell whether a Chicago steel customer chose to buy Pittsburgh steel because of a secret price cut by a Pittsburgh producer or for other reasons. Carlton avers that firms probably use delivered-price systems such as basing-point pricing not because it facilitates collusion, but because it is convenient (i.e., reduces transaction costs). If he and Haddock are right, the FTC's basing-point cases have probably done little to improve welfare and may have done some harm by forcing sellers to use more costly pricing mechanisms.

Morton Salt (1948)   The Supreme Court's first major decision regarding quantity discounts involved the Morton Salt Co., the largest producer of table salt in the United States. Morton charged its largest customers (major national supermarket chains buying in excess of 50,000 cases of salt per year) $1.35 per

<hr/>

[22]Dennis W. Carlton, "A Reexamination of Delivered Price Systems," *Journal of Law and Economics,* 26 (April 1983), pp. 51–70.

case, while purchasers of smaller quantities paid from $1.40 (for purchases of 5,000 or more cases per year) to $1.60 per case (for purchases of less than a rail carload). This meant that bulk buyers had a significant cost advantage over smaller buyers, a fact that damned the pricing scheme in the eyes of the Court:

> The legislative history of the Robinson-Patman Act makes it abundantly clear that Congress considered it to be an evil that a large buyer could secure a competitive advantage over a small buyer solely because of the large buyer's quantity purchasing ability. The Robinson-Patman Act was passed to deprive a large buyer of such advantages except to the extent that a lower price could be justified by reason of a seller's diminished costs due to quantity manufacture, delivery, or sale. . . .[23]

Further, the Court ruled that discounts can be cost-justified only by showing that the *full amount* of the discount is based on a seller's actual savings in cost. The Court found Morton's arguments that its discounts to large buyers were based on real cost savings unpersuasive.

Standard Oil (1951, 1958)   In the late 1930s and the 1940s, Standard Oil Co. sold gasoline to four large Detroit jobber-retailers at prices 1.5 cents per gallon below those charged to its service station customers. The FTC objected that this price structure put independent station operators at a disadvantage vis-à-vis the integrated jobber-retailers. Standard Oil argued that it cost less to serve the jobber-retailers since they took delivery in tank-car quantities, while independent retailers did not. But following the precedent of *Morton Salt*, Standard had to show that cost differences explained the entire 1.5 cents per gallon price difference, and this it could not do. Standard was successful, however, in arguing that the discounts reflected a good-faith effort to meet the competition. The four jobbers had been the target of competitors' "pirating" offers throughout the 1930s, and Standard's penny-and-a-half discount was a response to these rivals' bids. The Supreme Court opined that "Congress did not seek by the Robinson-Patman Act either to abolish competition or to so radically curtail it that a seller would have no substantial right of self-defense against a price raid by a competitor," and the Court ruled that "it is a complete defense to a charge of price discrimination for a seller to show that its price differential had been made in good faith to meet a lawful and equally low price of a competitor."[24] The Court sent the case back to the FTC for reconsideration of Standard's meeting-competition defense; the FTC decided Standard had not met the competition in good faith, but instead had used a simple (and illegal) quantity pricing system. The Supreme Court disagreed, and Standard finally was exonerated in 1958, fully 17 years after the case had begun.[25]

Borden (1962)   The two largest distributors of milk in Chicago, Borden Co. and Bowman Dairy, both had price schedules that gave volume discounts based on a customer's daily purchases. Both firms argued that these discounts

---

[23]*FTC v. Morton Salt Co.*, 334 U.S. 37 (1948), p. 43.
[24]*Standard Oil Co. of Indiana v. FTC*, 340 U.S. 231 (1951), p. 246.
[25]*FTC v. Standard Oil Co. of Indiana*, 355 U.S. 396 (1958).

were cost-justified, and both introduced voluminous cost studies into evidence at trial to justify their claims. The Supreme Court ruled, however, that simply demonstrating a difference between the average cost of selling to a few large customers and the average cost of all other customers was not enough to cost-justify a discriminatory pricing system. Neither Borden nor Bowman, the Court said, had shown that *all* its smaller customers were more costly to serve.[26] This was a heavy burden of proof, and it has made cost defenses exceedingly difficult to establish.

Utah Pie (1967)   In 1957, Utah Pie, a small producer of baked goods, began selling frozen pies in the Salt Lake City area, quickly winning about two-thirds of sales in this market. Three national firms, Pet Milk, Continental, and Carnation, also sold frozen pies in the area. Over 1958 to 1961, they tried to win some of Utah Pie's market share with substantial discounts on their various brands of pies. They succeeded, shaving Utah Pie's share from 66.5 percent in 1958 to about 34 percent in 1959 and about 45 percent in 1960–1961. Lower courts had dismissed the case, finding no evidence that the three national firms' pricing tactics had weakened competition. But the Supreme Court found that all three large firms at one time or another charged prices in Salt Lake City that were below average total costs and below those charged in other geographic markets. The Court decried a "drastically declining price structure" in the Salt Lake City market that it feared would eventually drive Utah Pie out of business. What is more, the Court found some evidence—including Pet Milk's use of an industrial spy to gather damaging information on Utah Pie's production process—to signal predatory intent on the part of the larger national firms.[27]

The decision has been a lightening rod for criticism; many feel it symbolizes all that is wrong with the Robinson-Patman Act.[28] First, although Utah Pie was small relative to the national firms, it was the dominant producer in the Salt Lake City market. Thus, the decision protected a seller with—in the words of Supreme Court Justice Stewart, who authored a dissenting opinion in the case—a "quasi-monopoly." Second, the Court's grief over the trend toward lower prices in the market should probably have been joy, for—in the words of Justice Stewart again—"lower prices are the hallmark of intensified competition."[29]

Borden Revisited (1966, 1967)   The Borden Co. was back in court in the mid-1960s in cases involving its pricing of *private-label products.* Borden had long sold its evaporated milk under its own label (with the identifiable "Elsie the Cow" symbol) and also under private or store-brand labels. Despite the fact that the production process for private-label milk was identical to that for

---

[26]*United States v. Borden Co.,* 370 U.S. 460 (1962).

[27]*Utah Pie Co. v. Continental Baking Co.,* 386 U.S. 685 (1967).

[28]See, e.g., Ward S. Bowman, "Restraint of Trade by the Supreme Court: The Utah Pie Case," *Yale Law Journal,* 77 (November 1967), pp. 70–85.

[29]*Utah Pie Co. v. Continental Baking Co.,* 386 U.S. 685 (1967), p. 706.

Borden's own brand, the private-label milk was sold at lower prices. The Supreme Court felt that the two products were "physically identical and of equal quality" and hinted that the price differences could therefore be illegal discrimination within the meaning of the Robinson-Patman Act. The Court therefore remanded the case to the circuit court for further consideration.[30] Had the circuit court taken the Supreme Court's cue, the private-label industry would have been turned upside down. But the circuit court appeared to sympathize more with the dissenting opinion of Justice Stewart than with the Court's majority opinion. Stewart had argued that the products were not of like grade and quality if consumer preference (i.e., willingness to pay a higher price for a branded product) demonstrated they were not. He had noted that Borden took extra precautions with its own brand to ensure that a "flawed product" did not reach the consumer. Accordingly, the circuit court found that "where a price differential between a premium and non-premium brand reflects no more than a consumer preference for the premium brand, the price difference creates no competitive [injury.]"[31]

Where We Stand Now

In the 1960s and 1970s, several committees and task forces, and even the Department of Justice, issued reports criticizing the Robinson-Patman Act and recommending its reform. On three separate occasions, however, Congress held hearings on the matter and concluded that no reform was necessary or desirable.

But federal enforcement of the act is weak, to say the least. According to former FTC chairman Earl Kintner and law professor Joseph Bauer,

> [A]lthough Congress continues to stand by the Robinson-Patman Act, the statute is being effectively repealed to some extent by the very agencies which have the duty of enforcing it. Indeed, the Justice Department has been the foremost critic of the act, and it has never engaged actively in enforcing its provisions. . . . [U]ntil 1968, the [FTC] engaged in vigorous enforcement of the act. Recently, however, it too has severely reduced its enforcement activities. . . . The present vitality of the Robinson-Patman Act has been sustained by private litigants.[32]

Thus is it likely to remain. Given the alacrity with which small business groups and the antitrust bar petition Congress whenever the topic of reform (or repeal) comes up, it seems clear that Robinson-Patman is a permanent feature of the antitrust landscape. But unless there is a significant change of direction at the Justice Department or the FTC, we are likely to see no more than a handful of federal Robinson-Patman complaints annually. And the incentive to bring private cases will likely be affected by a recent Supreme Court deci-

---

[30]*FTC v. Borden Co.*, 383 U.S. 637 (1966).
[31]*Borden Co. v. FTC*, 381 F.2d 175 (1967), p. 181.
[32]Earl W. Kintner and Joseph P. Bauer, "The Robinson-Patman Act: A Look Backwards, a View Forward," *The Antitrust Bulletin*, 31 (Fall 1986), pp. 605–607.

sion. Until 1981, private plaintiffs benefited from the courts' use of an *automatic damages rule* in price discrimination cases: Disfavored buyers, after proving they paid higher prices than favored buyers, could recover damages equal to the amount of the price difference times the volume of their purchases. In *J. Truett Payne v. Chrysler,* however, the Court ruled that a plaintiff must prove actual injury (i.e., prove the amount of sales or profits lost to the favored buyers) that resulted from the discrimination.[33] By raising plaintiffs' burden of proof in private Robinson-Patman cases, this decision may significantly reduce the volume of private litigation in this area. This does not mean, however, that business decision makers and the lawyers who advise them can safely ignore Robinson-Patman when they formulate their pricing or marketing strategies.

SUMMARY AND CONCLUDING REMARKS

Price discrimination exists when the ratio of price to marginal cost for a particular product differs from one consumer to the next or from one unit of the product to the next. Not all price differences, therefore, are evidence of discrimination; where costs of serving certain consumers (or groups of consumers) vary, so should prices. To successfully price-discriminate, sellers must, in general, (1) face a negatively sloped demand curve for their products, (2) be able to identify (if only roughly) how much consumers are willing to pay for their products, and (3) prevent reselling of their products.

There are many different price discrimination techniques. So-called perfect (or first-degree) price discrimination may involve a take-it-or-leave-it offer or a two-part tariff. In the former, a seller either offers a buyer a given amount of output at a price equal to the buyer's total valuation of this amount of output or refuses to sell the buyer any output at all. In the latter, a seller charges a lump-sum fee for the right to buy output at a certain price per unit. Both techniques can, in principle, enable a buyer to capture virtually all a buyer's surplus. In multipart pricing (or second-degree price discrimination), a seller charges two (or perhaps more) basic prices to a single consumer. Some volume discounts are, in fact, multipart pricing schemes. In a market segmentation scheme (or third-degree price discrimination), a seller sorts consumers into groups according to their demand elasticity, charging higher prices to consumers with low elasticity of demand and offering discounts to those with more elastic demand.

Price discrimination can actually enhance consumer welfare, i.e., can move the output of a monopolistic seller closer to the competitive level. In general, the more "perfect" a discrimination scheme is, the more likely is this result. Most price discrimination, however, is quite crude, often conforming to the market segmentation model. In such cases, the shape of the relevant demand curves will determine whether the discrimination will increase or decrease output.

---

[33] *J. Truett Payne Co. v. Chrysler Motors Corp.,* 451 U.S. 557 (1981).

Section 2 of the Clayton Act, as amended by the Robinson-Patman Act, guides the legal treatment of price discrimination. Charging buyers different prices for goods of like grade and quality is prohibited where the effect of such discrimination may be to weaken competition, either in the discriminating seller's market (i.e., the primary line) or in the buyer's market (i.e., the secondary line). Firms accused of price discrimination may argue that their prices differ because costs differ, because they are meeting the competition of other sellers, or because the price differences are necessary to stave off bankruptcy. Judicial interpretation of the Robinson-Patman Act has made the cost defense exceedingly difficult to employ successfully; defendants must show that every penny of a price difference results from cost differences. The courts have allowed greater latitude in cases where defendants argued that price differences between consumers stemmed from their good-faith effort to meet the competition of other sellers—although they must still show that their rivals' prices were lawfully set.

QUESTIONS FOR REVIEW AND DISCUSSION

9.1 Consider two customers A and B who (separately) came to your store to buy a new video camera. Customer A knew everything about video cameras and quickly bought a top-of-the-line model. Customer B knew nothing about such cameras and stayed for a full hour while you patiently explained the virtues of different models. Eventually customer B bought the same model as A, but you charged B a price $50 higher than you charged A. Based on the (refined) definition in this text, is this necessarily price discrimination? Based on what you know about the way the law has worked in this area, do you think you'd be found guilty of illegal price discrimination if you made a habit of this sort of thing? Suppose, on the other hand, you charged both A and B identical prices. Could this possibly be viewed as price discrimination? Explain.

9.2 List the various techniques for price discrimination discussed in this chapter. Try to give an example of each *from your own experience;* i.e., give examples other than those mentioned in the text.

9.3 Some stores give trading stamps in proportion to a customer's purchases at the store. For example, 10 stamps might be given for every $1 spent. The stamps can then be collected and subsequently exchanged for merchandise. The stamps typically are given (or at least offered) to *all* customers. Can this be price discrimination? Explain.

9.4 Airlines often have frequent-flyer programs in which travelers receive points for each mile they fly on a particular carrier. Once a certain number of points have been accumulated, they can be "cashed in" for "free" tickets. Are such programs part of a price discrimination scheme? Carefully explain why or why not.

9.5 Explain how a consumer's time value and income level might be related. Explain how a consumer's income level and demand elasticity for a particular product might be related. Then explain how sellers might take advantage of these connections to set up a price discrimination scheme, buttressing your analysis with real-world examples.

9.6 Evaluate the following quote, carefully correcting any errors or misstatements: "Price discrimination cases are very rare because the antitrust authorities know that prosecuting them invariably does more harm than good. A price-discriminating monopolist will produce more output than one forced to sell at a single price, so it should be tolerated."

9.7 What is a private-label brand? Sellers of private-label products are often fond of pointing out that these products were produced by a well-known manufacturer and are therefore identical to the manufacturer's own famous-label brands. Yet consumers often pay higher prices for these famous-label products. Why? Is this evidence of some irrationality on the part of consumers? Explain.

CHAPTER 10

TRADE PRACTICES

Harmony between two individuals is never granted—it has to be conquered indefinitely.

Simone de Beauvoir

Trade is seldom as simple as elementary market models imply. Sophisticated marketing and distribution strategies would be unnecessary in the frictionless, perfect-information world of economists' model of pure competition, but the fact is that in most instances the world does not conform to the assumptions of such a model. So, either to cope with real-world frictions and information problems or to profit from them, businesses use myriad tactics and practices that have drawn the scrutiny of the antitrust authorities. These practices will occupy us in this chapter.

We first discuss, in turn, tie-in sales, exclusive dealing arrangements, and vertical restraints such as resale price maintenance and exclusive territories. Our procedure is to describe these practices, list the standard antitrust objections to them, and summarize their legal status. Once this foundation has been laid, we move on to (1) identify some of the market conditions that might give rise to these practices, (2) analyze their welfare implications, and (3) critique, in some cases, the thrust of public policy. In the latter part of the chapter, we discuss some provocative new theories that identify several business tactics which may be aimed at disadvantaging rivals in ways that ultimately harm consumers.

TIE-IN SALES

In a *tie-in sale*, goods are sold with "strings attached." Specifically, the seller makes the sale of good X conditional on the buyer's promise also to buy good *Y*. For example, IBM for many years leased its tabulating machines on the condition that customers also buy their requirements of punch cards (used with the machines) from IBM rather than some other dealer.

In some cases, products are so closely tied together—and these ties so obviously efficient—that we don't even think of them as separate products. Shoes are typically sold with laces and new cars with tires, radios, etc. It would be possible to sell these goods separately; indeed, there is a well-developed "aftermarket" for replacement shoelaces, tires, automobile radios, and many other goods that are usually sold in combination with various primary goods. But "untying" such goods in all cases would clearly harm consumers. Buying, say, shoes and then identifying and purchasing the appropriate pair of shoelaces would involve higher transactions costs than buying these goods in combination. Thus, such a tie-in is natural and beneficial to buyers and unlikely to arouse the ire of antitrust authorities.

Antitrust Objections

Not all tie-ins are seen as innocent or benign, however. Many scholars view them with a fair amount of suspicion and are convinced that at least some tie-ins have anticompetitive effects. In brief, the major arguments raised against tie-in sales are as follows:

1 Tie-ins can be used to exclude or *foreclose* small sellers from a particular market. In one case, a firm pioneering community antenna television (CATV) systems tied its basic subscriptions to purchases of various connecting wires and to 5-year service contracts. Customers who wanted CATV had to agree to take the whole package and could not purchase connecting wires or service separately from independent dealers. The Antitrust Division argued that this unfairly kept such dealers from competing for this business and thus harmed consumers. Eventually, the firm was required to modify its practices, although the courts did recognize some circumstances in which tie-ins could be legitimate.[1]

2 Tie-ins can give a seller with monopoly power in one market sufficient leverage to extend this power into another. For some time, e.g., Kodak tied sales of film and film processing. After shooting a roll of film, customers simply mailed it to Kodak for developing "at no extra charge"—i.e., the price of the film included processing. Under this system, about 90 percent of the film shot by amateur photographers was sold and processed by Kodak. The antitrust authorities felt that Kodak had levered its film monopoly, which resulted in part from the superiority of Kodak's product and from various patents the firm held, into a film-developing monopoly. In 1956, Kodak agreed to sell its film and processing separately, to license its processing technology to new entrants, and to divest itself of much of its processing capacity.

---

[1] *United States v. Jerrold Electronics Corp.,* 187 F. Supp. 545 (1960), affirmed *per curiam,* 365 U.S. 567 (1961).

3 Tie-ins can create barriers to entry into markets. Some firms might be able to scrape up enough capital to enter the market for good X, for example, but not the market for good Y. When another seller ties purchases of X and Y together, potential entrants might find it necessary—but financially difficult—to produce and sell both goods. Thus, entry into the market for X is deterred, and competition suffers.

4 Tie-ins can aid cartel discipline. Suppose good X is sold by a cartel at a fixed price. One way to secretly shave this price would be to sell related goods Y, Z, etc., at a discount. The price of X would then appear to be uniform even though considerable price-cutting is going on. The cartel might solve this problem by requiring members to tie sales of X to sales of Y, Z, etc., quoting a single price for the bundle. It might then be easier to detect any deviations from the cartel price and so keep the cartel functioning.

5 Tie-ins can increase the profits associated with a monopoly. IBM's tie-in of tabulating machines with punch cards (mentioned earlier) is an often cited example. IBM's market share for both machines and cards exceeded 80 percent. Under the circumstances, IBM likely could set monopolistic prices for its machines. But, as we discussed in Chapter 9, a single monopoly price may not maximize a monopolist's profits. Price discrimination can raise profits if the seller can sort buyers according to their willingness to pay (and, in addition, keep low-price buyers from reselling to high-price buyers). Now a buyer's intensity of demand for tabulating machines may be highly correlated with the number of punch cards used. Those with high intensity (high-price) demand will likely use lots of cards; those with low-intensity (low-price) demand will use fewer cards. Thus, it is commonly argued that IBM tied machines to cards to price-discriminate. A customer's use of cards enabled IBM to "meter" the customer's demand almost perfectly. Even after setting machine prices equal to costs, IBM could earn profits in direct proportion to each customer's use of its machines by setting the price of punch cards slightly in excess of marginal costs. Such a scheme might raise total profits above the level yielded by a simple monopoly price on the machines.

Legal Treatment of Tie-ins

Although section 1 of the Sherman Act may be read to prohibit anticompetitive tie-in sales, section 3 of the Clayton Act is more explicit on the matter:

> It shall be unlawful . . . to lease or [sell] goods . . . on the condition, agreement, or understanding that the lessee or purchaser thereof shall not use or deal in the goods . . . of a competitor or competitors of the lessor or seller, where the effect . . . may be to substantially lessen competition or tend to create a monopoly in any line of commerce.

Over the years, the courts have almost—but not quite—construed this language to mean that tie-in sales are illegal per se. If it is clear that distinct products are being tied (i.e., that the tie-in is not of the innocent shoe-and-shoelace variety) and that the tie-in affects a substantial amount of commerce, then the courts are quite likely to look askance at tie-ins, especially when used by relatively large firms. In the *Northern Pacific Railroad* case, e.g., the Supreme Court ruled that tie-ins are "unreasonable in and of themselves" when used by firms with substantial market power or when they foreclose competing firms from a significant portion of a market.[2]

The evolution of this tough standard began with the aforementioned *IBM* case. At trial, IBM argued that it required customers to use IBM's own cards to ensure that its machines were not damaged by the use of cheaper, but inferior, cards. Since customers would be unable to distinguish whether a jam-up resulted from a poor-quality machine or bad cards, IBM asserted that a tie-in was necessary to protect the firm's reputation or "goodwill." This argument was undercut by the observation that IBM allowed the federal government to use non-IBM cards, apparently without ill effect. The Supreme Court concluded that IBM's goal was not the protection of its reputation, but rather "the elimination of business competition and the creation of monopoly."[3]

In a similar case, the International Salt Co. was forced to stop requiring users of its patented salt processing machines to use only International's salt in these machines.[4] Just as in *IBM*, the Court rejected International Salt's argument that the tie-in was aimed at ensuring high-quality performance of its machines. This goal, the Court ruled, could have been served by requiring customers to observe reasonable quality standards in the raw materials they purchased.

IBM and *International Salt* indicated that a blanket prohibition of tie-ins was in the offing, but two defenses were eventually recognized by the courts. In *Jerrold Electronics* (also briefly described earlier), the courts recognized that tie-ins were necessary to safeguard product quality in some circumstances. The CATV industry, then in its infancy, might never have developed had customers been frustrated by poor product quality resulting from inferior equipment or service. Thus, the courts judged Jerrold's decision to tie its CATV subscriptions to certain equipment and maintenance purchases to be defensible—for a time. Once the industry had been established, the courts ruled, the restraints would have to be dropped. In a similar vein, the courts ruled in *Carvel* that the parent firm, which sold ice cream franchises, could require franchisees to buy certain supplies and equipment from the parent in order to protect the reputation of the parent firm and ensure the quality of products sold at each outlet.[5] In *Chicken Delight*, however, the courts took a contrary view, enjoining Chicken Delight from requiring that its franchisees purchase certain inputs and equipment from the parent firm. In this case, the courts reasoned that product quality could be preserved simply by specifying certain standards that franchisees had to observe in buying supplies from

---

[2]*Northern Pacific Railroad Co. v. United States*, 356 U.S. 1 (1958).
[3]*International Business Machines v. United States*, 298 U.S. 131 (1936), p. 140.
[4]*International Salt Co. v. United States*, 332 U.S. 392 (1947).
[5]*Susser v. Carvel Corp.*, 332 F.2d 505 (1964).

independent dealers.[6] The key in *Carvel* was that the court was evidently convinced that such standards would not be effective in the circumstances of that case.

In *Fortner*, the Supreme Court established another defense. Plaintiff Fortner Enterprises, a real estate developer, had borrowed $2 million from the U.S. Steel Homes Credit Corporation to develop certain parcels in Kentucky. It agreed to use prefabricated homes manufactured by U.S. Steel on these parcels. Subsequently, Fortner accused U.S. Steel of using its market power in the market for credit (the "tying good") to advantage in the market for prefabricated housing (the "tied good"). But the Supreme Court found that U.S. Steel in fact had no market power in the credit market and, therefore, the tie-in could not violate the Clayton Act.[7]

In sum, when defendants can show (1) that they lack monopoly power in the market for the tying good or (2) that a tie-in is necessary to protect product quality *and* that alternative quality assurance mechanisms are unavailable, the tie-in may be judged reasonable. Where the defendant holds a large share of the market for the tying good or where the amount of foreclosure in the market for the tied good appears large, however, arguments about the reasonableness or business necessity of the arrangement are likely to be unavailing.

There is some hint, however, that both the courts and the antitrust authorities are inclined to relax this standard in the future. In a dissent in one recent case involving tying, four Supreme Court justices stated:

> The time has therefore come to abandon the "per se" label and refocus the inquiry on the adverse economic effects, and the potential benefits the tie may have.[8]

And the Antitrust Division of the Justice Department has issued "Vertical Restraints Guidelines," which state that "tying will not be challenged if the party imposing the tie has a market share of 30 percent or less in the market for the tying product," unless it can be established that the tie-in "unreasonably restrains competition" in the market for the tied good.[9]

VIGNETTE 10.1   Tie-ins in the Movie Industry: Block Booking

Tying was used in the marketing of motion pictures as early as 1916. In a practice dubbed *block booking*, distributors would agree to rent exhibitors one film on the condition that others in a specified block of films be rented as well. In *Paramount Pictures*,[10] which involved licensing of films for theatrical exhibition, and later in *Loew's*,[11] which involved licensing of films to TV stations, the Supreme Court brand-

---

[6]*Siegel v. Chicken Delight*, 448 F.2d 43 (1971).
[7]*Fortner Enterprises v. U.S. Steel Corp.*, 429 U.S. 610 (1977).
[8]*Jefferson Parish Hospital District No. 2 v. Hyde*, 466 U.S. 2 (1984), p. 35.
[9]U.S. Department of Justice, Antitrust Division, "Vertical Restraints Guidelines," January 23, 1985, p. 41.
[10]*United States v. Paramount Pictures, Inc.*, 344 U.S. 131 (1948).
[11]*United States v. Loew's, Inc.*, 371 U.S. 38 (1962).

ed the practice illegal. The Court's primary objection is that block booking extends monopoly power by adding "to the monopoly of a single copyrighted picture that of another copyrighted picture."[12]

The idea here is that the market power of certain popular movies can be used to create similar power for unpopular ones. But this is hard to credit. Consider, e.g., two films that were block-booked in the late 1970s, the popular *Star Wars* and *The Other Side of Midnight*, which was widely ignored. If exhibitor *X* is willing to pay $10,000 to show *Star Wars* and $500 to show *The Other Side of Midnight*, the maximum *X* will pay for the two movies combined cannot exceed $10,500. Block-booking cannot alter this fact: If the distributor asks a price of $11,000 for the block, exhibitor *X* will decline, the popularity of *Star Wars* notwithstanding.

Why, then, would a distributor bother with block booking? One possibility, formalized by George Stigler,[13] is that it facilitates price discrimination. If exhibitors differ widely in the amounts they will pay for various films, block booking might enable distributors to increase profits above those possible when films are rented individually at uniform rates. Suppose exhibitor *X* values the two films as we have discussed above, but exhibitor *Y*, who serves a viewing audience slightly less fond of science fiction and a bit more fond of soap opera, is willing to pay only $8,000 for *Star Wars* and $1,000 for *The Other Side of Midnight*. The distributor can get total revenues of $17,000 by renting each film separately at a price sufficient to induce both *X* and *Y* to rent both films (i.e., $8,000 for *Star Wars* and $500 for *The Other Side of Midnight*). Or the distributor can earn $18,000 by combining the films into a block at a price of $9,000. Both exhibitors would accept this all-or-none offer because both attach a total value of $9,000 (or more) to the two films. Thus, block booking enables some consumers' surplus to be converted to profit.

Roy Kenney and Ben Klein argue, however, that price discrimination is not the motive for block booking. In a remarkably detailed study of the behavior in the *Loew's* case, Kenney and Klein propose—and present evidence in support of— a more benign motive: the desire to reduce transactions costs in a most peculiar market.[14]

Note first that films, which vary widely in quality, are often booked into major theaters well before they are completed. Such precommitment makes it easier and cheaper for exhibitors to plan schedules, advertise, and budget resources. But it is impossible to predict the quality or commercial prospects of films yet unfinished. (Indeed, it is often hard to predict a film's reception by audiences even after previewing the finished product or reading critics' reviews!) Thus, a major studio will find it necessary to "average-price," i.e., set prices for films of given anticipated grade (*A*, *B*, etc.) equal to some average for all the films in that grade. With average pricing, some films may be underpriced and others overpriced, but on average, prices will be right.

But average-pricing without some limits can cause problems. As an analogy, consider a grocery store selling "loose" tomatoes in a bin at a price of, say, 50 cents each. Consumers will then have an incentive to search through the bin for tomatoes they value more than this, leaving smaller or bruised ones in the bin. Of course, this

---

[12]*Paramount*, 334 U.S. 131 (1948), pp. 156–157.

[13]George J. Stigler, *The Organization of Industry*, Irwin, Homewood, IL, 1968, pp. 165–170.

[14]Roy W. Kenney and Benjamin Klein, "The Economics of Block Booking," *Journal of Law and Economics*, 26 (October 1983), pp. 491–540.

search process will waste a good deal of time (each new consumer spends time learning what previous consumers already know—that the tomatoes left in the bin are less desirable than some others already at the checkout stand!) and will also cause some fraction of the tomatoes to be damaged while consumers pick through them. To avoid the waste associated with this over-searching by consumers, many grocers sell tomatoes in prewrapped packages of three or six.

If average-priced movies were unbundled, first-run film exhibitors might similarly over-search, demanding repeated screenings so they could "skim off" underpriced offerings. Prices on remaining offerings would then have to be reduced, and total licensing fees would fall. Or second-run exhibitors might use information gleaned from observing audience reaction to a film's first run to break (or renegotiate) contracts, leading to costly recontracting, rearrangement of schedules, and lost fees. Block booking, like packaging tomatoes in bunches, avoids such waste and perhaps lowers average prices to buyers. In the view of Kenney and Klein, it is hard to see what public purpose is served by banning the practice.

EXCLUSIVE DEALING

Closely related to tie-in sales are exclusive dealing arrangements, in which firm X (say, a manufacturer, supplier, or franchisor) sells to Y on the condition that Y will accept no goods from X's competitors. Generally, these arrangements are of two types. In *requirements contracts,* firms agree to purchase all their requirements of one or more of their inputs from a single supplier. In *franchising agreements,* local dealers use the trademark of a parent firm and often agree to purchase all their important supplies from that firm. Franchising agreements are commonly viewed as tying use of the parent's trademark to purchases of supplies. Indeed, the major cases involving franchising (*Carvel, Chicken Delight*) have already been mentioned in this context. Accordingly, in what follows, we focus on cases that involve requirements contracts.

Antitrust Objections

The major objection raised to exclusive-dealing arrangements is market foreclosure. As with tie-ins, it is argued that requirements contracts, by reserving a buyer's purchases of some input(s) to one supplier, prevent other suppliers from competing for some fraction of the buyer's business.

In addition, it is sometimes argued that such contracts inhibit entry at the supplier level. The idea here is that one firm might lock several buyers into exclusive long-term supply contracts. A potential entrant might therefore have to create new outlets (i.e., enter at more than one level of the production process) to participate in the market. This may be possible but will generally involve higher costs than entry at a single level.

Of course, it seems fair to ask why buyers would bind themselves into requirements contracts that limit entry and eventually enhance or generate market power for a supplier. Indeed, if requirements contracts augment a dominant supplier's market power, buyers not only would avoid such contracts, but also might offer actual (or potential) suppliers premium prices to induce them to remain in the market (or enter it) and keep the monopolistic wolf from their door. Ben Klein and Les Saft argue that requirements contracts enable franchisors to safeguard product quality more cheaply and effectively than alternative strategies.[15]

Legal Treatment of Exclusive Dealing

Even those most suspicious of exclusive dealing arrangements will admit that they can occasionally be efficient and helpful to both seller and buyer. With such arrangements in place, sellers may be able to cut marketing costs and plan production more easily and cheaply; such savings might be passed on to buyers. In addition, buyers may benefit from more certain and steady supplies or may save on inventory costs by specializing in one brand. Accordingly, there is little sentiment in favor of a per se ban on exclusive dealing; a rule-of-reason approach guides policy in this area.

The Supreme Court first considered the competitive impact of requirements contracts in *Standard Oil of California*. Standard required nearly 6,000 independent gasoline retailers in the southwest to buy all their gas from one company. On occasion, retailers were required to to buy their entire supplies of tires, batteries, and accessories from their gas supplier as well. While recognizing that these arrangements could produce benefits for refiners and dealers alike, the Court judged them a violation of section 3 of the Clayton Act. Although Standard's requirements contracts involved only about 6.7 percent of sales in the area, the Court ruled that widespread use of such contracts could "prevent a late arrival from wresting away more than an insignificant portion of the market."[16] Ironically, the judgment appears to have had a perverse competitive effect. The Justice Department hoped that ending requirements contracts in the gasoline business would encourage independent retailers to become "split-pump" stations, carrying more than one brand of gas, and encourage price competition and entry by new refining companies. Instead, the major refiners simply vertically integrated into gasoline retailing; independent (non-franchised) retailers and split-pump stations are far less common today.

In *Motion Picture Advertising*, the FTC attacked an exclusive dealing arrangement under the Sherman Act and FTC Act as well as the Clayton Act. Section 5 of the FTC Act prohibits "unfair methods of competition" whether or not such methods could yet be proved to have damaged competition; the idea is to stop "in their incipiency" practices which *might* be anticompetitive. The defendant, a producer of movie advertising films, held about 40 percent of the relevant market and usually required its customers to sign 1- to 5-year

---

[15]See Benjamin Klein and Lester F. Saft, "The Law and Economics of Franchise Tying Contracts," *Journal of Law and Economics,* 28 (May 1985), pp. 345–361.
[16]*Standard Oil Co. of California v. United States,* 337 U.S. 293 (1949), p. 309.

requirements contracts. The Supreme Court ruled that these contracts "sewed up a market . . . tightly for the benefit of a few" and were therefore "unfair" within the meaning of section 5.[17]

Such language appeared to make it much easier to attack requirements contracts and made many firms reexamine their supply practices. In one case, the Nashville Coal Co. had contracted to supply all the coal required by the new generators of a Florida utility company, Tampa Electric. Just before the first scheduled delivery, however, Nashville informed Tampa that the requirements contract violated antitrust law, and Nashville could not fulfill its conditions. Tampa was forced to buy higher-priced coal from another company and sued Nashville to force compliance with the contract. Two lower courts agreed with Nashville that antitrust law voided the contract, but the Supreme Court ruled in favor of Tampa. Adopting a fairly broad definition of the relevant market, the Court found that the contract would foreclose less than 1 percent of the market to Nashville's rivals. Any lessening of competition this produced, the Court reasoned, was amply offset by benefits to the parties of reduced selling expenses, protection against price fluctuations, and assurance of supply availability.[18]

Tampa Electric guaranteed that a rule-of-reason approach would be applied in all exclusive-dealing cases and made it more difficult for the antitrust authorities to win such cases. When requirements contracts are used by firms with large market shares, however, or appear to be "forced" on customers, it is quite likely such contracts will be viewed with suspicion by antitrust authorities and the courts.

VERTICAL RESTRAINTS

Producers often impose certain restrictions on the actions of wholesale or retail distributors of their products. These limits, dubbed *vertical restraints* because they involve firms that occupy different steps on the ladder of production and distribution, can be of many types, but two have attracted the interest of antitrust policymakers and scholars.

In *vertical price-fixing,* commonly called *resale price maintenance* (RPM), a producer specifies the prices that wholesalers or retailers may charge when reselling the producer's product. This involves more than mere "suggested retail prices." Some manufacturers, e.g., print a suggested price on the package of a product but are quite happy if a retailer ignores the suggestion and slaps a lower price on the package; after all, the lower the price, the more units will be sold and ordered from the manufacturer. In RPM, however, manufacturers punish such discounting, often by "cutting off" the discounter from future access to the product.

Some manufacturers also restrict the territories in which distributors may

---

[17]*FTC v. Motion Picture Advertising Service Co., Inc.,* 344 U.S. 392 (1953), p. 395.
[18]*Tampa Electric v. Nashville Coal,* 365 U.S. 320 (1961).

sell their products. Distributor X might be assigned an *exclusive territory* comprising one area (e.g., a county or state), while Y may be granted exclusive sales rights in the neighboring area. If either sells across territorial lines, the manufacturer may refuse to supply the "poacher" any further. This practice is often referred to as *vertical market division;* the upstream manufacturer divides markets geographically among its various distributors. Many franchise agreements include grants of territorial exclusivity. If you buy a fast-food franchise, e.g., there is a good chance your franchise contract would prevent the franchisor from trying to open a franchise under the same name within a given specified area, which may range from a few city blocks to several square miles.

Antitrust Objections

Whatever the practical differences between vertical price-fixing and vertical market division, the antitrust objections to the two practices are remarkably similar. Simply put, these restraints keep sellers of a particular brand of product from competing with each other. In antitrust jargon, the restraints reduce *intrabrand competition.* By removing dealers' discretion over prices on certain brands, vertical price-fixing keeps some dealers from offering more attractive prices to win customers from rivals. By protecting sellers in some territories from "invasion" by rival sellers, vertical market division similarly helps keep prices on certain brands high.

At first blush, it seems clear that consumers would pay much lower prices if such restraints were removed. But in this there is a bit of a puzzle. What interest does a manufacturer have in keeping its distributors from competing with each other? If one retailer is willing to sell at a lower price than another, why wouldn't the manufacturer applaud? It is possible that the high-price retailer is charging too high a markup on the manufacturer's goods, thus pocketing excessive profits, or is just plain wasteful. Subjecting such retailers to the discipline of competition should be a good thing—even from the manufacturer's point of view—because it will squeeze every penny of excess markup out of these retailers and force them to be lean and cost-efficient. As noted earlier, this will lower retail prices and increase quantity demanded, enhancing the manufacturer's sales. So why limit intrabrand competition?

One answer may be that the manufacturer is not, in fact, imposing the restraints, but merely responding to the entreaties of retailers who have formed a cartel and are getting the manufacturer to enforce it for them. That is, the retailers have jointly fixed prices or divided markets geographically, but to prevent cheating among themselves (i.e., secret price-cutting or poaching), they convince the manufacturer to punish cheaters, presumably in exchange for a slice of the cartel pie. In essence, the vertical restraints are not really vertical at all, but really horizontal in nature, originating in a conspiracy among retailers.

Or the restraints may be part of a horizontal conspiracy involving other manufacturers. A manufacturers' cartel may be difficult to police because it is so easy to secretly shave price by, say, throwing in favorable credit terms or free delivery. And if the number of buyers is small, it will be difficult to infer cheating by statistical means (i.e., by observing shifts in market share). Imposing vertical restraints may enhance cartel discipline. For one thing, it may be easier to identify price-cutting by checking retail rather than wholesale prices. In addition, some feel that protecting distributors from intrabrand competition may make them more loyal to a manufacturer and less likely to "jump" to another; such jumping is therefore stronger evidence of cheating.

Note, however, that manufacturers might be willing to limit competition among retailers of their brands for purely innocent—even essential—business purposes. Some products, e.g., cameras, stereo components, and cosmetics, are most effectively marketed by sales staff who can ask potential buyers questions about their individual needs, explain the attributes of various products, and make recommendations about specific brands or models. Manufacturers recognize that retailers will be reluctant to incur the costs of such activities if customers can walk out the door and buy the recommended merchandise at cut-rate prices elsewhere. Accordingly, they impose vertical restraints as a way of inducing retailers to learn about their products, display them attractively, and recommend them to customers. More will be said about this rationale later.

Legal Treatment of Vertical Restraints

Although many analysts see the motives and competitive effects of vertical price-fixing and vertical market division as quite similar, there are significant differences in how the two practices have been treated by antitrust authorities and policymakers.

Vertical Price-Fixing   In some eras it has been illegal per se for a manufacturer to fix resale prices, at other times perfectly legal, and still other times somewhere in between. This variation has resulted partly from waffling by the courts and partly from intervention by legislators.

In 1911, the Supreme Court branded the practice illegal per se in the *Dr. Miles* case. Miles, a drug company, had tried to specify the prices its dealers could charge. When one dealer refused to comply, Miles sued. The Supreme Court found Miles's actions to be a per se violation of section 1 of the Sherman Act because it restrained competition among dealers of the company's products.[19]

This strict standard was modified in 1919 in the *Colgate* case. Unlike the Miles Medical Company, Colgate had used no written agreements to fix its retail prices. Instead, it simply announced it would not supply any distributor failing to adhere to Colgate's prices. The Court ruled that the Sherman Act forbade restraints of trade but did not "restrict the long recognized right of trader or manufacturer . . . freely to exercise his own independent discretion as to

---

[19]*Dr. Miles Medical Co. v. John D. Park and Sons Co.*, 220 U.S. 373 (1911).

parties with whom he will deal."[20] This certainly appeared to create a nice loophole for manufacturers: As long as they didn't formalize a written agreement or coerce dealers to maintain resale prices, but just "independently" refused to deal with firms that did not adhere to preannounced conditions, they were in the clear.

Shortly afterward, however, the Supreme Court closed this loophole a bit, moving back toward the strict standard of *Dr. Miles*.[21] Upset that manufacturers could not protect them from price-cutting by large discounters and uncertain about the state of the law, many small retailers formed associations that lobbied for legislative relief. By the mid-1930s, at least 10 states had passed laws (euphemistically called *fair trade laws*) that legalized RPM. These laws, obviously in conflict with the *Dr. Miles* standard, compounded the legal uncertainty. In 1937, Congress stepped in and passed the Miller-Tydings Act, which amended the Sherman Act to permit states to pass laws that legalized vertical price-fixing and prevented the FTC from taking action against the practice. By 1941, 45 states had passed such laws. In 1952, Congress even widened the scope of Miller-Tydings. Under the McGuire Act, in states where RPM was legal even distributors that had not signed a formal RPM agreement with a manufacturer were bound to fix resale prices if *any* distributor in the state had signed such an agreement.

Economic forces soon eroded the reach of the Miller-Tydings Act and McGuire Act, however. Large discounters often defied RPM policies openly. Mail-order houses in states with no fair trade laws shipped merchandise into all states. And the growth of national discount chains gave them some political clout as well. By the mid-1970s, two dozen states had repealed their fair trade laws entirely, and many others had weakened them. And in 1976, Congress repealed the Miller-Tydings Act and McGuire Act, rendering vertical price-fixing illegal once again.

But the waffling did not end there. Convinced that vertical price-fixing was more likely to be beneficial to consumers than not, the head of the Antitrust Division announced in 1981 that the Justice Department would not initiate cases involving the practice—and would, in fact, appear on behalf of firms accused of vertical price-fixing by private plaintiffs! Congressional criticism limited such court appearances, but throughout the 1980s cases that involved RPM were almost exclusively initiated by private parties. Both the Justice Department and the FTC sat out these contests—or actually cheered the defendants from the sidelines.

In *Monsanto*, the Supreme Court tried to accommodate the precedents of both *Dr. Miles* and *Colgate*. The Court ruled that vertical price-fixing is illegal per se, but unilateral action by a manufacturer is permissible; i.e., cutting off a price-cutting dealer is illegal when there is evidence that tends to exclude the possibility that the manufacturer and nonterminated distributors acted inde-

---

[20]*United States v. Colgate and Co.*, 250 U.S. 300 (1919), p. 307.

[21]*United States v. Schrader's Sons*, 252 U.S. 85 (1920); *FTC v. Beech Nut Packing Co.*, 257 U.S. 441 (1922).

pendently.[22] Merely terminating a dealer following receipt of complaints from other dealers is not sufficient evidence of concerted action, however; "something more" is required. Unfortunately for Monsanto, the Supreme Court found evidence that the firm had not, in fact, acted unilaterally and had terminated one of its discount dealers as part of an agreement with its other distributors; the Court upheld a $10.5 million judgment against Monsanto.

In *Sharp Electronics*, however, the Court appeared to edge away from the per se standard of *Dr. Miles*. In a decision authored by Justice Scalia, the Court stated that a per se standard should apply only when there is a specific agreement about price between a manufacturer and one or more of its dealers. Absent evidence of such an agreement, the Court suggested that vertical price restraints ought to be judged under a rule of reason because they might serve legitimate business purposes or actually enhance competition between rival brands.[23] *Sharp* hints that the legal treatment of vertical price-fixing might be changed significantly in the future.

But where does this legal history leave business decision makers *today*? Quite likely it leaves them confused. Perhaps the best assumption to make is that while vertical price restrictions are not likely to arouse the interest of federal antitrust authorities (at least for now!), they *may* inspire private antitrust litigation. Whether a court will find such restraints illegal will hinge on the extent to which they appear to be the result of joint action by a manufacturer and some of its dealers rather than unilateral action by the manufacturer alone. Users of RPM are best advised to avoid any appearance of concerted action (e.g., referring to complaints of other dealers when informing a noncomplying dealer of termination) and avoid any appearance of coercion in dealing with noncomplying firms. In fact, it's probably better to terminate a dealer without comment than to try to convince a dealer to "shape up" and comply with resale price limits.

Vertical Market Division The degree of waffling regarding the legal status of exclusive territories has been only slightly less than that regarding RPM.

Prior to World War II, vertical territorial restrictions were common and unquestioned. After the war, however, the Justice Department took the position that such restraints were illegal per se under section 1 of the Sherman Act and negotiated several consent decrees that enjoined some firms from defining or enforcing them. But White Motor Co., a truck manufacturer, defended its use of exclusive dealer territories, claiming that they enabled White to compete more effectively against larger truck producers. A district court sided with the Justice Department, branding the restraints illegal per se, but the Supreme Court disagreed, stating

> We do not know enough of the economic and business stuff out of which these arrangements emerge to be certain, they may be too dangerous to sanction or they

---

[22]*Monsanto v. Spray-Rite Serv. Corp.*, 104 S. Ct. 1464 (1984).
[23]*Business Electronics Corp. v. Sharp Electronics Corp.*, 485 U.S. 717 (1988).

may be allowable protections against aggressive competitors or the only practicable means a small company has for breaking into or staying in business . . . and within the "rule of reason."[24]

The Court remanded the case to the district court for a full trial. But before the trial was held, White negotiated a settlement with the Justice Department. In two other cases, however, lower courts judged vertical market division reasonable. In *Snap-On Tools*, an appeals court found that a hand tool manufacturer's use of exclusive territories actually promoted competition with rival manufacturers by securing necessary sales, promotion, and service investments from dealers.[25] In *Sandura*, a flooring products manufacturer argued that it needed closed territories to secure "effective distributor assistance" in order to introduce a new product line, and an appeals court agreed.[26]

A rule-of-reason approach to territorial restraints seemed well established, and the courts appeared well down the road to recognition that such restraints could have affirmative business purposes. In *Schwinn*, however, the Supreme Court took a detour. The Court judged a bicycle manufacturer's use of territorial restraints to be a per se violation of section 1 of the Sherman Act in situations where title to merchandise had clearly passed from producer to dealers; it was only where title was retained by the producer (e.g., as part of an agency or consignment relationship) that such restraints were permissible under a rule-of-reason approach. The Court reasoned, apparently, that any limitation on the freedom of a trader comprises an illegal restraint of trade once a manufacturer has parted with "dominion over" an article.[27] This was a major departure from the pattern established since *White Motor*, and it aroused considerable scholarly criticism.

A decade later the Supreme Court overruled *Schwinn* in its *Sylvania* decision. A franchised dealer of Sylvania televisions had tried to sell outside its authorized territory. When Sylvania terminated the dealer's franchise, the dealer sued, arguing that Sylvania's territorial restrictions were identical to those which had been found per se illegal in *Schwinn*. In a decision authored by Justice Powell, the Court jettisoned the per se standard it had articulated in *Schwinn*, noting that vertical territorial restrictions could have certain redeeming virtues that dictated a rule-of-reason approach. Granting that the restraints could harm intrabrand competition, the Court recognized that the practice could also enable a firm to compete more vigorously with producers of rival brands, i.e., could enhance *interbrand competition*. The need to weigh any adverse intrabrand competitive effects against any interbrand competitive benefits called out for the rule of reason—whether title to merchandise had passed to dealers or not. Sylvania's exclusive territories were judged legal.[28]

---

[24]*White Motor Co. v. United States*, 372 U.S. 253 (1963), p. 263.
[25]*Snap-On Tools Corp. v. FTC*, 321 F.2d 825 (7th Cir., 1963).
[26]*Sandura Co. v. FTC*, 339 F.2d 847 (6th Cir., 1964).
[27]*United States v. Arnold, Schwinn & Co.*, 388 U.S. 365 (1967).
[28]*Continental T.V. v. GTE Sylvania*, 433 U.S. 36 (1977).

TABLE 10.1
ANTICOMPETITIVE TRADE PRACTICES—A SUMMARY

Practice	Antitrust objections and treatment
Tie-ins	May exclude or foreclose some sellers from market; may extend monopoly power into new market; may inhibit entry, aid cartel discipline, facilitate price discrimination. Likely to be judged illegal when user holds large share of market for tying good.
Exclusive dealing	May exclude or foreclose competition, raise entry barriers. Likely to be judged reasonable except when used by large firms or its use is "forced" on customers.
RPM	Eliminates intrabrand competition; may facilitate collusion at manufacturing level. Per se illegal when there is a specific agreement about price between manufacturer and one or more dealers; judged under rule of reason otherwise.
Exclusive territories	Eliminates intrabrand competition; may facilitate collusion. Judged under rule of reason; likely to be judged reasonable unless user large relative to the market.

Under the rule of reason, territorial restraints will generally be permitted unless the firm that imposed the restraints is large relative to the market. In such circumstances, impairment of intrabrand competition may involve some monopoly welfare losses for consumers, which would, of course, have to be weighed against any efficiencies associated with the restraints.[29] But when exclusive territories are used by a firm which is small relative to the market or in markets where entry is easy, it is clear that impairing intrabrand competition will have no adverse effects on consumer welfare and may benefit consumers by strengthening interbrand competition. In such circumstances vertical market division suits are unlikely, for defendants will almost surely win.

See Table 10.1 for a summary of anticompetitive trade practices.

VIGNETTE 10.2   Some Pro- and Anticompetitive Effects of Vertical Restraints

Is it possible that limiting competition between dealers of a particular brand can actually enhance competition between brands? In some circumstances, limiting intrabrand competition can have favorable *inter*brand competitive effects. But it is also clear that vertical restraints can adversely affect consumer welfare.

---

[29]In one fairly concentrated industry, cases against users of exclusive territories were resolved not by the courts, but by Congress. In the 1970s, the FTC filed complaints against eight major soft drink manufacturers (including Coca-Cola and Pepsi), but the industry responded by petitioning Congress for a special antitrust exemption. Congress obligingly passed the Soft Drink Interbrand Competition Act of 1980 (94 Stat. 939); the FTC then dismissed all its complaints against the bottlers.

Consider first the circumstances of the *Sylvania* case. In 1962, Sylvania was struggling to stay afloat. In an industry where the market leader, RCA, made 60 to 70 percent of television sales nationwide, Sylvania's market share was a bit above 1 percent. At the time, Sylvania sold its TVs to independent or company-owned distributors who in turn resold to a large and diverse group of retailers. Then the company hit on a new strategy. Phasing out its wholesale distributors, Sylvania began to sell directly to a smaller and more select group of franchised retailers who sold from designated locations. Limiting the number of retailers and granting them exclusive territories made them much more willing to promote the Sylvania brand name and invest in the kind of service and repair facilities necessary for the efficient marketing of the firm's products. By 1965, Sylvania's market share had climbed to 5 percent, and the company ranked as the eighth largest color TV manufacturer in the United States. Clearly, the restraints contributed to Sylvania's emergence as a credible rival in this market. As a result, the restraints made the market for televisions more competitive than it might have been had Sylvania not survived.

Vertical restraints do not always generate efficiencies in distribution, however, and where they do not, their effect may be to substantially reduce consumer welfare. Stan Ornstein and Dominique Hanssens have studied the use of resale price maintenance in the liquor industry and found no evidence that the practice enhanced efficiency in this market.[30] Ornstein and Hanssens hypothesized that if RPM made the distribution of liquor less costly, it would lead to increased consumption. They found, however, that where RPM was used, per capita liquor consumption fell by about 8 percent. In their view, use of RPM was not motivated by liquor manufacturers' desires to create an efficient distribution network for their products, but by retailers' interest in the formation of a cartel in the retail market. Political contributions in states where RPM was approved, they found, came primarily from retailers' groups. They concluded that RPM pushed retail liquor prices up by almost 5 percent and thus enabled liquor store owners to extract considerable wealth from consumers (over $225 million in 1978 alone).

ECONOMIC ANALYSIS OF VARIOUS TRADE PRACTICES

The courts and antitrust authorities have been much influenced by economic analysis in their treatment of tie-in sales, vertical price-fixing and market division, and other trade practices. It behooves us, then, to take a more thorough look at some of the economic rationales for these practices.

Quality Assurance and Maintenance of Brand Name

A company's brand name and the reputation that attaches to it are among its most important assets. Because this asset is intangible, however, attaching a precise value to it is difficult, and it often does not appear in accounting statements of a firm's net worth. But it would be wrong to conclude from this fact that a firm's brand name is so ephemeral that it can safely be ignored for policy purposes or that firms ignore it in their day-to-day production and market-

---

[30]Stanley I. Ornstein and Dominique M. Hanssens, "Resale Price Maintenance: Output Increasing or Restricting? The Case of Distilled Spirits in the United States," *Journal of Industrial Economics*, 36 (September 1987), pp. 1–18.

ing decisions. A good deal of effort is devoted to preserving and enhancing this asset, in the form of quality control procedures, advertising expenses, and on occasion restrictive distribution practices.

Clearly, some tie-in sales are motivated by the desire to "protect the integrity or reputation of a product."[31] When two or more goods are jointly used to produce some final good or service, substandard performance by *any* can affect the reputation of the others. Consider, as a hypothetical example, a new type of receiver of TV signals, a sophisticated new "satellite dish" small enough and cheap enough to appeal to a mass market. The quality of the final product (i.e., what you see on your set) will be affected by many things: the quality of the dish itself; the quality of any peripheral equipment used, such as wires or channel boxes; and perhaps your skill at manipulating the equipment. If you are disappointed in the results (e.g., picture quality is poor or the variety of selections appears small), whom will you blame? The dish manufacturer? The local dealer? The manufacturer of the peripherals? Yourself? All the above? Quite likely, the dish manufacturer will suffer some diminished regard if consumers feel that they are getting less than they bargained for from the new product. Accordingly, the dish manufacturer will try to keep mistakes made by others involved in the production process—including you—from damaging its reputation. For example, the manufacturer may tie dish sales to purchases of certain peripheral equipment or may offer such equipment, consumer training, or postsale service as part of a single package "at no extra charge" (as in the aforementioned *Jerrold Electronics* case).

In other circumstances, firms may protect their reputations or the value of their brand names by imposing certain restraints on dealers of their products. Such restraints may be especially useful when products are perishable or a distributor performs one or more functions in the production process (e.g., mixing, repackaging, or assembling). Consider distribution of draught (or keg) beer. The quality of such beer may be very sensitive to its treatment by distributors. Refrigeration may be required to keep it fresh. At the least, inventories of such beer must be carefully monitored and "rotated" to maintain uniform freshness. If a distributor lets some kegs sit around too long or fails to store them at a proper temperature, consumers of these kegs will be disappointed in the product's quality. They might blame the manufacturer instead of (or in addition to) the distributor.

In circumstances such as these, unscrupulous (or just lazy) distributors can seriously damage a manufacturer's brand name. A dealer's incentive to act in ways that are contrary to the manufacturer's interest can, however, be tempered in a variety of ways. As one possibility, the dealer might be required to sell the manufacturer's product exclusively, i.e., may be bound to an *exclusive-dealing* arrangement. Then if the manufacturer's reputation suffers and sales decline, the dealer suffers adverse long-term consequences as well. Alternatively, dealers may be granted exclusive territories (local monopolies) in the manufacturer's brand. The value of such monopolies will be greatly

---

[31]Department of Justice, "Vertical Restraints Guidelines," p. 39.

diminished if consumers become disenchanted with the brand; accordingly, dealers will have an incentive to preserve product quality.

Restrictions such as these are very common in *franchising* relationships. Often, a franchisor sells an independent owner not just a license to sell a particular product, but an entire system of doing business. For example, when you buy a McDonald's franchise, not only do buy the right to sell Big Macs, McNuggets, etc., but also you agree to sell these things the way the parent company specifies and often to buy your supplies from the parent or some authorized distributor. Some of these restrictions may help preserve product quality. A hamburger franchisee might be tempted to buy cheap, low-quality ground beef or buns, taking advantage of the fact that many customers will be lured to the shop (once, at least) by the reputation or advertising of the franchisor. Requiring the franchisee to buy supplies from specified sources—in combination with various other restraints—prevents conduct such as this which can damage the brand name of the franchisor and other franchisees. Of course, some requirements may have nothing to do with quality assurance. A requirement that a franchisee buy, say, napkins or paper bags from the franchisor may simply be a way to collect a royalty that is related to a franchisee's business volume. Franchisees may prefer such payments to lump-sum franchise fees because the payments ensure that the franchisor will have a continuing interest in the success of the overall enterprise.

The Problem of Free Riding

Free riding occurs when one individual takes advantage of the efforts of another without paying for them. Students who have had to work together on group projects are familiar with the problem. Commonly, each member of a group that produces a project gets the same grade. As a result, some group members may try to contribute as little as possible to the project in the hope that better-motivated (or smarter?) members of the group will "pull them along" to a high grade with little effort. At the least, this seems unfair: Those who work hard get the same reward as those who don't. And if *everyone* tries to take a free ride, the students and their instructor alike will be disappointed by the results: Group assignments will be useless, and a valuable learning tool will have to be discarded. It will be both equitable and efficient to devise a way to eliminate such behavior.

Free riding may be an especially severe problem when special sales or educational efforts are necessary to sell a product. Suppose, e.g., you produce a new variety of personal computer (PC). Your machine has many unique attributes; even PC aficionados will need to be educated about your product if they are to demand it and use it to its fullest potential. You might buy advertising to explain these attributes, but this is expensive (especially for a young start-up producer like yourself) and may be wasted on lots of people who will have no use for such specialized information. Alternatively, you might go to owners of independent computer stores. With a little training, the sales personnel in such stores should be able to identify potential buyers of your PC and explain its attributes to them. To compensate these dealers for their efforts, you allow them a generous markup over your wholesale price.

All appears to be well. Your PC starts catching on, winning favorable reviews in computer magazines, and curious customers are flocking to the showrooms. But then you start getting complaints from the store owners; yes, people are coming in to "test-drive" your machine, but they're not buying. You wonder how this can be—your factory is working overtime to fill orders. The store owners complain that people are using a "browse and buy elsewhere" strategy. They are learning about your PC in the showrooms but buying them from mail-order houses that advertise cut-rate prices in the back pages of computer magazines. These mail-order houses can cut markups because they have no showrooms or well-trained clerks and spend no time patiently teaching customers about your machine's unique capabilities; all they have is a phone, a warehouse, and a forklift. You check your records, and, sure enough, just about all your recent orders are from such dealers.

You realize that the mail-order houses are taking a free ride on the sales efforts of your full-service dealers. You also realize what will happen if you don't put a stop to it: No store owners will carry your products, customers will have no place to learn about and try these products, and soon even the mail-order houses' cut-rate prices will be insufficient to generate much sales activity. How can you solve the problem? You might simply refuse to deal with mail-order operations, announcing that distribution of your PCs will be limited to retail stores. But this may not prevent all free riding. Some discount dealers with "bare-bones" operations—no showroom, no trained sales staff, just stacks of PCs in cartons and a cash register—may still be able to take advantage of the sales effort of full-serv e dealers. (Some discounters, in fact, explicitly invite consumers to adopt a "browse elsewhere and buy here" strategy; their advertisements suggest that buyers check out equipment at department or specialty stores and then come to the discounter for the "lowest possible price.")

To fully protect against such free riding, it may be necessary to vertically fix prices, refusing to resupply any dealers that sell below a price sufficient to allow retailers to recover necessary selling costs, or allocate markets, granting distributors "local monopolies" of a particular brand. These restraints enhance the likelihood that those distributors who go to the trouble and expense of providing certain services necessary to the successful marketing of a product will reap the benefits of their activity. Once resale prices are fixed by a manufacturer, competition among distributors will be limited to nonprice dimensions, e.g., the kind of sales effort the manufacturer seeks to cultivate. And exclusive territories similarly insulate distributors from price-cutting, making poaching of customers from full-service dealers more difficult. Of course, there may be alternative means of protecting against free riding (e.g., cooperative advertising or careful monitoring of each distributor's behavior), but these alternatives might be excessively costly or ineffective in some circumstances.

But Ben Klein and Kevin Murphy point out that RPM and exclusive territories may still fail to induce free-riding retailers to supply desired sales effort.

They may, e.g., attempt to continue to free-ride by supplying nonprice services that are not desired by the manufacturer but are valued by consumers (e.g., a mail-order dealer may sell PCs at the price set by the manufacturer but win extra sales by "throwing in" a case of diskettes for free). Manufacturers will nevertheless find vertical restraints useful. With such restraints in place, returns to dealers will be greater than without them. Thus, manufacturers can use the restraints to ensure that dealers who supply desired promotional services are rewarded for their efforts; dealers who ride free are "punished" when manufacturers refuse to resupply them and they lose the higher stream of income they could have earned by satisfying the manufacturer's expectations.[32]

Successive-Monopoly Distortion

When there is monopoly at both the manufacturing level and the distribution level, vertical restraints (or, alternatively, vertical integration) can clearly have pro-consumer effects.

Suppose spring water is produced in two stages, bottling and retailing, and *both* stages are monopolized. Assume that the demand curve D and marginal revenue curve MR for spring water are as shown in Figure 10.1. For simplicity, assume also that the MC of bottling and the MC of retailing are both zero. The monopolist bottler knows that the profit-maximizing rate of output of spring water will be that which equates MR and MC. This is Q_m. Accordingly, the bottler sets a wholesale price of P_m. But the bottler has failed to consider the (downstream) monopoly held by the retailer. To the monopolist retailer, this wholesale price is now the marginal cost of retailing. That is, the retailer will decide how much to sell and what price to charge by equating MR and MC ($= P_m$). The retailer will conclude that it is profit-maximizing to sell Q_{sm} units of spring water at a retail price of P_{sm}.

Because there are *successive monopolies* here, the problem of monopoly distortion is amplified. Because each monopoly adds its own markup to the product, the final price is higher—and output lower—than would be the case if only one stage of the production process were monopolized. The welfare loss to consumers with successive monopolies is equal to the area bound by points $Q_{sm}AQ_c$; it would be only Q_mBQ_c with a single monopoly. Total profits in the industry are lower, too (equal to the area $0P_{sm}AQ_{sm}$ with successive monopolies, far less than the area $0P_mBQ_m$ with a single monopoly). Clearly, both producers and consumers will benefit if this successive-monopoly distortion can somehow be avoided.

One possible solution is a merger between the bottler and retailer. But this may be impossible (because of antitrust obstacles) or impractical (because the two firms may find it hard to agree to terms). Alternatively, the bottler might impose certain restrictions on the retailer. The bottler might, e.g., impose a

---

[32]See Benjamin Klein and Kevin M. Murphy, "Vertical Restraints as Contract Enforcement Mechanisms," *Journal of Law and Economics*, 31 (October 1988), pp. 265–297.

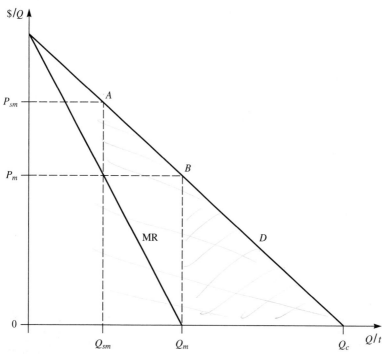

FIGURE 10.1
SUCCESSIVE-MONOPOLY DISTORTION. Monopoly at two stages of the production process amplifies the problem of monopoly distortion. Each monopoly adds its own markup to
the product, so price is higher $(P_{sm} > P_m)$ and output is lower $(Q_{sm} < Q_m)$ than if only one
stage were monopolized.

price ceiling, or maximum retail price, on the retailer. Fixing the retail price at a
maximum of P_m would force the retailer to act as a competitive firm, expanding output sold to Q_m. Of course, repeal of the Miller-Tydings Act and
McGuire Act has made it illegal for manufacturers to try to control the prices
of independent retailers.

Another strategy is to impose a *sales quota* on the retailer. The bottler might
require the retailer to sell at least Q_m units of output. The only practical way
for the retailer to accomplish this is to lower price to P_m—at least at the margin. Thus, the bottler controls the retailer's price without appearing to do so.

The most sophisticated way for the bottler to eliminate the distortion is
with a *two-part pricing scheme.* For example, the bottler might grant the retailer
a franchise to sell the spring water in exchange for (1) an up-front franchise fee
and (2) a per-unit charge for water. The bottler then sets the franchise fee at
$0P_mBQ_m$ and the price of water equal to MC (zero, in this example). The retailer
will mark the price of the water up to P_m and sell Q_m units, earning revenues
equal to $0P_mBQ_m$. But these are not profits to the retailer, since the bottler has
already captured this amount as the up-front franchise fee. By price-discrimi-

nating in this way, the bottler moves price and output to the levels which maximize industry profits, eliminates successive-monopoly distortion, and—not least—captures all the industry profits (in the form of franchise fees).

Tying and Price Discrimination

Tie-in sales may increase a monopolist's profits by facilitating price discrimination. In general, tie-ins of goods which are unrelated will not be profitable, but tying goods with related demands can enhance profits by enabling the seller to meter demand.

Recall IBM's tie-in of tabulating machines with the cards used in these machines. Presumably, the machines saved users money by reducing the amount of labor required to perform a certain number of calculations. But firms differed greatly in their intensity of use of such machines. Suppose, for simplicity, cards cost 1¢ to produce and each one used enables a machine to perform a calculation that saves a firm 2¢ on labor costs. If firm A performs 10,000 calculations per day while firm B performs only 5,000, firm A will be willing to pay a maximum daily rental for the machine of $100 (assuming it must buy cards at 1¢ each), while firm B will be willing to pay only $50. If IBM had perfect knowledge of each firm's intensity of demand for IBM machines, IBM could set different rental prices to each and allow them to buy cards competitively. But, of course, IBM will have no such knowledge, nor will it be able to anticipate changes or variation in each user's intensity of demand. Setting a single rental price will therefore cause IBM to forgo profits on its machines: The price may be too low to capture all the potential surplus of intense users or too high to induce users with less intense demand to rent machines.

By tying machine rentals to cards, however, IBM may have found a reliable way to meter use of machines and extract the lion's share of each consumer's surplus. In the extreme, IBM could lease its machines at a zero price and require users to use only IBM cards in the machines, setting the price of cards at 2¢ each (or a bit less). In our example, IBM will then sell 10,000 cards per day to firm A and 5,000 to B, earning gross revenue of $200 and profit of $100 (or a bit less) a day from firm A and gross revenue of $100 and profit of $50 (or a bit less) from B, capturing virtually their entire surpluses. Card purchases by A and B tell IBM exactly how much value each firm attaches to the tabulating machines and are the vehicle by which IBM charges those with different demands different prices.

Price discrimination of this kind may also be done via an explicit meter, of the kind used by gas and electric companies and producers of photocopiers. But such meters can be costly, and it may be possible to detach them. Also, charging customers different rental fees may be a sufficiently overt form of price discrimination to invite antitrust action. Of course, tie-ins are not foolproof either. In this example, card users will have a strong incentive to avoid IBM's upcharge by buying cards elsewhere at competitive prices. In practice, IBM policed its tie-in by having its technicians report whether a renter was using non-IBM cards when service calls were made. If so, IBM penalized the firms by charging them for repairs.

Leverage and Monopoly Extension

Recall that one of the prime antitrust objections to tying arrangements is that they are a tool by which monopolists in one market "lever" themselves into monopolies in markets for complementary goods. For example, in the 1950s, Kodak was accused of trying to extend its monopoly on film into the film processing market by tying its film sales to processing. In a case decided at about the same time, the Supreme Court stated its view:

> . . . the essence of illegality in tying arrangements is the wielding of monopolistic leverage; a seller exploits his dominant position in one market to expand his empire into the next.[33]

Economic analysis has since shown, however, that *in at least some circumstances* this theory makes no sense; i.e., tying will have nothing to do with a desire to expand or extend one's monopoly.

Fixed-Proportions Case   Consider first the case where complementary goods are used in fixed proportions. That is, using one unit of good X requires use of one unit of good Y; there are no good substitution possibilities for Y. The Kodak example probably applies here. Each roll of film bought requires developing, whether by Kodak or someone else.[34] Under these circumstances, it is easy to show that Kodak will gain no extra profits by extending its film monopoly into film processing. Kodak's film monopoly will enable it to capture all the possible monopoly profits in the film market, whether Kodak ties its film to processing or not.

Suppose the marginal cost MC of producing and developing film each equals $0.50 per roll, so that the MC of developed film equals $1 per roll. Given a demand curve D for developed film (and associated marginal revenue curve MR) as shown in Figure 10.2, industry profits will be maximized when the price of processed film is at the monopoly level P_m, say, $5 per roll. If, at this price, one million rolls per week are produced and consumed, a (nondiscriminating) firm with a complete monopoly on both film production and processing will earn profits of $4 million per week (equal to $5 minus $1 times 1 million rolls).

But the holder of a film monopoly alone can do just as well! The film producer could set a wholesale price P_w of $4.50 per roll. If processing is competitive, processors will add their MC ($0.50) to this price, and the final price will

---

[33]*Times-Picayune Publishing Co. v. United States,* 345 U.S. 594 (1953), p. 611.

[34]It is possible, of course, that some rolls may be bought and discarded (perhaps because they were improperly exposed). But we ignore this possibility as quantitatively insignificant. In what follows, we also omit retailing from the discussion.

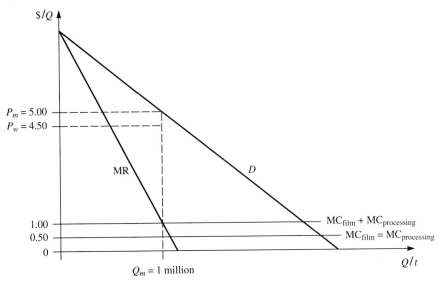

FIGURE 10.2
TIE-INS WITH FIXED PROPORTIONS. The holder of a monopoly on film production *and* processing will set price P_m = $5 and earn profits of $4 per roll. The holder of a monopoly on film production alone can set a wholesale price P_w = $4.50, earning the same monopoly profit per roll.

still be $5 per roll and the output 1 million rolls per week. When two or more complementary goods are used in fixed proportions, a monopoly of any is as good as a monopoly of all. (Note that if film production is competitive but processing is monopolized, the results are the same.) In tying its film and film processing together, Kodak was probably not seeking a film processing monopoly, since such a monopoly would have been redundant. From a policy perspective, then, there appears little reason to worry about tie-ins that extend monopoly when the goods involved are used in fixed proportions. When goods are used in fixed proportions, it is the total cost of the combination that matters, not their individual prices. If you are willing to pay at most $20 for a pair of gloves, the seller can charge $19 for the right glove and $1 for the left (or vice versa); whatever is done, whether the gloves are "tied" or priced separately, the price of the pair cannot exceeded $20. Tie-ins give a monopolist no power to raise the price of a complementary bundle of goods that the monopolist does not already have and thus are unlikely to reduce consumer welfare in such circumstances.

Variable-Proportions Case   Not all tie-ins involve goods that are used in fixed proportions, however. Consider, e.g., cameras and film. These are clearly complementary goods; film prices will affect the demand for cameras, and vice versa. But the two goods can be used in varying proportions. A camera

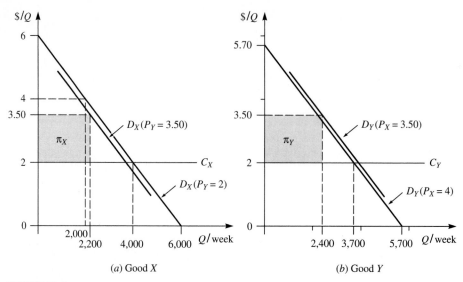

FIGURE 10.3
TIE-INS WITH VARIABLE PROPORTIONS. A monopolist seller of good *X* can earn profits of $4,000 per week by charging $4 for *X* alone. But tying *X* to good *Y* and charging $3.50 for each can raise weekly profits to $6,900.

may be used to shoot only one roll of film at a time, but photographers may choose to shoot many rolls or few over the useful life of a camera. In such circumstances, tying may enable a seller to lever a monopoly in one market into a monopoly in the market for a complementary good. That is, tie-ins can yield a second monopoly, damaging consumer welfare by increasing price and reducing output in the market for the tied good.

Suppose, e.g., product X is sold by a monopolist (protected perhaps by a patent) while complementary product Y may be produced and sold competitively.[35] Assume that X and Y each cost $2 to produce no matter how many are made and that the demand for X *when the price of Y is $2*, labeled $D_X(P_Y = 2)$, is as shown in panel *a* of Figure 10.3. That is, the demand curve $D_X(P_Y = 2)$ in Figure 10.3*a* shows how much X will be demanded at various prices of X when complementary good B is sold at the competitive price ($2). In such circumstances, the best the (nondiscriminating) monopolist seller of X can do is to set the price of X at $4, sell 4,000 units per week, and earn weekly profits of $4,000. Panel *b* of Figure 10.3 shows the demand for good Y *when the price of X is $4*, labeled $D_Y(P_X = 4)$. At the competitive price of $2 for Y, 3,700 units per week can be sold (generating zero economic profits for the sellers).

Now note the effect of the interrelated demands for X and Y. Suppose that the complementary relationship between X and Y is such that every $1

[35]This illustration is an extension of one devised by Ward S. Bowman, "Tying Arrangements and the Leverage Problem," *Yale Law Journal*, 67 (November 1957), pp. 25–26.

increase (or decrease) in the price of Y reduces (or increases) demand for X by 200 per week, while every \$1 increase (or decrease) in the price of X reduces (or increases) demand for Y by 400.[36]

Observe what happens when the monopolist *ties* sales of X to sales of Y. For example, the monopolist may insist that X be sold only on the condition that all the Y used with it also be purchased from the monopolist. In addition, the monopolist may charge, say, \$3.50 for each product. This \$1.50 increase in the price of Y will shift the demand for X to the left by 300 units; referring to the new demand curve for X, labeled $D_X(P_Y = \$3.50)$ in Figure 10.3a, we find that the monopolist now sells 2,200 units of X per week, netting weekly profits on X of \$3,300.

But that is not the end of the story. The monopolist now earns some profits in the market for good Y as well. Cutting the price of X from \$4 to \$3.50 shifts the demand curve for good Y to the right by 200 units; referring to the new demand curve for Y, labeled $D_Y(P_X = \$3.50)$ in Figure 10.3b, we find the monopolist now sells 2,400 units of Y per week, netting weekly profits on Y of \$3,600. Total profits on sales of X and Y are now \$6,900 per week, far higher than the \$4,000 the monopolist earned when the goods were not tied.[37] In this case, *the monopolist seller of X has a clear interest in monopolizing the market for good Y, and the tie-in provides the leverage to do it.* We conclude that (1) when goods are used in variable proportions, tying arrangements can harm consumers and competition and (2) such arrangements merit the scrutiny of antitrust authorities.

NONPRICE PREDATION

It is common in cases of alleged monopolization to argue that predatory tactics, especially predatory pricing, can be used to acquire market power. But, as we observed in Chapter 6, some scholars have challenged the logic of predatory pricing, and a few empirical studies have found that successful price predation is quite rare. Critics of predation theory argue that allegations of predatory price cuts are often made by firms burdened with relatively high production costs that have simply lost the competitive battle to lower-cost producers. Such views have affected antitrust policy; courts now tend to be far more skeptical of predatory pricing claims than in the past. In a 1986 decision, the Supreme Court rejected the claims of U.S. electronics manufacturers that a Japanese firm had engaged in predatory price-cutting, and the Court went on

---

[36]Given these relationships, the quantities of X and Y demanded (Q_X and Q_Y) will depend on the prices of X and Y (P_X and P_Y) in this example as follows:

$$Q_X = 6400 - 1000\,P_X - 200\,P_Y$$

and

$$Q_Y = 7300 - 1000\,P_Y - 400\,P_X$$

[37]Note that the monopolist's profits will be maximized at approximately \$6,992 per week when $P_X = \$3.456$ and $P_Y = \$3.813$.

to state its view that plaintiffs should probably bear a high standard of evidence in such cases:

> [C]utting prices in order to increase business often is the very essence of competition. Thus, mistaken inferences in cases such as this one are especially costly, because they chill the very conduct the antitrust laws are designed to protect.[38]

But as worry about predatory pricing has diminished among antitrust scholars and officials, their concern about other forms of predatory conduct—what we refer to as *nonprice predation*—has been on the rise. Indeed, if the volume of scholarly writing on the topic and the speeches of enforcement officials are any guide, the theory and policy of nonprice predatory behavior will be the focus of much activity through the 1990s and beyond.

Forms of Nonprice Predation

In predatory pricing theory, one firm (the predator) cuts price below cost to impose losses on rivals (the prey) and drive them from the field, whereupon the price-cutter may recoup its losses by ratcheting prices up to monopoly levels. The twin problems in this theory are that (1) the price-cutting may impose much larger costs on the predator than on the prey, especially as the predator's share of the market grows, and (2) unless the predator somehow erects barriers to entry (or reentry), setting monopoly prices will simply lure sellers into the field, push prices back to competitive levels, and leave the predator with nothing to show for its "investment." Unless a predator can successfully *bluff* firms out of the market and keep them out (i.e., can obtain the benefits of predatory conduct without actually paying the costs of such conduct), predatory pricing is a dubious strategy.

In principle, *nonprice predation,* i.e., embarking on strategies (other than price-cutting) aimed at imposing losses on rivals, avoids such problems. It is argued that when predators manipulate variables other than price, they will avoid incurring larger losses than their rivals. In fact, ways may exist for a firm to inflict costs on rivals at no (or little) cost to itself!

One possibility is that firms may change a product's characteristics in order to head off entry by a rival. Former law professor and now U.S. Congressman Thomas Campbell has offered a hypothetical example of such behavior.[39] Suppose (1) breakfast cereals differ from one another in only one dimension, sweetness, (2) consumers' tastes are uniformly distributed along a continuum ranging from least sweet to most sweet (i.e., there are equal numbers of consumers at each point on this continuum), and (3) consumers invariably choose the cereal closest in sweetness to their taste. Suppose further that, as in Figure

---

[38]*Matsushita Electric Industrial Co. v. Zenith Radio Corp.,* 475 U.S. 574 (1986), p. 594.

[39]See Thomas J. Campbell, "Predation and Competition in Antitrust: The Case of Nonfungible Goods," *Columbia Law Review,* 87 (December 1987), pp. 1625–1675. For a possible real-world example, see John C. Hilke and Phillip B. Nelson, "Nonprice Predation and Attempted Monopolization: The *Coffee (General Foods)* Case (1984)," in John E. Kwoka, Jr., and Lawrence J. White, *The Antitrust Revolution,* Scott, Foresman, Glenview, IL, 1989, pp. 208–240.

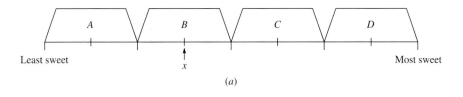

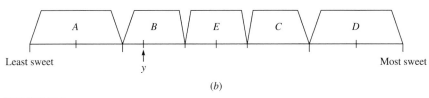

FIGURE 10.4
PREDATION AND CHANGING PRODUCT CHARACTERISTICS: A TASTE CONTINUUM.
In panel b, a fifth cereal maker (E) joins the four (A, B, C, D) shown previously in panel a.
Seller E expects to win one-half the customers preferring sweetness levels between B and
C, but B and C may respond to E's entry by changing their formulas to cause E's market
share to shrink.

10.4a, four sellers A, B, C, and D have formulated their cereals so that each
serves approximately one-quarter of the cereal market. Firm B, for example,
sells a cereal sweeter than that sold by A but less sweet than that sold by C; as
a result, B gets one-half the consumers whose tastes place them between A and
C on the taste continuum. Indeed, B's market share will be the same no matter
where it locates between A and C. If B moves closer to C by sweetening its
cereal, it will gain a customer (preferring greater sweetness) from C for every
customer (preferring less sweetness) it loses to A. As long as A and C do not
vary their formulas, B is indifferent about where it locates between the two.

Now suppose a fifth firm, labeled E in Figure 10.4b, enters, selling a cereal
sweeter than B's but less sweet than C's. Ordinarily, E could expect to win
one-half of the customers between B and C. But B or C can respond by *changing its formulas*. If either B or C moves closer to E (B by sweetening, C by
becoming less sweet)—moves which cost them nothing to make, in terms of
forgone market share—they can cause E's market share to shrink. Conceivably, E can be squeezed out of the market entirely by this strategy or
deterred from entering in the first place.

There are many possible forms of such a strategy. In addition to varying an
established product's characteristics, firms may introduce new brands, called
fighting brands, with characteristics close to those of a new (or potential) entrant. Conceivably, *brand proliferation* might fill up all available market niches,
leaving little room for entry by new rivals. If an entrant depends on consumers with particular tastes or characteristics, existing firms might target
special advertising or promotional programs (e.g., giveaways, coupons) solely
at these consumers to preempt entry. The key idea here is that such strategies

are supposed to be relatively cheap to undertake but impose large costs on potential rivals.

Before such theories are accepted too readily, however, note that they hinge on a variety of simplifying assumptions which may not apply. In the cereal example, it was posited that sweetness was the *only* factor affecting consumer demand. As Eric Rasmusen and John Wiley have pointed out, when other determinants of demand are introduced into the analysis, e.g., price, it can be demonstrated that varying product characteristics is *not* costless to the predator.[40] Suppose consumers are willing to pay a slight price premium for a product that more closely conforms to their tastes; i.e., a consumer preferring the sweetness level denoted by point *x* in Figure 10.4*a* would be willing to pay more for *B*'s cereal than for that offered by either *A* or *C*. Introducing this small bit of realism drastically affects *B*'s behavior. Given the formulas of *A* and *C*, seller *B* will no longer be indifferent about where to locate between them: It will choose a sweetness level exactly halfway between that of *A* and *C* because this formulation offers *B* the maximum protection from competition; i.e., consumers at or near point *x* are willing to pay the highest price for *B*'s product, since their tastes differ most from those consumers served by *A* and *C*, and that is the formula *B* will choose. Now when faced with the prospect of entry by *E*, seller *B* will *not* find it costless to alter its formula and move closer to *E*, for consumers with tastes at or near point *x* would not be willing to pay such a high price for *B*'s product if it did so. Seller *B* would sacrifice revenues to move (even temporarily) toward *E*'s position on the taste continuum. Indeed, it might be sensible for *B* to move *away* from *E*, staking out a new group of consumers with tastes at or near point *y* (which lies exactly halfway between the formulations of *A* and *E*) in Figure 10.4*b*. And if *B* does decide to move toward *E*, it might find that *A* sweetens its formulation to steal some of *B*'s former customers, adding to the costs of such a strategy.

When nonprice predation is costly, it is subject to the same sorts of questions commonly asked about predatory pricing. (Will a predator really be willing to pay such costs to drive out a rival? Will mere threats to pay such costs be credible?) In addition, it might be easy to confuse hard-nosed competition for predation. Altering a product's characteristics, introducing new brands, and targeting promotions toward a particular group of consumers may, after all, be "the essence of competition," just like price cuts. For these and other reasons, nonprice predation theories have not achieved universal acceptance among antitrust scholars and policymakers. This skepticism is probably wise, for as the Supreme Court has noted, mistaken inferences here will be very costly indeed.

Raising Rivals' Costs

Predatory behavior typically aims at reducing rivals' revenues. But a predator might also take actions which damage competition because they *raise rivals'*

---

[40]Eric Rasmusen and John Shepard Wiley, Jr., "Antitrust and Spatial Predation: A Response to Thomas J. Campbell," *Columbia Law Review,* 89 (June 1989), pp. 1015–1032.

costs, i.e., shift competitors' supply curves upward (to the left). Such actions, if feasible, may be profitable even when they do not drive rivals from the market. It is much easier to compete against high-cost rivals than against low-cost ones. A predator should be able to raise price or increase market share if rivals' costs can somehow be pushed up.

Blowing up a rival's factory or sabotaging a rival in other direct ways will, of course, accomplish this goal. But those instrumental in developing the theory of *raising rivals' costs* (RRC) have suggested several practices that may harm competitors in far more subtle (and thus less obviously illegal) ways.[41]

As one possibility, entrenched firms may try to make it more expensive for firms to enter or introduce new products by increasing the cost of acquiring market information, a tactic which has been dubbed *signal jamming*.[42] Before marketing of a new product is begun on a mass scale, it is common to test-market the product in selected areas to gauge consumer response, in order to plan a production and distribution strategy. An entrenched rival could reduce the reliability of such tests by cutting prices or embarking on a major advertising campaign in the rival's test-market cities. At the least, such tactics would make it harder (i.e., more expensive) to determine how consumers really feel about the competing products; at most, it might discourage entry entirely.

Alternatively, a dominant firm may try to affect input markets in ways that disadvantage rivals. Consider, e.g., the coal mining industry. Coal can be mined by using large amounts of labor and less capital or by using large amounts of capital and less labor. All firms' cost curves would rise if miners bargained for higher wages, of course, but firms that rely more on labor-intensive mining methods would be hurt most by such wage increases. Thus, firms that employ capital-intensive mining methods might actually support union efforts to win industrywide wage increases. By raising the labor-intensive firms' costs *relative* to their own, the capital-intensive firms may win sufficient extra market share to more than offset the extra wages they themselves pay. Oliver Williamson has suggested that several large (capital-intensive) coal producers conspired with the United Mine Workers (UMW) in the 1950s in just this way: By supporting the UMW's demand for high wages for miners across the whole industry, it is possible the large firms put smaller, labor-intensive coal companies at a competitive disadvantage and earned extra profits.[43]

RRC theorists have suggested—and bestowed very colorful names on—several other tactics firms might use to put rivals at a disadvantage. Using the *bottleneck method*, dominant firms buy up a key high-quality or low-cost input,

---

[41]See Steven C. Salop and David T. Scheffman, "Raising Rivals' Costs," *American Economic Review,* 73 (May 1983), pp. 267–271; Thomas G. Krattenmaker and Steven C. Salop, "Anticompetitive Exclusion: Raising Rivals' Costs to Achieve Power over Price," *Yale Law Journal,* 96 (November 1986), pp. 209–293; Steven C. Salop and David T. Scheffman, "Cost-Raising Strategies," *Journal of Industrial Economics,* 36 (September 1987), pp. 19–34.

[42]Drew Fudenberg and Jean Tirole, "A 'Signal Jamming' Theory of Predation," *Rand Journal of Economics,* 17 (1986), pp. 366–376.

[43]Oliver E. Williamson, "Wage Rates as a Barrier to Entry: The Pennington Case in Perspective," *Quarterly Journal of Economics,* 82 (February 1968), pp. 85–116.

forcing the remaining firms to obtain their requirements of this input from less preferred or higher-cost suppliers. For example, in the early 1900s a group of railroad operators obtained control of the only railroad bridges across the Mississippi River at St. Louis, letting other railroads use these bridges only on discriminatory terms.[44] Using the *cartel ringmaster* technique, a producer helps organize a cartel for her or his suppliers; in exchange, the producer gets a price break from the cartel that is not extended to the producer's rivals. In the late 1800s, e.g., John D. Rockefeller's Standard Oil Company may have helped form a cartel for railroads that linked Cleveland and New York. Rockefeller monitored all freight traffic between the two points by obtaining bills of lading from the railroads. When one railroad won more than its assigned share of the business (perhaps by shaving price below cartel levels), Rockefeller could easily shift some of his oil shipments from that railroad to another, punishing the cheater. For his trouble, some of his shipping charges were rebated, i.e., his rail costs were lower than those of his rivals.

Like other nonprice predation theories, these theories are new; there are still some doubts about their applicability. Whether they will seem plausible to antitrust enforcement authorities or to the courts remains to be seen.

VIGNETTE 10.3　Predatory or Strategic Use of Government

Even critics of the various RRC and nonprice predation theories are willing to grant that there exists at least one surefire method for putting a rival at a competitive disadvantage: use of government regulation to exclude rivals from a market or raise their costs of doing business. William Baumol and Janusz Ordover think antitrust policy has been used for this purpose in several high-profile cases.[45]

When, e.g., General Motors proposed to join with Toyota to build small cars in California, GM's rivals, Ford and Chrysler, pressed the FTC to prohibit the joint venture on the grounds that it would damage competition in the automotive market in general, particularly in the subcompact segment of this market. Baumol and Ordover noted a telling irony in this complaint: If the joint venture *really* would generate monopoly power for GM/Toyota, enabling this "dominant firm" to restrict output and raise prices, Ford and Chrysler would have applauded! As GM/Toyota raised prices, Ford and Chrysler would have been able to follow suit. Quite likely, Ford and Chrysler were simply worried that the joint venture would make their competitive lives more difficult by introducing economies in production or improving product quality. The FTC refused to block the venture, but did condition its approval on GM/Toyota's promise to limit production of their new vehicle to no more than 250,000 units per year. This output restriction, a most curious product of an effort to enforce antitrust laws, possibly prevented the joint venturers from taking advantage of all possible economies of scale, resulting in higher production costs than might have otherwise eventuated. Thus, the gambit by Ford and Chrysler did pay off, at least in part.

An earlier example concerns competition between AT&T and MCI Communi-

---

[44]*United States v. Terminal Railroad Association,* 224 U.S. 383 (1912).

[45]William J. Baumol and Janusz Ordover, "Use of Antitrust to Subvert Competition," *Journal of Law and Economics,* 28 (May 1985), pp. 247–265.

cations in the long-distance telecommunications market. Prior to entry by MCI, AT&T had this market to itself, and its rates in some areas did not correspond closely to the costs of service (in part because of regulatory exigencies). In high-density areas, prices were slightly above costs; in low-density areas, prices were well below costs. Predictably, MCI entered first in high-density areas, winning customers by offering discount rates. When AT&T responded with rate cuts not only in areas where MCI had entered but also in other areas (adjusting all rates to correspond more closely to costs), MCI responded with a lawsuit. MCI claimed the cuts were predatory and argued that AT&T's rate cuts in areas where MCI had yet to enter the market were "preemptive strikes." MCI sought to use the antitrust laws to limit a rival's pricing flexibility, seeking among other things a court order requiring AT&T to hold its prices at preentry levels. An appeals court decided against MCI on this point but did order AT&T to grant MCI access to its local telephone switching equipment on terms more favorable than AT&T had initially demanded.

In hostile takeover battles, it is common for managers of the target firms to initiate antitrust actions against their suitors. Such litigation was one of the reasons Marathon Oil was able to defeat a takeover by Mobil Oil in the early 1980s. Marathon's managers argued successfully that the takeover would damage competition in the marketing of gasoline to independent dealers in certain areas of the country.[46] If this were true, however, Marathon's executives might have welcomed the takeover by Mobil: If the combined entity would enjoy high (monopoly) profits, Marathon's executives might simply have bargained for their fair share of these spoils. It is possible, of course, that Marathon's executives were selfless individuals striving to ensure for car owners a supply of cheap, plentiful gasoline. But more likely than not, their lawsuit was simply a useful tactic in a battle they were determined—for other reasons entirely—to win.

SUMMARY AND CONCLUDING REMARKS

The reach of antitrust policy clearly extends far beyond the pricing behavior and merger plans of dominant firms or groups of firms, affecting a host of marketing and distribution practices commonly used by large and small businesses alike.

Many antitrust authorities and scholars fear that tie-in sales (conditioning the sale of one good on a buyer's promise to purchase another as well) will have anticompetitive effects, enabling practitioners to foreclose markets to smaller rivals, extend monopoly, bar entry, or accomplish other ends that will reduce consumer welfare. The courts have tended to take a dim view of the practice, and they will tend to excuse it only in cases where defendants lack market power or where a tie-in is clearly necessary to protect product quality and other quality assurance mechanisms are unavailable. Similar antitrust objections are often raised about exclusive-dealing arrangements, in which a seller conditions sales on a buyer's promise not to accept goods from the seller's rivals. Because such arrangements can yield significant savings (e.g., in the form of reduced marketing and inventory costs), they are judged under a rule-of-reason analysis; unless these arrangements are used by firms with

---

[46]*Marathon Oil Co. v. Mobil Corp.*, 669 F.2d 378 (6th Cir. 1982).

large market shares (thus posing the danger of significant market foreclosure) or appear to be forced on customers, they are likely to be judged reasonable.

Manufacturers sometimes require their downstream distributors or retailers to set certain prices on the manufacturer's products or to sell these products only in specified territories. The antitrust objections raised with respect to these restraints (dubbed vertical price-fixing and vertical market division, respectively) are identical: Each greatly reduces competition among competing sellers of a particular brand; i.e., they reduce intrabrand competition. Policy toward the practices differs, however. The courts appear to take a much dimmer view of vertical price-fixing (although this may be changing); if there is any hint that the practice is the result of joint action by a manufacturer and some of its dealers rather than unilateral action by the manufacturer alone, it is likely to be judged illegal. Vertical market division, however, is likely to be permitted unless imposed by a firm that is large relative to the market.

It is quite likely that the courts' more relaxed view of such vertical restraints in recent years is the product of scholarship showing that these restraints can have important efficiency rationales. For example, such restraints can help firms to protect product quality, overcome free-rider problems that might make it difficult to provide important pre- or postsale services to consumers of a particular product, or reduce welfare losses associated with successive-monopoly distortion. Some scholars have recently warned, however, that many common business practices may have anticompetitive effects. For example, strategic introduction of new brands or well-timed promotional campaigns may limit entry by new rivals or raise their costs of production. It remains to be seen how these new theories of predatory behavior will affect policy.

QUESTIONS FOR REVIEW AND DISCUSSION

10.1 One antitrust objection to tie-ins is that they might enable a seller to increase the amount of profit derived from a given amount of market power. What favorable consequences can this have? What unfavorable ones? Explain.

10.2 For some time, Coors Beer required tavern owners who sold Coors on draught to sell *only* Coors and no other light-color draught beer. The tavern owners were allowed to sell dark draught beers and any brand of beer in cans or bottles, but if they wished to carry Coors on draught, they could not also carry, say, Michelob on draught. The FTC obtained a court order to prevent this kind of exclusivity. What do you think the FTC was worried about? What do you think Coors was trying to do?

10.3 You regularly eat lunch at a hamburger franchise that always seems to be busy—too busy, in fact, with long lines during the noon hour. Sensing an opportunity to make money from this "overflow" demand, you contact the parent company and offer to buy a franchise down the block from the one you patronize. To your surprise, they refuse to sell you a franchise in that location, stating that to do so would violate the existing franchise's "exclusive territorial rights." The person you talk too even candidly admits that "we don't want you competing with one of our other people." This sounds like an anticompetitive restraint of trade to you, and you immediately contact a lawyer to bring a private antitrust suit. What arguments are you (or your lawyer) likely to make in bringing such a suit? What counterarguments can you anticipate from the franchisor? Given the current legal treatment of such issues, what are the chances you will prevail?

10.4a The examples of free riding discussed in the text involve circumstances in which one distributor incurs explicit costs of selling a manufacturer's product (e.g., local advertising expenses or the cost of training sales staff) while others avoid these costs and try to poach customers by offering lower prices. Is this really undesirable? Aren't lower prices always better for society? In your answer, consider the issue of product definition and bundling of complementary products. (*Hint:* Is a computer sold after a demonstration really the same as one sold via mail order? Are their prices comparable?)

b Some have suggested that free riding can be a problem even when a dealer incurs no extra costs in selling a manufacturer's product. Howard Marvel and Stephen McCafferty, e.g., have noted that some dealers have a reputation for carrying only high-quality merchandise; these dealers "certify" goods as being of high quality by their willingness to stock them.[47] For example, certain department stores are known for carrying only the hottest fashions; when other stores carry the same brands, they reap some benefits from the "certifying" stores' actions. Discuss whether this constitutes true free riding. Does a manufacturer face any dilemmas in such circumstances?

10.5 In the discussion of extension of monopoly via tie-ins, we noted that when goods are used in fixed proportions, acquiring a second monopoly will produce no extra profits for a (nondiscriminating) monopoly seller. The tying used by Kodak (film and processing) was used as an example. If Kodak's tie-in was not aimed at monopolizing the film processing market, why do you think Kodak used the practice?

10.6 In the spring of 1991, Congress considered an amendment to that year's highway appropriations bill. The Lautenberg/Chafee Amendment aimed to freeze trucks at their present size and prohibit use of longer single-trailers or double- or triple-trailers on federal highways. The Association of American Railroads lobbied vigorously for the amendment, and purchased full-page advertisements in various magazines and newspapers. The ads showed a triple-trailer truck passing a small car on the highway, and asked readers to "imagine the anxiety you'll feel when one of these doubles or triples goes rumbling by you."[48] The ads also urged readers to call their congressional representatives to express support for the amendment.

Why do you think the Association of American Railroads is so concerned that motorists not feel excessive anxiety? Do you think the Lautenberg/Chafee Amendment has any relevance to the "raising rivals' costs" or "predatory use of government" literature? Use graphs to explain your answer in detail.

---

[47]Howard P. Marvel and Stephen McCafferty, "Resale Price Maintenance and Quality Certification," *Rand Journal of Economics,* 15 (1984), pp. 346–359.

[48]Source: *The New Republic,* 204 (June 17, 1991), p. 5.

CHAPTER 11

SPECIAL TOPICS IN COMPETITION POLICY: ADVERTISING AND PATENTS

The only reason why every man does not know everything . . . is that no one has ever yet found it worth while to know so much.

Henry Ford

We have yet to address two important (if unrelated) topics in competition policy: advertising and patents. Suspicions that advertising *might* damage competition—by raising barriers to entry, by artificially differentiating products, or by some other means—have deep roots. Patents clearly *do* limit competition, although they apparently aim to do so for good reason: enhancing the rate of innovation. In this chapter, we aim to develop a better understanding of these activities by examining their purposes, their effects, and the public policies that surround them.

ADVERTISING

Economists are a notoriously contentious lot, so it should be no surprise that their opinions on advertising differ sharply. To many, advertising is a force for evil: It manipulates consumers, damages competition, and wastes enormous resources. Others view advertising in more favorable terms, arguing that it makes markets more competitive and/or provides valuable information that facilitates consumers' comparisons of price and quality across sellers.

On one point, however, there is no dispute: Advertising is big business. By the end of the 1980s, annual advertising expenditures in various media exceeded $100 billion—more than 2 percent of the gross national product

(GNP). It is interesting, however, that the fraction of national output devoted to advertising is actually lower now than in earlier eras. As Figure 11.1 shows, sellers spent well in excess of 3 percent of the GNP on advertising for many years during the early 1900s. Clearly, advertising has been important to U.S. business for a long time.

We begin this section by examining why firms might find it desirable or necessary to devote such considerable resources to advertising. We then summarize the evidence on the effects of these expenditures on competition and briefly discuss the policy treatment of advertising.

Economics and Advertising

Critical Theories   The first important economic critiques of advertising appeared in the early 1930s, when Edward Chamberlin and Joan Robinson published their theories of monopolistic competition. Unlike pure competition, where firms sell homogeneous products, in monopolistic competition firms sell *differentiated products*. Thus, each firm faces a negatively sloped

FIGURE 11.1
ADVERTISING AS A PERCENTAGE OF GNP, 1900 TO THE PRESENT. The fraction of national output devoted to advertising has actually fallen from the levels that prevailed in the early 1900s.

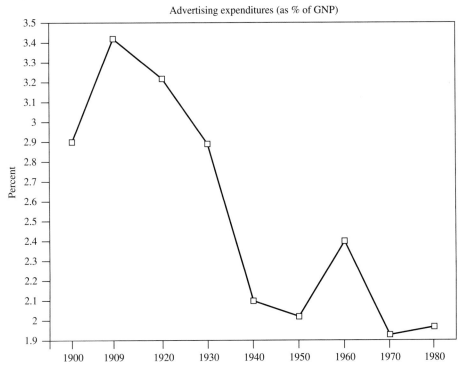

demand curve for its product and has the ability to raise price above marginal cost without losing all its customers. In long-run equilibrium, monopolistic competition begets the same sort of allocative and productive inefficiency associated with monopoly (recall the discussion in Chapter 3). And since advertising is clearly a way for sellers to differentiate their products from those offered by rivals, it must share some of the blame for such inefficiency. In the view of Chamberlin and Robinson and their followers, then, advertising helps create monopolistic market structures and gives firms latitude in pricing that they would otherwise not have; the result is that consumers pay higher prices for less output.

Joe Bain built on the theories of Chamberlin and Robinson, arguing that advertising could be an effective barrier to market entry by rival firms. If advertising involves significant scale economies (e.g., if it costs less to make each advertising message "stick" in the minds of consumers as the scale of an advertising campaign increases), new firms may find it necessary to enter on a fairly large scale in order to be cost-competitive with entrenched rivals.[1]

While Bain acknowledged that some advertising provides useful information to consumers, he also amplified Robinson's plaint that much advertising aims only to manipulate a gullible public. In this view, consumers are not sovereign. Producers guide consumers' preferences via clever advertising campaigns, convincing them to buy—at inordinately high prices—products for which they otherwise would have little use:

> [T]he bulk of advertising is . . . primarily "persuasive." It is aimed at creating product preferences through generally phrased praises of the attributes of various outputs . . . or simply through dinning into the potential buyer's mind an awareness of the product through endless repetition. Thus an important category of product differentiation is built primarily on a nonrational or emotional basis, through the efforts of the "adman."[2]

John Kenneth Galbraith soon took up this theme, stating explicitly that advertising's "central function is to create desires—to bring into being wants that previously did not exist."[3] This belief in the power of advertising to manipulate consumers rather than inform them soon took root. Today, it is common for business executives to assert that advertising no longer merely helps sell a product, but that advertising *is* the product. In this view, consumers choose products as much for the advertising-created aura or image that surrounds goods as for their intrinsic qualities. One advertising executive for a major British brewery put it as follows:

---

[1]To some, this is not a true entry barrier unless the unit costs of advertising are higher for new firms than for existing ones. See George J. Stigler, *The Organization of Industry*, Richard D. Irwin, Homewood, IL, 1968, p. 70. See also Harold Demsetz, "Barriers to Entry," *American Economic Review*, 72 (March 1982), pp. 47–57.

[2]Joe S. Bain, *Industrial Organization*, 2d ed., Wiley, New York, 1968, p. 227.

[3]John Kenneth Galbraith, *The Affluent Society*, Houghton Mifflin, Boston, 1958, p. 155. But it is impossible to conclude that a "want" is neither important nor real just because advertising contributed to its creation. See Friedrich A. Hayek, "The Non Sequitur of the 'Dependence Effect,'" *Southern Economic Journal*, 27 (April 1961), pp. 346–348.

The many competitive brands [of beer] are virtually identical in terms of taste, colour and alcohol delivery, and after two or three pints even an expert couldn't tell them apart. So the consumer is literally drinking the advertising, and the advertising is the brand.[4]

Indeed, our faith in the persuasive power of advertising is so strong that advertising campaigns lately have been used as weapons in the fight against some of our most costly and intractable social problems, e.g., drug abuse and teen pregnancy. The common worry, though, is that most often advertising promotes unwholesome and materialistic values. So widespread is this concern that David Ogilvy, a legendary adman and staunch defender of the industry, concludes his autobiography by granting that advertising, although it should not be abolished, "must be reformed."[5]

Friendly Theories   Many of the above critiques of advertising spring from economists' preoccupation with textbook models of perfect competition, in which information is freely available and transaction costs are zero. Spending resources on advertising in an attempt to convince consumers to buy brand X instead of Y seems utterly wasteful in the context of such models. In the real world, however, information is never free and transaction costs are often quite significant. Some economists have taken these complications into account to develop theories of advertising that are more sympathetic to the practice.

George Stigler was among the first to model the behavior of buyers and sellers when information about price (or other product characteristics) is costly to obtain.[6] Stigler pointed out that information is a good like any other. Often consumers must produce this good themselves, by sequentially searching among various sellers. As long as the expected reduction in price exceeds the cost of additional search, the search will continue. But it is reasonable to expect that sometimes buyers will find it efficient to pay prices above the minimum available, for the costs of finding out about a lower price (or the costs of transporting oneself to the lowest-priced seller) may exceed the potential savings. So in the real world we expect prices of even homogeneous goods to vary among sellers. Price advertising, in Stigler's formulation, can drastically reduce buyers' costs of search: "High-priced" sellers will find it harder to take advantage of consumers' ignorance about their alternatives when price advertising is common. We expect, therefore, that such advertising should reduce the mean and variance of selling prices in a particular market. And, in fact, the empirical evidence supports this view (recall Vignette 7.4). When advertising for such goods as eyeglasses and prescription drugs is allowed, the average prices of such goods are generally much lower.[7]

---

[4]Eric Clark, *The Want Makers,* Viking Penguin, New York, 1988, p. 24.
[5]David Ogilvy, *Confessions of an Advertising Man,* Atheneum, New York, 1985, p. 164.
[6]See Stigler, *The Organization of Industry,* pp. 171–190.
[7]See Lee Benham, "The Effect of Advertising on the Price of Eyeglasses," *Journal of Law and Economics,* 15 (October 1972), pp. 337–352; and John F. Cady, "An Estimate of the Price Effects of Restrictions on Drug Price Advertising," *Economic Inquiry,* 14 (December 1976), pp. 493–510.

Of course, critics of advertising generally agree that price advertising can benefit consumers. Their point is that most advertisements convey no information about product price nor, for that matter, any other information (e.g., directions on the proper use of a product, its performance specifications, or locations of dealers) that would truly be useful to consumers. But Stigler's followers would respond that even advertisements lacking such "hard" information can reduce search costs by letting consumers know what alternatives are available. And there is at least some evidence supporting this view: In the aforementioned study of the eyeglass market, e.g., it was found that prices were lower in states that allow advertising than in those that prohibited it, even where regulations expressly forbade mentioning prices in advertisements (although prices were found to be lowest in states where advertising was completely unregulated).

A more spirited defense of so-called image advertising originates in the work of Phillip Nelson and, later, Ben Klein and Keith Leffler. Nelson pointed out that most goods fall into one of two distinct categories and that advertising may serve different functions for each.[8] The key characteristics of some products can be judged prior to purchase; Nelson dubbed such products *search goods.* It is possible, e.g., to tell whether bananas are ripe or a jacket is fashionable before you bring such items to the checkout stand. *Experience goods,* however, are those whose key characteristics can be verified only after the purchase, generally following product use. The reliability of a major appliance, e.g., may be hard for even the most technologically sophisticated buyer to forecast before the purchase.[9]

In Nelson's view, there will be a major difference in the character of the advertising for search goods and experience goods. Consumers have substantial control over the content of advertisements for search goods because they can detect any differences between the advertised and actual properties of such goods before they buy them. Advertisements for search goods, therefore, are quite likely to contain direct (and truthful) information about these goods' attributes, information which will have substantial value to potential buyers. Consumers obviously exert less influence on the content of advertisements for experience goods, however, since they must buy such goods to determine if advertising claims are truthful. Thus, advertisements for experience goods are likely to contain minuscule amounts of direct information about these goods' real attributes, and in any case any claims about experience qualities ("tastes great!") are likely to be discounted as self-serving by rational consumers. Nevertheless, such advertisements can have some *indirect* informational value

---

[8]See Phillip Nelson, "Information and Consumer Behavior," *Journal of Political Economy,* 78 (April 1970), pp. 311–329; "Advertising as Information," *Journal of Political Economy,* 82 (August 1974), pp. 729–754; "The Economic Consequences of Advertising," *Journal of Business,* 48 (April 1975), pp. 213–241.

[9]In addition, it may be difficult for consumers to judge the quality of some goods even after purchase. For example, some consumers may be unable to tell whether their mechanic has performed a claimed automobile repair or done so with the highest-quality replacement parts. Such goods have been dubbed *credence goods;* see Michael R. Darby and Edi Karni, "Free Competition and the Optimal Amount of Fraud," *Journal of Law and Economics,* 16 (April 1973), pp. 67–88.

to consumers. According to Nelson, when an experience good is advertised, consumers are aware that the seller has gone to great expense to bring it to their attention:

> I contend that this is the useful information that the consumer absorbs from the endorsements of announcers, actors, and others who are paid for their encomiums. These and other advertisements for experience goods have no informational content. Their total informational role—beyond the relation of brand to function—is simply contained in their existence. The consumer believes that the more a brand advertises, the more likely it is to be a better buy.[10]

There are several reasons why the common assumption that heavily advertised brands are better buys might be valid. Noting that firms differ in their efficiency, e.g., Nelson argued that firms with lower costs (relative to the utility of their brands to consumers) will find that it pays to expand their sales by advertising. In addition, producers of high-quality brands will find that each dollar spent on advertising will generate more repeat purchases (relative to initial purchases) than for low-quality brands. Finally, brands that possess qualities likely to appeal to the greatest number of buyers will have a larger market for their advertising. In each case, then, *consumers are likely to observe a positive correlation between advertising intensity and the value they receive from a particular brand.* Advertising is a signal: A heavily advertised brand may be more likely to (1) be produced by a more efficient firm, (2) be of higher quality, or (3) possess desired attributes.

Klein and Leffler took this line of argument in a new direction.[11] In their view, advertising is an investment; it helps create an intangible asset that serves the same function as a *forfeitable collateral bond* might serve in other contexts. Imagine, e.g., you are a banker and need someone to transport large amounts of cash (for day-to-day transactions, payrolls, etc.) to various customers around town. Before you hire an armored car company for such duties, you'll want to make sure that the company will not profit by driving off to Mexico with your cash. Accordingly, you might insist the company deposit funds in some account that will be forfeited to you in the event it absconds with your money. If the deposit is big enough (i.e., if you demand sufficient collateral), the firm will have no incentive to head for the border. In the formulation of Klein and Leffler, sellers of various experience goods might (like the armored car company) try to reap a one-time gain by promising high-quality merchandise and charging premium prices, but instead delivering cheap, low-quality goods. Consumers need some mechanism to keep this from happening.

Consider the following example (summarized in Table 11.1). A brewery can sell beer that consumers assume "tastes great" for $0.50 per can; at this price, the demand per period is 1 million cans. The economic costs of producing such beer are also $0.50 per can, so economic profits will be zero (i.e., account-

---

[10]Nelson, "Advertising as Information," p. 732.
[11]See Benjamin Klein and Keith Leffler, "The Role of Market Forces in Assuring Contractual Performance," *Journal of Political Economy*, 89 (August 1981), pp. 615–641.

TABLE 11.1
USING ADVERTISING TO ASSURE CONSUMERS ABOUT PRODUCT QUALITY—AN EXAMPLE

Event	Result
1 One million cans (per period) of Great-Tasting Beer are produced at a cost of $0.50 per can and sold at that price.	Zero economic profits (per period).
2 One million cans (per period) of Mediocre-Tasting Beer are produced at a cost of $0.25 per can and sold (for *one* period) at a price of $0.50 per can.	$250,000 in economic profits for one period, zero economic profits afterward.
3 Consumers require firm to create a brand-name asset worth at least $250,000 *before* they will pay $0.50 per can for a beer claiming to "taste great."	Once such an asset exists, the firm will produce and sell Great-Tasting Beer.

If consumers are rational (i.e., skeptical about claims regarding "experience qualities" of a good), event and result 3 will occur.

---

ing profits will be normal) if the brewery produces and sells great-tasting beer. But a cheaper beer (one which "tastes mediocre") can be produced for $0.25 per can. Since this is an experience good, the possibility exists that consumers might still pay $0.50 per can for the mediocre-tasting beer—*once*, at least. After actually tasting this beer, consumers would conclude they were cheated and never buy it again.[12] But the firm might not care. After all, can it not score a one-time economic profit of $250,000 by cheating consumers in this way? Can it not then simply change the name of its product and earn zero economic profit forever after by behaving normally? (Or, alternatively, can it not change the name of its product every period and pile up huge long-term cheating profits by continuing to sell high-priced, low-quality merchandise to gullible consumers?)

Klein and Leffler would answer these questions with a resounding "no!" In their view, before rational consumers will take a chance on an experience good, they will require some signal that the seller has something to lose by cheating them. Advertising provides such a signal because the brand awareness (or *brand-name capital*) that it creates is a *nonsalvageable asset* that acts much as collateral. In the brewery example, consumers would not buy just any beer that is claimed to taste great; they would demand some assurance that this self-serving claim was likely to be valid. Such assurance might come from consumers' mere awareness—created by expensive, often-repeated

---

[12]Note that consumers have little recourse to the law in such circumstances. Given the high costs of litigation, we are unlikely to go to court over the disappointing taste of a single can of beer—and unlikely to convince the authorities to go to bat for us either. And if we did, it would be exceedingly difficult to win our case. After all, taste is a subjective matter, and if the defendant produces a few consumers who are willing to state that the mediocre-tasting beer pleased *their* palates, it would be hard to see how a jury could convict the brewery for making a false advertising claim or fraudulently diminishing the quality of its product.

advertising messages—of a product's brand name. If, in our example, this intangible asset is worth more than $250,000, then the brewery has no incentive to pursue the one-time gains from cheating, for to do so would involve greater costs than benefits. The brewery's brand-name asset will depreciate completely (i.e., will have no salvage value) if its customers recognize they have been cheated, so the firm's losses from cheating them would exceed its gains. And *unless* the brewery has created such collateral, rational consumers will avoid its product.[13]

Of course, Klein and Leffler do not claim that consumers can make precise calculations of the amount of brand-name capital a firm has at risk when they make all their purchases, or even that consumers are aware of all these considerations. They simply suggest that this model might explain why consumers are right to trust "famous-brand" products (i.e., why they attach a low probability to the prospect that they will be disappointed in the quality of such products) and are rational to pay higher prices for them. For example, many pay a premium price for Bayer Aspirin despite repeated assurances from consumer advocates that generic versions of this product are chemically equivalent to Bayer. Perhaps these buyers are aware that "aspirin is aspirin" but worry whether some unknown producer of an unbranded version of the product might choose to stint on quality (by failing to monitor the purity of the product or failing to put aspirin in the tablets at all!) in pursuit of the short-term gains from cheating. Or perhaps buyers reach for brand-name goods because clever advertising executives brainwash them into doing so. In either case, we will observe producers rushing to advertise to create the brand awareness necessary to successfully market a product. Once they have advertised, they will be reluctant to cheat consumers because this will depreciate the value of the asset they have gone to great expense to create. In the Klein-Leffler formulation, then, no matter what the informational content of advertising messages (and no matter what advertising executives *think* they're doing to the psyches of consumers), expenditures on advertising have value because they are part of a mechanism providing assurance that consumers are likely to get the level of quality they anticipate when purchasing experience goods.

VIGNETTE 11.1 Marketing a Legend

Today, the success of Honda Motor Company's Acura line is legendary. With the Acura, Honda proved that the Japanese could compete with the Europeans as producers of high-priced luxury cars. Indeed, Acura's success spawned imitators such as Nissan's Infiniti and Toyota's Lexus divisions. But it was not always so; for some months after the introduction of the Acura, sales were extremely slow, despite a vibrant economy. Some automotive industry analysts opined that Honda, reputedly invincible, had produced a flop.[14]

---

[13]Note that advertising is not the only way to accomplish this. Nonsalvageable investments in productive capacity or other selling expenses (e.g., expensive signs, giveaways of merchandise, or other promotional expenses) might do the job as well.

[14]See, e.g., Damon Darlin and Doron P. Levin, "Honda Hits Early Snags in Effort to Enter the Luxury-Car Market," *The Wall Street Journal*, 208 (September 24, 1986), p. 35.

The problem was not the car, which got excellent technical reviews, but a flawed marketing strategy. Convinced that upscale buyers would be put off by Honda's reputation for economical, reliable smaller cars, Honda had decided to sell its new luxury models through an entirely new division. In fact, Honda took pains to keep its connection to the new Acura line quiet; early Acura advertisements made no reference to Honda, and the company insisted the new car not be sold in Honda showrooms. Finally, the company's advertising budget was kept small, on the premise that the high-income, high-education buyers to whom the Acura might appeal were unlikely to be persuaded by mere advertising appeals.

But buyers were clearly unwilling to plunk down tens of thousands of dollars on a product they had never heard of. Before taking such a gamble, buyers want more than just a pleasant test drive or a favorable review in a magazine. They want to know that the product will not prove disappointing "down the road." They want to know that the seller has something to lose by cheating them. In this case, then, it probably wouldn't have hurt to have customers know that Honda—with its excellent reputation for quality—stood behind the Acura name. And it was crucial that the company devote more resources to advertising as a way of creating the kind of brand-name capital that would be a useful quality signal to consumers.

Fortunately, the company soon rectified these mistakes. In its second year, Honda doubled its Acura advertising budget from $20 million to $40 million. What is more, some advertisements began to include references to the Honda name, and sales staff were no longer discouraged from mentioning the Honda connection. Sales more than doubled.[15] The lesson was not lost on Honda's imitators. When Nissan and Toyota introduced their new luxury lines, they spent 3 times as much on advertising as Honda did during Acura's first year.

Some Empirical Evidence

There exists a mountain of empirical research on the welfare effects of advertising. We turn now to a brief survey of this work.

Entry Barriers   As we have noted, some economists have suggested that advertising fosters brand loyalty, that large advertisers benefit from scale economies, or that advertising confers benefits on incumbent firms in some other way. By contrast, others argue that advertising, by cheaply informing potential buyers about alternative products, actually reduces entry barriers.

Joe Bain was the first to make an empirical connection between advertising and entry barriers.[16] Bain identified the liquor industry as one where advertising and promotion costs produced "very high" barriers. Research by James Ferguson and Yale Brozen showed, however, that Bain's claims about entry barriers in this industry were not verified by the data: The record reveals significant new entry into this market, high turnover among the industry's lead-

---

[15]See Ruth Stroud, "The Acura Gambit Pays Off for Honda," *Advertising Age*, February 29, 1988, p. S-2.

[16]Joe S. Bain, *Barriers to New Competition*, Harvard University Press, Cambridge, MA, 1956, p. 296.

ing firms, and instability of firms' market shares throughout the post-World War II era.[17]

Jean Jacques Lambin performed an exhaustive study of brand loyalty for several products, using data from various European countries.[18] He found that there is indeed a consumer tendency toward "inertia" in brand purchase decisions: Once consumers buy a particular brand, there is a high probability they will do so again. But this inertia may have many causes. For example, once consumers have found one brand to be reasonably satisfactory, they may stick with it simply because switching carries some risk (i.e., switching may either raise *or lower* utility).

In assessing the hypothesis that advertising is a cause of consumer inertia, Lambin tested whether increases in various measures of advertising intensity produced increases in measured inertia. Surprisingly, he found they did not. In fact, they did the opposite: Increases in advertising intensity *reduced* brand loyalty. Evidently, intensive advertising lowers consumers' perceived costs of switching to new brands and reduces the likelihood they will be the captives of any particular seller.

Lambin's study also cast some doubt on the popular notion that there are scale economies in advertising that might impede entry. In fact, Lambin's data appear to be consistent with significant *diminishing* returns to scale in advertising: In his sample, a 10 percent increase in advertising intensity raised sales only 1 percent. He concluded that "large scale advertising has no built-in advantage of the power of the large purse."[19] Julian Simon found evidence of decreasing returns to advertising in a different sample of U.S. industries.[20] Studies by John Peterman and David Blank have also failed to find evidence supporting the view that large-scale TV advertisers reach potential customers at lower cost than smaller advertisers.[21]

Ioannis Kessides characterized advertising as a barrier because entrants must achieve a given level of consumer recognition before they can expect to sell any output.[22] The advertising dollars spent to do this are nonsalvageable or sunk costs and thus are irrelevant to the production and pricing decisions of firms already in the market. These incumbent firms therefore have a cost advantage over potential entrants.[23] Kessides analyzed the data from 266

---

[17]See James M. Ferguson, "Advertising and Liquor," *Journal of Business,* 40 (1967), pp. 414–434; Yale Brozen, "Entry Barriers: Advertising and Product Differentiation," in Harvey J. Goldschmid, H. Michael Mann, and J. Fred Weston (eds.), *Industrial Concentration: The New Learning,* Little, Brown, Boston, 1974, pp. 115–137.

[18]Jean Jacques Lambin, *Advertising, Competition, and Market Conduct in Oligopoly over Time,* North-Holland, Amsterdam, 1976.

[19]Ibid., p. 98.

[20]Julian L. Simon, "Are There Economies of Scale in Advertising?" *Journal of Advertising Research,* 5 (April 1969), pp. 15–20.

[21]See John L. Peterman, "The Clorox Case and the Television Rate Structures," *Journal of Law and Economics,* 11 (October 1968), pp. 321–422; and David M. Blank, "Television Advertising: The Great Discount Illusion, or Tonypandy Revisited," *Journal of Business,* 41 (January 1968), pp. 10–38.

[22]Ioannis N. Kessides, "Advertising, Sunk Costs, and Barriers to Entry," *Review of Economics and Statistics,* 68 (February 1986), pp. 84–95.

[23]Again we should note that there is some disagreement as to whether such an unavoidable cost of doing business constitutes a true entry barrier. See the articles cited in note 1.

manufacturing industries and found that this sunk cost barrier did impede entry. But he also detected a countervailing effect of advertising: Potential entrants perceive a greater likelihood of success in markets where advertising is important. He concluded that for the majority of industries studied, the latter consideration is more important than the former and that advertising seems, on balance, to facilitate entry.

Concentration and Profits Assessment of a possible link between advertising and market concentration or profitability began with a 1948 study by Nicholas Kaldor and Rodney Silverman. Using data for over 100 British industries, they concluded that there was a positive correlation between advertising intensity and industrial concentration.[24] Bain's work, cited earlier, reinforced the view that advertising contributed to the evolution of oligopolistically structured markets, but also provoked a surge of new research (using different data and more refined statistical methods) on this point.

The results here are mixed, but it is probably safe to say that most of the newer empirical studies conclude that advertising plays a small—and perhaps insignificant—role in promoting oligopoly. Peter Asch, e.g., examined whether changes in advertising intensity produced changes in market structure in the United States from 1963 to 1971, and he found they had not, concluding that "heavy advertising was at least as likely to accompany concentration *decreases* as increases [emphasis added]."[25]

Another line of inquiry, which began with William Comanor and Thomas Wilson, has examined the relationship between advertising intensity and profits. Comanor and Wilson found the average profit rate in industries that advertised heavily was significantly higher than that for their full sample of 41 consumer goods industries.[26] Later researchers pointed out, however, that the data used by Comanor and Wilson treated advertising outlays as current expenses rather than long-lived investments in brand-name capital. Some studies subsequently found that adjusting rates of return to account for this fact caused the positive relationship between advertising intensity and profit rates to weaken considerably or to disappear.[27] The picture here remains cloudy, however. Harold Demsetz has shown that the biased accounting data on which we must rely to examine the matter might produce a spurious causal link between advertising intensity and

---

[24]Nicholas Kaldor and Rodney Silverman, *A Statistical Analysis of Advertising Expenditures and Revenue of the Press,* Cambridge University Press, Cambridge, England, 1948.

[25]Peter Asch, "The Role of Advertising in Changing Concentration, 1963–1971," *Southern Economic Journal,* 46 (July 1979), p. 295. For a useful summary of the literature on both sides, see Stanley I. Ornstein, *Industrial Concentration and Advertising Intensity,* American Enterprise Institute, Washington, 1977.

[26]William S. Comanor and Thomas A. Wilson, "Advertising, Market Structure, and Performance," *Review of Economics and Statistics,* 49 (November 1967), pp. 423–440.

[27]See Harry Bloch, "Advertising and Profitability: A Reappraisal," *Journal of Political Economy,* 82 (March-April 1974), pp. 267–286; Robert Ayanian, "Advertising and Rate of Return," *Journal of Law and Economics,* 18 (October 1975), pp. 479–506. But see Leonard W. Weiss, "Advertising, Profits, and Corporate Taxes," *Review of Economics and Statistics,* 51 (November 1969), pp. 426–430.

profitability—or conceivably might mask a genuine entry barrier that is yet undiscovered.[28]

Price and Quality   As we pointed out earlier, evidence that informational advertising can lower product price has existed for some time.[29] Over time, the empirical literature on this point has grown rapidly. Advertising has been linked to lower prices not just for eyeglasses and drugs, but also for gasoline, legal services, and contact lenses.[30] One provocative study, however, found that even *noninformative* advertising could be associated with lower prices. Robert Steiner examined advertising by toy manufacturers, who started buying time on popular kiddie shows in the mid-1950s.[31] He found that before these campaigns began, toys generally sold at close to manufacturers' suggested retail prices. After advertising, toy prices often were 40 percent *below* suggested retail, although in cities where there was little or no advertising, prices continued to hover around the suggested retail. Evidently, advertising increased the number of known substitutes to consumers, facilitated comparison shopping, and lowered toy prices.

Some professional groups (e.g., the American Bar Association) have expressed concern that advertising and the tough price competition it can beget might be associated with diminished product quality.[32] So far, however, there is little empirical support for this view. One particularly careful study, by John Kwoka, analyzed the market for optometric services before and after removal of advertising restrictions. Kwoka found that while advertisers' prices and quality tended to be lower, nonadvertisers' quality was actually greater (even though their prices were lower!); further, nonadvertisers remained in the market in sufficient numbers to *raise* average market quality.[33] Studies of other markets similarly fail to detect an advertising-induced reduction in product quality.[34]

---

[28]See Harold Demsetz, "Accounting for Advertising as a Barrier to Entry," *Journal of Business,* 52 (July 1979), pp. 345–360.

[29]See note 7.

[30]See Alex R. Maurizi, "The Effects of Laws against Price Advertising," *Western Economic Journal,* 10 (September 1972), pp. 321–329; Howard Marvel, "The Economics of Information and Retail Gasoline Price Behavior: An Empirical Analysis," *Journal of Political Economy,* 84 (October 1976), pp. 1033–1066; Timothy J. Muris and Fred S. McChesney, "Advertising and the Price and Quality of Legal Services: The Case for Legal Clinics," *American Bar Foundation Research Journal,* 1979 (Winter 1979), pp. 179–207; Gary D. Hailey, Jonathan R. Bromberg, and Joseph P. Mulholland, "A Comparative Analysis of Cosmetic Contact Lens Fitting by Ophthalmologists, Optometrists, and Opticians," *Report of the Staff of the Federal Trade Commission,* Bureaus of Consumer Protection and Economics, Washington, 1983.

[31]Robert L. Steiner, "Does Advertising Lower Consumer Prices?" *Journal of Marketing,* 37 (October 1973), pp. 19–26.

[32]See, e.g., Richard Schmalensee, "A Model of Advertising and Product Quality," *Journal of Political Economy,* 86 (June 1978), pp. 485–503.

[33]John E. Kwoka, Jr., "Advertising and the Price and Quality of Optometric Services," *American Economic Review,* 74 (March 1984), pp. 211–216.

[34]See, e.g., Federal Trade Commission, Bureau of Economics, *Staff Report on Effects of Restrictions on Advertising and Commercial Practice in the Professions: The Case of Optometry,* Government Printing Office, Washington, 1980. See also the studies by Muris and McChesney and by Hailey et al. cited earlier.

Other Welfare Concerns   In sum, the conventional view that advertising renders markets less competitive appears to be on shaky empirical ground. There is little evidence that advertising binds consumers to sellers with sufficient strength to bar entry to new firms, nor is there much support for the idea that scale economies in advertising beget such barriers. While the research on the correlation of advertising intensity with market concentration or profitability is more mixed, it would be hard to argue that advertising commonly damages competition on the basis of this work, especially in view of the compelling evidence that advertising can significantly lower prices without having an adverse impact on product quality. This might explain why today most justifications of advertising regulation do not claim that it produces large competitive benefits, but instead rely on other public interest rationales. Specifically, such regulation is usually defended on grounds that (1) it enhances consumer welfare by limiting the amount of deceptive or fraudulent advertising claims, (2) it is necessary to protect certain classes of buyers (e.g., small children) who are unable to properly evaluate commercial messages, or (3) it can help achieve certain social goals (e.g., reduction of smoking).

Public Policy and Advertising

Formal authority to regulate the content of advertising messages was granted to the Federal Trade Commission in 1938, when the Wheeler-Lea amendment modified section 5 of the FTC Act to prohibit not only "unfair methods of competition" but "unfair or deceptive acts or practices." In fact, however, the courts had already recognized the FTC's jurisdiction in this area,[35] and the common law had long viewed fraud and deception in commerce with disfavor.

False or Deceptive Advertising   The FTC takes a fairly broad view of what might constitute false or deceptive advertising. The commission does not need to show that an advertisement has deceived anyone in particular but can simply determine, in its expert capacity, that an advertisement has a *tendency* to deceive. Further, the FTC may judge an advertisement to be deceptive because of what it *does not* say as well as what it says. Finally, the FTC often insists that advertisements be sufficiently clear that they not mislead even susceptible consumers. Where the FTC determines these criteria have been violated and a significant number of consumers are likely affected by a particular advertisement, it can either attempt to settle the matter informally, by seeking assurances that the campaign has been (or will be) discontinued and will not be resumed, or issue a formal complaint against the firm involved. The accused firm can then negotiate a consent settlement without formal litigation or can go to trial before an FTC administrative law judge or hearing examiner. The firm can appeal an adverse decision to the full commission. If the accused is judged guilty, the FTC issues an order to cease and desist from the unlawful

---

[35]See *FTC v. Winstead Hosiery Co.*, 258 U.S. 483 (1922).

practice. At this point, the accused firm can appeal for judicial review. If the order is final and the firm fails to comply, the FTC can seek civil penalties up to $10,000 per day for continuing violations. The commission can also order "corrective" advertising to undo any damage caused by claims shown to have been deceptive.

Obviously, the FTC's resources are limited; it cannot possibly validate all the claims made in the enormous number of advertising messages transmitted annually. To economize on enforcement costs in this area, the commission launched its "Ad Substantiation Program" in the 1970s. To a great extent, this program shifts the burden for proving the validity of advertising claims to firms. The commission can engage in "sweeps" in which advertisers are sent letters that demand authentication of their claims. FTC staff and consultants then review the submitted documents and press action in cases where claims appear unfounded.

Protecting Certain Buyers   In the 1970s, the FTC conducted a study of the effects of advertising on children, concluding the following:

> We have shown that television advertising addressed to young children, who do not yet understand the selling purpose of commercials, or who lack the ability to comprehend or evaluate such commercials, or *a fortiori* to preschool children who have even greater perceptual difficulties as to advertising, is inherently unfair and deceptive. The inherent unfairness and deceptiveness are so great that only a ban can effectively remedy them.[36]

The proposed ban would have restricted advertising of many specified products deemed harmful (e.g., sugary foods) during times when the bulk of the viewing audience was young children.

The strong language of the FTC report, and its even stronger recommendations, provoked a rancorous debate. On one side were nutritionists, child psychologists, and some prominent consumer advocates who argued that children were captives of TV advertisements, that these advertisements coaxed children into demanding many products that damaged health, and that these considerations required a broad view of "deception" in advertising. On the other side were large cereal and toy makers, advertising agencies, and networks who argued that First Amendment rights of free speech were sacrosanct, and that there was no evidence a ban would enhance welfare. The latter group eventually prevailed—either because their arguments were more persuasive or because they had more political muscle—and the "kid-vid" proposal was withdrawn.

The idea that some buyers deserve special protection from the tactics of sellers has taken root, however, and in the early 1980s the FTC implemented several rules aimed at controlling the flow of information to consumers. *Mandatory disclosure laws* which require firms to reveal truthfully to consumers

---

[36]Federal Trade Commission, Bureau of Economics, *Staff Report on Television Advertising to Children,* Government Printing Office, Washington, 1978.

certain information about their products apply in several markets. Used-car dealers, e.g., must post stickers that list any known defects and warranty terms for each car they sell. While such laws have the potential to benefit consumers who have low ability to determine product quality prior to purchase, the laws will not necessarily improve consumer welfare in aggregate. Under some conditions, e.g., such laws can induce sellers to gather less information about their products and actually reduce the extent of disclosure. And, in fact, empirical research shows little evidence that disclosure laws have tangibly helped buyers.[37]

Social Goals Prominent consumer advocates such as Ralph Nader believe that advertising contributes mightily to some of the greatest U.S. public health problems: alcoholism, heart disease, and cancer. In the mid-1980s, e.g., over two dozen groups (led by the Center for Science in the Public Interest) joined to petition the FTC for limits on advertising of alcohol, just as federal law had, in 1971, restricted cigarette advertising. The petition called alcohol use a *public health nightmare* and blamed it for numerous accidental deaths (especially automobile-related fatalities) and adverse health effects. It sought several remedies, including a total ban on advertising reaching small children, teens, or problem drinkers as well as health warnings and public service messages to offset the seductive effects of alcohol advertising.

The petition was not approved, in part because the FTC's own staff (at the Bureaus of Consumer Protection and Economics) weighed in with a memorandum opposing it:

> Protection of the principles of consumer sovereignty rests at the heart of the Commission's exercise of its unfairness authority. In the context of alcoholic beverage advertising, these principles will not support a finding of substantial injury solely in the promotion of this lawfully marketed product. To hold otherwise would permit the Commission to substitute its own tastes for that of the marketplace. Thus, a finding that the challenged practices are unfair would require evidence that the practices are likely to lead to abuse. It is abuse, not consumption per use, that leads to unavoidable consumer injury.[38]

In essence, the FTC staffers argued that the petition would take the commission beyond the regulation of messages that were deceptive or related to illegal activity. Such a step required evidence that such regulation would directly advance some "substantial government interest." Eliminating the social effects of alcohol abuse might comprise such an interest, of course, but the staffers wanted proof that advertising was linked to not only the consumption of alco-

---

[37]See, e.g., Gregg A. Jarrell, "The Economic Effects of Federal Regulation of the Market for New Security Issues," *Journal of Law and Economics*, 24 (December 1981), pp. 613–675; Michael D. Pratt and George E. Hoffer, "The Efficacy of State Mandated Minimum Quality Certification: The Case of Used Vehicles," *Economic Inquiry*, 24 (April 1986), pp. 313–318.

[38]Federal Trade Commission, Bureau of Economics, *Memorandum to the Federal Trade Commission on Omnibus Petition for Regulation of Unfair and Deceptive Alcoholic Beverage Advertising and Marketing Practices*, Government Printing Office, Washington, 1985, p. 12.

hol but also its *abuse*. When research produces some evidence of such linkage, it is quite possible such a petition will be revived.

VIGNETTE 11.2   The Cigarette Advertisement Ban

What is undoubtedly the single most important experiment in the history of advertising regulation—the federal ban on cigarette advertisements—has been underway for over two decades now, long enough for scholars to study its effects in some detail. These studies have shown some surprising (indeed, vexing!) results: There is little evidence that the advertising ban has contributed to a reduction in cigarette consumption or enhanced welfare.

James Hamilton produced the first major study of the advertising ban's effects.[39] He noted that the 1964 Surgeon General's report on the adverse health consequences of smoking, coupled with the antismoking advertisements that ran throughout the late 1960s under the fairness ("equal-time") doctrine, contributed to a health scare that reduced cigarette consumption well before the ban. In fact, Hamilton argued, the antismoking advertisements were more effective than the cigarette companies' own advertising campaigns. Thus, the ban had perverse effects: By taking cigarette advertisements off the air and rendering the fairness doctrine inoperative, the ban reduced the number of antismoking messages and actually increased cigarette consumption!

Hamilton's empirical results are broadly consistent with those obtained in later studies. In general, research tends to support the view that advertising does not increase overall cigarette demand—and eliminating advertising does not reduce demand. Rather, advertising affects the distribution of sales among competing brands and greatly facilitates the introduction of new brands.[40]

The latter issue may be particularly important. By making it more difficult for new firms to enter the market, the advertising ban clearly has competitive effects. Of course, if our goal is to reduce cigarette consumption, we hesitate to label these effects "adverse." That is, if the ban makes it easier for incumbent firms to form a cartel in this market and raise prices, the advertising ban might reduce consumption after all! But some researchers worry that the entry barriers will adversely affect the *mix* of products available to consumers.[41] For example, new entrants might be more likely to cater to consumers' growing concern about health by offering low-tar brands; the advertising ban will make such entry more difficult, reducing the likelihood that consumers will benefit from improved products.

If the evidence suggests that the advertising ban failed to improve the welfare of consumers, it benefited at least one group: the tobacco companies. Mark Mitchell

---

[39]James L. Hamilton, "The Demand for Cigarettes: Advertising, the Health Scare, and the Cigarette Advertising Ban," *Review of Economics and Statistics*, 54 (November 1972), pp. 401–411.

[40]See, e.g., Henry G. Grabowski, "The Effects of Advertising on the Interindustry Distribution of Demand," *Explorations in Economic Research*, (1976), pp. 21–75; Gideon Doron, *The Smoking Paradox*, Abt Books, Cambridge, MA, 1979; Eugene M. Lewit, Douglas Coate, and Michael Grossman, "The Effects of Government Regulation on Teenage Smoking," *Journal of Law and Economics*, 24 (December 1981), pp. 545–569; John A. Bishop and Jang H. Yoo, "Health Scare, Excise Taxes and Advertising Ban in the Cigarette Demand and Supply," *Southern Economic Journal*, 52 (October 1985), pp. 402–411.

[41]See Lynne Schneider, Benjamin Klein, and Kevin Murphy, "Government Regulation of Cigarette Health Information," *Journal of Law and Economics*, 24 (December 1981), pp. 572–612.

and Harold Mulherin examined the stock returns of the major cigarette producers around the time the advertising ban was implemented.[42] They found evidence that confirms the view that the ban—by lessening market entry and rendering the fairness doctrine inoperable—protected the tobacco companies from brand competition. Not only were the returns to holders of tobacco firms' stock abnormally high throughout this period, but also the riskiness of such investments (i.e., the variation in returns) was significantly reduced.

Conclusions   The empirical evidence on advertising is too sketchy to permit a final verdict on its usefulness in every case. We certainly should not rule out the possibility that it can be a strategic tool used to bar entry or create spurious product differentiation. But if advertising can reduce consumer welfare, so, too, can its absence. There is strong evidence that restrictions on advertising can render markets less competitive; on the other side, there is little evidence that regulatory attempts to *force* sellers to provide useful information about their products have truly benefited buyers.

Thus, we should be careful about installing new limits on advertising. It will be tempting to try to use such limits to correct informational disparities that can put consumers at a disadvantage in their dealings with sellers, or to contain the external costs associated with certain patterns of consumption (topics we will confront more directly later, in our discussion of social regulation in Chapters 16 and 17). But we must remember that advertising regulation, whatever its motivation, can affect competitive vigor. When we propose regulations that aim to achieve one objective, we should not fail to consider that these might produce secondary effects that can, when all is said and done, confound our efforts to enhance consumer welfare.

PATENTS

Antitrust policy is aimed at promoting competition and inhibiting monopoly. The patent system appears to do the opposite. Governments grant patent holders exclusive rights over any new and useful product or production process for some finite period (17 years in the United States). With a patent system in place, firms can use the courts to ward off imitators (i.e., competitors) and enforce their monopoly until their patent expires.

Although some might argue that this is a clear example of one government policy at war with another, most economists and policymakers would probably respond that there is no necessary contradiction. Both policies, in principle, aim to enhance welfare; antitrust policy aims to do this by avoiding the deadweight surplus losses associated with monopolistic conduct, while the patent system aims to expand surplus by encouraging an optimal amount of innovative activity. In this view, patents are one way (although by no means the only way) to solve a free-rider problem that might otherwise result in a

[42]Mark L. Mitchell and J. Harold Mulherin, "Finessing the Political System: The Cigarette Advertising Ban," *Southern Economic Journal*, 54 (April 1988), pp. 855–862.

world in which there is too little research and innovation. For while inventions are sometimes the result of sudden (and perhaps relatively cheap) "flashes of creative genius," rendering such inventions commercially useful is usually a costly endeavor. James Watt, e.g., devised his successful version of the steam engine in such a flash and made a working model of his engine in only 3 days, but he had to spend 11 years and the equivalent of 60 person-years of labor getting his invention ready for the marketplace. If imitators could have simply copied his engine once it was perfected, Watt would never have been able to recover his enormous research and development (R&D) investments. The imitators, burdened by none of Watt's sunk R&D costs, would have set a price equal to the marginal costs of manufacturing their copies. Watt would have had to match this price (and write off his R&D investments) or make no sales. Anticipating this, Watt probably would not have made these investments.

Clearly, a society that fails to innovate will be a poorer society. One study by Edward Denison found that nearly *half* the increase in output per worker in the United States between 1929 and 1969 was the result of advancements in scientific and technical knowledge.[43] As we shall see, however, not everyone agrees that patents are required to produce the optimal amount of innovation or that the current patent system is working as intended. Researchers have identified potential abuses of patents that have important antitrust implications. Before discussing some of these potential problems, however, we should learn a bit about where the patent system came from and how it works.

Background

The first formal patent code was promulgated in Venice, Italy, in 1474. The notion that protecting innovators from imitators could induce more innovation was embedded in the preamble to that code:

> We have among us men of great genius, apt to invent and discover ingenious devices. . . . Now, if provisions were made for the works and devices discovered by such persons, so that others who may see them could not build them and take the inventor's honor away, more men would then apply their genius, would discover, and would build devices of great utility to our commonwealth.[44]

Over the next century, this idea spread northward. Unfortunately, patent monopolies were often awarded not to stimulate genuine innovation but to reward favorites of the ruling monarch or to further mercantilist goals, especially in the England of Elizabeth I. After repeated clashes with the Crown on this issue, the British Parliament in 1623 passed the *Statute of Monopolies*, declaring patents illegal except for grants to the "true and first" inventor(s)

---

[43]Edward Denison, *Accounting for United States Economic Growth, 1929–1969,* Brookings Institution, Washington, 1974.

[44]As quoted in S. C. Gilfillan, *Invention and the Patent System* (Materials Relating to Continuing Studies of Technology, Economic Growth, and the Variability of Private Investment, Joint Economic Committee, U.S. Congress), Government Printing Office, Washington, 1964, p. 11.

of a new product or means of production. Such grants would expire after 14 years (the time it took a master to train two successive generations of apprentices).

The British patent code was copied by several American colonies, each making its own modifications. The desire to standardize these codes across states led to passage of the first U.S. patent law in 1790. The law required that, prior to issuance of a patent, an official examination be held to ensure that an applicant's invention was "new and useful." In 1793, this requirement was dropped, and the State Department was authorized to issue patents without inquiring into the novelty or usefulness of the inventions they covered. The result was a flood of dubious patents and a court system overflowing with patent litigation. In 1836, Congress reinstituted the more stringent requirements of the 1790 statute. Figure 11.2 shows the trend in patent activity in the United States since 1880.

Under current U.S. law, an invention must satisfy three criteria in order to be patentable. First, the invention must be new; the public cannot have known of the invention before the inventor completed it or for more than 1 year prior to the date of application for the patent. Second, the invention must be useful. Since conclusive evidence of practical usefulness often hinges on future developments, the patent authorities tend to be quite lenient in applying this test. Third, the invention must be nonobvious. If the product or process in question would have been "obvious to a person having ordinary skill in the art," it is not patentable.

Most other countries apply similar conditions for patentability. There are some important international variations in patent law, however. For example, in several countries (most notably Japan, Germany, and Brazil), it is possible to obtain full-term patents covering major innovations, called *petty patents*— lasting as little as 3 years—on minor inventions and product improvements. The International Patent Cooperation Treaty of 1970 greatly simplified the process of acquiring patent protection internationally, allowing an inventor to start the process of obtaining patents in a large group of participating nations by filing a single application at one of four major patent offices (in Europe, Japan, the United States, and the former U.S.S.R.—now the Commonwealth of Independent States) that conduct international patent searches.

So that issuing authorities may apply their patentability tests, applicants are required to describe their inventions in considerable detail. Given the large number of patent applications (about 130,000 per year in the United States) relative to the small number of examiners, however, the reality is that most applications receive only a cursory review. Still, the queue is sufficiently long in the United States that an inventor can expect to wait nearly 2 years to have her or his application acted upon. (This is not altogether bad from the applicant's view, however. Since the "clock" timing the period of patent protection does not start until a patent is formally awarded, this delay effectively lengthens the period of protection to almost 19 years.)

Even after a patent is awarded, its validity is far from certain. The patent office provides no assistance to inventors who suspect that other individuals

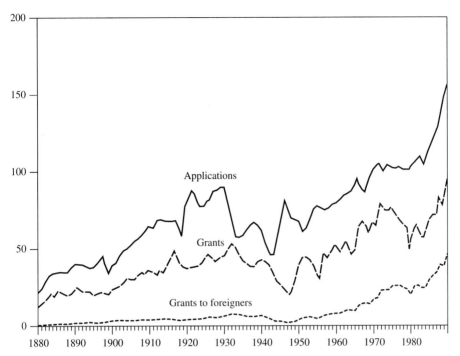

FIGURE 11.2
U.S. PATENT APPLICATIONS AND GRANTS, 1880–1989 (IN THOUSANDS). Did the decline in
U.S. patent grants in the 1970s contribute to the productivity slowdown of that era?
Source: Zvi Griliches, "Patent Statistics as Economic Indicators: A Survey," *Journal of Economic
Literature,* 28 (December 1990), p. 1664.

or firms are infringing on their patent rights. Patent holders often must litigate
(at their own expense) to enforce their claims. In many cases, inventors have
sued those using their patented products or processes without authorization
only to find that the courts considered their inventions obvious and therefore
not worthy of patent protection.

VIGNETTE 11.3   The Productivity Slowdown and Patent Activity

Productivity growth is central to enhanced human welfare. If we can coax more output from a given amount of input, we can enjoy a steadily improving standard of living. In the 1970s and early 1980s, however, productivity growth slowed considerably. For example, output per hour worked in the United States grew 32 percent in
the 1960s but only 15 percent in the 1970s, and in some years it actually fell. This
obviously did not bode well for the U.S. economy, and researchers have been
searching for clues to the origin of this productivity crisis for some time.

   One of the early suspects in the case was an apparent decline in the rate of innovation. As Figure 11.2 shows, patent awards in the United States dipped appreciably over this period, falling by nearly 40 percent from 1970 to 1979. What is more,
patent applications from U.S. citizens or corporations fell by 11 percent during this
period, so an increasing fraction of patent awards were to foreigners. Was the
United States losing its competitive inventive edge?

Not necessarily. It turns out that our indicator of technological decline was, in the words of economist Zvi Griliches, a "bureaucratic mirage."[45] Patent Office resources declined sharply during this period; the number of examiners fell by nearly 30 percent from 1974 to 1980, creating a major bottleneck in the patenting process. And in 1979 the number of awards dipped sharply because there was no budget for printing approved patents!

But if the appearance of a decline in inventive activity during the 1970s was *largely* a statistical mirage, it was not *entirely* one. There has been a genuine decline in patenting relative to the growth of R&D expenditures for some time now. That is, the number of patents awarded per dollar spent on R&D has fallen by about 1 to 2 percent per year since the mid-1950s. What is more, foreign patent applications have indeed been crowding out domestic applications. Are these trends cause for worry?

Griliches thinks not. First, he argues, the decline in patent awards relative to R&D may simply reflect an *improvement in the quality of patented inventions.* Many patents turn out to be worthless. If the decline in awards (relative to R&D) simply reflects an unwillingness to pay the costs of patenting inventions with low expected value, then it is probably not worth worrying about. There is some evidence, at least, that the average value (or quality) of patents is rising. Griliches also notes that it is not clear whether we need a growing number of inventions to sustain our current economic growth rates. As to the rising rate of foreign inventions, he says simply that "we are likely to be their ultimate beneficiaries."[46]

But if the productivity crisis did not originate in a real decline in innovation, what did cause it? As we will see in later chapters, some researchers blame cost-ineffective government regulation for at least *part* of the decline. But the bulk of the decline remains unexplained, a mystery yet to be solved.

Patents, Innovative Activity, and Welfare

Rationales   Over the years, scholars have devised several rationales for a patent system. Some of these are rather philosophical. For example, it is sometimes argued that under *natural law* an inventor is entitled to the use of her or his own ideas and that appropriating the ideas of another is theft. Or a patent may be thought of as a reward that is morally due to an inventor for her or his work.

Most arguments for patents are more mundane and utilitarian, however. We have already outlined the most common one: that granting patent rights will encourage the development of useful new products and processes by increasing the likelihood that an inventor will be able to recover the costs of innovative activity. Alternatively, patent rights are presumed to create market power that will yield above-normal profits; such profits will incite a race to be first to invent a new product or process. There is some empirical evidence that patent protection makes imitation more difficult or costly, thus enabling

---

[45]Zvi Griliches, "Patent Statistics as Economic Indicators: A Survey," *Journal of Economic Literature,* 28 (December 1990), pp. 1661–1707.
[46]Ibid., p. 1702.

inventors to recover costs or earn monopoly profits. While it is certainly possible for imitators to "invent around" patents or copy innovations in other ways, at least two major surveys have found that patents raise the costs of imitating innovations and lengthen the time it takes to bring an imitation to market, especially for "major" inventions.[47] And other surveys have found that, at least in some sectors (especially the chemical and pharmaceutical industries), there would be a substantial reduction in R&D effort if patents did not exist.[48] Of course, it is possible that a patent system may produce *too much* innovation. If the rewards to patent holders are too high, too many individuals may devote their time and energy to inventive activity (at the sacrifice of the alternative output they might have otherwise produced), or too many resources might be expended to ensure a first-place finish in the inventive race (since second-place finishers get no rewards).[49]

Another utilitarian argument is that patents, by encouraging inventors to disclose their ideas in exchange for protection from competition with imitators, will increase the overall pace of innovation by enabling inventors to build on each others' work. Absent a patent system, the chief way to discourage imitation in order to recover the costs of (or derive monopoly returns on) inventions would be to jealously guard "trade secrets." The detailed descriptions required in patent applications, however, may aid researchers working in areas related to the patented product or process, enlarging the fund of human knowledge.

Welfare Effects   Whether consumers perceive significant benefits from a particular patented invention may depend on the extent to which the invention is a significant improvement over existing products or processes. Suppose, e.g., one firm in a competitive industry devises a more efficient, cost-saving production process and patents this process. If the cost savings are large, consumers' surplus may grow appreciably, even if the inventing firm is able to price its product monopolistically. Consider panel a of Figure 11.3, which shows a market demand curve D and an initial (horizontal) cost curve C_1. Competition among firms with such costs will yield a market rate of output (per period) of Q_c and a price P_c, with associated consumers' (and social) surplus equal to the area bound by points P_cAB. If the invention reduces the inventing firm's costs all the way to C_2, the firm will find it possible—and profitable—to monopolize this industry. The intersection of the inventing firm's cost curve with the market marginal revenue curve MR dictates a rate of

[47]See Edwin Mansfield, "R&D and Innovation: Some Empirical Findings," in Zvi Griliches (ed.), *R&D, Patents and Productivity,* University of Chicago Press, Chicago, 1984; Richard C. Levin, Alvin K. Klevorick, Richard R. Nelson, and Sidney G. Winter, "Appropriating the Returns from Industrial Research and Development," *Brookings Papers on Economic Activity* (Special Issue on Microeconomics), 3 (1987), pp. 783–820.

[48]See, e.g., Charles T. Taylor and Z. Aubrey Silberston, *The Economic Impact of the Patent System,* Cambridge University Press, Cambridge, England, 1973. See also Richard C. Levin, "A New Look at the Patent System," *American Economic Review,* 76 (May 1986), pp. 199–202.

[49]The classic welfare analysis of patents and the optimal amount of innovation is by William D. Nordhaus, *Invention, Growth, and Welfare,* M.I.T. Press, Cambridge, MA, 1969.

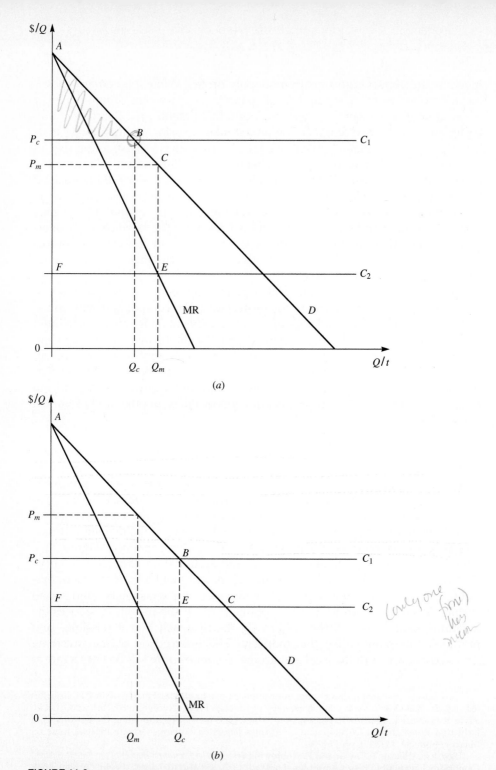

FIGURE 11.3
WELFARE EFFECTS OF A COST-REDUCING PATENTED PROCESS. When an invention produces a large cost reduction (panel *a*), consumers will see their welfare enhanced even as they
pay a monopoly price. Small cost reductions (panel *b*) may be associated with trivial rises in consumers' surplus, although social surplus will grow.

output (per period) of Q_m and an associated price P_m. Because the cost reduction here is so large, however, the new monopoly price is actually below the old competitive one, and consumers' surplus grows to area P_mAC. Further, social surplus grows even more, for the cost saving implies that fewer resources will now be used in this industry. These savings are captured as producers' surplus, equal to area P_mCEF.

But if the cost savings associated with a patented process are small, consumers may notice no great improvement in their well-being. Consider panel *b* of Figure 11.3, which shows a much smaller downward shift in production costs from C_1 to C_2. Here the inventing firm might *like* to monopolize the industry and set a rate of output (per period) equal to Q_m and a price P_m, but this is not possible because the firms using the unpatented production process associated with cost curve C_1 could always beat this price. The inventing firm has two choices: Either it can set a price just an eyelash below P_c in order to win sales from its rivals (perhaps eventually driving them all from the industry), or it can license the patented invention at a per-unit price just below P_c minus F (the amount the invention saves its users). Either way, consumers' surplus will be only trivially greater than its initial level P_cAB. But, of course, *social* surplus grows by area P_cBEF (by the amount the inventing firm earns as producers' surplus). Further, we should remember that once the patent expires and *all* firms' costs fall to C_2, consumers' surplus will expand to area ACF. Thus, even inventions that produce no (short-term) increase in consumers' surplus are likely to generate significant social welfare gains.

Some research suggests that patents on new and superior consumer products (as opposed to patents on processes for producing known products) will necessarily increase consumers' surplus.[50] Whether patents on such inventions will enhance overall social welfare, however, will depend on the cost of the innovation and several other factors. Patents on cost-saving production processes in monopolistic markets will also enhance consumer welfare. At the theoretical level, then, most scenarios associate the patent system with welfare gains. What worries many people, however, is that the system does not work in practice as it might in theory.

Abuses of Patents

Researchers have identified several schemes by which the current patent system might be used anticompetitively. The fear here is not simply that patent holders might charge monopoly prices for their patented products, an action which is quite legitimate under the current system, but that firms might use the system to handicap rivals, lever their patent monopoly into a monopoly in other markets, divide up markets, or otherwise conspire against consumers.

Preemptive Patenting and Patent Suppression   As we have noted, it is often possible for firms to invent around an important patent, devising alter-

---

[50]See Dan Usher, "The Welfare Economics of Invention," *Economica*, 31 (August 1964), pp. 279–287.

native products or processes that imitate the patented one without actually infringing on patent rights. To forestall such activity and strengthen patent rights, an inventing firm may attempt to create a *patent thicket*, obtaining patents not just one central product or process, but on a host of related products or processes. Firms that try to compete with the inventing firm will find their attempts to duplicate the central product or process blocked by the inventing firm's grip on alternative technologies. Many of the firm's patents on related products or processes may never be used or licensed; such *sleeping patents* are held only to raise the costs of entry or imitation by potential rivals.

The idea that enormously valuable inventions are commonly suppressed by evil monopolists is widely accepted and has even inspired a few popular films. The existence of sleeping patents appears to support such a view: The presumption is that holders of such patents are suppressing inventions in order to protect their monopoly positions. Under most plausible assumptions, however, suppression of superior inventions will not make sense. Since such inventions reduce a monopolist's costs of providing consumers with a given level of service, profits will be maximized by introducing rather than suppressing inventions.[51] In truth, then, most sleeping patents apply to products or processes that are inferior to inventions which are ultimately used.

It can be argued, however, that suppression of even inferior patents damages welfare. It might be worth exploiting such patents if the holder of the superior patent is charging a monopoly price for the associated product or amassing inferior patents to help sustain a dominant market position. Accordingly, many countries require compulsory licensing (at "reasonable" royalty rates) of unused patents.

Patents and Market Leverage　Another concern is that patents can give firms the leverage they need to monopolize markets for other, unpatented products. This might be accomplished via *tie-in sales*, in which the sale of a patented product is conditioned on a customer's agreement to buy a related product as well. An often cited example is IBM's requirement (during the 1930s) that purchasers of its patented tabulating machines use only unpatented IBM punch cards in the machines. As we discussed in Chapters 9 and 10, tie-ins such as this are often aimed at increasing—via price discrimination—the profits associated with a monopoly of the tying good rather than the creation of a new monopoly of the tied good. If so, the arrangement may actually enhance welfare by expanding output of the tying good (depending on the degree to which the discrimination is perfect). Under certain circumstances, however, the tie-in may lead to a monopoly of the tied good, thus diminishing welfare.

Patents and Collusion　The suspicion is strong that pooling or cross-licensing of patents sometimes conceals cartel activities that, absent the patent

---

[51]For a detailed exposition of this point, see Jack Hirshleifer, *Price Theory and Applications*, 4th ed., Prentice-Hall, Englewood Cliffs, NJ, 1988, pp. 274–276.

system, would be clearly illegal. Often, one firm may hold a patent on a particular process, e.g., and several other firms may hold patents that accomplish much the same purpose in slightly different ways. In such circumstances, the various firms may pool their patents in order to avoid the uncertainty and costs of litigating to determine which patent(s) will be enforceable. The pooling agreement may specify mandatory selling prices for goods manufactured under the various patents or may otherwise limit competition by barring new entrants from membership in the pool. Alternatively, patents for complementary products or processes may be held by competing firms. Cross-licensing agreements among such firms may provide them with the pretext they need to meet and specify final product prices, allocate territories, or otherwise conspire against consumers.

Extending the Lives of Patents   Since patents are awarded even for improvements to existing products or processes (provided the improvements are "new and useful"), clever patent holders may artificially lengthen the life of basic patents by amassing improvement patents that will continue to constrain imitators once the basic patent expires. If the life of the basic patent has been optimally set (i.e., if the term of the patent provides rewards commensurate with the optimal rate of innovation), such activities will (1) enable the patent holder to impose deadweight monopoly welfare losses for too long and (2) induce a rate of innovation that is excessive by rewarding innovation too well.

Some Case Law

Although early antitrust cases involving patents were aimed at determining whether patent holders were exempt from the Sherman Act's section 1 ban on price-fixing, most later cases were aimed at combating many of the abuses discussed above.

General Electric (1926)   GE held the basic patents for use of tungsten filaments in light bulbs. Alternative technologies were generally inferior, so GE had considerable monopoly power in this market. The company could have refused to license its patents and thus maintained its monopoly, but chose instead to license a rival, Westinghouse, to produce tungsten filament bulbs. Westinghouse promised not to undercut wholesale and retail prices fixed by GE—an agreement that, if not complicated by patent issues, would have been in clear violation of the antitrust laws. The Supreme Court ruled, however, that a patent holder's exclusive right to "make, use, and vend" a discovery included the right to fix the sale price on a patented good even when the good was produced under license by another firm.[52]

---

[52]*United States v. General Electric Co.*, 272 U.S. 476 (1926).

Tying Cases   As we saw in Chapter 10, the courts are likely to judge tie-in sales illegal (under section 3 of the Clayton Act) whenever the defendant holds a large share of the market for the tying good or where the amount of foreclosure in the market for the tied good appears large. In both the *IBM* and *International Salt* decisions,[53] the Supreme Court rejected defendants' arguments that their tie of unpatented to patented goods was motivated by the desire to ensure quality performance by the latter. Thus, where tying is concerned, patents confer on their holders no extra protection from antitrust prosecution.

Hartford-Empire (1945)   In the *General Electric* decision, the Supreme Court expressed its willingness to allow a patent holder to fix prices charged by licensees in cases that involve a single patent holder who licenses a single patent. Its *Hartford-Empire* decision showed, however, that the Court would not allow a group of firms to pool their patents and use patent licenses as a way of circumventing the antitrust laws. The case is extremely complicated. The story starts with the invention of automatic glassmaking machinery in the early 1900s. Several different processes were patented by different firms, and as improvements were made, the number of patents multiplied rapidly. Some firms began to exchange cross-licenses in order to use each others' processes. Often, the cross-licensing agreements explicitly divided markets, reserving certain types of glass or equipment production to each firm. The largest firms formed a patent pool; by 1938, 94 percent of the glass containers manufactured in the United States were made on machinery licensed under the pooled patents. Hartford-Empire, which held over 600 of 800-odd patents in the pool, began to coordinate production decisions for the industry, assigning to each manufacturer a strict output quota on each type of container. What is more, Hartford-Empire refused to license its patents to potential entrants. A district court found that such actions suppressed competition in the industry. The Supreme Court agreed, ruling that the pool's members "employed their joint patent position to allocate fields of manufacture and to maintain prices of unpatented glassware."[54]

U.S. Gypsum (1948)   From 1912 to 1929, U.S. Gypsum Company held a patent for producing wallboard with enclosed edges (which kept the gypsum core from crumbling). The company licensed rivals to produce its patented wallboard as long as they agreed to sell at prices fixed by U.S. Gypsum. Under the *General Electric* precedent, this was probably quite legal. But as the expiration date on its primary patent neared, U.S. Gypsum met with its licensees and laid out a new strategy. The company had applied for patents on a new type of wallboard ("bubble board," which was supposedly lighter and less expensive than the older variety). It offered to license its patents if licensees agreed

---

[53]*International Business Machines v. United States*, 298 U.S. 131 (1936); *International Salt Co. v. United States*, 332 U.S. 392 (1947).
[54]*Hartford-Empire Co. v. United States*, 323 U.S. 386 (1945).

to pay a royalty on *all* wallboard of *every* kind, whether or not made under patent protection. Under the agreement, U.S. Gypsum controlled prices on all wallboard products, adopting a basing-point method of fixing prices. To prevent cheating on the agreement, U.S. Gypsum established product standards and prohibited sellers from granting favorable credit or delivery terms to buyers (to curtail nonprice competition) and set up a subsidiary company to investigate any complaints that a licensee had violated the agreement. The Supreme Court found such arrangements to be "overwhelming evidence of a plan of the licensor and licensees to fix prices and regulate operations in the gypsum board industry."[55] The key here is that U.S. Gypsum, unlike GE, had acted in concert with other members of the industry, effectively suppressing competition in the markets for both unpatented and patented products.

Suggestions for Reform

Do the social benefits of the U.S. patent system (more innovation) exceed the social costs (monopoly welfare losses, abuses like those in the *Hartford-Empire* and *U.S. Gypsum*)? Unfortunately, a definitive answer to this question is impossible. We can't know what would have been invented *absent* a patent system, and we certainly don't know what *remains* to be invented! Many think the system can be improved, but there is not much sentiment to scrap it entirely. The reason has probably been best summarized by Fritz Machlup:

> If one does not know whether a system "as a whole" (in contrast to certain features of it) is good or bad, the safest "policy conclusion" is to "muddle through"—either with it, if one has long lived with it, or without it, if one has lived without it. If we did not have a patent system, it would be irresponsible, on the basis of our present knowledge of its economic consequences, to recommend instituting one. But since we have had a patent system for a long time, it would be irresponsible, on the basis of our present knowledge, to recommend abolishing it. . . .[56]

One improvement economists had been suggesting for some time was implemented in the United States in 1980. Since that time, patent holders have had to pay periodic renewal fees to keep their patents in force. Three and a half years after the granting date, the fee is $450; after 7½ years, the fee is $890; after 11½ years, the fee is $1,340. As of the end of 1988, about one-sixth of the patents granted from 1981 to 1984 had expired.

Additional suggestions for improving the current system are aimed at lessening the amount of market power a patent confers or at curbing some of the above-named abuses of patents. In this group are proposals to (1) beef up the review process so that patents are granted only for truly significant inventions, (2) shorten the life of a patent, and (3) require patent holders to license their patents at a "reasonable" royalty rate (usually defined as a rate based on the

---

[55]*United States v. U.S. Gypsum Co.,* 333 U.S. 364 (1948), p. 389.
[56]Fritz Machlup, *An Economic Review of the Patent System,* 85th Cong. 2d Sess., Senate Judiciary Committee, Subcommittee on Patents, Trademarks, and Copyrights, Study No. 15, Government Printing Office, Washington, 1958, pp. 79–80.

inventor's costs of perfecting the process or product). Of these, the last is the most controversial. It is common in many European countries, but attempts to change U.S. law in this direction have been met with the implacable opposition of industrial groups and the patent bar. Compulsory licensing has, however, been ordered as a remedy in some antitrust cases.

Other suggestions are aimed at strengthening patent rights (in part because of a fear—recall Vignette 11.3—that the United States is losing its technological edge). Two such proposals were adopted in the early 1980s. One enabled small businesses and universities to retain exclusive rights to products developed under federal research grants; the other made it possible to solidify a patent grant by having the Patent Office "recheck" it. Another proposal, to lengthen the life of patents (especially on pharmaceutical products), regularly comes before Congress but has yet to be adopted.

Finally, some suggest greater reliance on various alternative means of enhancing a society's rate of innovation. We could, e.g., diminish patent rights and make up for any resulting deficiency in the incentive to invent with greater government funding of R&D or bounties or prizes to successful innovators.

Reliance on federal funding for R&D has actually been diminishing in recent years. In 1970, about 57 percent of R&D spending came from the federal government; by the late 1980s, this fraction was down to about 48 percent. Boosting the federal role in R&D would not be without drawbacks, however. Critics of this approach note that a centralized grant-making authority might be highly bureaucratized and slow to respond to changes in the technological landscape, might ignore promising new researchers in favor of "known quantities," or might fail to diversify its activities properly, thus wasting considerable resources when it "backs the wrong horse." It is also interesting to note that the award approach was long used in the Soviet Union, where certificates of invention were given to individuals whose ideas were used industrially. These individuals were then entitled to a share of the resulting cost savings (up to a ceiling of 20,000 rubles). The resulting pace of innovation in Soviet industry was not notably rapid, however.

SUMMARY AND CONCLUDING REMARKS

There are two classes of theories about advertising. Critical theories hold that while advertising *can* sometimes provide useful information to consumers, it rarely does so. Instead it often persuades them to buy products they do not need at excessively high prices. In addition, sellers use advertising to artificially differentiate their products or to bar entry by rivals, rendering markets less efficient than is otherwise possible. Friendly theories hold that even image advertising can have indirect informational value to consumers, signaling higher product quality or comprising a nonsalvageable asset that can help forestall cheating by sellers. The empirical evidence tends to support a more sympathetic view of advertising than was common a few decades ago. There is little evidence that intensive advertising helps bind customers to sellers or otherwise raises entry barriers. Studies of advertising and market concentration, although mixed, tend to suggest that advertising plays a small, perhaps insignificant, role in promoting oligopoly. And there is strong evidence that advertising can beget lower prices without adversely affecting product quality.

Patents clearly can have adverse competitive effects in a static sense: By granting inventors monopoly rights over their new products or processes, prices for these goods may be set above competitive levels. The hope is, however, that granting such rights will increase dynamic efficiency, enhancing welfare by calling out a greater volume of inventions. A complicating factor is the abuse of the patent system: preemptive patenting to curb entry by rivals, tying patented goods to unpatented ones, pooling or cross-licensing patents to facilitate collusion, and artificially extending the lives of patents by amassing patents for improvements to existing products or processes. A good deal of antitrust law has been aimed at curbing such abuses. In general, the courts will not limit a single patent holder's right to fix prices on the patented good, but when patents are used as part of a tying arrangement or when pooling or licensing appears to support a price-fixing conspiracy among several firms, the arrangements are quite likely to be ruled illegal.

QUESTIONS FOR REVIEW AND DISCUSSION

11.1 Advertising is expensive. We should expect, then, that once advertising costs are added to the costs of producing a product, the full costs of advertised products should exceed those of similar nonadvertised products. Yet there is statistical evidence that, in at least a few markets, the onset of advertising reduced prices to consumers. How can this be? Develop a detailed analysis of this issue, using graphs to support your discussion.

11.2 Suppose there are scale economies in advertising; e.g., a campaign that can get your message to 1,000 potential buyers is cheaper (per buyer) than one that gets your message to 500. How might such scale economies be considered a barrier to entry? Can such scale economies adversely affect competition? What, if anything, should policymakers do in such circumstances? Explain your views.

11.3 Two of your friends decide to open a business, selling homemade snacks and beverages in the dorms during evening hours, when the campus store is closed. One wants to announce the new venture with a big splash: a large advertisement in the school paper, a big party where samples of your products will be given away free, and a custom-printed menu and price list put in every student's mailbox. The other friend says these ideas are ridiculously expensive, that it would be months before such sizable start-up costs could be recouped, and that it would be better to just sell the products from door to door without any big promotional expenses. Which strategy do you think is better? Why?

11.4 In recent decades, federal authorities have devoted greater resources to enforcing truth-in-advertising regulations. As a result, it is possible consumers are less skeptical of advertising claims than they were years ago. It is now common to hear consumers remark that "they couldn't say it if it wasn't true" after viewing an advertisement. But the volume of advertising messages is so large that only a fraction of these are ever rigorously reviewed by the authorities. What problem does this fact pose for consumers? Will these regulations necessarily enhance consumer welfare?

11.5 Imagine a world in which patents do not exist. In such a world, can you think of any ways inventors might recover the costs of their inventive effort? Suppose at least one such way exists, but it is costly to employ. Analyze (using graphs) the welfare effects of this alternative compared to a patent system.

11.6 In 1986 the Supreme Court ruled that patents could be awarded for new "genetically engineered" organisms, and in 1988 researchers at Harvard University received the first patent on an animal, a genetically altered mouse. Work is now underway to engineer hogs that will yield low-cholesterol pork and cows that will give more milk. Farmers' groups argue, however, that if they have to pay royalties on the *offspring* of such animals, many farmers (especially smaller ones) will be bankrupted. They have asked for special exemption from charges of patent infringement if they breed or sell patented animals' offspring. Evaluate farmers' claims that patent royalties would force many of them out of business. Then discuss the welfare implications of the exemption they desire. Clearly state any assumptions you make to facilitate your discussion, and use graphs to illustrate your analysis.

11.7 Most countries award a patent to the first inventor to *file* a patent application. The United States and Canada, by contrast, use a *first-to-invent* rule in awarding patents. Under such a rule, company X may file a patent application prior to company Y, but if Y can document that it actually made the invention prior to X, then Y will be awarded the patent. Assuming that at least one of the reasons we have a patent system is to encourage disclosure of inventions, are there any shortcomings to the system used in the United States and Canada? Explain.

ECONOMIC REGULATION

CHAPTER 12

NATURAL MONOPOLY AND ECONOMIC REGULATION

[P]ublic utility status was to be the haven of refuge for all aspiring monopolists who found it too difficult, too costly, or too precarious to secure and maintain monopoly by private action alone.

Horace Gray

Antitrust aims to secure the benefits of competitive conduct for consumers. In general, such conduct will produce the largest possible amount of output at the lowest possible social cost. Quite often (indeed, too often, in the view of critics of the structure-conduct-performance paradigm), we associate such conduct with a particular kind of market structure: many sellers, all so small that they behave as price takers.

Under certain cost and demand conditions, however, such a structure will be grossly *in*efficient. It is possible, e.g., for a single firm to produce a product (or group of products) more cheaply than two or more firms can. In such a case, we have what is usually described as a *natural monopoly*: Conditions favor the concentration of production in the hands of a single seller. Trying to impose the structural conditions associated with pure competition in such circumstances will waste considerable resources.

Economists recognized very early that "competition policy" could be useless or counterproductive where conditions conducive to natural monopoly prevail. In 1848, John Stuart Mill observed that if the many gas and water companies then serving London were replaced by "only one establishment, it could make lower charges" yet still earn "the rate of profit now realized."[1] In 1887, Henry Carter Adams went the next step. Adams sorted industries into three basic classes: those with decreasing, constant, or increasing returns to scale (i.e., those with rising, constant, or declining unit-cost curves). Granting that competition is workable in industries that fall into the first two classes, Adams argued that state regulation was necessary for industries that fall into the third class:

> [W]here the law of increasing returns works with any degree of intensity, the principle of free competition is powerless to exercise a healthy regulating influence. This is true because it is easier for an established business to extend its facilities for satisfactorily meeting a new demand than for a new industry to spring into competitive existence. . . . The control of the state over industries should be coextensive with the application of the law of increasing returns in industries. . . . Such businesses are by nature monopolies. . . . If it is for the interest of men to combine, no law can make them compete.[2]

In Adams's view, state control or oversight of natural monopolies would enable society to benefit from the advantages of large-scale production but protect consumers from the abuses of monopoly power. This view has long served as the chief public-interest rationale for *economic regulation.*

Economic regulation may involve state control of (1) the price a seller may charge for one or more products, or the rate of return a seller may earn; (2) the mix of products a seller may offer, the quality of these products, or the conditions under which they are sold; and (3) the conditions of entry into (or exit from) a particular market. Of course, some economic regulation may affect only one or two of these variables and can affect them all to varying degrees. For example, the Federal Communications Commission (FCC) tightly regulates entry into radio and TV broadcasting, but says nothing about pricing in these industries. In general, however, once an industry has been singled out for economic regulation, the relevant regulatory body, whether a federal agency or a local public utility commission, will have a great deal to say about how firms in that industry are run.

Which industries will be so singled out? This is a complicated question, having as much to do with the vagaries of the political marketplace as with economic models of natural monopoly. It is easier to say which industries legally *can* be selected for economic regulation: just about any the state pleases. This sweeping authority to regulate developed slowly. At first, only those industries "affected with a public interest" could be regulated. English common law imposed on certain occupations deemed vital to the well-being of society (e.g.,

---

[1]John Stuart Mill, *Principles of Political Economy*, Longmans, London, 1926, p. 143, as quoted by William W. Sharkey, *The Theory of Natural Monopoly*, Cambridge University Press, Cambridge, England, 1982, p. 14.
[2]Henry Carter Adams, "Relation of the State to Industrial Action," in Joseph Dorfman (ed.), *Two Essays by Henry Carter Adams*, Augustus M. Kelly, New York, 1969, as quoted in Sharkey, *The Theory of Natural Monopoly*, p. 15.

blacksmiths, innkeepers, millers, bakers) an obligation to charge reasonable fees. In 1877, the Supreme Court relied on this tradition in ruling that price regulation by a state did not violate the U.S. Constitution:

> Property does become clothed with the public interest when used in a manner to make it of public consequence, and affect the community at large. When, therefore, one devotes his property to the use in which the public has an interest, he, in effect, grants to the public an interest in that use and must submit to be controlled by the public for the common good. . . .[3]

For the next several decades, the Supreme Court tried to distinguish those industries "affected with a public purpose" from those not so affected. Clearly, this was an impossible task. Why, e.g., was it clear to the Court that transport firms could be regulated, but not food or apparel manufacturers? In 1934, the Court threw up its hands, ruling in *Nebbia v. New York* that "a state is free to adopt whatever economic policy may reasonably be deemed to promote the public welfare" provided the regulations imposed are not "arbitrary, discriminatory, or demonstrably irrelevant to the policy the legislature is free to adopt. . . ."[4] Since *Nebbia*, legislatures have had broad power to regulate business conduct, and the Supreme Court has rarely second-guessed the wisdom of legislatures in this area.

The theory and practice of economic regulation will occupy us for the next few chapters. We begin in this chapter by outlining the theory of natural monopoly, which economists have refined a bit over the past decade. Not all economic regulation can be plausibly explained by this single public-interest rationale, however. Accordingly, alternative rationales are discussed in turn. We conclude this chapter with an analysis of the difficulties faced by economic regulators, whatever their motivation. In succeeding chapters, we examine in detail some of the strategies used by regulators to address specific policy problems, we review some possible alternatives to economic regulation, and then we advance to specific case studies to assess the performance of economic regulation and deregulation.

THE THEORY OF NATURAL MONOPOLY

An industry is a natural monopoly if a single firm can meet market demand more efficiently than two or more firms can. To help determine whether an industry is a natural monopoly, economists use the concept of *subadditivity of costs*. Suppose all firms in an industry use the same technology, and each has a cost function denoted by $C(q)$, which is to say that any firm can produce q units of output for $C(q)$ dollars. Let us take the simplest case: There are two firms in the industry, and we denote the output of firm 1 as q_1 and the output

---

[3]*Munn v. Illinois,* 94 U.S. 113 (1877), p. 126.
[4]*Nebbia v. New York,* 291 U.S. 502 (1934), p. 536.

of firm 2 as q_2. We say that costs in this industry are *subadditive* at the level of output $Q = q_1 + q_2$ if

$$C(Q) = C(q_1 + q_2) < C(q_1) + C(q_2) \qquad (12.1)$$

for all possible combinations of q_1 and q_2 summing to Q. Where the inequality in (12.1) holds, it is cheaper to concentrate industry output in a single firm than to share it among two or more firms. Such subadditivity is a necessary condition for the existence of a natural monopoly.

Let us consider a concrete illustration. Suppose all widget manufacturers (using similar technologies) have long-run cost schedules like those shown in Table 12.1. The table shows long-run total and long-run average total costs (LTC and LATC, respectively) as widget production is increased from 1 to 20 units per day when production is organized within a single firm and when production is shared equally by two firms. Figure 12.1 shows the LATC curves associated with the data in Table 12.1. Observe that LATC reaches a minimum of $200 per unit when a single firm produces 10 units per day; the single firm thus produces 10 widgets per day at a total cost of $2,000 per day. If, however, two firms occupied this market (each producing 5 widgets per day), then the

FIGURE 12.1
SUBADDITIVITY OF COSTS. Given costs like those shown in Table 12.1, it will be cheaper to organize production of up to 14 units in one firm. Production of 15 or more units is best organized in two firms.

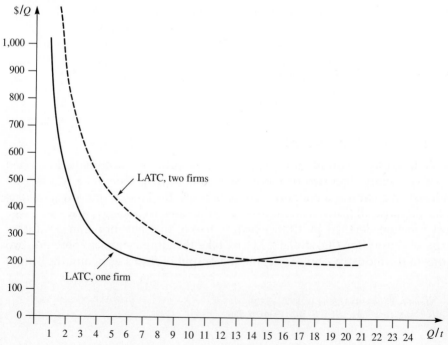

TABLE 12.1
PRODUCTION COST FOR A HYPOTHETICAL FIRM AND INDUSTRY

Production organized in one firm				Production organized in two firms			
Q	Q per firm	LTC, $	LATC, $	Q	Q per firm	LTC, $	LATC, $
1	1	1,010	1,010	1	0.5	2,005	2,005
2	2	1,040	520	2	1	2,020	1,010
3	3	1,090	363.33	3	1.5	2,045	681.67
4	4	1,160	290	4	2	2,080	520
5	5	1,250	250	5	2.5	2,125	425
6	6	1,360	226.67	6	3	2,180	363.33
7	7	1,490	212.86	7	3.5	2,245	320.71
8	8	1,640	205	8	4	2,320	290
9	9	1,810	201.11	9	4.5	2,405	267.22
10	10	2,000	200	10	5	2,500	250
11	11	2,210	200.91	11	5.5	2,605	236.80
12	12	2,440	203.33	12	6	2,720	226.67
13	13	2,690	206.92	13	6.5	2,845	218.85
14	14	2,960	211.43	14	7	2,980	212.86
15	15	3,250	216.67	15	7.5	3,125	208.33
16	16	3,560	222.50	16	8	3,280	205
17	17	3,890	228.82	17	8.5	3,445	202.65
18	18	4,240	235.56	18	9	3,620	201.11
19	19	4,610	242.63	19	9.5	3,805	200.26
20	20	5,000	250	20	10	4,000	200

cost per widget would climb to $250 and it would cost $2,500 per day for the same industry output. If we want 10 widgets per day, we save $500 per day by concentrating output in one firm rather than two. Clearly, this cost function is subadditive at a rate of output of 10 widgets per day (and all smaller rates of output). If 10 or fewer widgets are to be produced per day, it will be efficient to organize widget production within a single firm.

Subadditivity and Scale Economies So far, subadditivity appears related to the familiar concept of economies of scale, in which we observe declining LATC as we expand a firm's scale of operation. We might be tempted to conclude that natural monopoly exists as long as—and only as long as—there are scale economies in production. To do so, however, would be wrong and would overlook some outputs for which natural monopoly conditions hold.

To see why, extend the above example to consider levels of output greater than 10 widgets per day. Refer once again to Table 12.1 and Figure 12.1. Given our hypothetical cost schedules, there are no scale economies beyond an output rate of 10. Suppose, e.g., we want to produce 12 widgets per day. At this scale, a single producer's total costs rise to $2,440 per day, and unit costs rise to $203.33 per widget. Thus, the single producer experiences *dis*economies of scale as output is increased from 10 to 12 widgets per day. But note that *costs remain subadditive* at the higher rate of output; i.e., it costs less to produce 12 widgets with one firm than with two or more firms. If two firms combined to produce 12 widgets per day (each producing 6 widgets per day), total industry costs would be $2,720 per day, a per-widget cost of $226.67![5]

Thus, if we want 12 widgets per day, we can save $280 per day (or $23.34 per widget) by concentrating production in one firm rather than two—despite the fact that the firm will be experiencing some diseconomies of scale at this output rate. In fact, costs remain subadditive in this example up to a rate of output in excess of 14 widgets per day. A single firm can produce 14 widgets per day at a total cost of $2,960 per day, while two firms sharing this daily rate of output would have combined total costs of $2,980. Thus, we would save $20 per day by concentrating output in a single firm even if the desired rate of output were 14. If, however, we desire 15 widgets per day, we can save $125 per day by organizing production in two firms, each producing 7.5 widgets per day.

We conclude: *A cost function that is subadditive at some output Q does not necessarily exhibit scale economies at Q.* We may find, therefore, that it is efficient to concentrate all industry output in a single firm even where that firm is experiencing diseconomies of scale. This may seem, at present, to be a minor point. But as we shall see later, it will have important implications for policy when the *sustainability* of a natural monopoly is considered.

The Multiproduct Firm

The discussion above assumes that firms produce a single product. Often, however, a firm will produce two or more goods, often because it is cheaper to produce certain products jointly. A steer, e.g., yields both beef and hide. While it's possible to use a steer for beef while discarding its hide (or vice versa), it certainly seems impractical. When, as with the production of beef and hides, it is cheaper to produce two products together rather than separately, an *economy of scope* exists.

Such economies are often linked to the existence of certain common or shared inputs, i.e., inputs that, once obtained for the production of one good, may also be available (in whole or in part) to aid in the production of another. Certain raw materials (the aforementioned steer), physical capital (a generator usable at different times to power different productive processes), or human

---

[5]Note that when two firms have identical cost curves (as they do in this example), total industry costs are minimized when output is shared equally between them. To test this assertion, calculate total industry costs if one firm produces 10 widgets and the other produces 2, or various other output combinations.

capital (the know-how of certain individuals) may fit this description. Indeed, when one is producing and selling related products, knowledge will be a particularly important shared input. For example, once you have learned how to make (or sell) corn flakes, you may also be able to apply some part of this knowledge to making (or selling) bran flakes or some other cereal. Producing and selling such goods together will be efficient; the knowledge acquired in the production of one good will not have to be duplicated in the production of the other(s). Such factors likely explain why, in an advanced economy, virtually all large firms are multiproduct firms.

As in the case of single-product firms, *cost subadditivity is required for the existence of a multiproduct natural monopoly.* In the multiproduct case, firms produce an output *vector* composed of various quantities of various goods. We say that a cost function is subadditive for a particular output vector *q* when *q* can be produced more cheaply by a single firm than by any combination of smaller firms.

Unfortunately, in a multiproduct setting subadditivity can be a rather elusive concept. It's often difficult to tell whether a particular cost function is subadditive just by looking at it (or its graph). Things were much simpler in the single-product case, where the presence of scale economies at a particular rate of output (e.g., at $q \leq 10$ in Figure 12.1) *guaranteed* that costs were subadditive at that rate of output, i.e., was a sufficient condition for subadditivity.[6] In the multiproduct case, we may observe product-specific scale economies, but costs may not be subadditive.

Consider the following numerical example. Suppose that two goods X and Y can be jointly produced and that the total cost function $C(q_X, q_Y)$ for these goods is

$$C(q_X, q_Y) = 10q_X^{0.5} + 10q_Y^{0.5} + (q_X q_Y)^{0.5} \qquad (12.2)$$

Table 12.2 shows how production costs behave as we vary the production of X and Y from 0 to 5 units per period. When X or Y is produced separately, significant economies of scale are present (i.e., there are product-specific scale economies). If, e.g., a firm produces no Y, its per-unit costs of producing X will fall steadily, from \$10 when 1 unit of X is produced to \$4.47 when 5 units are produced. Per-unit costs of producing Y similarly fall if X production is held constant. But this cost function exhibits no economies of joint production; in fact, it exhibits scope *dis*economies. Suppose a single firm produces both one X and one Y; its total costs will then be \$30. But if, instead, a separate specialty firm produced one X (and no Y) while another produced one Y (and no X), their total costs would be only \$20. We would save \$10 by producing X and Y separately rather than jointly in a single firm. As Table 12.2 shows, the cost disadvantage associated with joint production climbs rapidly in this example:

---

[6]It is important to remember that, in the single-product case, costs may be subadditive even after all scale economies are exhausted.

TABLE 12.2
PRODUCTION COSTS FOR MULTIPRODUCT FIRMS DISPLAYING
DISECONOMIES OF SCOPE

One firm produces only X				One firm produces only Y			
Q_X	Q_Y	LTC_X, $	$LATC_X$, $	Q_X	Q_Y	LTC_Y, $	$LATC_Y$, $
1	0	10	10	0	1	10	10
2	0	14.14	7.07	0	2	14.14	7.07
3	0	17.32	5.77	0	3	17.32	5.77
4	0	20	5	0	4	20	5
5	0	22.36	4.47	0	5	22.36	4.47

One firm produces both X and Y			Two specialty firms produce X and Y separately		
Q_X	Q_Y	LTC_{X+Y}, $	Q_X	Q_Y	$LTC_X + LTC_Y$, $
1	1	30	1	1	20
2	2	48.28	2	2	28.28
3	3	64.64	3	3	34.64
4	4	80	4	4	40
5	5	94.72	5	5	44.72

If we produced 5 units each of X and Y, costs would be $50 higher per period than if we produced the same amount of output in separate firms.

Thus, when scope *diseconomies* exist side by side with scale economies, natural monopoly will exist only for each product produced separately. In the above example, there will be a natural monopoly in X and one in Y, but no natural monopoly of X and Y together, i.e., no multiproduct natural monopoly.

As an example of a long-run total cost function that would give rise to a multiproduct natural monopoly, consider the following:

$$C(q_X, q_Y) = 10q_X^{0.5} + 10q_Y^{0.5} - (q_X q_Y)^{0.5} \qquad (12.3)$$

Table 12.3 shows how costs vary for this new cost function as we vary production of X and Y from 0 to 5 units per period. Producing, say, 5 units of X and 5 units of Y in a single firm costs $39.72, while producing an equivalent amount of output in two separate specialty firms (one producing 5 units of X and no units of Y, the other producing no units of X and 5 units of Y) costs $44.72. Thus, if we desire 5 units of X and 5 units of Y, we can save $5 per period by organizing production in a single firm. This cost function is subadditive at $q_X = 5$, $q_Y = 5$ (and, in fact, at every output level).

In practice, it can be extremely difficult to verify whether a given cost func-

TABLE 12.3
PRODUCTION COSTS FOR A MULTIPRODUCT
FIRM DISPLAYING BOTH SCALE AND SCOPE
ECONOMIES

	Produce X and Y separately			
Q_X	LTC_X, $	Q_Y	LTC_Y, $	$LTC_X + LTC_Y$, $
1	10	1	10	20
2	14.14	2	14.14	28.28
3	17.32	3	17.32	34.64
4	20	4	20	40
5	22.36	5	22.36	44.72

	Produce X and Y jointly		
Q_X	Q_Y	LTC_{X+Y}, $	$LTC_X + LTC_Y$ minus LTC_{X+Y}
1	1	19	1
2	2	26.28	2
3	3	31.64	3
4	4	36	4
5	5	39.72	5

tion is subadditive in a multiproduct setting. There are no convenient short-cuts. As we have seen, the presence of product-specific scale economies is not a sufficient condition for subadditivity and natural monopoly. Economies of joint production—of which scope economies are but one measure—are necessary for multiproduct natural monopoly. But the presence of scope economies is not a sufficient condition for such monopoly. As William Baumol, John Panzar, and Robert Willig have shown, even the appealing combination of economies of scale *and* scope is no *guarantee* of subadditivity and natural monopoly. In their words,

> [T]here apparently exist no straightforward mechanical criteria that permit us to test whether or not a particular function is subadditive, short of checking the applicability of the definition itself. That is, there exist no conditions necessary *and* sufficient for subadditivity that are analytically simpler than the definition.[7]

Testing for subadditivity, then, requires a good deal of backbreaking econometric toil, forcing researchers to sift through lots of data to estimate cost functions under alternative market structures. Without such effort, however, poli-

---

[7]William J. Baumol, John C. Panzar, and Robert D. Willig, *Contestable Markets and the Theory of Industry Structure*, rev. ed., Harcourt Brace Jovanovich, New York, 1988, p. 170.

cy makers may misdiagnose the appropriate structure of a particular industry, concluding there is natural monopoly where none really exists or overlooking it when it does exist, or they may make other serious policy errors.

VIGNETTE 12.1   Economies of Scale and Scope in U.S. Industries: Some Empirical Evidence

In recent years, scholars have been hard at work studying the nature of costs and the optimum configuration of firms in several key U.S. industries.

Analysts have long presumed that domestic production of automobiles is concentrated in only three major firms—General Motors, Ford, and Chrysler—because there are significant scale economies in automobile manufacturing. In a careful study of industry costs from 1955 to 1979, Ann Friedlaender, Clifford Winston, and Kung Wang confirmed the importance of scale economies.[8] In fact, by their estimates, as of 1979 the typical automaker would have enjoyed significant savings had scale been increased further (while maintaining the same mix of products): A 10 percent rise in output could have been attained with only an 8.1 percent rise in costs. Friedlaender et al. also found that scope economies are important determinants of firm costs. Ford, e.g., reduced its costs by 22 to 34 percent by combining production of its large cars with the production of small cars and trucks. Friedlaender et al. concluded, however, that the U.S. automobile industry cost function did not exhibit subadditivity for the relevant sample period, and the industry was not, therefore, a natural monopoly. For example, in 1979 industry production costs were $96.6 billion; if the industry had been completely monopolized, costs would have been $127.8 billion.

David Evans and James Heckman tested for subadditivity in local and toll telephone services from 1958 to 1977, during which these markets were the exclusive domain of the Bell System.[9] They rejected the hypothesis that Bell's costs were subadditive at the output levels produced over this period: In each year, they estimated that there would have been appreciable savings had the industry been organized with multiple firms.

Thomas Gilligan, Michael Smirlock, and William Marshall estimated multiproduct cost functions for banks, using data from 1978.[10] They found that, contrary to popular belief, the data did not indicate the existence of scale economies in banking beyond relatively low output levels; in fact, they found evidence of product-specific diseconomies of scale. They did find significant savings from joint production in banking, but concluded that the industry is not characterized by natural monopoly. Nevertheless, they recommended that regulators pay close attention to these joint production considerations: In a multiproduct setting, attempts to regulate one aspect of banks' operations will necessarily spill over to others and might preclude banks from attaining their lowest-cost output vector.

---

[8]Ann F. Friedlaender, Clifford Winston, and Kung Wang, "Costs, Technology, and Productivity in the U.S. Automobile Industry," *Bell Journal of Economics*, 14 (Spring 1983), pp. 1–20.

[9]David S. Evans and James J. Heckman, "A Test for Subadditivity of the Cost Function with an Application to the Bell System," *American Economic Review*, 74 (September 1984), pp. 615–623.

[10]Thomas Gilligan, Michael Smirlock, and William Marshall, "Scale and Scope Economies in the Multi-product Banking Firm," *Journal of Monetary Economics*, 13 (May 1984), pp. 393–405.

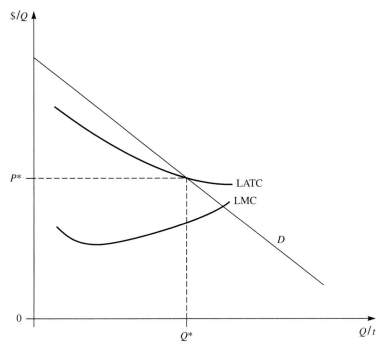

FIGURE 12.2
A SUSTAINABLE NATURAL MONOPOLY. If a natural monopolist sets a price of P^* and no entrant can serve any consumer at LATC lower than P^*, there is no incentive to enter this market and the natural monopoly is sustainable.

Sustainability of Natural Monopoly

For a long time, economists presumed that natural monopolies would be immune to profit-seeking entry. Recent research has shown this presumption to be false.[11] It is possible, given certain demand and cost conditions, that it will be efficient to concentrate an industry's entire output in a single firm, yet such a firm might not be able to prevent entry by a rival.

A natural monopoly where entry can be prevented is said to be *sustainable*.[12] Figure 12.2 shows long-run cost (LMC, LATC) and demand (D) curves for a sustainable natural monopoly. We assume these cost and demand conditions would prevail for any seller in this industry, i.e., that no seller will have lower cost curves than any other.[13] As long as the natural monopolist sets a

---

[11]See Baumol et al., *Contestable Markets and the Theory of Industry Structure*, Chapters 8, 11.

[12]More formally, Baumol et al. state that the announced prices of a monopolist are sustainable if the monopolist is financially viable at these prices and if no potential entrant can find a marketing plan the expected economic profits of which cover the costs of entry; a monopoly is sustainable if and only if there exists for the firm at least one sustainable price vector. See *Contestable Markets and the Theory of Industry Structure*, pp. 192–194.

[13]We restrict our discussion here to the case of a single-product firm.

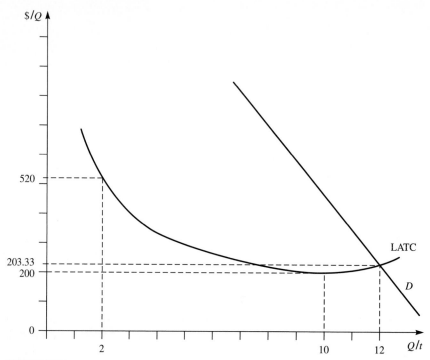

FIGURE 12.3
AN UNSUSTAINABLE NATURAL MONOPOLY. With a natural monopolist setting P = $203.33 and Q =12, an entrant might try to serve a subset of this market, offering to sell 10 units at a price of $200. Although such entry is feasible, it is socially undesirable in this case.

price equal to (or no higher than) P^*, there can be no profitable entry by any rival. Since no entrant could serve any consumer or group of consumers at LATC lower than P^*, there is simply no incentive to enter (i.e., no lure of profits). The key to sustainability here—and in general—is the fact that the LATC curve is falling over the relevant range of demand. A natural monopoly will be *un*sustainable when the LATC curve is rising over some portion of the relevant range of demand.

Figure 12.3 shows an unsustainable natural monopoly (using the same hypothetical cost schedule that appeared earlier in Table 12.1 and Figure 12.1). Here demand curve D intersects the natural monopolist's LATC curve at an output of 12 units per period. LATC at this rate of output equals $203.33 per unit. But even if the monopolist sets this price and earns zero profits—perhaps because a regulator tells it to—a rival with an identical cost function may see an opportunity for profitable entry. An entrant may, e.g., try to serve a subset of consumers in this market, producing and selling 10 units per period at a price between $200 (its LATC at that scale of operation) and $203.33, earning some positive profits. This leaves the incumbent firm with only 2 units per period (assuming it doesn't respond with a price change), which could only be produced at a LATC of $520 per unit! Because costs are subadditive at $Q = 12$, entry is clearly inefficient here: It disturbs the natural monopoly, leading to higher average and total costs of production in the industry. Of course, the incumbent firm may not take the rival's entry lying down; it may try to respond with price cuts or some other strategy (collusion?). But (refer once again to Table 12.1) there is *no* way, given this cost function, that two firms can produce 12 units of output per period as cheaply as a single firm can. Even if the two sellers figure out a way to live with each other in this example, there is a compelling public interest in getting one of them out of the market.

What to do? It might appear that the answer is simple: Set up a regulatory authority to bar entry in any and all markets that appear to be unsustainable natural monopolies. For two reasons, however, this may be unwise. First, if demand shifts to the right (so that it intersects LATC at an output rate of 15 or higher in Figure 12.3), this may no longer be a natural monopoly, and entry might be socially desirable. Clearly, demand can fluctuate a great deal over time, and it will be difficult for a regulator to install or lift barriers appropriately. Second, once entry is barred, the protected natural monopolist might become lazy about controlling costs, allowing LATC to drift upward (i.e., might become "X-inefficient"). Thus, a lean and hungry potential entrant might be able to enter with lower costs than those of the incumbent—and save society resources—but is prevented from doing so by government-erected entry barriers. For these reasons and because there is little empirical evidence (so far) that sustainability problems are important in very many cases of natural monopoly, scholars are reluctant to endorse entry barriers as a solution to the problem.

OTHER RATIONALES FOR ECONOMIC REGULATION

Not all economic regulation can be explained by the desire to enhance efficiency by coping with the problems of natural monopoly. The demand for economic regulation can arise—and certainly has arisen—from a variety of other factors as well. In this section, we outline a few of the most prominent factors.

Destructive Competition

When a natural monopoly is unsustainable, competitive entry may be said to be *destructive*. It "spoils the market" for the incumbent firm and wastes resources. But some scholars and policymakers conceive of *destructive competition* more broadly. In this view, competitive *pricing* (i.e., setting $P = MC$) will occasionally be destructive in industries where fixed costs are large[14] and demand is highly variable or cyclical. In such circumstances, competition may keep prices below average total costs long enough to drive many firms into

---

[14]The presence of fixed costs indicates that the discussion of destructive competition tends to focus on short-run behavior.

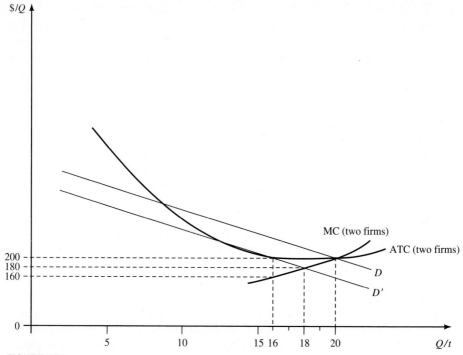

FIGURE 12.4
DESTRUCTIVE COMPETITION. If demand falls from *D* to *D'*, competition may force price down to $180, which is below ATC. This might bankrupt one of the two sellers. Given these costs, however, it will be inefficient to concentrate production in a single firm.

bankruptcy. The outcome will not be in the interests of either producers or consumers.

Consider, for example, the situation described by Figure 12.4, which shows an ATC curve (similar to the one for 2-firm production in Figure 12.1) and associated MC curve for representative firms in a hypothetical industry. If normal demand in this industry is such that the optimum rate of industry output is 20 units per period, it will be efficient to have two firms in this market, each producing 10 units per period. At this rate of output, $P = MC = ATC_{min} = \$200$ per unit for each firm. All is well.

But now suppose the industry demand curve shifts to the left, to D'. Now D' intersects the industry ATC curve ($ATC_{n=2}$) at an output rate of 16 units per period. The cheapest way to produce this rate of output, given these cost functions, is for each of the two firms to produce 8 units per period. Total costs would then be $3,280 per period, or $205 per unit. (Note that if a single firm tried to produce 16 units per period, total costs would be $3,560 per period; thus, given demand conditions in this example, we do not have a natural monopoly.) But note that at this rate of output, *price exceeds marginal cost.* As

Figure 12.4 shows, MC at an output rate of 16 equals $160. Thus, there is an incentive for each firm to cut price slightly in order to make additional sales (either to steal customers from the other firm or to reach customers who will only buy at prices less than $205). Unless such price-cutting is prevented, however, price will be driven *below average costs*. If both firms behave competitively, producing additional output until $P = MC$, then price will be driven down to $180 per unit and industry output will expand to 18 units per period. That is, competitive behavior will yield a combination of price and output determined by the intersection of D' and $MC_{n=2}$ (the industry supply curve) in Figure 12.4. At this price and quantity combination (assuming, again, that the firms share industry output equally), ATC equals $201.11 per unit and each firm loses $21.11 per unit. As long as demand remains at D', one (or both) producers will eventually go belly-up.

Of course, firms in perfectly competitive markets can sometimes earn losses and go bankrupt, too. Yet economists shed nary a tear over this competitive process, much less refer to it as destructive. Indeed, such a process is praised as a mechanism for properly allocating resources: If demand falls in a competitive market, some firms *should* exit so that their productive assets can be reallocated to higher-valued uses. Why doesn't the same cold logic apply here? The key is the nature of costs relative to market demand. In this example, costs are lower when two firms share production, whether the output rate is to be 16 or 18 (indeed, any rate we choose between 14.14 and 28.28 units per period). Resources would be wasted, i.e., production costs would rise, if one firm went bankrupt and output were concentrated in a single firm. Further, there may be other social costs of this process of destructive competition. Once there is a single producer, monopolistic pricing may ensue. Or there may be "instability costs" associated with the cycles of exit and entry that result from fluctuations in demand.

Thus, there may be a public interest in forestalling price competition in such circumstances. Formally regulating prices so as to ensure that the optimum number of firms survives, or tolerating collusion that achieves the same goal, may save resources.

VIGNETTE 12.2   Destructive Competition in Transportation Industries?

It has long been argued that competition can be destructive in railroading, trucking, and other transportation industries. The main preconditions for destructive competition appear to be present: Production in such industries is often very capital-intensive, involving sizable fixed costs, and demand can fluctuate seasonally or over the business cycle.

Rate wars were a problem (from the point of view of stockholders, if not consumers) from the earliest days of railroading, and they were especially severe during periods of depressed business activity. As William Ripley summarized in 1913, "[p]eriods of abject demoralization incidental to the most furious rate wars have alternated with periods of peace, characterized by more or less faithful observance of agreed rates."[15] For example, during the depression of 1876–1877, rates on east-bound, first-class freight fell 85 percent, from $1.00 to $0.15 per 100 pounds, while westbound rates fell 67 percent, from $0.75 to $0.25.[16] It is true that during a depression the general level of prices often falls, but according to one measure wholesale prices fell only 7 percent in 1876 and 4 percent in 1877.[17] The rate wars continued to break out even after creation of the ICC in 1887. For several weeks in 1888, the cost of shipping dressed beef from Chicago to New York fell to $0.06 per 100 pounds; in 1895, the cost of shipping grain from Kansas City to Chicago fell to $0.02 per hundredweight, although the published (and therefore the legal) rate was $0.17. Clearly, real freight rates fell drastically during these rate wars. Unless rates were initially far above average and marginal costs (perhaps because the railroads were successfully colluding), it seems reasonable to conclude that the wars drove rates well below average total costs. Until the ICC was granted authority to set minimum rates in 1920, such demoralizing episodes would be a central feature of the industry.

Examination of the structure of railroad costs tells why. One detailed study using operating data for 1969 found that the long-run elasticity of cost with respect to output for the industry as a whole was 0.87; i.e., a 10 percent increase in output would increase costs only about 8.7 percent. For some individual railroads, scale economies were far greater. The Western Pacific, e.g., would increase costs by only 5.2 percent if it found a way to raise output 10 percent.[18] Such scale economies and the sunk nature of the railroads' capital costs (i.e., once track has been laid, it is hard to apply it to some alternative use or transfer it to serve some new market) produce a strong and enduring incentive to embark on periodic price-cutting strategies to win extra freight volume.

It seems unlikely the same can be said of certain other transport industries, however. The great majority of regional and interregional trucking firms face scale diseconomies. For regional carries, e.g., a 10 percent output increase would raise costs by about 10.9 percent.[19] And clearly most capital costs in the trucking industry are not sunk as they are for railroads; trucks can easily be transferred from one market to another in response to sudden changes in industry demand, so that prolonged excess demand should not be a problem in trucking.

Equity Considerations

Proponents of economic regulation often invoke *equity considerations* rather than efficiency arguments to justify a particular regulatory regime. Indeed, on occasion it has been acknowledged that some types of regulation may be inefficient (at least in some dimensions) but are nevertheless worthwhile because they enhance *fairness.* Of course, fairness can be an elusive concept; fairness to me may be oppression to you. In addition, fairness arguments can dis-

[15]William Z. Ripley, *Railroads: Rates and Regulation,* Longmans, Green, New York, 1913, p. 431.

[16]Ari Hoogenboom and Olive Hoogenboom, *A History of the ICC,* W. W. Norton, New York, 1976, p. 3.

[17]Source: George F. Warren and Frank A. Pearson, *Prices,* Wiley, New York, 1933, as reported in U.S. Bureau of the Census, *The Statistical History of the U.S.,* Basic Books, New York, 1976, p. 201.

[18]Ann F. Friedlaender and Richard F. Spady, *Freight Transport Regulation,* M.I.T. Press, Cambridge, MA, 1981, pp. 145–147.

[19]Ibid., p. 174.

guise some remarkably cynical (and selfish) motives. But it is undeniable that such arguments have often been employed sincerely and have indeed affected policy.

In the early debates about regulation of the railroads, public furor about unfair price discrimination loomed large. Absent rate regulation, the pattern of freight rates that evolved from the 1850s to the 1880s appeared to unduly favor certain types of shippers and disadvantage others. Large shippers often used their buying power to win lower rates or rebates from railroads. And shippers in large cities served by several carriers benefited from intense price competition, while those off the beaten track paid much higher rates. Prices appeared unrelated to the mileage a particular type of cargo might travel, which struck many as both unfair and inefficient. Thus, the stated goals of the Interstate Commerce Act of 1887 were chiefly to eliminate discriminatory rates and achieve a rate structure that would be "just and reasonable."

Ironically, however, equity considerations have also been invoked to justify the imposition of a discriminatory rate structure rather than its elimination. When airline fares were regulated by the Civil Aeronautics Board (CAB), e.g., prices were sometimes kept *above* costs in some markets in order to keep them *below* costs in some others; i.e., regulated rates delivered *cross-subsidies*, implicitly taxing consumers in certain markets in order to subsidize those in others. Typically, fares on routes that involved smaller cities (with relatively low or highly variable demand and high unit costs) were set below costs, so that lines that served such markets earned losses. These losses were made up, however, by setting fares above costs on routes that involved larger cities (with stronger and more dependable demand and lower unit costs). Proponents of such cross-subsidies argue that it is unfair to burden those in smaller towns with higher transportation costs even if it costs more to serve such markets. Acknowledging that cross-subsidies redistribute income among consumers, these proponents maintain that such redistribution can enhance overall equity. Economists have, in general, taken a dim view of such arguments and suggested that if cross-subsidies are truly desirable for equity reasons, they should be delivered via explicit tax-and-spend programs rather than hidden in this way.

Income distribution considerations have also played a role in the regulation of certain industries where *economic rents* might be earned. Recall that rents are payments in excess of the minimum necessary to induce a seller to offer a good for sale. Suppose, e.g., you own an oil well holding 1,000 barrels of oil. If it costs $1 per barrel to pump the oil, any price over $1 ensures that you will pump all 1,000 barrels and earn rents. If the price of oil is $5 per barrel (perhaps because this is the cost of pumping oil from the *marginal* well), your rents will total $4,000.

Earning such rents strikes some as inherently unfair: Just because you happen to own a well from which it is easy to remove the oil, why should you grow richer than someone out drilling new wells or, for that matter, producing other goods entirely? Such rents seem especially unfair when the price of the relevant good rises appreciably due to factors out of your—or anyone else's—control. When the Organization of Petroleum Exporting Countries (OPEC) formed a worldwide oil cartel and raised the price of oil many fold in the early 1970s, owners of wells in the U.S. "oil patch" (Louisiana, Texas, Oklahoma) might have earned enormous rents, had regulators not stepped in specifically to prevent such a redistribution of income from oil consumers to producers. First, price controls aimed to keep oil produced in the United States cheaper than OPEC oil. When it became obvious that this created a powerful disincentive to produce domestic oil, a *windfall profits tax* (i.e., a tax on that portion of the oil revenues deemed to be a pure rent) was instituted instead.

Economists have been very critical of this kind of *rent control* (of which limits on the prices landlords can charge their tenants is but one example!), noting that the equity effects of such policies may or may not be favorable, but that they involve huge efficiency costs. Specifically, such price controls generate allocative inefficiency (over- or underproduction of affected goods) even in the short run, and in the long run they create all sorts of perverse incentives to over- or underallocate inputs in affected markets.

Finally, some argue that economic regulation enhances equity because, by taking decisions out of the cold, hard economic marketplace and putting them in the political marketplace, the poor are empowered. When market forces alone guide resource allocation decision, dollar votes count most—and the wishes of those with few dollars receive little consideration. But in the political sphere, this reasoning goes, everyone is on a roughly equal footing, and the poor have a better chance of getting what they want. In addition, more democratic economic decision making (or, at least, instituting relatively "open" administrative procedures which enable many individuals or groups to influence regulatory outcomes) may be seen as a good in itself; i.e., people will "feel better" about a system in which they have a clear mechanism for voicing their opinions.

Of course, supplanting market forces with political ones may reduce as well as enhance the degree to which certain groups, especially the poor, feel empowered. Wealth and income carry influence in the political marketplace just as in the economic one. It is entirely possible that regulators will be more attentive to the wishes of the well-to-do than to those of the poor in regulating economic activity, and at times regulators may choose to serve their own interests rather than those of the public at large.

Rationing

In some cases, it is argued that economic regulation is necessary to ration or limit access to a valuable *common-property resource*. The usual example of such a resource is the spectrum of radio or television broadcasting frequencies. Although this spectrum is a continuum, reception is best if broadcasters are dispersed along it. If access to frequencies were free and unlimited, broadcasters might flood the airwaves, with more than a single broadcaster sending signals over a particular bandwidth or channel. Consumers would find the results unsatisfactory: The competing signals would be garbled. Thus, competition for the common resource could destroy its value. Clearly, some way of delineating exclusive rights to use such a resource is needed. It is unclear, however, whether the form of regulation currently used (in which the government grants broadcasting licenses to those who satisfy various arbitrary criteria) accomplishes this purpose very equitably or efficiently.

VIGNETTE 12.3   Rationing the Broadcast Spectrum

In the early days of radio, rights to the electromagnetic broadcast spectrum were allocated on a first-come, first-served basis. Ever since passage of the Federal Radio Act in 1927, potential broadcasters have had to apply to the government for a license to use a particular portion of this spectrum at specific times.

No one doubts the need for some sort of system to assign and enforce rights to this resource. Critics of the government's regulatory approach have focused on the way it assigns licenses. Applicants must convince the Federal Communications Commission (FCC) that their programming serves the "public interest, convenience, or necessity," a requirement that is commonly met by adhering to certain guidelines about program content and the amount of public service programming that is scheduled. Then licenses are granted (or renewed) *at no charge to the licensee.* The critics point out that this zero-price licensing system confers enormous windfall gains on those lucky enough to be granted rights to (scarce) broadcast frequencies, at a huge opportunity cost to the federal Treasury. Economists have estimated that if broadcast rights were auctioned off in the same way as offshore drilling rights or mineral rights to federal lands are, the Treasury could bank an extra $1 billion a year; rights to the total spectrum are probably worth about $200 billion.

That the government has not rationed the broadcast spectrum via the price system is commonly assumed to be an accident of history. No one thought of it back in the 1920s, the story goes, and now we simply continue the system put in place back then. The mistake may cost taxpayers a bundle, but, in this view, it is an innocent mistake.

But economist Thomas Hazlett has recently challenged this notion.[20] In Hazlett's view, the zero-price licensing scheme adopted in 1927 did not result from ignorance of superior alternatives, nor was regulation itself aimed simply at preventing interference problems associated with broadcasters crowding each other's frequencies. Rather, he argues, the approach taken was aimed at creating rents in this market and distributing them among the key constituencies in the policymaking process.

Significant rents were created by restricting the portion of the spectrum available to broadcasters to less than 5 percent of that technologically feasible for broadcast use. In Europe, significantly more of the broadcast spectrum was in use, but U.S. legislators knowingly rejected this option. By thus limiting the number of licenses issued, the government created an effective entry barrier in broadcasting that ensured each license would have significant value.

Why not capture these rents for taxpayers by auctioning these artificially scarce licenses? Hazlett argues that legislators understood that a money auction for broadcast rights would not have been in their personal interests. Broadcasters would sim-

---

[20]Thomas W. Hazlett, "The Rationality of U.S. Regulation of the Broadcast Spectrum," *Journal of Law and Economics,* 33 (April 1990), pp. 133–175.

ply pay the market-clearing price for their frequencies and go merrily on their way, beholden to no one. Better to create a situation where legislators and regulators held near life-and-death power over broadcasters. Competition for valuable licenses in the political marketplace would then produce significant benefits for incumbent politicians in the form of campaign contributions or programming sympathetic to interest groups the incumbent held dear (or, for that matter, to the incumbent).

Market Stabilization

Some markets will be inherently unstable; others will be unstable if producers behave in certain (perhaps irresponsible) ways. In either case, it is often argued, social welfare will improve if government intervenes and stabilizes such markets with policies to tame wild price fluctuations, limit entry or control output, or otherwise regulate producer conduct.

Inherent instability has long been thought to afflict agricultural markets. The culprits here are highly inelastic demand and supply conditions, coupled with unpredictable external circumstances that can cause sudden shifts in either demand or supply. Figure 12.5 illustrates the problem. Large price changes do not cause us to change the amount of food we consume all that much; i.e., we wouldn't eat 20 percent more just because food was 10 percent cheaper. (Of course, demand elasticity will be considerably greater for a single commodity: If chicken prices fall 10 percent and steak prices remain unchanged, I may buy considerably more chicken and less steak, while keeping my total intake of calories about the same.) On the supply side, it will take farmers some months—or perhaps years—to significantly alter their output to take advantage of a price rise or to avoid the ill effects of a fall in price. Once crops are planted, an individual farmer can alter final yields per acre (by varying the amounts of water or fertilizer the crops might get) only a small amount in the short run. Accordingly, in Figure 12.5 the relevant demand curve D and short-run supply curve S are both quite steep. For purposes of comparison, a more elastic demand curve, labeled D_e, is also shown. If erratic weather, crop disease, or pestilence suddenly shifts supply from S to S', price will shoot up from P_0 to P_1. If weather is unusually good or input prices fall unexpectedly, so that supply shifts from S to S'', price will fall like a stone, from P_0 to P_2. If such supply shifts are normal or common, we will observe prices ranging up and down over the broad range from P_1 to P_2 in this market. If only demand were more elastic (as with demand curve D_e), however, such supply shifts would lead to price fluctuations over the much narrower range of P_3 to P_4.

Farmers' lagged responses to changes in market conditions can compound the problem. The best-known historical example is known as the "hog cycle," aptly described by agricultural economist Geoffrey S. Shepherd:

> A large corn crop that depresses the price of corn leads farmers to breed more sows and feed their pigs more heavily. When these pigs reach the market in large volume a year or two after the large crop has been harvested, they depress the price of hogs. Farmers then find hog production relatively unprofitable; they breed fewer sows;

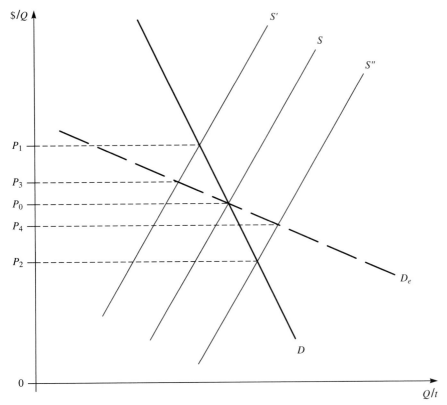

FIGURE 12.5
PRICE SWINGS IN AGRICULTURAL MARKETS. Given the highly inelastic demand curve D, supply shifts from S' to S'' will cause price to vary widely, from P_1 to P_2. If demand were more elastic, such as D_e, such shifts would produce smaller price changes, from P_3 to P_4.

within a year or two, fewer pigs reach the market, and hog prices rise. Then the cycle starts all over again.[21]

In fact, hog prices moved up and down in a remarkably regular 4-year cycle over the late 1800s and into the early 1900s. Clearly, significant resources are wasted over such cycles, as fixed capital and other inputs flow in and out of the affected markets and are used to varying degrees; it would be efficient to "smooth out" such fluctuations and save these resources. What is unclear is whether agricultural price stabilization of the kind that is typically used is truly necessary to accomplish this purpose.

The specter of market instability is also used to explain entry restrictions, price controls, and other regulations in markets where the above considera-

[21]Geoffrey S. Shepherd, *Agricultural Price and Income Policy*, 3d ed., Iowa State College Press, Ames, 1952, pp. 15–16.

tions may not apply at all, e.g., the financial and insurance industries. The idea here is that business failures in certain markets can produce negative spillover effects. For example, when one bank fails, it is argued that confidence in other banks is shaken as well. This might lead consumers to withdraw their cash and bury it in coffee cans in their backyards, a turn of events which will not only cause "innocent" banks to experience difficulties but, far more important, produce ill macroeconomic effects as well. Thus, in this view, there is a much greater public interest in ensuring the solvency of banks and insurance companies than of the corner shoe store. We must be careful here, however. It is possible that public-interest rationales that apply in very limited circumstances can be used to justify regulatory policies that are neither efficient nor particularly equitable.

Regulation Not in the Public Interest: Capture and Rent Seeking

We discussed the economic theory of regulation and introduced some principles of public choice analysis in Chapter 4. In both frameworks, regulation is seen as something that produces goods demanded by self-interested groups or individuals who transact in the political marketplace. By way of brief review, three central insights of this approach are as follows:

First, since information and transactions costs are high in the political marketplace, many individuals will be rationally ignorant about policies that affect them in minor ways and/or will choose not to participate in the process of framing these policies. In addition, free-rider problems will make it difficult to mobilize large groups, while numerically compact groups will be easier to manage. Accordingly, it is often possible for a numerical minority to rule a majority of transactors in the political marketplace.

Second, vote-maximizing politicians will often deliberately blur distinctions between themselves and their rivals and will be most anxious to serve the interests of the median voter. In addition, logrolling or vote trading in the political arena can produce policies that either enhance welfare by enabling the production of goods which are intensely demanded by only a minority of the electorate or, alternatively, diminish welfare by serving such a minority. Election cycles may also lead politicians to weigh short-run policy effects more heavily than is socially optimal.

Third, normal principal-agent problems will be exacerbated in bureaucracies because (1) the intangible nature of much government output makes monitoring the bureaucracy and gauging its efficiency more difficult than in private firms, (2) such bureaucracies rarely face competing agencies that might spur improved performance, and (3) absence of any well-defined "owner" or residual claimant, and the concomitant failure to tie managers' rewards to performance in the government sphere, implies that government managers will rarely have an incentive to enhance efficiency, since they will derive little benefit from doing so.

Application of the public choice approach can obviously make one very pessimistic about the likelihood that the political marketplace will produce results which coincide with the public interest. Often public choice analysts presume that regulation is industry-inspired and quite profitable. In general, there are four basic categories into which we put attempts to use regulation for selfish ends: (1) attempts by producers to gain at the expense of consumers, (2) pursuit of cross-subsidies, (3) attempts by some producers to put other producers at a competitive disadvantage, and (4) alliances between producers and unrelated public interest groups aimed at gaining certain benefits at consumers' expense.

The last category merits special attention. Interest in certain regulatory policies often brings together groups that otherwise have little in common. An industry group that seeks to extract wealth from consumers or somehow disadvantage rivals might link arms with an independent group that seeks a regulatory solution to what it perceives to be some social ill; with the consumers that will be affected by the regulation, these groups comprise a *regulatory triad.* Bruce Yandle has (more colorfully) dubbed this the *Baptists-and-bootleggers phenomenon.*[22] Some religious groups, e.g., object to widespread distribution of alcohol on moral grounds. In some areas (especially the south), these groups have most unexpected allies: bootleggers and moonshiners who expect to win higher prices when legal barriers to entry are erected in their local markets.[23]

When private interest is joined to a credible public-interest rationale, a formidable political force often results for two reasons. First, of course, the public-interest rationale will often be persuasive *even if it is false or spurious;* the population that opposes the regulation is thereby thinned. Second, if the costs of proving that such a rationale is false or spurious are nontrivial, fewer opponents will choose to participate in the debate about the policy *even if they are convinced it is counter to the public interest.* At some point, it can simply be too costly to lobby on a particular issue; even bogus public-interest arguments serve to up the ante and discourage players in the policy game. Such arguments, then, are very useful strategic tools. We should be surprised when a plea for regulation is *un*accompanied by some appealing public-interest rationale. But we should dig hard to discover whether such rationales are valid and applicable to the situation at hand.

VIGNETTE 12.4   Early Regulation of Electric Utilities: Who Gained?

The electric power industry has been regulated, in at least some form, from its infancy. Retail distribution of power requires that wires pass over (or under) public thoroughfares, inviting either municipal or state oversight of operations. Thus, the long

---

[22]Bruce Yandle, "Bootleggers and Baptists," *Regulation,* 7 (May/June 1983), pp. 12–16.
[23]For empirical evidence that such alliances help explain why various states regulate liquor sales in the ways they do, see Janet Kiholm Smith, "An Analysis of State Regulations Governing Liquor Store Licensees," *Journal of Law and Economics,* 25 (October 1982), pp. 301–319.

history of government intervention in this industry provides a golden opportunity to study the origins and effects of economic regulation.

George Stigler and Claire Friedland were particularly intrigued by one question: Does regulation keep prices low? On the surface, it certainly appears that it does. For example, in 1917 the price of electricity (as measured by utilities' average revenues per kilowatt-hour generated) was 70 percent lower in states that had established commissions to regulate public utilities (such as electric and gas companies) than in states without such commissions. But many factors other than regulation might account for these differences. It is cheaper to provide electric power where the density of population is greater, e.g., and where sources of hydroelectric energy are abundant.

Stigler and Friedland looked at electricity prices after correcting for the influence of such variables and reached a rather surprising conclusion: Rates in states with public utility commissions were only a tiny bit lower (and differences were not large enough to be statistically significant) than in states without regulatory commissions for the period from 1917 through 1932. Data for the year 1937 showed a negative and significant effect of state regulation on electricity prices, but primarily for commercial and industrial consumers—not exactly the group that regulation is typically thought necessary to protect. Stigler and Friedland also found no statistically significant differences in profit rates between firms subject to state regulation and those not subject.[24]

These findings are puzzling. Under the public-interest rationale for regulation, state commissions might be expected to significantly reduce rates by protecting consumers from monopolistic pricing. Alternatively, under the economic theory of regulation, in which regulated firms comprise a numerically compact, narrowly focused (and therefore more politically successful) interest group than consumers, state commissions might enable utilities to earn rents by raising prices above competitive levels. But shouldn't there should be *some* difference?

Research by Gregg Jarrell solved the puzzle.[25] Jarrell noted that Stigler and Friedland overlooked the fact that even absent a state utility commission, electric firms were usually subject to regulation by municipalities. Such regulation was often very strict in the late 1800s and early 1900s, with some municipalities fostering competitive conditions in their markets by awarding duplicative franchises. Indeed, the tendency of municipalities to award multiple franchises was criticized by many observers of the day as overlooking the naturally monopolistic character of the industry and creating *excessive* competition, leading often to bankruptcies or consolidations. Replacing municipal regulation with state regulation was usually offered as a way to correct such misguided behavior.

Stigler and Friedland's findings could now be qualified: It was not necessarily the case that state regulation had no effect on the price of electricity, but state and municipal regulation did differ little in their effects on price over the period from 1917 to 1937. But Jarrel raised another interesting issue. State regulation came in a great rush; 25 states substituted state commissions for municipal regulation between 1912 and 1917. Why? Was this an attempt to eliminate misguided or ineffective local regulation and to secure *lower* prices for consumers, as the public-interest

[24]George J. Stigler and Claire Friedland, "What Can Regulators Regulate? The Case of Electricity," *Journal of Law and Economics,* 5 (October 1962), pp. 1–16.
[25]Gregg A. Jarrell, "The Demand for State Regulation of the Electric Utility Industry," *Journal of Law and Economics,* 21 (October 1978), pp. 269–295.

approach to regulation would suppose? Or was this an attempt to replace pro-competitive municipal regulation with (more compliant) state regulation, as the economic theory of regulation might suggest?

The evidence is not friendly to the public-interest view. Holding all other determinants of costs and demand constant among states, Jarrell found that in 1912 prices were 46 percent *lower* in the 25 states that adopted state regulation between 1912 and 1917 than in states that adopted such regulation later. What is more, profits of firms in these "early-regulated" states were 38 percent lower, and output 23 percent higher, than in the "later-regulated" states. Between 1912 and 1917, prices in the 25 early-regulated states *rose* by 26 percent relative to the later-regulated states. Jarrell argues, therefore, that state regulation came early in those states where *producers* had the most to gain from such regulation (i.e., where municipal regulation was least friendly to producers) and that producers did in fact gain in the form of higher prices and profits.

The idea that economic regulation can be pro-producer rather than pro-consumer may seem surprising. It is interesting, however, that policy analysts of the day understood what was going on. Political scientist Delos Wilcox wrote in 1914:

Most corporations have come to see advantages in regulation itself and very great advantages in state as opposed to local regulation. By means of state regulation, they escape from the annoyance of local nagging and immediate political pressure for lower rates, and appear to feel that they are stealing a march on the municipal ownership forces.[26]

DILEMMAS FOR REGULATORS

As we have seen, determining whether a particular market is a natural monopoly can be a nontrivial task. But suppose we have done it. Figure 12.6 shows demand D and marginal revenue MR in this market. The (single-product) producer's long-run marginal costs are rising, but suppose D intersects the long-run average total cost curve in its declining portion. Clearly, we want one producer in this market so that these scale economies can be fully exploited. We fear, however, that such a producer will (as monopolists typically do) find the profit-maximizing rate of output by equating MR and LMC and set price far above costs. In Figure 12.6, such behavior generates a price and output rate of P_m and Q_m, respectively, and profits of $(P_m - \text{LATC}_m)Q_m$ per period.

Obviously, this result is unsatisfactory. There is a large deadweight welfare loss, and a good portion of the scale economies available to the monopoly remain unexploited. Economic regulation appears to offer a straightforward solution. We can create a regulatory body to grant monopoly status to some seller (thereby obtaining the benefits of all possible scale economies), and in addition we can regulate prices so the seller cannot behave monopolistically (thereby avoiding deadweight losses). But unfortunately this solution is not as simple as it seems.

[26]Delos F. Wilcox, "Effects of State Regulation upon the Municipal Ownership Movement," *Annals of the American Academy of Political and Social Science*, 53 (1914), pp. 85–86, as quoted in Jarrell, *"Demand for State Regulation,"* p. 294.

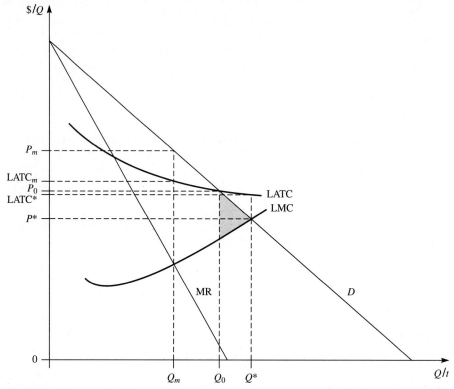

FIGURE 12.6
ECONOMIC REGULATION OF A NATURAL MONOPOLY. Fearing the natural monopolist will set price P_m, we regulate. But a price equal to marginal cost, at P^*, will not enable the firm to cover its costs. However, $P_0 =$ LATC involves some deadweight welfare loss (the shaded area).

The Pricing Problem

The first question that must be answered concerns the appropriate price to specify. Economic theory tells us that social welfare can be increased as long as the marginal benefit attached to a particular unit of output exceeds the marginal cost of producing it. This is why perfectly competitive markets, in which firms produce until price (our measure of how much value people attach to a particular unit of a good) equals marginal cost, are said to maximize welfare.

In the market shown in Figure 12.6, welfare is maximized only when price is set at P^* and output is Q^*. At this price and rate of output, social surplus (measured by the area between the demand and marginal cost curves from the origin out to the quantity produced Q^*) is as high as it can possibly be. But all is decidedly not well from the producer's point of view. At this price, the firm will be unable to cover its production costs; that is, $P^* <$ LATC* at Q^*. If the regulatory authority simply specifies that price must equal P^*, the monopoly may not produce Q^* but may prefer to shut down (or never open at all) rather than show losses of $(LATC^* - P^*)Q^*$ per period.

If the regulator chooses a price sufficient to allow the firm to recover its costs, such as P_0 in Figure 12.6, welfare will not be maximized. At P_0, the firm can cover its costs (i.e., earn zero economic profit or a normal rate of return on invested capital) by producing output Q_0. But at Q_0, consumers value additional output by more than it would cost to produce; we forfeit social surplus (the shaded area in Figure 12.6) on the produced units between Q_0 and Q^*.

There are some things regulators can do to address this dilemma. One possibility is that price can be set at P^* and any losses can be made up with a subsidy from the government. But the money for this subsidy must come from somewhere. If money is raised via income or sales taxes (as it commonly would be), this will imply some distortion of resource allocation in other markets: Such taxes (unless they are "lump-sum" and therefore do not affect transactors' marginal considerations) will raise prices and reduce quantities exchanged in the taxed goods' markets. And, often, employing *any* tax revenues to subsidize a monopoly will be politically unpopular. For this reason, some natural monopolies may be publicly owned, for then operating subsidies do not appear to be benefiting private owners.

Alternatively, regulators can allow the monopolist to price-discriminate, fixing high rates for one class of consumers to cover losses incurred when prices equal marginal costs for another class. But this may be unpopular as well; it transfers income from consumers to the monopoly and treats different consumers unequally. Clearly, the pricing decision for a regulated natural monopoly can be a very complicated matter.

The Incentive Problem

Assume, for simplicity, that the regulatory authority "solves" the pricing problem by setting a price that allows the monopoly to recover its costs but earn no economic profits; i.e., assume price equals P_0 in Figure 12.6 (although the discussion that follows would be unaffected if the regulated price were P^*). Now there is a problem of another sort: The firm may perceive that the route to higher prices is *higher costs*! If costs are allowed to drift upward, the regulated price P_0 will produce losses; the natural monopoly can then appeal to the regulatory authority for a price increase to cover its (unexpectedly high) costs. Unless the authority can distinguish wasteful expenditures from useful and necessary ones, it may have no choice but to grant the request. Thus, the monopoly might be rewarded for wasting resources.

But would the monopoly actually do such a thing? After all, returns to the firm's owners will be normal as long as $P = LATC$; allowing costs to rise doesn't put money in their pockets. It might, however, make the lives of the managers (agents) hired by these owners more pleasant. We see, then, that this is a special case of the principal-agent problem. Agents always may be suspected of having an interest in feathering their own nests to the extent that they can get away with it, i.e., to the extent that such activity is too costly for their principals to detect. Avoiding extravagant expenditures on facilities or staff is a potential problem whenever firm ownership and control are separate. It is especially severe here, however, because rate regulation assures stockholders they will earn a normal return no matter what their agents do (well, almost). Accordingly, principals are likely to devote fewer resources to monitoring agents' behavior.

It is interesting to note the welfare effects of resource waste by a regulated monopoly. Suppose, as in Figure 12.7, a natural monopoly faces demand curve D and marginal revenue curve MR and is capable of producing output along long-run marginal cost curve LMC under ordinary circumstances, i.e., when unregulated. A regulatory authority initially sets price equal to $P^* =$

FIGURE 12.7
WELFARE EFFECTS OF A WASTEFUL REGULATED MONOPOLY. If regulation causes costs to drift up to LMC_w, the regulated firm wastes areas A, B, and C. Unregulated monopoly may involve deadweight welfare loss equal to areas B, C, and E. Thus, regulation produces surplus gains only if area E is greater than area A.

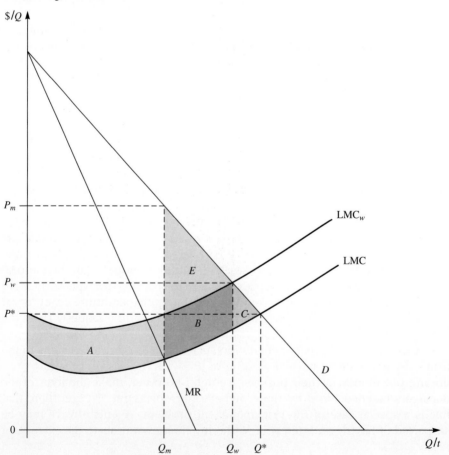

LMC (the firms' LATC curve is not shown, to keep the diagram a bit clearer). But this incites wasteful behavior; the monopoly firm soon allows its costs to drift upward to LMC_w (e.g., the firm's managers hire redundant staff for the sheer thrill of bossing more people around or because it is tiresome to keep the existing staff working at peak efficiency and extra hands are needed just to get the work done). Unable to determine whether these higher costs are useful and necessary, the authority raises price to P_w, and output falls to Q_w. As a result, social surplus diminishes by the sum of the areas labeled A, B, and C in Figure 12.7. Areas A and B measure the resources that are wasted as a result of the firm's diminished efficiency; area C measures the deadweight loss associated with the reduction of output from Q^* to Q_w.

At this point, students (and not a few policymakers) might be tempted to say, "Well, we don't like losing areas A, B, and C, but it's better than getting gouged by an unregulated monopoly. Then price would be much higher—way up at P_m instead of P_w." But notice: Having an unregulated monopoly in this market would reduce social surplus by the sum of areas B, C, and E. The monopolist would have no incentive to allow costs to drift up from MC, since such waste would, absent regulation, reduce profits. Accordingly, output would be determined by finding the intersection of MR and MC, at Q_m, and areas B, C, and E sum to the deadweight welfare loss associated with this rate of output. Now the difference between an unregulated monopoly and a wasteful regulated one can be seen clearly. Areas B and C will be lost in either case; an unregulated monopoly generates an additional loss equal to area E, while the wasteful regulated monopoly loses area A. If area E is smaller than area A, it might actually be better to have an unregulated monopoly than a wasteful regulated one! (This assumes, of course, that we are indifferent to the distributional effects of the income transfer from consumers to producers in the form of the unregulated monopoly's profits.) The final regulated price P_w may be far below the prospective monopoly price P_m, but if area A exceeds area E, society might be best served by *de*regulating this monopoly (unless, of course, a regulatory regime that eliminates resource waste can be found).

Clearly, economic regulation can be a vexing and complicated task. And, so far, we have barely begun to enumerate the problems that can arise in regulated industries and the strategies that have been developed to try to solve these problems. That will be the agenda for the next chapter.

SUMMARY AND CONCLUDING REMARKS

Federal, state, and local governments have sweeping authority to engage in economic regulation that is not "arbitrary, discriminatory, or demonstrably irrelevant" to some legitimate public interest. Such regulation can involve control of prices or rates of return, product quality, and/or entry conditions.

The most compelling public-interest rationale for economic regulation is the theory of natural monopoly. A single-product industry is a natural monopoly when total industry output can be produced more cheaply by one firm than by two or more, i.e., when costs are subadditive at the relevant rate of output.

Scale economies need not be present at the relevant rate of output for this condition to hold. Not all natural monopolies will be sustainable. Sustainability will be a problem when the market demand curve intersects a natural monopolist's unit-cost curve along its upward-sloping portion. Some argue that government-erected entry barriers will be desirable in such cases.

There are several other public-interest rationales for economic regulation. In some industries, e.g., competitive behavior is thought to be destructive. When fixed costs are large relative to variable costs and demand is variable, competitive pricing (i.e., setting $P = \text{MC} < \text{ATC}$) may be unhealthy for both firms and consumers. In addition, fairness considerations are commonly invoked to explain economic regulation. Removing (or, ironically, sometimes enforcing) discriminatory pricing and redistributing income via cross-subsidies are thought, by some, to be justified on equity grounds. Finally, economic regulation is sometimes justified as a way to allocate a scarce common-property resource or to avoid the waste associated with instability of certain markets. But some argue that much regulation occurs because it creates economic rents, that some groups simply will be more successful than others in using the political or regulatory apparatus to benefit from these rents, and that such redistribution has little to do with distributional equity.

Economic regulation in a market which is a natural monopoly poses two key dilemmas for regulators. The first relates to pricing. The welfare-maximizing price in any market will be that which equates price and marginal cost; in a natural monopoly, however, such a price may not enable a firm to recover all its costs. Alternatively, setting a price equal to average costs will, in a natural monopoly, impose some deadweight welfare losses on society. The second, perhaps more difficult, problem is that if a regulator fixes prices with reference to costs or guarantees a firm a particular rate of return, the firm may have perverse incentives to inflate costs and waste resources.

QUESTIONS FOR REVIEW AND DISCUSSION

12.1 Define economic regulation. Some feel that antitrust policy is a form of economic regulation. Is your definition consistent with this interpretation? How are antitrust policy and economic regulation the same, and in what key respects do they differ?

12.2 Define cost subadditivity. Suppose the joint production of goods X and Y is described by the following cost function:

$$C(q_X, q_Y) = \begin{cases} 0 & \text{if } q_X, q_Y = 0 \\ 100 + q_X^{0.5} + q_Y^{0.5} + (q_X + q_Y) & \text{if } q_X, q_Y > 0 \end{cases}$$

Over what values of q_X and q_Y, if any, will $C(q_X, q_Y)$ be subadditive?

12.3 Evaluate the following quote: "In a natural monopoly, it is inevitable that there will be but a single seller. Whether we start with two or two hundred sellers in such a market, it is certain we will finish with only one."

12.4 Define scope economies. List three major industries in which you think scope economies are important, and discuss in detail how such economies affect production and marketing strategy.

12.5 Evaluate the following quote: "If we define predatory pricing to be setting any price below average costs in order to win market share from a rival, then enforcing laws against this kind of predatory pricing makes sense only as a way of forestalling destructive competition."

12.6 Economic regulation often delivers cross-subsidies, implicitly taxing some consumers so that others receive tangible benefits. Show how such cross-subsidies typically work, using a diagram equipped with appropriate cost and demand functions to illustrate your discussion. Carefully delineate the efficiency implications of such cross-subsidies. Proponents of such cross-subsidies argue that they enhance equity. What conditions must hold for this to be true with respect to *vertical equity* (discussed in Chapter 3)? With respect to *horizontal equity?*

12.7 Suppose a hypothetical natural monopoly seller faces a demand curve described by the function

$$Q_d = 500 - 50P$$

Ordinarily, this seller has constant marginal costs equal to $5 per unit. If the seller is regulated, however, it will be able to engage in *featherbedding* (i.e., will inflate costs via extravagant expenditures on superfluous staff, etc.), raising costs by 20 percent, to $6 per unit. Is social welfare maximized by regulating this firm and setting price equal to marginal costs or by leaving the firm unregulated and (presumably) allowing it to set a monopoly price?

CHAPTER 13

REGULATORY STRATEGIES AND ALTERNATIVES

Never tell people how to do things. Tell them what you want them to achieve and they will surprise you with their ingenuity.

George S. Patton

As we saw in the last chapter, there are many possible reasons why we might prefer not to leave some industries entirely to the tender mercies of competitive market forces. If one or more of these reasons applies in a particular market, policymakers have some difficult choices to make.

They must determine first whether public intervention in such markets is truly desirable and, if so, then what type of intervention is best. It is certainly possible that some forms of intervention will come at a higher social cost than the potential problems they aim to solve. And even well-designed regulatory programs can produce ill side effects, some so severe that they dissipate a good portion of the potential gains from such programs. Once the decision to intervene is made, we must choose the institutional form it will take.

One possibility is *judicial regulation*. Since colonial times, those firms "affected with a public interest" have been required, under common-law traditions, to provide the public "adequate service at reasonable and nondiscriminatory rates." (Alternatively, a state legislature may make more specific requirements of firms in a statute, leaving interpretation and enforcement of such requirements to court action.) Those who believe that they have been overcharged or otherwise unfairly treated by certain sellers (often those with some local monopoly power) can litigate. Obviously, however, relying on the courts to regulate such matters involves high transactions costs and considerable uncertainty.

By about the mid-1800s in the United States, many localities and states were experimenting with regulation via *franchising* of individual sellers. Under this approach, a particular firm would be awarded a franchise (often an exclusive one) to operate in a certain area. In return, the firm would promise to provide a specified level of service at specified rates. Many cities relied on franchising for provision of water, power, and transportation services during the late 1800s and early 1900s.

Eventually, however, reliance on franchising waned, and most public utilities in the United States came to be either *publicly owned* or privately owned but operated subject to the oversight of some *regulatory commission.* The general tendency has been for regulatory authority to be concentrated at higher and higher levels of government over time. At first, when many utilities operated within city boundaries, municipal oversight was feasible. As technology changed and firms expanded to serve larger regions, state or federal regulatory bodies were often formed to oversee these industries.

Those who regulate public utilities have to address some vexing problems related to the pricing and investment practices of the firms under their jurisdiction. Identifying these problems and discussing possible solutions are the first tasks of this chapter. Then we discuss some of the complications posed by regulation of a firm's profit rate or rate of return. Such regulation produces some subtle but important perverse managerial incentives. A discussion of possible curatives, dubbed *incentive-compatible regulation,* follows. We conclude the chapter by detailing some of the problems and potentialities involved in the various alternatives to direct economic regulation, such as public ownership, franchising, and deregulation.

THE PRICING DILEMMA: POSSIBLE SOLUTIONS

Figure 13.1 (which differs from Figure 12.6 only slightly, with numerical values used to make the discussion more concrete) reviews the dilemma that typically arises in regulating the prices of a natural monopoly. Here we have a demand curve D that intersects the long-run average cost curve LATC in its declining portion.

Average-cost pricing, with price set equal to LATC at, say, $1.50 per unit, allows the firm to earn a normal rate of return on sales volume of 100,000 units per day. Total revenues equal total costs at $150,000 per day. But because this price exceeds marginal cost, we know it is allocatively inefficient; i.e., there is some unrealized social surplus under this pricing scheme (equal to the shaded area in Figure 13.1). There are still some units that consumers value in excess of production costs; unless price falls to equality with long-run marginal cost (LMC) at $1 per unit, the potential gains from exchange in this market will not be maximized. But such *marginal cost pricing* will produce a different problem for regulators: The firm no longer earns a normal rate of return. When $P = \text{LMC} = \$1$, $Q = 120,000$ units per day and LATC = $1.30; thus, total revenues are $120,000, and total costs are $156,000 per day. Few firms can survive very long in such circumstances. Unless we're willing to pay the firm a direct sub-

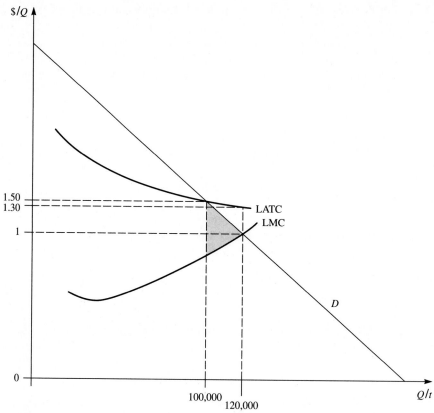

FIGURE 13.1
THE PRICING DILEMMA AND PRICE DISCRIMINATION IN A NATURAL MONOPOLY. Setting a single price equal to long-run ATC, such as $1.50, enables the firm to earn normal returns, but forgoes social surplus equal to the shaded area. When price equals marginal cost at $1, surplus is maximized but the firm earns losses. Price discrimination (e.g., a two-part tariff) may resolve the dilemma.

sidy of $36,000 per day to cover its losses, we've got a problem: A workable pricing scheme (P = LATC) is inefficient, and an efficient pricing scheme (P = LMC) appears unworkable.

Many scholars have grappled with this dilemma and proposed some pricing schemes that will move output toward the surplus-maximizing level yet enable regulated firms to cover their costs.

Price Discrimination

In Chapter 9, we said price discrimination exists when the ratio of price to marginal cost for a particular product (or kind of product) differs from one consumer to the next or from one unit sold to the next. As we saw then, price discrimination can take many forms and can often enhance welfare by moving a monopolist's output closer to that which would occur under perfect competition. Some forms of the practice might be useful in a natural monopoly setting as well.

Let us return to Figure 13.1. As we have noted, the problem here is that the surplus-maximizing price, $1 per unit, generates daily economic losses of $36,000. Making up these losses with operating subsidies raised via taxation may be politically infeasible, but covering the losses with revenues generated via price discrimination may not.

Regulators may, e.g., propose a modified *two-part tariff*, in which consumers pay a lump-sum fee for the right to buy as many or few units of the product as they choose at some specified per-unit price. Suppose Figure 13.1 describes a local market for natural gas service. The regulatory authority might set the price of gas at $1 per unit consumed (e.g., per 100 cubic feet), ensuring that the efficient rate of output (120,000 units per day) is demanded. To ensure that the company can afford to produce this amount of output, however, the authority might allow it to charge all consumers connected to the gas system a flat fee sufficiently high that the firm nets the additional $36,000 per day it needs to cover all its costs. (If, e.g., there are 12,000 consumers in this market, each demanding an average of 10 units per day at the price of $1 per unit, then a flat fee of $3 per day will do the job.) The up-front charge is really a disguised lump-sum tax that transfers enough surplus from consumers to keep the producer in business at the optimal rate of output. Note, however, the care with which such a charge must be levied; it cannot extract so much of any individual consumer's surplus that the consumer decides not to obtain the service at all, for then the quantity exchanged would fall below the optimum level.

Suppose, alternatively, that each consumer in the market described by Figure 13.1 wants but one unit of output, and each is willing to pay a different price for it. Once again, a price of $1 results in the optimum amount of output (120,000 units). But there are many consumers who would have been willing to pay far more than $1 for the single unit of output each wants. Assuming that the regulators can sort consumers according to their willingness to pay (or will allow the firm to do so) and that reselling is impossible, the firm might extract sufficient consumers' surplus to cover its total costs by setting a price of, say, $1.50 to the consumers of the first 100,000 units of output, and then cutting the price to $1 so that an additional 20,000 units are sold to those with less intense demand. (In fact, such a price schedule would generate economic profits of $14,000 per day while simultaneously ensuring that the allocatively efficient rate of output was produced and consumed.)

In practice, of course, it will be hard to implement such discriminatory pricing schemes with perfect precision. In most cases, firms and regulators will lack the kind of detailed information about demand and cost conditions that is embodied in Figure 13.1. In addition, we may find that there are some defections from the market under our two-part tariff scheme or that our alternative scheme is confounded by the defection of some potentially high-priced buyers to the low-priced group. In at least some circumstances, however, some form of price discrimination will be the only practical means of maintaining both allocative efficiency and the solvency of regulated firms.

Value-of-Service Pricing

In practice, regulated prices commonly are set sufficiently high to allow regulated firms to break even; i.e., most regulators rely on average-cost rather than marginal cost pricing. While it is true that setting any price above marginal cost will involve some allocative inefficiency, it is also true that the amount of welfare loss associated with average-cost pricing can be reduced by considering the elasticities of demand for the various products sold by the regulated firm and setting prices accordingly. This strategy, which is simply a special example of price discrimination, is variously called *value-of-service pricing, optimal pricing with a break-even constraint,* or *Ramsey pricing* (after economist Frank P. Ramsey, who worked extensively in this area).

The main conclusion of the value-of-service approach is that the amount by which regulated prices for the firm should exceed marginal costs (assuming they *must* do so for the firm to break even) will be in inverse proportion to the price elasticities of demand for the products involved. Some more arithmetic will reinforce the point.

Consider Figure 13.2, which shows the markets for two distinct goods produced by a regulated multiproduct firm. Panel *a* shows the demand curve for product X, labeled D_X; panel *b* shows the demand curve for product Y, labeled D_Y, which is considerably less elastic. For simplicity, we suppose each good can be produced at constant (and identical) long-run marginal cost, say $1. Clearly, social surplus is maximized if regulators set a price of $1 for both goods, yielding sales of $Q_X = 60,000$ and $Q_Y = 60,000$. But, once again, this may be unworkable. The firm's total revenues of $120,000 when price equals $1 may not cover all its costs; making up losses with direct subsidies may be impossible for political reasons. So regulators may specify a uniform price sufficiently above LMC to allow the firm to cover average costs, say, $1.50. At this price, there will be some loss of social surplus for both goods—but *this loss will be greater as the demand is more elastic.* Demand for X is relatively elastic; when price is raised to $1.50, quantity demanded in this market falls to $Q'_X = 40,000$ and social surplus of $5,000 is lost.[1] Demand for Y is relatively inelastic; when price is raised to $1.50 here, quantity demanded falls only to $Q'_Y = 50,000$, so the amount of lost social surplus is only $2,500.[2] Setting a uniform price of $1.50, then, enables the firm to raise its revenues from $120,000 to $135,000 (which we assume equals its costs), but at the cost of a total of $7,500 in lost social surplus.

---

[1]The surplus loss is the triangle bound by points *ABC* in Figure 13.2. The area of this triangle (one-half the triangle's base times its height) is ½ × 20,000 units × $0.50 = $5,000.

[2]Here, the surplus loss is the triangle bound by points *EFG*, which has area ½ × 10,000 units × $0.50 = $2,500.

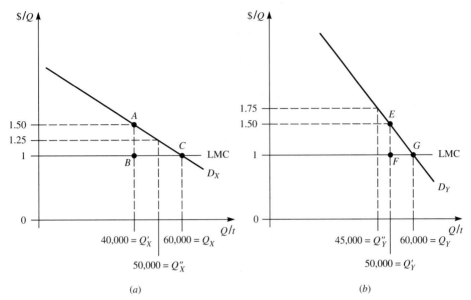

FIGURE 13.2
SURPLUS LOSSES WITH UNIFORM PRICING WHEN DEMAND ELASTICITIES DIFFER. A price of $1 for both X and Y will be efficient, but may not allow the firm to break even. A price of $1.50 for both goods will cover costs, but will impose large surplus losses. Setting price closer to LMC for X, for which demand is elastic, and farther from LMC for Y, for which demand is inelastic, reduces surplus loss.

These surplus losses can be reduced if the price of good X is set closer to LMC and the price of good Y set farther from LMC. Consider setting the price of X at $1.25 and the price of Y at $1.75. Given the linear demand curves in Figure 13.2, this will yield sales of $Q_X'' = 50,000$ and $Q_Y'' = 45,000$. This price structure will actually produce more total revenue than the uniform price of $1.50 for both goods, at less cost in forgone social surplus: Revenues are now $141,250 and surplus losses $6,875.[3]

In general, welfare may be enhanced when regulators recognize that buyers do not attach the same value to goods that may cost the same amount to produce. Specifically, *welfare will be maximized when prices exceed marginal production costs in direct proportion to the value buyers attach to a particular good or service* (i.e., social surplus is maximized when P exceeds MC to a degree that varies inversely with buyers' elasticity of demand).[4]

---

[3]Surplus losses in the market for good X are equal to $\frac{1}{2} \times 10,000$ units $\times$ $0.25 = $1,250. For good Y, surplus losses are $\frac{1}{2} \times 15,000$ units $\times$ $0.75 = $5,625.

[4]In precise terms, we can maximize social surplus by fixing the proportion by which price exceeds marginal cost for some good or service i, denoted $(P_i - MC)/P_i$, so that

$$(P_i - MC)/P_i = k(1/E_i) \tag{13.1}$$

where E_i is the elasticity of demand for good i and k is a multiplier reflecting the surplus loss resulting from the break-even constraint. See William J. Baumol and David F. Bradford, "Optimal Departures from Marginal Cost Pricing," *American Economic Review*, 60 (June 1970), pp. 265–283.

VIGNETTE 13.1   Value-of-Service Pricing in the Rail and Trucking Industries

Ramsey pricing has a long history in transportation industries. In the early days of the Interstate Commerce Commission, rail rates for agricultural commodities and certain raw materials were much lower than those charged on manufactured goods. These rates varied inversely with demand elasticity. Since transit costs were a large portion of the final value of low-value agricultural products, shippers of these commodities were very sensitive to transit prices, i.e., had very elastic demand for transportation. Manufactured goods, however, had a high value relative to the cost of transporting them, so shippers of these goods had relatively inelastic demand for transit services. It is doubtful, however, that regulators were attuned to such factors; the rate structures they devised were likely aimed at placating certain political constituencies (e.g., farmers and miners) or achieving certain social objectives (e.g., aiding economic development of the west).

Well and good so far. But time and the rise of interstate trucking have rendered this approach obsolete. Once manufacturers could ship via truck, their demand for rail transit became far more elastic, and this should have led to rate cuts on their goods and rate hikes on bulk commodities. Instead, the ICC allowed truckers to copy the system used by railroads. This seems puzzling: There is no public interest served by value-of-service pricing absent conditions of natural monopoly, and the trucking industry clearly lacks these conditions. Did the ICC err in copying this approach from the rail industry? More likely, the ICC was simply more attentive to the interests of both rail and trucking firms than to the interests of consumers. Allowing truckers to imitate railroads' value-based rates minimized the degree of competition between the two modes of transit and, in turn, kept both modes' markups on shipments of manufactures high. This struck many scholars as a perverse and unwarranted application of value-of-service rate making, and it would eventually be widely cited as evidence of the need for fundamental reform of transportation regulation.

Pricing, Capacity, and Peak-Load Problems

We have yet to address thoroughly an important fact about many industries that will be subject to rate regulation: The particular pricing policy used will affect how much capacity regulated firms will choose to create. Decisions about price and capacity will be *interdependent*. What is more, decisions about optimal capacity will be greatly affected by regular fluctuations in demand over time. An electric company, e.g., must decide how much generating capacity to install based on the rate structure it will be allowed to use, and regulators must find the rate structure that induces the company to select the socially optimal capacity level. These tasks will be greatly complicated by the fact that the demand for electricity can vary considerably over the course of a day (higher demand during business hours), a week (higher demand on weekdays), or a season (higher demand during summer).

Uniform-Demand Case   Consider first the relationship between pricing and capacity decisions when demand is uniform over the relevant market period. Figure 13.3 shows a hypothetical town's demand curve D for electric

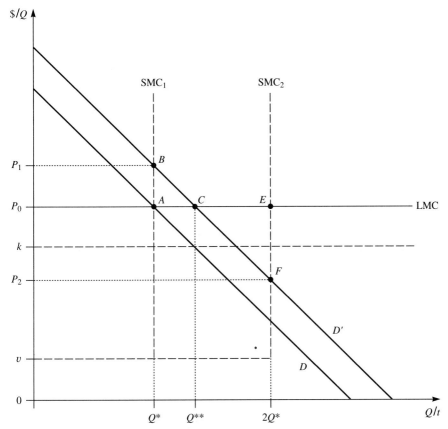

FIGURE 13.3
PRICING AND CAPACITY DECISIONS WITH UNIFORM DEMAND. Given initial demand curve D and costs LMC, the optimal amount of capacity to build is Q^*. If demand then shifts to D', capacity should be increased to Q^{**} in the long run. Until this is done, however, it will be efficient to raise price to P_1 to ration available output Q^*.

power, in units per day. Suppose, for simplicity, that the cost of building generating capacity is a constant k per unit per period, and operating costs (chiefly for fuel) are a constant v per unit per day, so that the long-run marginal cost curve is horizontal and equals the sum of $k + v$. (Note that this assumption of constant LMC makes graphical illustration of this example simpler and neater, but does not seriously alter our conclusions.) The optimal amount of capacity to build is then Q^*, the rate of output at which D and LMC intersect. Building less or more capacity will not maximize welfare, i.e., will either forgo or dissipate some social surplus. A price P_0 will equate quantity demanded to the available amount of capacity Q^*.

What if the demand for electricity shifts somewhat, to D' in Figure 13.3? Optimal capacity should then be expanded to Q^{**} (the rate of output at which D' and LMC intersect) *if* capacity can be created instantaneously and is fully divisible (i.e., there are no discontinuities in LMC). But these conditions may not apply. In the short run, it may be impossible to add any new capacity at all; in the long run, it may be possible to add capacity only in discrete lumps (e.g., in integer multiples of Q^*). What then?

If capacity is fixed at Q^* in the short run, we have a short-run marginal cost curve SMC_1 that is an inverted L: horizontal at v up to the capacity Q^*, vertical afterward. Price must therefore rise to P_1, at which D' and SMC_1 intersect. If we leave price at P_0 (or, indeed, at any level below P_1), there will be excess demand for power, and we can't be sure the Q^* units available will be allocated efficiently (i.e., will go to the users who value these units the most). In the short run, price (rather than output) should be changed to ensure that all the available capacity—and no more—is demanded.

If expansion of capacity in the long run can come only in discrete lumps, the decision about optimal capacity becomes more complicated. Suppose, e.g., that we can add generating capacity (beyond Q^*) in our hypothetical town only by constructing an entirely new power plant, doubling capacity to $2Q^*$. Should we respond to the increase in demand to D' by building this second plant? If we did so, we would capture extra social surplus equal to the area bound by points ABC in Figure 13.3. This is the amount by which consumers' valuations of the extra units between Q^* and Q^{**} exceed the long-run costs of providing them. But all units beyond Q^{**} actually cost more to produce than they are worth to consumers. The area bound by points CEF measures the amount by which production costs exceed consumers' valuations of the extra output from Q^{**} to $2Q^*$ in Figure 13.3. Only if area ABC is greater than area CEF will social surplus be enhanced by building the second plant and expanding capacity to $2Q^*$. (We would then have a new short-run marginal cost curve SMC_2, which intersects D' at a price P_2. Since $P_2 <$ LMC, regulators would once again face the dilemma of either covering all the firm's costs *or* setting allocatively efficient prices.) But if, as it appears in Figure 13.3, area CEF exceeds area ABC, we are better off staying with a single plant (and letting price rise to P_1 to allocate this capacity efficiently).

Variable-Demand Case   What if the demand for electricity in our hypothetical town varies considerably over the day, with high demand during peak hours and low demand during off-peak hours? Such variations will complicate the task of setting the price and capacity still more.

Assume once again that generating capacity costs a constant amount k and operating costs are v (both per unit per day), so that long-run marginal costs are horizontal at LMC $= k + v$ in Figure 13.4. Assume also that we need not add capacity in discrete lumps; i.e., capacity is fully divisible. Now suppose there is high demand for power during peak hours (say, the 12 hours from 8 a.m. to 8 p.m. each day) and much lower demand during off-peak hours (the remaining hours of the day). In Figure 13.4, D_p and D_o, respectively, describe peak and off-peak demands; each is drawn to show how much power would be demanded per day at each possible price if the relevant curve prevailed over the *entire* day. For example, if D_p prevailed over the entire day and price was P_0, then Q_0 units would be demanded. Since D_p applies only half of the time, however, a price of P_0 would actually generate only $Q_0/2$ units per day. (Note that at P_0 no power would be demanded during off-peak hours!) Which demand curve should we consider in making decisions about price and optimal capacity in this market? If we consider only D_p and ignore D_o, we may "overbuild," wasting resources by creating capacity we need only half the time. If we consider only D_o, we will likely be very frustrated by power shortages during peak periods.

Oliver Williamson has suggested a way to make welfare-maximizing decisions about price and capacity that considers both demand curves.[5] In Williamson's method, the various peak and off-peak demand curves are aggregated into an *effective demand-for-capacity* curve. The aggregation method is a rather tricky three-step process:

1 Find the vertical difference between each demand curve and the short-run marginal cost curve. In the example described by Figure 13.4, this involves subtracting v from the demand curves D_o and D_p.

2 Multiply this difference by the fraction of the relevant market period over which this demand prevails. In our example, each demand curve prevails for half the day; multiplying the vertical difference between each curve and v by 0.5 yields the curves labeled $0.5(D_o - v)$ and $0.5(D_p - v)$ in Figure 13.4.

3 Add vertically the resulting weighted demand curves *and* the short-run marginal cost curve to obtain the effective demand-for-capacity curve. In our example, the curve thus obtained is labeled D_E in Figure 13.4.

Once we have calculated the effective demand for capacity in this way, choosing optimal capacity and the efficient price structure is easy. First, find the intersection of the demand-for-capacity curve and the long-run marginal cost curve. In Figure 13.4, D_E and LMC intersect at a rate of output labeled Q^*; this is the optimum scale. Given this capacity, we now have a new short-run marginal cost curve (labeled SMC in Figure 13.4) that is an inverted L, horizontal at the firm's unit operating costs (v in our example) and then vertical at the given capacity level. The allocatively efficient prices will be those that equate the quantity of power demanded and supplied in each period. They can be determined by finding the intersection of the new short-run marginal cost curve and the demand curve that prevails in each period. In Figure 13.4, the resulting peak-period price is labeled P_p, and the off-peak price is P_o.

How can we be sure this method produces an efficient result? Consider first the effect of small increases in scale above Q^*. Increases in output will cost $k + v$ per unit per day; by construction, our effective demand-for-capacity curve D_E reveals how much value consumers attach to such output. Clearly,

[5]Oliver E. Williamson, "Peak-Load Pricing and Optimal Capacity under Indivisibility Constraints," *American Economic Review*, 56 (September 1966), pp. 810–827. For precursors, see Marcel Boiteaux, "Peak-Load Pricing," *Journal of Business*, 33 (April 1960), pp. 157–179, and Peter O. Steiner, "Peak Loads and Efficient Pricing," *Quarterly Journal of Economics*, 71 (November 1957), pp. 585–610.

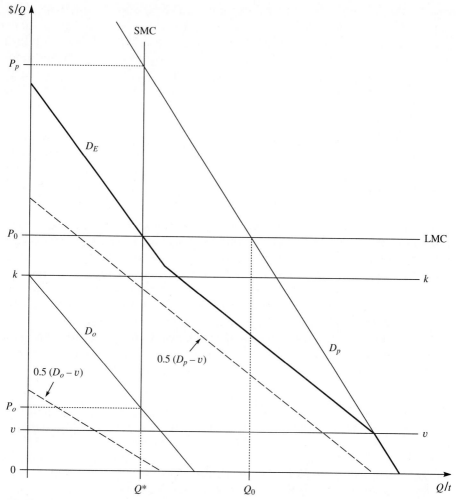

FIGURE 13.4
PRICING AND CAPACITY DECISIONS WITH VARIABLE DEMAND. When peak-period demand D_p and off-peak demand D_o vary widely, firms should construct an effective demand-for-capacity curve D_E. The optimum capacity Q^* is then found at the intersection of this curve and the firm's long-run marginal cost curve (LMC).

beyond Q^* the extra cost of output exceeds its value to consumers: LMC = $k + v$ lies above D_E beyond Q^*. Social surplus will be dissipated if we expand beyond Q^*. If, however, capacity is set below Q^*, the cost of adding extra capacity is less than the value consumers attach to such capacity: D_E lies above LMC between the origin and Q^*. We are forgoing some social surplus. We maximize social surplus by setting capacity precisely at Q^*.

This solution has some interesting properties. Note first that total revenue equals total cost; i.e., economic profits are zero. With output at Q^* in both peak and off-peak periods, the total daily cost of operating our hypothetical electric utility will be Q^* times the firm's per-unit capacity and operating costs,

LMC $= k + v$. That is, total daily cost equals $(k + v)Q^*$. Total daily revenue, however, equals $0.5P_pQ^* + 0.5P_oQ^*$, or $0.5(P_p + P_o)Q^*$. By construction, $k + v$ equals the average of our peak and off-peak prices, or $0.5(P_p + P_o)$, so

$$\text{Total revenue} = 0.5(P_p + P_o)Q^* = \text{total cost} = (k + v)Q^* \qquad (13.2)$$

Thus, although off-peak revenues do not cover the full costs of providing service during this period (because $P_o <$ LMC), the deficit incurred here is exactly made up by the surplus incurred during peak hours (because $P_p >$ LMC by the exact amount by which $P_o <$ LMC). In other words, the way we have constructed D_E and determined capacity ensures that surpluses earned during peak hours just offset deficits during off-peak hours, so that the enterprise breaks even.

This need not always be the case, however. If, e.g., the cost of adding capacity is not constant, the revenue generated under this (or another) peak-load pricing program may or may not cover total costs. Relaxing other assumptions can make peak-load pricing and capacity decisions more complicated still. We have assumed here that peak and off-peak demands are independent of each other—that changes in prices in one period do not cause consumers to shift their consumption to another period. In the real world, such shifting is quite likely to occur—indeed, encouraging users to change their consumption patterns so that costly expansion of capacity might be avoided or postponed is often a central goal of a peak-load pricing scheme. Although modeling such behavior is more complex than what we discussed here, the basic thrust of policy should be the same: Determine capacity at the intersection of an LMC curve and an effective demand-for-capacity curve, and set prices in each subperiod by finding the intersection of an SMC curve and the relevant subperiod demand curve.

RATE-OF-RETURN REGULATION IN THEORY AND PRACTICE

If we are to judge by the rhetoric surrounding the implementation of a particular regulatory regime, there are three basic goals of economic regulation: (1) Hold prices down to costs (including an allowance for "reasonable" profits), (2) avoid allocative inefficiency, and (3) eliminate inefficient and excessively costly production methods.[6] But these are rather fuzzy targets for policymakers, and as we have seen, trying to hit all three simultaneously can be difficult or impossible in some circumstances. In competitive markets, however, these goals are all met. Some argue, therefore, that economic regulation should aim to duplicate the results of a competitive marketplace.

In long-run competitive equilibrium, economic profits are zero because total revenues exceed all *explicit* costs (e.g., for wages, raw materials, etc.) by

---

[6]Of course, we should not necessarily judge the *true* motivation for a particular public policy by the rhetoric that surrounds it. It is sad but true that those who seek to use the regulatory process to serve only their own ends may invoke plausible—but perhaps spurious—public-interest rationales to curry popular favor and/or raise the costs of opposing these ends.

an amount just equal to a firm's *implicit* costs (chiefly, the opportunity cost of capital, or the yield which could have been earned by investing the firm's capital in some alternative instrument of equal risk). If invested capital equals K and the opportunity cost of capital equals r_o, then the firm's implicit costs are $r_o K$; if we denote the firm's explicit (or operating) costs as OC, then in equilibrium total revenues (TR) equal total costs (TC), or

$$TR = TC = OC + r_o K \tag{13.3}$$

What is more, competitive firms will maximize their profits by choosing the rate of output where price and marginal cost are equal (thus ensuring allocative efficiency) and will have an incentive to choose the configuration of inputs that will minimize the cost of producing this rate of output.

If regulators have as their goal duplication of these competitive results, then the process of regulating prices appears simple. The regulatory authority must (1) determine the firm's operating costs OC, (2) add to this amount an allowance for profit equal to $r_o K$, and (3) set price(s) so that the firm's total revenues are just equal to this sum. Setting rates so that the firm covers its costs (including a normal return on invested capital) certainly seems to be what the Supreme Court had in mind when it rendered its *Bluefield* decision in 1923:

> A public utility is entitled to such rates as will permit it to earn a return . . . equal to that generally being made at the same time and in the same general part of the country on investments and in other business undertakings which are attended by corresponding risks and uncertainties; but it has no constitutional right to profits such as are realized or anticipated in highly profitable enterprises and speculative ventures. The return should be reasonably sufficient to assure confidence in the financial soundness of the utility and should be adequate, under efficient and economical management, to maintain and support its credit and enable it to raise the money necessary for the proper discharge of its public duties.[7]

As we shall see, however, such *cost-of-service rate making* or *rate-of-return regulation* is not nearly so simple in practice as textbook discussions make it seem. A regulatory authority will face several difficulties in determining the appropriate values (e.g., a firm's operating costs or the opportunity cost of capital) to use in setting rates. What is more, once rates have been set, managers of regulated firms may have strong incentives to behave in ways that defeat the public-interest purpose of the regulatory regime in place. Let us look at each set of problems in turn.

Practical Difficulties

If regulators had unlimited budgets and/or cared not at all for their own comfort and well-being, it is possible they could make the kinds of perfect opti-

---

[7] *Bluefield Water Works and Imp. Co. v. Public Service Commission of West Virginia*, 262 U.S. 679 (1923), p. 692.

mizing decisions described by theory. But neither condition holds. Regulators often are unable to buy all the information they need to set optimal rates, and often they adopt procedures with an eye more to administrative ease than economic efficiency. In consequence, economic regulation involves a good deal of imperfection.

Determining the Cost of Capital   One of the more controversial decisions regulators will have to make concerns what rate of return to allow on invested capital. In principle, investors must be granted a "fair" return. (But, as one might suspect, determining what is fair is both difficult and mighty important to consumers and stockholders of regulated firms. As a result, the rate-setting process, which normally involves quasi-judicial hearings before the relevant regulatory authority, is usually contentious and lengthy—and so gives lucrative employment to many lawyers, economists, and other industry "experts.") In addition, regulators must set a rate of return sufficiently high to attract the new investment that will fund new projects or expansion of capacity in the industry.

In principle, the appropriate rate for both these tasks is the opportunity cost of capital. But fixing a precise value to this economic concept can be complicated. Note first that a capital investment in a particular firm might take many forms, including various classes of bonds and types of stock. There will not be a single measure of opportunity cost that we can apply to all these. Figuring out the yield which must be paid to bondholders is relatively easy, since bondholders are usually paid a fixed coupon rate of interest. Calculating a fair return on stockholders' equity is more difficult. If this rate is not chosen properly, a firm's shareholders will suffer huge wealth losses or receive windfall gains.

Consider the following example. A hypothetical regulated firm has zero operating costs and attracts capital by selling stock (for simplicity, we assume it issues no bonds). It sells 100,000 shares for $10 each, raising $1 million. The investors anticipate they will receive dividends of $1 per share per year (i.e., a 10 percent rate of return on their shares), since this is the rate they judge they can earn on comparably risky instruments. If regulators set rates sufficiently high to generate $100,000 per year in net revenue, investors' anticipations will be realized. If, however, regulated rates generate less (more) than $100,000 for this purpose, the value of the shareholders' investment must fall (rise) by enough to make the effective rate of return on these shares equal to that of comparable investments. Let us say the regulatory authority decides that a fair annual return to shareholders is $80,000, or $0.80 per share. Anyone who tries to sell the shares of this firm at a price of $10 would be disappointed to find no takers, for at this price the annual dividends yield a rate of return of only 8 percent, while (we have assumed) shares in comparable firms yield 10 percent. Until the price of shares in this firm falls to $8, these shares will not sell. At this price, however, total shareholders' equity is $800,000—and shareholders have lost $200,000. However, investors would reap a windfall if regulators set rates which yielded, say, $120,000 in revenues. With dividends at $1.20 per share, each share in this firm would likely fetch $12; total stockholders' equity would therefore rise by $200,000, to $1.2 million.

The importance of setting a rate of return that is equal to that of comparable investments should be clear. But no two firms, no matter how similar they might appear, will ever be *identical* with respect to the risks they face or their prospects for the future. No two firms can ever inhabit exactly the same market or, therefore, ever face identical underlying business conditions. Reading off the rates of return earned by some sample of comparable firms may or may not be a reliable guide to a truly fair rate of return for the relevant regulated firm. The problem here is compounded by the fact that the firms that seem most comparable to a regulated firm may themselves be regulated. This introduces an element of *circularity* to the process: The performance of comparable firms may be merely a guide to what other regulators have done rather than a reliable indicator of the opportunity cost of capital.

Some unfortunate characteristics of financial markets will also affect the ability of regulators to divine the appropriate rate of return to allow investors. Risk will vary not only across industries, but also over time. Investors' expectations about growth in earnings will be imprecise and will depend in part upon ever-changing underlying economic conditions. Finally, the choice of regulatory policy itself will affect investors' expected return; i.e., there is a "feedback loop" between regulators and investors. When, e.g., regulators decide investors in a particular industry merit a rate of return of 10 percent, investors may conclude that the industry is (by virtue of this regulatory rule) less risky and therefore may be willing to accept a lower rate of return. In sum, choosing the rate of return to allow regulated firms is far from an exact science.

Determining the Rate Base   Determining the value of a regulated firm's capital assets (the *rate base*) on which a fair rate of return might be earned will be an imprecise—and therefore contentious—matter as well. Note first that differing rates of return can generate similar revenues if the rate base is adjusted appropriately. For example, required revenues with a rate base of $1 million and an allowed rate of return of 6 percent will be the same as with a rate base of $1.2 million and a 5 percent rate of return. Predictably, then, regulators and regulated firms do constant battle over which assets belong in the rate base and the value that should be attached to these assets (e.g., what about property soon to be abandoned by the firm? construction in progress? intangible property such as patents?).

Since the Supreme Court's 1944 *Hope* decision,[8] the most common method of valuing the assets in a firm's rate base is to deduct accumulated depreciation from the original cost of these assets. But estimating depreciation is a difficult proposition, often carried out according to seemingly arbitrary accounting rules. Normally, the market is a reliable guide to asset values: We can judge what something is worth by finding what someone might pay for it in

---

[8]*Federal Power Commission v. Hope Natural Gas Company*, 320 U.S. 591 (1944).

an arm's-length transaction. Using market-based asset values in the rate-making process involves two problems, however. First, calculating such values is difficult and will entail fairly high costs; exchanges of all or part of a regulated firm's real property are rare, and most regulatory commissions would find it impossibly expensive to make reliable market-based estimates of asset values from such sales. Second, there is another feedback loop here: What someone will pay for the assets of a regulated firm will invariably be influenced by the rates regulators set. To avoid such problems, most commissions use the original-cost-less-depreciation method of determining the rate base despite some fairly important shortcomings.

Consider the following example. There are two power plants X and Y subject to rate regulation. They are as close to identical as can be, given the fact that X was built many years ago while Y has just been completed. In the years between the construction of X and Y, the cost of land in the areas surrounding *both* has risen. But if we use *historical cost* to attach a value to the two plants, X will appear to be worth far less than Y, even though the opportunity cost (or current market value) of the resources used is the same for both. So, X's rate base will be less than Y's, and its regulated rates will be lower, too. This will produce some economic distortions: We will see a tendency toward overconsumption of X's power and underconsumption of Y's. And, despite the fact that the opportunity costs of the resources that X and Y use are identical (or nearly so), firms will prefer to locate near X rather than near Y to take advantage of X's lower rates. These shifts—unwarranted with respect to the true underlying social costs of X's power—may affect the distribution of employment opportunities, real estate values, and numerous other variables. Of course, the shifts could favor Y if building plants became cheaper over time, perhaps because of technological advances. Then X's rate base (and rates) would exceed Y's, and the kinds of distortions discussed above would be reversed.

Other Problems   The desire to make a regulatory regime cheap and easy to administer may conflict with the desire for greater economic efficiency in several other areas.

In principle, cost-based rates should be set according to what costs *will be* rather than what they *have been*. But predicting future costs with precision is impossible. The regulatory authority that tries to do it will have to sort through widely differing opinions and will be tied up in proceedings of great length and complexity. So even though last year's prices and quantities will likely differ from next year's, they are commonly used in rate making because such data are easy to obtain.

In addition, positive information costs will complicate the task of translating a particular revenue requirement into an efficient *rate structure*. Regulators sometimes overlook the kinds of efficiency-enhancing pricing strategies discussed earlier (e.g., value-of-service pricing) because of the high costs of obtaining accurate estimates of the price elasticity of demand in regulated markets. In practice, regulators often make rather arbitrary assumptions about demand elasticity. In some industries, such as electric power, regulators implicitly assume elasticity is zero (although this is starting to change, especially in telephone regulation). In deciding an appeal for a rate increase, e.g., regulators may find that a particular electric company requires an additional $10 million in revenue to cover its increased costs. It is common practice to divide $10 million by the number of kilowatthours produced and consumed in some prior year (the *test year*) to estimate how much extra must be charged per kilowatthour to yield the desired additional revenue. Thus, the regulators assume that the demand curve for electricity is vertical, i.e., that the higher rate per kilowatthour will not reduce quantity demanded. This is, of course, a false assumption. It will produce flawed estimates of the extra revenue that will result from the price hike and may encourage the firm to make inefficient investments in plant and equipment or to hire redundant staff.

Periodically reassessing and restructuring rates will also be expensive. As a result, many regulatory authorities have no regular schedule for such revisions; rate reviews are commonly initiated by the regulated firm(s). In general, cost increases lead the firm(s) to appeal for rate increases. If, however, costs should fall, the firm(s) have little interest in bringing this to the attention of regulators. Until regulators catch on to the cost reduction and revise rates downward, the firm(s) keep the savings as extra profits. Interestingly, such *regulatory lag* may not be all bad. Indeed, some researchers have cited this lag as one of the means by which we may ameliorate some incentive problems inherent in rate regulation. To such issues we now turn.

Incentive Problems

In truly competitive markets, both a carrot and a stick motivate firms to behave efficiently. The carrot is the higher profits that can be realized if costs are reduced below those of rivals. The stick is the threat of bankruptcy if costs rise above those of rivals. Rate-of-return regulation and cost-plus rate making whittle down both carrot and stick, perhaps to negligible proportions.

The central problem is that regulators will not (cannot, given positive information costs and their status as outsiders) be as well informed about the internal workings of their subject firms as the firms' managers are. As a result, it will occasionally be possible for these managers to incur costs—and have these costs become part of firms' revenue requirements—that are not strictly necessary for the conduct of the firms' business. Managers may be willing to incur these costs to make their lives more pleasant or their surroundings more comfortable. Alternatively, managers may simply make mistakes in judgment (perhaps resulting from a regulation-diminished incentive to be careful) which result in excessive operating costs. Whatever the cause, once these higher costs are incorporated in the rate base, the outcome will be resource misallocation and reduced welfare.

Regulators can, of course, disallow expenditures they consider unreasonable in determining a firm's reasonable operating costs or its rate base. At various times, regulatory commissions have tried to pare excessive executive salaries or disallow certain expenses entirely (e.g., extravagant costs of attending conventions). But these attempts have not always been successful, and the Supreme Court has warned that commissions ought not to meddle excessively in the day-to-day activities of a regulated firm:

> The Commission is not the financial manager of the corporation and is not empowered to substitute its judgment for that of the directors of the corporation; nor can it ignore items charged by the utility as operating expenses unless there is an abuse of discretion in that regard by the corporate officers.[9]

It has been easier to show an abuse of discretion with respect to expenditures for charitable contributions, lobbying, and some forms of advertising and promotion than for operating expenses that are more obviously a part of the production process. As long as a firm's expenditures are plausibly linked to production (e.g., "Our staff deserves to be well paid because they are highly productive and possess special skills," "We need a new fleet of company cars to ensure that our managers can get where they're needed promptly and reliably," "We need a new corporate headquarters because it will improve managers' morale and make them more productive"), it is unlikely a regulatory authority will attempt to prove such "abuse."

Interestingly, the aforementioned *regulatory* or *rate-setting lag*—a gap in time between the realization of some cost savings and an accompanying reduction in the rate base—may curb such behavior. If, e.g., prices set in one year will remain in effect for some months or years afterward and the firm is allowed to keep any higher-than-expected profits earned in the interim, it may actually have an incentive to try to lower its costs in order to realize such higher profits. Depending on other elements of the regulatory process, however, regulatory lag alone will not eliminate some important perverse incentives in regulated industries.

The Averch-Johnson Effect Firms combine inputs (e.g., land, labor, and capital) to produce output. Ordinarily, firms will try to minimize production costs by combining inputs in such a way that the *marginal product per dollar spent on all inputs is the same.*[10] Suppose, e.g., a given firm uses labor and capital in such proportions that hiring an additional unit of labor will yield incremental output of 1,000 units, while buying an additional unit of capital will have a marginal product of 900 units. If both cost the same amount, say $100, we can conclude that the firm's present use of inputs is inefficient: The firm would get 10 units of output per extra dollar spent on labor, but only 9 units of output per extra dollar spent on capital. The firm could get more output without increasing its total costs by using more labor and less capital. Observe: Spending $100 to hire another unit of labor yields an extra 1,000 units; saving $100 by buying one less unit of capital involves the sacrifice of

---

[9]*Missouri ex rel. South Western Bell Telephone v. Public Service Commission of Missouri*, 262 U.S. 276 (1923), p. 289.

[10]That is, $MP_K/P_K = MP_L/P_L = MP_N/P_N$, where MP and P denote the marginal product and price, respectively, of capital K, labor L, and land N.

only 900 units. Thus, this simple substitution nets the firm 100 extra units of output at no extra cost! Alternatively, the firm could cut its production costs and still produce its former rate of output by making a similar substitution: One more unit of labor will produce sufficient additional output to enable the firm to buy about 1.11 fewer units of capital, saving the firm about $11 without reducing output. Additional savings may come as the firm continues to substitute labor for capital, but of course hiring additional labor will (according to the law of diminishing returns) reduce labor's marginal product, while using less capital will raise labor's marginal product. Production costs will reach a minimum when the marginal product to price ratios of all inputs are equal.

Harvey Averch and Leland Johnson theorize, however, that rate-of-return regulation might induce a firm to combine inputs in a nonoptimal way.[11] Specifically, regulating a firm's rate of return on capital might, under certain circumstances, induce the firm to overinvest in capital relative to other inputs and operate at a rate of output where cost is not minimized.

This tendency, dubbed the *Averch-Johnson* (or *A-J*) *effect*, will be present if the *allowed* rate of return set by regulators r_a exceeds the true opportunity cost of capital r_o. Recall that under rate-of-return regulation, the firm's allowed total revenues TR_a will equal operating costs OC plus the allowed return on invested capital $r_a K$. The firm's real underlying costs TC, however, will equal OC plus the true cost of invested capital $r_o K$. When $r_a > r_o$, the firm can earn positive economic profits π_e :

$$\pi_e = TR_a - TC = (OC + r_a K) - (OC + r_o K) \qquad (13.4)$$
$$= (r_a - r_o)K$$

Thus, for every dollar of capital K the firm buys, it earns economic profits equal to $r_a - r_o$. If, say, r_o is 0.10, but r_a is set at 0.20, then each $1 of invested capital will net the firm $0.10. For example, the allowed return on invested capital of $1 million here will be equal to $200,000, of which only $100,000 is the true opportunity cost of capital; the remaining $100,000 is economic profit.

This will do more than just put money in the pockets of the firm's shareholders. It will cause resource misallocation. To see how, return to the numerical illustration discussed above, in which (initially) a hypothetical firm's marginal product per dollar spent on labor was 10 (or 1,000/$100), while its marginal product per dollar spent on capital was 9 (or 900/$100). As we saw, such conditions should induce the firm to substitute labor for capital. If r_a exceeds r_o, however, the firm may not do so, for whenever r_a exceeds r_o, the price of capital will, *in the view of this regulated firm*, appear lower than its true market price. If again r_a exceeds r_o by 0.10, each $1 spent on capital nets the firm $0.10 in profits; thus, a unit of capital with a market price of $100 appears, to this firm, to cost only $90 (or $100 minus the $10 that each unit of capital contributes to profits). To this firm, then, substituting labor for capital does *not*

---

[11]Harvey Averch and Leland L. Johnson, "Behavior of the Firm under Regulatory Constraint," *American Economic Review*, 52 (December 1962), pp. 1052–1069.

appear to make sense: The apparent marginal product per dollar spent is the same for each input ($1,000/\$100 = 900/\$90 = 10$). The firm will accordingly combine its inputs in a way that is socially inefficient and wasteful, using too much capital (sometimes called *gold-plating* the rate base) and too little labor. The firm's costs will be too high, as will the price, and the rate of output produced and consumed in this market will be too low (although it will exceed that of the unregulated monopolist). Social surplus will not be maximized.

Some economists, notably William Baumol and Alvin Klevorick, doubt the quantitative significance of the A-J effect, however.[12] Tiny differences between r_a and r_o will not change a regulated firm's view of the relative prices of capital and other inputs very much. Empirical evidence on the existence of the A-J effect is somewhat mixed. While three studies of the electric power industry detected significant overcapitalization,[13] one study found none.[14]

This apparent conflict might be explained by the fact that regulatory commissions often set r_a without careful regard to underlying economic conditions. Thus, it is possible that the incentive to overcapitalize, which hinges on an excess of r_a over r_o, has been strong in some periods and weak (or absent) in others; that is, r_o has varied up or down while r_a has been relatively inflexible. Indeed, it is possible that in some periods (e.g., when general price inflation is severe and/or unanticipated) r_a might fall below r_o, leading to a *reverse A-J effect*, i.e., inefficient substitution of other inputs for capital.[15]

Other Perverse Incentives   That rate-of-return regulation or cost-plus pricing can lead firms to be wasteful is probably no surprise to students; regulators, we can assume, are aware of this fact as well. What if well-meaning regulators try to overcome their ignorance of the minutiae of their subject firms' day-to-day operations by simply *assuming* these firms will overstate their costs and so deliberately set rates that will yield revenues less than firms' true total costs? Perhaps the authority will disallow a portion of firms' expenditures for some items and allow full recovery only for those expenditures it is *sure* are necessary for production. For example, regulators may allow full recovery for an electric utility's fuel expenses or the repair costs for an old generator, but (suspecting gold-plating) may not allow the utility to recover the full costs of a new generator. Clearly, this poses the kind of problem (the reverse A-J effect)

[12]William J. Baumol and Alvin K. Klevorick, "Input Choices and Rate-of-Return Regulation: An Overview of the Discussion," *Bell Journal of Economics and Management Science*, 1 (Autumn 1970), pp. 162–190.

[13]Robert M. Spann, "Rate of Return Regulation and Efficiency in Production: An Empirical Test of the Averch-Johnson Thesis," and Leon Courville, "Regulation and Efficiency in the Electric Utility Industry," *Bell Journal of Economics and Management Science*, 5 (Spring 1974), pp. 38–74; H. Craig Petersen, "An Empirical Test of Regulatory Effects," *Bell Journal of Economics*, 6 (Spring 1975), pp. 111–126.

[14]William J. Boyes, "An Empirical Examination of the Averch-Johnson Effect," *Economic Inquiry*, 14 (March 1976), pp. 25–35.

[15]For a suggestion that this phenomenon was important during the late 1960s and early 1970s, see Paul L. Joskow and Paul W. MacAvoy, "Regulation and the Financial Condition of the Electric Power Companies in the 1970's," *American Economic Review*, 65 (May 1975), pp. 295–301.

hinted at above: Subject firms will now have an incentive to use only those inputs for which cost recovery is ensured and may avoid investing in other types of inputs even where such investments are—absent regulation—sensible. Our electric company may continue to use a generator that guzzles fuel and breaks down often when a more cost-effective one is available, but is induced to prolong the life of the old generator by overzealous regulation. Another problem is that the firm may respond to regulation of this kind by inefficiently reducing product quality in order to bring costs down to equality with allowed revenues.

There is a suspicion (although unverified empirically) that regulated firms will have a diminished incentive to innovate, or to adopt existing innovations, at a socially optimal rate even where regulators have very good information about costs and allow full cost recovery. Unregulated firms reap the benefits of cost-reducing innovations in the form of extra profits or are punished with losses if they fail to adopt such innovations when rivals do so. But regulated firms may not be able to keep the gains from innovation. Indeed, if the regulatory authority quickly adjusts allowed revenue downward whenever costs fall, there is no reason for the firm to innovate at all. Given that the authority is unlikely to know what a firm *might* have done but didn't, there will be nothing pushing the firm to adopt or originate cost-saving ideas or equipment. Regulatory lag might partially cure this tendency: For at least the period between the time an innovation is put in place and the next rate revision, the firm will get to keep the gains from innovation.

Finally, when companies that are subject to rate-of-return regulation are allowed to diversify into other (unregulated) sectors, new problems loom. For example, when some of a firm's assets jointly produce output for regulated and unregulated markets, the firm will have an obvious incentive to misreport costs, allocating excessive portions of the costs of such assets to the regulated market. This will enable it to raise price in the regulated market; if price in the unregulated market does not change, the firm's profits must rise. Thus, rate-of-return regulation can induce firms to diversify into unrelated markets when it is socially inefficient to do so. See Table 13.1 for a summary.

Clearly, rate-of-return regulation is a vexing and imprecise undertaking. (As evidence, consider that regulatory lag, which we might a priori think is a symptom of the inefficiency of the regulatory process, is sometimes cited as medicine for some of regulation's true illnesses!) Anyone who presumes that economic regulation will necessarily correct market failure, or will do so cheaply and easily, is advised to think again.

INCENTIVE-COMPATIBLE ECONOMIC REGULATION

That rate-of-return regulation involves incentive problems is no just-discovered secret. Participants in the regulatory process have long been aware of such problems and have occasionally offered suggestions aimed at (1) improving firms' incentives to behave in socially beneficial ways and (2) enhancing

TABLE 13.1
PROBLEMS IN RATE-OF-RETURN REGULATION—A SUMMARY

---

1 *Determining the correct allowable rate of return is difficult.* If allowed rate of return differs from true opportunity cost of capital, shareholders will experience windfall gains or losses; this also may induce firm management to alter mix of inputs in inefficient ways.

2 *Determining correct rate base is difficult.* Circularity in rate making and asset valuation (i.e., feedback loop between rate structure and value of productive assets) and unreliability of accounting data complicate calculation of correct rate base, resulting in allocative and/or productive inefficiency.

3 *Information problems make it difficult to translate the revenue requirement into an efficient rate structure.* Regulators often know far less about firms' true costs and demands than managers, and even managers may not have sufficient knowledge of these variables to make efficient pricing schemes workable in practice. The result: allocative inefficiency.

4 *Incentive problems make productive inefficiency likely.* Principal-agent problems in both the regulatory process and firm management are likely to cause regulators to stress administrative ease over efficiency and firm managers to mix inputs nonoptimally or otherwise waste or overcompensate for factors of production.

---

the likelihood that regulators will have as their central goal the maximization of social welfare rather than some other objective.

In recent years, there has also been a flurry of theoretical work in this area.[16] So far this scholarly research has failed to yield any simple cures. If anything, it has highlighted the difficulties regulators face in trying to ensure that firms make efficient production and investment decisions. Some researchers have attempted to derive optimal bonus plans and compensation schemes regulators can use to induce firms to make an optimal effort to control costs. In simple static models of this kind, where regulators and firms make decisions in but one period, regulators require large—perhaps unrealistically large—amounts of information to induce optimal firm behavior. Of course, regulation is not static but dynamic; regulators might use repeated observations of firm performance over many periods to fine-tune rewards and penalties. But this merely means firms may have an incentive to deceive regulators, perhaps sacrificing some profits today to make tomorrow's reward structure even more favorable. In the face of deceptive or strategic behavior, designing an optimal regulatory regime becomes even more difficult. Such difficulties have not paralyzed scholars with despair, however. Scholars have used the lessons of history and economic theory to devise several proposals that may occasionally improve incentives under rate-of-return regulation.

The Sliding Scale   One way to induce firms to attempt to control costs is to allow them to keep some portion of the profits they earn if their realized

---

[16]For a useful summary of this literature, from which much of the following discussion is drawn, see Paul L. Joskow and Richard Schmalensee, "Incentive Regulation for Electric Utilities," *Yale Journal on Regulation*, 4 (1986), pp. 1–49.

rate of return exceeds that initially set by the regulatory authority. Suppose, e.g., the opportunity cost of capital is 10 percent and the authority specifies that the allowed rate of return r_a should equal this amount. Superior management, however, results in cost reductions so that the firm's realized rate of return r_r turns out to be 12 percent. If the regulatory authority responds by adjusting rates downward by the full amount of the cost reductions, fixing the allowed rate of return once again at 10 percent, the firm's managers will soon learn that there is little reason to control costs, for they get to keep higher-than-anticipated profits for but a single period. As an alternative, however, the authority might use a *sliding scale* to adjust rates, setting the new price structure to allow a rate of return higher than the old one by some fraction of the difference between the old allowed rate of return and the realized rate of return. That is, the authority might set a new allowed rate of return r_a' such that

$$r_a' = r_r + b(r_a - r_r) \tag{13.5}$$

where b is some fraction between 0 and 1. In our example, if the authority sets $b = 0.5$, then r_a' will be 11 percent (that is, 12 percent minus one-half of 2 percent, the difference between the allowed and realized rates of return). Here the sliding scale allows the firm to keep half the savings yielded by decisions that permanently lower its costs. Accordingly, it has a stronger incentive to pursue such savings.

Of course, realized rates of return may differ from those allowed for reasons having nothing to do with management efficiency. Changes in underlying economic conditions (e.g., fuel cost changes, business cycles) may produce such differences as well. In this sense, the sliding-scale approach is both a *reward-sharing* and a *risk-sharing* mechanism. Firms share some of the rewards resulting from cost savings with consumers, but also burden consumers with some of the risks associated with cost increases. Suppose, as an alternative example, some exogenous factor raises costs so that the firm's realized rate of return is only 8 percent. If again r_a is 10 percent and b is 0.5, then r_a' will be 9 percent. Just as the firm was only partially rewarded for reducing costs under this regime, it is partially protected from the consequences of cost increases.

Although the sliding-scale approach meshes nicely with existing regulatory processes and accounting conventions, it does have some deficiencies. The most important is that persistent changes in underlying economic conditions will yield rates that are either too high or too low for too long. Consider a prolonged bout with inflation (as in the United States in the 1960s and 1970s). Such inflation causes realized rates of return to fall below allowed rates for an extended period. Even if the regulated firms produce efficiently, they are "punished" with rates of return below the cost of capital and may fail to invest optimally. Clearly, business conditions must be monitored regularly and the sliding-scale formula adjusted appropriately if this approach is to enhance performance in regulated sectors.

Partial Cost Adjustment   Another proposal is to allow recovery of only some fraction of the amount by which a firm's *unit costs* exceed an allowed benchmark, presumably the firm's minimum attainable costs. Firms will then have no incentive to allow costs to drift upward since they will be unable to recover the full amount of such cost increases. Just as with the sliding-scale approach, however, it must be recognized that underlying economic conditions will change over time. Thus, implementing this approach requires regulators to forecast how minimum costs will change as input prices, output, and technology change. This will pose some formidable—perhaps insurmountable—conceptual and practical difficulties. For example, cost estimates should be based on the opportunities faced by firms rather than the actual choices they made; i.e., regulators will need to know what their subject firms *could have paid* for inputs rather than what they actually paid. It will usually be the case that regulators lack the knowledge and information needed to employ this method successfully.

Rate Indexing or Price Caps   The favorable incentive effects of regulatory lag have been noted. In an inflationary environment, however, frequent rate adjustments will be necessary to keep regulated firms viable; as the frequency of rate adjustments increases, the incentive benefits of regulatory lag may be lost. To preserve regulatory lag in an environment where input prices are rising, some have proposed tying rates to some general price index. Prices would then be adjusted automatically as input prices rose, without the need for a new rate base that would "take back" any gains from enhanced efficiency or innovation. In practice, this method requires base prices to be set ("capped") at some initial proceeding, after which subsequent changes are automatic and equal to the change in some specified price index (e.g., the consumer price index) less some fixed allowance for expected productivity growth. Suppose, e.g., the chosen price index rises by 5 percent over the relevant period, while the productivity growth allowance is 1 percent. The regulated firm's price cap would then be automatically revised upward by 4 percent in the next period. By fixing the productivity growth allowance, this scheme creates an incentive for firms to improve productivity by more than this allowance. In our example, if input prices rise by 5 percent but productivity rises 2 percent, the allowed 4 percent rate increase will leave the firm with 1 percent of its revenues as compensation for its success in raising productivity above the prespecified norm. Of course, selecting appropriate price indices and productivity norms may be difficult, and over long intervals it may be necessary to revise the price-cap formula. In principle, however, this method can lead to improved pricing and investment decisions by regulated firms.

VIGNETTE 13.2   Price Caps in the Telephone Industry

In recent years, many states have been experimenting with rate indexing or price caps in their regulation of intrastate long-distance telephone service. In 1982, to settle an antitrust suit brought by the Justice Department, the telephone industry was restructured significantly: AT&T spun off various "local operating companies" to provide all local service, while what remained of AT&T (with various competitors) focused on long-distance service. Initially, most regulation of intrastate long-distance charges by AT&T and other firms followed the traditional rate-of-return approach, but by 1987 enough states had adopted variants of the price-cap approach to enable fruitful comparisons between states.

According to Alan Mathios and Robert Rogers, AT&T's prices are significantly lower in those states which have gone to some sort of price-cap regulation of intrastate long-distance rates.[17] The price of a 5-minute daytime call in states that allowed AT&T and its competitors some degree of pricing flexibility was (as of 1987) an average of 7 percent lower than in states that maintained strict rate-of-return regulation. Further, the longer the newer approach had been used, the greater was its apparent price advantage. There are several possible explanations for this, of course. For example, AT&T may have been playing an elaborate strategic game, cleverly arranging its intrastate long-distance prices to make it appear that price-cap regulation at the *state* level has advantages for consumers, so that some day such regulation will be adopted at the *federal* level. But it is also possible that the results obtained by Mathios and Rogers validate theorists' expectations that AT&T and its rivals have a stronger incentive to control costs and innovate under price-cap regulation than under more traditional schemes, and that competition eventually forces firms to share these savings with consumers in the form of lower prices.

Using Yardsticks   Rate-of-return regulation is most commonly applied to firms deemed natural monopolies; thus, within a given area, there will usually be no close rivals that we may use as *yardsticks* against which to measure a subject firm's relative performance. If, however, we can identify comparable firms that operate in other areas, i.e., firms of similar size in markets with similar demand and cost characteristics, then such comparisons may be feasible. Calculating the average of these comparable firms' unit costs and setting the subject firm's prices equal to this amount are called *yardstick competition,* an approach which (in theory at least) creates strong incentives for efficiency.[18] Under this method of rate setting, the regulated firm's prices are independent of its own costs. The firm that can cut unit costs below the average of its group of "comparables" reaps economic profits; the firm that can't suffers losses. The effect is the same as if all the regulated firms were competing with each other, and the expected result is that the costs of all will converge to some minimum level.

But there are some hurdles to jump before implementing yardstick competition. First there must be a sufficiently large sample of comparable firms. Given the imperfect nature of the accounting cost data available for regulated industries, it will be difficult to know for certain whether firms are truly com-

---

[17]Alan D. Mathios and Robert P. Rogers, "The Impact of Alternative Forms of State Regulation of AT&T on Direct-Dial, Long-Distance Telephone Rates," *Rand Journal of Economics,* 20 (Autumn 1989), pp. 437–453.

[18]Andrei Shleifer, "A Theory of Yardstick Competition," *Rand Journal of Economics,* 16 (Autumn 1985), pp. 319–327.

parable or merely appear so. Further, market conditions and local regulatory policies will differ significantly from place to place, and it will be hard to statistically adjust for such differences. It is possible, then, that the yardstick approach will be flawed in practice, introducing a system of highly random rewards and punishments to subject firms. See Table 13.2.

Noncomprehensive Approaches   The methods described thus far are comprehensive in that they apply to a subject firm's overall performance or cost structure. But some approaches apply only to certain portions of a firm's operations—generally those which appear most crucial to operations or those for which data are most accurate or readily available. In electric utilities, e.g., fuel costs account for 40 percent of total costs, and measuring these costs is quite easy. Accordingly, incentive plans tied to fuel costs or fuel use are reasonably common. Also popular are incentive plans which reward electric utilities that achieve specific performance targets for certain generating units, e.g., those that keep their nuclear reactors (which usually have the lowest unit costs) operating near full capacity. The problem with such noncomprehensive approaches is that firms might "cheat" and meet the specific targets by incurring extra costs in areas where deviations from industry norms are harder to detect. For example, a utility might meet its fuel-use targets by spending more on generator maintenance or on new technology than it saves in fuel costs. Capacity targets for nuclear plants are especially worrisome: It is conceivable a firm will then have an incentive to compromise safety to achieve the target.

ALTERNATIVES TO REGULATION

Although direct economic regulation is clearly the approach most commonly used to deal with natural monopoly or address other issues discussed in Chapter 12, it is by no means the only approach. Proponents of at least two alternative approaches—government ownership and franchise-bidding schemes—

TABLE 13.2
INCENTIVE-COMPATIBLE REGULATION: A SUMMARY

---

1 *Sliding scale:* Adjusts allowed rate of return upward (or downward) by some fraction of difference between former allowed rate and realized rate, letting firms keep some portion of profits earned from cost savings (or avoid some losses realized as result of circumstances beyond management's control).

2 *Partial cost adjustment:* Sets a benchmark for firm's unit costs (presumably equal to firm's minimum attainable costs), allowing only partial recovery of amount by which actual costs exceed this level.

3 *Price cap:* Base prices set at initial hearing; subsequent price changes are automatic and equal to changes in some general price index less allowance for expected productivity growth.

4 *Yardstick competition:* Base prices set by reference to costs of comparable firms; subject firm then gets to keep any profits earned if its costs are kept below average of comparables.

---

argue that these methods can be superior to direct regulation in some circumstances. Proponents of another alternative—outright *de*regulation of some industries—argue that in some cases economic regulation either has been misapplied or has worked so badly that net welfare would be enhanced by simply eliminating it in whole or in part.

Public Ownership

Three arguments are commonly invoked to justify public or government ownership of a firm. First, such ownership is a substitute for regulation of a private firm by a commission or another authority. Instead of addressing the basic dilemma of natural monopoly by creating a layer of bureaucracy to supervise the pricing and output decisions of managers acting on behalf of private shareholders, the government acts as owner and directly hires managers to achieve its objectives. We would hope—but probably should not assume—that these objectives will center on the maximization of social welfare.

Second, putting publicly owned firms side by side with private ones might force the private firms to behave more efficiently or competitively. If we suspect the firms in a particular market are wasteful or colluding, creating a model public firm to compete with them might enhance welfare by inducing better performance or ending collusion. The Tennessee Valley Authority, a federally owned producer of electric power, is an often-cited example of a public firm that has forced private rivals to become more efficient and reduce prices.

Third, when a product has the peculiar characteristics that qualify it as a *public good*, it may be undersupplied if left to private producers. Because public goods are both nondepletable and nonexcludable (recall Chapter 3), private firms will find it very difficult to make a go of producing and selling such goods. Consumers will have an incentive to understate their true preferences for such goods (hoping they can consume them freely once they are produced), and the high costs of excluding nonpayers will make it hard to recover costs if the good is produced privately. In any event, given their nondepletability, the allocatively efficient price of public goods is zero. Thus, it is argued, public provision of public goods (e.g., national defense) financed via taxes is both inevitable and desirable.

But public ownership poses some serious problems. Most important, public ownership involves principal-agent problems at *two* levels. As we saw in Chapter 8, such problems often arise when the ownership and day-to-day management of an enterprise are separated. Owners (principals) want maximum return on their investments. But managers (agents) may have somewhat different interests; they may wish to enhance their own utility in ways that will reduce profits. If information about all the decisions that managers make were freely available to owners, there would be no principal-agent problem, for managerial misbehavior would be easily detected and punished. But we live in a world where information is neither perfect nor freely available, so managers will have some latitude to indulge their tastes for greater security or comfort on the job. Owners may try to use various tactics, e.g., bonus plans and stock options, to ensure that managers have strong incentives to maximize their firms' long-run profits, but such tactics may simply reduce principal-agent problems to tolerable levels rather than eliminate them.[19]

To see the first source of principal-agent problems that affect the performance of public enterprises (or, for that matter, direct regulation), consider political officeholders, their appointees, and government functionaries (so-called bureaucrats) as the agents of voters. Whether these voters (as principals) have as their objective maximum efficiency or equity, their agents will have some latitude to pursue other goals because it is very costly to detect such behavior. And, more important, even when inefficient or unresponsive behavior is detected, it will be very hard to modify. Transacting in the political marketplace is not cheap, and serious free-rider problems will confound attempts to make political representatives truly accountable for their actions. Finally, the political marketplace is notably lacking in the kinds of institutional devices (the aforementioned bonuses or stock options) that might make political agents' incentives conform more closely to their principals'.

When public enterprises are created, officeholders and bureaucrats become principals as well, and the managers they hire are their agents. This adds another layer of principal-agent problems; whatever objectives these political principals transmit to their agents, the agents will have some latitude to disregard them and pursue their own objectives. Since public enterprises are typically not for profit and issue no ownership shares, the value of which will rise or fall depending on the firm's performance, limiting such behavior might actually be harder in public enterprises than in private ones. Owners of private firms can, as we have noted, tie a significant portion of their managers' compensation to firm profits. In public firms, this option is usually unavailable. Managers of public enterprises, therefore, are often given less managerial autonomy than their private-sector counterparts and often must manage subject to a set of bureaucratic rules aimed at limiting their opportunities to indulge their preferences. Of course, such rules may merely cause managers to take more circuitous routes to enhance their well-being (e.g., a cap on a manager's salary may cause the manager to spend company resources on a larger support staff or more comfortable surroundings).

In sum, there is reason to suspect a priori that public enterprises will perform inefficiently relative to private ones. The empirical literature seems to confirm this suspicion. But making meaningful comparisons of the performance of public and private enterprises is not as easy as you might think. In naturally monopolistic markets, there will be no (or few) private firms to which we can compare existing public firms. Where private and public firms exist side by side, the private firms are usually regulated, and disentangling the effects of regulation from those of ownership can be difficult. Finally, it is

---

[19]On the optimal amount of "agency costs" owners will pay, see Michael C. Jensen and William H. Meckling, "Theory of the Firm: Managerial Behavior, Agency Costs, and Ownership Structure," *Journal of Financial Economics,* 3 (1976), pp. 305–360.

possible that public enterprises will have social objectives (e.g., affecting the distribution of income), the pursuit of which renders normal measures of corporate performance meaningless.

There appears to be strong evidence that public firms are less efficient than private ones in sectors where competition is strong or where government oversight of regulated private producers takes relatively uncomplicated forms.[20] Many studies show that private trash collection, transit, firefighting, and health service firms have lower production costs than their public counterparts. But the evidence from other sectors, where competition is more limited and the hand of regulation heavier, is more ambiguous. While several researchers have found superior efficiency in private electric and water utilities and airlines, others have found no differences or mixed results, and a few have even found greater efficiency in public enterprises.

VIGNETTE 13.3 Neither Rain Nor Sleet Nor Competitors . . .

With over 800,000 employees, the U.S. Postal Service (USPS) is the nation's largest employer and best-protected monopoly: Technically, even dropping a valentine into your neighbor's mailbox is a violation of USPS's legal monopoly on the delivery of first-class mail. This privileged status dates back to Revolutionary War days, when the Continental Congress kept competitors out of the postal business in order to generate much-needed revenues for the war effort. Recently, of course, the USPS has been no cash cow. During the 1980s, federal operating subsidies averaging nearly $1 billion a year were necessary to keep it afloat.

Why maintain this government monopoly in the face of such losses? The most common rationale is that postal service is an unsustainable natural monopoly. The idea is that industry costs are lowest when first-class mail delivery is handled by a single firm. If rivals were allowed to enter this market, they would merely "skim the cream," serving only low-cost customers and leaving high-cost ones to USPS, keeping USPS from exploiting scale economies and thus wasting resources.

This is a respectable argument (although several econometric studies, including one commissioned by USPS itself, have found no evidence of significant scale economies in postal operations[21]). But note: Even if it is desirable to have but a single firm in this market, it does not follow that this firm must be government-owned and-operated. The question thus arises: Could *privatizing* postal service make the mail go through faster and/or more cheaply?

There is ample evidence suggesting it might.[22] In markets where USPS does compete with private firms, it seems woefully inefficient by comparison. United Parcel Service, e.g., charges lower rates, makes faster deliveries, and has a dam-

[20]For an overview of the empirical literature, see Anthony E. Boardman and Aidan R. Vining, "Ownership and Performance in Competitive Environments: A Comparison of the Performance of Private, Mixed, and State-Owned Enterprises," *Journal of Law and Economics*, 32 (April 1989), pp. 1–33.

[21]See, e.g., Satinder N. Gupta and Jatinder N. D. Gupta, "Economies of Scale and Economies of Scope in the U.S. Postal Service," *Engineering Costs and Production Economics*, 8 (July 1985), pp. 269–280.

[22]See, e.g., Peter Ferrara (ed.), *Free the Mail: Ending the Postal Monopoly*, Cato Institute, Washington, 1990, from which much of the following information is drawn.

age rate one-fifth that of USPS. And on certain rural routes, USPS contracts out delivery service to private carriers, saving up to 60 percent of the cost of serving these routes itself.

USPS is saddled with extraordinarily high labor costs. It has been slow to automate many of its functions and pays its employees about one-third more than workers in comparable jobs elsewhere.[23] In the words of one former postal commissioner, USPS workers are "the highest paid semiskilled workers in the world." It does not appear these premium wages are tied to superior performance. One internal audit found that the average letter carrier wastes 1.5 hours each day, which costs USPS about $650 million annually. Another audit found that USPS damages half the packages marked fragile that it carries. Yet another found properly addressed mail dumped in the trash at 76 percent of post offices sampled. A survey by U.S. Congressman Bill Green found that 32 percent of the mail delivered in his Manhattan district was delivered late by USPS's own (rather modest) standards.

In sum, USPS appears to be a graphic illustration of the kinds of incentive and monitoring problems that arise in public enterprises. Absent the lure of profits or the threat of bankruptcy, USPS managers are slow to innovate, overgenerous with employees, and tolerant of inefficiency. But we should not expect reform any time soon. USPS managers, unionized workers, and certain classes of mailers who benefit from special postal subsidies make up potent interest groups with a joint interest in maintaining the status quo. Although they may be outnumbered by those grumbling about high costs and poor service, they are far more likely to be influential in the political marketplace.

Franchise Bidding

There is yet another approach to the natural-monopoly problem which avoids both formal regulation and public ownership: a system of competitive bidding for privately owned utility franchises. The key here is to recognize that markets served most cheaply by a single firm need not be afflicted by monopolistic conduct as long as there is *meaningful competition for the rights to the monopoly franchise*. If competition *within* a market is impossible, it may still be feasible to have competition *for* the market by auctioning off the rights to a monopoly franchise.

How would such an auction work? We are accustomed to auctions in which bidders offer a seller some price for a good or service, with the highest bid winning. But if a monopoly franchise were awarded in this way, competitive bidding would simply drive the franchise price up to an amount equal to the present value of expected future monopoly profits in the relevant market. Monopoly pricing—and the associated loss of social surplus—would surely ensue, and that is the very thing we want to avoid. Thus, bidding for the franchise must take a different form: *The rights to the monopoly franchise should go to whichever bidder promises the best price (or, for nonstandardized goods, the best combination of price and quality) to consumers.* The winner of this auction, then,

[23]Douglas K. Adie, *An Evaluation of Postal Service Wage Rates,* American Enterprise Institute for Public Policy Research, Washington, 1977.

would be the *low* bidder. Competition would drive bid prices down to the lowest possible levels for each possible level of product quality. As long as the auction is open and noncollusive and as long as inputs to the relevant production process are available in open markets as well, there will be no need to fear monopolistic results even though a single firm would indeed be granted rights as an exclusive seller. Further, once the franchise is awarded, the winning firm will have every incentive to control costs, invest efficiently, and adopt innovations optimally, since it will get to keep all resulting cost savings.

The real world has a way of confounding schemes that sound good in theory, however, and scholars such as Richard Schmalensee have expressed reservations about the feasibility of franchise bidding.[24] One set of problems relates to the bidding process itself. Selecting a winner (i.e., determining an optimal price structure and mix of products) may be a complex process, requiring the franchise-granting authority to have the same kind of expertise one hopes to find in a regulatory commission. In addition, there is no guarantee that the bidding will be truly competitive. In particular, many new firms may be reluctant to bid on a franchise that has expired when the previous franchisee is also in the bidding, since the previous winner is almost certain to be better informed about actual cost and demand conditions than are the potential bidders.

Another set of problems relates to the likely behavior of the winning bidder under the franchise contract (which, given the uncertainty about the future, will be of finite duration). If the contract is for a relatively long term, there must be some formula to allow for rate changes as costs, demands, and technologies change over time—or renegotiation must be allowed. If a formula approach is infeasible and renegotiation allowed, the need for some sort of agency similar to a regulatory commission—again—becomes apparent. Some sort of agency may also be needed to police the franchise contract, unless this is simply left to the courts. Finally, short-term contracts may involve *maintenance externalities*. That is, as the end of a contract term approaches, the franchise may stint on maintenance and underinvest in new assets, leaving the next operator to cope with any resulting problems.

These are important problems, but they may not be intractable ones. The degree of technological complexity and the swiftness of change in the relevant industry are crucial variables. If it is possible to specify a limited number of service standards, the bidding process will be of manageable dimensions. If technological change is not too rapid, it may be possible to agree on a formula for periodic rate increases, and the problems associated with midcontract renegotiation may never arise. Enforcing such a contract—seeing that the franchisee is charging promised prices and providing adequate service—will be much simpler than performing all the tasks involved with direct rate regulation. Finally, if the fixed assets of the operation may feasibly be inspected and

[24]Richard Schmalensee, *The Control of Natural Monopolies*, Lexington Books, Lexington, MA, 1979, pp. 68–73.

evaluated when a contract expires, the maintenance externality problem may be solved by having the franchisee post a bond that would be forfeited if problems with the fixed equipment were detected (just as tenants pay a security deposit when renting an apartment).

VIGNETTE 13.4   Franchise Bidding and Waterworks

It appears that practitioners detected advantages in franchise bidding well before theoreticians did. The French have used the system for local water supply for more than two centuries. The first franchise contract for water distribution dates to 1782, when the Perier brothers were given exclusive distribution rights in Paris for a period of 15 years. The Perier firm was later nationalized, however, and by 1854 the real price of water in Paris had quintupled. In other population centers, private water franchises were common from the 1850s onward, although many municipalities opted to build and manage their own systems. Since 1950, however, most municipalities (including Paris) have turned to private companies to manage their systems. Today, about 70 percent of France's drinking water is supplied by private companies.

The water supply industry is well suited to the franchise-bidding approach. The technology of water supply is well known and relatively static, and specification about service standards and quality are readily formulateable. Some French cities and towns therefore grant private firms exclusive rights (called *concessions*) to both build and operate the local water system. The concessionaire advances all capital for construction, assumes full responsibility for management and maintenance of facilities, and collects payments from users. The concession is usually granted for a lengthy period—commonly 30 years—to enable amortization of the original capital outlay. Often the concession contract sets the price of water sold with a formula including a fixed and variable component (i.e., a two-part tariff) in which users pay a fixed monthly fee for access to a supply pipe of a certain diameter plus a variable charge based on the number of cubic meters consumed. In other cities, the expenses for the initial installation of facilities are borne by the local government, while a private firm then manages the facilities and provides working capital. The management contract commonly includes detailed specifications requiring maintenance and upgrading of facilities. Although no detailed studies exist to compare the costs of private and public water systems in France, the trend toward increased privatization (in a country not noted for its fondness for the private sector) suggests an efficiency advantage for the private systems. Indeed, private French water suppliers are widely viewed by professionals in the industry as being at the leading edge in waterworks management and technology, and French concessions have branched out and set up systems in cities in Italy, Peru, Morocco, Indonesia, Kuwait, and a dozen or more African nations.

Deregulation

Successive Presidents since Gerald Ford have had regulatory reform somewhere on their economic agendas, usually quite high. By the mid-1970s, some regulatory efforts had become unpopular, and thus there was at least some political hay to be made by advocating reform. But both popular opinion and the reform process got their initial impetus from scholarly work dating to the late 1950s and 1960s that was highly critical of the nature and performance of much economic regulation.

Some researchers took aim at the theory of regulation itself. Others evaluated the performance of specific industries and/or the agencies that regulated them. The empirical work accumulated steadily through the late 1960s and 1970s. It sounded a remarkably consistent theme. By 1981, two eminent economists could, after surveying this literature, conclude:

> In an era when economists are often accused of being unable to agree on anything, we find comfort in the virtually unanimous professional conclusion that price and entry regulation in several multifirm markets is inefficient and ought to be eliminated.[25]

Such findings undermined the presumption that regulation existed only to serve the public interest. Whatever its goals, it seemed clear that much federal regulation diminished rather than enhanced social welfare. Specifically, scholarly studies of various regulatory industries showed that (1) economic regulation existed in several industries where none of the normal public-interest rationales truly applied, (2) regulation often was responsible for both allocative and productive inefficiency, and (3) much economic regulation appeared to be inspired by rent-seeking or redistributive motives. In several industries, outright deregulation—substitution of competitive market forces for government oversight—was recommended. In others, major modification of existing regulatory institutions was suggested.

If informed scholarship inspired the regulatory reform movement that swept Washington in the late 1970s and 1980s, many other sources of energy were needed to sustain it. Several high-profile events dramatized the need for reform (e.g., the 1970 failure of Penn Central, the nation's biggest railroad, shed discredit on the regulatory practices of the ICC). The popular press gave ample play to horror stories of regulatory excess. Consumer advocacy groups seized on evidence of capture of regulators by business groups. Hearings chaired by Senator Edward Kennedy in 1975 won wide press coverage, focusing public attention on the anticonsumer effects of much rate regulation and the less-than-stellar performance of several federal agencies. Several academic economists moved into positions where they could greatly affect the course of federal regulation—or end it entirely.

Major changes began in 1975. The Securities and Exchange Commission ended fixed brokerage fees for stock market transactions, and the ICC modified rate setting for both trucking and railroad firms. In 1977, the Civil Aeronautics Board instituted several changes that ultimately led to airline rate deregulation. In 1980 and 1981, the Federal Communications Commission deregulated cable TV and partially deregulated the radio industry, and the ICC further loosened its grip on rail and truck rates. Although the pace of

---

[25]Paul L. Joskow and Roger G. Noll, "Regulation in Theory and Practice: An Overview," in Gary Fromm (ed.), *Studies in Public Regulation,* M.I.T. Press, Cambridge, MA, 1981, p. 8.

deregulation slowed afterward, continued reform and modification of federal regulatory institutions remain a prominent feature of economic life in the United States. In Chapters 14 and 15 we examine the effects of this regulatory tinkering on several major industries.

SUMMARY AND CONCLUDING REMARKS

Regulating prices in a natural-monopoly setting is not a simple matter. Marginal-cost pricing is allocatively efficient but poses the possibility that regulated firms may earn subnormal profits and so wither and die. Yet average-cost pricing may not maximize social surplus. In the single-product case, various price discrimination schemes (e.g., two-part tariffs) may be used to bring prices close to marginal costs yet enable the regulated firm to cover its full costs. The surplus loss from average-cost pricing can be minimized if value-of-service pricing is used; under this approach, prices vary according to the elasticity of demand, with price set closest to marginal cost when demand is elastic and farthest from marginal cost when demand is inelastic.

Pricing regulation will affect firms' decisions about investing in productive capacity, and vice versa. When demand does not vary systematically by time of day (or week or month), optimal capacity can be determined by finding the intersection of the product demand and long-run marginal cost (LMC) curves. If demand shifts, price should rise (or fall) to equate quantity demanded to existing capacity until the optimal capacity can be adjusted. When demand does vary by time of day, optimal capacity can be determined by deriving an effective demand-for-capacity curve from the separate demand curves that pertain in peak and off-peak periods and finding this curve's intersection with the LMC curve. Prices in each subperiod can be set by finding the intersection of the relevant subperiod demand curve and the short-run marginal cost curve.

Attempts to duplicate the results of competitive markets via rate-of-return regulation involve myriad practical difficulties and can produce many perverse incentives in subject firms. Determining the appropriate cost of capital and the subject firm's rate base is a complicated and contentious matter, and error in either estimate can result in major distortions in resource allocation. More important, a cost-plus approach to rate setting can induce firms to waste (or pay too much for) factors of production, to overinvest in fixed capital, and perhaps to be slow to innovate. Several schemes to improve incentives under regulation have been devised. The most promising attempt to sever the tie between firms' allowed revenues and their costs so that managers will be more interested in reducing costs and innovating optimally.

There are three basic alternatives to economic regulation. Proponents of publicly owned enterprises argue that such firms can be effective substitutes for private firms and can eliminate a costly extra layer of bureaucratic control of such firms. Empirical evidence suggests, however, that public firms are burdened by significant managerial incentive problems. Franchise bidding seeks to streamline economic regulation by auctioning off monopoly rights (in markets where this is appropriate) to firms that promise consumers the best combination of price and quality. This approach will involve some practical difficulties where costs or technology are changing rapidly, however. Finally, frustration with the poor performance of regulatory agencies and their subject firms has led many to suggest abandoning regulation entirely in some areas, leaving market forces to guide decisions.

QUESTIONS FOR REVIEW AND DISCUSSION

13.1   Return to Figure 13.1. Here there is a pricing dilemma because the market demand curve D intersects the long-run average total cost curve LATC while the latter is downward-sloping. Describe this dilemma. Will such a dilemma exist if D shifts rightward, so that it intersects LATC while the latter is upward-sloping? Explain. What other (or additional) problems will arise in this circumstance?

13.2   Humongous State University has 20,000 commuter students and only 10,000 parking spaces. Each year, some students occupy the provost's office and demand that a new garage be built so that the parking "crisis" will be alleviated. The provost hires your consulting firm to resolve the issue. You estimate that total student demand for parking (in spaces per year) is described by the equation

$$Q_d = 16{,}000 - 40P$$

where P is expressed in terms of the rental price per year. The (amortized) social cost of creating additional parking capacity is $100 per space per year, *assuming* a garage holding 5,000 spaces (or some multiple of 5,000 spaces) is built. Otherwise, the per-space cost is far higher. What do you advise? Should HSU build one garage? Two? In answering, assume the goal here is to maximize social surplus, not merely to get the angry students out of the provost's office.

13.3   The demand for commuter rail service between Suburban Acres and downtown Megalopolis varies considerably over the day. Off-peak demand is given by the (inverse) demand function

$$P_o = 20 - 0.6Q$$

peak demand is given by

$$P_p = 40 - 0.2Q$$

where Q is in trains per day and P is price per trip. Each demand curve applies over half the day. Short-run marginal cost is constant and equal to 0; long-run marginal cost is constant and equal to 18. Using geometry and algebra, calculate the optimal level of rail capacity in Megalopolis and the optimal peak and off-peak subway fares.

13.4a   Suppose you have just been promoted to a managerial position in a government agency or a government-owned firm. You discover that the previous manager has hired several redundant staff in your department and that these people can be fired without adversely affecting efficiency. What factors will affect whether you fire these workers? How will your department's budget likely be affected if you do fire them?

b Now suppose you face the same situation in a privately owned but regulated firm. Are your incentives any different? Specifically, how will the nature of regulation affect your incentive to fire the redundant workers? Discuss how the various incentive-compatible regulation schemes discussed in the text might affect your decision to fire the workers.

13.5 Suppose you own a large company that develops residential and commercial real estate. Your current project involves building an entire planned community, called Newtown, which will place hundreds of residences, retail establishments, and employment centers on currently barren land. Obviously, Newtown will require electric power, natural gas, sewer and water service, telephone service, and perhaps cable TV. What are your alternatives in securing such goods for Newtown? What are the advantages and disadvantages of each? If you don't protect the residents of Newtown from monopolistic overcharging by providers of these goods, what are the consequences for your wealth?

CHAPTER 14

ECONOMIC REGULATION AND NATURAL MONOPOLY: THE ELECTRICITY, NATURAL GAS, AND TELECOMMUNICATIONS INDUSTRIES

I never knew a pollytician to go wrong ontil he's been contaminated by contact with a businessman.

Finley Peter Dunne

It is impossible to appreciate what economic regulation can and cannot do without seeing how it has actually been applied in a selection of key industries. That is what will occupy us next. In this chapter, we examine three industries in which natural-monopoly considerations have played a key role in defining the scope and nature of regulation, although, as we shall see, other factors have also influenced regulators' actions. In turn, we look at electric utilities, natural gas production and distribution, and telephony. Our discussion in each case begins with a look at the nature of the industry itself and a description of the historical development of regulation. We then proceed to an assessment of how regulation has worked (or not worked) and some discussion of contemporary issues. In Chapter 15 we will look at a sample of industries where characteristics of natural monopoly, although possibly present, simply do not adequately explain why economic regulation has occurred or the form it has taken.

ELECTRIC UTILITIES

The theory of natural monopoly is the oldest and most widely accepted public-interest rationale for economic regulation, and the market for electricity seems to be one to which it clearly applies. In this section, we acquire some basic knowledge of the workings of this market, examine the practical application of regulatory theory, and discuss some proposals for regulatory reform.

Overview

The electric power industry began in the late 1870s, with numerous private producers selling power for street lighting and electric railways. Service areas were small for technological reasons; with electricity supplied at first as direct current, efficiency losses were enormous if power was transmitted very far. Technological advance (e.g., development of the alternating-current system by George Westinghouse in 1886) soon made transmission over long distances feasible, however, making the use of large, centralized generators possible.

As the industry evolved, its three stages of production (power generation, transmission of power to distribution centers, and subsequent delivery of power to final consumers) tended to be integrated in a single firm. Scale economies were quickly apparent in at least the first two stages of the production process. As engineers built and designed ever-larger generators, the cost per unit of electric power (generally, dollars per kilowatthour[1]) fell appreciably. Scale economies in transmission result from the fact that as the voltage of a line increases, larger quantities of usable energy can be transmitted over longer distances with a smaller loss of energy.

Production and financing scale economies led to a merger movement in the industry throughout the 1910s and 1920s. By 1932, 16 large holding companies (i.e., companies holding sufficient stock in other companies to affect their management) accounted for more than three-quarters of the electricity generated in the United States. Such concentration, financial scandals that surrounded several consolidations, and the use of holding companies to defeat state regulation led to demands for more stringent regulation of electric utilities. Although most states had commissions for this purpose by 1930, the holding companies usually crossed state boundaries and thus were not entirely within the jurisdiction of the state commissions, who could determine the retail rates at which interstate companies sold to local consumers but not the wholesale rates these firms charged out-of-state customers. This provided a golden opportunity for abuse under the cost-plus regulatory schemes employed within states. Suppose, e.g., utilities X and Y, in neighboring states, were owned by a single holding company. Within each state, commissions would try to keep retail rates equal to costs (including a normal return to capital). But if X sold power across state lines to Y, the price of X could not be legally regulated by either state. If X charged a monopoly price to Y, then Y would have little reason to object, since regulators in Y's state would likely allow it to recover its

---

[1]A watt is a measure of the energy drawn by an appliance or piece of equipment. One kilowatt is 1,000 watts. The flow of energy from a generator to a piece of equipment over time is measured in kilowatthours. For example, a 75-watt light bulb left on for 1 hour will use 0.075 kilowatthour. Generator capacity is often measured in megawatts; 1 megawatt is 1 million watts.

costs (and, in any case, X and Y were ultimately controlled by the same owners). The net result is that the holding company could earn high profits on this transaction by circumventing state regulation.

Congress responded in 1935 by passing the Public Utility Holding Company Act and the Federal Power Act. The former extended the authority of the Securities and Exchange Commission (SEC) to many of the financial affairs of public utilities and forced a major reorganization of the industry by providing that holding companies more than twice removed from their operating subsidiaries were to be abolished. Starting in 1938, SEC-ordered divestitures created various "integrated systems" that were generally nondiversified and confined to a single area (usually, a single state). The Federal Power Act gave the Federal Power Commission, which had been created in 1920, the power to regulate rates on interstate transmission of power. Together, the acts removed most obstacles to regulation of electric rates and service by state and federal commissions. In 1977, the Federal Power Commission was abolished and its functions transferred to the newly created Federal Energy Regulatory Commission (FERC), which has broad authority to regulate electricity and natural gas prices, oil pipeline fees, and mergers in energy industries.

Today, there are upward of 3,500 electric systems in the United States, although the largest 200 hold almost 90 percent of industry generating capacity. Almost 80 percent of industry capacity is in privately owned firms. Ten percent originates in federal agencies, and the remainder originates in state- or city-owned systems and cooperatives. The great majority of the smaller systems today generate no power of their own, instead purchasing it wholesale from other utilities. In recent years, the industry has become increasingly coordinated. After the great northeast blackout of November 1965, the industry established nine *regional reliability councils* to coordinate bulk power supply and prevent further large-scale blackouts. Intersystem connections and *power pools* have developed, and continue to be developed, throughout the country. There are now three large networks of interconnected systems; one covers 39 states and two Canadian provinces. Pools can vary in terms of their formality. In some, groups of utilities simply commit themselves to common principles for interconnected operation. In others, requirements are more formalized, and there may be joint ownership of generating plants.

The post-World War II era saw considerable technological progress and low fuel prices, resulting in falling rates and rapid industry expansion. For regulators, this was a tranquil period largely free of controversy. But when oil prices rose significantly in the 1970s, electricity rate regulation became a contentious matter. Rate hearings attracted considerable publicity, and the extent to which public utility commissioners appeared to favor business interests or consumer interests was the subject of considerable debate—especially in the dozen states where such commissioners are elected rather than appointed by governors. In general, utilities' requests for rate hikes drew much closer scrutiny during this period, and interest in new approaches to rate setting grew.

The energy crisis also made it economically feasible to tap a variety of alternative energy sources such as the wind and sun. One new source of power was *cogeneration*, i.e., simultaneous production of electricity and heat from the same primary energy source. For example, an industrial plant might produce surplus heat in the course of its normal operations. Rather than let this heat go up the chimney, the firm might try to recapture it and use it to generate electricity. But there must be a buyer for this power, and the only logical candidate is the local electric utility, which might exercise its monopsony power to dictate unfavorable terms. With this issue in mind, Congress passed the Public Utilities Regulatory Policies Act (PURPA) in 1978, requiring that utilities buy power from independent suppliers at a price equal to the utilities' savings from reduced generation costs. FERC provides guidelines for determining what these costs are, and the actual prices can be regulated by the state utility commissions.

Current Rate Regulation

State commissions' regulation of electric rates usually takes the classic form: Regulators determine a utility's revenue requirement as the sum of its operating costs (including an allowance for depreciation and taxes) and a fair return on its assets, and then they set the level and structure of electricity prices to satisfy this requirement. There are several alternative rate structures.

Electricity usage meters had not been invented when firms first began selling power to retail customers, so most charged a fixed price regardless of the quantity purchased—obviously an inefficient pricing scheme. With metering came, first, *flat rates* (per kilowatthour) which remained the same no matter how many or few units were consumed. Eventually, however, most utilities began to charge residential customers *declining block rates.* In this system, rates are constant within specified blocks of units; e.g., price may be set at $0.08 per kilowatthour for the first 500 kilowatthours used per month, $0.04 for the next 500 kilowatthours, and so on, with the unit price falling until a final, open-ended block is specified. Often, declining block rates are accompanied by fixed monthly *customer charges* unrelated to usage. Whether accompanied by such fixed charges or not, however, declining block rates can approximate the kind of price discrimination (recall Chapters 9 and 13) that will enable both marginal cost pricing and normal returns to the subject firm. In practice, however, neither regulators nor the firm is likely to have the kind of information needed to ensure that output will be precisely at the allocatively efficient level.

Declining block rates may be justified by either cost-of-service or value-of-service considerations. Charging lower prices as usage increases appears to make sense if scale economies are present. In addition, most customers presumably use power to satisfy their most inelastic (and therefore high-priced) demands first and their more elastic (low-priced) demands afterward. But some important criticisms of such rates have recently been made. First, scale economies appear to be less important in the industry today than they once were. In most locales, market demand has grown sufficiently that an efficient generating plant is small relative to total market output. And although generating costs decline as plant size rises, maintenance costs and unreliability problems increase, limiting exploitation of new scale economies in power plant construction. Further, it is argued that in an era of increased energy scarcity and environmental sensitivity, we should not encourage large-quantity energy consumption. Finally, placing the highest rates on those who use the smallest quantities of electricity—usually, the poor, who own few appliances—is decried on equity grounds.

Perhaps in response, there is increasing use of *inverted rates* and *lifeline rates.* In an inverted rate scheme, the price per kilowatthour rises rather than declines over successive blocks, so that increased consumption is punished with higher prices. In lifeline schemes, prices not only rise over successive blocks, but also begin at a level below the supplier's per-unit costs. In principle, this helps the poor pay for a "subsistence" quantity of electricity. Since the costs of this program must be made up elsewhere, it will redistribute income among consumers. But it is anyone's guess whether this redistribution will really enhance vertical equity. Not all users of small amounts of electricity are poor. In some cases, high-income individuals who divide time between residences may benefit from such rates. And many poor will never benefit from such a program. Most of the poor are renters. In many apartment buildings, electricity usage in individual units is not metered. Instead, a single meter measures use in the entire building, and landlords recover electricity costs in monthly rent payments. Buildingwide, the lifeline rates will be of little import.

For commercial and industrial customers, declining block rates are supplemented with *demand charges* or *kilowatt charges.* From time to time, industrial users will have huge power requirements. Arranging to have sufficient capacity to meet such demands will involve costs. Thus, utilities will monitor such users' maximum demand for power and levy extra charges based on users' instantaneous rate of consumption at a particular time.

As an extreme example, suppose you have one appliance that requires 10 kilowatts that you operate 100 hours per month, for a total monthly consumption of 1,000 kilowatthours. However, I have a machine that requires 100 kilowatts, but I operate it only 10 hours per month. My monthly consumption of 1,000 kilowatthours matches yours, but it will be very costly to install sufficient capacity to supply the larger load I require. Demand charges, which also might follow declining block rate patterns, are rationalized as attempts to help recover such costs. They may or may not do so in practice, however, since they do not take account of the time of day I switch on my machine. Extend the example above. Suppose now there are 10 people in this market with demands for power like yours, and me. To serve the 10 people like you, the local utility needs to be able to produce 100 kilowatts at any one time, since you all might be operating your appliances at once. If I turn on my machine as well, the utility needs to double its capacity to 200 kilowatts, which will obviously be expensive. But suppose I only turn on my machine at 3 a.m., when you and all the rest of the customers are asleep. The utility could get by with a capacity of only 100 kilowatts, and my demand for large gulps of power need not impose significantly higher costs on the utility. Thus, whether demand charges are efficient will depend on whether individuals' demand peaks are correlated with the system's peak.

Such considerations have increased interest in peak-load pricing schemes, or *time-of-use (TOU) rates*. In the mid-1970s, the Department of Energy sponsored several experimental applications of TOU electricity pricing. In general, these experiments confirm that (1) TOU rates reduce electricity consumption during peak periods, (2) high-use customers are more sensitive to TOU rates than low-use customers, (3) responsiveness is greater as the ratio of peak to off-peak prices increases, and (4) demand shifts from peak to off-peak periods are greater as the peak period is defined more narrowly.

VIGNETTE 14.1   Peak-Load Pricing and Consumer Behavior

Sometimes noneconomists are surprised by the power of basic economic principles. When energy prices rose during the 1970s, it was literally front-page news that consumers responded with energy-conserving changes in behavior (e.g., investments in home insulation). Many observers evidently felt that ingrained consumption habits were too hard to break or that consumers paid little attention to prices in making their buying decisions.

Similar skepticism often greets economists' suggestions that resources can be saved by adopting peak-hour pricing schemes to level out demand for certain goods. Price signals are especially weak in the electricity market, the skeptics argue: People turn appliances on or off when they "need" them and do not think about the cost per kilowatthour at such times.

Recent experiments with peak-hour pricing of electricity, however, put the lie to such assertions. One experiment in Wisconsin, evaluated by Douglas Caves and Laurits Christensen, was conducted particularly carefully.[2] About 700 participants were chosen by stratified random sampling; participation was mandatory (i.e., there were no special incentive payments that might bias results). Some participants were confronted with peak to off-peak price ratios of 2:1, while this ratio was set at 4:1 or 8:1 for others. The length of peak periods varied from 6 to 12 hours. In all cases, rates were structured so that a participant's bill would not rise or fall if electricity usage did not change. Thus, participants who ignored the new price structure would not notice a change in their utility bills if they continued their prior consumption habits; there were no penalties for failing to shift demand to off-peak periods.

Nevertheless, considerable shifting did occur. Caves and Christensen calculated that, where the ratio of peak to off-peak prices was 2:1, consumers reduced electricity usage during peak summer months by an average of 11 to 13 percent (depending on the length of the peak period). Higher ratios of peak to off-peak prices yielded greater reductions in consumption during peak periods: An 8:1 ratio yielded reductions of 15 to 20 percent for summer months.

Some critics argue that even if peak-load pricing shifts consumptions on most

---

[2]For an accessible summary of results, see Douglas W. Caves and Laurits R. Christensen, "Time-of-use Rates for Residential Electric Service: Results from the Wisconsin Experiment," *Public Utilities Fortnightly*, 111 (March 17, 1983), pp. 30–35.

days, it will not shift consumption on certain "critical days," e.g., during lengthy summer heat waves, when air conditioners are used most extensively. But Caves and Christensen found that the experimental results refuted this conjecture. For summer months, there was actually greater shifting on critical days (up to 31 percent reduction in consumption when the price ratio was 8:1) than on nonpeak days.

Some environmental groups have opposed peak-load pricing of electricity on the grounds that it might lead to increases in the total consumption of electric power and, thus, added degradation of the environment. But consumers actually consumed *less* total electricity in this experiment. Although usage in off-peak periods did rise, this was more than offset by usage reduction in peak periods.

In sum, the Wisconsin experiment shows that consumers do respond to price signals in the sophisticated ways that economic theory predicts, and it suggests that peak-load pricing has great potential to alter the intertemporal pattern of demand.

Wide application of TOU rates clearly can save some resources by enabling a utility to avoid investing in excessive peak-period capacity, but will also involve some added metering and administrative costs. Doubts about the cost-effectiveness of time-of-*day* price schemes have slowed their adoption in the United States, but seasonal differentials (e.g., higher rates for summer to smooth peak demands) are now used in almost all states.

Effects of Regulation

Economists have been studying electric utility regulation for a long time, during which they have written countless books and articles that outline how regulation should work or criticize the way it does work. Most of these writings were ignored by policymakers until the 1970s, when the energy crisis seemed to increase interest in finding ways to mollify consumers by controlling electricity prices more effectively while at the same time ensuring that utilities would be able to attract sufficient investment to satisfy future demands for power.

Economists' complaints about electricity rate regulation have generally taken two forms: (1) The overall *level* of regulated rates is incorrect, because regulatory authorities are captured by firms, because cost-plus rate setting induces such waste that some of (or all) the gains from regulation are offset, or because regulators are captured by consumers, and (2) the *structure* of rates is inefficient (i.e., widespread use of average-cost pricing is unwarranted and should be abandoned in favor of marginal cost pricing).

Rate Level We discussed some of the empirical work related to the first criticism in Chapter 12 and need not rehash it here. Two more recent studies merit mention, however. Using similar methods, they assess whether regulation has favorably affected electricity prices. They measure the demand for electricity and the marginal cost of providing it, calculate the prices that unregulated monopolies might charge, and compare these to actual prices. Thomas Gale Moore applied this method to 1962 data for 69 regulated utilities, 62 private and 7 municipal. He concluded that regulation did not exert much of a favorable effect on prices: "We can safely say that it appears that regulation has not reduced prices more than 5 percent and probably less than that."[3] Robert Meyer and Hayne Leland applied a similar approach to a richer pool of data (for 1969 and 1974) so that they could take account of differences in demand and regulatory impact across states. They found larger favorable price effects—at least in some states—than Moore had, but they concluded that states vary greatly with respect to the effectiveness of regulation, that there was some cross-subsidization evident (at least in 1969), with business customers favored at the expense of residential users, and that actual prices charged did not appear to be welfare-maximizing.[4]

We should note, however, that even if regulation keeps prices below monopoly levels, it may be that welfare gains from lower prices are more than offset by higher production costs which result from the perverse incentives inherent in cost-plus rate regulation (refer once again to Figure 12.7 and the accompanying text). Unfortunately, estimating the current extent of any productive inefficiency due to regulation is problematic because today virtually all private utilities in the United States are regulated. Thus, interfirm comparisons are impossible; international comparisons are probably meaningless because underlying conditions vary so much from country to country. It is generally agreed that there are some short- and long-run production inefficiencies in the industry, however. Thus, while regulation does—under normal circumstances—keep electric prices below monopolistic levels, any net gains are probably smaller than they could be.

The Moore and Meyer-Leland studies both pertain to a period when utilities' input prices were relatively stable. Once fuel prices and capital costs started to rise sharply in the inflationary mid-1970s, however, regulators were slow to grant rate increases, effectively pushing real rates *below* optimal levels. This *rate suppression* depressed utilities' net earnings below the opportunity cost of capital, giving rise, some argue, to a reverse A-J effect.[5] Starved for capital, many utilities failed to expand capacity at optimal rates, stinted on maintenance, or made other decisions that reduced their operating efficiency.[6] What is more, artificially low rates encouraged overconsumption of power and led many consumers to postpone desirable energy-conserving investments.

Eventually, as fuel prices eased in the 1980s, this problem was mitigated. But it seems clear that the regulatory apparatus has a very tough time adjusting its sights to hit a moving target: When costs rise, rates lag behind and margins are squeezed; but when costs fall, lagging rate reductions allow margins

[3]Thomas Gale Moore, "The Effectiveness of Regulation of Electric Utility Prices," *Southern Economic Journal,* 36 (April 1970), p. 374.

[4]Robert A. Meyer and Hayne E. Leland, "The Effectiveness of Price Regulation," *Review of Economics and Statistics,* 62 (November 1980), pp. 555–566.

[5]See Peter Navarro, *The Dimming of America,* Ballinger, Cambridge, MA, 1985.

[6]Marie R. Corio, "Why Is the Performance of Electric Generating Units Declining?" *Public Utilities Fortnightly,* April 29, 1982, pp. 3–8.

to recover. In sum, then, often regulators will have chosen the wrong rate level. Whether they are erring on the upside or downside will depend on economic circumstances and perhaps political considerations.[7]

Rate Structure Economists have had relatively good luck convincing regulators of the wisdom of marginal cost pricing. In France, where the electricity industry is government-owned, the utility's staff economists (led by Marcel Boiteaux, author of several important theoretical papers on peak-load pricing) implemented a marginal cost pricing system for industrial customers as early as 1956. Great Britain adopted marginal cost pricing for industrial customers in the late 1950s and applied a form of it to residential customers in the early 1960s.

Marginal cost pricing of electricity did not come to the United States until 1974, when the Wisconsin Public Service Commission—the first state public utility commission and long acknowledged as a consistent innovator—applied it to that state's utilities.[8] The commission specified that rate levels should differ in summer and winter, declining block rates should be eliminated in summer, and rates throughout the state should be based on marginal costs. In later decisions, the commission ordered utilities to base demand charges to industrial users on maximum power used during the *utilities' peak periods* (generally, daytime in hot summer months) rather than the users' peaks. Such charges were easy to implement because most industrial customers already had meters recording their power usage by time of day. And since the estimates of marginal cost used to formulate new price schedules were forward-looking, based on current or future plant costs, conversion to marginal cost pricing generally proceeded without imposing financial losses on the utilities. The results: Wisconsin utilities steadily reduced the amount of excess capacity they were forced to maintain, and growth in peak demand fell throughout the 1970s.

By the late 1970s, many other state commissions had moved toward marginal cost pricing, with almost all adopting seasonal peak-load pricing and many encouraging elimination of declining block rates and employing some variation of TOU rates for industrial customers. In 1978, in the Public Utility Regulatory Policy Act (mentioned earlier), the federal government joined the trend toward reform, requiring state commissions to hold hearings to consider factors related to marginal cost pricing.

In sum, the theoreticians have made major strides in altering the way electricity rate structures are typically devised. Although no estimates of the

---

[7]Navarro, *The Dimming of America,* pp. 107–109, found that states where public utility commissioners were elected rather than appointed were far more likely to have rate suppression problems.

[8]*Application of Madison Gas and Electric Company for Authority to Increase Electric and Gas Rates,* Wisconsin Public Service Commission (1974). For a detailed discussion, from which much of the following is drawn, see Leonard W. Weiss, "State Regulation of Public Utilities and Marginal-cost Pricing," in Leonard W. Weiss and Michael W. Klass (eds.), *Case Studies in Regulation,* Little, Brown, Boston, 1981, pp. 262–291.

allocative efficiency gains associated with these reforms yet exist, it is quite likely they are substantial. But these reforms may just be the beginning; many of the incentive-compatible regulatory schemes discussed in Chapter 13 have yet to be applied to this industry. What is more, technological advances may make even more radical reorganization of the industry feasible.

Deregulate Electricity?   Some economists feel that full or partial deregulation of the electric power industry is now warranted. As mentioned above, it appears that economies of scale have been exhausted in most major markets. In addition, technological improvements in power transmission have made it possible for producers in different locations to compete in the same markets. Large-capacity lines now carry current so efficiently that utilities in southern California, e.g., can obtain power from hydroelectric sources in Oregon and Washington.

Reform proposals vary considerably. One option is complete deregulation, with all price and entry regulations eliminated at all levels. The deregulated industry would simply be subjected to tough antitrust scrutiny. Other proposals are more structured. For example, it might be feasible to separate power generation from power distribution, eliminate price and entry regulation in power generation, and remove territorial restrictions on sales to distributors. Price competition could then rule at the generation level, and firms would have optimal incentives to control costs, innovate, invest in new generating capacity, etc. The distribution level might then be organized with independent firms subject to traditional price regulation, or franchise bidding used to control retail prices.

These are provocative proposals. They hint that the utility industry, long one of the more staid sectors in the U.S. economy, might be in for some massive and wrenching changes in the years ahead.

VIGNETTE 14.2   Competitive Electric Utilities?

One day in 1968, University of Illinois economist Walter Primeaux was teaching the standard theory of natural monopoly, explaining that competition is neither likely nor desirable in such situations, when a student remarked, "That's not the way it is in Lubbock, Texas."[9]

Intrigued, Professor Primeaux investigated. He found that Lubbock, a city of about 160,000, did indeed have two electric utilities, one city-owned, the other private. Consumers were free to select service from either, with no service charge for making changes. Although there was duplication of facilities throughout Lubbock (e.g., the two firms do not share poles), the city's commercial and industrial rates were the lowest in Texas and residential rates were lower than other cities in the Texas plains. Unsurprisingly, citizens in Lubbock were quite happy with their electricity duopoly, viewing the situation as healthy and preferable to monopoly.

Similar direct competition exists (or has existed) in many other locales, from

[9]This section is drawn from Walter J. Primeaux, Jr., *Direct Electric Utility Competition: The Natural Monopoly Myth*, Praeger, New York, 1986.

small towns like Sikeston, Missouri, to large cities like Portland, Oregon. After carefully studying such situations over many years, Primeaux concluded that consumers benefit substantially from direct electric utility competition. He found evidence that such competition yielded lower rates and better service and was unaccompanied by the kind of destructive rate wars many allege are inevitable in such situations. He argues that any social losses from unexploited scale economies in such markets are more than offset by competitive firms' tighter control over costs and superior management.

These are challenging views. They may not lead to a rush to dismantle utility monopolies, but they should spur interest in ways to improve the efficiency of standard forms of regulation. If current modes can dissipate all the gains from economies of scale in this industry, there is clearly much room for improvement. Professor Primeaux's work also reinforces two other lessons. First, even the most plausible public-interest rationales for regulation must be subjected to careful empirical evaluation; second, students should never be afraid to raise their hands in class.

NATURAL GAS

Natural gas is a crucial part of the U.S. energy supply. Today about as much energy is produced from gas as from petroleum or coal, and since it is such a clean-burning fuel, reliance on natural gas is likely to grow in the future. Our experience in regulating the market for gas at the federal level has not been a happy one. We examine it here to illustrate some of the problems that can arise under economic regulation and the difficulties that may be encountered in altering a well-established regulatory regime.

Overview

In the early part of this century, before pipeline networks were established to deliver natural gas from wellhead to buyer, gas was regarded as a useless by-product of oil production. Quite costly to store, it was often burned ("flared off") at the wellhead or simply released into the atmosphere. The development of seamless pipe, which could withstand the high pressures necessary to transport gas long distances, made pipeline networks feasible and greatly increased the value of natural gas. Drilling and exploration increased, production soared, and gas began moving in volume from fields in the southwest (chiefly Texas, Louisiana, Oklahoma, New Mexico, and Kansas) to markets in the north and east.

It is common to distinguish three levels of the gas industry: exploration and production, pipeline delivery to local utilities or large industrial users, and delivery to retail consumers. At the local utility level, the industry appears to have many of the same characteristics that lead to state regulation of retail rates on electricity. Gas delivery, like electricity delivery, requires large amounts of fixed capital, and it is quite likely that a particular area is most cheaply served by a single distributor, for this avoids the expense of installing parallel gas lines. Accordingly, local gas companies have generally been granted exclusive franchises within specific markets and subjected to rate regulation just as electric power companies have. Municipal and state regulation of gas utilities dates from the 1920s. Most of the same principles and problems discussed earlier regarding electric utility regulation apply here as well; for this reason, little more needs to be said about this level of the market.

Problems upstream—at the production and pipeline delivery levels of the industry—led in the early 1930s to demands for federal regulation of gas distribution. Since they had no legal power to regulate prices paid for gas piped across state lines, state and local officials argued that their regulation of retail prices was bound to be ineffective. Pipelines, the argument went, are naturally monopolistic.[10] Unless the wholesale prices that local utilities paid to the pipeline companies were regulated, consumers would pay monopoly prices for gas despite local regulation. In addition, the kind of financial abuse and concentration of ownership that had afflicted the electric industry in its early days was present here, with several large holding companies coming to dominate gas production and distribution. In 1935, a Federal Trade Commission report revealed that more than half the gas produced in the United States and three-quarters of interstate pipeline mileage were controlled by 11 holding companies.

After considerable debate, in 1938 Congress passed the Natural Gas Policy Act, granting the Federal Power Commission (FPC) considerable authority over the interstate sale of natural gas, including power to set "just and reasonable rates" for its transmission. The FPC set about applying rate-of-return regulation to interstate pipelines, but did *not* try to control the price that producers charged distributors at the wellhead, assuming it had no power to do so. This was a defensible view: The 1938 act stated that it did "not apply . . . to the production or gathering of natural gas."[11] The language of the act, however, was sufficiently vague to support other interpretations. In any case, the FPC soon found itself in the midst of an interregional conflict. Many in the gas-consuming states of the north wanted the FPC to regulate wellhead prices, while those in gas-producing states opposed such regulation.

In 1954, the issue went to the Supreme Court. The state of Wisconsin argued that the Phillips Petroleum Company had monopoly power in gas production that it used to jack up prices to pipeline companies and thus to final consumers. Phillips replied that it had no monopoly power and that, with thousands of independent gas suppliers selling to pipelines, gas production was very competitive. The FPC had decided not to intervene. But stating that Congress had intended in 1938 to extend FPC control to "all wholesales of nat-

---

[10]This argument has at least some merit. There are scale economies related to the diameter of pipe used: The cost of pipe is roughly proportional to its diameter, but its capacity is proportional to the *square* of its diameter. Thus, it will likely be cheapest to have a single pipeline (using the widest available pipe) linking city X with field Y. In large markets, however, there may have been (or may now be) room for more than one line from field to market, given existing limits on the maximum pipe size available. Further, pipelines connect fields and markets in many scattered locales; lines can crisscross, and many areas can therefore be served efficiently by more than one line. In sum, scale economies will not require a single supplier for the entire national market or, for that matter, for some large regional markets.
[11]15 U.S.C. 717 (b) (1964).

ural gas in interstate commerce," the Court ordered the FPC to judge the reasonableness of Phillips' prices and, in effect, regulate all wellhead prices of all natural gas sold interstate.[12]

The decision mystified many. It was far from clear that the Court's assertions about congressional intent were valid. And many (including the FPC) doubted that public utility principles applied to natural gas production. According to several studies, concentration here was lower than in the average manufacturing industry. In 1954, there were over 4,500 independent producers selling gas in interstate markets.[13] One fact was clear, however: Despite the Court's feeling that the FPC should regulate wellhead prices of natural gas, the agency was ill equipped to do so.

Before the *Phillips* decision, the FPC regulated fewer than 100 pipeline companies and acted on about 700 rate filings a year. In the first year after *Phillips*, the FPC received about 11,000 rate filings from producers. In addition, regulating prices at the wellhead was more complex than fixing pipeline rates; gas and oil are often joint products of a particular well, and allocating costs is difficult. Costs vary widely from region to region. Hearings on the reasonableness of the Phillips Petroleum Company's rates took 18 months, and a decision was not rendered until 1959 (when, to the chagrin of Wisconsin officials, the FPC found Phillips' rates reasonable). A huge backlog of cases soon developed. The FPC estimated it would not finish its 1960 case load until the year 2043! The commission threw in the towel. To speed up the process, it announced in 1960 that prices would be set by an *area rate* method. Dividing the United States into 23 geographic areas, the FPC aimed to set uniform prices based on average production costs within each area. The commission used a two-tier price structure in each area: It set one (lower) price ceiling for "old" gas (i.e., gas already in production or gas associated with oil) and a second (higher) ceiling for "new" gas (gas either discovered or first committed to production after January 1, 1961).

Adoption of area rates and the two-tier system was an important watershed. It indicated that federal policy in this market had moved beyond standard utility regulation (aimed at securing the benefits of scale economies while at the same time avoiding monopolistic pricing) and was now animated by *redistributive goals*. The public-interest rationale invoked on behalf of the two-tier system had nothing to do with natural monopoly, but with *rent control*; i.e., it aimed to avoid bestowing "windfalls on the owners of reserves discovered and developed at lower costs in the past."[14] In practice, the area rates promulgated by the FPC were significantly lower than those which had prevailed earlier, redistributing billions of dollars from gas producers, public treasuries in producer states, and producers of rival fuels to large industrial

[12]*Phillips Petroleum Company v. Wisconsin et al.*, 342 U.S. 672 (1954).

[13]See Clark A. Hawkins, "Structure of the Natural Gas Producing Industry," in Keith C. Brown (ed.), *Regulation of the Natural Gas Producing Industry*, Johns Hopkins University Press, Baltimore, MD, 1972.

[14]See Alfred E. Kahn, *The Economics of Regulation: Principles and Institutions*, vol. 1, Wiley, New York, 1970, p. 43.

users, local gas utilities and their customers, and pipelines in gas-importing states.

But even the area rate system proved too complex for the FPC to administer effectively. By 1974, the commission had completed rate hearings in less than half of the areas it had designated. So, in that year, the FPC resorted to *nationwide ratemaking,* fixing a "uniform just and reasonable national base rate" on all interstate sales of natural gas.

The seeds of disaster had been sown. From the early 1960s, the FPC's interstate price ceilings were below the costs of producing gas in many areas. This discouraged efforts to find and exploit new sources of gas, encouraged producers to sell what they did have intrastate, and stimulated consumption. By 1968, annual consumption had started to exceed new additions to reserves. Shortages in many areas began in 1970. By 1971, the FPC began to specify *curtailment procedures*—essentially orders for rationing available gas on a nonprice basis. When the OPEC cartel coalesced and raised oil prices in 1973, causing the demand for substitute fuels such as gas to increase, shortages became more widespread and acute. Curtailments grew. By the winter of 1976–1977, quantity demanded exceeded quantity supplied by about 20 percent. But curtailments were uneven; some areas saw supplies cut 50 percent, while others were relatively unaffected. Since supplies were generally curtailed to industrial users first, many jobs were lost; indeed, some estimate job losses in the hundreds of thousands.

VIGNETTE 14.3   The Dual Market for Natural Gas

Suppose you build a home for $100,000. It's soon clear that, whether by luck or superior foresight, you chose a great neighborhood in which to invest. People from all over want to buy houses there, and the price of houses like yours is bid up to $200,000. Wonderful, you say. But then regulators decide that this is unfair. "Your house cost only $100,000 to build," the regulators say, "and if you sell it for $200,000, you'll reap an unjustified windfall." They put a ceiling price of $100,000 on your house and other houses of similar vintage, "to protect consumers from price gouging." You and many other homeowners respond, quite rationally, by refusing to sell, and soon consumers face an acute shortage of housing in your area.

The situation in the natural gas market in the 1970s resembled this fable—but there was an interesting wrinkle in the gas market. Some gas buyers were outside federal regulators' jurisdiction. Gas that didn't cross state lines wasn't subject to price controls. It was as if, in the example above, you could sell your house for $200,000 to in-state buyers and only $100,000 to out-of-state buyers. You'd have to be a fool to sell to an out-of-state buyer. So once (unregulated) intrastate gas prices moved significantly above (regulated) interstate prices, more and more gas began to stay home in producer states. The results: economic inefficiency and political tension.

In 1973, Louisiana governor Edwin Edwards announced that a large gas field had been discovered in Plaquemines Parish, in southern Louisiana, containing enough gas to fill New Orleans' requirements for 50 years. The problem was that the only pipeline near the field headed north—to New York and Washington. The governor announced, therefore, that the gas field would not be developed until it could be reached by an intrastate pipeline. From the viewpoint of those in producer states, regulators wanted to force them to sell their gas for a fraction of its true market value, and their response was well expressed in bumper stickers reading, "Let the Yankee bastards freeze in the dark."[15]

Such stories convinced many in the consuming states of the north that the gas curtailments they were experiencing were unnecessary and part of a conspiracy to win price decontrol that would see gas prices rise to monopolistic levels. Stories abounded of secret storage tanks where gas was hoarded; cartoons showed rotund, cigar-smoking capitalists shutting off the gas to poor, shivering wretches in northern cities.

In the media, there was an ongoing debate between those who believed the gas crisis was real and those who thought it artificial. The former were convinced that we were about to run out of gas and advocated programs to stimulate conservation and convert to alternative fuels. In one *Newsweek* cover story in 1973, for example, the headline read, "U.S. Fuel Reserves: How Long Will They Last?" The answer, for natural gas, was deemed to be 11 years. Of course, 1984 has come and gone, and we still have ample supplies of gas. So those who were convinced the shortages of the 1970s were artificial clearly were right—but not in the sense they meant. There was no conspiracy of producers against consumers. The withholding of supplies was not a plot by a handful of fat-cat monopolists, but the inevitable response of literally thousands of independent gas producers to the incentives inherent in the FPC's system of price controls.

Although the FPC tried to raise ceiling prices to alleviate the shortages, it did not raise prices to market-clearing levels. By 1978, (unregulated) prices on gas sold intrastate were still more than twice those on interstate sales. A bruising battle over price decontrol was waged in Congress. The contending parties were familiar. Those from gas-consuming areas, arguing the shortages were artificially contrived, favored continued regulation, while those from areas where gas and rival fuels were produced argued that decontrol was necessary to end the crisis.

Public choice theory predicts that no single group or interest will get everything desired from regulation. Congress's resolution of the matter, the Natural Gas Policy Act of 1978, illustrates this principle perfectly. Each contending interest group in the policy debate could take comfort from some portion of the act. Consumers were happy that the act gave federal regulators (now the FERC) authority over the intrastate market as well as interstate sales. Gas producers gained phased deregulation of newly discovered gas and higher prices for flowing gas. Producers of rival fuels such as coal won certain protective provisions and the assurance that higher gas prices would make their products relatively more attractive to buyers. Even bureaucrats won new powers to manage industrial and utility fuel use patterns.

Decontrol of newly discovered or hard-to-get gas (that in wells over 5,000 feet deep) was phased in over the period from 1978 to 1985. By 1984, the wellhead price of gas was almost 3 times its 1978 level. Since 1984, however, wellhead prices of gas have been declining significantly. There are two reasons.

[15]See Tom Bethell, "The Gas Price Fixers," *Harper's*, 258 (June 1979), pp. 37–44, 104–105.

First, as proponents of decontrol had forecast, higher gas prices gave producers an incentive to find and sell more gas. Second, when the OPEC cartel began to unravel, falling oil prices put downward pressure on other fuel prices.

Effects of Regulation

Stephen Breyer has argued that our experiment with federal regulation of natural gas prices is an example of a *regulatory mismatch*.[16] That is, economic regulation was asked to do a job for which it was ill suited: redistribute income (or engage in rent control) rather than cope with the natural-monopoly problem.

To see why most economists think redistributing income via price controls is a bad idea, consider Figure 14.1, which shows demand (*D*) and supply (*S*) curves for natural gas in interstate markets. For illustrative purposes, prices and quantities in this diagram are labeled with the approximate values prevailing circa 1975. A wellhead price of about $0.60 per 1,000 cubic feet just clears the interstate market. Quantity demanded and quantity supplied are equal at 16 trillion cubic feet. Consumer surplus is equal to the area bound by points *ABI*, producer surplus equals area *BEI*, and total social surplus equals area *AEI*.

A price of $0.40 shifts considerable surplus from producers to consumers. Consumers save $0.20 per 1,000 cubic feet of gas sold, but the price cut also reduces quantity supplied to 13 trillion cubic feet, so the transfer from producers to consumers is $2.6 billion per year (the area bound by points *BCFG* in Figure 14.1). Consumer surplus expands to area *ACFH*, and producer surplus shrinks to *CEF*. But a key by-product of our transfer of surplus from producers to consumers is that *total social surplus shrinks*, too. It now equals area *AEFH*. The triangular area bound by points *FHI* is lost. The precise size of this area is determined by the shapes of the market demand and supply curves. If, say, supply is inelastic and demand is elastic, it may be that this area of deadweight loss will be rather small. In 1975, however, gas curtailments were about 3.8 trillion cubic feet out of about 13 trillion cubic feet sold interstate. Clearly, this is not a trivial reduction. It is safe to say that the surplus losses resulting from price controls during this period were significant.

Some might argue, of course, that these efficiency losses are justified by equity gains. That is, converting some gas producers' surplus to consumers' surplus enhances vertical equity if we assume consumers are poorer than producers. But this greatly oversimplifies the nature of the transfer. Not all stake holders (owners, managers, and workers) in gas companies are wealthy, and not all the beneficiaries of price controls are poor. Indeed, over 60 percent of gas output normally flows to industrial users, who, we should probably assume, are on just about the same rung of the economic ladder as gas companies. Thus, a good deal of the redistribution is not vertical at all, but horizon-

---

[16]Stephen Breyer, *Regulation and Its Reform*, Harvard University Press, Cambridge, MA, 1982, pp. 240–260.

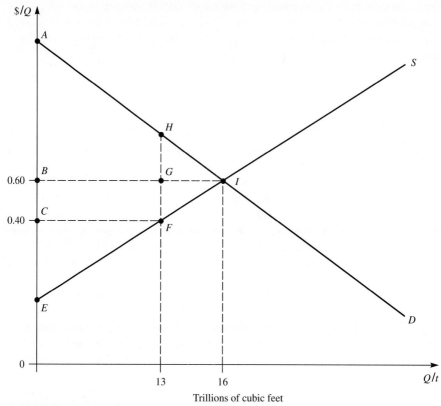

FIGURE 14.1
REDISTRIBUTION VIA GAS PRICE CONTROLS. Setting a price of $0.40 per unit instead of the market-clearing price of $0.60 per unit reduces quantity supplied from 16 to 13 trillion cubic feet, transferring producers' surplus equal to area *BCFG* (about $2.6 billion per year) to consumers and imposing a deadweight welfare loss equal to area *FHI*.

tal. In addition, price controls (and resulting curtailments) leave some consumers without gas entirely. These consumers must pay to search out other sources of energy; the higher costs they pay must be counted as part of the costs of this redistribution. It is anyone's guess, then, whether this type of transfer really enhances vertical equity.

Also note that deadweight losses (area *FHI* in Figure 14.1) are not the only kind of efficiency losses produced by price controls. There is also an *exchange inefficiency;* i.e., there is no assurance that gas is flowing to those who value it most highly. It is quite possible that some consumers getting no gas value it more than those who are getting adequate supplies. Given the bureaucratic rules for rationing available supplies, however, exchanges that could enhance welfare (i.e., those who attach a low value to gas trading it to those who value it more highly) are prohibited. In addition, (1) some consumers will spend some real resources to lobby the officials who are writing the curtailment procedures to ensure they are among the lucky recipients of the redistributed producers' surplus; (2) some (unscrupulous) producers will spend some real resources trying to figure out ways to evade the controls; and (3) the authorities will have to spend resources trying to detect such evasions and to police the system. All these resources (the time and talents of lobbyists, managers, lawyers, and bureaucrats) have alternative uses. The output they might have produced if used alternatively must be counted as a cost of the program. Clearly, redistributing surplus in this way is more expensive than meets the eye.

TELECOMMUNICATIONS

Most people are aware that the telecommunications industry of today differs profoundly from that of a decade or so ago. In 1982, a momentous antitrust settlement completely restructured the industry. It split the American Telephone & Telegraph Company (AT&T) into smaller (though still large) parts, radically changed industry pricing policies, and brought competition to markets that had known only regulation for decades. In this section, we examine how regulatory policy toward this industry evolved over time, discuss the reasons why changes in market structure were desirable, and outline the effects of the restructuring that did occur.

Overview

On February 14, 1876, Alexander Graham Bell applied for a patent on a device permitting the electrical transmission of vocal sounds. Although some were skeptical about the commercial potential of the device (in fact, one of Bell's backers offered all rights to the telephone to Western Union for $100,000 in 1877—and Western Union declined!), it soon became clear that Bell's ideas and gadgets were enormously valuable. Once some lawsuits over the validity of Bell's patents were cleared up, the Bell Telephone Company held a patent-protected monopoly on telephony until 1894.

Somewhat underfinanced, Bell Telephone Company opted to franchise local operating companies, granting them territorial monopolies in key metropolitan areas. Local investors supplied the capital necessary to build a system for effective local service: phones, wires, central switches, etc. Bell provided equipment and set certain specifications and guidelines and in exchange received annual per-telephone licensing fees and a large block of stock in each local operating company. These licensed companies could construct long-distance lines within their territories, but could not connect their local networks with franchises in other territories. Bell reserved this activity for itself, creating a subsidiary (AT&T) to operate the long-distance network that tied together the various local exchanges. In addition, Bell integrated vertically, establishing Western Electric Company as its exclusive manufacturing arm. The idea was that these arrangements would help Bell control the local franchises and deter entry by rivals once the patents expired.

The telephone industry proved so lucrative, however, that entry was inevitable. Independent companies, lured by rates of return on invested capital approaching 50 percent per year, grew like mushrooms in rural areas Bell had overlooked or where its service was unsatisfactory. By 1902, there were more than 4,000 independent telephone companies operating about 44 percent of all telephones then in existence in the United States. At first, Bell tried to compete directly with these independents, reducing rental rates on its telephones and expanding facilities rapidly. In 1907, following some financial difficulties that saw a change in top management, Bell changed its strategy. Led by new president Theodore Vail, Bell tried to buy up many of the companies and exchanges that were key links in regional independent systems. In addition, Vail became a forceful and articulate advocate of government regulation of the industry.

Vail maintained that the telephone industry was a natural monopoly. His slogan, which AT&T revived in the late 1960s and early 1970s, was "one policy, one system, and universal service." He argued that having even two competitors in this market involved wasteful duplication of facilities, which would force the public to pay "double rates for service, to meet double charges, on double capital, double operating expenses and double maintenance."[17] It was by no means clear that these assertions were valid. While the quality of services provided by the independent companies varied widely, prices had fallen sharply as a result of their entry and they had spurred some important technological advances. The Columbus, Ohio, market was an often cited example of the effects of side-by-side competition between phone companies. Prior to entry by an independent company, consumers paid $96 per year for connection to a system of about 2,000 phones. When an entrant charged $40 for service, Bell lowered its charge to $54, so a consumer connected to both paid $94 per year—$2 less than Bell had previously charged—and the system grew to some 22,000 phones.[18]

By 1913, however, the presumption that telephony was at least a local monopoly began to be established in policy. In that year, the Justice Department resolved some independents' antitrust complaints against AT&T with an agreement, dubbed the *Kingsbury commitment*, in which AT&T agreed to let independents interconnect into its system. In exchange, the government allowed for reduced competition between the two. By the early 1920s, the idea that the industry was naturally monopolistic had taken firm root in Congress, which in 1921 passed the Willis-Graham Act, granting AT&T antitrust immunity and giving the ICC authority over consolidations in the industry.

By 1932, with its market share grown to almost 80 percent, AT&T clearly dominated the telephone industry. Regulatory control over the industry was minimal, however. The ICC, far more comfortable with and interested in rail-

---

[17]As quoted in Robert Bornholz and David S. Evans, "The Early History of Competition in the Telephone Industry," in David S. Evans (ed.), *Breaking Up Bell: Essays on Industrial Organization and Regulation*, North-Holland, New York, 1983, p. 18.
[18]Ibid., pp. 19, 21.

road matters than in telecommunications, exercised little of its statutory over-sight authority. Some state public utility commissions tried to set phone rates, but local operating companies generally appealed these rates to federal courts. The reviews were often sufficiently lengthy and costly that state commissions began to avoid telephone rate cases altogether. Thus, AT&T had the benefits of a sanctioned monopoly without any offsetting control by regulators. From the firm's point of view, this was the ideal form of regulation. From a consumer's viewpoint, however, it may have been something else entirely.

In 1934, Congress created the Federal Communications Commission (FCC) to oversee the development of "a rapid, efficient, nationwide, and worldwide wire and radio communication service with adequate facilities at reasonable charges." The FCC's primary responsibility was clearly to regulate the emerg-ing radio industry, but it was also charged with regulating so-called common carrier activities, including telephony. Congress's major worry was that AT&T, as a vertically integrated monopoly, could inflate charges for its equip-ment (manufactured by its Western Electric subsidiary), thus boosting the rate base used to set rates by state regulatory authorities. According to a 1935 report by a special investigative committee, overcharges by Western Electric cost subscribers about $51 million per year.[19] But AT&T successfully resisted attempts by Congress (and later the Justice Department) to divest it of Western Electric and its research arm, Bell Laboratories.

The structure of the industry posed other complications. Most long-distance calls must begin and end in a local exchange. When a voter in Boise, Idaho, calls her senator in Washington, D.C., the call first goes through a local exchange central switching center in Boise. The signal then is switched onto long-distance lines, routed to the Washington central switching center, and finally delivered to the senator's office via the Washington, D.C., local exchange. Thus, although the FCC's jurisdiction was limited to interstate wire and radio transmissions, either end of such interstate calls involved the use of facilities—the local exchanges—which were under the authority of state utility commissions. The two layers of regulatory authority had to get together to allocate costs between the interstate and intrastate jurisdictions. The proce-dures devised for this purpose were dubbed *separations*. Similarly, AT&T Long Lines, which operated the long-distance system, and the local operating com-panies had to work out procedures, dubbed *settlements*, for allocating among them the revenues on long-distance calls.

Local regulators had a strong interest in allocating a large share of the costs of the local exchanges to long-distance service. In this way, local costs would appear lower, local rates could be set lower, and the state regulators would look good to their constituents. Of course, federal regulators had exactly the opposite interest. The resulting friction over separations was the dominant regulatory issue of the 1930s and early 1940s. Evidently, the state regulators' interests were more compelling; by 1943, separations policy clearly favored

[19]FCC, *Investigation of the Telephone Industry in the U.S.*, Government Printing Office, Washington, 1939.

local users. An unrealistically high share of local exchange costs were allocated to long-distance service, so that local rates were lower and long-distance rates higher than they should have been; i.e., *local users were the recipients of a subsidy from long-distance users.* By some estimates, long-distance service was priced at 2 to 3 times its marginal cost, and local service was priced at half its marginal cost. By the early 1980s the subsidy to local operating companies was about $7 billion yearly. Of course, separating costs when facilities are shared isn't easy. But it is quite clear that the FCC had little stomach for the job. After investigating AT&T's rate base from 1935 to 1939, the FCC refused to do so again for three decades, explaining it was just too big a job. Instead, the FCC regulated by negotiation: The FCC would watch AT&T's earnings and ask for a rate adjustment if it felt returns were excessive.

Regulation at the local level also yielded some cross-subsidies. For example, charges for basic service (a single no-frills telephone used for local calls) were kept below costs and the resulting deficits made up by charges in excess of costs for nonbasic service (extension phones, toll calls, transmission of data). In addition, above-cost prices were set on some services in order to defray costs associated with others (e.g., directory assistance) that were given away.

Clearly, post-World War II regulation had strayed considerably from the task of protecting consumers from pricing abuses by a natural monopoly. Especially at the federal level, regulators seemed little interested even in ascertaining producers' costs so that prices could be set equal to them. Much policy was aimed at redistributing surplus among classes of consumers. Forces were in motion, however, that would eventually cause this regulatory structure to crumble.

By the mid-1950s, AT&T's dominant market position was under attack at two levels. First, rival producers of attachments that could be used with AT&T's equipment began to chip away at AT&T's monopoly of phone system hardware. In 1956, a federal appeals court (overruling the FCC, which had sided with AT&T) decided in *Hush-A-Phone* that AT&T had no right to keep subscribers from using an independently made cuplike device which, when snapped onto telephone mouthpieces, muffled background noise and ensured greater privacy over what was said.[20] In 1968, the FCC ruled that AT&T could not prevent subscribers from using their telephones with an independently made device that enabled telephone calls to be "patched into" mobile radio systems.[21] These decisions brought the first small measures of competition to the telephone equipment industry in a long time. The move toward competition received a further boost in 1980, when the FCC forced AT&T to change its policy of renting, rather than selling, all its phone equipment and allowed other producers to compete in this market. Henceforth, consumers would have a much expanded menu of phone equipment from which to choose, all competitively priced.

---

[20]*Hush-A-Phone Corp. v. United States and FCC,* 238 F.2d 266 (1956).
[21]*In the Matter of Use of the Carterfone Device in Message Toll Telephone Service,* 13 F.C.C. 2d 420 (1968).

Second, and perhaps more important, some independent firms had begun to assault AT&T's long-distance service monopoly. During World War II, defense-oriented research had rapidly advanced microwave technology, which could be adapted to long-distance telecommunications. In the years immediately following the war, this industry was reasonably competitive, with several firms constructing microwave facilities to transmit TV signals. But the FCC reversed this trend, protecting AT&T by limiting access to microwave broadcasting frequencies and upholding AT&T's refusal to interconnect with the facilities of rival companies. In 1956, however, the FCC reconsidered these policies, and in 1959, in the *Above 890* decision, the FCC opened the door—a crack, at least—to private microwave systems and competitive long-distance service.[22] Now private firms could have permanent frequency allocations to set up microwave facilities for their own use, although they could not sell services to others and AT&T could still refuse to interconnect its local networks with these new systems. Years later, a tiny but persistent company, Microwave Communications, Inc. (MCI), would push the door open wide.

Heavy users of long-distance service between two points (e.g., a company headquarters and a branch office) found private microwave systems extraordinarily attractive. Under the pricing structure prevailing at the time, for example, AT&T often charged 4 times as much for large-scale services as a microwave hookup would cost. When firms began to convert to private microwave systems, AT&T responded with significant discounts to large users (under its "Telpak" rate structure), cutting its old prices by as much as 85 percent (for users who leased a bundle of 240 private lines). This kept large users in AT&T's fold, but smaller users who needed few or no private lines still paid high charges. And if a carrier other than AT&T proposed to serve such customers with a microwave system, they would need to be interconnected with AT&T's local system.

Enter MCI, which in 1963 asked the FCC to allow it to build a microwave system between Chicago and St. Louis that would interconnect with AT&T's local networks in those cities and offer small customers "leased private lines" at half the price charged by AT&T. The resulting legal wrangle took until 1969 to resolve. When the FCC ruled in favor of MCI,[23] it was flooded with similar applications. In 1971, the FCC stated its goal of bringing more competition in long-distance markets more generally, requiring interconnection to support that policy. AT&T resisted interconnection as long as it could, arguing that firms like MCI were *cream skimmers,* serving only the most lucrative (high-volume, low-cost) markets. Allowing this, the argument went, would make it impossible for AT&T to subsidize less profitable operations in the hinterlands and would increase the costs of the system as a whole. In 1978, however, the Supreme Court upheld the FCC's decisions.

MCI took advantage of the FCC's initial order to expand its offerings to

[22]*Allocation of Microwave Frequencies Above 890 Mc.*, 27 F.C.C. 359 (1959).
[23]*In the Matter of Microwave Communications, Inc.*, 18 F.C.C. 953 (1969).

include dial-up, long-distance service to individual customers (its "Execunet" service). AT&T once again protested and this time had the FCC as an ally. But an appeals court overturned the FCC's rejection of Execunet, and the Supreme Court found no reason to question this decision.[24] For the first time in its history, AT&T faced the prospect of significant potential entry in the long-distance telecommunications market.

In the meantime, the Justice Department had become increasingly concerned about AT&T's aggressive responses each time rivals made even the smallest assaults on AT&T's market dominance. (In North Carolina, for example, AT&T sued to prevent a tiny company from distributing advertising in the form of plastic covers that consumers could slip over their phone books, arguing that this was an "unauthorized attachment" to its equipment!) In addition, the equipment and long-distance controversies had encouraged many private antitrust actions against AT&T. By 1974, about three dozen such suits had been filed. Then the Justice Department filed its own mammoth suit, alleging AT&T had monopolized the markets for telephone equipment, long-distance service, and local service. The government's suit alleged that regulation had been ineffective and sought a massive restructuring of the company as a remedy. It was this suit that led to the historic 1982 consent decree alluded to earlier. But we should summarize the effects of regulation on the industry as it *was* before we outline how it has come to be structured.

Effects of (Predivestiture) Regulation

State and federal regulation of telecommunications prior to AT&T's 1982–1984 restructuring produced massive efficiency losses. In general, these losses took four forms: deadweight losses from mispricing of services, overbuilding and gold-plating of local facilities in response to these misspecified prices, resource waste from uneconomic *bypassing* of the public network by heavy users frustrated by overpriced services, and wasteful backward integration into unregulated equipment supply in order to avoid rate-of-return regulation.

Of course, while economists regarded such distortions in the allocation of resources with disfavor, others took exactly the opposite view. Theodore Vail's rhetoric about universal service had strong appeal, and setting high prices to some consumers in order to subsidize others, e.g., rural customers or the urban poor, was often applauded. Consider, e.g., the way Senator Clifford Hansen summarized the effects of cross-subsidization on a small town in Wyoming:

> It has hardly more than 100 people living there. This year [1977], about 40 families— whose phone service had been coming to them on an eight-party line—will have, for the first time, a choice of single-party, two-party or four-party service. Now, that might not sound like much to city folks, but it's much appreciated out there. The

---

[24]*MCI v. FCC*, 561 F.2d 365 (1977), *cert. denied*, 434 U.S. 1040 (1978).

phone company had to spend about $8,000 per subscriber to update that service, and to me, it's a classic example of how beneficial a regulated monopoly can be. In a competitive environment, no company would've invested that kind of money on such a small town.[25]

Under the type of regulation that prevailed prior to 1982, the Senator's key conclusion—that certain investments wouldn't have been made in a competitive market—applied to markets all over the United States and to many of the services and facilities AT&T provided. Let us assume, for the sake of argument, that the statement is correct. Why do economists grumble about such cross-subsidies?

Consider first the effects of such subsidies on total social surplus. The two panels of Figure 14.2 show separate markets for a particular kind of service, say, hookup to a local network. Panel *a* shows the demand and supply curves in a small market, labeled D_s and S_s, respectively. Panel *b* shows demand D_l and supply S_l in a large market. The surplus-maximizing prices in each market will be those that equate quantity demanded and quantity supplied. In the small market, this will be P_s (so that Q_s hookups are made); in the large market, this will be P_l (so that Q_l hookups are made). Note that the market-clearing price of hookups in the small market exceeds that in the large market— perhaps because the smaller market has a more dispersed population, requiring more wire (or other equipment) per hookup to the local network.

It was (and, in some markets, still is) quite common for regulatory authorities to ignore such cost differences, instead setting prices by referring to some *average* of relevant costs in all markets. In our example, an authority might set a price for hookups equal to P_a in both the small and large markets. This delivers a subsidy to consumers in the small market at the expense of consumers in the large market. It also reduces social surplus appreciably in *both* markets. In the small market (Figure 14.2*a*), consumers now choose to buy Q_{as} hookups; the cost of each unit between Q_s and Q_{as} exceeds the value consumers attach to it, so there is a deadweight loss measured by the shaded area. In the large market (Figure 14.2*b*), consumers buy Q_{al} units; they value additional units up to Q_l by more than these units would cost to produce, so surplus measured by the shaded area is forgone.

These losses may be small if, e.g., the relevant demand and supply curves are very inelastic. Some argue, therefore, that cross-subsidies of this kind are desirable, for they may enhance equity and create only minor efficiency losses. But James Griffin has found evidence that suggests that the losses associated with at least one cross-subsidy—from long-distance users to local callers— have been anything but minor. According to Griffin's estimates, such losses ranged from $1.1 to $1.5 billion (in 1975 prices) annually, certainly nothing to

---

[25]R. Burke Stinson, "Congress Focuses on Telecommunications Policy," *AT&T Long Lines,* September/October 1977, p. 38, as quoted in William S. Reece, "Consumer Welfare Implications of Changes in Interstate Telephone Pricing," *Journal of Consumer Affairs,* 21 (Summer 1987), p. 150.

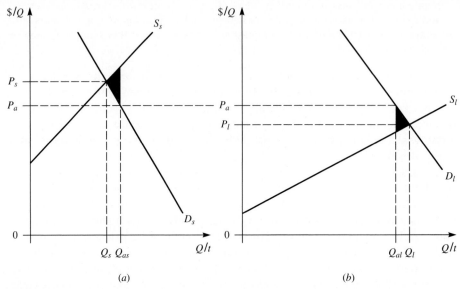

FIGURE 14.2
WELFARE EFFECTS OF CROSS-SUBSIDIES. The surplus-maximizing price of hookups is P_s in the small market (panel *a*) . In the large market (panel *b*) it is P_l. Setting a uniform price P_a equal to the average cost of hookups in the two markets wastes surplus equal to the shaded areas.

sneeze at.[26] And it must be stressed that this cross-subsidy is but one of many under the mode of regulation that generally prevailed prior to 1982. In another study, Bridger Mitchell estimated the nationwide welfare losses from widespread use of *flat-rate pricing* of phone service (in which consumers pay a flat monthly rate for telephone rental that does not vary with phone usage) at about $250 million (in 1978 prices) annually.[27]

What about the equity effects of eliminating inefficient pricing and cross-subsidies in telecommunications service markets? We expect that raising local rates closer to the true costs of local service would, all other things remaining unchanged, adversely affect the poor. Several studies in the mid-1970s confirmed this forecast. Table 14.1 shows one such. According to this source, raising the price of basic monthly service from below $5 to $6.50 or more reduces the percentage of the poorest households (those with incomes of less than $3,000, in 1975 prices) that possess phones from 80 to 72 percent, while such price hikes reduce the percentage of the richest households with phones only trivially, from 98 to 97 percent. But raising the flat rate for basic service is not

[26]James M. Griffin, "The Welfare Implications of Externalities and Price Elasticities for Telecommunications Pricing," *Review of Economics and Statistics*, 64 (February 1982), pp. 59–66.
[27]Bridger M. Mitchell, "Optimal Pricing of Local Telephone Services," *American Economic Review*, 68 (September 1978), pp. 517–537.

TABLE 14.1
PERCENTAGE OF HOUSEHOLDS WITH A TELEPHONE
AVAILABLE, BY HOUSEHOLD INCOME CLASS AND PRICE
OF BASIC SERVICE, 1970.   Setting the price of basic service
closer to marginal cost likely will reduce poorest households'
access to phone service significantly. Two-part tariffs can
ameliorate this problem, however.

	Price of basic service, $		
Income, $	< 5	5 to 6.50	> 6.5
< 3,000	80.4	76.3	71.9
$3,000–5,999	85.6	79.3	74.8
$6,000–8,999	90.1	88.2	84.6
$9,000–11,999	94.1	93.1	90.4
> 12,000	97.9	96.8	96.9
All households	90.6	86.7	86.2

Source: L. J. Perl, "Economic and Demographic Determinants of FCC
Telephone Availability," National Economic Research Associates, Inc.,
April 5, 1975, Table 12 (filed by AT&T Co., FCC Docket No. 20003, Bell
Exhibit 21).

the only policy option. If we adopt more creative pricing structures, we might
avoid reducing the poor's access to phone service. The aforementioned study
by Mitchell, e.g., noted that adopting a two-part tariff for local phone service
(i.e., combining a flat monthly connection charge with a per-call usage charge)
in lieu of a simple flat-rate scheme can actually increase the likelihood that
poor households will have access to phone service. With a two-part tariff, the
flat monthly connection fee could actually be *reduced,* enabling more poor
households to afford a phone, although coupling this with a usage fee would
mean that all households (including poor ones) would make fewer calls per
month.

It should also be pointed out that cost-averaging and cross-subsidization
will not always have favorable equity effects. Consider the equity effects of
charging a zero price for certain goods or services. In some states, e.g., local
operating companies could not charge a separate fee for each phone jack
installed in subscribers' homes. Costs of jack installation were recovered as
part of the basic monthly fee charged to all customers. Since each customer
privately viewed the price of an extra jack as zero, many households, including or especially well-to-do ones, had extra jacks installed even when they
attached a trivial value to them. The costs of installing redundant phone jacks,
multiplied across many thousands of households, were anything but trivial,
however. Thus, this scheme produced both inefficiency and inequity: Those
consuming less housing (the poor) benefited relatively little from zero-price

extra phone jacks, but paid part of the costs of serving those who did (wealthier inhabitants of larger homes) in their basic monthly bills.

VIGNETTE 14.4   The Welfare Effects of a Zero-Price Lunch

It's a cliché that "there's no free lunch"—all economic goods are costly, even those given away at a zero price. In general, economists prefer to see things sold at prices that reflect their true social cost, but on occasion it *can* be efficient to give some things away "free." It's costly to collect fees; when there are many transactions for a good that is cheap to produce and for which demand is inelastic, the welfare gains from efficient pricing may be more than offset by these collection costs.

From the first days of telephony to the mid-1970s, no phone company in the United States charged for information or directory assistance calls. It may be that in the industry's infancy, charging for this good was uneconomical. Identifying users of the service, metering usage, and billing users would have been difficult and costly. Providing "free" directory assistance and recovering the costs of the operators and equipment needed to provide it by adding a few cents to all subscribers' monthly bills probably seemed efficient. By the 1950s, however, advances in automatic message accounting equipment (and later computer technology) had certainly made charging for directory assistance economically feasible and efficient. Yet it was not until 1974 that a company—Cincinnati Bell—introduced the first charging plan. Although companies in many other states soon petitioned their regulatory authorities for permission to institute similar programs, the pace of conversion to a price system was slow, and a few state legislatures even passed laws prohibiting charging for directory assistance.

George Daly and Thomas Mayor studied the economic effects of this "missing market" carefully.[28] Figure 14.3 summarizes their approach. The demand curve for directory assistance calls, labeled D, shows that when calls are free, Q_0 calls are made per period. If the cost of handling such calls is C_0 per call, the socially optimal number of calls per period is Q_2. The calls from Q_2 to Q_0 cost more than consumers value them, and the shaded area labeled A measures the social surplus that is wasted by this system. Charging for calls is not costless, however; it involves some extra expenses for billing and accounting. Cost curve C_1 (which equals C_0 plus these billing costs) shows the cost per call when directory assistance calls carry some price. If this price P_1 is set equal to the cost per call, the number of calls per period will fall to Q_1. The added billing costs, equal to the shaded area labeled B, must then be subtracted from area A to obtain a measure of the *net* social benefits from instituting directory assistance charging (or, looked at from the other side, the losses from *not* charging). According to Daly and Mayor, these net benefits were equal to approximately $750 million in 1978—a bit more than half of the annual costs of providing the service nationwide.

That's not chicken feed. So why were companies and regulators so slow to adopt charging? It may have been that the individuals who benefited from zero-price directory assistance were able to coalesce as a special interest and preserve their subsidies. Daly and Mayor found that usage of directory assistance service was enormously concentrated. In Cincinnati, prior to the initiation of charging, about 82 percent of subscribers used the service fewer than 3 times per month—and 49 per-

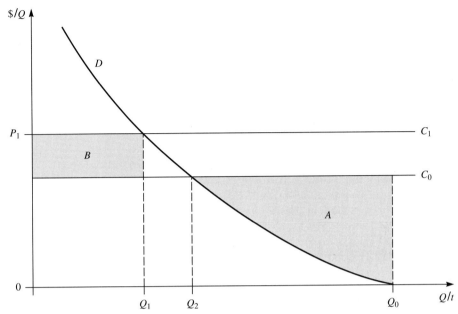

FIGURE 14.3
THE MARKET FOR DIRECTORY ASSISTANCE. Zero-price directory assistance wastes social surplus equal to area A. Charging for directory assistance calls raises the total social cost of Q_1 such calls by area B. Thus, the surplus gain resulting from instituting a charging system equals area A minus area B.

cent of subscribers used the service not at all in an average month. In other words, a small fraction of subscribers, generally commercial entities such as real estate and telephone sales firms, accounted for the great bulk of directory assistance calls. These intense users clearly liked the in-kind subsidy they received under a no-charge system and wanted it to continue. So did the labor unions representing the workers who might have been displaced once the volume of calls fell under a price system. Although inefficient (and inequitable, given the identities of the beneficiaries of the old system), the status quo had staunch defenders, and these groups greatly slowed the adoption of directory assistance charging.

Restructuring the Industry

As we have seen, the trend toward increased competition in the telecommunications industry had started well before the Justice Department filed its antitrust suit against AT&T in 1974. Technological advances and an FCC that had gradually become less favorably disposed to AT&T's interests chipped away at the firm's monopoly power in the long-distance market and in equipment manufacture from the 1960s onward. By the 1970s, the company regarded its position as untenable. It faced increased competition in what it regarded as the most lucrative fields of the telecommunications business, and a consent decree it had negotiated in 1956 prevented it from entering the booming field of data processing. As litigation of the antitrust case proceeded, it seemed to AT&T that the government would win at least some of the structural changes it sought. AT&T began to negotiate a settlement with the Justice Department; the resulting agreement was announced on January 8, 1982. The presiding judge in the case, District Court Judge Harold Greene, approved the consent decree with some changes in 1983 and has since made additional modifications to its terms.

The decree (or Judge Greene's subsequent orders) has greatly transformed the industry. As a result,

• AT&T divested its local operating companies, consolidating these 21 firms into seven regional holding companies (NYNEX, Bell Atlantic, Bell South, Ameritech, Southwestern Bell, U.S. West, and Pacific Telesis).

• The local operating companies were required to provide "equal access" to all competing long-distance companies (the three largest were AT&T, MCI, and GTE Sprint).

• AT&T was allowed to maintain ownership of its Western Electric and Bell Laboratories subsidiaries, although divestiture of the local operating companies meant Western Electric no longer had a captive market for its goods.

• AT&T was allowed to enter the market for computer and data processing equipment.

• The regional holding companies have been allowed to diversify their operations into nontelecommunications markets such as real estate and financial services (but not into equipment manufacturing).

In general, scholars and policymakers welcomed the divestiture. Clearly, the long-distance and equipment markets were no longer (if they ever truly were) natural monopolies. Eliminating entry barriers and opening these markets to competition should pay long-term dividends. Old-style economic regulation is now limited to the only level of the industry where natural-monopoly considerations appear relevant—local service.

Consumers have responded to the restructuring of the industry more coolly, however. A 1986 poll found that almost two-thirds of the individuals sampled thought the breakup of AT&T was a "bad idea." Table 14.2 suggests a reason why. It shows that opening the interstate long-distance market to competition (a process that started, of course, prior to the divestiture) had the predicted effect: By 1986, interstate rates were 41 percent lower (in real, inflation-adjusted terms) than they had been in 1977 and 21 percent lower than they had been in 1982. But local rates, which fell from 1977 to 1980, rose 26 percent from 1982 to 1986. In total, the long-term decline in phone rates from 1965 to 1981 was reversed in 1982; since that year, rates have risen about 10 percent.

So consumers' complaints about the divestiture are quite understandable. Hikes in local rates exceeded the reductions in long-distance rates, so all but intense users of long distance are, on net, paying more for phone service. But the divestiture is not the real culprit here. As Table 14.2 shows, hikes in local rates began prior to the divestiture, in 1981. In fact, the real reductions in rates from 1977 to 1980 were—at least partly—an artifact, a by-product of a regula-

TABLE 14.2
INDEX OF REAL AVERAGE TELEPHONE RATES, 1965 to 1986.
Consumers tend to think that the breakup of AT&T was a bad idea,
perhaps because they blame it for the real increases in local phone
rates observed during the 1980s.

	Real average telephone rates (base year = 1977)		
Year	Total	Interstate	Local
1965	147	Unavailable	Unavailable
1977	100	100	100
1980	76	73	77
1981	75	72	78
1982	78	75	82
1983	80	74	86
1984	83	69	94
1985	84	64	98
1986	86	59	103

Source: Robert W. Crandall, "Local Telephone Rates Catch Up with Costs,"
Wall Street Journal, February 17, 1987, p. 10.

tory process that relied on historical-cost accounting practices. As inflation raged in the late 1970s, regulatory lag kept phone rates artificially low. Some of the increases recorded from 1981 to 1986 had nothing to do with the divestiture, but were simply catch-up increases left over from the earlier inflationary period. In addition, in the early 1980s consumers began paying for past accruals of "inside-wiring" costs, which had been deferred under previous regulatory policy, as well as new inside-wiring costs. In sum, it is easy for consumers to blame divestiture for problems that did not originate there and to ignore its beneficial effects. For example, by some estimates, competition in the telephone equipment market has reduced prices there by 20 to 25 percent and greatly expanded consumers' range of choice.

Current Issues This does not mean, of course, that the restructured industry is problem-free. The local operating companies are subjected to the same kind of rate regulation that, we have seen in various contexts, can yield gold-plating and other forms of productive inefficiency. In addition, the local regulators have lately tinkered with new cross-subsidies. Lifeline rates have been especially popular.

Perhaps more important, technological advances have made it possible for large customers to bypass the local network. For example, a business with several offices in a city can link them via microwave transmitters or fiber-optic lines (assuming it can obtain rights-of-way for the latter) for voice or data transfer. When coupled with high-speed computer switching equipment, this effectively takes all the business's internal communications out of the local exchange. Such bypass can create serious problems for the local operating companies. They lose revenue from these large subscribers and must then cover common capital costs and (depending on the type of local rate regulation imposed) any subsidies for smaller, residential subscribers from a depleted earnings pool. In addition, long-distance companies—even AT&T, now that it is independent of the local operating companies—might compound the bypass problem by using these alternative technologies to link large customers in different cities, thus avoiding the local companies' charges for access to their local networks. To reduce long-distance firms' incentives to bypass, the FCC has already imposed a set of flat monthly *subscriber line charges* on both residential and business customers in order to reduce access charges. This policy has not been popular; it accounts for some part of the real increase in rates alluded to earlier. Groups representing low-income and elderly subscribers have been particularly vocal opponents of these higher rates to local subscribers.

In sum, there are many issues that remain for policymakers to address in this industry, and the pace of technological change will doubtless produce more in short order. In general, the changes made thus far have been beneficial. By bringing prices closer to costs in the various levels of this market, allocative efficiency has been enhanced. And by introducing competition where feasible, productive efficiency has been enhanced.

SUMMARY AND CONCLUDING REMARKS

This chapter summarized the organization and regulation of three industries which, at least at some levels, are naturally monopolistic: the markets for electric power, natural gas, and telecommunications services.

In the electric power industry, there are prospective scale economies at each of the three levels of the production process (power generation, power transmission, and retail delivery). For this reason, the industry has been subjected to local or state regulation virtually from its earliest days; federal regulation of interstate sales of power came in the 1930s. Rate regulation usually takes the classic form: State commissions determine a utility's revenue requirement as the sum of its operating costs (including an allowance for depreciation and taxes) plus a fair return on the value of its assets, and they set the level and structure of electricity prices in order to satisfy this requirement. Rates may be constant as usage rises (flat), fall with increases in usage (declining block), or rise as usage rises (inverted block). Commercial users also pay demand charges based on their peak demands for power. In recent years, regulators have moved more toward marginal cost pricing of electricity, and many states now authorize utilities to employ time-of-use rates to level peak and off-peak demands for power. Some also require utilities to offer lifeline rates to make power more affordable to the poor. In general, this kind of regulation has worked tolerably well, if far from perfectly. In some periods, rates have been set above utilities' costs (although not at monopolistic levels), while in inflationary periods the rate suppression squeezed utilities' rate of return below the opportunity cost of capital. In sum, rate regulation has yielded both allocative and productive inefficiencies in the industry, leading to recommendations for reforms to bring competition to some levels of the production process and to improve the incentives of the industry's managers and regulators.

In the natural gas market, regulation has worked less well. While the local (retail delivery) level of this market is naturally monopolistic, it is not clear that pipeline transmission of gas is so, and it is clear that gas production is *not* monopolistic. Federal regulation of gas prices at the wellhead, then, had redistributive motives. Once federally mandated prices on gas sold interstate moved below market-clearing levels, shortages of gas (curtailments) were inevitable. In the mid-1970s, such shortages led to significant welfare losses, economic dislocation (e.g., job losses), and wasteful conversion to other sources of energy. Since most gas is used by industry, it is not clear that the redistribution enhanced equity either.

The early history of the telecommunications industry in the United States is the history of AT&T, which embraced regulation as a way to maintain its monopoly status (which had originated in patents). Early federal regulation of AT&T was extraordinarily friendly; oversight was minimal and attempts to force AT&T to divest itself of its equipment manufacturing division met with failure. The system of separations devised by federal and state regulators to allocate costs between intrastate and interstate jurisdictions produced massive cross-subsidies, with long-distance callers paying above-cost prices in order to deliver below-cost service to local callers. By the 1980s, these cross-subsidies amounted to about $7 billion per year. But technological advances and changes in attitude at the FCC soon began to erode AT&T's dominance of the industry and limit these and other cross-subsidies. By 1982, under seige from the antitrust authorities, AT&T agreed to divest itself of its local operating companies, which would then provide local access to competing long-distance companies. The local/long-distance cross-subsidy was thus reduced; long-distance rates fell, and local rates rose closer to costs. While this and other aspects of the restructuring have been controversial, most observers credit it with increasing allocative and productive efficiency in the telecommunications market.

QUESTIONS FOR REVIEW AND DISCUSSION

14.1 Explain why, in the 1930s, federal regulation of interstate sales of power was necessary to make state and local regulation of rates effective. Now that it is technologically feasible to "ship" power long distances, will competition among interstate sellers of power be sufficient to make federal regulation unnecessary?

14.2 Define a reverse A-J effect. What conditions are necessary for such an effect to occur? What will happen if such an effect persists over a lengthy period?

14.3 Suppose the demand for electricity in a hypothetical market is described by the equation $Q_d = 1,000 - 50P$. The cost of producing electricity is constant at $5 per unit. Identify the price and rate of output that an unregulated monopolist will set. Now suppose regulation comes to this market, but regulators are unable to accurately measure the seller's costs; they set a price of $7.50 and tell the firm that if any profits are subsequently earned, prices will be revised downward to eliminate those profits. Accordingly, the firm quickly finds ways to raise its production costs to $7.50 per unit. Is welfare enhanced by regulation?

14.4 During the mid-1970s, some argued that curtailments in supplies of natural gas to interstate buyers were a result of diversions of gas to the intrastate market (since price controls did not apply to intrastate sales) and that extending federal authority to control prices on intrastate sales would have solved the problem. Do you agree? Explain your reasoning thoroughly, using graphs where necessary.

14.5 When I bought my home, I noticed there were phone jacks in every room, including two in the basement and one in the garage! The previous owner happily explained that the phone company had installed all these phone jacks "for free" some years earlier. Obviously, phone jacks are not free. So who paid for them? Do you think this payment system is economically efficient? Did the previous owner derive any benefit *other* than increased convenience from this system? Explain your answers fully.

CHAPTER 15

ECONOMIC REGULATION IN A NONMONOPOLY SETTING: TRANSPORTATION, AGRICULTURE, AND SAVINGS INSTITUTIONS

When the corruption of American politics was laid on the threshold of American business—like a bastard on the doorstep of his father—a tremendous disturbance resulted.

Vernon Louis Parrington

In Chapter 14 we examined the effects of economic regulation in industries where natural-monopoly considerations are clearly important—at least at some stages of the production process. In this chapter, we look at industries in which other rationales for economic regulation have generally been offered. Only in the case of railroads, where customers in small markets will generally not benefit from competition between lines, have natural-monopoly arguments been invoked to explain the onset of regulation. Even here, however, most acknowledge that railroads' desire to be saved from "destructive competition" had a good deal to do with the decision to regulate this industry—and to similarly regulate trucking and airlines. In the case of agricultural markets, many argue that economic regulation will enhance efficiency by stabilizing inherently volatile markets, enhance equity, or accomplish both ends. The first of these rationales is also commonly used to explain regulation of savings institutions, where, it is said, unwise actions (or just plain bad luck) in a few firms can have adverse effects on an entire industry or economy.

RAIL AND TRUCK TRANSPORTATION

Structurally, the rail and trucking industries have little in common. Railroading involves substantial fixed costs and, at least for small markets, appears to possess some characteristics of a natural monopoly; trucking does not. Entry into and exit from railroading is difficult; in trucking, just the opposite is true. Most areas are (today, at least) served by one or a few rail lines, most quite large; in trucking, there are many firms, most very small. Yet for much of its history, the Interstate Commerce Commission (ICC) has applied many of the same regulatory approaches to these two industries. As we shall see, these approaches have not always served the interests of consumers. By the 1980s, this had become sufficiently clear that significant reform of rail and trucking regulation—long desirable—became politically feasible.

Overview

Even before there was an ICC, there was substantial government involvement in railroading. At the federal level, the desire to link the various regions of the country and to promote economic development in the wake of the Civil War's devastation led to generous subsidies for those willing to invest in new rail lines. State and local governments also competed among themselves to attract rail lines to their communities. The result was a near trebling of track mileage in the United States from 1865 to 1887. It is quite likely the generous subsidies had led to overbuilding of rail lines. Most major cities were linked by several lines (there were, for example, 20 railroads connecting Atlanta and St. Louis by 1880), and competition among them was fierce. Attempts to prop up freight rates via cartels almost invariably failed, and by the mid-1880s rail industry leaders were calling for government intervention to "bring order to the industry." They were joined by shippers in smaller markets served by a single line, who complained of "unfair rate discrimination." The (monopoly) prices they paid on short hauls from small towns to major cities often exceeded the (competitive) rates that applied on longer hauls between cities. Thus, from the outset rail regulation has had conflicting goals, aimed at duplicating the results of competition in some markets but at suppressing competition in others.

The ICC, created in 1887, had limited authority. It required carriers to publish rates and reviewed these charges to see that they were "reasonable and just" and nondiscriminatory, but the ICC could do little more. It was soon clear that the commission lacked the tools to do all that its proponents hoped. Price-cutting and rebating remained common. In 1920, Congress judged that railroading was chronically depressed and explicitly charged the commission with ensuring that carriers earned a "fair return." More important, it gave the ICC a way to do so, granting the commission the power to fix both maximum and minimum rail rates.

Nevertheless, rail companies' average rates of return were below those set by the ICC throughout the 1920s. The problem, at least in part, was a new source of competition: trucks and buses. Railroad interests pressed to have these new modes of transportation regulated, first at the state level and eventually federally. Until the mid-1930s, there was a political deadlock (the ICC, railroads, and the state utility commissions on one side with shippers, motor carriers, and vehicle manufacturers on the other). But the American Trucking

Association, recognizing that federal oversight of their industry might have certain benefits, eventually dropped their opposition to federal regulation.

Under the Motor Carrier Act of 1935, existing motor carriers were required to document their previous service and apply for operating licenses from the ICC. The commission granted fewer than one-third of the applications for licenses and restricted motor carriers' operations significantly. Proposals for entry or expansion of operations were considered only if no existing carrier yet offered service in the relevant market. Rates were tightly controlled. If rivals—whether motor carriers, railroads, or water carriers (which were brought under the ICC's authority in 1940)—protested a carrier's proposed tariff, the ICC would investigate and suspend the proposal if it found the rate to be less than the carrier's estimated full costs.

In short, the ICC had become a perfect cartel enforcement device for motor carriers. Carriers formed *rate bureaus* to fix prices (and after 1948 these bureaus were exempt from the antitrust laws under the Reed-Bulwinkle Act). The ICC punished those who deviated from these prices and prevented entry by firms attracted by the high rates of return that resulted from such prices. Note that no convincing public-interest rationale for the ICC's activities in this market had been advanced. No one seriously believed that trucking was naturally monopolistic or that the arguments used to justify entry restrictions and rate-of-return regulation in railroading applied here. Rather, regulation was extended to trucking to protect railroads' interests. If trucks (and barge lines) were able to compete freely for freight, the end result would clearly be a much smaller and less prosperous rail industry. The ICC, by now quite adept at protecting railroads from the consequences of competing with each other, slipped easily into the role of protecting railroads from the consequences of competition from other modes of transit, applying the same regulatory tools to all.

Effects of Regulation

Railroads   It is possible that the first few decades of ICC regulation of railroads enhanced social welfare. To comply with the ICC act's stipulation that prices on short hauls be lower than those on long hauls along the same tracks, the commission generally lowered short-haul prices and raised long-haul prices. The most reasonable estimates, by Richard Zerbe, are that the surplus gains from the reduction in short-haul prices more than offset the surplus losses in the long-haul market, so on net the total surplus grew.[1] And, as Ann Friedlaender has pointed out, the structure of rates used in the early years of the ICC served certain social goals. The railroads used value-of-service pricing extensively, charging low rates to shippers of agricultural products and raw materials (who, given the low value-to-weight ratios of their commodities, had fairly high elasticities of demand for rail transit) and higher rates to shippers of manufactured goods (whose demand for rail transit was more inelastic).

---

[1]Richard O. Zerbe, Jr., "The Costs and Benefits of Early Regulation of the Railroads," *Bell Journal of Economics*, 11 (Spring 1980), pp. 343–350.

This enabled the railroads to break even (or perhaps do even better than that) with minimum loss of social surplus. And it spurred economic development in the west in two ways. The low rates on eastbound farm output encouraged settlement of western lands, and the high rates on manufactured goods encouraged industrial development in the west, protecting its infant industries from more efficient eastern rivals.[2]

As rival modes of transportation emerged, however, this policy became less desirable, and, indeed, the standard public-interest rationales for regulation became less applicable. Where pipelines, barge lines, and trucking companies could compete with railroads, the rationales for the old pricing structure no longer applied. Consider the relatively high markups on shipments of manufactured goods. Absent competition, such markups are justified by value-of-service principles. With competition, the markups invite resource waste. Even though the most efficient way to ship, say, machinery between two cities might have been by rail, the high markups meant that some manufacturers would choose to ship their goods by truck. Had they been free to cut prices in order to compete, the railroads could have prevented inefficient shifts to rival modes. But the ICC was evidently less concerned with efficiency than with distributional concerns; the commission feared that lower rates on manufactured goods would mean higher rates to farmers and producers of raw materials, and it very much wanted to deliver subsidies to these constituencies. The desire to deliver cross-subsidies also made the ICC loath to allow carriers to abandon money-losing routes and led it to formulate many rules (regarding the rates one railroad paid another for use of its freight cars) that adversely affected operating efficiency. The results were bad for many railroads and for society at large.

Many economists have attempted to quantify the efficiency losses associated with ICC regulation of railroads. Although the estimates differ from study to study, there is wide agreement that ICC policies have produced sizable surplus losses.[3] The studies have identified three major sources of loss:

1 Losses from the inefficient diversion of freight from rail to trucks that results from minimum-rate rail regulation. Estimates here vary widely, with some approaching $3 billion per year. The most reasonable estimates, however, are much smaller—around $1 billion annually in the late 1970s.[4] The lower estimates are more realistic because much freight would travel by truck even if rail rates had been cut substantially, for rail transit is typically slower than trucking and often results in more damage to shipments.

---

[2]Ann F. Friedlaender, *The Dilemma of Freight Transport Regulation,* The Brookings Institution, Washington, 1969.

[3]For an excellent review, see Theodore E. Keeler, *Railroads, Freight, and Public Policy,* The Brookings Institution, Washington, 1983, pp. 80–96. For a recent study suggesting that earlier work exaggerated the direct costs of railroad rate regulation, see Kenneth D. Boyer, "The Costs of Price Regulation: Lessons from Railroad Deregulation," *Rand Journal of Economics,* 18 (Autumn 1987), pp. 408–416.

[4]Clifford Winston, "The Welfare Effects of ICC Rate Regulation Revisited," *Bell Journal of Economics,* 12 (Spring 1981), pp. 232–244.

2 Losses from maintenance of excess capacity in railroading. This was partly a by-product of federal and state regulation that kept railroads from abandoning routes where costs exceeded revenues. Again, some estimates here are quite high, but the most reasonable projections are that annual savings of between $500 million and $1 billion would have resulted had the ICC allowed railroads to abandon uneconomical lines.[5]

3 Losses from inefficient use of freight cars. The ICC set rates on cars that were used. For example, a Santa Fe Railroad freight car that carried lettuce to the east coast might be used by the Boston and Maine Railroad to ship manufactured goods west; the B&M would simply pay the Santa Fe Railroad a mileage charge plus a per-diem charge for each day it used the car. Typically, these rates were kept below the market-clearing price, forcing railroads that owned many cars to subsidize the operations of those owning few cars. But this system led to periodic shortages of freight cars and inefficient utilization of existing cars (since they could be used for less than their true social cost). The best estimates are that the welfare costs associated with this pricing policy and with other, related rules regarding car utilization range from $1.5 to $1.7 billion annually.[6]

Clearly, these are nontrivial losses. A more encompassing estimate of the costs of ICC regulation of the railroads during the 1960s and 1970s has been provided by Douglas Caves and Laurits Christensen. They noted that Canada's railroads were substantially deregulated in 1967 and compared various measures of output per unit of input for railroads in Canada and the United States in subsequent years. Although the Canadian railroads were at lower productivity levels than U.S. railroads before 1967, their productivity grew very rapidly in the deregulated environment and by 1977 had achieved higher productivity levels than their U.S. counterparts with respect to several measures. Caves and Christensen argue that, had U.S. railroads not been regulated in the mid-1970s, higher productivity would have cut their costs by as much as $6.7 billion annually.[7]

Trucking   Economists criticized the Motor Carrier Act of 1935 the moment it was passed. It seemed clear that price and entry restrictions were unwarranted in this market. Scholars feared that prices would soon rise above competitive levels and result in huge welfare losses. Evidence that these fears were realized is abundant and compelling.

One of the most convincing studies of the effect of regulation on trucking rates was authored by staff economists at the Department of Agriculture. Not all commodities were subject to rate regulation, and in the mid-1950s several

---

[5]Ann F. Friedlaender and Richard H. Spady, *Freight Transport Regulation: Equity, Efficiency, and Competition in the Rail and Trucking Industries*, M.I.T. Press, Cambridge, MA, 1981.

[6]Jason Sumner and Allen Ferguson, *Deregulation and Fleet Efficiency*, Public Interest Economics Center, Washington, 1980.

[7]Douglas W. Caves and Laurits R. Christensen, "The High Cost of Regulating U.S. Railroads," *Regulation*, 5 (January-February 1981), pp. 41–46.

goods—fresh and frozen poultry and frozen fruits and vegetables—were newly exempted from regulation, making an interesting before-and-after study possible. The results: Following deregulation, trucking rates on poultry fell by one-third, while rates on fruits and vegetables fell by almost one-fifth—and service quality actually improved.[8]

That regulated trucking rates were far above costs is confirmed by the observation that the certificates issued by the ICC permitting entry into certain markets were bought and sold for large sums of money. In ordinary circumstances, where expected returns in a particular market are approximately normal, the right to enter would have no value. When entry is restricted, however, and prices are set above costs, higher-than-normal expected returns will be capitalized into the value of whatever asset enables the receipt of such returns. In the case of trucking, the key asset was the ICC-issued *certificates of necessity and convenience*. By 1977, certificates worth about $600 million had been exchanged, while the total value of all certificates outstanding was probably in excess of $3 billion.[9]

According to some estimates, by the 1970s trucking rates exceeded competitive levels by as much as 20 to 25 percent, transferring considerable surplus from consumers to producers. But producers did not capture all the surplus extracted from consumers; they shared some of their gains with their unionized employees. Members of the Teamsters' Union received wages approximately 50 percent higher than they would have in a competitive market.[10] And, of course, these rates produced sizable deadweight surplus losses.

But ICC regulation also produced efficiency losses in other areas. The high rates charged by regulated *common carriers* induced many producers to buy their own trucks and carry their own goods to market (i.e., become *private carriers*) even when this was economically inefficient. Often these private carriers operated well under full capacity. For example, a South Carolina furniture company might ship two truckloads of its goods to New York per week, its trucks returning empty. A New Jersey paint producer might ship two truckloads of its goods to Georgia per week, its trucks also returning empty. The total mileage for these private carriers exceeds 300,000 annually, and trucks are empty for one-half of it. But the ICC prohibited intercorporate private hauling, preventing such firms from getting together and coordinating their shipments. The result: Needless waste of capacity, labor, and fuel.

In addition, the ICC's insistence on setting uniform rates—even where market conditions yielded decidedly nonuniform costs of service—generated considerable waste. One example concerned uniform prime-haul and back-haul

---

[8]James R. Snitzler and Robert J. Byrne, *Interstate Trucking of Fresh and Frozen Poultry under the Agricultural Exemption,* USDA MRR-224 (March 1958); *Interstate Trucking of Frozen Fruits and Vegetables under the Agricultural Exemption,* USDA MRR-316 (March 1959).

[9]John W. Snow and Stephen Sobotka, "Certificate Values," in Paul W. MacAvoy and John W. Snow (eds.), *Regulation of Entry and Pricing in Truck Transportation,* American Enterprise Institute, Washington, 1977, pp. 153–156.

[10]Thomas Gale Moore, "The Beneficiaries of Trucking Regulation," *Journal of Law and Economics,* 21 (October 1978), pp. 327–343.

rates. Consider trucks hauling merchandise from a large, urban market, the *prime haul*, to a small, rural market. Since there is less freight originating in the smaller market, there will be excess capacity and lower costs on back hauls. The ICC refused to permit lower back-haul rates, however. Again, the result was that many trucks carried no freight at all on their return trips, wasting resources. What is more, the ICC's uniform prices generated important distortions in firms' location decisions. Lower back-haul rates would have induced firms to locate in such a way as to take advantage of these favorable rates. Over time, traffic imbalances might have been reduced. The ICC's system produced the opposite incentive, encouraging growth in prime-haul traffic that added to imbalances.

In sum, ICC regulation of motor carrier rates generated enormous inefficiency in this market. By the late 1960s, it was clear that consumers would benefit greatly from deregulation. One study, extrapolating the experience of deregulated Canadian trucking firms, estimated that similar deregulation in the United States would lower trucking rates by almost 7 percent.[11] Another study, based on the observed effects of deregulation in European markets, forecast even greater reductions.[12] Such findings gave impetus to an emerging regulatory reform movement.

Deregulation

The advocates of partial deregulation of railroads and trucking (some shippers' groups, some large railroads, and a few pro-competition academics) faced some formidable political obstacles (the opposition of trucking firms and labor unions in both industries). The first (small) deregulatory action did not come until 1975, when the ICC ruled that rail and trucking rate bureaus could not protest independent rate filings by members. In 1976, momentum began to build: Congress passed the Railroad Revitalization and Regulatory Reform ("4-R") Act, which limited the grounds under which rates could be challenged as "unreasonable," and the ICC effectively deregulated a portion of the trucking industry by widening specified commercial zones around major cities in which truckers escaped ICC jurisdiction. Changes in the composition of the commission, with a few pro-competition appointees taking seats, accelerated the pace of change. Senator Edward Kennedy, Chairman of the Antitrust and Monopoly Subcommittee of the Senate Judiciary Committee, held hearings on rate setting in trucking that received considerable attention. In 1979, President Jimmy Carter proposed deregulating all rail rates over a 5-year period. Later that year, Carter and Kennedy proposed a joint bill to deregulate trucking, and the President appointed three new pro-competition commissioners to the ICC. Politically, the balance had tilted; the advocates of deregulation had carried the day.

---

[11]James Sloss, "Regulation of Motor Freight Transportation: A Quantitative Evaluation of Policy," *Bell Journal of Economics and Management Science,* 1 (Autumn 1970), pp. 334–347.
[12]Thomas Gale Moore, *Trucking Regulation: Lessons from Europe,* American Enterprise Institute, Washington, 1976.

What the newly oriented ICC began, Congress completed, passing a new Motor Carrier Act in June 1980. The act greatly liberalized entry into the trucking industry. Before, a prospective entrant had to prove that (1) there existed an unmet need in the market and (2) no existing carrier wanted to meet that need. Now, the burden of proving that new entry was not in the public interest was on any party that *protested* granting an entrant permission to operate, and the diversion of revenue from existing carriers was no longer (by itself) evidence that entry was undesirable. In addition, the act authorized the ICC to liberalize procedures in many areas, including restrictions on return hauls.

Also in 1980, Congress passed the Staggers Rail Act, which made it far easier for railroads to abandon unprofitable routes. In addition, Staggers gave the railroads new pricing freedom, limiting ICC jurisdiction to those rates where railroads exercise "market dominance." As a result, almost two-thirds of rail rates were effectively deregulated. State regulations that affected the use of caboose, crew composition, and crew size were also loosened at about the same time.

The results of this regulatory reform effort are, according to just about all accounts, quite favorable.[13] Rail rates in many (but not all) markets have fallen. Western railroads took advantage of their new pricing flexibility to cut rates on fresh fruits and vegetables when economic conditions permitted, increasing their carriage of these commodities enormously. Some captive shippers of bulk commodities, e.g., coal and grain, have faced higher rates, however. On net, though, railroads' revenues per ton-mile—a crude measure of overall rates—fell in real, inflation-adjusted terms in the early 1980s, suggesting that most shippers benefited from lower rates. Yet railroads actually improved profitability in the years that followed deregulation, largely by eliminating inefficient operations, trimming payroll costs, and more fully utilizing their facilities.

Regulatory reform in the trucking market has, if anything, yielded bigger dividends. Rates have fallen, service has improved, and complaints from shippers have declined. Entry into the industry soared, and existing firms spread out into many new territories in the months that followed passage of the Motor Carrier Act of 1980. In a survey of 2,200 manufacturers in 1981, nearly two-thirds reported paying lower trucking rates. Surveys by the ICC found that rates charged by regular-route, less-than-truckload carriers typically fell by 10 to 20 percent and often by as much as 40 percent. And surveys of service quality found that rate cuts were not accompanied by poorer service quality—as trucking interests had forecast in debates prior to deregulation. But perhaps the best evidence that deregulation had transformed the trucking industry to a far more competitive industry is the fact that the market for entry certificates soon dried up. Such certificates fetched an average price in excess of $500,000

---

[13]For a detailed summary, see Thomas Gale Moore, "Rail and Trucking Deregulation," in Leonard W. Weiss and Michael W. Klass (eds.), *Regulatory Reform: What Actually Happened*, Little, Brown, Boston, 1986, pp. 14–39.

in 1976–1977. By 1981–1982, almost no sales of certificates were taking place, and the few that were sold went for small change.

It is possible, of course, that the gains in consumer welfare associated with these reforms are destined to be short-lived and that some of the ill effects forecast by critics of rail and trucking deregulation will eventually arrive. We should continue to study the effects of deregulation with care. For now, however, it seems that regulatory reform has eliminated many of the inefficiencies that had resulted from the ICC's earlier handling of these vital industries.

AIRLINE TRANSPORTATION

As we have seen, it is often hard to tell whether regulation is working as it should. Even when scholars provide clear evidence that it is not, it is hard to whip up much interest in regulatory reform because most consumers have little interest in this impenetrable subject and those who will be harmed by reform will strive mightily to convince policymakers that tinkering with the status quo poses grave danger to everyone from Main Street to Wall Street.

Our experience with the airline industry has been a little different, however. By the 1960s and 1970s, the ill effects of airline regulation were obvious and dramatic, making it possible to generate political momentum for reform more readily here than in almost any other industry. Thus, deregulation of the airlines was accomplished more quickly and completely than in either railroading or trucking. Indeed, it actually was a spur to reform in these and other industries. A close examination of the industry should prove fruitful.

Overview

In the 1920s, Congress tried to promote the nascent airline industry by transferring the task of carrying the mail from the U.S. Army to private air carriers. Mail contracts would, it was hoped, provide the carriers with a dependable stream of revenue that they could invest in new equipment in order to expand passenger service. Unfortunately, the ICC (which held the U.S. Post Office's contracting authority and initially oversaw the industry) encouraged airlines to carry mail below their full costs in order to win new routes. As a result, many carriers began experiencing financial difficulties despite the growing demand for air transport. Congress responded with the Civil Aeronautics Act of 1938, creating the Civil Aeronautics Board (CAB).

The CAB was modeled after the ICC. It had broad powers to allocate air routes, set fares, ensure safe operations (although air safety regulation became the domain of the Federal Aviation Administration in 1958), and control many other aspects of airlines' operations. From the outset, it was clear that Congress wanted the CAB to promote the growth of aviation; at its birth, its main job was to administer subsidies to the industry. At the same time, however, the CAB was supposed to keep fares low enough to allow the public access to air travel.

Whether because of Depression-era suspicion about the virtues of unfettered competition or other factors, from its birth the CAB was very protective of the firms in its charge. There were 16 existing airlines at the time (subsequently dubbed *the trunks*), and their route authority was "grandfathered." Henceforth, any airline (whether existing or new) that wished to offer new service in a market had to petition the CAB for authority. For the next 50 years, the CAB gave ironclad protection to the incumbent carriers: It did not allow one new entrant to commence service on a major route! In addition, the board had an unofficial ceiling on the number of carriers it would allow to serve a particular route. Often, it awarded lucrative routes to financially ailing carriers regardless of whether these carriers had submitted the best service proposals. In setting fares, the top concern was airline profitability rather than consumer welfare, although the CAB did deliver cross-subsidies to some consumers. Rates on long-haul service were kept above costs in order to keep fares below costs in some short-haul markets (especially ones in which traffic was light). The CAB was a bit more flexible with respect to entry into small markets. More than a dozen local service carriers, benefiting from CAB subsidies in the years after World War II, established a market niche for themselves and eventually grew into regional carriers. Yet none were allowed to become as large as the trunk carriers.

The industry grew rapidly in the postwar years. Total revenue-passenger miles increased about tenfold between 1950 and 1970, from under 10 billion to nearly 100 billion. Technological improvements improved airline safety and convenience and lowered average fares. Air travel changed from an exotic luxury to a commonplace of modern life.

By the early 1970s, however, there were troubling signs that CAB regulation was not working all that well. Mergers had shrunk the number of major trunk airlines to 10. These carriers provided more than 90 percent of scheduled flights in the United States. Given the CAB's limits on entry and its protective pricing and route allocation policies, these trunks' domestic operations should have been quite profitable. Yet they were not. The CAB's target rate of return for the major airlines was set equal to returns in the manufacturing sector—roughly 10.5 percent in the 1960s and 12 percent in the 1970s. But in only 4 of the 20 years from 1957 to 1976 did the major airlines' average rate of return on stockholders' equity equal that for all manufacturing firms, and those were years in which new-generation aircraft were introduced that substantially lowered carrier costs.

Some airlines complained that higher fares were needed to yield them a "fair return." But there was compelling evidence that fares—at least on some routes—were already higher than they needed to be. The evidence came from the *intra*state market.[14] Like other federal agencies, the CAB lacked authority over transactions within each state. Two states, California and Texas, were

---

[14]Michael E. Levine, "Is Regulation Necessary? California Air Transportation and National Regulatory Policy," *Yale Law Journal,* 74 (July 1965), pp. 1416–1447.

large enough to support flourishing intrastate carriers. In California, these intrastate carriers offered fares that were *less than half* those charged by CAB-certificated lines, and one (Pacific Southwest) grew to become the dominant intrastate carrier by the early 1960s. In Texas, the start-up of an unregulated intrastate carrier was fought for several years in the courts, but by 1971 Southwest Airlines began operations. The new line experimented with several new pricing, scheduling, and service strategies, including peak and off-peak pricing, more frequent out-and-back flights, and "no frills" service. Its fares were generally one-third lower than those of regulated carriers during peak periods and *two-thirds* lower off-peak. Indeed, off-peak fares were so low that Southwest's advertisements claimed it was cheaper to fly than to drive!

What is more, the financial health of these intrastate carriers was excellent. Their rates of return on equity usually exceeded those of the regulated major airlines, often by a considerable margin. This seemed to put the lie to the argument that competition in the industry would—as in the early days of railroading—invariably be "destructive." In fact, the airline industry bore no characteristics of natural monopoly, and there was no real reason to believe that any model of destructive competition applied to it. Entry into the industry is (or would have been, had the CAB allowed it) relatively easy, for the market for new and used airline equipment is quite competitive and it is possible to keep start-up costs down by leasing rather than buying planes. Entry into new regions by existing carriers is easier still. Thus, although demand for air travel can vary greatly over the business cycle, it is generally not true that the industry is so capital-intensive that regulation is needed to forestall "ruinous" price-cutting in periods of downturn. The long history of competitive intrastate service in California appeared to establish that.

So if the CAB was producing neither high profits for carriers nor low fares for consumers, what *was* it doing? That question became the focus for widely publicized hearings convened by Senator Edward Kennedy's Administrative Practices Subcommittee of the Senate Judiciary Committee. Senator Kennedy, ably assisted by Stephen Breyer, a former Harvard law professor, focused a bright spotlight on the CAB's failings.[15] The hearings drummed home the message that CAB policies led to high prices and injury to consumers. Examples from California and Texas were highlighted, with comparisons drawn to similar interstate flights on which fares were much higher, as shown in Table 15.1. All industry and CAB attempts to explain away the differences appeared lame or evasive. During the hearings, President Gerald Ford's staff weighed in with comprehensive proposals that reduced the CAB's authority over prices and routes. The reform process was underway; within a few years, the CAB would be gone.

---

[15]For a most entertaining and enlightening account of these hearings and of the regulatory reform process in general, see Stephen Breyer, *Regulation and Its Reform,* Harvard University Press, Cambridge, MA, 1982, especially pp. 321–339.

TABLE 15.1
INTRASTATE AND INTERSTATE FARE COMPARISONS, 1975.   In the 1970s, regulated
interstate airfares were often twice those on unregulated intrastate routes.

City pair	Distance, miles	Fare, $	Fare per mile, $
Dallas/Houston	239	13.89*	0.058
Las Vegas/Los Angeles	236	28.70	0.122
Los Angeles/San Francisco	338	18.75	0.055
Chicago/Minneapolis	339	38.89	0.115
Los Angeles/Sacramento	373	20.47	0.055
Boston/Washington, DC	399	41.67	0.104
San Francisco/San Diego	456	26.21	0.058
Detroit/Philadelphia	454	45.37	0.100

*Off-peak price.
Source: Subcommittee on Administrative Practice and Procedures, U.S. Senate Judiciary Committee, *Civil Aeronautics Board Practices and Procedures*, 1975, p. 41.

Effects of Regulation

It is doubtful that the classic kind of economic regulation administered by the CAB was ever appropriate in the airline industry, where competition was quite feasible. Congress's obvious desire to promote the development of the industry (even assuming this desire was in the public interest) could certainly have been satisfied via subsidies alone. In any case, it turned out that the authority Congress gave the CAB over entry and prices was not enough to truly control the industry. Lacking authority over other elements of air transportation (e.g., schedules, equipment, in-flight services), the CAB was ultimately powerless to keep airlines from competing in *nonprice dimensions*. The result was that many of the CAB's goals were unattainable, and many of its dictates simply resulted in resource waste and diminished consumer welfare.

To see why, consider a hypothetical air route between two cities served by carriers A and B. Suppose, given the current level of traffic, the average cost per passenger on this route for both A and B equals $50. Suppose also the CAB—whether to stimulate growth of A and B or to provide them with sufficient revenues to cover losses on other, less lucrative routes—sets a fare of $75 on this route, so that each passenger now generates $25 in profit. Both A and B will therefore knock themselves out to win new passengers on this route. They would, absent CAB regulation, probably offer cut-rate fares to win more business. But the CAB won't allow this kind of competition. So the carriers will simply compete in other dimensions. There are lots of possibilities—so many, in fact, that the CAB couldn't have controlled them all even if it had wanted to. Carrier A starts off by offering wider seats, better meals and snacks, and free movies, and B counters with newer planes, free champagne, and more appealing flight attendants. On and on it goes. Each line advertises more, schedules more frequent departures, buys speedier reservation systems, and hires more and better staff to win those extra passengers. Naturally, it all gets pretty expensive after a while. In fact, this nonprice competition will stop only when costs have climbed to equality with CAB-specified fares.

Of course, the CAB doesn't have to leave fares alone. In fact, the CAB often responded favorably to carriers' pleas for cost-justified fare hikes. In practice, then, CAB rate setting was a bit like a dog chasing its tail: High rates begot nonprice competition that raised costs, which eventually led to higher rates, which produced more nonprice competition, and so on. Each time rates rose, consumers were pushed farther backward along the demand curve for air travel. Thus, industry load factors (the occupied fraction of available seats) fell consistently through the 1950s and 1960s. For example, in 1952, the major trunks' average load factor was 68 percent. By 1969, it was down to 50 percent, and in 1971 load factors on transcontinental flights averaged 39 percent. Meanwhile, load factors on the intrastate lines commonly exceeded 70 percent.

What were the welfare costs of all this? Some researchers have attempted to calculate how much fares would have been reduced absent CAB regulation, i.e., how much lower fares might have been had the major trunk airlines behaved as the unregulated carriers in California and Texas. In one study, Ted Keeler found a wide variance in the extent to which regulated fares in 1968 exceeded those that might have prevailed under competition, from as little as 20 percent on short-haul routes to 95 percent on long-haul routes.[16] These estimates are reasonably consistent with other studies of the day. Unfortunately, translating such figures to precise estimates of surplus lost is impossible. It is clear that higher-than-competitive fares inflicted large deadweight losses on society and that airlines' costs of service were excessive in the regulated era. But some of the airlines' extra costs produced services valued by consumers, reducing net surplus losses a bit. While it seems fair to say that the welfare costs of CAB regulation were several billion dollars per year, it is hard to pin down these losses. Fortunately, however, the complete deregulation of the industry in the 1980s has given scholars ample opportunity to compare the industry before and after regulation.

Deregulation

Following the Kennedy hearings, a chastened CAB moved to open entry into the industry and to allow existing carriers to compete more freely. The pace of reform was hastened when Alfred E. Kahn, an eminent economist committed to bringing greater competition to the industry, was appointed to chair the CAB in 1977. In 1978, Congress passed the Airline Deregulation Act, which formalized the CAB's policy of freer entry and exit and gave carriers greater pricing flexibility. Most important, the act specified that CAB's control of fares

---

[16]Theodore E. Keeler, "Airline Regulation and Market Performance," *Bell Journal of Economics and Management Science,* 3 (Autumn 1972), pp. 399–424.

and routes would end entirely in 1983 and that the agency would be abolished by 1985. On the last day of 1984, the CAB officially ceased to exist.

Scholars and policymakers observed the results of deregulation with great interest. As with all empirical work, real-world complications made precise measurement and attribution of effects difficult. Immediately after deregulation, e.g., the energy crisis pushed fuel prices up sharply, leading to fare hikes instead of cuts. In general, however, researchers have given deregulation high marks.[17] Various authors have noted several direct effects:

1 Easier entry—and exit. Several regional carriers that had been prevented from expanding into major routes immediately did so, and several new lines (some offering "budget" fares, others offering premium service at higher fares) sprouted. Some older, less efficient lines that had saddled themselves with high labor costs went belly-up, as did some of the new entrants that had tried to expand too far too fast.

2 Price competition. Average fares on major routes that linked large cities fell from 9 to 15 percent over 1976 to 1983. However, fares in smaller markets sometimes climbed steeply. (Thus, deregulation eliminated the cross-subsidies that had prevailed under the CAB.) On net, average fares fell about 9 percent over this period.[18] Once competition focused on price, average service quality declined, with fewer freebies on flights, more crowded planes, and more lost luggage. But it's important to stress that a decline in service quality was probably *efficient*. In the regulated era, nonprice competition had likely pushed quality well beyond the level where marginal value equaled its marginal cost.

3 Improved factor utilization. Airlines began to scramble to find ways to deploy their capital and labor more efficiently. They experimented with new fare structures to push load factors up, used new routing procedures (e.g., *hub-and-spoke networks*), and squeezed wage and work-rule concessions from their employees to reduce operating costs and boost productivity. Of course, this has not been a blessing to all. Some passengers today (especially those on expense accounts) long for the days of empty planes and luxurious in-flight services. And some unionized airline employees found that a more competitive industry was also a less remunerative one in which to work—although many more people are now employed in the industry.

Steven Morrison and Clifford Winston have totaled the benefits and costs of deregulation to calculate its net welfare impact. They estimate that under deregulation, travelers have saved in excess of $6 billion annually in lower fares and that airlines' annual profits are $2.5 billion higher than they would have been under regulation.[19] A Federal Trade Commission study reached

[17]See Elizabeth E. Bailey, David R. Graham, and Daniel P. Kaplan, *Deregulating the Airlines*, M.I.T. Press, Cambridge, MA, 1985; Alfred E. Kahn, "Surprises of Airline Deregulation," *American Economic Review*, 78 (May 1988), pp. 316–321.

[18]Thomas Gale Moore, "U.S. Airline Deregulation," *Journal of Law and Economics*, 29 (April 1986), pp. 1–28.

[19]Steven A. Morrison and Clifford Winston, *The Economic Effects of Airline Deregulation*, The Brookings Institution, Washington, 1986.

similar conclusions, suggesting that the total social savings after a decade of deregulation of air transport exceeded $100 billion.[20]

Some argue, however, that these gains are illusory or temporary. They suggest that the industry will eventually be monopolized or that the largest airlines will successfully collude and send fares skyward. They invoke concerns about diminished safety in an environment where competition is *too* fierce (recall Vignette 2.3). At this writing, however, it seems unlikely that calls for reregulation of the industry will go very far, although heightened antitrust scrutiny of several airlines' marketing and scheduling practices has already begun.

VIGNETTE 15.1   Are Airline Hubs Anticompetitive?

In the first decade after deregulation, over 200 new airlines were organized. Less than one-third of these survived, however; the others wound up in bankruptcy court or were acquired by other, larger carriers. Indeed, an airline merger wave in the late 1980s produced an industry that is more concentrated today than in the days when the CAB barred entry: The eight-firm industry concentration ratio for the entire United States is now 94.

Concentration is even greater in cities where one line has established a hub through which its connecting flights (spokes) to other cities are channeled. In the view of some, such as Senator John Danforth, a line's hub city can become a fortress that other carriers cannot enter, leaving consumers captives of the dominant line.[21] Trans World Airlines, e.g., runs so many flights through its St. Louis hub that it has locked up (via long-term leases) 52 of the 76 gates at the airport there and controls 83 percent of the St. Louis seat capacity. This, in the view of Senator Danforth, is a significant barrier to entry and challenges the presumption that the airline industry is tolerably contestable (refer once again to the discussion of contestability in Chapter 2, especially Vignette 2.4).

Why do airlines use hub-and-spoke routing? It is simply the most cost-effective way to produce connections to a wide array of cities. Consider the following example, illustrated in Figure 15.1*a* and *b.* A carrier wishes to link five east coast cities with five west coast cities. There are two ways to offer travelers in each city daily round-trip flights to any of the five cities on the opposite coast. The first, shown in panel *a,* is via direct flights between all pairs of eastern and western cities. The line would originate five daily flights from Boston (to Seattle, Portland, San Francisco, Los Angeles, and San Diego), five from New York, and so on, for a total of 50 flights per day. Clearly, this will require a lot of equipment and personnel—and, as panel *a* illustrates, lead to rather crowded airways. The alternative is to create a hub in some midwestern city, say, St. Louis. Then a single flight from each coastal city to the hub can effectively connect travelers to all other cities, as shown in panel *b.* This cuts the number of flights needed to provide the desired linkups to 20 per day (and adds another city—the hub—to the carrier's list of cities served). This will save a lot of equipment and personnel, although it will also lengthen each passenger trip (by 1

[20]J. D. Ogur, C. L. Wagner, and M. G. Vita, *The Deregulated Airline Industry: A Review of the Evidence,* Federal Trade Commission, Washington, January 1988.

[21]John C. Danforth, "Endangered Airline Competition," *Journal of Commerce,* 379 (March 9, 1989), p. 8A.

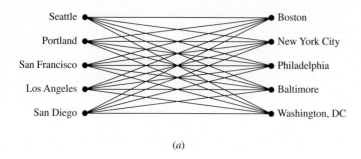

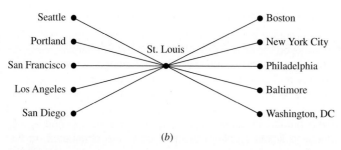

FIGURE 15.1
TWO HYPOTHETICAL AIRLINE ROUTE MAPS. Hub-and-spoke systems (panel *b*) enable carriers to provide linkups between a given number of cities with far less equipment.

hour or so) as connections are made at the hub. For most purposes, however, this will be a favorable trade-off. In the words of transportation expert Michael Messner,

As the number of spokes in a hub and spoke network grows, service increases at a geometric rate while costs increase arithmetically. The major hubs in the U.S. provide connecting transportation service to 2,500 origin-destination pairs in an extremely cost-effective manner. American Airlines offers transportation to 3,074 city pair combinations through its Dallas/Fort Worth hub with just 170 dedicated aircraft.[22]

In Messner's view, any competitive evils associated with "fortress hubs" are more than offset by these efficiencies and by the fact that hub-and-spoke routing enables small- and medium-sized carriers to rival the service of much larger firms, enhancing competition in the industry.

AGRICULTURE

In principle, agricultural markets have most of the key characteristics of the models of perfect competition found in introductory economics textbooks. In

[22]Michael G. Messner, "Hubs Aid Airline Efficiency," *Journal of Commerce*, 379 (March 15, 1989), p. 14A.

just about all agricultural markets there are many sellers, most quite small, producing homogeneous products. Students may be puzzled, therefore, to find that these markets are among the most heavily regulated in the U.S. economy. If much economic regulation aims to duplicate the results of perfect competition where markets are not competitively structured, what are regulators doing here? In what follows, we suggest some answers to this multifaceted question.

Overview

Federal intervention in agricultural markets goes all the way back to 1789, when tariffs were specified on sugar. By ensuring that domestic sugar prices would exceed those on world markets, these tariffs provided an implicit subsidy to domestic sugar producers. While there was some agitation for explicit federal subsidies for many other crops in the late 1800s, political pressure diminished in the early 1900s as farm prices soared, especially during World War I. When the war's close brought price declines, however, there were renewed calls for government assistance to agriculture. Proponents of support programs offered many reasons why farming merits special attention, among them that (1) national economic prosperity depends on farm prosperity; (2) farmers are "squeezed" by monopolistic farm equipment sellers and monopsonistic commodity buyers; (3) the national defense requires a large agricultural sector; (4) most farms are too small to conduct or finance vital research activity; (5) farm incomes are low relative to nonfarm incomes and remain so because farm workers refuse to abandon their cherished way of life in the face of declining farm prices; (6) agricultural markets are inherently unstable, and price fluctuations and wasteful economic dislocations can be easily and cheaply avoided with appropriate federal intervention.

By the late 1920s, Congress was committed to some sort of farm support program. The legislation that emerged, signed in 1929 by President Herbert Hoover, was called the Agricultural Marketing Act. The act created the Federal Farm Board (an eight-member board whose original appointees included tobacco, grain, dairy, citrus, cotton, and fruit producers plus, as chair, the president of the International Harvester Company, the nation's largest producer of farm equipment) and provided it with a fund of $500 million to make subsidized loans to farm cooperatives and to set up *stabilization corporations* to "prevent and control surpluses." Within a few months, the Great Depression of the 1930s began. Farm prices began to fall sharply, but the Federal Farm Board strove mightily to prop up farm incomes. It made loans to cooperatives at very favorable rates, with farm output as collateral. Defaults were common. By mid-1931, the Federal Farm Board had accumulated over 230 million bushels of wheat—about one-quarter of annual production—and had spent about one-third of its entire fund trying to stabilize prices on this one crop. It spent another one-third of its fund in the cotton, butter, grape, and wool markets before it threw in the towel, having slowed, but not stopped, a

57 percent decline in farm prices in the early years of the Depression. Bankruptcies and foreclosures in the farm belt were rampant; it seemed clear something more needed to be done.

"Increasing agricultural purchasing power," i.e., raising farm prices, was an explicit goal of the Agricultural Adjustment Act signed into law by newly elected President Franklin Delano Roosevelt in 1933. The act introduced the concept of *parity prices*. The basic idea was that price supports and output controls should be used to raise prices to parity with those in a base period, which the act specified as the 5 years from August 1909 to July 1914. Not coincidentally, that period has sometimes been referred to as the *golden age* of farming in the United States. Although many crops had already been planted by the time the bureaucracy required to administer the act was in place, the Agricultural Adjustment Administration moved quickly to curtail supplies, offering cash payments to farmers who would plow under their growing crops or slaughter young pigs and pregnant sows. Since many people were going hungry at the time, such policies were extremely unpopular. In the following year, less visible supply reduction programs were implemented: Rental payments were made to farmers who agreed to take acreage out of production, and guaranteed prices were fixed for crops grown on the acres for which farmers had *allotments. Price supports*[23] and production controls have been a central feature of many U.S. agricultural markets ever since.

Support prices were only modestly above free-market levels at first. With global food supplies reduced during and immediately after World War II, there was minimal accumulation of surpluses. In the late 1940s and 1950s, however, government stockpiles of surplus foodstuffs began to grow alarmingly. Setting above-market prices gave farmers strong incentives to expand output by enhancing yields per cultivated acre, and myriad technological advances (hybrid seeds, chemical fertilizers, mechanization) gave them the means to do it. Although "flexible" (i.e., lower) support prices were introduced and other demand and supply management policies implemented, surplus accumulation slowed but did not stop. By 1961, stockpiles were at record levels, and the government spent about $1 billion just to *store* the surplus commodities it had to purchase at supported prices.

The 1960s saw a major change in the system of payments to producers of some crops. The government began to move from fixing prices on certain farm products to making transfer payments to farmers. Direct payments were made to farmers who retired acreage from cultivation and complied with several

---

[23]Technically, most price supports take the form of "nonrecourse loans," in which the government sets a price on a particular commodity and then lends farmers money by using crops valued at this price as collateral. For example, the price of wheat may be set at $2 per bushel; a farmer can then use 10,000 bushels of wheat as collateral for a $20,000 loan. If the price of wheat turns out to be $2.50 per bushel, the farmer can sell the wheat on the open market at this price, pay back the loan, and keep the difference as profit. If, however, the market price turns out to be $1.50 per bushel, the farmer can default on the loan and turn over 10,000 bushels of wheat to the government, effectively "selling" it to Uncle Sam at the previously set support price.

additional conditions. *Target prices* were set on certain crops, and payments were made to producers to bridge any gap between target and market prices. These reforms had some favorable effects for consumers. For example, under the target price system, consumers paid less for food and U.S. farm products became more competitive in world markets. There were some political costs: Once the government began writing some fairly sizable checks to farmers—many of whom were quite wealthy—the programs were scrutinized more closely. In 1974, a ceiling of $20,000 (later raised to $50,000) was placed on the direct payments. In general, though, the 1970s were quite prosperous years for farmers. Domestic demand for foodstuffs was stimulated by rapid expansion of the Food Stamp program. Poor weather in many areas of the globe and lagging agricultural production in Communist-bloc countries stimulated U.S. exports of farm output. Farm incomes rose, and prices of agricultural land boomed.

In the early 1980s, however, this situation reversed itself. Export demand fell significantly, a result of improved weather patterns and expanded output in industrialized countries (some of which subsidized agricultural production even more heavily than the United States) and less developed countries alike. In addition, an unanticipated decline in inflation rates had contributed to a farm debt crisis. Buoyed by the expansion of the 1970s, many farmers had borrowed large sums (at federally subsidized interest rates) to bring new land under cultivation. But tight-money macroeconomic policies that commenced in 1980 wrung most inflation from the economy and precipitated a recession, leaving farmers in dire financial straits. Their loans carried interest rates that, in the inflationary late 1970s, looked reasonable. It makes sense, e.g., to pay 12 percent interest on money borrowed to buy land that may appreciate by 20 percent or more per year (as farmland had from 1975 to 1980); after repaying the loan, the farmer is left with a tidy profit. Once the recession hit, however, the price of farmland fell by an average of 6 percent a year from 1980 to 1985. Many farmers could not repay their loans. (Their land was collateral; when the value of the collateral fell below a certain percentage of the loans' balances, the banks called the loans and forced the farmers to settle.) The value of farm loan foreclosures by life insurance companies, which had been less than $30 million in 1980, climbed to over $800 million by 1986. It was the hardest period "down on the farm" since the Depression era.

Demands for relief took many forms. Several Hollywood movies and considerable TV news exposure dramatized the plight of the family farm and made it seem that every one was on the brink of failure. The response was a dramatic expansion of federal outlays for farm support programs. In 1983, the Payment-in-Kind (PIK) program began. Under PIK, growers of wheat, corn, cotton, and rice were paid *not* to plant these crops. To reduce federal outlays, the farmers' payments were not in cash but in kind, i.e., taken from the government's bulging stockpiles of surplus commodities. The $50,000 ceiling on payments was waived. Price supports on milk were so far above free-market levels that by 1983 the government was buying nearly one-eighth of total domestic production, at an annual cost that commonly exceeded $2 billion. Generous price supports on other commodities pushed federal outlays for "farm income stabilization" way up, from $7.4 billion in 1980 to $23.8 billion by 1985.

Even these increases were not sufficient to end financial distress in the farm sector; a resurgence of rural populism led to calls for more federal aid. But tax cuts and the recession of the early 1980s had produced mammoth federal budget deficits, and there was also sentiment to trim farm programs. Congress grappled with numerous proposals throughout 1985, finally passing the Food Security Act in December of that year. As public choice theory predicts, no group got all it wanted in the act. There were some market-oriented reforms (e.g., phased-in reductions in milk prices and in some target prices) and some innovations (e.g., limits on cultivation of new lands and swamp drainage), but many programs emerged largely unchanged. One controversial feature was the Dairy Termination Program, which paid over $1.8 billion to dairy farmers who "retired" from the business and slaughtered their herds (which, of course, made ranchers unhappy, for the surge in the supply of beef lowered prices in their market). Federal income supplements to farmers, which peaked in 1986 at $29.6 billion (over $10,000 for every child, woman, or man living or working on a farm), have fallen beneath $20 billion per year since. Still, this can represent one-quarter or more of the annual net income of farmers. Clearly, the well-being of farmers now is linked as much—or perhaps more— to what happens in the halls of Congress and the U.S. Department of Agriculture as to the weather or other natural factors.

Effects of Regulation

We should reiterate that the outlays discussed above are *transfers* from taxpayers to farm owners, others in the agricultural sector, and the bureaucrats who administer the programs. Price supports also transfer additional income from consumers to farmers. Pure transfers are not objectionable by themselves— assuming they satisfy certain fairness criteria—because losses to some are fully offset by gains to others. The central problem with many agricultural programs is that they transfer income very inefficiently, promoting considerable misallocation of resources and deadweight loss of social surplus.

Figure 15.2, which shows demand D and supply S in a hypothetical agricultural market, illustrates how just one type of income support program—the *target price system*—affects net welfare. When the government guarantees farmers a target price equal to P_t, they produce Q_s. The price that will clear the market of this amount of output is P_c. Total farm income is P_t times Q_s, of which P_c times Q_s comes from consumers and $(P_t - P_c)$ times Q_s comes from taxpayers. One problem with this system is that all the surplus output beyond Q_e is worth less to consumers than it actually costs to produce. The difference between the total cost of producing this additional output and its total value to society, shown as the shaded area in Figure 15.2, is one measure of the net social losses of this kind of program. Resources are misallocated because there

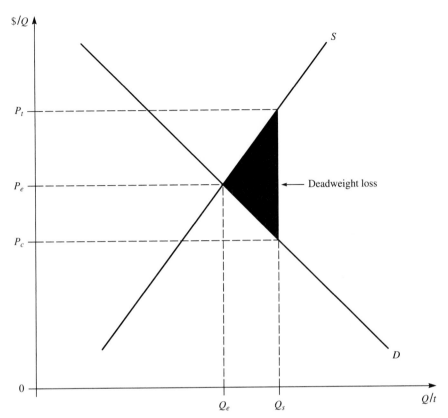

FIGURE 15.2
WELFARE EFFECTS OF A TARGET PRICE SYSTEM. When the government sets a target price
P_t, farmers produce Q_s. At this rate of output, the price to consumers will be P_c, but taxpayers will
pay $(P_t - P_c)Q_s$ to farmers, and surplus equal to the shaded area is wasted.

is excessive production and consumption in this market; i.e., resources that are
more highly valued in other uses are wastefully expended here.

Other farm income programs impose additional types of welfare losses.
Simple price supports, e.g., impose deadweight surplus losses of the kind discussed above plus costs associated with storing surplus output. When acreage
controls are used to try to restrict output, farmers devote extra resources
(labor, machinery, chemical fertilizers) to boosting yields on the land they are
allowed to cultivate. And any program that creates rents for some group
invites expenditures on unproductive activities (e.g., lobbying) that dissipate
some of or all these rents. In sum, all programs that move farm prices significantly from levels that would have prevailed in unregulated markets have net
social costs, i.e., produce smaller benefits for farmers than they cost society at
large.

Over time, the net social costs of all the various farm income support policies have varied widely, from trivial levels to the billions of dollars per year. In

TABLE 15.2
ANNUAL NET LOSSES FROM INCOME SUPPORT PROGRAMS (INCLUDING TRADE
RESTRICTIONS) UNDER THE 1985 FOOD SECURITY ACT.   Even if optimistic measures
are used, the annual social loss from farm programs for just eight basic crops exceeds
$4 billion.

Commodity	[Billions of dollars]			
	Consumer loss	Taxpayer cost[1]	Producer gain	Net loss
Corn	0.5–1.1	10.5	10.4–10.9	0.6–0.7
Sugar I[3]	1.8–2.5	0	1.5–1.7	0.3–0.7
Sugar II[3]	1.1–1.8	0	1.0–1.4	0.1–0.4
Milk	1.5–3.1	1.0	1.5–2.4	1.1–1.7
Cotton	—[2]	2.1	1.2–1.6	0.5–0.9
Wheat	0.1–0.3	4.7	3.3–3.6	1.4–1.5
Rice	0.02–0.06	1.1	0.8–1.1	0.06–0.32
Peanuts	0.2–0.4	0	0.15–0.40	0.0–0.05
Tobacco	0.4–0.7	0.1	0.1–0.2	0.4–0.6

[1]Includes CCC expenses after cost recovery.
[2]Less than $50 million.
[3]Case I assumes U.S. policies do not affect world sugar prices. Case II takes into account the fact that U.S.
policies reduce world sugar prices. The value of sugar import restrictions to those exporters who have access to
the U.S. market (that is, value of quota rents) is $250 million.
   Note: All figures reflect Gramm-Rudman-Hollings.
   Source: Compiled by the Council of Economic Advisers from various sources.

1987, the President's Council of Economic Advisors tried to estimate the annual net social costs of income support programs under the 1985 Food Security
Act for eight major agricultural commodities.[24] Their figures are reproduced
as Table 15.2. Clearly, program costs vary widely. Net losses in the peanut
market are quite low, while those in the milk and wheat markets likely exceed
$1 billion per year. Even summing the low-end estimates for these products,
however, puts the annual net cost over $4 billion per year. When we add the
welfare costs of other federal programs or of federally sanctioned cartel
arrangements in domestic agriculture, the projected efficiency losses mount
still higher.

There are two reasons that such efficiency losses may be justified. One possibility is that stabilizing this market requires intervention of the sort we have
discussed, that these losses are an inevitable by-product of this intervention,
and that the welfare gains from stabilization far exceed these losses. There are
reasons to be suspicious about this rationale, however. First, we don't really
know if there are any nongovernment alternatives (e.g., private insurance) to
this kind of intervention, for the intervention is so massive that there has been
little room for such alternatives to evolve. Second, it is not clear that agricul-

[24]*Economic Report of the President, 1987,* Government Printing Office, Washington, January 1987,
pp. 147–178.

tural markets really require special stabilization efforts. Several lesser commodity markets have escaped regulation without apparent ill effect. Finally, it
is far from clear that stabilization efforts alone require such massive subsidies—or any subsidies at all, for that matter.

This brings us to the second rationale for intervention: equity considerations. It may be that farmers are so poor relative to the rest of the population
that price supports, acreage controls, and other ways of delivering subsidies to
them are justified as necessary (although costly) ways of enhancing vertical
equity. But there are reasons for suspicion about this rationale as well. It is certainly true that farm laborers' earnings lag behind those of workers in some
other sectors: Average annual wages in farming are typically more than 40
percent below the national average. Retail workers' salaries, however, are 35
percent below the national average, and no similar programs are aimed at
them—indeed, they pay some of the costs of agricultural subsidies in the form
of higher food prices.

In any case, it is not clear that farm income support policies affect *laborers'*
incomes much; indeed, it is not clear that farm subsidies raise returns to current farm *owners* very much. This is because future anticipated subsidies will
be *capitalized* into the value of whatever fixed assets are required to qualify for
the subsidies. In agriculture, this means that the price of land (or, more precisely, land on which appropriate acreage allotments are held) will rise to capture any subsidies associated with its use. Suppose, e.g., that subsidies on
tobacco add $50 to a tobacco farmer's expected annual profits per acre of
tobacco cultivated. If the subsidies are expected to last indefinitely and if the
interest rate is, say, 10 percent, then these subsidies simply make the farmer's
land worth an extra $500 per acre.[25] The farmer can sell, retire on the capital
gain, and leave it to the next owner to earn an approximately normal rate of
return in tobacco farming. In short, those who own farmland at the time subsidies are put in place are enriched; subsequent owners simply earn competitive
returns on the land forever after (unless there are unanticipated increases or
decreases in the subsidies).

Finally, it is evident that income support payments are often distributed in
ways that do not serve the goal of equity enhancement. As Figure 15.3 shows,
the largest farms (those with annual sales over $500,000) get payments that
average $40,000 per year; the smallest farms often get trivial direct payments.
Rice producers, e.g., received $814 million in direct payments in 1986, and 61
percent of that total went to payees who received checks in excess of $50,000.
One beneficiary was the crown prince of Liechtenstein, a partner on a Texas
rice farm that received a subsidy of $2 million. Over $1.5 billion was paid to
cotton producers in 1986, and 55 percent of that total went to payees receiving
$50,000 or more; one California farmer received a check for $12 million.[26]

---

[25]Recall that the present value of a perpetuity equals the annual payment divided by the relevant interest rate. Here $50/0.10 = 500; this is the amount someone would pay for an asset that
yields $50 per year indefinitely.

[26]*Economic Report of the President, 1987*, pp. 156–157.

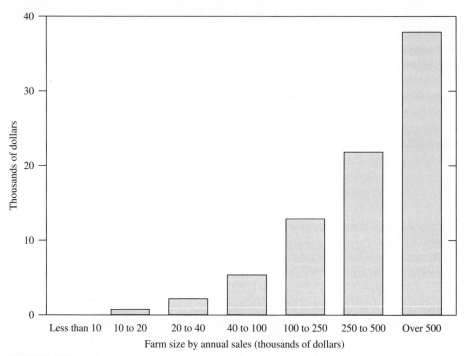

FIGURE 15.3
AVERAGE DIRECT GOVERNMENT PAYMENTS PER FARM, BY SALES CLASS, 1985. Farm income support programs are not limited to small farms; indeed, the largest payments go to the largest farms.

Prospects for Reform

If public choice theory does not entirely explain why farm programs exist, it certainly helps explain why these programs have taken the form they have. Public choice analysis also suggests that these programs are likely to be very hard to change in substantive ways, much less eliminate. Agricultural producers form a compact and cohesive interest group—relative to consumers and taxpayers at least—and are very well organized politically. There is every reason to suspect they will succeed in keeping government support flowing to them indefinitely.

Perhaps the most promising approach to reform, therefore, aims not to eliminate subsidies but to ensure that they are directed to those most in need. The key to this approach, called *decoupling,* is to break the linkage between subsidies and production. Basing subsidies on criteria other than output and avoiding interference with market prices will stop the transmission of false signals to producers and will reduce resource misallocation. Targeting aid on the basis of need will end the regressive redistributions (from relatively poor eaters to wealthy producers) that occasionally occur under the current system.

Another approach is to wean farmers off federal money by stimulating export demand for their products. In effect, this keeps prices at or near current support levels by substituting foreign demand for government purchases. The obstacle here is that many foreign governments (especially Japan and the European Economic Community) subsidize and protect their farmers every bit as generously as the United States, and lowering tariff barriers to these markets will require some complicated diplomatic wheeling and dealing.

In sum, there is little reason for optimism that major reform of federal farm policy is around the corner. As the experience with airline deregulation showed, however, the right mix of circumstances and political actors *can* turn things around if given sufficient time.

VIGNETTE 15.2   Sweet Deal or Bitter Harvest?

In 1985, when Congress supported the price of domestic sugar at $0.215 per pound, sugar was selling on world markets for about $0.04 per pound. Setting prices so high above market levels had predictable effects. Considerable wealth was transferred from consumers to producers ($3 billion a year by some estimates, $930 million by more conservative estimates), and there was a large deadweight surplus loss and misallocation of resources. So high were sugar prices that it became profitable to use corn syrup as a sweetener in many products, and acreage devoted to sugar beet cultivation soared (by 26 percent from 1982 to 1988).

To keep domestic prices high while minimizing federal outlays for the program, the government has sharply cut sugar import quotas. This has taken a huge toll on the impoverished sugar-producing nations of the Caribbean and elsewhere. Some estimate that 400,000 jobs have been lost in these countries since 1983. Ironically, in 1983 the United States had begun a program, dubbed the *Caribbean Basin Initiative,* to alleviate poverty (and thereby enhance political stability) in Caribbean and Latin American nations by promoting trade with the United States. In the wake of the sugar program, however, imports from these nations fell 63 percent.[27]

Domestically, the program has strained relations in previously harmonious farming communities. With sugar prices so high, sugar beets often bring growers 4 times more per acre than wheat and corn. Thus, beet producers are outbidding other farmers for land, driving up rental prices, and crowding less fortunate farmers off the land. Some farmers have formed a group, called *Fair Farm Policy,* to protest the inequities of sugar subsidies. In many small towns, tensions run high between the well-heeled beet growers and growers of other crops; childhood friends shun each other, families refuse to sit near each other in church, and farm women no longer get together for weekly coffee klatches.[28]

But given the distribution of costs and benefits of the program, no significant changes are likely. Even using high-end estimates, the supports cost each consumer about $12 per year. However, there are relatively few beneficiaries of the subsidies, and each has a very large stake in the program, which increases each grower's annual profits by an average of $100,000 to $200,000. With the increased demand for substitute sweeteners such as corn syrup, growers of corn also benefit

---

[27]Paul Magnusson, "U.S. Consumers, and the Caribbean, Are Getting a Sour Deal on Sugar," *Business Week,* 3104 (May 8, 1989), p. 41.

[28]Bruce Ingersoll, "Small Minnesota Town Is Divided by Rancor over Sugar Policies," *Wall Street Journal,* June 26, 1990, pp. A1, A12.

from the program. We shouldn't be surprised, then, that consumers aren't organized on this arcane issue, while the farm lobby bestows large sums on key legislators.

And, of course, foreign sugar workers—no matter how destitute—don't weigh into the political calculations of U.S. elected officials at all. As Senator Bennett Johnston of Louisiana (the nation's second-largest sugar producing state) has said, "I see reform as a job-for-job loss to Latin America. You say I have a vested interest? You're damn right I do." And those who presumably must look at issues in a broader perspective have, so far, declined to do so. The reason? Logrolling. As one aide to republican President George Bush has said, "Fact is, we need the support of Democrats like Bennett, which makes sugar the lowest of low priorities."[29]

SAVINGS INSTITUTIONS

Banks and related financial intermediaries may be the most heavily regulated institutions in the United States. Several federal agencies and at least one agency in each state oversee the industry's many subsectors. Describing the origins and impacts of the various layers of regulation in this industry probably merits book-length treatment. Our goal here is far more modest. We want to see how regulation and deregulation have affected behavior and performance among the firms in this industry called *savings* or *thrift institutions*: savings and loan associations (S&Ls), mutual savings banks, and credit unions. The principal source of these institutions' funds is the savings of the public. The principal destination of their funds is mortgage loans for housing or personal loans for other durable goods such as automobiles. In the mid-1980s, the confluence of several factors—of which partial deregulation is commonly named as the most important—created a crisis in this industry. A significant fraction of S&Ls became insolvent. Since their deposit liabilities were federally insured, Uncle Sam was left holding a very large bag indeed. In 1989, the present value of the future cost of the S&L bailout was put at $167 billion—about $700 for each person in the United States. Clearly, it's worth spending some time figuring out how this regulatory catastrophe happened—and whether it can happen again.

Overview

Modern U.S. savings institutions are descendants of what were called *building and loan associations*, modeled after British *building societies*. From their origins in the 1830s, these associations specialized in providing funds for purchases of housing. Indeed, the earliest of these associations raised capital by levying dues on their members, made mortgage loans only to members, and disbanded when all the initial members' housing demands had been met. Eventually, though, these associations evolved into true financial intermediaries, encouraging saving by offering interest payments on various types of depository accounts in order to make mortgage or home improvement loans to borrowers.

---

[29]Michael Kramer, "The Free-Trade Hypocrisy," *Time*, 135 (April 16, 1990), p. 24..

Significant federal regulation of these institutions did not come until the early 1930s. Thousands of thrifts failed in the first years of the Great Depression, and a crisis of confidence spread rapidly. As customers withdrew their deposits, virtually all banking institutions—no matter how stable or carefully managed—eventually experienced difficulties. Regulation of the industry, it was argued, could produce great welfare gains by ensuring that (1) financial intermediaries behaved in accordance with sound business principles and (2) the insolvency of any individual institution did not sow seeds of financial panic, destabilizing financial markets and causing problems for other institutions. To ease cash flow problems among savings institutions, Congress created the Federal Home Loan Bank Board (FHLBB) in 1932 and granted it extensive power to charter and regulate thrifts in 1933. In 1934, Congress expanded these regulatory powers and created (as part of FHLBB) the Federal Savings and Loan Insurance Corporation (FSLIC) to insure deposits at both federally and state-chartered institutions. *Deposit insurance* was an especially important innovation. It greatly comforted depositors, for now money placed in an insured institution would be recoverable even in the event of the institution's insolvency. But as it made depositors less interested in monitoring the financial condition of their S&Ls, it shifted virtually all responsibility for regulatory oversight of the activities of these institutions to regulators. This would turn out to be very important indeed.

Nevertheless, all was quiet for the next three decades or so. Savings institutions were expected to "borrow short" (i.e., acquire deposits from savers who could withdraw them on short notice) to "lend long" (make long-term, fixed-interest-rate mortgage loans), and that is what they did. As long as the structure of interest rates remained stable, with short-term rates paid to depositors below the long-term rates on mortgage loans, the industry prospered. In the mid-1960s, however, inflation pushed interest rates up, putting thrifts in a financial squeeze. Much of their income came from long-term mortgage loans, made years earlier, carrying fixed interest rates below the rates they were now paying depositors. Profits took a beating.

In 1966, Congress obligingly placed ceilings on the interest rates that thrifts had to pay depositors. Since similar (and slightly lower) ceilings already applied to commercial banks, most depositors had nowhere else to go, and the problem eased. True, the unanticipated inflation of the 1960s had cost the S&Ls a lot of money, but the new rate ceilings increased profit margins on new lending and offset these losses, at least in part.

By the late 1970s, interest rates were again rising, even more steeply than they had before. But this time, rate ceilings couldn't solve financial intermediaries' problems. A new innovation—the money market mutual fund—existed. By pooling their money in such funds, even small savers could take advantage of the higher rates paid on credit market instruments such as government bonds or short-term commercial paper. As interest rates on such instruments rose well above the deposit rate ceilings, money began to flood into these funds—and away from financial intermediaries, a process that came to be called *disintermediation.*

Many thrifts began to experience large operating losses. With no new deposits flowing in, no new loans could be made. The institutions were tied to a portfolio of poorly performing assets: loans they had made years earlier which carried yields that were now below market. By 1981, the industry in aggregate was operating at a net loss. The river of red ink caused the net worth of many thrifts to fall alarmingly. In 1980, the aggregate value of thrift institutions' tangible net worth (i.e., their total assets, not including intangibles such as goodwill, minus total liabilities) had exceeded 5 percent of assets. By 1982, tangible net worth for the industry as a whole was less than 1 percent of assets.

This time FHLBB, Congress, and some state agencies responded not with a series of new controls or regulations, but with the opposite. In 1980, Congress passed the Depository Institutions Deregulation and Monetary Control Act (DIDMCA), which, among other provisions, phased out interest rate ceilings and raised the limit on coverage of an insured deposit from $40,000 to $100,000. In 1982, with the Garn-St. Germain Act, Congress authorized federally chartered thrifts to make investments well beyond their traditional bailiwick of residential mortgage loans: Henceforth, thrifts could, e.g., make commercial real estate loans and even make a small amount of direct equity investments.

All these steps were, by themselves, eminently sensible. They eliminated many regulations that were inefficient or inequitable or both. Ceilings on interest rates, e.g., imposed sizable deadweight welfare losses and caused banking institutions and depositors to waste considerable resources in finding ways to avoid them. For example, institutions raised effective yields by offering gifts to those who opened new accounts or purchased large certificates of deposit. In addition, they built many more branch offices than they might have if they had been allowed to compete for deposits by offering customers a better price. And the ceilings transferred substantial sums from smaller (and likely poorer) depositors. According to David Pyle, the ceilings cost small savers $5.2 billion just for the years from 1968 to 1970.[30]

Unfortunately, however, these changes did not take place in a vacuum. They took place in a market where other regulations had profound effects—some quite perverse—on the behavior of both producers and consumers. And they took effect at an incredibly inopportune time, a time when many producers had a strong urge to engage in risky behavior and federal regulators had neither the tools to temper this urge nor the resources to monitor conduct very closely. As we now know, this was a disaster waiting to happen. It soon did.

Effects of Regulation and Deregulation

Let us engage in a bit of role-playing. Imagine you are vacationing in Las Vegas, where casino gambling is legal. Normally, you are a very straight-

---

[30]David H. Pyle, "The Losses on Savings Deposits from Interest Rate Regulation," *Bell Journal of Economics and Management Science,* 5 (Autumn 1974), pp. 614–622.

laced, risk-averse person. But, guided by a "when in Rome, do as the Romans do" philosophy, you step up to the tables. At first, you hold your own quite nicely; then, at the blackjack table, you are wiped out. You simply encountered a bad run of cards—your losses, you are sure, had nothing to do with your playing strategy. Nevertheless, you are disconsolate. Your empty purse ends your plans for luxurious meals and entertainment for the remainder of your stay. As you get up to leave, however, a smiling employee of the casino courteously informs you that "the house" would be delighted to extend you credit. Normally, of course, you would refuse their generous offer. You've already lost enough, you think, and further losses would be unconscionable. But then you remember something you once read: Gambling debts to casinos are, for all practical purposes, unrecoverable. It seems that casinos are reluctant to invite bad publicity by suing people who have already lost their shirts, and many courts refuse to order repayment of the debts even when suits are filed. In any case, you know they are not going to get much even if they do sue you: Your only possessions are a 20-year-old Ford Pinto, some used textbooks, and a broken-down stereo. Your credit rating can't be ruined because it doesn't exist. You therefore realize that if you accept the credit and win, you get to keep the booty; if you lose, you're no worse off than you are now.

If, after considering your options, you are sorely tempted to disregard any pangs of conscience and accept the casino's offer of credit in order to take another crack at that blackjack dealer, then you know how it must have felt to be the owner or manager of an insolvent thrift institution in the early 1980s. A large number of thrifts had no remaining tangible net worth by 1981 and thus had a strong incentive to try to recover by seeking high-return, high-risk investment instruments. They were in a "heads I win, tails I break even" situation: If the investments paid off, they were in the chips once again; and if they didn't, FSLIC would have to pick up the pieces. And deregulation gave them a host of new instruments in which to invest. They could make loans for beachfront condominiums, office buildings, and golf resorts as well as good, old single-family homes—or invest directly in stocks, bonds, or currencies. Finally, the removal of interest rate ceilings meant that they could go out and compete aggressively for funds to finance these escapades. Many thrifts pulled deposits from all over the country by advertising their interest rates—often *higher* than prevailing market yields—in national publications. Even consumers who'd never heard of the institutions that offered these lucrative rates were willing to send their money along as long as they saw the magic words *FSLIC insured* in the advertisements.

Since deposit insurance reduced consumers' interest in assaying the solvency of the institutions that invested their money, this task fell almost entirely to regulators. But the regulators were not up to the job. First, FHLBB accounting standards were ill designed to signal problems and to protect the insurance fund from liability. FHLBB judged net worth by using *historical*-cost measures rather than measures based on current market value. As a result, thrifts could have negative net worth—and a very strong incentive to roll the dice on risky projects—without the FHLBB's even knowing about it. And

DIDMCA actually authorized FHLBB to revise its net-worth standards *downward*, making it easier for insolvent thrifts to limp along, accumulating greater deficits by the day.

More important, the premiums that FSLIC charged member thrifts for deposit insurance coverage were a flat percentage of deposits and were not keyed to risk at all. Thus, thrifts were not penalized for holding a portfolio of risky investments. We would not consider charging drivers with dozens of speeding tickets and/or accidents the same automobile insurance rates as drivers with perfect safety records; we recognize that it would be both unfair and inefficient and would invite reckless behavior. Somehow, we overlooked the same fact here.

Finally, the regulatory apparatus in place was left over from a simpler, inherently safer era. It was ill equipped to oversee all the new activities that thrifts would undertake in the 1980s. In fact, the number of examiners and supervisors at FHLBB actually fell each year from 1981 through 1984. The system was simply overwhelmed. And when regulators sounded the first notes of alarm, they often were met with little sympathy from members of Congress, to whom the thrift industry had been generous campaign contributors.

VIGNETTE 15.3   Constituent Service or Influence Peddling? Congress and the S&L Crisis

As an example of the kind of high-risk investment strategy pursued by thrifts in the wake of deregulation, consider Lincoln Savings & Loan Association, a state-chartered institution in Irvine, California. By 1985, fully 80 percent of Lincoln's assets were tied up in common stocks, "junk" bonds (high-yield, high-risk debt instruments often used to finance corporate takeovers), foreign currencies, and various commercial real estate developments. Lincoln's owner, Charles F. Keating, had even invested $100 million of depositors' money in an arbitrage fund run by Ivan F. Boesky (later convicted of insider trading) and $132 million in a single stock, that of Gulf Broadcasting Co.

At the time, regulators proposed that S&Ls should put no more than 10 percent of their assets into such speculative ventures. When they refused to waive this limit for Lincoln, Keating began to lobby several influential members of the Senate Banking Committee.

He lavished campaign contributions on Senators Alan Cranston, Dennis DeConcini, John Glenn, John McCain, and Donald Riegle, who would subsequently become known as the *Keating five*. For example, Cranston (or various foundations he controlled) received $163,000 from Keating or his associates during 1986, when he faced a tough reelection fight, and another $850,000 in contributions during 1988. During one stay at the Phoenician, a lavish Arizona resort in which Lincoln held a large stake, Keating gave Cranston a check for $400,000 to fund the Center for Participation in Democracy, a voter registration group directed by Cranston's son.[31]

---

[31]Paula Dwyer, "The Seduction of Senator Alan Cranston," *Business Week*, 3136 (December 4, 1989), pp. 82–84.

In April 1987, the senators—at Keating's request—met with FHLBB Chairman Edwin J. Gray to express their interest in the Lincoln case, and later they met with four top officials of the San Francisco Federal Home Loan Bank. For their part, the senators denied that the visits were attempts to convince regulators to bend the rules to benefit Lincoln. They argued that their efforts were a perfectly proper form of constituent service.

But others found it hard to believe that the meetings could do anything other than transmit a strong signal to handle Lincoln with kid gloves. And the large sums of money that changed hands made it appear that influence was being sought, even if it were not officially for sale. When asked if his contributions to the five senators had gone to buy influence, Keating declared: "I want to say in the most forceful way I can, I certainly hope so."[32] Mr. Keating has been sentenced to ten years in federal prison for his conduct while head of Lincoln Savings.

For many, the most troubling aspects of the scandal are that elected officials' definition of "proper constituent service" is now so wide and money is so important in electoral politics. A record $28 million was spent during Cranston's reelection campaign; an acute need for cash might explain why this liberal Democrat would be receptive to overtures from an arch-conservative Republican. But attending to the affairs of well-heeled potential campaign contributors is not all that unusual in Washington. As one of the top staffers on the Senate Banking Committee admitted, "Every member has someone they carry amendments for. That's what this committee is all about. It represents a lot of special interests."[33]

All might have been well had the thrifts' gambles paid off with greater frequency. Unfortunately, they encountered a bad run of cards. The unraveling of the OPEC oil cartel depressed oil prices sharply, and the "oil patch" economy became depressed. Thrifts in the southwest that had invested in office buildings and other projects which depended for their viability on a robust local economy plunged deep into insolvency. Not a few kept making larger, more desperate wagers in the hopes of recovering; they only enlarged FSLIC exposure to loss. Some thrifts outside the southwest found that the Tax Reform Act of 1986 rescinded many of the tax breaks on the real estate developments in which they'd invested. Soon these institutions were in deep trouble, too.

FSLIC, which typically had to liquidate fewer than five insolvent thrifts per year throughout its history, now found it had to dispose of dozens of insolvencies per year. In 1988, FSLIC disposed of over 200 insolvent thrifts, which had held about 7.5 percent of all thrift assets, at a cost to the insurance fund of $31.7 billion. (These sums either paid off depositors, in the case of liquidations of failed thrifts, or, in some cases, paid acquirers an amount equal to an insolvent thrift's negative net worth in order to keep it running.) Most of the failed thrifts were state-chartered (and thus subject to less stringent net-worth requirements), and most had done what theory predicted they would as they approached insolvency: They had invested in extraordinarily high-risk invest-

---

[32]Ibid., p. 84.
[33]Ibid.

ments, including holding direct equity stakes in various development projects, and had often exceeded regulatory limits on loans to one borrower. And in a disquietingly large number of cases, there was evidence of self-dealing or outright fraud.

In August 1989, Congress and President George Bush committed $167 billion to the chore of cleaning up the mess, creating the Resolution Trust Corporation (RTC) to sell off thrift assets and manage insolvent institutions. Yet the process was far more expensive than initially imagined, and the RTC has returned to Congress several times to request additional appropriations. Clearly, this is the most spectacular regulatory failure in U.S. history.

What is especially worrisome is that several of the factors that contributed to this failure have yet to be completely corrected. FHLBB has been beefed up significantly (with more than twice as many examiners and supervisors as in the mid-1980s) and has tightened controls on the kinds of investments that thrifts can make. But, e.g., thrifts still are not required to use market values in their accounting statements, and deposit insurance premiums are still not risk-based. Thus, it is possible that, given the "right" set of economic circumstances, the crisis could flare anew.

SUMMARY AND CONCLUDING REMARKS

In this chapter we examined how economic regulation of railroads, trucking, airlines, agriculture, and savings institutions has affected these industries and the public.

Regulation of railroads has always had conflicting goals. Some demanded regulation to duplicate the results of competition in markets served by a single line; others demanded regulation to suppress competition in markets served by several lines. Since the surplus gains from the lower rates that the ICC set in the single-line markets exceeded the surplus losses from higher rates in the multiple-line markets, regulation likely enhanced welfare, at least in its early years. Over time, however, the ICC's protective attitude toward railroad interests posed problems. When the ICC extended rate and entry regulation to trucking, a market which was structurally competitive, welfare losses from inefficiently high rate levels, inflexible rate structures, and other policies began to mount. Regulation induced inefficient diversion of traffic from railroads to trucks, led to losses from excess rail and truck capacity and inefficient utilization of rolling stock, and even had an adverse impact on business location decisions. Deregulation, embraced by many railroads but fought by truckers and the unions that benefited from the status quo, finally got underway in the late 1970s and culminated in 1980, with the passage of the Motor Carrier Act and the Staggers Rail Act. In the years since, both rail and trucking rates have fallen (although not in all markets), productivity has improved, and customer satisfaction has increased.

Regulation of the airline industry was motivated by Congress's desire to stimulate growth in this industry and perhaps by Depression-era suspicion about the virtues of competition. For the 50 years following the creation of the

CAB in 1938, it allowed no new entrants to commence service on a major route. Further, it greatly limited competition among existing carriers in order to provide them capital for growth and for subsidies to consumers in small, less lucrative markets. Limits on price competition were not sufficient to accomplish all the CAB's goals, however: nonprice competition caused airlines' costs to rise and load factors to fall. By the 1970s, it was clear that regulation was at the root of some serious problems in the industry. By contrast, unregulated intrastate carriers offered lower fares, had lower costs, and were more profitable than the regulated interstate carriers. Congress passed the Airline Deregulation Act in 1978, although the CAB had already begun to liberalize entry conditions and give carriers more pricing flexibility. The results of deregulation have generally been favorable: Fares on most (but not all) routes are now lower than they would have been under regulation, and carriers have enhanced productivity enormously. By one estimate, the welfare gains of airline deregulation amount to over $8 billion annually.

While there are many possible public-interest rationales for government intervention in agricultural markets, none convincingly explains why such massive federal subsidies flow to this sector or why these subsidies flow to the individuals they do. For such explanations we must employ the theory of public choice, which predicts that numerically compact groups will generally be more successful at using the political apparatus for their benefit than large, diffuse groups. Thus, while some farm programs may help stabilize otherwise volatile markets and others redistribute income to worthy recipients, most simply transfer wealth or income from large numbers of consumers and taxpayers to relatively small numbers of growers (many of whom are very wealthy indeed). Unfortunately, these programs also involve considerable loss of social surplus and induce significant misallocation of resources, at a net cost in the billions of dollars per year.

The 1980s saw the greatest regulatory/deregulatory failure in history: the U.S. savings and loan crisis. The crisis originated in a confluence of several factors, including macroeconomic conditions and deregulatory initiatives undertaken in 1980 and 1982. The inflation of the late 1970s, coupled with the interest rate ceilings then in effect, caused deposits to flow out of savings institutions in pursuit of higher yields. As a result, many thrifts showed earnings losses that eventually pushed their net worth to zero—or below. At this point, they had little to lose by gambling on high-risk, high-yield investments, for if these investments paid off, they would profit handsomely, and if they didn't, federal deposit insurers would have to make up losses to depositors. Partial deregulation (although thrifts remained heavily regulated) made it easier for thrifts both to seek higher-risk investments and to compete for deposits by offering consumers high (often above-market) rates. When the economic recession of the early 1980s struck, many thrifts became insolvent. Flawed accounting practices and ineffective regulatory oversight disguised these insolvencies for a time, adding to the overall costs of paying off customers of failed thrifts, now approaching $200 billion (in present-value terms). Surprisingly, some of the factors that contributed to this failure (e.g., deposit insurance premiums that are not related to the risks of an institution's investment portfolio) are, as this is written, yet to be corrected.

QUESTIONS FOR REVIEW AND DISCUSSION

15.1 Suppose that in the early years of the ICC rail rates were cut on short hauls and raised on long hauls in order to eliminate "unfair rate discrimination." Using graphs, show and discuss how such changes in rates likely affected welfare in these two distinct market segments.

15.2 Suppose you had been a trucking industry executive in the early part of this century. Could you have conceived of any public-interest rationale for regulation of your industry? Any private-interest rationale? Explain. Did the kind of trucking regulation that eventually came about support the public- or private-interest rationale?

15.3 Suppose you are a policy analyst assigned to study the effects of airline deregulation. You are convinced that hub-and-spoke networks lower airlines' costs, but you also observe that carriers charge slightly higher fares on flights originating in their "fortress hubs" than on flights of similar length originating elsewhere. Would you favor banning such hubs? What factors would you consider, and what facts would you need to know, to make such a decision?

15.4 Consider a hypothetical agricultural market. Suppose a government-supported price is set above the equilibrium level. Trace the welfare effects of this policy in a diagram, identifying all transfers and any losses of social surplus. Assume the government enforces the price support by buying any output not bought by consumers at the supported price. Now suppose the government tries to minimize its outlays in this market by setting output quotas (i.e., fixing the rate of output below the equilibrium level) instead of support prices. Trace the welfare effects of this policy, and discuss any differences between the two types of programs.

15.5 Suppose the legislature of your state passes a law that says that automobile insurance rates should be based strictly on the number of miles an insured automobile is driven. Insurers are not allowed to consider where these miles are driven, who is doing the driving, or any other factor in setting rates. How do you think this would affect automobile safety? Do you think such a system would be equitable? How does this example apply to the S&L crisis?

PART FOUR

SOCIAL REGULATION

471

CHAPTER 16

ENVIRONMENTAL PROTECTION AND PUBLIC POLICY

The most important thing about Spaceship Earth [is that] it didn't come with an instruction manual.

R. Buckminster Fuller

So far, we've been preoccupied with the reasons that governments try to affect prices and output rates in markets for various economic goods and with the methods (chiefly, antitrust policy and economic regulation) they use to do so. We now turn down another important avenue of inquiry: why and how governments try to influence market behavior to ensure that production and consumption of goods does not entail excessive environmental degradation, excessive risk to consumers, and excessive risk to workers.

Government policies aimed at protecting the environment, consumers, or workers, commonly discussed under the heading of *social regulation,* are certainly not new. In the 1300s, for example, Londoners who violated that city's smoke pollution ordinances were beheaded. In the United States, laws that regulated the purity or quality of certain goods date from colonial times, and state and federal efforts to control water pollution began in the late 1800s. It is clear, however, that social regulation has been a growth industry since about 1970, when the Environmental Protection Agency (EPA) and Occupational Safety and Health Administration (OSHA) were created and the National Commission on Product Safety recommended creation of the Consumer Product Safety Commission (CPSC).

These and other agencies devoted to social regulation are fundamentally different from those that we have examined so far. First, the social regulatory agencies are concerned not with firms' pricing and output decisions but with how firms produce goods and/or how buyers might use them. As a result, these agencies often must delve deeply into the details of the production process, approving or disapproving of specific manufacturing methods or product designs. Clearly, this will reduce the autonomy of managers (and occasionally of consumers), so the actions of social regulators will often be controversial. Second, social regulation is not industry-specific. Agencies such as the EPA and OSHA affect just about all industries at least a little bit, in contrast to economic regulatory agencies (such as the Interstate Commerce Commission) which affect relatively few industries (e.g., railroads) a great deal. It is argued, therefore, that social regulatory agencies are less susceptible to *capture* by the firms or industries they oversee, since no single firm or industry has a terribly large stake in the decisions of such agencies. It is not clear, however, whether social regulatory agencies might often be *more* susceptible to capture by groups organized around a single issue (e.g., environmental activists, labor unions).

In this chapter and Chapter 17, we examine the theory and practice of social regulation in some detail. We begin in this chapter with a discussion of public policy toward environmental quality. We discuss the economic problem of externalities, which much environmental policy aims to solve. Next we examine the nature of EPA policy, assess its performance, and discuss some actual and suggested policy reforms. In Chapter 17 we discuss regulatory policies designed to protect the health and safety of consumers and workers.

ECONOMICS AND THE ENVIRONMENT

It is common to express skepticism about mixing economics with ecological issues. Some consider environmental matters to be the proper and exclusive domain of natural scientists or engineers (who may identify processes that either degrade or enhance the ecosystem) or perhaps lawyers (who may write, interpret, or enforce laws to preserve the environment). Others recognize that economic calculation *can* play a role in the discussion of environmental policy, but argue (on normative grounds) that such calculation is inappropriate given the difficulty of assigning dollar values to things they regard as "priceless," e.g., human health, aesthetics, or the survival of rare animal species.

We can sidestep a philosophical debate on whether economists *should* be involved in environmental policy-making by simply noting the obvious fact that they *are* deeply involved and, in fact, have been so from the outset. This is so because economics provides both a welfare justification for environmental regulation and a framework that regulators can use to plot strategy and weigh options. Thus, anyone interested in contributing to policy in this area must understand how economists approach environmental issues.

The foundation for this approach is the theory of *externalities*, introduced in Chapter 3. In this section, we advance that discussion, pinning down the problems associated with externalities more precisely and moving on to a discussion of ways in which economists of various stripes might address these problems.

VIGNETTE 16.1   Capitalism, Socialism, and Pollution

Environmental issues are lightning rods for controversy. It is safe to say that most people do not see them in the dispassionate way economists do. In general, economists tend to view environmental quality much as they view other goods. For various reasons, they tend to think markets will provide less of this good than is socially optimal, but by and large are unwilling to abandon market organization to try to correct the problem. Instead, economists aim to improve markets' performance in this area.

Others, however, take the view that markets and capitalist organization are at the root of most of our environmental problems. Barry Commoner, long a leading light of environmentalism, recently wrote:

The origin of the environmental crisis can be traced back to the capitalist precept that the choice of production technology is to be governed solely by private interest in profit maximization . . . Environmental improvement can occur only if we implement . . . socialism, classically defined as social ownership and control of the means of production.[1]

While many might shrink from radically restructuring society along socialist lines in order to address environmental problems, the idea that government will be a better steward of the environment than private individuals is quite common. It is interesting to note, therefore, that where state ownership of the means of production is common, environmental quality is no better—and in many cases is substantially worse—than in market-oriented economies.

Marshall Goldman, a renowned expert on the Soviet economy, was the first to document this fact.[2] He found examples of astounding environmental degradation in his travels through the U.S.S.R. (now the Commonwealth of Independent States). Even by the late 1960s, most Soviet cities lacked sewer systems, and only a tiny fraction made any attempt to treat sewage before dumping it into nearby rivers. Irrigation projects divert so much water from the Aral and Caspian Seas that these bodies of water have been gradually disappearing. The Volga River, estimated to carry one-half of all discharged effluent in Russia, is so polluted that steamboats carry signs warning passengers not to toss cigarettes overboard, for fear the river might ignite.

Part of the problem is the fact that government planners and factory managers are so desperate to fulfill economic development goals and output quotas that, in Goldman's words, there is "a political as well as an economic imperative to devour idle resources in the U.S.S.R."[3] But it is also clear that communal or government ownership is no environmental panacea: When *everyone* owns a resource, it is difficult or impossible to exclude those who would abuse or overuse the resource. For example, since everyone—or no one—owns the gravel along the shores of the Black Sea, construction crews for many years just hauled it away to use in building projects. Massive beach erosion has been the result, with numerous landslides causing several buildings to slide into the sea.

The situation is no better in China and eastern Europe. Air pollution is so bad in China's Sichuan province that 90 percent of the trees in its pine forests have died.

---

[1]Barry Commoner, *Making Peace With the Planet*, Pantheon Books, New York, 1990, pp. 217, 219.

[2]Marshall Goldman, *The Spoils of Progress: Environmental Pollution in the Soviet Union*, M.I.T. Press, Cambridge, MA, 1972.

[3]Ibid., p. 188.

And according to the United Nations' Global Monitoring Program, pollution in eastern Europe "is among the worst on the Earth's surface." In Poland, "a third of the nation's 38 million people live in areas of ecological disaster," according to the Polish Academy of Sciences. In East Germany, 80 percent of surface waters are unsuitable for fishing, swimming, or drinking, and one-third of all lakes are declared "biologically dead" from decades of absorbing untreated chemical wastes.[4]

Of course, most of these societies have many grand-sounding environmental laws and regulations on the books. But, as Goldman wrote, "passage of a law does not mean it will be enforced, especially when the interests of the governing officials do not coincide with the intent of the law."[5]

The Externality Problem: Welfare Effects Reviewed

As we observed in Chapter 3, market results may be less than perfect even where perfect competition rules. A major problem is externalities, also known as spillover or neighborhood effects. *Negative externalities* are defined as costs that market transactors impose on third parties (those "external" to a transaction) without these parties' consent. *Positive externalities* are defined as benefits that transactors confer on third parties without their consent.

Pollution is the most often cited example of a negative externality. But note that economists' objection here is not simply that pollution occurs, for in an industrial society (or even a preindustrial one) some amount of pollution is inevitable and—dare we say it?—even optimal. Rather, the problem is that unfettered markets may, in certain circumstances, contribute to *excessive* production of pollution and/or of goods which degrade the environment when they are produced or consumed. Thus, when pollution externalities are present, the allocation of resources is distorted and social welfare is not maximized.

To identify the welfare losses associated with a pollution externality, consider the following scenario. A paper mill locates along the banks of a river. The mill inhabits a perfectly competitive market, in which the going price of paper is, say, $10 per unit. Thus, the mill faces a demand curve for its product, labeled D in Figure 16.1, that is horizontal at this price. Its marginal costs of production, labeled MC_p, rise with output, by $0.10 for each extra unit produced.[6]

Soon it is clear, however, that the mill produces something besides paper: pollution. Some of the chemicals used in the manufacturing process seep into the adjoining river, making it unfit for swimming and fishing for some distance downstream. We say, therefore, that the mill is imposing external costs on swimmers and fishers. Suppose that these external costs are constant at $4 per unit of paper produced. Thus, the total social costs of each unit of paper

---

[4]Thomas DiLorenzo, "Does Capitalism Cause Pollution?" Center for the Study of American Business, Washington University, St. Louis, Mo, Contemporary Issues Series 38, August 1990, pp. 8–12.

[5]Goldman, *The Spoils of Progress*, p. 190.

[6]That is, $MC_p = 0.10Q$.

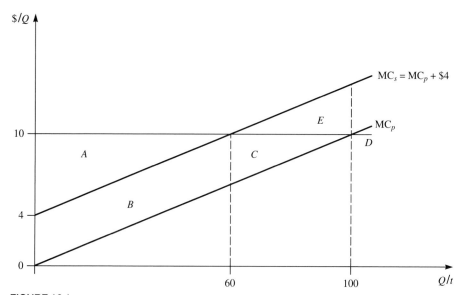

FIGURE 16.1
WELFARE EFFECTS OF A POLLUTION EXTERNALITY. Unless the external costs of production
(here, $4 per unit) are considered, the firm will produce 100 units of output per period instead of
60. As a result, social surplus equal to area *E* will be wasted.

produced, labeled MC_s in Figure 16.1, are MC_p + $4. That is, the amount the
mill privately pays to produce each unit of paper (MC_p) is but a part of what
society as a whole pays ($MC_s = MC_p + $4), which includes both the mill's production costs and the external costs that the mill's activities impose on swimmers and fishers.

If, as we might expect, the mill ignores the well-being of swimmers and
fishers and considers only its private costs in making its production decision,
the mill will expand output until $P = MC_p$ and will produce 100 units per
period. (For brevity, let *per period* be understood in all succeeding references to
output rates or values that depend on such rates.)

Let us calculate the total social surplus that results from this decision. Given
our assumption that the demand curve *D* is horizontal, there is no consumers'
surplus here (or, more precisely, this tiny mill's activities do not add to total
consumers' surplus in the paper market). The mill does earn some producer's
surplus, however, equal to $500, or the sum of areas *A*, *B*, and *C* in Figure 16.1.
But to calculate the *net* social surplus, the external costs that the mill's activities impose on swimmers and fishers must be deducted from this amount.
These external costs are $400, or the sum of areas *B*, *C*, and *E*. Thus, net social
surplus, if the mill is guided only by its private costs, is $100. Geometrically,
net social surplus when output is 100 units is $(A + B + C) - (B + C + E)$, or
area *A* minus area *E*.

If the mill behaved in a more public spirited fashion, social welfare would be enhanced. Suppose, e.g., the mill included in its calculation of costs the external costs that its activities impose on swimmers and fishers. If this were the case, the mill's calculation of its *private* costs would coincide with that of *social* costs. It would expand output only until $P = MC_s$, producing 60 units. Although its output would fall, *net social surplus would rise*. Producer's surplus when output is 60 is $420, or the sum of areas A and B in Figure 16.1. The external costs imposed on swimmers and fishers are now $240, or area B. Thus, net social surplus here is $180—or $80 higher than before. Geometrically, net social surplus when output is 60 is $A + B - B$, or area A alone, higher than before by area E, which we may call the deadweight welfare loss associated with this pollution externality.

Of course, the problem is that the mill has little incentive to consider the welfare of swimmers and fishers in deciding its rate of output. Given that producer's surplus falls from $500 ($A + B + C$) to $420 ($A + B$) when output is reduced from 100 to 60, it is quite unlikely the mill will, on its own, "do the right thing" from the standpoint of social welfare. A good deal of environmental policy is aimed at addressing this problem in one way or another.

Before moving on to a discussion of some proposed solutions to the externality problem, however, we note an important fact: Avoiding the welfare losses associated with externalities will reduce—but not necessarily eliminate—pollution. In our example, even if the mill chooses to reduce its output from 100 to 60 units, the extent to which the river is polluted falls, but not to zero. The river is still sufficiently polluted that swimmers and fishers lose goods or services they value by $240. Social welfare is enhanced not because pollution is eliminated, but because it is reduced to efficient levels. The key here is to realize that the social value of each of the first 60 units of paper produced equals or exceeds the social cost of producing it, *including the environmental cost*. By contrast, each unit produced beyond the sixtieth one costs society more to produce than it is worth. In the context of this example, we can maximize welfare by ensuring that the mill produces no more (or less) than 60 units of paper, i.e., that it does not overproduce (or underproduce) either paper or pollution. We do not—at least given the values assumed here—want the mill to shut down in order to please swimmers and fishers.

Of course, it would be nice to have both the right amount of paper and zero pollution, but we'd need to know more about the specifics of this example to tell whether this is possible. Perhaps we can, at some cost, install equipment that will keep the mill's chemicals from seeping into the river, so that the mill, swimmers, and fishers can all live peacefully together. Whether we should install such equipment, however, will depend on its cost. Total social welfare will not be enhanced if we spend more for the equipment than it saves us in avoided external costs (just as, on a personal level, your welfare is not enhanced if you spend $10 for something that yields you $5 worth of benefits). Obviously, the circumstances that will affect our choice of the optimal solution to an externality problem can differ greatly from case to case. As we shall see, designing policy *rules* that will reliably ensure the maximization of social welfare over a broad range of circumstances won't be easy.

Liability Rules and Pigou Taxes

One possible solution to the pollution problem posed in the example outlined above fairly leaps out at us: Make the paper mill *legally liable* for any damage that its activities inflict on its neighbors. Under such a liability rule, the mill is forced to consider the costs that it imposes on swimmers and fishers as part of its total production costs; i.e., the swimmers' and fishers' losses will no longer be external to the mill. Once the externality is "internalized" in this way, the mill will expand output only until $P = MC_s$, at $Q = 60$ units in Figure 16.1. This result is efficient, for (as we saw above) social surplus is at a maximum when $Q = 60$. It also appears more equitable, for swimmers and fishers are now compensated for the damages that the mill's activities inflict on them.

Another way to describe this liability rule is to say that it grants swimmers and fishers a *property right* to use the river for recreational purposes. In effect, all externality problems can be viewed as conflicts between parties over the right to use a scarce resource in a particular way. In our example, the paper mill's desire to use the river to dispose of its chemical wastes conflicts with swimmers' and fishers' desires to use the river for recreation. This rule establishes the primacy of the swimmers' and fishers' rights. In some sense, they then own the river for certain purposes and are entitled to payments from those who seek to use it for other purposes.

An equivalent way to internalize externalities is with taxes. For example, once we observe that the mill's activities generate external costs equal to $4 per unit of paper produced, we could charge the mill a per-unit output tax equal to this amount. Once again, the mill will then consider that its private production costs now include the costs its activities impose on its neighbors. Accordingly, it will expand production only until $P = MC_s$ (which equals $MC_p + \$4$), at $Q = 60$ in Figure 16.1. Taxes that require payments equal to the amount of external costs that a transactor's actions impose on others are called *Pigou taxes* (or, alternatively, *Pigovian taxes*) in honor of the British economist A. C. Pigou, who suggested the idea in the early 1900s.[7] Conceivably, the proceeds of the tax could be used to compensate swimmers and fishers for the damages they experience as a result of the mill's activities. The Pigou tax in this example will produce receipts just sufficient to compensate swimmers and fishers fully for their damages ($4 × 60 units = $240). But it is important to note that whether the receipts are paid out in this way or not, the Pigou tax achieves the goal of ensuring that the firm produces welfare-maximizing amounts of paper and pollution.

The Coasian Critique

For some time, scholars and policymakers almost unanimously believed that most any externality problem could be solved via a simple two-step process: (1) Determine who or what is the cause of the problem, and (2) make that

---

[7]A. C. Pigou, *The Economics of Welfare*, Macmillan, New York, 1920.

party legally liable for damages or subject to Pigou taxes of the kind discussed above. In 1960, however, Ronald Coase, a lawyer trained in economics, pointed out circumstances in which this analysis required modification.[8] Coase found that simple liability rules or tax schemes were, in some cases, not necessary to internalize an externality. In other circumstances, he found, such approaches might actually lead to inefficient results.

The Zero-Transaction-Costs Case   Let us return to our paper mill by the river. Suppose now the swimmers and fishers are represented by a single party: the owner of the land through which the river flows downstream from the mill. Swimmers and fishers pay this landowner an admission fee for the right to enter and use the river for recreational purposes. (In fact, such fees probably provide us with the only reliable way to calculate the external costs associated with the mill's activities: We can observe how much admission revenues fall as the mill's output of paper and pollution rise.) Suppose further that the landowner and the paper mill owner can get together and transact business *at zero cost* to themselves.

Given suppositions like these, Coase said, the externality problem we have been discussing will disappear—on its own, no matter how we assign legal liability! This result, known as the *Coase theorem*, can be stated formally as follows:

> Absent transaction costs, the private and social costs of actions involving externalities will be equal; thus, the assignment of legal liability (or property rights) will have no effect on social welfare.

According to the Coase theorem, whether we grant the mill owner the right to use the river for the disposal of chemical wastes or the landowner the right to a clean river flowing through her property will make no difference. The result will be the same—and will coincide with the social optimum—in either case.

This finding seems surprising, to say the least. It is easy to see how welfare is maximized if the mill owner is made liable for damages. Forcing the mill owner to pay damages to the landowner internalizes the externality. The mill owner will make production decisions based on full social costs (MC_s in Figure 16.1) rather than private costs (MC_p in Figure 16.1). We can rest assured that the right amount of paper will be produced.

But what if the mill owner is *not* liable for damages? On the surface, this appears to invite the mill owner to behave in a socially damaging fashion, boosting output beyond optimal levels again. Since the landowner cannot legally recover her revenue losses from the mill owner, won't the latter make production decisions with reference to MC_p rather than MC_s? The surprising answer is no, if the two parties can transact costlessly with each other.

---

[8]Ronald H. Coase, "The Problem of Social Cost," *Journal of Law and Economics*, 3 (October 1960), pp. 1–44.

Return to Figure 16.1 and imagine that the mill owner is producing only 60 units even though he is *not* liable for any costs that the mill's pollution inflicts on the landowner. Would the mill owner like to raise output to 100 units? On the surface the answer is yes: An extra 40 units of output will add $80 (area C) to the mill owner's profits. But if the mill owner raises output from 60 to 100, the landowner will lose an additional $160 (C + E) in revenues from swimmers and fishers. Thus, the increase in output will benefit the mill owner $80 (area E) less than it costs the landowner. Clearly, there is the possibility of a mutually beneficial agreement here: If the landowner offers to pay the mill owner, say, $120 (or area C plus one-half area E) to keep his output at 60 rather than raise it to 100 units, *both* will be better off. The offer clearly benefits the landowner, for she will save $40 if it is accepted. But it will benefit the mill owner, too. His producer's surplus is $420 (A + B) if output is 60 and $500 (A + B + C) if output is 100. If he accepts the landowner's offer and produces 60 units, however, he earns $420 in producer's surplus *plus* the landowner's payment of $120, for a total of $540. Given the landowner's offer, the mill owner will not choose to overproduce at all!

In sum, even though the mill owner has the right to ignore the external costs that his activities impose on the landowner, the fact that the two parties can get together and rearrange property rights (at zero transaction costs) leads to an efficient allocation of resources anyway. Note the key: Wherever there is an externality problem, there is a deadweight welfare loss (like area E in Figure 16.1). Avoiding this loss will enlarge the social pie so that everyone can enjoy a larger slice. Naturally, everyone will want a larger slice of pie, and our assumption of zero transaction costs simply guarantees that an agreement about how to get it will be easy to reach. In our example, keeping the mill's output at 60 yields $80 more in social surplus, and the mill owner and landowner both recognize the gains from an agreement between them and reach such an agreement cheaply and quickly.[9] Whether we make the mill owner liable for damages or not won't affect welfare: We'll get the same result either way (although the decision about liability will, of course, affect the distribution of income between the mill owner and landowner).

In general, when the costs of transacting are zero, it is impossible for the private and social costs of an action to diverge; i.e., all external costs can be internalized when transacting is costless. When actions by A impose costs on B, C, D, etc., these parties can, in a zero-transaction-costs world, offer payments up to the amount of the damages they experience to induce A to cease such actions. Since payments forgone are *costs* (specifically, *opportunity costs*), A will consider such offers as part of his total costs of production even when he is not legally liable for the costs his actions impose on third parties. Suppose, e.g., an action by A costs B $1 and B offers A $1 to cease the action.

---

[9]Of course, the actual distribution of gains from such an agreement might vary over a wide range. The mill owner might be willing to accept a side payment as small as $80 from the landowner; the landowner might be willing to pay as much as $160 to get the mill owner to keep output at 60 units.

This offer forces *A* to consider the effects of his actions on *B*. If *A* declines the offer and engages in the action, we will know the action's benefits exceed his private costs *plus* the $1 offer from *B*. In other words, where negotiations are costless, they will produce efficient results because they force private and social costs together: *A* will consider *B*'s offer exactly as a Pigou tax.

Solving externality problems by negotiation will not be practical in all—or perhaps most—circumstances, however. Suppose, e.g., it costs more than $80 for our mill owner and landowner to get together, negotiate a deal, and hire lawyers to draft a contract. Such transaction costs would more than offset the gains from trade, and the externality problem could not be resolved in this way. Or the landowner might be unsure whether another mill owner might come along and demand similar payments in exchange for a promise not to overproduce paper. Or, finally, there may be many landowners involved here rather than just one, and negotiations might take considerable time and effort. In such cases, *how we assign liability will matter a great deal*; Coase offered a suggestion about how we should do so.

VIGNETTE 16.2   The Land of Fruit and Honey

We live in a world of positive transaction costs. This does not mean, however, that Coase-style transactions can never solve externality problems.

Consider the interaction between beekeeping and farming. If bees are kept near certain fruit crops, greater cross-pollination occurs and more fruit is produced. Similarly, proximity to many crops increases bees' honey production. There's a *positive externality* problem here: If beekeepers do not consider the external benefits their bees confer on growers and growers do not consider the external benefits their crops confer on beekeepers, there will be underproduction in both markets. Disciples of Pigou, assuming transaction costs were so high that markets would fail to solve this problem, argued that government intervention—in the form of subsidies or taxes that would bring the parties' private and social costs of production together—were necessary to ensure the optimum allocation of resources.[10]

But Steven Cheung climbed down from the academic ivory tower long enough to learn something about these markets, and he found that beekeepers and growers get together to solve this problem without the government's help. According to Cheung, beekeepers and growers are well aware of the benefits each can bring to the other, and they use Coasian side payments, specified in oral and written contracts, to reimburse each other for increasing output to socially optimal levels.[11]

The financial terms of these contracts depend upon the relative values of the interacting external benefits. For example, placing hives in apple orchards yields almost no extra honey but does enhance apple production. Thus, apple growers paid (in 1971, when Cheung performed his research) about $10 per hive to "rent bees." Putting hives in blueberry fields, however, increases both honey and blueberry

---

[10]J. E. Meade, "External Economies and Diseconomies in a Competitive Situation," *Economic Journal*, 52 (March 1952), pp. 54–67.

[11]Steven N. S. Cheung, "The Fable of the Bees: An Economic Investigation," *Journal of Law and Economics*, 16 (April 1973), pp. 11–33.

production. Accordingly, blueberry growers paid only about $5 per hive to obtain the pollination services of bees; beekeepers received an additional $5 per hive in extra honey output. For some crops, such as mint, hives are used only to extract nectar. In such cases, beekeepers pay growers rent.

Cheung also found that beekeepers consider their bees' external (pollination) benefits in deploying hives. When hives are deployed for both pollination service and nectar extraction, the density of hives is about 2.5 times what would be employed for nectar extraction alone. That is, hives are clustered so densely that the extra honey produced per hive (hives' "marginal nectar product") is zero or negative; but because the beekeepers capture hives' external benefits in the form of pollination fees paid by farmers, they deploy the efficient number of hives.

In Cheung's view, the market for nectar and pollination services puts the lie to the assertion that solution of externality problems *requires* government intervention. His work is a warning to those who would devise policy to solve *theoretical* rather than *real* problems. Before we start writing regulations or laws to correct market failure, we had better be sure that the relevant market is indeed failing.

The Positive-Transaction-Costs Case   For years economists dismissed Coase's analysis by saying, more or less, "OK, fine. In a zero-transaction-costs world, we could negotiate externality problems away. But this is the real world, and transaction costs are so high that it is practically impossible to solve pollution problems with Coasian transactions. So let's get down to business and start taxing polluters (Pigou-style), or making them liable for the costs they impose on society." Coase pointed out, however, that this Pigovian approach is dangerously incomplete and can lead to serious policy errors.

First, observed Coase, sometimes it will be difficult to determine who is really to blame for an externality problem. In the example we've been using so far, it may seem obvious that the mill owner is responsible for the polluted river. But consider a slightly different example: the noise pollution that is a by-product of your fondness for heavy metal rock 'n' roll. The inhabitant of the next apartment considers you to be the source of a major externality problem and calls the police every time you crank up your stereo to enjoy your favorite music. You, however, consider your neighbor to be the source of the problem. It is his desire for peace and quiet that imposes costs on you. In fact, you're both right. It takes *two* to have an externality problem: If *either* you *or* your neighbor moved (or otherwise changed your behavior), the problem would evaporate.

Even in our paper mill example, it might be difficult to say that the mill owner is "at fault" in all cases. Suppose the mill has been in existence for generations, while the landowner has only recently opened the river to swimmers and fishers. Is the mill owner then guilty of imposing costs on the landowner, or is it the other way round? In Coase's view, externality problems between two parties are almost always *reciprocal; both* must bear some responsibility for them. Externality problems arise because both parties wish to use the same resource for different purposes.

Building on this point, Coase suggested that if policymakers are preoccupied with laying the blame for externality problems, they might overlook the cheapest (i.e., welfare-maximizing) way to solve such problems. And *that*, said Coase, is how any externality problem should be addressed in the positive-transaction-costs world in which we live: *We should try to determine which party can avoid (or cope with) the problem at least cost and specify property rights or liability rules so that this party has an incentive to do so.*

Let us return to our paper mill example. This time negotiations between the concerned parties have completely broken down. Imagine you are the judge in a lawsuit brought against the mill owner. Naturally, the plaintiffs—a coalition of landowners, swimmers, and fishers—want the court to force the mill owner to pay all damages resulting from his pollution of the river, while the mill owner replies that he has been on that river far longer than the plaintiffs and therefore owes them no compensation. (The mill owner, aware of the need for a public interest justification for his actions, may also argue that if he is judged liable for damages, he will be forced to lay off many local townspeople.)

The basic economic facts of the case are embodied in Figure 16.1, which should by now be quite familiar. To these facts, however, let us now add another: Suppose in the course of the trial the lawyer for the paper mill points out (and the attorney for the plaintiffs does not deny) that abundant pollution-free swimming and fishing opportunities are available *upstream* from the mill. All the plaintiffs have to do is build a road to this alternative recreational area, which can be done at a cost of, say, $300. Now, how should you rule? If you find for the plaintiffs, the mill will reduce its rate of output to 60 (and the aforementioned layoffs will occur), since its liability to pay damages here acts just as a Pigou tax. If you find for the defendant, the mill will likely continue to produce 100 units of paper.

Assuming that you wish to make society as well off as possible, i.e., you want to maximize social surplus, you should rule in favor of the paper mill! To see why, examine Figure 16.1 once again. Ordinarily, making the mill liable for the external costs that it imposes on swimmers and fishers would be a good idea, for the mill would then reduce output from 100 to 60 and the net social surplus would rise from $100 (producer's surplus of $500 minus external costs of $400) to $180 (producer's surplus of $420 minus external costs of $240). Thus, making the mill pay damages produces a surplus gain of $80 (area *E*). Now, however, we know that we can *eliminate* the external costs entirely by spending $300 to build the road to the alternative recreational area. Once this is done, the mill can produce 100 units and earn producer's surplus of $500. Even after deducting the cost of building the road (thus replacing the recreational opportunities of swimmers and fishers), we are left with a net social surplus of $200. Thus, net social surplus is $20 greater if we rule in favor of the mill owner and leave it to the plaintiffs to build the road to the upstream location. Faced with either a loss of $400 in external costs or a $300 expenditure to build the road, the plaintiffs will have an incentive to build the road, and net social surplus will be maximized. (Of course, equity considerations may lead us to force the mill owner to pay part of or all the cost of building the road—although we must be careful in writing our decision. We want to ensure that swimmers and fishers relocate upstream; we don't want the mill owner's contribution to these relocation costs to be misconstrued as damage payments or Pigou taxes.)

Of course, different facts could have dictated that we make a different judgment. Suppose it came out at trial that the mill could buy, for $280, special waste disposal equipment that would eliminate the pollution problem. Now we should rule in favor of the plaintiffs. The mill owner would then have a strong incentive to install the special equipment. He could produce 100 units and earn net producer's surplus of $220 ($500 minus $280, the cost of the equipment), higher by $40 than the $180 in net surplus he would earn if he produced 60 units and paid plaintiffs' damages. Given that the mill owner can (in this case) avoid the external costs associated with his activities more cheaply than users of the river can, making the mill owner liable for damages will produce the desired (welfare-maximizing) outcome.

In sum, our decision should depend on the circumstances of the case at hand, and it will have a major effect on welfare. If we are concerned with welfare maximization, we shouldn't simply try to figure out who is to blame for a particular problem and make that party liable for the damages they inflict. We must sift through the facts attendant to each particular externality problem to discover the party that can avoid any external costs most cheaply, and we should rule in such a way that they have an incentive to do so. If we make a mistake and assign liability to the wrong party and if transaction costs are so high that a rearrangement of legal rights cannot occur, we will misallocate resources and forfeit considerable social surplus.

Over the years, many economists have built on Coase's insights to develop a distinctive approach to environmental problems, often described as the *property-rights approach*. Where Pigou and his followers tend to focus on the consequences of externality problems, devotees of the property-rights approach tend to ask why the externality problem exists at all. Commonly, they ascribe such problems to an incomplete specification or assignment of rights to certain property. They sometimes recommend that certain environmental problems be best addressed by assigning these rights more completely, or reassigning them. In other cases, they will look for ways to reduce transaction costs so that the parties involved may negotiate efficient solutions to externality problems.

Few scholars believe this approach is fruitful in all contexts. Indeed, some even question whether Coasian prescriptions are ever useful.[12] Ample research has shown, however, that the law of torts (which involves actions—intentional or unintentional—that cause damage to other parties) has indeed evolved in a way that is at least loosely consistent with Coasian precepts.[13]

---

[12]Robert Cooter, "The Cost of Coase," *Journal of Legal Studies*, 11 (January 1982), pp. 1–34.

[13]William Landes and Richard Posner, *The Economic Structure of Tort Law*, Harvard University Press, Cambridge, MA, 1987.

And, as we will see later, policymakers are considering market-based approaches to pollution problems with greater frequency these days. Clearly, there is much of value in Coase's analysis of externality problems.

VIGNETTE 16.3   The Common Law on Pollution Externalities

Under the common law, those harmed by pollution have long been able to sue for compensatory damages or, less often, injunctive relief. It is interesting to note that decisions in such cases do *not* uniformly make polluters liable for damages à la Pigou. In fact, they often use reasoning that appears designed to produce efficient results.

Consider the case of *Folmar v. Elliot Coal*.[14] Defendant Elliot ran a coal-cleaning plant that polluted the air nearby, eventually provoking a lawsuit from two homeowners whose domiciles were within 1,500 feet of the plant. It was clear that the defendant's actions had imposed costs on the plaintiffs in the form of discomfort and annoyance and probably reduced values for their properties.

However, both the trial and appeals courts refused to find the defendant liable for damages. They were guided by tort law principles which held that

[T]he owner of private property is entitled to damages due to injury occurring from a nontrespassory invasion of his premises if the defendant's conduct is the legal cause of the invasion and the invasion is (a) substantial, and (b) intentional and unreasonable, or unintentional negligent, reckless or ultrahazardous conduct.

Although the damages were substantial, the courts found them *not unreasonable*. In deciding this issue, the appeals court was guided by the tort law principle that "[a]n actor's conduct is unreasonable . . . unless the utility of his conduct outweighs the gravity of the harm." The defendant had already invested in some pollution abatement equipment; further investments were not, in the appeals court's view, "economically feasible." In other words, the courts weighed the costs of allowing the defendant to continue polluting against the costs of further limiting him from doing so—exactly the kind of comparison Coase might have recommended— and found the latter to exceed the former. The homeowners' losses went uncompensated.

Setting Standards

Most of the pollution problems with which state and federal environmental agencies grapple are a bit more complex than those we have been discussing so far. These problems commonly affect many parties over broad areas, so direct negotiations among these parties are clearly out of the question. But simply defining a broad right to pollute (or to be free from pollution) may not maximize welfare. Most often, neither the costs associated with pollution nor the costs of avoiding it will vary directly and uniformly with output, as in our earlier example. In such cases, it may be necessary to divide rights to resources among parties contending for them.

To see why this might be necessary and how it might be done, consider the

---

[14]*Folmar v. Elliot Coal Mining Co.*, 441 Pa. 592, 272 A.2d 910 (1971).

following scenario. A power plant burns coal to produce electricity. As a by-product, various pollutants (e.g., sulfur dioxide or particulate matter such as soot) are released into the air near the plant, imposing health and disamenity costs on those in the vicinity. For simplicity, let us assume this plant is the only source of air pollution in the area.

Figure 16.2 shows a cost-benefit approach to abatement (i.e., removal) of this pollution. The horizontal axis plots the amount of pollution removed from the air. We are currently at the origin, and the farther right we go, the cleaner the air gets. The question, of course, is how far we should go. The vertical axis

FIGURE 16.2
POLLUTION ABATEMENT: A COST-BENEFIT APPROACH. Social surplus is maximized if we remove or abate any units of pollution for which marginal benefits of abatement exceed costs. Here, the efficient abatement standard is 50 units of pollution removed. Additional units of pollution would cost more to remove than to tolerate.

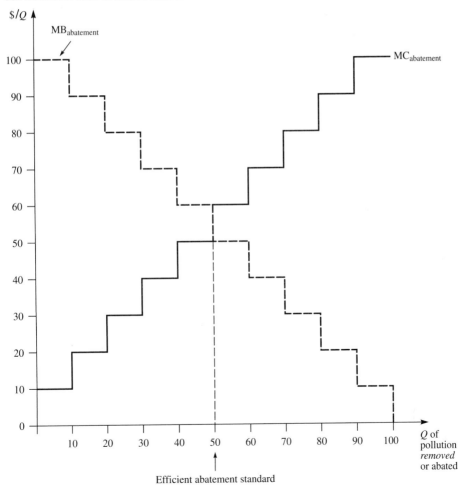

measures dollar costs and benefits (per unit) of removing particular units of pollution.

The upward-sloping step function in Figure 16.2 depicts the marginal cost (MC) of pollution abatement, labeled $MC_{abatement}$. It shows that the level of pollution can be reduced by 10 units at a cost of $10 per unit, so the total cost of removing these first 10 units of pollution is $100. But reducing pollution another 10 units costs $20 per unit, adding $200 to the total abatement cost. Reducing pollution a further 10 units costs $30 per unit, and so on. This rising $MC_{abatement}$ curve illustrates the fact that typically it is very cheap to eliminate the first few units of pollution. In our example, we might need only to place a tarpaulin over our coal storage bins to keep dust from blowing into the air. Reducing emissions further is more expensive, however, requiring us to buy more expensive (low-sulfur) coal or install smokestack scrubbers, etc.

The downward-sloping step function in Figure 16.2 shows the *marginal benefit* (MB) of removing each unit of pollution, labeled $MB_{abatement}$. These benefits are really the health and disamenity costs we avoid with each extra unit of pollution abated. In this example, abating the first 10 units of pollution confers a sizable benefit, enabling society to avoid health and disamenity costs of $100 per unit. Thus, the total benefit of removing the first 10 units of pollution is $1,000, perhaps because this generates a significant reduction in the incidence of serious pollution-related illness. Abating the next 10 units of pollution, however, carries a smaller incremental benefit ($90 per unit), as does abating the next 10, and so on, perhaps because we now avoid fewer (or less serious) illnesses or the grossest forms of disamenity. As we remove more and more pollution (i.e., as the air gets closer to pristine purity), the added benefit (per unit) of still cleaner air approaches zero.

Suppose we declare that the surrounding populace has the right to breathe pure air, and so we require the electric company to abate 100 units of pollution. We will find that achieving this goal costs a total of $5,500 (that is, $100 for the first 10 units abated, plus $200 for the next 10, and so on to $1,000 for the last 10). But this policy will generate total benefits of $5,500 as well (that is, $1,000 for the first 10 units abated, plus $900 for the next 10, and so on to $100 for the last 10). Thus, society is left with no *net* gain: We spend as much on pollution abatement as we get in health cost savings, enhanced amenity, etc. We simply substitute, dollar for dollar, the costs of controlling pollution for the costs of tolerating it.

If we want to maximize social welfare, we should not tell the electric company to eliminate its output of pollution completely, but to reduce it by 50 units. It's easy to see why this policy is efficient. Consider reducing the level of pollution by 10 units. As noted before, this costs a total of $100. But it avoids health and disamenity costs of $1,000, thus saving society $900. Similarly, eliminating a second 10 units of pollution costs $200 more, but avoids pollution costs of $900, saving society $700. As long as $MC_{abatement}$ lies below $MB_{abatement}$, in fact, there is social surplus (i.e., net social benefit) associated with further pollution abatement. If, however, $MB_{abatement}$ lies below $MC_{abatement}$, then further reduction of pollution costs more than it is worth.

After we have abated 50 units of pollution, further abatement is actually wasteful: Abating the next 10 units (for a total of 60 units abated) costs $600 but generates health and amenity benefits of only $500, so society would be $100 poorer as a result.

In sum, we can set *efficient standards* for pollution abatement by finding the intersection of curves measuring the marginal benefit and marginal cost of pollution abatement. (Note that we can look at our $MB_{abatement}$ curve as a demand curve for pollution abatement, and our $MC_{abatement}$ curve is like an abatement supply curve. Thus, the surplus-maximizing amount of the good in question—pollution abatement—will be found at the intersection of demand and supply curves, just as in "normal" markets.) If the benefits of eliminating a particular unit of pollution exceed the costs, we should eliminate it; if the costs of eliminating it exceed the benefits, we should tolerate it. In our example, the efficient standard is 50 units of pollution abated; removing any more or less pollution will not maximize social welfare. In this case, we achieve a welfare optimum by granting the plant a limited right to pollute (or, to look at it from the other side, granting those in the vicinity a limited right to pure air).

Note that if transactions were costless, the efficient standard is exactly the result that would be obtained via negotiations among the affected parties. In our example, those experiencing adverse health and amenity affects would be willing to pay up to $1,000 to get the plant to reduce pollution by 10 units, while the plant would be willing to do so for as little as $100. Clearly, there is room for mutually beneficial exchange here—and for other exchanges that would reduce the level of pollution by 50 units. Although high transaction costs may forestall any such exchanges, we might view the pollution standards set by environmental regulators as attempts to duplicate the results that would ensue from market exchange in a zero-transaction-costs world.

Note also that our example, in which we call upon a firm to reduce—but not eliminate—pollution, should not be taken to mean that it will *always* be best to "split the difference" in allocating rights to a scarce resource among competing parties. It is quite possible that the benefits of avoiding exposure to a certain type of pollution may be so high, or the costs of abating it so low, that the efficient standard for such pollution is complete abatement (or zero exposure). Figure 16.3a illustrates this possibility. On the other hand, a particular kind of pollution may impose such negligible costs on society, or would be so costly to abate, that it is inefficient to abate it at all, as in Figure 16.3b.

And, of course, it is difficult in some cases to measure the costs or benefits of pollution abatement, as we shall see when we examine environmental policy in practice. Such measurement difficulties should not, however, lead us to throw our hands up and disregard cost-benefit considerations entirely in setting pollution standards. If we are able to calculate a reasonable range of abatement costs and benefits, e.g., we will be able to specify a corresponding range for an efficient standard, as in Figure 16.3c. Depending on circumstances and our attitudes toward risk, we may set the final standard closer to one limit of this range or another.

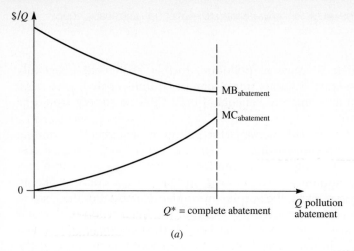

(a)

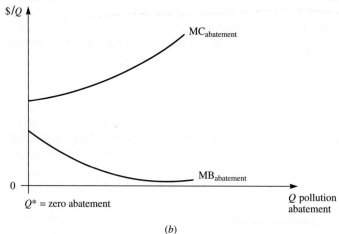

(b)

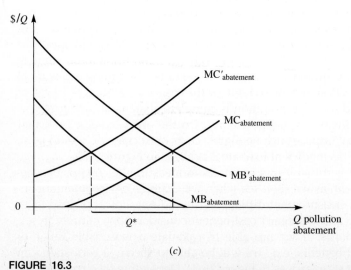

(c)

FIGURE 16.3
EFFICIENT STANDARDS UNDER VARYING COST-BENEFIT ASSUMPTIONS. (*a*) Complete abatement is efficient. (*b*) No abatement is called for. (*c*) Uncertainty about cost and benefit estimates leads to specification of a range of possible efficient abatement standards.

PUBLIC POLICY AND ENVIRONMENTAL QUALITY

Our discussion thus far has centered on how policymakers *might* address environmental issues. It is time to examine how they actually do it. We begin with a brief survey of the problems that have become the focus of regulatory action.

Environmental Problems: An Overview

The air, water, land, and species of the earth sustain our lives, give us materials useful in production and consumption, and—not least—have amenity values of their own. Given a large population of diverse preferences, it is inevitable that there will be conflicts about how these environmental resources should be used. When resources are owned, conflicts about their use can be easily resolved by market bidding. If I want the lot next door to my house to remain vacant (perhaps to ensure greater peace and quiet), I can try to buy it. If I am unwilling or unable to bid enough for this purpose, that is society's way of deciding that the lot's value in some other use or to some other user exceeds my own. As we have seen, however, many environmental resources are not amenable to ownership and exchange. When resources are *unpriced*, conflicts about their use go unresolved, and their misuse or abuse becomes common.

We misuse the air, water, and land around us when we use these resources excessively for waste disposal, rendering them unusable (or less usable) for other purposes. The villain is not always the manufacturing firm dumping soot or various gases into the air, chemical wastes into waterways, or toxic substances into landfills. Often *we* are the problem. When we drive rather than walk to our destination, we use an unpriced resource—the air—to dispose of the carbon monoxide and nitrogen dioxide (among other things) that our vehicle produces. In similar ways, we often disregard the effects of our consumption activities on water quality or land pollution because these resources are generally unpriced or underpriced.

Our consumption of energy—to power our cars and appliances, heat our homes, and manufacture other goods—is a major source of polluted air. According to the National Commission on Air Quality, combustion of fossil fuels accounts for nearly one-half of emissions of particulates and hydrocarbons and 85 to 95 percent of emissions of sulfur dioxide, nitrogen dioxide, and carbon monoxide. The largest single source of water pollution is government-owned wastewater treatment plants. Other *point sources* (sources that discharge piped or channeled effluent into waterways from an identifiable point or points) have generally become sufficiently controlled that today *nonpoint sources* such as runoff from farms, roads, and urban land uses are a more significant cause of water pollution. Most *toxic substances* that make their way into our air, water, or land (e.g., asbestos or pesticides such as DDT, which can be poisonous when exposure exceeds some minimal level) are by-products of industrial processes or agricultural production.

Fortunately, some common pollutants, such as domestic sewage or other organic wastes, are *biodegradable*: Through chemical and biological processes, they can be broken down into harmless substances and absorbed by the environment—provided that we do not dispose of them in excessive quantities or concentrations. But many toxic pollutants do not change in this way or do so very slowly. In some cases, they can accumulate in human or animal tissues, leading to adverse health effects many years after their release into the ecosystem.

Of course, not all pollutants carry the costs of diminished health. Some merely annoy us or reduce our enjoyment of the natural world. But even those who are indifferent to annoyance or take little pleasure from nature may be provoked to act when informed about the health effects of many forms of pollution. One widely cited study, e.g., by Lester Lave and Eugene Seskin, concluded that a 50 percent reduction from 1960 levels of key air pollutants in a metropolitan area would add about 1 year to the life expectancy of every individual in the area.[15] It is hard to suggest, in the face of such findings, that nothing needs to be done to ameliorate pollution problems.

Finally, we note that some environmental policy aims not at the conservation of air, water, or land resources but at the *preservation of species*. As in other contexts, well-specified and enforceable ownership rights can ensure that a species will avoid extinction. There is little likelihood that Longhorn cattle or Siamese housecats will ever be classified as endangered species. But not all species yield useful economic products, enhance private owners' utility levels, or are even amenable to private ownership. Such species' chances for survival are commonly ignored when economic agents determine their actions (recall Vignette 3.3 on overhunting of the buffalo in the Old West and, today, overhunting of the African elephant). With this externality problem in mind, government may intervene to prevent or redirect some economic activities in order to limit the likelihood that certain species will become extinct.[16]

Structure and Policies of the EPA

The EPA was established in 1970 to coordinate a unified, national policy on environmental issues and enforce old and new legislation that deals with air and water pollution, toxic substances, waste disposal, pesticides, and radioactive substances. We cannot enumerate here all its duties or the programs it has devised to discharge them, but we summarize its main activities below.

Air Pollution   The Clean Air Act of 1970 identified several common air pollutants (called *criteria pollutants*) and empowered the EPA to establish national *ambient air quality standards*, or maximum allowable levels of exposure to these pollutants. The EPA established two sets of standards. *Primary stan-*

---

[15]Lester B. Lave and Eugene P. Seskin, *Air Pollution and Human Health*, The Johns Hopkins University Press, Baltimore, MD, 1977.

[16]Alternatively, the survival of rare species may be seen as a pure public good. Many individuals may place a positive value on this good. That is, they may derive utility from the knowledge that a species exists—even if they never actually observe a member of the relevant population in the wild. But free-rider problems or other complications may mean that it will be underproduced by the market. Accordingly, intervention to ensure species survival may be justified.

dards aim to protect the health of the most sensitive group in the population, while *secondary standards* are more stringent and aim to clean the air of visible pollutants and prevent corrosion or any other effects of polluted air. The EPA also divided the nation into several hundred *air quality control districts* and made each state responsible for attaining the standards within its jurisdiction.

By 1975 it was obvious that many regions were not in compliance with the primary standards, and in 1977 Congress amended the Clean Air Act, extending the deadline for compliance but designating all areas that did not meet the original deadlines as *nonattainment regions*. These regions were subjected to particularly stringent controls. State agencies were required to limit new construction of large sources of pollution through the use of a permit program. Permits could not be issued unless the agency could show that the source (1) did not jeopardize attainment and (2) employed equipment designed to ensure that emissions of pollutants would be kept to the lowest attainable rate. In regions that had attained the standards, the EPA imposed controls aimed at *prevention of significant deterioration* (PSD). PSD policies set limits on allowable increases in pollutant levels beyond the district's baseline. Once these limits were reached, no new sources of pollution were permitted, even if the district had cleaner air than that required by the prevailing ambient standard. In addition to the ambient standards, the EPA established uniform national emission standards for mobile (e.g., trucks and automobiles) or stationary (e.g., power plants) sources that emitted hazardous pollutants or for new sources of criteria pollutants.

The EPA enforces these standards by issuing permits or certificates to new sources of pollution, monitoring compliance, and determining appropriate penalties or remedies when noncompliance is detected. For example, automobile manufacturers obtain certificates to produce certain models when prototypes pass EPA inspection. Follow-up assembly-line monitoring and on-road testing ensure continuing compliance. The majority of states now require periodic smog inspections as a central feature of their attainment plans. When violations are detected, the EPA can recall products, levy fines, and, for severe offenses, impose criminal penalties.

Water Pollution Congress's 1972 Water Pollution Amendments were remarkably ambitious. They urged that "the discharge of pollutants into the navigable waters be eliminated by 1985." Congress set 1977 as the deadline for achieving the *best-practicable control technology* (BPCT) in industry and secondary treatment of municipal sewage and 1983 as the deadline for achieving the *best-available control technology* (BACT) in industry. By 1977, it was obvious that these goals were unrealistic. They would have cost hundreds of billions of dollars to achieve and, given the large volume of pollutants coming from nonpoint sources (which were not directly affected by the EPA standards), would not have ensured that waterways were "swimmable and fishable," as Congress wanted. Accordingly, Congress postponed the BPCT standards until 1979 and relaxed the BACT standards for pollutants such as human waste and organic debris, although tightening them for toxic wastes.

From these broad standards the EPA derived maximum allowable emission levels for tens of thousands of point sources. A specific factory, e.g., may be allowed to dump X pounds of suspended solids for every Y units of output. The pollutants that are covered and the limits that are set can vary from industry to industry. Every facility that discharges wastes into U.S. waters is subject to such limits and must obtain a permit from the EPA before beginning operations. EPA monitoring focuses on "major" permit holders, although firms that make small discharges are more likely to be monitored closely the more toxic are the substances they discharge. Penalties for violations range from slaps on the wrist ("notices of violations") to heavy fines. Note, however, that city governments are some of the biggest violators of water pollution standards, and the EPA has relatively little leverage to keep cities to any kind of timetable. The practice now is to get cities to sign consent decrees, whereby they agree to meet pollution targets by specified dates. If a consent decree is violated, cities answer to federal district judges rather than the EPA.

Toxic Substances   The EPA is also authorized to regulate *hazardous products* (e.g., pesticides) or *hazardous wastes* (i.e., toxic chemicals that are by-products of industrial processes) that are not dumped into the air or water.[17]

The EPA must be notified of all new potentially hazardous products prior to their manufacture, and it may require makers of these products to prove, via scientific tests, that their products are "reasonably" safe in their intended uses. If the EPA is not satisfied that a product is safe or considers it unsafe in certain uses, it may ban a product (as it did with the pesticide DDT), require the recall of products, or impose labeling requirements.

The tragedy at Love Canal focused policymakers' (and the public's) attention on the hazards of chemical wastes dumped in landfills or other sites. Until 1953, Hooker Electrochemical had dumped waste chemicals into what was then considered impermeable clay near the canal, in the Niagara Falls area. Then Hooker deeded the land to the Niagara Falls Board of Education, which built a school there. Later—despite the fact that Hooker had specifically warned against developing the site for residential uses—the board sold parcels to a homebuilder, and people began moving into the area. By 1978, residents were complaining of chemicals leaking to the surface and vapors in their basements, and medical reports suggested that residents had abnormally high rates of liver disease, miscarriage, and birth defects.

In 1980, Congress responded to this and other notable incidents with the *Superfund Bill,* authorizing the EPA to require that sites afflicted by toxic waste problems be cleaned up by the "responsible parties." In addition, the bill set aside $1.6 billion (raised by taxes on petroleum and chemical production) to finance cleanup in areas where liability was unclear or resources unavailable.

---

[17]Authorization for these activities came with the Toxic Substances Control Act of 1976; the Resource Conservation and Recovery Act of 1976; the Comprehensive Environmental Response, Compensation, and Liability Act (often called the "Superfund Bill") of 1980; the Hazardous and Solid Waste Amendments of 1984; and the Superfund Amendment and Reauthorization Act of 1986.

The EPA then embarked on a program to identify all uncontrolled waste sites in the United States, classify them according to the seriousness of the hazard there, and begin cleaning up these sites.

The Effects of Environmental Policy

Benefits   It is quite clear that federal and state efforts to improve environmental quality are bearing some fruit. In 1970, when the EPA was created, significant portions of the Atlantic coast and Great Lakes shorelines were closed to swimmers and fishers, many rivers near urban areas were little more than open sewers, and the air over many industrial cities was often thick with smoke and redolent of various foul-smelling pollutants. Today, there are stories of environmental triumph from coast to coast. It is actually pleasant to fish and boat on waterways passing through the heart of industrial Detroit; the air over Chattanooga, once gray with soot, is now crisp and clear; salmon have returned to the Willamette River in Oregon, once one of the nation's most polluted.

But we need not rely on mere anecdotal evidence to conclude that the quality of the environment has improved in important ways. By 1984, the President's Council on Environmental Quality (CEQ) could write that

> [T]he nation's air quality is improving. Federal standards have been achieved for four of the six criteria air pollutants in most areas of the country. The two criteria air pollutants that persist as problems are carbon monoxide . . . and ozone . . . ; a downward trend is evident for both of these pollutants.[18]

According to the *pollution standard index* (PSI) developed in 1976 to provide a common, well-understood measure of local air quality, most metropolitan areas have experienced steady declines in the number of days per year in which air quality was unhealthful (UNH1), very unhealthful (UNH2), or hazardous (HAZ). Figure 16.4 shows the trends in four major cities. The declines shown for St. Louis and Washington are fairly representative of those for other large commercial centers. In some cities, such as Atlanta, unhealthful air was never much of a problem. In others, such as Los Angeles, it remains a severe problem. Nationwide, sizable declines in the levels of lead (down 87 percent from 1977 to 1986), sulfur dioxide (down 37 percent), and carbon monoxide (down 32 percent) have been reported, with smaller—but still measurable—declines in other pollutants.

Water quality is similarly improved. Table 16.1 shows the percentages of waterways that met the Clean Water Act's "fishable and swimmable" goal for a sample of 20 states in 1984. While the statutory goal was not achieved everywhere, it was achieved in the great majority of cases, and most rivers and lakes showed substantial improvement during the 1970s and 1980s. In 1972,

---

[18]Council on Environmental Quality, *Environmental Quality 1984*, Government Printing Office, Washington, 1984, p. 11.

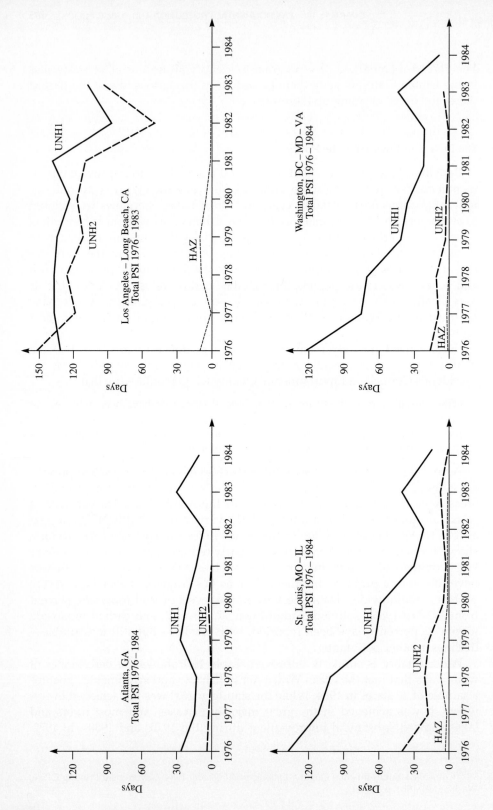

for example, only 36 percent of the nation's rivers and streams supported the uses designated for them (e.g., fishing, swimming, drinking). By 1982, that figure had risen to 64 percent. And 84 percent of the lakes in the United States supported their designated uses in 1982.[19]

In addition, there is evidence that the levels of various environmental contaminants that accumulate in human and animal tissue has been declining. For example, DDT levels in walleye found in Lake Erie fell by about 50 percent, and DDT levels fell by about 60 percent in trout found in Lake Ontario from 1977 to 1983. The level of polychlorinated biphenyls (PCBs) found in herring gull eggs in colonies near eastern Lake Superior fell by about 70 percent from 1974 to 1986. And the percentage of the human population with PCB concentrations exceeding 1 part per million fell from 68.4 percent in 1972 to 8.6 percent by 1983.[20]

Clearly, these are heartening results. But an important question remains: How much are these improvements *worth*? It is certainly nice to have cleaner, more healthful air and waterways more amenable to recreational uses. Economists are notoriously utilitarian, however. We always like to know whether something is worth more than it costs. This requires some accounting of benefits.

In the case of environmental quality, this accounting is quite difficult. It requires us to make laborious calculations of enhanced property values, reduced cleaning bills, health care costs saved, etc., and to somehow estimate the value of aesthetic improvement and of lives saved. This is clearly a complicated—and controversial—undertaking. Yet it can be done and must, if we are to monitor the social utility of our pollution control programs.

The most commonly cited estimates of the benefits of air and water pollution control have been produced by A. M. Freeman.[21] Summing the benefits to human health, recreational values, enhanced commercial values, and other sources of benefit, Freeman concluded that the annual benefits from air pollution control range from $7.6 billion to $79.7 billion, with a "most reasonable" point estimate of $32.4 billion (all values expressed in 1982 dollars). The annual benefits from water pollution control are estimated at $5.3 billion to $25.5 billion, with a point estimate of $13 billion.

---

[19]Ibid., p. 83.
[20]Council on Environmental Quality, *Environmental Quality 1986*, pp. C-46, C-47; *Environmental Quality 1987–88*, p. 417.
[21]A. Myrick Freeman III, *Air and Water Pollution Control: A Benefit-Cost Assessment*, Wiley, New York, 1982.

FIGURE 16.4
TRENDS IN AIR QUALITY IN ATLANTA, LOS ANGELES–LONG BEACH, ST. LOUIS, AND WASHINGTON, DC. In some cities (e.g., Atlanta) air quality has never been much of a problem; in others (e.g., Los Angeles) poor air quality remains a problem. But in many cities (e.g., St. Louis, Washington), the 1980s saw marked improvement in air quality.

TABLE 16.1
PERCENTAGES OF RIVER MILES IN 20 REPORTING STATES MEETING GOAL OF "SWIMMABILITY AND FISHABILITY." While the Clean Water Act's goal has not been achieved everywhere, it was achieved in a majority of the nation's rivers by the mid-1980s.

State	Total river miles	Assessed river miles	Percent fishable	Percent swimmable	Percent swimmable or fishable
Arkansas	11,202	11,202	94	53	—
Delaware	—	491	—	—	43
Maine	31,806	2,652	—	—	66
Maryland	9,300	7,440	—	—	92
Massachusetts	10,704	1,630	—	—	47
Minnesota	91,871	2,708	94	39	—
Mississippi	10,274	10,274	—	—	90
Missouri	18,750	18,670	99	21	—
Montana	19,168	17,251	95	96	95
Nebraska	24,000	7,152	74	19	—
New Hampshire	14,544	14,544	—	—	93
New Mexico	3,500	3,500	100	—	—
North Carolina	40,207	37,378	—	—	81
Ohio	43,919	4,949	—	—	62
Oregon	90,000	3,500	—	—	74
Rhode Island	724	724	—	—	81
South Carolina	9,679	2,489	—	—	57
Texas	80,000	16,120	—	—	90
Vermont	4,863	2,325	—	—	93
Virginia	27,240	4,964	81	46	—

Source: U.S. Environmental Protection Agency, *National Water Quality Inventory: 1984 Report to Congress,* Washington, 1985.

Costs The benefits discussed above are not trivial sums. But neither are the costs of complying with state and federal pollution control regulations. According to Kit Farber and Gary Rutledge, in 1986 expenditures by business, government, and individuals for pollution abatement had reached $70.8 billion—or about $300 for every woman, man, and child in the United States. Of this amount, $56.6 billion (again, in 1982 dollars) was for control of air and water pollution.[22]

This causes us to furrow our brow: If Freeman's point estimates are credited, the total annual benefits of air and water pollution control programs ($45.4

[22]Kit D. Farber and Gary L. Rutledge, "Pollution Abatement and Control Expenditures, 1983–86," *Survey of Current Business,* 68 (May 1988), pp. 22–29.

billion) are less than their costs by over $11 billion! Of course, this is not a fair comparison. Freeman's numbers are mere approximations, and perhaps his upper-range estimates are more credible than his point estimates.

But it is also true that direct expenditures for purchase of pollution control equipment and other *compliance costs* are but a portion of the total costs of pollution abatement efforts. Many scholarly studies have identified EPA regulations as a major cause of the slowdown in productivity experienced by U.S. manufacturing firms during the 1970s.[23] One study found that manufacturing output in 1976 was about $11 billion (in 1982 dollars) below what it would have been absent mandated pollution control expenditures.[24] Compliance with EPA regulations in some cases caused firms to close plants entirely,[25] imposing both economic and psychic costs on affected workers. Diverting investment funds to pollution abatement equipment from other uses such as research and development may also have unmeasured effects on the rate of innovation and international competitiveness. If the benefits of pollution abatement programs are higher than we have so far measured, so, too, are the costs.

Cost-effectiveness   It is possible to conclude, in any case, that the aggregate benefits of pollution control *might* exceed the aggregate costs. But this is probably a flawed approach in any case, for in aggregating costs and benefits across programs, we overlook the fact that some programs may be wildly cost-ineffective while others may be sound investments. And when we look closely at specific elements of our overall environmental protection program, it is clear that in some cases we spend huge sums to produce negligible environmental benefits and in others we could produce the kinds of tangible benefits we now enjoy at far lower cost.

Consider the programs aimed at controlling pollution from automobiles. The standards devised for this purpose are extremely stringent. By 1981, for example, a new car had to meet limits for certain pollutants that were about 5 percent of the unregulated 1966 levels. The standards aim (1) to reduce smog, which reduces visibility and can cause coughing, wheezing, and chest discomfort at high concentrations as well as crop damage; (2) to reduce carbon monoxide, which can impair the nervous system or heart function; and (3) to reduce particulates, which can lead to cardiac and pulmonary ailments. The health and amenity benefits associated with the *complete* elimination of manufactured smog through automobile emissions controls, certainly a laudable goal (although an unrealistic one, given that some smog originates in other sources), have been estimated at $8.3 billion per year. But under current stan-

---

[23]See, e.g., Wayne B. Gray, "The Cost of Regulation: OSHA, EPA and the Productivity Slowdown," *American Economic Review*, 77 (December 1987), pp. 998–1006.

[24]Robert W. Crandall, "Pollution Controls and Productivity Growth in Basic Industries," in Thomas G. Cowing and Rodney E. Stevenson, *Productivity Measurement in Regulated Industries*, Academic Press, New York, 1981.

[25]See Council on Environmental Quality, *Environmental Quality 1978*, p. 433.

dards, these regulations impose annual costs of about $16.8 billion.[26] This is hardly a good return on our investment. The problem is that we are employing *national* standards to treat *local* problems. Urban smog is largely concentrated in southern California, Houston, and the New York area. The benefits of automobile emissions reductions fall almost exclusively in these areas, while under our national approach costs are imposed everywhere.

Many scholarly studies demonstrate that the benefits derived from other programs can be obtained in a far less costly manner. Scott Atkinson and D. H. Lewis, e.g., showed that controls of particulate emissions in the St. Louis area in the 1970s were 6 to 10 times more expensive than the minimum-cost approach.[27] Eugene Seskin et al. found controls to be 10 times more expensive than a cost-minimizing strategy in controlling nitrogen oxide emissions in the Chicago area in the late 1970s and early 1980s.[28] In the mid-1980s, Frank Gollop and Mark Roberts estimated that electric utilities could save about 47 percent of the cost of complying with then-current clean air regulations if allowed to trade pollution rights among themselves (an approach that will be discussed more fully later).[29] After a broad survey of air pollution policy, the General Accounting Office concluded in 1982 that more sensible policies could yield the same benefits at savings of 40 to 90 percent of prevailing compliance costs.[30]

Not all pollution control programs are cost-ineffective, of course. There is evidence that the benefits of controls on many stationary sources of air pollution and point sources of water pollution have exceeded the costs. It is clear, however, that there is considerable room for improvement in our pursuit of greater environmental quality.

REGULATORY REFORM

Over the years, economists have offered several important criticisms of the EPA's centralized, bureaucratic approach to regulation; what is more, they have devised several novel approaches that might produce better results at lower cost.

---

[26]Robert W. Crandall, Howard K. Gruenspecht, Theodore E. Keeler, and Lester B. Lave, *Regulating the Automobile*, The Brookings Institution, Washington, 1986, p. 114. Freeman, *Air and Water Pollution Control*, also concluded that the costs of controlling emissions from mobile sources exceed the benefits associated with the *complete* elimination of ozone and carbon monoxide pollution.

[27]Scott E. Atkinson and D. H. Lewis, "A Cost Effective Analysis of Alternative Air Control Strategies," *Journal of Environmental Economics and Management*, 1 (1974), pp. 237–250.

[28]Eugene P. Seskin, Robert J. Anderson, Jr., and Robert O. Reid, "An Empirical Analysis of Economic Strategies for Controlling Air Pollution," *Journal of Environmental Economics and Management*, 10 (1983), pp. 112–124.

[29]Frank M. Gollop and Mark J. Roberts, "Cost-Minimizing Regulation of Sulfur Emissions: Regional Gains in Electric Power," *Review of Economics and Statistics*, 67 (February 1985), pp. 81–90.

[30]U.S. General Accounting Office, *A Market Approach to Air Pollution Control Could Reduce Compliance Costs without Jeopardizing Clean Air Goals*, Government Printing Office, Washington, 1982, p. ii.

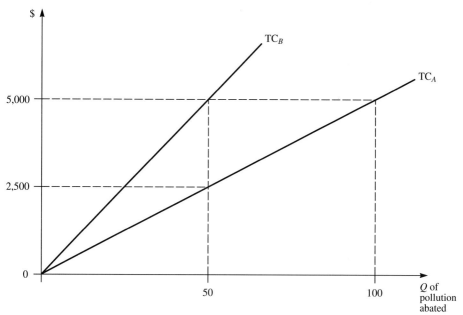

FIGURE 16.5
AN ACROSS-THE-BOARD APPROACH TO POLLUTION ABATEMENT. In this example, removing 100 units of pollution by forcing each of two plants (*A* and *B*) to cut pollution by 50 units would cost $7,500. We could achieve the same level of abatement at a cost of $5,000 by telling plant *A* to cut pollution by 100 units and leaving *B* alone.

Criticisms

The EPA most often relies on a *command-and-control* method of addressing environmental problems; i.e., it identifies sources of pollution and tries to control emissions from each source by imposing stringent standards or, in some cases, mandating the use of specific abatement equipment. There are several flaws in this approach.

Knowledge and Information Problems The amount of knowledge and information required to correct even a modest pollution problem is staggering. While most regulators are highly intelligent, well-educated individuals, they usually will not have access to the crucial bits of information necessary to make truly cost-efficient abatement decisions.

Consider the following example. A firm operates two plants, *A* and *B*, that are a town's sole source of a certain air pollutant. The EPA determines that emissions of this pollutant must be cut in half if the town's air is to be rendered healthful. Lacking any reason to do otherwise, it directs each plant to cut its emissions of the pollutant by 50 percent. While this will achieve the EPA's goal of healthful air, it may not do so in a cost-effective manner. Figure 16.5 illustrates the reason: The two plants may not have identical costs of pollution abatement. In Figure 16.5, the total costs of abating pollution at plant A, labeled TC_A, rise by \$50 for each unit of pollution eliminated, while the total costs of abating pollution at plant B, labeled TC_B, rise twice as fast.[31] If the EPA follows an across-the-board approach and requires the elimination of, say, 50 units of pollution at each plant, we will spend a total of \$7,500 on pollution abatement. But note: We could obtain the same level of air quality by having plant A eliminate 100 units of pollution and B eliminate none, and the total costs of abatement would fall to \$5,000.

In general, it is unlikely that a regulator in some far-off location will know how the costs of abating pollution vary among discharge points within plants, across plants, or across firms. There are nearly 30,000 major stationary sources of air pollution in the United States; each usually has several discharge points. The number of sources of water pollution is even greater. It is inconceivable that the EPA will be able to custom-tailor its emission standards to all these sources. But its reliance on the command-and-control approach means that those who do have good information about the most cost-effective means of abatement, such as firm or plant managers, have little opportunity to put this information to constructive use.

Incentive Problems   On occasion, the EPA sets emissions limits based on "the best available technology economically achievable." This creates something of a perverse incentive for polluters: If they come up with a new technology to reduce pollution, they are handing regulatory authorities a way to impose more costly restrictions on them. Thus, the command-and-control approach may retard innovation in pollution abatement.

Since the EPA often applies stricter standards to new rather than old equipment, firms may also have an incentive to keep obsolete plants and equipment running longer than they otherwise would, which may actually damage environmental quality (or impose other social costs, e.g., they may reduce worker safety). And since the EPA often requires sources to reduce their pollution from some previous "base" level, firms have an incentive to drag their feet. If one firm ambitiously "cleans up its act" before the EPA strictly requires it to, subsequent across-the-board requirements to reduce emissions levels by $X\%$ will (assuming rising marginal costs of abatement) hit it harder than its foot-dragging rivals.

More generally, the EPA's reliance on direct controls means firms will be passive and reluctant to search for ways to do more than is strictly required. Suppose a firm is required to cut its emissions level by 50 percent, and it can do so for \$1 million. It has little reason to point out, under the current system, that it can cut its emissions 80 percent for an outlay of \$1.1 million. Once the firm satisfies the standard, it has no reason to try to exceed it—even if it can do so very cheaply.

---

[31]That is, $TC_A = 50Q_A$, while $TC_B = 100Q_B$, where Q_A and Q_B denote the quantity of pollution abated at plants A and B, respectively.

Problems in the Political Process   Some of the problems with our environmental policy do originate not in the EPA, but in Congress. In a nutshell, some interest groups have occasionally succeeded in manipulating environmental legislation to generate benefits for themselves. These efforts have usually inflated the costs of enhanced environmental quality; on occasion, they have *diminished* environmental quality.

Perhaps the best example has to do with the 1977 amendments to the Clean Air Act dealing with coal. Environmental activists wanted to force public utilities in western states to install smokestack scrubbers to remove at least 70 to 90 percent of the sulfur dioxide in stack gases. They found strong allies in legislators from eastern coal-mining states. The reason? Eastern coal contains a great deal of sulfur (as much as 8 percent), while western coal is low in sulfur (as little as 0.5 percent). Eastern coal producers knew that if the law required the installation of scrubbers rather than merely specifying how much sulfur dioxide could be *emitted* from stacks, their cheaper, high-sulfur coal would be easier to sell. Despite an EPA report noting that compliance costs *and sulfur emissions levels* would be higher under a scrubbing requirement than under a feasible alternative, the requirement passed.[32]

Several other studies have documented that environmental regulation has been used to affect competition among firms and regions. The key here is *enforcement asymmetries*. Simply put, while EPA regulations raise all firms' private costs, they raise some firms' costs more than others. New plants, e.g., must often meet tighter standards than old, and plants in cleaner areas must meet tighter standards than those in dirty areas. One study by Ann Bartel and Lacy Glenn Thomas concluded that EPA regulation is sometimes used as a predatory device, conferring cost advantages on some firms by handicapping others.[33] Another study by Peter Pashigian found that certain regulations have been promoted by some states (e.g., those in the north and east) in order to reduce the competitiveness of others (in the south and west).[34]

Market-Based Policies

The EPA has not ignored the criticisms of economists and other analysts. Since the late 1970s, it has experimented with a variety of reforms aimed at making environmental policy more flexible and cost-effective. Most of these reforms involve some form of *emissions trading*, in which additional emissions in one area or from one polluter are allowed as long as they are equaled or exceeded by reductions from some other source.

---

[32]Bruce A. Ackerman and William T. Hassler, *Clean Coal/Dirty Air or How the Clean Air Act Became a Multi-Billion Dollar Bail-Out for High-Sulfur Coal Producers and What Should Be Done about It*, Yale University Press, New Haven, CT, 1981.

[33]Ann P. Bartel and Lacy Glenn Thomas, "Predation through Regulation: The Wage and Profit Effects of the Occupational Safety and Health Administration and the Environmental Protection Agency," *Journal of Law and Economics*, 30 (October 1987), pp. 239–264.

[34]B. Peter Pashigian, "Environmental Regulation: Whose Self Interests Are Being Protected?" *Economic Inquiry*, 23 (October 1985), pp. 551–584.

Offsets   As noted earlier, new sources of pollution in regions which have not attained the EPA's ambient air quality standards can obtain a permit to operate only if the state control authority can demonstrate that progress toward attainment would not be jeopardized. In the mid-1970s, this put many nonattainment regions in a bind: Unless they somehow reduced emissions from already existing sources, new development would grind to a halt. But how to find the existing sources that could cut emissions most efficiently, and how best to convince them to do so? The EPA's *offset program*, expressly authorized in the 1977 amendments to the Clean Air Act, provided solutions. New emissions sources were allowed to purchase offsetting reductions (or, actually, slightly *greater* than offsetting reductions) in emissions from existing sources. Since the new sources naturally wanted to hold down their costs, they had an incentive to search for the existing sources that could achieve reductions most cheaply—exactly the process that would ensure efficient allocation of reductions. Uncertainties about evolving EPA policies made offset transactions somewhat less common than hoped; most of those that did occur were internal, involving adjustments of emissions within a firm. Still, by 1980 at least 32 external transactions had occurred,[35] and market-based methods of reducing pollution in a cost-effective fashion had a toehold.

Banking   In 1979 the EPA initiated its *banking program*: Firms in compliance with applicable standards were authorized to store the rights to pollution allowed at a plant until they wished to use them for offsets or trade them to other firms in offset transactions. This helped reduce firms' incentives to drag their feet in replacing obsolete facilities with newer, less polluting ones. Formerly, they might have delayed replacing such facilities because they would have forfeited the "right to pollute" (within the limits of applicable EPA standards) these facilities carried with them. Allowing these rights to be stored corrected this problem. Since emission reductions beyond EPA standards could also be banked and thus advertised for sale to new sources, the program also stimulated excess emission reduction and gave a boost to the market for offsets.

Bubbles   Later in 1979, the EPA gave existing emissions sources greater flexibility in how they could comply with applicable standards. Previously, the EPA had tried to force each source to produce specified emissions reductions at every discharge point. Under the *bubble policy*, the EPA allowed each source to choose its own mix of reductions as long as the overall air quality effects were up to par. By giving firms discretion to act within the hypothetical "bubble" surrounding their facilities, this policy enabled those with the best information about the costs of controlling pollution at various discharge points to allocate reductions in a cost-effective manner (neatly solving the

---

[35]Wes Vivian and William Hall, *An Examination of U.S. Market Trading in Air Pollution Offsets,* University of Michigan, Institute of Public Policy Studies, Ann Arbor, 1981.

problem posed earlier in Figure 16.5). Although the program was very limited in application, by 1985 about 50 bubble trades had been approved, producing capital savings estimated at $700 million and another $10 million per year in reduced operating costs (compared with the command-and-control approach).[36] In almost all cases, emissions reductions equaled or exceeded those that would have occurred without the trades.

Technology Forcing Although implementation of these reforms clearly improved the efficiency of environmental policy, they have had less impact than many environmental economists had hoped. In some cases, the rigidity of various statutes has halted extension of the emissions trading approach; adverse court decisions have limited the EPA's ability to build greater flexibility into the abatement process. In addition, since emissions trading programs appeared rather late in the game, many sources that might have benefited from this approach had already invested in equipment to comply with the command-and-control regulations. Finally, the idea that firms have a property right in surplus emission reductions has been hard for some to swallow. Thus, many programs are very limited in their applicability. In some states, confiscation of banked credits is a distinct possibility, limiting the incentive to create such credits.

Movement toward a full-fledged market for discharge rights that would allocate emissions reductions cost-effectively and produce strong incentives to reduce emissions has been hampered by a commitment to the concept of *technology forcing* in the pursuit of further progress. Many environmental activists are convinced that the best way to ensure long-term improvement in emissions levels is adoption of ever-stricter standards for new sources of pollution. That is, requiring new cars, power plants, or factories to use the best-available pollution control technologies will eventually lead to a cleaner environment, since older equipment and facilities must eventually be replaced. Much of the resistance to offsets, bubbles, and banking comes from those who fear that these programs—and emissions trading in general—enable new sources to escape the lowest technologically achievable emissions rate and thus will have unfavorable long-term effects on environmental quality. What this overlooks, however, is that technology forcing itself has perverse effects. Making new cars, plants, or factories subject to stricter standards significantly increases their costs, slowing the substitution of new for old. One study, by Howard Gruenspecht, showed that slightly *weaker* emissions standards for automobiles would have increased substitution of new cars for old sufficiently to reduce pollution for several years.[37]

---

[36]T. H. Tietenberg, "Uncommon Sense: The Program to Reform Pollution Control Policy," in Leonard W. Weiss and Michael W. Klass (eds.), *Regulatory Reform: What Actually Happened*, Little, Brown, Boston, 1986, p. 298.

[37]Howard Gruenspecht, "Differentiated Regulation: The Case of Auto Emissions Standards," *American Economic Review*, 72 (May 1982), pp. 328–331.

Recent Trends

In at least a few respects, market-based pollution control methods received a boost from the most recent piece of federal environmental legislation, the Clean Air Act amendments of 1990. This update of the 1970 Clean Air Act includes

- New compliance deadlines, ranging from about 6 to 20 years, for the cities which have thus far failed to comply with standards for ozone, carbon monoxide, and particulate matter
- More stringent standards for automobile tailpipe emissions of hydrocarbons, carbon monoxide, and nitrogen oxides beginning in the 1994-model year
- A requirement that reformulated gasolines producing fewer pollutants be devised and sold by 1995 in the nine cities with the worst ozone problems
- New standards for reduced emissions of 189 toxic pollutants over the next 10 years
- A two-phase, market-based system to reduce sulfur dioxide (SO_2) emissions by more than 50 percent by the year 2000
- New restrictions on the use, emission, and disposal of certain chemicals (e.g., chlorofluorocarbons) thought to deplete the ozone layer in the atmosphere

Perhaps the amendments' most innovative feature relates to SO_2 emissions, chiefly from power plants, which have long been thought to be linked to acid rain, damaging lakes and forests in the northeast and Canada. Under the new law, power plants will be given allowances to dump a certain amount of SO_2 based on their output of electricity between 1985 and 1987. Plants will be allowed to trade their allowances—each of which grants the right to dump 1 ton of SO_2 per year—in a national market. Such a system directly addresses the problem described in Figure 16.5. Now plants that can reduce emissions most cheaply will do so and will sell their surplus pollution allowances (for an amount economists expect will range from $250 to $1,100 each) to those whose costs of abatement are greater than the price of an allowance. In this way the costs of achieving the EPA's goal of a 50 percent reduction in SO_2 emissions will be achieved in a cost-effective fashion. In addition, the system may provoke a more intense search for new means of limiting SO_2 emissions than might have occurred under the old command-and-control approach.

It is possible that the emissions trading program for SO_2 may serve as a useful model, eventually expanding to encompass other pollutants (e.g., chlorofluorocarbons and other greenhouse gases thought to be damaging the ozone layer). But if the 1990 amendments are encouraging to those who believe in the value of market-based approaches to environmental problems, they are far from immune to economic criticism. Many provisions of the 1990 legislation (e.g., the automobile emissions controls) are likely to produce relatively small health and amenity benefits at high cost. While future costs and benefits are, of course, difficult to estimate with precision, environmental economist Paul R. Portney has remarked:

[B]ased on the studies that have been done, my back-of-the-envelope calculation suggests that the law, once it's fully phased in, will impose costs on the economy of $30 billion a year and generate benefits of $15–20 billion.[38]

Such forecasts may turn out to be in error, of course. The experts may underestimate the benefits of cleaner air and water. But so may they underestimate the social and economic costs (e.g., lost jobs, higher prices for fuel, automobiles, homes, etc.) of attaining these goals. If these figures are even approximately correct, though, it is clear we still have a lot of work to do in designing policies that meet our environmental goals in a manner that sacrifices as little as possible of alternative economic output.

SUMMARY AND CONCLUDING REMARKS

Economists tend to view most environmental problems as examples of negative externalities, i.e., costs that producers or consumers impose on third parties (those external to a transaction) without these parties' consent. When property rights or legal responsibilities are specified so that such externality problems can occur, it is commonly argued that private markets will fail to maximize welfare. Specifically, it is argued that when production or consumption involves some uncompensated external costs, there will be overproduction and dissipation of social surplus. The usual policy prescription in such cases is to "internalize the externality" by making the party imposing these costs liable for compensating victims or, equivalently, making this party pay a (Pigou) tax equal to the amount of external costs imposed.

Coase noted, however, that internalizing the externality in this way will be unnecessary in some circumstances and could lead to inefficient policies in others. If by chance it is costless (or very cheap) to transact, the problem might be solved by voluntary agreements among the affected parties. In the more realistic case where positive transaction costs prevent such agreements, Coase argued that a devotion to simple Pigou-style taxes or liability rules (i.e., "make the polluter pay") could lead policymakers to overlook the cheapest way to address externality problems. In Coase's view, we should try to determine who can avoid or cope with such problems at least cost, and then we should specify property rights or liability rules so that this party has an incentive to do so.

Federal efforts to cope with pollution externalities began with the creation of the EPA in 1970. The EPA sets maximum allowable levels of exposure to several common air pollutants (ambient air quality standards), sets maximum allowable levels for emission of pollutants into waterways, and regulates the discharge and cleanup of hazardous wastes by responsible parties.

It is clear that these efforts are improving overall air and water quality. Measures of air and water quality, although far from perfect, showed steady

---

[38]As quoted in Timothy Tregarthen, "Clean Air Act Boosts Costs, Markets," *The Margin,* 7 (Fall 1991), p. 41.

improvement during the 1970s and 1980s. It is possible, however, that the value of these improvements is exceeded by the costs of generating them—at least for some programs. Perhaps the least cost-effective pollution control program has been that for automobiles, where waste results from using national standards to treat local problems. However, programs aimed at controlling stationary sources of air pollution and point sources of water pollution have probably produced sizable net benefits. To overcome information and incentive problems associated with the EPA's current reliance on a command-and-control regulatory approach, many scholars have suggested that the agency make greater use of policies involving emissions trading, an approach which has been incorporated into the 1990 Clean Air Act's program to reduce sulfur dioxide emissions.

QUESTIONS FOR REVIEW AND DISCUSSION

16.1 The text outlines the welfare effects of negative externalities when the producer inhabits a competitive market. Discuss the welfare effects of such externalities when the producer is a monopolist. Use graphs to illustrate your analysis.

16.2 Professor Cheung's "fable of the bees" (Vignette 16.2) suggests that at least some externalities can be internalized by Coase-style transactions among affected parties. E. J. Mishan, however, argues that market transactions of this kind have little relevance to many environmental problems:

> [T]he possibilities of protecting the citizen against such common environmental blights as filth, fume, stench, noise, visual distractions, etc. by a market in property rights are too remote to be taken seriously.[39]

Do you agree with Professor Mishan? Can you think of *any* environmental problems that can be addressed without government intervention? Can government be viewed as an intermediary through which property rights are exchanged in Coase style? Explain.

16.3 Suppose widget production involves a peculiar form of pollution that affects only nearby sprocket producers. Every widget produced imposes $5 in costs on nearby sprocket producers, who must install special equipment to reduce this form of pollution to tolerable levels. Suppose, however, that the widget and sprocket producers can transact costlessly. Now the government (having read Pigou but not Coase) imposes a $5 tax per widget to solve this externality problem. Suppose, finally, that the beneficiaries of this tax cannot transact costlessly with either widget or sprocket producers. How will this tax affect welfare? Use graphs to illustrate your analysis.

16.4 Return to the paper mill example discussed in the text. The external costs imposed on downstream users of the river on which the mill is located, and the mill's cost and demand conditions, are as shown in Figure 16.1. Imagine you are judging whether the mill owner must pay compensatory damages to these downstream users. What factors will you consider in rendering your decision? Suppose you learn in the course of the trial that the mill can completely eliminate these external

---

[39]E. J. Mishan, "A Reply to Professor Worcester," *Journal of Economic Literature,* 10 (March 1972), p. 62.

costs by installing special pollution abatement equipment at a cost of $350. How will you rule? Explain your decision. Suppose the installation of such pollution abatement equipment is the only practical way to eliminate the external costs associated with the mill's activities. What is the maximum cost of such equipment that would make you rule in such a way that the mill installs it?

16.5 After hearing a prominent economist criticize federal environmental policy on the TV news one night, your roommate says, "I'm disgusted with these economists. They're completely fixated on dollars and cents, cost-effectiveness, and efficiency. Don't they know you can't put a price on some things? When it comes to ecology, we shouldn't worry about how much things cost—we should just slap on as many regulations as it takes to clean things up." Write an essay evaluating your roommate's views.

16.6 Distinguish the EPA's offset program from its bubble policy. Show, using graphs if necessary, how these policies can improve the efficiency of pollution abatement efforts.

CHAPTER 17

PROTECTING THE HEALTH AND SAFETY OF CONSUMERS AND WORKERS

Safety is a pretty poor marketing device, which is why the government has to get involved.

Lee Iacocca

A great deal of human activity involves risk. Many of these risks are familiar to us. If we canoe down a river, take a car trip, or dig coal in a mine, we are probably aware that an accident could cause us injury or even kill us.

The risks of other actions, however, may be completely unknown to us. Most of us probably do not consider eating peanut butter, drinking tap water, or sitting in a brick building to be risky. But when peanuts are improperly stored, they can develop a mold which produces a potent carcinogen, aflatoxin. The chlorine used to purify the tap water in many areas can react with organic matter in the water to produce hazardous compounds such as chloroform. And the natural radioactivity in stone or bricks can cause cancer.

Even when aware of such subtle risks, we probably would have a tough time weighing one against another. Most of us would probably be surprised to learn that each of the following activities carries the same risk:

- Traveling 6 minutes by canoe
- Traveling 300 miles by car
- Spending 3 hours in a coal mine
- Eating 40 tablespoons of peanut butter
- Drinking the tap water in Miami, Florida, for 1 year
- Living for 2 months in an average stone or brick building[1]

---

[1]Each activity increases the probability of death by 0.000001, or 1 chance in 1 million. See Richard Wilson, "Analyzing the Daily Risks of Life," *Technology Review,* 81 (February 1979), pp. 40–46.

Given the pace of change in modern times, we face new hazards almost every day. Will we have enough information to evaluate these hazards? Will we be capable of making wise decisions about which risks to bear and which to avoid? What characteristics of markets will aid or hamper us in our decisions? What should government do to ensure that the products we consume or the places in which we work are safe and healthful?

These are the questions that occupy us in this chapter. In Chapter 3, we found that product and labor markets, if left to their own devices, might fail to control risks to our health and safety effectively, suggesting a positive role for government regulation. In the next section, we lengthen the list of reasons why we might regulate product and workplace safety and explore some of the issues we must address when we attempt to do so. We then outline the methods used by several federal agencies—and the courts—to regulate consumer product safety and assess how well they have worked. Finally, we discuss the policies and performance of the federal agency charged with enhancing safety in the workplace, the Occupational Safety and Health Administration (OSHA).

HEALTH, SAFETY, AND THE MARKET

In Chapter 3 we discussed two sources of "market failure" relevant to health and safety concerns. Both have to do with an economic good—information—which has some interesting and important peculiarities.

Sources of Market Failure

Information as a Public Good Information about safety has the characteristics of nondepletability and nonexcludability identified with public goods in Chapter 3. Once I learn a particular fact, there is no less of this fact available for you to learn. Further, once knowledge about something exists, it may be difficult to keep those who did not pay to generate this knowledge from acquiring it.

Most economists feel that these characteristics mean that private markets will not supply public goods efficiently—or at all. Suppose, e.g., I determine via a series of expensive tests that a particular kind of car, brand X, is only half as safe as others of similar size and price (i.e., the probability of injury is twice as high in X as in other brands). I might try to recover my costs of learning this fact by charging potential car buyers a small fee to advise them about the safety of relative brands. I am likely to find, however, that my revenues fall far short of my costs. The first few people to buy the information I have produced will pass it on to their friends free of charge; it probably won't be long before my findings are written up in newspapers and magazines or broadcast on radio and TV. From my point of view, this *free riding* on my research may be an outrage, but from a social standpoint it may be efficient. After all, the information I have produced can be consumed (given its nondepletability) at zero marginal cost. Unless it is literally given away, less of it will be consumed than is optimal (review Figure 3.5). In sum, excludability problems may make free-lance research such as my automobile safety study economically infeasible, while its nondepletable nature makes selling information about safety at any positive price undesirable.

This does not mean that private markets will always fail to produce valu-able information about safety. For example, Consumers' Union of the United States, Inc., publishes road tests of automobiles and trucks in its monthly mag-azine *Consumer Reports*. In the mid-1980s Consumers' Union found that the Suzuki Samurai, a sport truck, was dangerously unstable when cornering and warned its subscribers of this fact. Predictably, the warning received wide press coverage (the nonexcludability trait again). Sales of the Samurai dropped so much that Suzuki soon withdrew the vehicle from the market. But this happy outcome may not be typical: Because Consumers' Union cannot be sure it will recapture all the costs of producing safety information from its subscribers, it probably engages in less research about safety than it otherwise would. Consumers' Union cannot afford to do crash tests on the vehicles it reviews, for example. That task is performed by a federal agency which makes its findings available free of charge. Indeed, in discussion of the *public-good problem*, this is the solution economists recommend most: Where private pro-ducers supply public goods in insufficient quantities, the government should step in, produce the goods (or at least contract with a private producer), and give them away.

Information Asymmetries Sometimes there is good information about the risks associated with a particular product or job, but it is not available to prospective transactors in equal measure. We can assume, in many cases, that a seller knows more about the risks associated with a product than a prospec-tive buyer and that an employer knows more about the potential hazards in some job than a prospective employee.

When one party to a transaction is *aware* of such an informational disadvan-tage, it may pose no problem. If, e.g., I am pondering a job offer from the local chemical plant, I will probably realize that the employer knows more about the dangers posed by the job than I. Accordingly, I will be skeptical about the employer's claims regarding the safety of the job and will have an incentive to investigate the issue myself, perhaps by making inquiries of more experienced workers or union representatives.

In some cases, however, transactors *may not be aware they are at a disadvan-tage*. Some of the health costs associated with the hypothetical chemical plant job may take many years to show up; my investigation may miss this fact. I might therefore accept a job that is riskier than I would prefer, or I might accept it at a wage that is lower than I would have demanded had I known I was shouldering such risk. The former result involves inefficiency, for my ser-vices are allocated to the wrong use (review Figure 3.6); the latter involves inequity, since I am not compensated for a cost I bear. Avoiding this kind of thing is the motive for various labeling requirements for consumer goods or "full disclosure" laws that cover employment relations. The basic idea here is

lators the chore of evaluating risks and determining which are tolerable and which are not. As we shall see, this can be a very vexing chore.

Externalities   Occasionally externality or spillover effects are invoked to justify certain kinds of safety regulation. Consider laws that require motorcyclists to wear helmets. Many bikers know that they face far greater risk of severe head injury when they ride without a helmet, but they still object to mandatory helmet laws. (Indeed, one famous actor who suffered a head injury in a motorcycling accident recently testified against a proposed helmet law in California, while admitting that a helmet would have prevented or reduced the severity of his injury!) It's difficult to say that there is an information problem here, although perhaps there is a bounded rationality problem. Proponents of helmet laws and similar policies, however, suggest there is an additional reason to regulate: the *shared* health and disability costs incurred by those who suffer serious avoidable injuries. Those who suffer such injuries and any resulting disability will not pay all the costs associated with their choices. If they are insured against such losses, other members of their insurance pool pay as well (in the form of higher premiums); if they are not insured, society at large pays the hospital bills and writes the disability checks.

At the least, this seems inequitable. Why should you pay some of the costs of my decisions to cycle, smoke, sky-dive, etc.? It may also be inefficient. We expect that the demand for risk—like the demand for all goods—is negatively related to its price. If people can shift some of the costs of risk to others, they might choose to consume too much of it. Safety regulation is thus aimed at avoiding welfare losses associated with overconsumption of risk, just as environmental regulation aims to prevent overproduction of pollution.

But we should invoke this rationale with care. Lots of choices can be said to produce spillover effects of some type. Our voting behavior, the decisions we make in raising our children, and choices we make about our diet or other aspects of our lifestyles can clearly shift some costs to other parties. A society that attempts to prevent all such cost shifting on equity or efficiency grounds will, however, look a great deal like a police state.

Optimal Exposure to Risk

Before we proceed to a discussion of the various ways in which regulators have sought to make goods or jobs safer, we should make clear two points. First, the ideal level of safety for a particular product or job may *not* be the *maximum* level of safety technologically attainable, for this level of safety may simply be too costly to achieve. In general, our goal will be the *optimal* level of safety, not maximum safety. Second, the information we glean from markets will be extraordinarily valuable in our pursuit of this goal.

Suppose, for a moment, that you are an all-seeing, all-knowing World Controller with the authority to determine how much of every good will be produced. You have access to the most precise data concerning the costs of producing various goods, and, more important, you know precisely how much value people attach to each unit of each good, including the one called *safety*.

Figure 17.1 shows the marginal production costs of, and marginal value attached to, particular levels of safety (for consumer goods or in the workplace). It is probably not surprising that extra units of safety cost more and more to produce, i.e., that MC_{safety} has a positive slope. As the quantity of safety produced approaches a maximum (labeled the no-risk level of safety in Figure 17.1), we simply must pay more to squeeze out the remaining sources of risk. It may, however, be surprising that the value attached to extra units of safety MV_{safety}, while high at first, tends to decline, reaching fairly low levels as the quantity of safety produced approaches the no-risk level. Isn't this at odds with common sense? Don't people attach an *infinite* value to all units of safety, from the first to the last? Don't we avoid *all* risks we know about?

The answers to these questions, if we contemplate real-world behavior even briefly, are clearly in the negative. Yes, we try to avoid the grossest sources of risk. But we do not avoid *all* known sources of risk, as we would have to if we placed an infinite value on safety. Most of us take car trips, and some of us smoke, hang-glide, work in coal mines, or become police officers even though

FIGURE 17.1
THE OPTIMAL LEVEL OF SAFETY AND RISK. It will be efficient to produce each unit of safety for which the marginal value exceeds marginal cost. Here, the optimal level of safety is Q^*, far less than the no-risk quantity.

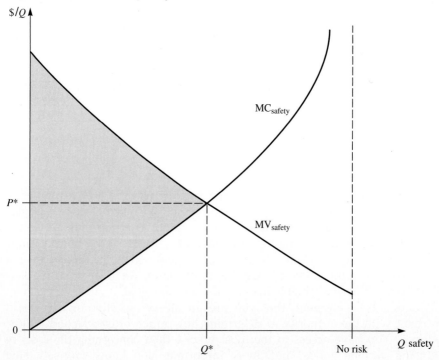

we know these activities are risky. *We take risks when we judge the potential benefits to exceed the costs.*

In your role as World Controller, you will likely choose the amount of safety to produce in the same way. You will eliminate risks where the benefits of doing so (MV_{safety}) exceed the costs (MC_{safety}). You will find the optimal level of safety to be Q^* in Figure 17.1. If you continued eliminating risks until reaching the maximum (no-risk) level of safety, you would produce many units of safety that cost more than they were worth (i.e., units for which $MC_{safety} > MV_{safety}$). This would not be efficient; it would dissipate the social surplus associated with safety. This surplus is maximized (and equals the shaded area in Figure 17.1) when the level of safety is Q^*.

We conclude: When risks are known and quantifiable and when the value of safety is similarly known and quantifiable, it is easy to determine the optimal level of safety to produce. This will be the level that equates the marginal cost and the value of safety (i.e., sets $MC_{safety} = MV_{safety}$). In general, *the optimal level of safety will be less than the maximum level of safety technologically attainable* (unless the cost of producing extra safety is extremely low or the value attached to extra safety is very high).

Markets and Risk

This is all well and good, you say, and quite obvious. But no regulator will be as omniscient as our hypothetical World Controller; i.e., no one will ever have access to the kind of information needed to determine the optimal level of safety in the example above. Even if we have precise data on the costs of engineering greater safety into a particular product or job, how can we ever calculate how much people *value* greater safety? This will surely be a complex task that involves considerable potential for error. But the task can be made more manageable thanks to the information gleaned from observing market transactions involving certain known risks.

Compensating Differentials   Consider the following example. The circus has two types of jobs available to entry-level personnel like yourself: risky (e.g., target for the knife thrower, human cannonball) and safe (e.g., popcorn vendor, ticket taker). Obviously, if both jobs carried the same wage rate, everyone would volunteer for the safe jobs and no one for the risky ones. The circus's personnel manager will have to offer more money to get people to accept the risky jobs. That is, those who accept risky jobs will earn wage premiums or *compensating wage differentials*.

The concept is illustrated graphically in Figure 17.2a and b. Panel a shows a hypothetical labor market, with a labor demand curve labeled D_L and two curves showing the supply of workers in risky and safe jobs, labeled S_{risky} and S_{safe}, respectively. At the market-clearing wage for safe jobs W_s, the quantity of workers offering their services for risky jobs is zero. Only if offered higher wages will some workers volunteer for the risky jobs, and only at the wage

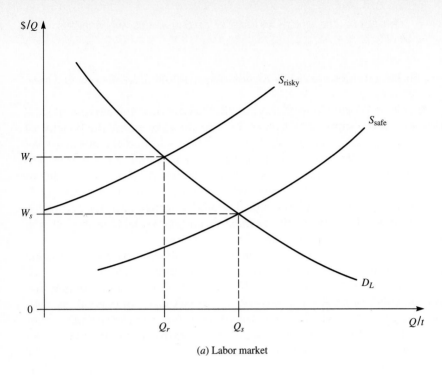

(a) Labor market

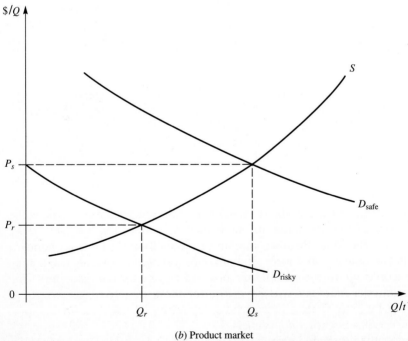

(b) Product market

FIGURE 17.2
COMPENSATING DIFFERENTIALS IN LABOR AND PRODUCT MARKETS. (*a*) Labor market in which workers receive a wage premium equal to $W_r - W_s$ as compensation for risky work. (*b*) Product market where consumers of risky goods receive a compensating differential $P_s - P_r$.

rate W_r will the quantities of workers demanded and supplied in such jobs be equal. In this labor market, the compensating differential for risk is $W_r - W_s$.

Figure 17.2b shows a hypothetical product market, with two curves that show the demand for risky and safe versions of the product, labeled D_{risky} and D_{safe}, respectively, and a supply curve labeled S. At the market-clearing price for the safe version of the product P_s, the quantity demanded of the risky version of the product is zero. Only if offered a discount will some buyers choose to bear the risk associated with this version of the product, and only at price P_r will the quantities of the risky product demanded and supplied be equal. Consumers of the risky version of the product receive the compensating differential $P_s - P_r$.

Risk premiums are quite common in labor markets; hazardous-duty differentials are explicit features of many union contracts. But will such differentials *fully* compensate workers for the risks they bear? The answer to this question will be yes if and only if workers are fully cognizant of the risks and their implications. Many job-related risks are obviously difficult to assess (e.g., hazards associated with exposure to carcinogenic substances, where there are time lags of a decade or more between exposure and observation of health problems). In such cases, we may observe no (or an inadequate) compensating differential, and we will have the kind of inefficiency (and inequity) problems discussed earlier.

Surveys of workers in occupations of varying riskiness suggest a general awareness of many of the hazards they face. There is a strong correlation between the risk level in an industry and workers' awareness that their jobs are dangerous in some respect.[6] But awareness that there is *some* risk is not the same as awareness of the full *degree* of risk. One study aimed at assessing whether workers' assessments of risk are at all accurate was conducted by Kip Viscusi and Charles O'Connor.[7] Their surveys of workers at four chemical plants found that workers' estimates of their risk of job-related injury conformed very closely to published accident rates for the industry as a whole. Further, workers' estimates of the overall job-related risks they faced were almost twice the actual accident rate for the industry, which Viscusi and O'Connor judged a reasonable allowance for other health hazards (e.g., long-term exposure to carcinogenic substances) not reflected in the published data. In sum, there seems to be evidence that at least some workers have reasonable perceptions of the risks they face.

No comparable surveys exist to assess whether consumers similarly weigh risks when they evaluate different products or different versions of the same product. There is anecdotal evidence that consumers are not indifferent to risk (e.g., the aforementioned Suzuki Samurai case). But the degree of risk associated with most consumer goods is very small, and tests of our cognitive abilities

---

[6]W. Kip Viscusi, *Employment Hazards: An Investigation of Market Performance*, Harvard University Press, Cambridge, MA, 1979.

[7]W. Kip Viscusi and Charles O'Connor, "Adaptive Responses to Chemical Labeling: Are Workers Bayesian Decision Makers?" *American Economic Review*, 74 (December 1984), pp. 942–956.

suggest that when probabilities of certain events fall below some threshold, we have great difficulty making reasonable and consistent choices among alternatives. We suspect, then, that product markets are less likely to be characterized by appropriate compensating differentials than labor markets.

Effects of Compensating Differentials   Workers' demands for adequate wage premiums in exchange for their acceptance of risky jobs will have efficiency-enhancing effects. Note first that employers have two choices about the risky jobs they must fill. They can pay workers a wage premium sufficient to induce them to bear the risk, or they can invest in equipment or procedures to reduce the risk (and, by doing so, reduce the compensating differential they have to pay). A profit-maximizing employer will naturally choose the cheaper alternative and so invest in such equipment or procedures until the wage reductions generated by improved safety no longer exceed the cost of such improvements. That is, the firm will improve safety until safety's value to workers falls below its cost. Thus, the existence of compensating differentials will induce firms to seek the optimal level of safety in various job classifications.

In addition, the size of the compensating differential will be the device by which workers sort themselves into various jobs according to their differing preferences for safety. Not everyone will be willing to bear certain known risks in exchange for the same wage premium. The most risk-averse will hold out for high premiums—and will tend, therefore, to select relatively safe jobs. The least risk-averse will accept lower premiums and find their way to riskier jobs.

Of course, the same generalizations apply where products carry compensating differentials. Producers will build safer products until extra units of safety add more to costs than to revenues. And consumers will sort themselves out according to their relative preferences for risk, some buying riskier but cheaper products, others paying higher prices for safer products.

Guidance for Regulators   Just because compensating differentials can, under certain circumstances, induce employers or producers to enhance safety—perhaps even to optimal levels—should not lead us to conclude that the market will magically solve all problems related to risk in product or labor markets. The fact is that the information problems discussed earlier will mean that some form of regulation will have great potential to enhance welfare in many labor and product markets. Data on compensating differentials will be of enormous value in this effort, for the data can be used to draw inferences about how much people value increments in safety and to help regulators set efficient standards for exposure to risk.

Suppose, e.g., we have a population of 100,000 police officers. Available historical evidence indicates that about 80 officers will be killed in the line of duty annually. Thus, each officer faces an annual probability of (job-related) death of 0.0008. Suppose further we find that police officers earn $2,000 more per year than those with comparable skills in similar—but risk-free—jobs. That is, police officers' compensating differential is $2,000 per year per person. We can then calculate the value of a statistical life. Our population of officers will be paid a total of $200 million (= $2,000 × 100,000 officers) in compensation for the 80 expected deaths. The rate of compensation per expected fatality is therefore $2.5 million (= $200 million/80).[8]

Many researchers, using differing data sources and methods, have used labor market data to estimate workers' implicit value of life in precisely this fashion. The estimates vary widely, from a low of about $700,000 to a high of $6.2 million (in 1987 dollars).[9] Statistical imprecision and methodological differences explain some of this variation, but not all. As we noted earlier, preferences about risk differ. Workers sort themselves into job-risk classes according to their preferences. We expect that those most willing to bear risk will accept the lowest wage premiums and find their way to the riskiest jobs, while those least willing to bear risk will demand much higher premiums and populate safer jobs. The studies are consistent with this expectation: Those finding the lowest implicit value per life generally are based on data from the riskiest occupations.

Such estimates can be used to assign dollar values to the impacts of regulations aimed at enhancing product or workplace safety. Continuing the example above, suppose it is found that requiring police officers to wear bulletproof vests will save 20 lives per year, i.e., reduces the probability of fatal injury from 0.0008 to 0.0006. Using officers' own implicit valuation of life, we can estimate the benefits of this requirement to be $50 million annually (= $2.5 million per life × 20 lives). Thus, if we can outfit our population of 100,000 police officers with vests for less than $500 per vest per year, the regulation will be efficient.

Many find such explicit valuations of life and limb to be repugnant. It is common to say that we should spare no expense to save lives. But this overlooks the fact that resources have alternative uses: Dollars spent to save police officers' lives cannot be used to save the lives of cab drivers, electricians, or coal miners, all of whom face even greater risks of fatal job-related injury. Similarly, dollars spent to engineer greater safety into automobiles cannot be spent to make safer toys, drugs, or tools. If we are to regulate intelligently, we must have some way to allocate scarce safety-enhancing resources. Accordingly, we cannot shrink from the seemingly macabre task of quantifying the benefits, and weighing these against the costs, of various programs and regulatory standards. In cases where it is impossible to estimate the benefits of some regulations, we should at least try to ensure that the regulations are formulated so that a given level of safety is achieved as inexpensively as possible, i.e., that the regulations are *cost-effective*.

It is time now to turn to an examination of the ways in which federal regu-

---

[8]Alternatively, we can calculate the value of a statistical life by dividing the wage premium per individual by the probability of a fatality; in this example, $2,000/0.0008 = $2.5 million.

[9]Michael J. Moore and W. Kip Viscusi, *Compensation Mechanisms for Job Risks*, Princeton University Press, Princeton, NJ, 1990, p. 14.

lators try to enhance the safety and health of consumers and workers. We begin with the oldest federal agency devoted to this purpose, and then we proceed to more modern inventions.

THE FOOD AND DRUG ADMINISTRATION

Background

Although Congress did not outlaw the adulteration and misbranding of food and drugs sold in interstate commerce until 1906 (with the Food and Drug Act), research on these matters had been conducted in the Bureau of Chemistry of the Department of Agriculture since the 1880s. The bureau examined various foodstuffs, food preservatives, and patent medicines and used the power of publicity to combat abusive practices.

The 1906 law was relatively toothless, but major new initiatives were passed in 1938 and 1962, and lesser amendments were passed in other years. The Bureau of Chemistry was reorganized as the Food and Drug Administration (FDA) in 1931. The 1938 Food, Drug, and Cosmetic Act (a response to a tragedy in which 70 died from a medicine that contained a poison) extended the coverage of the 1906 statute and required drug manufacturers to obtain a permit from the FDA before they marketed new products. Permits could be issued only after producers presented evidence that their new drugs were safe. The 1962 drug amendments (a response to a tragedy in which West German women who used a sleeping pill called thalidomide subsequently gave birth to deformed babies) gave the FDA authority to regulate the testing of new drugs and required that these drugs be proved not only safe, but also effective.

The modern FDA, a division of the Department of Health and Human Services, has an annual budget in excess of $500 million and a staff of about 7,300. It conducts research on the safety and efficacy of drugs and medical devices, sets standards for the safety and purity of the thousands of food and cosmetic products under its jurisdiction, and regulates both the cleanliness of the production process and the labeling of products.

Methods

Given the breadth of its responsibilities, it is no surprise that the FDA uses a wide variety of methods to achieve its goals.

In setting *safety standards* for drugs and medical devices, the FDA employs considerable flexibility, weighing risks against benefits case by case. Drugs that carry a high risk of harmful side effects may be approved for sale if they are also fairly effective in treating serious conditions, e.g., various cancers. Standard setting for food and cosmetics, however, is far less flexible; in general, the goal here is zero risk. This stringency is a result of statutory language (in the 1958 Delaney Amendment to the Food, Drug, and Cosmetic Act) that states "no [food] additive shall be deemed to be safe . . . if it is found . . . to induce cancer in man or animal." Under this approach, common food additives such as cyclamates, saccharin, and red dye no. 2 were banned following laboratory tests that showed they could induce cancers in laboratory animals (although Congress later exempted saccharin where used as an additive, requiring only that it be accompanied by a warning label). This approach is a bit controversial, for some doubt that what causes cancer in animals in an experimental setting (where exposure levels are extremely high) will cause it in humans in a natural setting (where exposure levels are much lower).

The FDA also sets various other standards. *Purity standards* aim to ensure that the composition and potency of drugs are as claimed. *Contamination standards* prohibit adulteration of food or drugs with "filthy, putrid, or decomposed" substances. *Product identity standards* establish criteria that a product must meet to be labeled in a certain way (e.g., to qualify as "beef with gravy," a product must contain at least 50 percent beef). To reinforce its contamination standards, the FDA also has *production cleanliness standards* that detail the proper way to maintain sanitary conditions in the manufacture or processing of food, drugs, and cosmetics. Finally, the FDA sets *efficacy standards* for drugs and medical devices. Even if harmless in and of themselves, ineffective drugs may involve health costs to the extent that they supplant more effective treatments.

Enforcement and Remedies

The FDA enforces its various standards in two basic ways. It attempts to head off problems with a certification program for new drugs and medical devices. Under this program, FDA staffers evaluate research conducted by producers concerning the safety and efficacy of products and must grant a permit before these products can be marketed. Certain food additives must also be certified as safe before they can be used. Once products are marketed, the FDA tries to enforce compliance with its standards by testing samples gathered from the field and by sending its own staffers into the field to inspect premises and analyze products or production processes.

If the FDA finds violations of its standards, it can seize products or order product recalls, obtain court injunctions against the activities of specific producers, or initiate civil or criminal prosecutions of violators. While most violations are misdemeanors, presence of "intent to mislead or defraud" means the violations are felonies punishable by up to 3 years' imprisonment and fines of up to $10,000 for each occurrence. In a representative year, the FDA will seize or order the recall of literally hundreds of products; prosecutions or injunctions are far more rare. Clearly, the agency is very busy, and many who are familiar with its operations feel that it deserves a larger budget and staff to carry out its duties more thoroughly.

Performance

The FDA has undoubtedly saved many lives and prevented considerable illness and suffering. The thalidomide tragedy mentioned earlier is an excellent example of the agency's beneficial effects on public health and safety. Approved for use in several European countries in the late 1950s, the drug was linked to severe birth defects in over 7,000 babies. But the FDA, enforcing the 1938 law requiring premarket drug safety clearance, kept thalidomide off the U.S. market. It is quite likely that FDA policing efforts have avoided many other horrors as well, although perhaps none so dramatic.

Nevertheless, the FDA has come in for considerable criticism from some quarters. These critics grant that the FDA produces many social benefits, but argue that the agency sometimes sets standards that are excessively stringent, i.e., aims at achieving levels of safety far beyond the optimal one. And they heap special criticism on the FDA's enforcement of the 1962 drug amendments, arguing that the delays and costs of proving new drugs to be safe and effective are keeping many useful drugs off the market for too long—or off the market entirely.

Figure 17.3 shows that new-drug introductions did indeed fall after passage of the 1962 amendments. Between 1950 and 1962, the FDA approved an average of 46 new drugs per year. From 1963 to 1975, the average fell to 16 new approvals (although the average is up to about 25 in the years since 1975). What is more, the longer, more complicated approval process pushed up the real costs of developing a drug in the United States (to over $125 million, by some estimates), which has made the industry more concentrated, has inflated prices, and has reduced the availability of therapies.[10]

Of course, reducing the rate of introduction of new chemical entities was the *goal* of the 1962 amendments. The presumption at the time was that drugs kept off the market by the new regulations were of dubious safety and effectiveness and that the amendments therefore enhanced welfare. A study by Sam Peltzman challenges this view, however.[11] According to Peltzman, a relatively small proportion (about 10 percent) of new drugs prior to 1962 were ineffective, and this proportion has remained roughly the same since. He concludes that the amendments led to a large decline in the introduction of effective drugs, with an associated reduction in consumers' surplus in excess of $350 million per year—equivalent to the effect of a 5 to 10 percent tax on drug purchases.

The FDA has not ignored such criticisms. In the 1980s, the agency modified its procedures on several occasions to hasten the drug approval process. The agency no longer requires submission of raw data from experimental studies (a requirement that had produced some applications in excess of 100,000 pages), and it now accepts data from clinical tests in foreign countries. In addition, the agency will grant expedited *compassionate approval* in cases where a drug shows promise in treatment of fatal ailments or where no alternative therapies are yet available. The changes have the potential to trim the approval process considerably.

[10]Henry G. Grabowski, *Drug Regulation and Innovation,* American Enterprise Institute, Washington, 1976.

[11]Sam Peltzman, "An Evaluation of Consumer Protection Legislation: The 1962 Drug Amendments," *Journal of Political Economy,* 81 (October 1973), pp. 1049–1091.

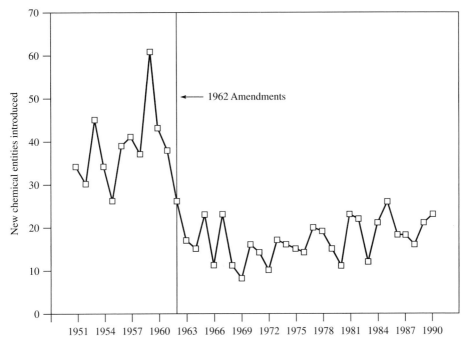

FIGURE 17.3
NUMBER OF NEW CHEMICAL ENTITY (NCE) DRUGS INTRODUCED ANNUALLY INTO THE
UNITED STATES,1951–1990. The 1962 drug amendents clearly reduced the rate of introduction
of new drugs in the United States. Introductions fell from about 38 per year over 1951–1962 to
less than 17 per year over 1963–1990.

VIGNETTE 17.2   Bureaucratic Lag and Drug Availability

New drugs are first tested in the laboratory and in animals to determine whether
they are biologically active and safe. If so, human trials are normally conducted in
three phases. Phase 1 lasts several months and aims to gauge safety and appropriate dosage. Phase 2, which compares the drug's effectiveness against established
treatments or an inert placebo, can last from 6 months to 2 years. Phase 3, which
lasts 1 to 4 years, verifies the drug's effectiveness and monitors adverse reactions
from long-term use. Following this, the FDA takes an average of $2\frac{1}{2}$ years to
review test data and grant final approval. All told, it can take 7 to 10 years to move a
drug from laboratory to market. But under the FDA's new rules, drugs that show
promise in the treatment of life-threatening diseases are tested more intensively in
phase 2, and phase 3 is eliminated. This can cut the approval process to less than
2 years.

  Why so long? Part of the "drug lag" stems from the fact that the FDA is over-
worked and understaffed. But part stems from the agency's extraordinary caution. In
the words of Harvard Medical School Professor Jerome Groopman, "the FDA lives
in fear of approving a drug and later learning it has an unrecognized toxic side
effect. Potential risk, rather than benefit, attracts most of the FDA's attention."[12]

[12]Jerome Groopman, "Rx for the FDA," *The New Republic*, 200 (February 13, 1989), p. 18.

When one is dealing with potentially toxic substances, caution is clearly warranted. But there is such a thing as excessive caution. Consider an ambulance taking a heart attack victim to the hospital. We do not expect the ambulance to observe speed limits and other traffic laws because we recognize that some risks may be necessary when time is of the essence—we trade an increase in one type of risk to reduce another. So it is with certain kinds of drugs.

Consider, e.g., flutamide, which shrinks prostate tumors. The FDA weighed the merits of the drug from 1981 to 1988, during which time 201,000 men in the United States died of prostate cancer.[13] It is possible that many of these lives might have been prolonged or saved had the FDA acted more quickly. Some argue, in fact, that the agency has an incentive to act too slowly. If patients suffer from ill side effects or die from a drug that was approved too hastily, the FDA will be blamed. But when patients die from cancer, AIDS, or some other malady while therapies are working their way through the approval pipeline, blame will likely fall on the disease, not the FDA.

To a very great extent, this all changed with the spread of AIDS. With large numbers of patients with life expectancies measured in months, a frantic search for therapies put the FDA's approval process under intense scrutiny. Once it became clear that drugs (for example, AZT) with potential to improve AIDS sufferers' lives were hung up in lengthy trials, activists put intense pressure on the FDA to speed up its procedures, and the agency responded. AZT was approved in record time—18 months. Not everyone is happy with the changes made, of course. Some want even more deregulation, while others argue that the hastened approval process will make it harder to test therapies rigorously. In the FDA's view, however, the modifications balance humanitarian concerns with the demands of "good science."

THE NATIONAL HIGHWAY TRAFFIC SAFETY ADMINISTRATION

Background

By the mid-1960s, it was obvious that America's love affair with the automobile was bittersweet; over 1.5 million people had died in automobile accidents, with the annual number of fatalities exceeding 50,000. The held wisdom had been that the blame for this carnage rested entirely with drivers, who caused accidents by their own recklessness, inattentiveness, or just plain incompetence. By the late 1950s, however, that mindset began to change. Some researchers had been working for years to design more forgiving automobile interiors that would minimize injuries when accidents did occur. Several writers—most notably Daniel Patrick Moynihan, now a U.S. Senator, and Ralph Nader—offered scathing criticisms of U.S. automakers' neglect of safety issues.[14] The issue made good copy, for it had horror stories in abundance, some heroes (consumer advocates), and villains (automobile companies); as a result, the media gave it big play.

By 1966, Congress responded with the National Traffic and Motor Vehicle

---

[13]Sharon Begley, "Desperation Drugs," *Newsweek*, 114 (August 7, 1989), pp. 48–51.

[14]Ralph Nader, *Unsafe at Any Speed: The Designed-in Dangers of the American Automobile*, Grossman, New York, 1965, updated 1972.

Safety Act, creating the National Highway Traffic Safety Administration (NHTSA, commonly pronounced "nit-sa"). The new agency, housed in the Department of Transportation, was authorized to devise and enforce specific standards to "enhance motor vehicle safety." Subsequent legislation such as the Highway Safety Acts of 1966 and 1970 and the Energy Policy and Conservation Act of 1975 have expanded the agency's authority slightly. It now regulates automobile fuel economy standards and oversees enforcement of speed limits on interstate highways in addition to setting safety standards for motor vehicles and related equipment such as motorcycle helmets. NHTSA's annual budget is about $225 million, and it employs in excess of 500 staffers.

Methods

NHTSA's equipment safety standards fall into one of three basic groups. *Precrash standards* are aimed at eliminating equipment-related causes of crashes or at enhancing the capacity of drivers to avoid crashes. These standards set certain engineering specifications for tires, brakes, and other equipment and impose design restrictions aimed at ensuring that drivers will be able to see and reach essential controls. *Crash standards* are aimed at protecting drivers, passengers, or pedestrians during a crash. Examples include requirements for headrests (to reduce whiplash), padded dashboards and steering wheels, and shatterproof glass. *Postcrash standards* are aimed at keeping injuries and losses to a minimum in the period immediately following a crash. Examples include specifications for fire resistance of fuel tanks, fuel lines, and materials in the passenger compartment.

Other standards relate to the ways in which vehicles and related equipment are manufactured and distributed. The goal here is to ensure that if a product is defective and must be recalled, manufacturers and purchasers can be identified and the problem rectified.

Note as well that many of the regulations that affect automobile safety are implemented by states, often after prodding by NHTSA. For example, all 50 states require the use of child-restraint devices, i.e., "kiddie safety seats." And various laws which require drivers to *use* the safety belts that NHTSA required manufacturers to install all originated at the state level.

Enforcement and Remedies

NHTSA relies on manufacturers to test their own products for compliance with NHTSA's standards and then certify to the agency that its standards are met. NHTSA then selects a small sample of the various models marketed and performs follow-up tests to monitor compliance. In addition, NHTSA encourages consumers to register any complaints they might have about safety (via a toll-free hotline). If these calls or the agency's field inspection efforts reveal any disturbing patterns that suggest a safety hazard, NHTSA may launch a formal investigation into possible product defects.

Far and away the most common remedy for safety-related defects or violations of standards are product recalls. Most recall campaigns are "voluntary," i.e., are initiated by manufacturers themselves. But firms are fully aware that NHTSA will make a recall compulsory if it is not satisfied with any actions taken.

Performance

NHTSA's effectiveness in reducing automobile-related death and injury rates has been the subject of much lively debate. As Table 17.1 shows, deaths from traffic accidents rose steadily in the years following World War II, peaked in the late 1960s and early 1970s (when NHTSA imposed most of its safety standards), and have been significantly lower in the years since. However, the fatality rate *per mile driven* had begun to decline well before NHTSA (and many state-level laws affecting automobile safety) existed. The relevant question, then, is how much—or whether—NHTSA *accelerated* this downward trend.

There are some who believe that the various regulations aimed at enhancing automobile safety have produced few benefits in this regard. One of the most prominent skeptics, in fact, argues that these regulations have been *counterproductive*. In a much debated article, Sam Peltzman observed that mandating installation of safety equipment could induce drivers to modify their behavior in *un*safe ways, possibly offsetting the benefits of the equipment.[15] Some drivers, e.g., might be falsely lured by the presence of seat belts, padded dashboards, etc., to believe that they are invulnerable to harm and drive more aggressively and have more accidents. Peltzman found some statistical support for this view: In the years following imposition of NHTSA's standards, fatality rates fell much less than engineering studies of the mandated safety equipment had predicted, and observed *in*creases in accident rates, extent of property damage, and pedestrian deaths are consistent with the notion that driver recklessness increased in this period.

Part of the problem here is that many factors affect automobile accident rates. For example, the age composition of the driving population (very young and very old drivers tend to have more accidents), consumption of alcohol, and the number of trucks on the highways will all affect the rate and severity of accidents. Perhaps the most thorough attempt to sort through such factors and quantify the effects of NHTSA's regulations on fatality rates was conducted by Robert Crandall, Howard Gruenspecht, Theodore Keeler, and Lester Lave. The authors analyzed more variables and a longer span of data than had been available to Peltzman. While they found some evidence that increases in driver aggressiveness had offset some of the potential gains of safety regulations, they concluded that there was still "a very large effect of the improved

---

[15]Sam Peltzman, "The Effects of Automobile Safety Regulation," *Journal of Political Economy*, 83 (July-August 1975), pp. 667–725.

TABLE 17.1
TRENDS IN TRAFFIC FATALITIES, 1951 TO 1987.   The downward trend in deaths per 100 million vehicle miles predated NHTSA.

Year	Number of deaths	Deaths per 100 million vehicle miles
1951	36,996	7.60
1953	37,955	7.04
1955	38,426	6.32
1957	38,702	5.95
1959	37,910	5.40
1961	38,091	5.15
1963	43,564	5.41
1965	49,000	5.52
1967	52,924	5.52
1969	55,032	5.27
1971	53,761	4.61
1973	55,113	4.26
1975	45,500	3.46
1977	47,878	3.35
1979	51,093	3.40
1981	49,301	3.27
1983	42,589	2.70
1985	43,795	2.47
1987	46,385	2.41

Source: U.S. Department of Transportation, Federal Highway Administration, *Highway Statistics,* GPO, Washington, various years.

safety design of automobiles since 1966."[16] Using the statistical model they had devised to sort out the various influences on fatality rates, the authors tried to estimate the number of highway deaths that might have occurred for the year 1981 *had all cars then on the road been built to pre-1966 safety specifications.* They found that between 13,000 and 23,400 additional traffic deaths would have been likely.[17] Clearly, if these estimates are at all accurate, NHTSA can take credit for saving many lives. In addition, the authors concluded that the total annual benefits from NHTSA's regulations likely exceed the costs of complying with them (which can add several hundred dollars to the price of a new car), perhaps by a considerable margin.

There is also evidence that NHTSA's educational efforts and states' efforts to ensure that drivers actually *use* the safety equipment available to them are

[16]Robert W. Crandall, Howard K. Gruenspecht, Theodore E. Keeler, and Lester B. Lave, *Regulating the Automobile,* The Brookings Institution, Washington, 1986, p. 66.
[17]Ibid., p. 75.

bearing fruit. One NHTSA survey showed that over 83 percent of infants and toddlers were observed traveling *un*restrained, i.e., without benefit of safety belts or car seats, in 1979. That figure fell steadily through the 1980s, and by 1987 only 15 percent of children were observed traveling unrestrained. And opinion polls show that public attitudes toward seat belt use are improving. In 1973, a Gallup poll showed only 28 percent of adults used seat belts, and by 1982 only 17 percent did so. But this figure rose steadily afterward, and by 1988, 69 percent of adults reported using belts.[18] Organized efforts to eliminate drunken driving are at an all-time high as well. Perhaps our greatest progress in reducing automobile-related death and injury is yet to come.

VIGNETTE 17.3   Unintended Effects of Regulations: Fuel Economy Standards and Automobile Safety

In 1975, in the wake of the Arab oil embargo, Congress passed the Energy Policy Conservation Act, which specified minimum fuel economy standards for all new cars sold in the United States. Called the *corporate average fuel economy (CAFE) standards,* the limits are a good example of the *technology-forcing* approach common to much social regulation. The presumption was that automakers had inadequate incentives to improve fuel efficiency on their own—especially since then-prevailing government controls kept prices of crude oil and gasoline artificially low—and needed a shove from Uncle Sam. Since 1985, all automakers have had to maintain at least a 27.5 miles/gallon rating for their fleets.

Unfortunately, Congress failed to consider that the chief way to make cars more fuel-efficient is to make them *smaller* and *lighter.* And there is a substantial body of evidence that, in crashes of all types, occupants of smaller, lighter cars are much more susceptible to serious injury and death than are occupants of larger, heavier cars. In general, a 500-pound reduction in vehicle weight is associated with a 14 to 27 percent increase in occupant fatality risk.

A study by the Insurance Institute for Highway Safety found that the 1989 fatality rate for the smallest cars on the road was 3 deaths per 10,000 registered vehicles, compared with 1.3 deaths per 10,000 large cars. Fatality rates have climbed after certain models were downsized for fuel economy. For example, the fatality rate for 1980–1981 Chevy Camaros and Pontiac Firebirds was 2.3 (per 10,000 vehicles). After downsizing in 1982, the fatality rate for 1982–1983 Camaros and Firebirds climbed to 3.3.[19]

Robert Crandall and John Graham attempted to quantify the effects of the CAFE standards on automobile safety. After first determining how much the CAFE standards contributed to reductions in vehicle weight, they then estimated what fatality rates would have been absent CAFE standards. They concluded that without CAFE standards there would have been 2,200 to 3,900 fewer automobile-related deaths and 11,000 to 19,500 fewer serious injuries over the 10 years of a given model

---

[18]Sources: George Gallup, Jr., and Alex Gallup, "Seat Belt Use Quadruples since 1982," *The Gallup Poll,* June 26, 1988, as reported in John D. Graham, *Auto Safety: Assessing America's Performance,* Auburn House, Dover, MA, 1989, pp. 222–223.

[19]Laurie McGinley, "Gas Savings vs. Safety Stirs Debate," *The Wall Street Journal,* 216 (September 6, 1990), pp. B1, B12.

year's useful life.[20] Of course, it might be argued that the fuel savings that have resulted from CAFE standards are worth such costs. But, using very conservative estimates about the value of life and limb, Crandall and Graham estimated that the adverse safety effects of CAFE standards for 1989 cars translate to a social cost of $1.9 billion to $3.4 billion, while the value of fuel saved by CAFE standards ranges from $1.8 billion to $2.2 billion. In other words, the CAFE standards are cost-ineffective.

Ironically, enforcing the CAFE standards fell to NHTSA. Thus, at the same time as the agency promulgated some standards that saved lives and avoided injuries, it enforced others that did the opposite.

THE CONSUMER PRODUCT SAFETY COMMISSION

Background

After allowing for FDA regulation of food, drugs, cosmetics, and medical devices; NHTSA regulation of motor vehicles and accessories; and other agencies' regulation of nuclear materials, pesticides, aircraft, boats, tobacco products, and firearms; about 10,000 different products remain. These products, and the 3 million firms that produce them, are under the jurisdiction of the Consumer Product Safety Commission (CPSC), created by Congress in 1972. Congress had been moved to act by the 1970 report of the National Commission on Product Safety, which had found that "20 million consumers are injured each year through the use of consumer products, of which 110,000 are permanently disabled and 30,000 killed."[21] The commission argued that much of this harm could be avoided if more attention were paid to hazard reduction.

Congress's creation of the CPSC signaled a change in strategy with regard to consumer safety issues. Previously, Congress had responded to specific problems with narrowly targeted legislation. For example, in 1953 Congress passed the Flammable Fabrics Act (first administered by the Federal Trade Commission), which restricted the sale of flammable apparel. The Child Protection Act of 1966 (first administered by the FDA) prohibited the sale of toys that could harm children. The 1972 Consumer Product Safety Act represented a more comprehensive approach. It gave the CPSC broad responsibilities to "protect the public against unreasonable risks of injury associated with consumer products" and various tools to achieve this objective. CPSC's resources, however, are a fraction of those of the consumer protection agencies discussed so far; its annual budget of $34 million is about one-seventh that of NHTSA, and its staff of about 500 is one-fourteenth that of the FDA.

Methods

Given the broad array of products and firms under its jurisdiction, one of the things CPSC has to decide is how to allocate its limited resources.

---

[20]Robert W. Crandall and John D. Graham, "The Effect of Fuel Economy Standards on Automobile Safety," *Journal of Law and Economics,* 32 (April 1989), pp. 97–118.
[21]*Final Report of the National Commission on Product Safety,* Government Printing Office, Washington, 1970, p. 1.

Accordingly, the agency tries to identify the most common and costly product-related injuries and to isolate their causes. It maintains a National Electronic Injury Surveillance System (a network of computer terminals in a sample of hospital emergency rooms throughout the country) for this purpose, and it supplements these injury data with information culled from examination of consumer complaints, a screening of death certificates, and its own laboratory tests. After hazards are identified, the agency assigns to each a priority ranking that depends on the severity and frequency of injury, the probability of future injuries, the degree to which consumers can foresee the risk involved, and other factors. Then CPSC devises a strategy to address its highest-priority problems.

The strategy generally takes one of three forms: a product ban, a design standard, or a labeling requirement or public education campaign. The agency has imposed relatively few bans, and some of these were subsequently overturned by the courts for procedural reasons (e.g., a ban on aerosols containing vinyl chloride was overturned because CPSC had failed to file a required environmental impact statement). CPSC's power to enforce strict design standards was weakened by the 1981 Product Safety Amendments, which required the agency to defer to "voluntary" safety standards that were devised by the affected industry (provided that these standards are likely to provide adequate protection to consumers) and to weigh benefits and costs before imposing its own "mandatory" standards. As a result, CPSC has come to impose such standards less frequently over time and to rely primarily on public education efforts to achieve its goals.

Enforcement and Remedies

Like NHTSA, CPSC requires manufacturers to foot the bill for certifying that their products meet specified standards. The agency then conducts field inspections and gathers product samples for laboratory tests to ascertain compliance. When safety-related defects or violations are detected, CPSC can seize or recall products, obtain injunctions or cease-and-desist orders against certain practices of manufacturers, and seek civil and criminal penalties.

Over the years, the agency has required recalls of well over 1,000 products, ranging from toy blow guns to coffee makers. One problem is that so many recalls are made in a typical year that many consumers never hear—or choose to disregard—a large fraction of them. A 1978 CPSC study of three dozen recall campaigns that involved over 2 million small appliances found that only about 1 in 8 were brought in for repair or replacement.

Performance

The CPSC argues that its efforts save more than 300 lives and prevent more than 250,000 injuries each year. Those outside the agency, however, tend to regard this as an overoptimistic assessment. Some critics view the CPSC as a rather timid regulator, reluctant to use its authority aggressively enough to produce significant gains in product safety. They acknowledge, however, that the data gathered by the agency are extremely useful in product liability suits brought on behalf of those damaged by faulty products. Fear of such suits, many feel, can lead producers to build greater safety into their goods.

Other critics argue that many of the standards the CPSC has imposed have been ineffective or actually counterproductive. One familiar CPSC regulation, e.g., is its requirement that some products (e.g., aspirin, furniture polish, turpentine) be covered with "childproof" safety caps to prevent accidental poisoning. The demand for such a standard arose in part from an erroneous perception that the poisoning rate for children was on the rise during the 1960s, when in fact it had been decreasing rapidly—indeed, even more rapidly than its established trend. The fatal poisoning rate for children under age 5 fell from 2.52 per million in 1950 to 2.19 per million in 1960 to 1.32 per million in 1970. Nevertheless, and despite widespread industry efforts to reduce the problem with warning labels, educational campaigns, and voluntarily introduced safety caps, mandatory standards were imposed in 1972. Regulators were confident that the safety benefits from protective caps would justify their higher costs and their inconvenience for some consumers (elderly or arthritic consumers, e.g., often find them impossible to open).

Unfortunately, these safety benefits have failed to materialize. In fact, after carefully examining the evidence on accidental poisonings, Kip Viscusi concluded that total poisoning rates (i.e., those for products not covered by the regulations as well as rates for covered products) were *higher* than would have been the case absent the regulations.[22]

The culprit here is what Viscusi has dubbed the *lulling effect*. Simply put, some regulations can lull consumers into a false sense of security about the hazards they face; as a result, they modify their behavior in ways that actually increase risk. In the case of drugs or other potentially poisonous substances, the safety cap regulations led some parents to be less careful about where they stored these products. Or the caps' inconvenience caused some users to leave caps off entirely. Finally, absence of caps on some goods led users to (wrongly) assume they were totally safe, leading to reduced vigilance. On net, the likelihood that children would be exposed to hazardous substances was greater after the regulations than before.

Viscusi is also skeptical that other CPSC standards have produced safety benefits. After analyzing trends in the overall home accident rate (death or injury from falls, fires, or other hazards), he concluded that "[t]here is no evidence in the aggregative data of any beneficial effect on product safety."[23] He found that the CPSC's flammability standards for carpets have actually been associated with a doubling of carpet-related injury rates, and he even concluded that the CPSC's much celebrated crib safety standards have been associated with a smaller reduction in crib-related injury rates than would have been pre-

---

[22]W. Kip Viscusi, "Consumer Behavior and the Safety Effects of Product Safety Regulation," *Journal of Law and Economics*, 28 (October 1985), pp. 527–553.

[23]Ibid., p. 537.

dicted by an extrapolation of the preregulation historical trend.[24] Other studies reach similar conclusions. Peter Linneman, e.g., found no safety benefits of the CPSC's mattress flammability standards.[25] And Ross Petty detected no reduction in bicycle-related injuries resulting from the agency's bicycle safety standards.[26]

In sum, the CPSC must be rated an underachiever among federal regulatory agencies. Its early efforts were tentative and not notably successful, and its later years have been characterized by passivity. While it counts a few prominent consumer advocates as friends and political allies, it can point to little hard evidence that its efforts have been fruitful and cost-effective. As a result, it has had to fight hard even to stay in business. Through the 1980s, its budget and staffing levels were trimmed back repeatedly. This, of course, makes it even less likely that the agency will emerge as a major force in the future.

PRODUCT LIABILITY LAW

The CPSC is not the only institution that affects product safety. The courts play a key role as well. *Product liability law,* a subarea of the law of torts, deals with the financial responsibility for damages that result from the use of consumer goods. Legal rules about liability are important in two ways. Since they determine who will pay the costs of product-related accidents, they clearly affect distributional equity. But they may also affect efficiency, for they can set forces in motion that will alter the number or severity of such accidents. In recent years, the courts have been modifying long-standing product liability rules, bringing new interest and controversy to a field that had long been regarded as an obscure legal byway.

Product Liability Rules

In theory, we can choose from an infinite variety of rules to guide decision making in product liability lawsuits. At one extreme, we may hold that sellers are never responsible for harm that results from the use of their goods. Under such a rule, which we may refer to as a *no-liability* or *caveat emptor* ("let the buyer beware") standard, the costs of product-related accidents are concentrated among a relatively small group: those to whom the accidents occur. Often, however, this will be objectionable on equity grounds. For example, in a tiny fraction of cases certain vaccines produce the very malady against which inoculation was sought. It seems grossly unfair to leave victims uncompensated for damages in such cases. In addition, a no-liability rule may be inefficient. Often product defects will be very difficult for buyers to detect,

---

[24]Ibid., pp. 551–552.

[25]Peter Linneman, "The Effects of Consumer Safety Standards: The 1973 Mattress Flammability Standard," *Journal of Law and Economics,* 23 (October 1980), pp. 461–479.

[26]Ross D. Petty, "The Consumer Product Safety Commission's Promulgation of a Bicycle Safety Standard," *Journal of Products Liability,* 1987, Vol. 10, Issue 1, pp. 25–50.

while manufacturers can detect and/or correct them more easily. Insulated from liability for defects, however, producers may have an inadequate incentive to exercise due care, and the degree of risk to buyers may therefore be inefficiently high.

At the other extreme, we might hold sellers strictly liable in all cases that involve product-related damages. Such a rule, which we might call a *strict liability* or *caveat venditor* ("let the seller beware") standard, is appealing to many on both equity and efficiency grounds. First, such a rule spreads the costs of accidents very widely. In principle, allowing those to whom a product-related accident has occurred to recover damages from the seller will force the seller to include anticipated damage costs in the prices of all goods sold. Thus, all consumers of the seller's products (and perhaps the firm's stockholders) will share in these costs, a situation which strikes most people as eminently fair. Second, such a rule will likely yield safer products. A seller who is strictly liable for damage costs has every incentive to spend extra dollars on safety if they will avoid larger court-ordered payouts down the road.

But a strict liability standard will not be efficient in all circumstances. Sometimes, it is buyers rather than sellers who can avoid a hazard most cheaply. When this is true, it will generally be more efficient to place liability on consumers, strengthening their incentive to avoid accidents. Compare, e.g., the following two scenarios: (1) Your brakes fail, and you have an accident shortly after you drive your new car off the dealer's lot. (2) Your brakes fail, and you have an accident after driving your car 150,000 miles, having ignored instructions in the owner's manual to have the brakes serviced every 50,000 miles. It is clearly efficient to place liability for the first type of accident on the manufacturer, for it is unrealistic to expect consumers to be able to assess whether their new cars' brakes are defective. But it may be reasonable to expect consumers to see that their brakes are maintained. It is impossible (or prohibitively costly) to manufacture brakes that will last forever. Given this fact of life, we want to ensure that consumers have the proper incentive to avoid risks that are under their control.

To cope with such circumstances, we may employ a liability rule that is somewhere between the two extremes discussed above. For example, we might employ a standard of *strict liability with contributory negligence*. Under this rule, the seller will be found liable for accident costs provided the consumer has taken due care, i.e., has used or maintained the product as a "reasonably prudent person" would have in the circumstances. A similar standard involves *breach of implied warranty*, in which sellers are liable for damages if a product is found to be unfit for the purpose for which it was intended or for other "reasonably anticipated" uses. Alternatively, we might hold sellers liable for damages only if plaintiffs can show that there was *negligence*—i.e., failure to take reasonable precautions—in the design, manufacture, or sale of the product.

Scholars have produced countless analyses of the implications of these and other liability rules. Some can be shown to be more likely than others to lead to the efficient level of risk or safety in product markets. But these findings often depend on the assumptions made about the amount of information about risk that is available to consumers, how this information is used, consumers' preferences about risk, or the propensity of those suffering product-related harm to bring lawsuits. In addition, there is much disagreement about the way that efficiency considerations should be weighted vis-à-vis equity concerns. There is, then, no consensus about the optimal liability standard, and states' product liability laws vary greatly. Further, the thousands of judges and juries who have had to interpret these laws have not always done so in a consistent or coherent fashion. Thus, generalizations about the current status of product liability law are difficult to make.

Trends in Case Law

Well into the 20th century, victims of product-related accidents in the United States had little hope of recovering damages from manufacturers. The doctrine of *privity* limited claims to those with a direct contractual relationship with the maker of a product (and even for this group, there were many legal obstacles to recovery). Consumers who suffered damages from defective automobiles, e.g., usually could not recover their losses from the manufacturer because they had dealt contractually with independent dealers, not the manufacturer. Since dealers were generally not responsible for product defects, consumers were left holding the bag. The landmark *MacPherson v. Buick* decision[27] dealt a severe blow to the privity doctrine. Still, plaintiffs faced many obstacles to recovery. Courts commonly barred recovery unless there was proof of irresponsible manufacturer behavior (i.e., negligence). Acquiring evidence of such behavior was often hard: Consumers commonly have limited access to information about the conditions under which goods are produced. But even where such evidence was available, courts often barred recovery where a product had been misused or where injury resulted from some danger of which the consumer was—or should have been—aware.

In recent years, however, U.S. courts have been moving closer to a strict liability standard in product liability suits. Today, establishing producer negligence is usually unnecessary. Consumer misuse of a product will not bar recovery if such misuse was foreseeable to the manufacturer. Even the presence of an obvious or "patent" risk may no longer be a bar to recovery. And the qualifications for a product defect, which still must be demonstrated, have loosened considerably. Formerly, defects were errors in the manufacturing process (e.g., failure to assemble a product correctly). Now, products may be judged defective if manufacturers *fail to warn* users of possible risks or if products contain *design defects* that expose users to "unreasonable danger." And full compliance with FDA, CPSC, or other agencies' safety regulations often counts for little in subsequent liability lawsuits.

---

[27]*MacPherson v. Buick*, 111 N.E. 1050 (1916).

Effects

As we might expect, enhancing accident victims' prospects for damage recovery has made product liability lawsuits a growth industry. Between 1974 and 1986, the annual number of product liability cases filed in federal courts jumped from 1,579 to 13,595, an increase of 761 percent. Data on claims in state courts (where most liability cases are filed) are sketchy, but available figures for two large urban counties (Cook County, Illinois, and San Francisco County, California) suggest a sharp upward trend in both the number of claims and the size of judgments. As Table 17.2 shows, the average award increased (in real, inflation-apart terms) over threefold in Cook County from the early 1960s to the early 1980s and over elevenfold in San Francisco County during the same period.

But what have been the effects of this trend toward more and bigger product liability lawsuits? Have stricter liability standards enhanced efficiency and equity? Unfortunately, there are no clear answers to these questions. There is, of course, good reason to *assume* that firms today produce safer products than they would have, had liability standards remained less strict. After all, investments in product safety now have a much higher payoff—in terms of damage awards and litigation costs avoided—than under earlier standards. And there is at least some evidence that product liability considerations loom large in firms' decisions to market certain products. One survey of 500 large corporations found that more than one-quarter had removed one or more products from the market for product liability reasons.[28]

But firms' incentives to produce safer products—or withdraw some risky products from the market—may not contribute to lower accident rates for at least three basic reasons:

1 Remember that firms will recover the costs of paying higher damage awards or producing safer products by charging higher prices. Some consumers, unwilling or unable to pay these higher prices, will substitute cheaper, lower-quality, less safe products. For example, once car prices include a higher safety or liability premium, some consumers may choose smaller, lighter models, while others may hold on to their older vehicles longer. In a similar vein, once ladder prices incorporate a liability premium, more people will be unwilling to spend the extra money for ladders and will stand on boxes or chairs to perform certain chores.

2 The products withdrawn from the market because of liability concerns may or may not be safer than available alternatives. As Peter Huber has observed, juries tend to regard risks from old and familiar products with more tolerance than risks from new and complicated ones.[29] Thus, they are far more likely to judge newer products "defective in design" or hold makers of these products liable for failure to warn about hazards. Because of this asymmetry,

---

[28]Alison Kittrell, "Tort System Costly Burden, Survey Finds," *Business Insurance*, May 9, 1988, pp. 3, 32.

[29]Peter Huber, "Safety and the Second Best: The Hazards of Public Risk Management in the Courts," *Columbia Law Review*, 85 (March 1985), pp. 277–337.

TABLE 17.2
AVERAGE AND MEDIAN JURY AWARDS IN PRODUCT LIABILITY CASES IN TWO LARGE
URBAN COUNTIES, 1960–1984. The data (in thousands of 1984 dollars) suggest a sharp
upward trend in the number of claims and size of judgments as a result of enhancing victims'
prospects for damage recovery.

	Cook County		San Francisco County	
Years	Average	Median	Average	Median
1960–1964	265	103	99	27
1965–1969	287	118	191	72
1970–1974	578	178	145	51
1975–1979	597	196	308	81
1980–1984	828	187	1,105	200

Source: Mark Peterson, *Civil Juries in the 1980s,* Rand Corporation, Santa Monica, California, Institute for Civil Justice, R-3466-ICJ, 1987, p. 22.

new products may be pulled from the shelves and the market left to older substitutes that are actually less safe.

3 A lulling effect (similar to that which offset the safety benefits of the
CPSC's childproof caps for drugs and other products) may be at work here. If
consumers assume that stricter liability standards must yield safer products
(or alternatively that they will always be fully compensated for any product-
related damages), they may change their behavior in ways that offset some of
the safety gains of such products, or they may become less vigilant about risks
that are actually under their control.

Because liability standards differ from state to state and because juries'
interpretations of these standards have been far from consistent over time, it
will be extraordinarily hard to sort through the accident rate data to ascertain
whether tightened liability rules have enhanced aggregate safety. So far, no
researchers have been up to the task. As a result, we simply don't know
whether the new rules have made the world a safer place or, if they have done
so, whether any safety benefits have been worth the cost.

But if the efficiency effects of the legal changes are unknown, can we not
rest content that the equity effects are favorable? Perhaps. According to a 1987
survey by the National Center for Health Statistics, about 13 percent of people
in the United States lack private health insurance; higher fractions lack disability or wage-loss insurance. We can presume that most of those who lack such
insurance protection are relatively poor. Since stricter liability rules extend
insurance coverage for the costs of product-related accidents to such individuals, it seems clear that we can chalk up a significant equity gain for these rules
relative to older, no-liability standards. A key question, however, is whether the
new rules are as equitable as alternative victim compensation schemes.

Consider the way in which stricter liability standards work. Damage awards to those harmed in product-related accidents typically are paid by producers' insurance carriers. As we have noted, the costs of liability insurance premiums are included in product prices. In fact, some have dubbed the new liability rules a "third-party insurance system," since consumers now get accident insurance from a third party—the manufacturer—with everything they buy. Note, however, that the liability premium will not vary among consumers; it will be the same amount (equal to average expected damage awards and litigation costs) for poor and rich buyers alike. But, as George Priest notes, damage awards will vary positively with income:

> The major components of tort damages are past and future lost income (obviously related to wealth), medical expenses (also typically wealth-related; the affluent person patronizes more expert doctors), and pain and suffering (highly correlated with lost income, since it is typically sustained job loss, rather than short though intense hospital expense, that signals disruption of the victim's life).[30]

The result, concludes Priest, is a regressive redistribution of income:

> With each damage element linked positively to income, a uniform premium will undercharge the rich and overcharge the poor for the given coverage. In effect, the system forces those with low incomes to subsidize the insurance costs of those with high incomes.[31]

Unhappily, then, the net efficiency and equity effects of the current liability rules are either unknown or ambiguous. One thing *is* clear, however. The new rules have excited great controversy. During the late 1980s, some charged that stricter liability rules had led to an insurance "crisis" in which premiums soared or liability coverage became unavailable altogether. Scholars were (and are) divided on whether such a crisis was real, and, if it was, whether it had anything to do with changing legal standards. Nevertheless, about one-third of the states responded with hasty legal reforms. These included arbitrary ceilings or caps on awards for pain and suffering and on assessments for punitive damages, changes in the standards of proof needed to establish a defendant's guilt, and limits on the fees paid to plaintiffs' lawyers (which often are a flat one-third—or more—of awards).

Demands for reform at the federal level have come from several manufacturers' and insurers' groups. These groups argue that varying—and rapidly changing—state liability rules make it very difficult to predict risk exposure. They want to establish uniform federal product design standards and do away with "joint-and-several liability" rules under which each contributor to an accident—no matter how small his or her role—can be held fully liable for all the costs of an accident. Such proposals have met determined opposition from various consumers' groups and the plaintiffs' bar, however. So far, Congress has declined to act.

---

[30]George L. Priest, "Understanding the Liability Crisis," in Walter Olson (ed.), *New Directions in Liability Law,* The Academy of Political Science, New York, 1988, p. 210.
[31]Ibid., pp. 210–211.

REGULATING THE WORKPLACE: OSHA

Background

In 1970, the National Safety Council estimated that each year workplace accidents were responsible for more than 14,000 deaths and another 2.2 million disabling injuries. Subsequent studies suggested that job-related illnesses were an even larger problem. In response, Congress created the Occupational Safety and Health Administration (OSHA) "to assure so far as possible every working man and woman in the nation safe and healthful working conditions."[32] At the time, few questioned whether the regulatory approach was the best way to address job safety issues, and few doubted that it would pay large dividends. One of the coauthors of the OSHA legislation expressed confidence that within a decade accident rates in the workplace would be cut by 50 percent or thereabouts.

In the years since 1970, OSHA has become one of the best known of federal regulatory agencies. With annual outlays of about $240 million and a staff of over 2,400, it is one of the larger ones as well. Unfortunately, OSHA's prominence has resulted as much from controversy as from accomplishment. Although organized labor defends it staunchly, OSHA has been the target of scathing criticism from employers—and even a few workers—who accuse it of issuing misguided, excessively picky or cost-ineffective regulations, inconsistent enforcement, and (most damning of all) a failure to get results. Indeed, the rate of lost-workday injuries actually *rose* through the 1970s, and by 1979 the rate was 30 percent higher than it had been when OSHA was created. Although the incidence of serious accidents has fallen since, the image of OSHA as an underachiever remains.

Methods

Congress authorized OSHA to set standards for occupational exposure to risk, but gave only vague guidance as to the nature or stringency of these standards. Much of the controversy that surrounds the agency's performance has arisen because of the way it has interpreted Congress's charge to enhance workplace safety and health *so far as possible.* In general, OSHA has taken that phrase to mean that it need not weigh the benefits of risk reductions against their costs. In practice, the agency does consider compliance costs in devising its standards, especially when a particular standard might force affected firms to shut down entirely. But it does not feel compelled to compare costs and benefits when discussing the reasons for its policies.

This interpretation was upheld by the Supreme Court in *American Textile Manufacturers v. Donovan* in 1981.[33] OSHA had imposed stringent standards for exposure to cotton dust, which can cause a lung disease called byssinosis. Textile manufacturers claimed that the standards were wildly cost-ineffective.

---

[32]OSHA Act of 1970, Section 2(b), 29 U.S.C. 651 (1976).
[33]*American Textile Manufacturers v. Donovan,* 452 U.S. 490 (1981).

OSHA disputed this claim, but also argued that Congress did not want the agency to weigh costs and benefits in setting standards. The Supreme Court took OSHA's side. It found no express calls for cost-benefit analysis in the congressional debate on the OSHA Act, and it interpreted Congress's suggestion that standards should be no more stringent than "feasible" to mean *technologically feasible* (i.e., capable of being done) rather than *economically feasible* (i.e., cost-effective). Although the High Court held in another case that OSHA must show that its standards will produce at least *some* benefits,[34] its decision in the cotton dust case left no doubt that OSHA could, if it wished, ignore costs in deciding how stringent to make its standards.

OSHA has been criticized for relying on *design standards* rather than *performance standards* and on *engineering controls* rather than *personal protective equipment*. The agency typically addresses safety problems by devising narrow and uniform rules that, in effect, prescribe the design of the workplace. Performance standards would, by contrast, specify certain results that the agency wanted firms to achieve (e.g., a 20 percent reduction in accident rates) and leave it to the firms to determine the best way to meet this goal.

Especially in OSHA's first decade, its prescriptions struck many as either trivial or excessively rigid. Among its early standards, e.g., were detailed specifications about the design of portable toilets for cowboys. And one famous case involved penalties against an employer who had failed to force his employees to wear life jackets while working on a bridge—even though the creek running under the bridge had long since dried up. Such examples made OSHA the target of considerable ridicule in the press, and the agency has learned to choose its battles more judiciously in recent years. Nevertheless, the agency maintains a partiality toward design standards and engineering controls even when more cost-effective alternatives exist. OSHA's standards for exposure to occupational noise are a relevant example. According to one study, OSHA's prescription that engineering controls be used to reduce the noise to which workers could be exposed in an 8-hour day to 90 decibels would have cost about $940,000 per hearing impairment avoided. By contrast, a similar reduction could have been obtained via protective equipment at a cost of $10,300 per hearing impairment avoided.[35] Yet, until the standards were overturned in the courts, OSHA insisted that noise reductions should result primarily from engineering controls and that personal protective devices (e.g., earplugs, earmuffs) should be used only as a last resort.

Economists also criticize OSHA's overemphasis on reducing workplace accidents and its underemphasis on health concerns. While writing 140-odd standards that apply to ladders, e.g., and formulating detailed specifications on the proper characteristics of handrails, the agency largely ignored health hazards posed by occupational exposure to many toxic or carcinogenic sub-

---

[34]*Industrial Union Department, AFL-CIO v. American Petroleum Institute*, 448 U.S. 607 (1980).

[35]John F. Morrall III, "Exposure to Occupational Noise," in James C. Miller III and Bruce Yandle (eds.), *Benefit-Cost Analyses of Social Regulation*, American Enterprise Institute, Washington, 1979, pp. 33–58.

stances. By some estimates, such exposure accounts for as many as 100,000 deaths per year—far more than the work-related fatal accident rate. In addition, the health risks of occupational exposure to dangerous substances are far more difficult for workers to evaluate on their own because the effects of exposure are postponed for long periods. Thus, it is here that the market is least likely to develop its own risk control mechanisms (e.g., compensating differentials). In sum, it is health standards that are likely to have the greatest pay-off per dollar spent on compliance—yet, by the mid-1980s, OSHA had issued only a dozen health standards, but hundreds of safety standards. In recent years, OSHA has recognized this imbalance and devoted greater attention to health concerns. Many feel, however, that an even greater shift of resources is warranted.

Enforcement and Remedies

To enforce its standards, OSHA has a large staff of inspectors who make visits to the workplace, determine whether there are any violations, and penalize violators. Many states also have their own inspectors who perform similar tasks.

Inspections can be triggered in several ways. Most commonly, a small sample of firms in high-risk industries are scheduled for *programmed inspections.* In recent years, these inspections have been targeted more narrowly in order to better husband staff resources. A large portion of U.S. manufacturing companies with good safety records are now exempt from scheduled inspections. Less frequently, inspections arise from *employee complaints.* (Surprisingly, such inspections generally turn up few violations, suggesting perhaps that disgruntled workers may be using the threat of OSHA inspection as a tool of collective bargaining or as a means of harassing employers.[36]) *Fatalities and catastrophes* trigger immediate investigations, and *follow-up inspections* are made where there is a pattern of serious, willful, or repeated violations of standards.

The annual number of inspections generally exceeds 70,000. Although this number seems large, only a tiny fraction of all enterprises ever see an OSHA inspector, and only about 3 million employees are covered annually by OSHA inspections. In addition, penalties for violations are often quite small. Even in 1980, when total OSHA penalties were at their highest level ever ($25.5 million), the average penalty per violation was a mere $193. During the Reagan Presidency, when OSHA adopted a less confrontational approach to business, penalties were lower still—down to an average of about $50 per violation by the late 1980s.

This raises troubling questions about the likely effectiveness of OSHA regulation. Simply put, firms will have little incentive to comply with OSHA's standards. The probability of an inspection is low, and the size of any penalty

---

[36]See W. Kip Viscusi, "Reforming OSHA Regulation of Workplace Risks," in Leonard W. Weiss and Michael W. Klass (eds.), *Regulatory Reform: What Actually Happened,* Little, Brown, Boston, 1986, p. 253.

will be small, so the expected costs of noncompliance are likely to be negligible. Perhaps, under these circumstances, we should be surprised if OSHA is anything *but* an underachiever.

VIGNETTE 17.4   To Lumberjacks, OSHA Is Not OK

Logging must rate as one of the more dangerous occupations on earth. For every 1,000 lumberjacks, there are about two injuries *per day*—often involving serious multiple fractures or gashes so deep they sever muscle—and a fatality about every 6 months.

One might think, therefore, that lumberjacks would regard OSHA regulators as their allies. Just the opposite appears to be the case, however. Many loggers openly defy OSHA specifications about safety equipment, and a few inspectors have literally been run out of the woods. In a most entertaining *Wall Street Journal* feature, William Blundell wrote of loggers reciting a poem about "the idiocies of the safety people" that concludes, "Who's going to protect us against our protection?" One safety official admitted that, in loggers' views, "We're a bunch of dirty S.O.B.'s for trying to jam safety down their throats."[37]

Some ascribe such behavior to loggers' sense of machismo or their stubborn resistance to change. But there may be other reasons as well. Many loggers evidently feel that some of the safety equipment mandated by OSHA will have no effect on the likelihood of a serious accident—or might even increase it. Requirements for heavy leg protectors, e.g., were criticized as counterproductive. Their mobility reduced by such equipment, many loggers felt more vulnerable to serious risks from falling trees or boulders.

There is also evidence that lumberjacks are quite concerned with sources of risk that *are* under their control. Loggers often work in teams, and any individual's safety will be crucially related to the conduct of teammates. Well aware of this fact, loggers act quickly to discipline unfit or lackadaisical coworkers. Characteristically blunt, loggers will first communicate displeasure with a team member verbally—"one on one, no dancing around, no politics," according to one Weyerhauser Co. employee. But if such warnings fail to improve behavior, the offender may become the target of hazing, which can range from the destruction of a logger's lunch to an invitation to step behind a tree for a faceful of knuckles.

Note also that the dangers of logging are no secret, so lumberjacks receive sizable compensating differentials for their willingness to bear risk. This suggests another reason for loggers' lack of fondness for OSHA: Cost-ineffective regulations may lower lumberjacks' effective wage rates and even reduce employment. To see how, consider Figure 17.4, which describes the market for lumberjacks. The initial demand and supply curves, labeled D_L and S_L, intersect at a wage rate w_0 and a quantity employed q_0. Now suppose an OSHA regulation that *we assume to be cost-ineffective* (without implying that all or most such regulations have this characteristic) is imposed. Specifically, we assume the regulation produces $u in safety benefits per period, but the employer's compliance costs are $v per lumberjack employed, where $u < $v. The supply of lumberjacks increases to S_L' because more people are willing to undertake such work now that it is safer. Since the extra safety

[37] William E. Blundell, "To Loggers, the Woods Are Dark and Deep—But Far from Lovely," *The Wall Street Journal*, 198 (December 8, 1981), p. 1.

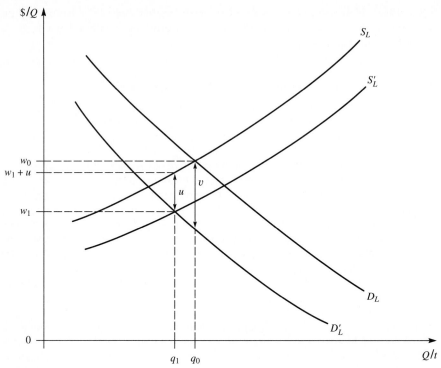

FIGURE 17.4
WAGE AND EMPLOYMENT EFFECTS OF A COST-INEFFECTIVE SAFETY REGULATION.
A cost-ineffective regulation reduces the demand for labor (to D'_L) by more than it increases the supply of labor (to S'_L). Thus, equilibrium employment falls (to q_1), and the effective wage falls (to $w_1 + u$, the added value of safety).

is valued at $\$u$, by assumption, S'_L lies below S_L by exactly this amount. Employers, however now reduce their demand for lumberjacks to D'_L because compliance costs add $\$v$ to the cost of hiring each lumberjack; if lumberjacks' marginal value to employers was initially given by D_L, their new value to employers is now $D_L - \$v$, or D'_L. The new equilibrium in this market, where D'_L and S'_L intersect, will be at a money wage rate w_1 and quantity employed q_1. Of course, to get lumberjacks' effective wage rate, we must add the value of the enhanced safety ($\$u$) to the lower money wage (w_1), but the resulting total is still less than their initial wage rate w_0; that is, $w_1 + \$u < w_0$. What is more, total industry employment falls as well; that is, $q_1 < q_0$. Perhaps, then, lumberjacks' antipathy toward "the safety people" is based on economic rationality as much as machismo.

Performance

Assessing OSHA's effectiveness is complicated by three factors. First, many things other than regulation affect workplace accident rates. The behavior of workers obviously plays a key role. One survey found that workers' actions were a major contributor to 63 percent of the fatalities and injuries in the National Safety Council's 1970 measure of workplace safety.[38] Sorting out the relative importance of these various factors won't be easy. Second, at its inception OSHA instituted a host of new injury-reporting procedures, making the interpretation of the data before and after OSHA problematic. Some changes in reported accident rates may result more from these new reporting or classification requirements than from anything else. Third, data on occupational diseases are sketchy and difficult to interpret because nonoccupational factors (e.g., smoking) may be responsible for, or contribute to, the incidence of a particular illness. As a result, we must be skeptical of claims (sometimes advanced by labor unions) that OSHA regulations have saved thousands of lives and avoided tens of thousands of serious injuries, for these claims are usually based on a superficial examination of injury rate trends, which showed steady declines (of about 2 percent per year) for decades prior to OSHA's creation.

Most scholarly studies find no significant effect of OSHA regulation on injury rates, especially in the agency's early years. John Mendeloff studied the period up to 1974 and found no statistically significant decline in overall lost-workday injuries either at the national level or for a more detailed data set for California.[39] Robert Smith studied lost-workday accidents at firms that had been inspected by OSHA in 1973–1974. He found that inspections reduced lost-workday accidents only for small plants, and he hypothesized that because small plants are less able to afford safety experts, they benefit most from inspections.[40] This effect was not found in 1974, however; a follow-up study by Daniel McCaffrey also found no reductions in inspected firms' injury rates for the period from 1977 to 1978.[41]

The most extensive research on OSHA's impact is by Kip Viscusi. One study that covered the 1972–1975 period found no evidence that OSHA had any favorable effect on workplace safety.[42] A later study that covered 1973 to 1983 found no significant impact of OSHA on overall injury and illness rates, but did find some evidence (although tenuous) that OSHA inspections over the later part of the decade studied had reduced lost-workday injuries slightly. He estimated that OSHA inspections may prevent from 1 to 2 lost workdays per 1,000 workers annually.[43]

These are remarkably small gains in safety, especially when they are weighed against the costs of complying with OSHA regulations. Although

[38]Viscusi, in Weiss and Klass, *Regulatory Reform*, p. 260.

[39]John Mendeloff, *Regulating Safety: An Economic and Political Analysis of Occupational Safety and Health Policy*, M.I.T. Press, Cambridge, MA, 1979.

[40]Robert S. Smith, "The Impact of OSHA Inspections on Manufacturing Injury Rates," *Journal of Human Resources*, 14 (Spring 1979), pp. 145–170.

[41]Daniel P. McCaffrey, "An Assessment of OSHA's Recent Effects on Injury Rates," *Journal of Human Resources*, 18 (Winter 1983), pp. 131–146.

[42]W. Kip Viscusi, "The Impact of Occupational Safety and Health Regulation," *Bell Journal of Economics*, 10 (Spring 1979), pp. 117–140.

[43]W. Kip Viscusi, "The Impact of Occupational Safety and Health Regulation, 1973–83," *Rand Journal of Economics*, 17 (Winter 1986), pp. 567–580.

most survey estimates of these compliance costs are now dated, educated guesses are that firms spend anywhere from \$500 million to \$2.5 billion annually on OSHA-mandated safety equipment and rules.[44] And given OSHA's reluctance to employ rigorous cost-benefit analysis in devising its programs, it is not surprising that scholarly evidence suggests that these costs are far in excess of those necessary to enhance occupational safety or health by some target amount. For example, a study of OSHA regulation of the railroad industry by Michael French concluded that current regulation needlessly adds as much as 1.7 percent to firms' operating costs.[45] Finally, a study of OSHA's standard for exposure to vinyl chloride gas concluded that its costs were about \$9 million per life likely to be saved—far higher than the cost per life saved of agencies such as the EPA, NHTSA, and the CPSC.[46] Clearly, it will be inefficient to spend \$9 million to save a single life in one sector when a similar expenditure can save several lives in some other.

It is apparent, however, that OSHA is determined to improve its performance. In the last decade, it has eliminated many of its least effective (and least popular) regulations, has better targeted its enforcement efforts, and has introduced several promising regulations. What is more, it has begun to shift its emphasis from safety toward health standards, where its activities are most warranted and can have the greatest payoffs. Some critics suggest, however, that health hazards should receive still more emphasis and that OSHA's emphasis on design standards rather than performance standards must change as well. Other critics argue that new legislation is required to compel the agency to explicitly balance benefits and costs in devising its standards. There is little support among scholars for deregulation, however; the consensus seems to be that health and safety regulation is necessary, but there are ample opportunities to improve it.

SUMMARY AND CONCLUDING REMARKS

If we lived in a world where we were perfectly (and costlessly) informed about all the risks that confront us in product or labor markets and if we were capable of flawlessly analyzing all this information, then health and safety regulation would be unnecessary. Consumers and workers would demand compensating differentials before they would bear any risk, and producers and employers would then have incentives to make goods or provide working conditions of optimal safety. In the real world, however, the underproduction of information in markets, information asymmetries, and the bounded rationality of transactors often make such regulation desirable.

The FDA sets various standards to enhance the safety and purity of food, drugs, medical devices, and cosmetics. It seeks to ensure the safety and effica-

---

[44]See Mendeloff, *Regulating Safety,* p. 88.

[45]Michael T. French, "An Efficiency Test for Occupational Safety Regulation," *Southern Economic Journal,* 54 (January 1988), pp. 675–693.

[46]H. R. Northrup, R. L. Rowan, and C. R. Perry, *The Impact of OSHA,* University of Pennsylvania, Philadelphia, 1978.

cy of new drugs with a costly (and time-consuming) review process. This clearly makes its harder (but not impossible) for unsafe or ineffective treatments to make it to the market, but also delays marketing of safe and effective ones. Responding to criticisms that such delays have cost lives, the FDA has lately modified its approval process for promising drugs aimed at treating fatal ailments where no alternative therapies are yet available.

NHTSA sets automobile safety standards aimed at reducing the number of crashes and protecting passengers should a crash occur. The best estimates are that NHTSA has been quite successful in achieving its goals. By one estimate, if all cars on the road by 1981 had been built to pre-1966 safety specifications, the annual traffic fatality rate would likely have been from 13,000 to 24,000 higher.

The CPSC has been less successful in reducing injuries resulting from other products. In some cases, in fact, researchers have found that some CPSC safety standards might actually have increased certain accident rates, perhaps because the standards induced consumers to modify their behavior in unsafe ways. Consumer product safety might also be affected by recent changes in product liability law. Many courts have moved closer to a strict liability standard for product liability, making it far easier today for consumers to recover damages resulting from a product-related accident. Worries about expensive liability lawsuits have led many manufacturers to withdraw some products from the marketplace. To date, however, there is no evidence that more stringent liability rules have reduced accident rates.

OSHA regulation of the workplace has been controversial because the agency tends to emphasize safety issues over health concerns and to rely on expensive design standards and engineering controls rather than more cost-effective performance standards and personal protective equipment. Early studies of OSHA's performance tended to conclude that it had no discernible effect on accident rates in the workplace. The agency has, however, made strides in shifting its emphases and adopting more flexible standards, and studies of its performance in more recent years find some evidence that OSHA inspections contribute to reductions—albeit small ones—in the rate of lost-workday injuries.

QUESTIONS FOR REVIEW AND DISCUSSION

17.1 Define an information asymmetry, and give a real-world example. In your example, how does the passage of time affect the asymmetry?

17.2 Suppose you work at a regulatory agency devising standards for exposure to a life-threatening substance. Your job is to measure the economic value of life and limb. How might you go about your task? What types of information might you need?

17.3 An FDA commissioner has stated, "the more desperate a disease, the more willing we are to trade on safety and efficacy." Interpret and evaluate this remark, using graphs if necessary.

17.4 Cars built after 1989 are required to have costly "passive restraint" devices such as air bags or safety belts that automatically lock into place. These requirements are aimed at protecting those who routinely fail to use the safety belts that have been mandatory equipment on new cars since the mid-1960s. Evaluate the efficiency and equity implications of the new requirements.

17.5 Define the lulling effect. Can you give any examples of this effect other than those discussed in the text?

17.6 To what does the legal phrase *privity of contract* refer, and how has it played a role in product liability law? Can you think of any circumstances in which the privity doctrine seems desirable, at least from an economic standpoint?

17.7 In spite of the best efforts of federal regulators and airlines themselves, there is still some risk associated with air travel. (Apparently, it is unreasonable to expect pilots, mechanics, or aeronautical engineers to be failsafe and impossible to control variables such as weather.) Under current standards of liability, those harmed by aircraft accidents (i.e., injured passengers or survivors of those killed in air disasters) may sue to recover damages. Suppose, instead, the airline industry successfully lobbied for federal legislation exempting it from liability as long as it had satisfied federal safety regulations. Would the exemption necessarily leave victims uncompensated in the event of an air disaster? How do you think the exemption would affect the safety of air travel? State clearly any assumptions you make, and use graphs to facilitate your analysis.

17.8 What is the difference between the optimal level of safety and the maximum level of safety? Which level does OSHA commonly seek in its standard-setting procedures? Why?

17.9 Empirical evidence seems to suggest that many of OSHA's safety standards yield tiny benefits, yet impose large compliance costs. Such cost-ineffective regulations can (recall Vignette 17.4) reduce workers' wages and levels of employment. Yet labor unions are typically staunch supporters of OSHA. Enumerate possible reasons why. (*Hint:* Consider the possibility that workers vary in their valuations of the safety benefits of OSHA regulations.)

CONCLUSION

CHAPTER 18

ANTITRUST AND REGULATION POLICY: RETROSPECT AND PROSPECT

Don't get the idea I'm knocking the American system.

Al Capone

We have completed a lengthy survey of the key ways that government affects the conduct of enterprise in the United States. We have identified some policies that have greatly enhanced social welfare, others that have diminished it, and many more that have done a little of both.

Now it is time to take stock, to gauge how well regulators have done in the past and discuss what they might do in the future. It would be nice if there were uniform views or consensus opinions on these matters. But, of course, there are not. Whether the topic is antitrust policy, economic regulation, or social regulation, opinions on past performance and visions of the future are many and diverse. As we have seen, the individuals or groups most affected by a specific policy will view it through the lens of self-interest, a lens which can often distort perceptions of the relative size of a policy's *social* benefits and costs. But the range of opinion among disinterested parties may be no narrower. Quite naturally, different people will attach different weights to the various effects of a particular policy. The importance I attach to fairness may lead me to brand ``successful'' a policy which sacrifices considerable efficiency in the pursuit of equity, while you may be unwilling to make such a trade-off. In sum, reasonable people may differ, even when the facts of a particular case are easy to uncover and well known to all. And, of course, often they will not be. Many of the data we need to weigh the benefits and costs of various policies are imprecise or nonexistent, making it hard to know whether we've done the right thing or how we may do it better the next time.

One goal in this concluding chapter is to sample these varying opinions on regulation's past and future. We'll start by seeing what ``the woman and man on the street'' seem to think.

GOVERNMENT REGULATION AND POPULAR OPINION

In 1990, the National Chamber Foundation (the research affiliate of the U.S. Chamber of Commerce) commissioned the Gallup organization to survey public opinion about the effects of government regulation. The poll (of about 1,000 randomly selected individuals) suggests that people in the United States are surprisingly skeptical about the effectiveness of much government regulation. When asked whether ``government regulations are worth the extra costs they impose,'' only 40 percent of the sample said yes; 51 percent said no (the remainder had no opinion). In addition, 72 percent of the sample agreed that ``current business regulations have caused the United States to be less competitive in world markets.'' Finally, only 34 percent of the sample agreed that regulation enhances the welfare of the public *as a whole*; 62 percent felt that ``most regulations benefit the interests of some special groups *at the expense of the public as a whole*.''

These results are broadly consistent with those of earlier polls.[1] Just after World War II, 54 percent of respondents in a *New York Herald Tribune* survey agreed that it was ``a good idea'' to have less government regulation of business, versus only 26 percent who thought this was ``not such a good idea.'' A 1952 Roper poll reported 49 percent of respondents saying there was ``too much'' regulation of business activity, with 29 percent saying the amount was ``about right'' and only 7 percent saying there was ``not enough.'' Even in the 1970s, when regulation was clearly a growth industry, the proportion of survey respondents who favored increases in regulation continued to be a minority. And toward the end of that decade, antiregulatory sentiment grew, with much larger numbers agreeing that regulation had made them worse off, as Table 18.1 shows. In sum, then, while most everyone agrees that some government regulation of enterprise is essential, by the early 1980s increasing numbers seemed to hold the view that some *de*regulation was desirable.[2] And by the late 1980s, there was evidence that consumers considered they had received tangible benefits from deregulation, in the form of greater competition in a variety of markets.[3]

One aspect of the 1990 National Chamber Foundation poll that merits spe-

---

[1]For an interesting review from which the proceeding data are drawn, see Seymour Martin Lipset and William Schneider, *The Confidence Gap: Business, Labor, and Government in the Public Mind*, Free Press, New York, 1983, especially pp. 223–230.

[2]Burns W. Roper and Thomas A. W. Miller, ``Americans Take Stock of Business,'' *Public Opinion*, 8 (August/September 1985), pp. 12–15.

[3]Thomas A. W. Miller, ``Is Deregulation Working?'' *Public Opinion*, 11 (March/April 1989), pp. 9–11, 59.

TABLE 18.1
GALLUP POLL RESULTS, 1966 TO 1981: HAS GOVERNMENT REGULATION OF LARGE CORPORATIONS MADE YOU BETTER OR WORSE OFF?   By the early 1980s, the public's opinion of regulation had reached a low ebb.

Percentage responding:	1966	1970	1977	1981
"Better off"	37	43	28	24
"Worse off"	21	15	26	40
"No difference"	18	22	26	17
"Don't know"	24	20	20	19

Source: Reprinted with the permission of The Free Press, a division of Macmillan, Inc., from *The Confidence Gap: Business, Labor, and Government in the Public Mind* by Seymour Martin Lipset and William Schneider. Copyright © 1983 by Columbia University in the City of New York.

cial comment is that respondents' answers varied strongly with their income and education. In general, those with higher income and more education tended to be more favorably disposed toward regulation. For example, Table 18.2 shows that only 32 percent of those with incomes below $20,000 thought that government regulations were worth the extra costs they impose, but a clear majority (54 percent) of those with incomes in excess of $75,000 thought so. And the fraction of respondents who thought regulation was generally worth the cost rose steadily with amount of education, from 25 percent of those with less than a 12th-grade education to 54 percent of those with some postgraduate education.

TABLE 18.2
1990 NATIONAL CHAMBER FOUNDATION SURVEY RESULTS ON WHETHER GOVERNMENT REGULATIONS ARE WORTH THE EXTRA COSTS THEY IMPOSE, BY INCOME AND EDUCATION.   High-income, high-education individuals tend to be more favorably disposed toward regulation.

	Percentage of sample who agree regulations are worth extra costs they impose
Income class	
< $20,000	32
$20,000 – $75,000	43
> $75,000	54
Education level	
Less than 12th grade	25
12th grade	32
Some college	44
College graduate	46
Some postgraduate	54

Source: National Chamber Foundation, "Gallup Survey of Opinion on Government Regulation," April 1990.

There are two ways to interpret these results. We might (arrogantly) discount the opinions of low-income, low-education respondents, on the assumption that such individuals are poorly informed about such an obscure topic as government regulation. Clearly, we need to take the results of polls on regulation with a grain of salt.[4] But there is probably little reason to single out the responses of low-income, low-education respondents; indeed, it is just such respondents who are likely to observe the effects of at least some forms of regulation on a daily basis. After all, blue-collar workers are much more likely to encounter OSHA regulations or be affected by EPA-mandated plant closures than higher-income, better-educated individuals.

So let us entertain an alternative interpretation: that high-income, high-education individuals respond as they do *because they attach greater value to the benefits generated by much regulation and are far more willing to pay regulation's costs.* In this view, those things regulation—at least, *social* regulation—is usually thought to provide, such as a cleaner environment or greater safety in product or labor markets, can be classified as *luxury goods.* (This is not to say that such things are mere frills. In economic parlance, luxury goods are simply those which have a high income elasticity of demand: A given percentage increase in consumers' incomes will produce a greater percentage increase in quantity consumed. The demand for many goods that we do not consider frills— e.g., private education—is highly income-elastic.) For *necessities,* however, income increases produce less than proportionate increases in consumption.

Figure 18.1 illustrates the nature of the relationship between income and demand for a hypothetical luxury and necessity. Here, when income doubles from Y to $2Y$, demand for the necessity rises 50 percent, to $1.5Q_0$, but demand for the luxury good triples, from Q_0 to $3Q_0$. It's probably reasonable to classify many of the goods that regulation aims to provide as luxuries. Many environmental problems, e.g., were more serious (or at least more obvious) generations ago, but our willingness to do something about them—to trade some economic output in exchange for greater environmental amenity—has clearly expanded as we have become more affluent. And less affluent countries seem less willing to sacrifice tangible output or to endanger jobs in exchange for environmental quality than we are.

Thus, our poll results suggest some important lessons. Although average citizens may be skeptical about the cost-effectiveness of many forms of government regulation, they will likely demand more of at least *some* of the things regulation can provide as time goes by and as incomes rise. It is true that we want policymakers to be careful about what they do; bureaucratic waste and

---

[4]As political scientist Everett Ladd has remarked,

> People have views on specific regulations which they encounter, of course, but they cannot apply any "overarching conceptual dimension" to regulation as a general issue or proposition. In this context, it is so very easy to err in asking the general public questions on regulation that are essentially meaningless since they fall outside the experience and cognitive world of most respondents.

Everett C. Ladd, "Opinion Roundup," *Public Opinion,* 3 (June/July 1980), p. 37.

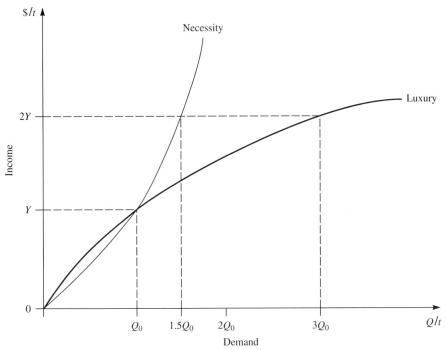

FIGURE 18.1
THE RELATION BETWEEN INCOME AND DEMAND FOR NECESSITIES AND LUXURIES. For
a necessity, income increases (from, say, Y to $2Y$) produce less than proportionate increases in
quantity (from Q_0 to $1.5Q_0$). For a luxury, income increases produce greater than proportionate
increases in quantity (from Q_0 to $3Q_0$).

inefficiency have few defenders. But this does not mean business decision
makers are likely to be given greater freedom from regulation in the future.
Indeed, the demand for regulation that promises greater personal safety, environmental quality, and equity is likely to show significant growth as we
become a more prosperous society.

THE JUDGMENTS OF SCHOLARS AND POLICYMAKERS

Those who have devoted their lives to the study of government intervention
in markets, or to guiding that intervention, have a great deal to say about the
way regulation has actually worked (in contrast to textbook discussions of the
way it is *supposed* to work). We cannot do full justice to the richness and diversity of their views about the effectiveness of regulatory policy in this brief
chapter. We can, however, summarize some research findings, offer some representative samples of opinion, highlight areas of agreement, and list some of
the controversies that remain.

Antitrust Policy

Well into the 1960s, antitrust enjoyed broad support among scholars, government officials, and even many business leaders. At least in some measure, this support arose from populist instincts. A common presumption was that antitrust could be used to protect small businesses from harm inflicted by larger ones. It was often said that antitrust existed to "keep the playing field level" for U.S. business and to provide a bulwark against "corporate giantism." It soon became clear, however, that using antitrust in this way posed some perils: Giving small businesses special protection often meant withholding the benefits of more efficient organizational forms or practices from consumers.

Two cases illustrate the point. In its *Foremost Dairies* decision, the FTC stated its belief that proof of violation of section 7 (the antimerger provision) of the Clayton Act "consists of . . . evidence showing that the acquiring firm possesses significant power in some markets *or* that its overall organization gives it a decisive advantage in efficiency over its smaller rivals."[5] Such indifference—nay, hostility—to the possible efficiencies that stem from a merger reached a climax in the Supreme Court's *Procter & Gamble* decision in 1967, where the Court stated baldly that "[p]ossible economies cannot be used as a defense to illegality."[6] Refusing to consider possible efficiency gains of some mergers or nonstandard business practices made enforcement easy—Justice Potter Stewart remarked in one case that "the sole consistency that I can find under Section 7 is that the government always wins"[7]—but took antitrust far from the goal of maximizing consumer welfare. As scholars such as Oliver Williamson had pointed out in 1968,[8] the welfare gains from even small cost savings can offset potential welfare losses from significantly higher oligopolistic prices.

By the 1970s, criticism that antitrust had become counterproductive, eradicating business practices or preventing mergers of tangible benefit to consumers, was widespread. Economists—especially those of the "Chicago school" (i.e., those who taught or had received their training at the University of Chicago)—began to take a lead role in redirecting antitrust theory and policy. The scholarly journals were filled with critical analyses of the approach to antitrust that prevailed at the time: the preoccupation with structure that would bar horizontal mergers between all but the tiniest of rivals, the deep suspicion that attached to virtually any tampering with price, and the presumption that most vertical restraints were attempts to foreclose competition. Although many economists would make major contributions to the reform effort, the research and writing of two law professors who would eventually

---

[5]*In re Foremost Dairies, Inc.,* 60 F.T.C. 944 (1962), p. 1084, emphasis added.
[6]*FTC v. Procter & Gamble Co.,* 386 U.S. 568 (1967), p. 580.
[7]*United States v. Von's Grocery, Inc.,* 384 U.S. 270 (1966), p. 301.
[8]Oliver E. Williamson, "Economies as an Antitrust Defense: The Welfare Tradeoffs," *American Economic Review,* 58 (March 1968), pp. 18–35.

become federal judges—Richard Posner and Robert Bork—were especially influential. Bork summarized his view of the status of antitrust with characteristic flamboyance:

> [M]odern antitrust has so decayed that the policy is no longer intellectually respectable. Some of it is not respectable as law; more of it is not respectable as economics; and . . . a great deal of antitrust is not even respectable as politics. The trends observable in antitrust . . . are four: (1) a movement away from political decision by democratic processes toward political choice by courts; (2) a movement away from the ideal of free markets toward the ideal of regulated markets; (3) a tendency to be concerned with group welfare rather than the general welfare; and (4) a movement away from the ideal of liberty and reward according to merit toward an ideal of equality of outcome and reward according to status.[9]

Such sentiments were not shared by the majority of antitrust scholars and practitioners. But the reformers had established a beachhead; in 1973, the Economic Policy Office was established within the Antitrust Division of the Justice Department, and economic analysis took on an increasingly important role in determining the kinds of cases that would be brought and the way they would be conducted. As Figure 18.2 shows, a massive shift of emphasis began in the 1970s and continued into the 1980s. Challenges to conglomerate and vertical mergers became more and more rare. Judicial thinking changed as well. In 1975 the FTC repudiated the antiefficiency reasoning of *Foremost Dairies* in its *Budd Co.* decision, branding as *procompetitive* an acquisition that made the merged firm stronger.[10] In its *General Dynamics* decision, the Supreme Court acknowledged for the first time that "other pertinent factors" might outweigh the higher concentration resulting from a merger.[11] And in its *GTE Sylvania* decision in 1977, the Court explicitly overturned its 1967 *Schwinn* ruling that vertical territorial restrictions were illegal per se, noting that "there is substantial scholarly opinion and judicial authority supporting [such restrictions'] economic utility."[12]

This efficiency orientation was strengthened—and market structure considerations were deemphasized—in the first Reagan term. Officials well versed in economic theory took the reins at the Justice Department and FTC and implemented more of the policy reforms that Bork and other critics had recommended. With the development of the Justice Department's merger guidelines in 1982, there was greater leniency with respect to horizontal mergers. The bulk of enforcement resources went to detection and prosecution of horizontal price-fixing agreements. Hostility to vertical restraints all but disappeared (although the courts did not buy the Antitrust Division's argument that vertical price restraints should, like vertical territorial assignments, be presumptively lawful).

---

[9]Robert Bork, *The Antitrust Paradox: A Policy at War with Itself,* Basic Books, New York, 1978, pp. 418–419.

[10]*Budd Co.,* [1973–1976 Transfer Binder] Trade Regulation Reporter CCTT (FTC No. 8848, Sept. 18, 1975).

[11]*United States v. General Dynamics Corp.,* 415 U.S. 486 (1974).

[12]*Continental T.V., Inc., et al. v. GTE Sylvania, Inc.,* 433 U.S. 36 (1977), pp. 57–58.

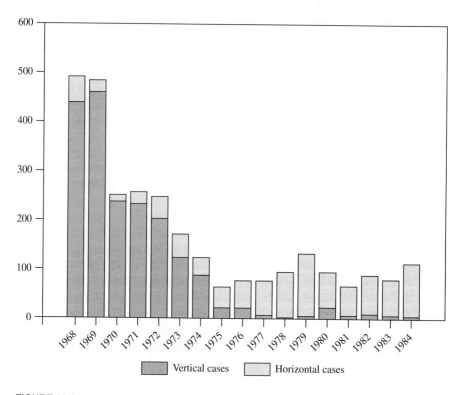

FIGURE 18.2
SHIFTING EMPHASIS AT THE JUSTICE DEPARTMENT: INVESTIGATIONS OF HORIZONTAL
AND VERTICAL RESTRAINTS OF TRADE, 1968–1984. Starting in the early 1970s, the Justice
Department greatly deemphasized vertical cases and increased the number and proportion of hor-
izontal cases it brought.
Source: Richard L. Johnson and David D. Smith, "Antitrust Divisions Merger Procedures and
Policy, 1968–84," Department of Justice Discussion Paper, 1986.

There was at least some empirical evidence in support of stepped-up
enforcement in horizontal collusion cases. In a 1981 paper, Michael Block,
Frederick Nold, and Joseph Sidak devised a model which suggested that in
the presence of antitrust enforcement efforts, a cartel's optimum price would
be at neither pure monopoly nor competitive levels, but at an intermediate
level depending on the authorities' enforcement capacity and the magnitude
of antitrust penalties.[13] They tested their model by examining local markets for
baked bread, long prone to price-fixing conspiracies and often the target of
Justice Department prosecution. They found that increases in the Justice
Department's enforcement capacity or the filing of a price-fixing complaint

---

[13]Michael Kent Block, Frederick Carl Nold, and Joseph Gregory Sidak, "The Deterrent Effect of
Antitrust Enforcement," *Journal of Political Economy,* 89 (June 1981), pp. 429–445. See also Michael
K. Block and Jonathan S. Feinstein, "The Spillover Effect of Antitrust Enforcement," *Review of
Economics and Statistics,* 68 (February 1986), pp. 122–131.

had the deterrent effect of reducing markups industrywide. Since government-imposed price-fixing penalties tended to be trivial, however, Block, Nold, and Sidak found that the most effective deterrent was the threat of large damage awards in the private class-action suits that usually followed successful government-initiated cases.[14]

Not everyone was happy with the reforms of the 1970s and 1980s, of course. To those of a "structuralist" orientation, the reforms represented a major retreat from the goals of antitrust; the shifts of emphasis during the Reagan years were virtually a policy of nonenforcement. Because structuralists tend to equate competitive vigor with low concentration, they longed for a return to the enforcement policy of the 1960s, which had most certainly kept industrial concentration well below the level that otherwise might have prevailed. Indeed, William G. Shepherd, a leading structuralist, concluded in 1982 that "the scope of competition increased substantially during 1958 to 1980," and antitrust policy deserved the lion's share of the credit for this trend.[15] Thus, the structuralists were especially critical of the more relaxed merger policy that prevailed in the 1980s. In the words of Walter Adams and James Brock, "the Reagan Administration created a hospitable environment for one of the most voracious corporate feeding frenzies and mass `corpocide' movements in American history."[16]

On the other side there were critics who felt that the reforms had not gone far enough—and, in fact, that antitrust should be abolished entirely! Some, like libertarian Dominick Armentano, had long viewed antitrust as a means by which true competition is subverted—a tool some businesses use to protect themselves from their more efficient rivals.[17] Others, such as mainstream liberal Lester Thurow, simply argued that the antitrust laws are unnecessary or undesirable in a global economy. "If competitive markets are desired," Thurow argued, "the appropriate policy should be to reduce barriers to free trade. . . . If[the antitrust laws] do anything, they only serve to hinder U.S. competitors who must live by a code their foreign competitors can ignore."[18]

It is probably fair to say, however, that most antitrust analysts—and especially most economists—find much to applaud in the approach to antitrust that now prevails. Many would like to see merger policy or the standards on predatory pricing tightened a bit, but relatively few would argue that the Justice Department's 1982 merger guidelines are inferior to the 1968 guidelines they replaced, or that key cases such as *General Dynamics* or *GTE Sylvania* were wrongly decided. Arguments that the antitrust authorities should bust up

---

[14]Note, however, that research by Craig Newmark casts some doubt on the strength of the deterrent effect found by Block et al. See Craig M. Newmark, "Is Antitrust Enforcement Effective?" *Journal of Political Economy,* 96 (December 1988), pp. 1315–1328.

[15]William G. Shepherd, "Causes of Increased Competition in the U.S. Economy, 1939–1980," *Review of Economics and Statistics,* 64 (November 1982), pp. 613–626.

[16]Walter Adams and James W. Brock, "Reaganomics and the Transmogrification of Merger Policy," *Antitrust Bulletin,* 33 (Summer 1988), p. 310.

[17]Dominick T. Armentano, *Antitrust Policy: The Case for Repeal,* Cato Institute, Washington, 1986.

[18]Lester C. Thurow, *The Zero-Sum Society,* Basic Books, New York, 1980, p. 146.

firms that exceed some arbitrary size threshold, attack mergers of small firms, or challenge all vertical restraints and mergers are seldom heard today. In large measure, this is so because economic analysis is now indisputably a crucial part of any antitrust case. Economics has clearly narrowed the bounds of what is considered acceptable discourse on antitrust policy. As a result, there is a much higher probability than ever that a particular antitrust decision will enhance consumer welfare.

Economic Regulation

Although regulation of prices and entry conditions in specific industries has a long history, it wasn't until the early 1960s that scholars began to empirically examine the effectiveness of this regulatory effort. Their findings were less than encouraging. With startling frequency, researchers concluded that the effects of economic regulation differed substantially from those predicted by *public-interest* models of market intervention, which presume that regulation is aimed at enhancing efficiency by correcting various market imperfections.

In markets that appear naturally monopolistic (e.g., electricity, local telephone service, natural gas distribution, water and sewer service), most studies concluded that regulation keeps price below the level that would be chosen by a single seller with an exclusive franchise. This is not to say, however, that regulated prices are approximately equal to those of some competitive ideal. Often the extent to which regulation constrains the pricing decisions of natural monopolists will vary with economic conditions: In times of constant or declining nominal costs, price regulation may be nonbinding, but in inflationary periods regulators often attempt to limit or delay price increases, forcing regulated prices closer to costs or, on occasion, below them. What is more, prices are often set at different levels for different classes of customers, not because such distinctions are economically efficient, but because such rate structures redistribute income in ways that satisfy certain political objectives.

In some markets populated by multiple firms, there is clear and abundant evidence that price regulation and entry regulation have often been used not to protect consumers from overcharges, but to protect incumbent firms from competition. Numerous studies of the airline, rail, and trucking industries and of several agricultural markets have fingered regulation as the culprit for higher consumer prices and major efficiency losses. It is interesting to note, however, that higher prices generally did not translate to persistently high rates of profit for regulated firms: Nonprice competition and sharing of rents with various interest groups—most often the firms' labor unions—generally bid returns down to normal levels.

Fortunately, these scholarly studies of regulatory failure did not merely gather dust on library shelves; they were used as ammunition in a regulatory reform movement that started in the late 1970s and continued into the 1980s. Since much of the damning evidence on regulation made good headlines (e.g., researchers' comparisons of high regulated *inter*state airfares with lower unregulated *intra*state fares), it was possible to enlist broad support for reform, which often included outright deregulation of some markets. So far, the evidence is that regulatory reform has produced significant benefits for consumers. Airline fares, e.g., are 10 to 15 percent below the levels that would have prevailed had regulation continued as before, saving consumers billions of dollars per year.[19] Reform in other markets has been less dramatic, but there is clear evidence that relaxing both price regulation and entry limits has produced consumer gains in the trucking and rail industries as well.[20]

In some markets, however, it is clear that federal regulation has kept prices *below* optimal levels. The rate-making approach used in the 1960s for natural gas, e.g., kept field prices too low to clear the market, causing regional gas shortages and inefficient substitution of other forms of energy. Subsequent attempts to correct these problems with more refined pricing regulations created new distortions. Similar problems arise from time to time in the health care industry. We tend to find, however, that regulation of this kind is self-limiting. Once shortages occur and/or service quality deteriorates, intense pressure for regulatory reform usually develops.

Efficiency losses associated with nonoptimal prices are just one of the problems researchers have linked to economic regulation, however. Perhaps more important is the tendency of regulation to increase costs—by distorting subject firms' input choices, encouraging waste or inefficiency, or failing to induce firms to adopt new and superior technologies in a timely fashion.

Several studies of public utilities have found evidence consistent with the prediction of economists Harvey Averch and Leland Johnson that rate-of-return regulation leads to wasteful overinvestment in capital when the allowed rate of return exceeds a firm's opportunity cost of capital.[21] Cost-plus utility regulation clearly eliminates firms' incentives to minimize costs or improve efficiency, although the rate-making process often incorporates mechanisms (e.g., investment prudency reviews, regulatory lag) that restore, at least in part, such incentives for public utilities.

Many studies conclude that rate regulation and entry regulation have raised costs in a variety of multifirm industries. Civil Aeronautics Board regulation of airlines, e.g., caused airlines to maintain inefficient route structures and underutilize aircraft and personnel. Interstate Commerce Commission regulation forced railroads to maintain service on thousands of miles of uneconomical routes and reduced incentives to use freight cars efficiently. Similarly, arcane route and commodity restrictions often forced truckers to return from a destination empty or with a partial load. Estimates of the annual

---

[19]Steven Morrison and Clifford Winston, *The Economic Effects of Airline Deregulation,* The Brookings Institution, Washington, 1986.

[20]Roger D. Blair, David L. Kaserman, and James T. McClave, "Motor Carrier Deregulation: The Florida Experiment," *Review of Economics and Statistics,* 68 (February 1986), pp. 159–164; James M. MacDonald, "Competition and Rail Rates for the Shipment of Corn, Soybeans, and Wheat," *Rand Journal of Economics,* 18 (1987), pp. 151–163.

[21]A few studies, however, are more equivocal, and all the empirical work in this area seems subject to some important limitations; for a brief review, see Paul L. Joskow and Nancy L. Rose, "The Effects of Economic Regulation," in Richard Schmalensee and Robert Willig (eds.), *Handbook of Industrial Organization, vol.* 2, North-Holland, New York, 1989, pp. 1477–1480.

costs of such waste total many billions of dollars. In addition, there is evidence, both anecdotal and econometric, that regulated industries showed lower rates of productivity growth and technological innovation than comparable unregulated industries.[22]

In sum, it is difficult to argue that economic regulation has commonly served the public-interest ends that have been advanced for it—at least prior to the reforms commencing in the 1970s. But neither is it accurate to say that regulators are commonly *captured* by firms and used to enforce their cartels. The story is far more complicated than that. Regulation has often served a variety of redistributive or political goals, often enhancing neither efficiency nor equity. Depending on the industry or time period studied, one can find examples of regulation-induced transfers of income from consumers to owners of firms[23] or to factors of production such as firms' managers or workers[24] or transfers *among* various classes of consumers[25] or producers.[26] As we have learned more about regulation's potential to reduce efficiency and redistribute income, we have certainly made some strides to ameliorate its least wholesome effects, at least in some industries. Clearly, however, much remains to be done.

Social Regulation

Although some social regulation has been around for a long time, most social regulatory agencies are just two or three decades old. To a large extent, the existence of these agencies is a testament to the power of ideas. The forceful writings of advocates such as Rachel Carson and Ralph Nader were instrumental in increasing public demand for environmental, health, and safety regulation in the late 1960s and early 1970s. As Figure 18.3 shows, the federal government responded to this demand with large increases in spending on social regulatory agencies in the 1970s, a trend that was only briefly interrupted during the Reagan years.

When we created agencies such as the Occupational Safety and Health Administration in 1969, the Environmental Protection Agency in 1970, and the Consumer Product Safety Commission in 1972, we had high hopes (expressed in these agencies' authorizing legislation) that soon workers would no longer "suffer diminished health, functional capacity, or life expectancy as a result of

[22]Aaron J. Gellmann, "Surface Freight Transportation," in William M. Capron (ed.), *Technological Change in Regulated Industries,* The Brookings Institution, Washington, 1971, pp. 166–196; Douglas W. Caves, Laurits R. Christensen, and Joseph A. Swanson, "Economic Performance in Regulated Environments: A Comparison of U.S. and Canadian Railroads," *Quarterly Journal of Economics,* 96 (November 1981), pp. 559–581.

[23]Thomas Gale Moore, "The Beneficiaries of Trucking Regulation," *Journal of Law and Economics,* 21 (1978), pp. 327–343.

[24]Ronald G. Ehrenberg, *The Regulatory Process and Labor Earnings,* Academic Press, New York, 1979.

[25]Roger G. Noll, "Let Them Make Toll Calls: A State Regulator's Lament," *American Economic Review,* 75 (May 1985), pp. 52–56.

[26]Joseph P. Kalt, *The Economics and Politics of Oil Price Regulation: Federal Policy in the Post-Embargo Era,* M.I.T. Press, Cambridge, 1981.

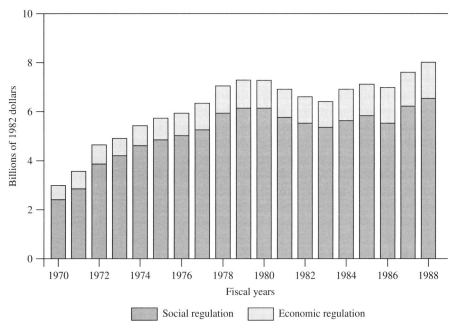

FIGURE 18.3
REAL FEDERAL OUTLAYS FOR ECONOMIC AND SOCIAL REGULATORY AGENCIES. Apart from a brief pause during the first Reagan term, regulatory spending has been growing strongly since 1970.

[their] work"; that there would be "zero [waste] discharges into the waterways"; that air quality would improve enough to "protect the most sensitive group in the population with an ample margin of safety"; that consumers would face no "unreasonable risks of injury" from the products they purchased. Thus far, however, it seems clear that most of these hopes, and others expressed for various other new agencies, are largely unrealized.

Of course, progress has been made. There are some wonderful triumphs to report. It is likely, e.g., that if we had done nothing to tighten the automobile safety standards that prevailed in 1965, the number of annual automobile fatalities would now be in the neighborhood of 60,000 rather than 45,000.[27] After surveying the scholarly research on the effects of much social regulation, however, one cannot help but conclude that the overall performance in this area has been disappointing. On occasion, scholars have failed to detect any favorable effect of regulation at all or have found perverse effects. OSHA's performance has been most vexing; many early studies found no significant impact of OSHA regulation on occupational illness and injury rates, although

[27]Robert W. Crandall, Howard K. Gruenspecht, Theodore E. Keeler, and Lester B. Lave, *Regulating the Automobile,* The Brookings Institution, Washington, 1986.

some more recent studies have detected small gains.[28] Where social regulation has produced measurable gains, these have often come at a very high cost—often higher than any reasonable estimate of the benefits or higher than would have been the case had a more reasonable regulatory mechanism been employed. Automobile pollution controls afford an excellent example. Such controls have certainly reduced smog in some areas, but at an annual cost that has been estimated at twice the benefits produced. The central problem is that the costs of this program are imposed everywhere while its benefits are limited to a few high-density, high-pollution areas such as Los Angeles and New York City; as a result, economists have observed, "it is difficult to conclude that the expenditures on emissions control for automobiles are well spent."[29] Finally, regulations imposed for one purpose often work at cross-purposes to those imposed for another. The classic example here is the corporate average fuel economy (CAFE) program, which aims to reduce our consumption of fossil fuels but, in addition, reduces automobile safety by inducing automakers to produce lighter vehicles.[30]

Why is social regulation so often inefficient? There are probably three basic reasons. First, the legislation authorizing such regulation generally was not written with cost-effectiveness and efficiency in mind. The OSHA Act is probably the best illustration. It directs OSHA to "assure *so far as possible* every working man and woman in the nation safe and healthful working conditions." It says nothing about ensuring safety only when it can be done cheaply, and it does not direct OSHA to use the most cost-effective regulatory scheme to achieve its goals. Many of OSHA's dictates thus appear to be *paternalistic* in nature; i.e., they aim to make individuals safer than they themselves would choose. For example, OSHA often favors lowering the concentration of harmful substances around a worker rather than permitting workers to wear personal protection devices. The latter course is often cheaper, but OSHA fears that even well-informed workers will choose not to wear the devices; thus, OSHA usually requires the more expensive program that eliminates more hazard than workers apparently want.

Another reason why social regulation sometimes diminishes welfare is that special interest groups occasionally invoke social goals as a guise for more cynical ends. Several empirical studies have demonstrated that OSHA and EPA regulations often have the effect (if not the purpose) of enhancing the profits of some firms relative to others; such gains are often shared with labor unions as a way of enlisting their support in the policy debate.[31] For example,

---

[28]W. Kip Viscusi, "The Impact of Occupational Safety and Health Regulation, 1973–83," *Rand Journal of Economics,* 17 (Winter 1986), pp. 567–580.

[29]Crandall et al., *Regulating the Automobile,* p. 114.

[30]Robert W. Crandall and John D. Graham, "The Effect of Fuel Economy Standards on Automobile Safety," *Journal of Law and Economics,* 32 (April 1989), pp. 97–118.

[31]Ann P. Bartel and Lacy Glenn Thomas, "Predation through Regulation: The Wage and Profit Effects of the Occupational Safety and Health Administration and the Environmental Protection Agency," *Journal of Law and Economics,* 30 (October 1987), pp. 239–264.

northern and eastern firms joined environmentalists in supporting tighter EPA air quality standards in southern, western, and rural areas because this put firms located in these areas (where air quality is already superior to national standards) at a competitive disadvantage.[32] William Niskanen, who saw such behavior first hand as an economic adviser in the Reagan administration, concluded in 1988 that "much [social] regulation in effect is a web of international tariffs—protecting old products against new products, declining industries against growing industries, and declining regions against growing regions."[33]

Finally, even the best-intended and most carefully written social regulations sometimes fail to improve welfare because consumers themselves defeat them, often by changing their behavior in ways regulators find extraordinarily frustrating. The requirement that automakers install seat belts, e.g., would have been highly cost-effective had everyone used the seat belts. But with only 10 to 15 percent of occupants buckling up, the practical benefits of the policy were negligible.[34] And because drug safety bottle cap regulations lulled consumers into a false sense of security and induced them to take less care in the handling of these products, these regulations actually *increased* total poisoning rates.[35]

It would be easy, then, to frown in dissatisfaction at social regulation's failure to fulfill its considerable promise to enhance welfare. But we should take note: Most social regulatory agencies are mere adolescents, and it would be unusual indeed if the behavior of any adolescent did *not* involve some failure and disappointment—and even wrongheadedness. As with most human endeavors, however, greater experience and maturity should improve our performance. In fact, there is already evidence that we are learning from our mistakes.

For example, at OSHA a highly adversarial command-and-control approach was replaced, in the Reagan years, with a more performance-oriented set of goals and enforcement procedures. OSHA now uses risk-assessment and cost-effectiveness tests in the promulgation of new regulations, and encourages managers and employees to work together to identify and eliminate conditions most likely to lead to serious workplace injuries or illnesses. And, as Figure 18.4 illustrates, these reforms appear to be paying off. Lost-workday injuries generally have been declining since 1980.

The EPA has also been moving—although less decisively—away from its traditional command-and-control approach toward market-based pollution control programs such as emissions trading (i.e., netting, offset, bubble, or

---

[32]B. Peter Pashigian, "Environmental Regulation: Whose Self Interests Are Being Protected?" *Economic Inquiry*, 23 (October 1985), pp. 551–584. See also Bruce A. Ackerman and William T. Hassler, *Clean Coal/Dirty Air*, Yale University Press, New Haven, CT, 1981.

[33]William A. Niskanen, *Reaganomics: An Insider's Account of the Policies and People*, Oxford University Press, New York, 1988, pp. 125–126.

[34]Daniel Orr, "Incentives and Efficiency in Automobile Safety Regulation," *Quarterly Review of Economics and Business,* 22 (Summer 1982), pp. 43–65; Lester B. Lave, "Conflicting Objectives in Regulating Automobiles," *Science*, 212 (1981), pp. 893–899.

[35]W. Kip Viscusi, "Consumer Behavior and the Safety Effects of Product Safety Regulation," *Journal of Law and Economics*, 28 (October 1985), pp. 527–553.

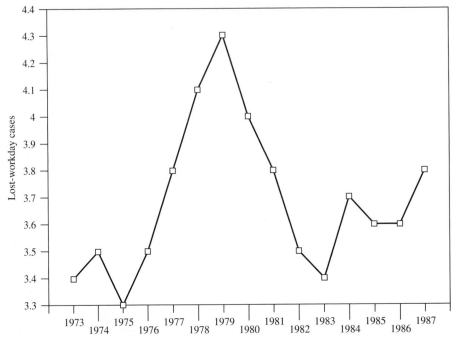

FIGURE 18.4
OCCUPATIONAL INJURIES AND ILLNESSES: LOST-WORKDAY CASES, 1973–1987. After peaking in 1979, lost-workday injury and illness rates were generally lower in the 1980s.

banking programs). Several studies, the results of which are summarized in Table 18.3, suggest that these programs are already saving over $1 billion annually without sacrificing environmental goals—although the savings could be greater if the programs were more widely used.[36]

These may seem like small victories, especially compared to social regulation's huge costs. But they signal something important: that the conduct of social regulation now involves greater attention to efficiency considerations—to economic analysis—than ever before. In the view of former FTC Chairman Michael Pertschuk, an ardently pro-regulation "cost-benefit draft resister," this means regulators can no longer simply *assume* that their actions will benefit the public, as they commonly did in the 1960s and 1970s:

> The economists earned my grudging respect . . . for their dogged insistence that we *think through* the reality of what we believed we were achieving with our intervention in the marketplace.
>   . . . We have learned from them that even where the impulse to regulate springs from deep wells of resentment at corporate abuse or neglect, we can end up punish-

---

[36]Robert W. Hahn and Gordon L. Hester, "Where Did All the Markets Go? An Analysis of EPA's Emissions Trading Program," *Yale Journal on Regulation*, 6 (Winter 1989), pp. 109–153.

TABLE 18.3

EMISSIONS TRADING ACTIVITY AND ITS IMPACT.   The use of market-based methods of pollution control is still limited, but has produced some significant savings without compromising environmental quality.

Activity	Estimated number of internal transactions	Estimated number of external transactions	Estimated cost savings (millions)	Environmental quality impact
Netting	5,000–12,000	0	$25 to $300 in permitting costs; $500 to $12.000 in emission control costs	Insignificant in individual cases; probably insignificant in aggregate
Offsets	1,800	200	Probably large but not easily measured	Probably insignificant
Bubbles:				
Federally approved	40	2	$300	Insignificant
State approved	89	0	$135	Insignificant
Banking	<100	<20	Small	Insignificant

Source: Robert W. Hahn and Gordon L. Hester, "Where Did All the Markets Go? An Analysis of EPA's Emissions Trading Program," *Yale Journal on Regulation*, 6 (Winter 1989), pp. 109-153, at p. 138. © Copyright 1989 by the *Yale Journal on Regulation*, Box 401A Yale Station, New Haven, CT 06520. Reprinted from Volume 6 by permission. All rights reserved.

ing not just the miscreants, but their victims, the consumers, upon whom the costs of regulatory compliance are most often loaded.

So the central lesson is, simply, regulatory humility. This does not mean unblinking reverence for unregulated markets. It does mean acknowledging the need for enhanced understanding of the structure and dynamics of markets and of the cause, or causes, of market failure.[37]

With this lesson learned, there appears reason for optimism that continued improvement in regulatory performance is likely.

THE FUTURE: EMERGING TRENDS

Anyone who attempts to divine the future will be wrong a good deal of the time, as weather forecasters, economists, and their clients well know. To elude blame for such failures, one can be either probabilistic (the old "40 percent chance of rain" gambit) or deliberately vague. We adopt the latter strategy. Rather than attempt to plot the future course of regulatory policy, we will sim-

[37] Michael Pertschuk, *Revolt against Regulation*, University of California Press, Berkeley, 1982, pp. 139–140.

ply identify some salient issues or policy stances that are likely to arise—some time. Often, we will rely on the guidance of experts or policymakers in this endeavor (the better to share the blame if our forecasts are hopelessly wrong).

Antitrust

As the 1990s commenced, it seemed clear that the antitrust reforms of the 1970s and 1980s, although well entrenched, were in for some fine-tuning. At the Antitrust Division of the Department of Justice, the emphasis on horizontal conspiracies and merger enforcement remained, but the Justice Department's policies and procedures were under review.[38] In brief, the Department sought

- To clarify its merger guidelines in order to eliminate ambiguities and be consistent with new learning.
- To incorporate *entry analysis* more fully in its merger enforcement policy. In this analytic framework, ease of entry would rebut an inference of anticompetitive effect drawn from market concentration data *if and only if* entry that results from a merged firm's higher price would likely occur (given its risks and sunk costs) within 2 years and would render the price increase unprofitable.
- To consider more fully the "noncoordinated effects" of a merger in highly concentrated markets. In such mergers, possible collusion, i.e., "coordinated action," is an obvious concern. Now, greater scrutiny will be given to the effects a merger might have on firms' noncoordinated decisions about price, output, or other key variables.

At the FTC, the contemplated changes seemed to be more wide-ranging.[39] The commission promised (1) to be more vigorous in its merger enforcement policy and to embark on some major studies of the competitive effects of mergers it had not challenged, (2) to spend more of its enforcement resources on *non*merger initiatives, and (3) to improve cooperation with state antitrust officials in order to intensify enforcement efforts in local cases.

The last point highlights one of the important new trends in antitrust policy in the late 1980s and early 1990s: the emergence of state attorneys general as prominent features of the antitrust enforcement landscape. Formerly viewed as mere in-house counsel to state governments, the state attorneys general have lately become far more aggressive about prosecuting antitrust violations — and violations of environmental and workplace safety laws as well. Nor is their effort limited to purely local bid-rigging conspiracies or complaints about unfair trade practices. In 1988, for example, 19 states jointly alleged

---

[38]"60 Minutes with the Honorable James F. Rill, Assistant Attorney General, Antitrust Division, U.S. Department of Justice," *Antitrust Law Journal*, 59 (1990), pp. 45–61.

[39]"60 Minutes with the Honorable Janet D. Steiger, Chairman, Federal Trade Commission," *Antitrust Law Journal*, 59 (1990), pp. 3–23.

(unsuccessfully, it turned out) that several national insurance companies had conspired to fix their rates,[40] and a 1989 multistate case accused Panasonic of illegal resale price maintenance on its electronics products.[41] The state attorneys general have even put forth their own merger guidelines.[42]

Not everyone endorses this trend, of course. Some hold that state attorneys general, many of whom are popularly elected, will let political considerations affect antitrust case selection, challenging mergers that do not damage competition but might discomfit an influential local firm or, alternatively, looking the other way when a merger might be anticompetitive but will benefit an in-state firm. The attorneys general naturally deny such charges and argue that their efforts have been even-handed and consumer-oriented, and that they fill a void created by federal authorities' failure to bring sufficiently many cases—especially with regard to vertical restraints—to deter anticompetitive conduct. Who's right? The jury is still out. There simply hasn't been enough time to evaluate the nature and consequences of stepped-up state-level enforcement. Clearly, however, these new players are here to stay and have the potential to significantly alter the direction of policy. In evaluating mergers or business practices, e.g., state enforcers are less inclined to accept efficiency rationales and are more preoccupied with market concentration data than federal authorities. In the words of one official:

> We require efficiency justifications to be demonstrated by hard evidence and to be quantified. We have severely limited the number of factors beyond market concentration that we consider: we have 3, the Department of Justice has 13.[43]

Are such criteria merely throwbacks to the standards and practices of the 1970s or harbingers of a new era of antitrust enforcement? We can only wait and see.

In academic research, there are two emerging trends of note. First is the rising prominence of game theory or the analysis of strategic firm behavior. Over the last decade, the academic journals on antitrust and industrial organization have swelled with game-theoretic analyses of firm conduct. Although many unresolved questions remain, this work has already answered several important questions relevant to antitrust policy. As Oliver Williamson has summarized:

> (1) severe structural preconditions in both concentration and entry-barrier respects need to be satisfied before an incentive to behave strategically can be claimed to exist; (2) attention to investment and asset characteristics is needed in assessing the condition of entry—specifically, nontrivial irreversible investments of a transaction-specific kind have especially strong [entry-deterring] effects; (3) history matters in

---

[40]*In re Insurance Antitrust Litigation,* 723 F. Supp. 464 (N.D. Cal. 1989).

[41]*In re Panasonic Consumer Elecs. Antitrust Litigation,* Civ. Action No. 89 Civ. 0368 (S.W.K.) (S.D. N.Y. 1989).

[42]See "Horizontal Merger Guidelines of the National Association of Attorneys General," *Antitrust and Trade Regulation,* Special Supplement, 52 (March 12, 1987), no. 1306.

[43]"Interview with Robert Abrams, New York State Attorney General," *Antitrust,* 4 (Summer 1990), p. 15.

assessing rivalry—both with respect to the leadership advantage enjoyed by a sitting monopolist as well as in the incidence and evaluation of comparative costs; and (4) reputation effects are important in assessing the rationality of predatory behavior.[44]

Whether scholarly theorizing about strategic behavior much affects the course of antitrust enforcement will, of course, depend on the courts' receptivity to this type of reasoning. Thus far, instances where strategic theories have been used as the foundation of an antitrust case are extremely rare; there are no cases where judges or juries have found such theories persuasive and crucial to their decisions. But we should be patient. As the "Chicago school" antitrust critics showed in the 1960s and 1970s, trends in the academic literature can be leading indicators of antitrust revolutions to come.

Another issue that has received increasing scholarly attention is the globalization of the marketplace and the implications of this trend for antitrust. To some, heightened international competition means that U.S. antitrust policy is (except in purely localized markets) redundant—or worse. In this view, even highly concentrated domestic markets can be very competitive when the specter of foreign competition looms. Or vigorous antitrust enforcement might actually *hinder* U.S. firms in the global economy, perhaps by keeping them from merging to realize certain economies or by preventing their adoption of certain business practices that are available to their foreign rivals. In particular, some worry that antitrust enforcement prevents U.S. firms from cooperating and planning in order to make the kinds of complementary investments needed to develop and commercialize new technologies.[45]

So far, the view that antitrust enforcement should be relaxed or modified to enable U.S. firms to gain some prospective advantage in international markets has yet to be endorsed by any enforcement authority or the courts.[46] Academic research on the topic proceeds, however, and given Congress's attentiveness to concerns about the international competitiveness of U.S. firms, it is unlikely that we have heard the last of the matter.

Regulation

We concluded earlier in this chapter that the demand for many of the things that social regulation can provide is quite likely to rise over time, as incomes rise. The wealthier we become, the more likely we are to want the benefits of a cleaner environment and greater workplace and product safety and the more willing we will be to bear the costs of these goods.

---

[44]Oliver E. Williamson, "Antitrust Enforcement: Where It Has Been; Where It Is Going," in John V. Craven (ed.), *Industrial Organization, Antitrust, and Public Policy*, Kluwer-Nijhoff, Boston, 1983, p. 63.

[45]Thomas M. Jorde and David J. Teece, "Innovation, Cooperation, and Antitrust," *High Technology Law Journal*, 4 (1989), pp. 1–112.

[46]In *United States v. Ivaco, Inc.*, 704 F. Supp. 1409 (W. D. Mich. 1989), the court rejected an argument that anticompetitive effects in the United States could be offset by making the defendant firm a more credible rival in its Canadian market.

If recent budgets are any guide, the federal government already is tooling up to satisfy this increased demand. Despite the pressure of enormous deficits, the 1991 budget included funding for 7,500 new staffers at federal regulatory agencies. What is more, budgetary trends show that social regulation is clearly where most of the action promises to be in coming years. The EPA alone now accounts for about one-third of the total spending of federal regulatory agencies—double its share of two decades ago.

Of course, it would be wrong to say that regulatory growth is always an efficient response to the demand for some public good. Often, as Sam Peltzman has observed, new government programs are simply a response "to the articulated interests of those who tend to gain or lose from politicization of the allocation of resources."[47] So we must ask, how much will the expanded regulatory effort that we expect in the future serve the broad public interest, and how much will it merely serve narrower interests who seek to use the power of government for its own ends?

There is at least some cause for optimism. First there is the matter of momentum. The regulatory reform movement that drastically altered the nature of economic regulation still has considerable force. Although agencies such as the Interstate Commerce Commission or Federal Communications Commission may never suffer the same fate as the now-defunct Civil Aeronautics Board, the reformers probably have assured that such agencies can survive only by paying far greater attention to the welfare implications of their policies. In the realm of social regulation, the reformers have succeeded in establishing that cost-benefit considerations are an integral part of any regulatory program. Such accomplishments are likely to endure, simply because it will take considerable time and energy to chip away at the essential logic that lies at their core.

But there are several reasons for worry. First, the aforementioned federal budget deficits will put pressure on political entrepreneurs to search for "off-budget" means of serving certain constituencies. As Murray Weidenbaum has remarked, regulation is an appealing alternative to direct spending programs:

> Regulation is a hidden tax with a double payoff for politicians. First, they can crow to their constituents that they voted for clean air and in favor of people with disabilities and so forth. . . . The second political payoff is that the same members of Congress can berate "greedy" companies for raising prices even though they are merely passing on the costs of complying with the new federal mandates.[48]

Second, the globalization of the marketplace, and the transitional pains this will imply, may lead to a demand for protectionist policies. Often it is politically inexpedient to employ the most obvious and direct barriers to interna-

---

[47]Sam Peltzman, "The Growth of Government," *Journal of Law and Economics,* 23 (October 1980), p. 287.

[48]Murray Weidenbaum, "The New Wave of Business Regulation," Center for the Study of American Business, Washington University, St. Louis, MO, Contemporary Issues Series 40, December 1990, p. 2.

tional trade (e.g., higher tariffs, import quotas), but regulation can often achieve similar results more subtly. By drawing up rules related to product safety or environmental impact which foreign countries find difficult to meet, imported goods can be kept out of the domestic market and domestic firms implicitly subsidized.

Third, not all the effects of the deregulation of the 1970s and 1980s have been favorable; in some cases, deregulation has been linked to some considerable and obvious pain. Market instabilities in the airline industry, e.g., or fraud and corruption in financial services industries have discomfited many and therefore have provoked calls for *re*regulation in these and other areas. Scholarly studies concluding that particular regulatory reforms have produced net benefits for the public will be of little consequence if it is widely believed that these reforms have failed.

Of course, these trends are all manifestations of what we have called the *public choice calculus* that affects the efficiency of the political marketplace. Given the high costs of transacting in this marketplace, often the representatives of narrow interests will get what they wish at the expense of broader, more diffuse interests. And often the narrowly focused groups will succeed in part because they "raise the ante" to other players by invoking spurious public-interest rationales that make it difficult and costly to figure out what really is the best policy alternative.

This is more than frustrating—it is costly. So it would be nice if we could promise that inefficient "private-interest regulation" is less likely to occur in the future than it has in the past, but we cannot. It would be nice if we had some formula to render the political marketplace more efficient, but we do not. Some, such as Weidenbaum, suggest that businesses take a more active role in the public policy arena, beefing up their Washington, D.C., offices to deal with pending legislation and new regulations:

> Often the most effective form of influence is making available to government decision makers prompt, factual, and detailed analyses of the impacts of proposed legislation. Every member of Congress listens when someone describes how a bill will affect his or her district.[49]

But there is no reason to believe that such efforts, were they to be undertaken, would necessarily enhance *social* welfare: Remember that businesses are just as apt to use the political marketplace for their own ends—to be *rent seekers*—as are other groups. And as Gordon Tullock has remarked, "[u]nfortunately, if we all engage in rent-seeking, we will all be worse off than if all of us pursued the public interest. It is the classic `prisoners' dilemma.'"[50] If there is hope for a brighter future, Tullock continues, it is this: "I have no definite answers to the problem of the prisoners' dilemma in this case or in others.

---

[49]Ibid., p. 13.
[50]Gordon Tullock, "Concluding Thoughts on the Politics of Regulation," in Robert J. Mackay, James C. Miller III, and Bruce Yandle (eds.), *Public Choice and Regulation: A View from Inside the Federal Trade Commission*, Hoover Institution Press, Stanford, CA, 1987, p. 342.

Nevertheless, in general we are more likely to be effective if we understand the problem than if we do not."[51]

Of course, understanding the problem is not enough. If we hope to solve it, then we must be willing to act on our knowledge. We must temper our own urge to use regulation for selfish ends and must expose and sanction others' self-interested use of government. Or we must devote some time and energy to devising institutional rules that will limit the incentive to try to use government to achieve inefficient or inequitable ends. Clearly, this calls for some altruistic behavior on the part of each of us. Learning about key public policies and transacting with our elected officials and their regulatory agents to ensure that they serve the broad public interest will be costly. But the likelihood of improvement in regulatory performance will hinge entirely on our willingness to pay this price.

[51]Ibid.

INDEXES

NAME INDEX

SUBJECT INDEX